A MODERN BOOK OF ESTHETICS

An Anthology

Fourth Edition

Edited with Introduction and Notes by

MELVIN RADER

University of Washington

HOLT, RINEHART AND WINSTON, INC.

New York   Chicago   San Francisco   Atlanta
Dallas   Montreal   Toronto   London   Sydney

Copyright © 1973, 1960, 1952, 1935 by Holt, Rinehart and Winston, Inc.
All rights reserved
Library of Congress Catalog Card Number: 72–86536
ISBN: 0–03–001756–4
Printed in the United States of America
   5 6   038   9876543

Acknowledgments

Grateful acknowledgment is made to the following persons and publishers who have kindly granted permission to quote from copyrighted works:

George Allen & Unwin Ltd. for British Empire rights to reprint from *Introductory Lectures on Psycho-Analysis* by Sigmund Freud, 1922, Revised Second Edition, 1929; and from *Ways of Knowledge and Experience* by Louis Arnaud Reid.

The American Philosophical Quarterly and Maurice Mandelbaum for permission to reprint "Family Resemblances and Generalizations Concerning the Arts" by Maurice Mandelbaum, *The American Philosophical Quarterly*, Vol. 2 (1965).

The American Society for Aesthetics and George Boas for permission to reprint "In Defense of the Unintelligible" by George Boas, *The Journal of Aesthetics and Art Criticism*, Vol. 9 (1950–1951); "Art and the Language of Emotions" by Curt J. Ducasse, *The Journal of Aesthetics and Art Criticism*, Vol. 22 (1964); and Morris Weitz for permission to reprint "The Role of Theory in Aesthetics" by Morris Weitz, *The Journal of Aesthetics and Art Criticism*, Vol. 15 (1956).

Art International and Clement Greenberg for permission to reprint "Counter-Avant-Garde" by Clement Greenberg, *Art International*, May 1971.

Basic Books, Inc., for permission to reprint from *Collected Papers* by Sigmund Freud, 1925.

Basil Blackwell & Mott Ltd. and G. E. M. Anscombe for permission to reprint from *Philosophical Investigations* by Ludwig Wittgenstein, 1953.

Bolligen Foundation, Inc., for permission to reprint from *The Nude: A Study in Ideal Form* by Kenneth Clark, copyright 1956 by the Trustees of the National Gallery of Art, Washington, D. C.

The British Journal of Aesthetics and John Kemp for permission to reprint "The Work of Art and the Artist's Intentions" by John Kemp, *The British Journal of Aesthetics*, Vol. 4 (1964); and Harold Osborne for permission to reprint "The Quality of Feeling in Art" by Harold Osborne, *The British Journal of Aesthetics*, Vol. 3 (1963).

The British Journal of Psychology for permission to reprint " 'Psychical Distance' as a Factor in Art and an Aesthetic Principle" by Edward Bullough, *British Journal of Psychology*, Vol. V (1913).

Cambridge University Press for permission to reprint from *The Beautiful* by Vernon Lee, 1913; and for British Empire rights to reprint from *Science and the Modern World* by Alfred North Whitehead, 1925.

Chatto & Windus, Ltd., and Professor Quentin Bell for British Empire rights to reprint from *Art* by Clive Bell.

The Clarendon Press, Oxford, for permission to reprint from *The Principles of Art* by R. G. Collingwood, 1938; and from *On the Aesthetic Education of Man* by Freidrich Schiller, translated by Elizabeth M. Wilkinson and L. A. Willoughby, 1967, Letter 27.

Constable & Company, Ltd., for British Empire rights to reprint from *The Sense of Beauty* by George Santayana.

Thomas Y. Crowell Company for permission to reprint from *Aesthetic Analysis* by D. W. Prall, 1936.

Crowell Collier and Macmillan, Inc., for permission to reprint "Aesthetics, Problems of" by John Hospers from *The Encyclopedia of Philosophy*, Paul Edwards, editor. Vol. 1, pages 36–39. Copyright © 1967 by Crowell Collier and Macmillan, Inc.

Doubleday & Company, Inc., for permission to reprint from *Design and Nature* by Ian McHarg. Copyright © 1969 by Ian McHarg.

Harcourt Brace Jovanovich, Inc., for permission to reprint from *Technics and Civilization* by Lewis Mumford, copyright, 1934, by Harcourt Brace Jovanovich, Inc.; renewed, 1962, by Lewis Mumford.

Harvard University Press, Cambridge, for permission to reprint from *The Basis of Criticism in the Arts* by Stephen C. Pepper. Copyright 1945 by the President and Fellows of Harvard College.

The Hogarth Press, Ltd., for British Empire rights to reprint from *Collected Papers* by Sigmund Freud, 1925.

Humanities Press Inc. for permission to reprint from *The Hidden God* by Lucien Goldmann, translated by Philip Thody, copyright 1964.

Lund Humphries Publishers Ltd. and Rudolf Arnheim for permission to reprint "Gestalt Psychology and Artistic Form" by Rudolf Arnheim in *Aspects of Form*, edited by Lancelot Law Whyte. Copyright 1951 by Percy Lund Humphries and Company, Ltd.

International Publishers for permission to reprint from *Illusion and Reality* by Christopher Caudell, 1947.

The Journal of Philosophy and Monroe C. Beardsley for permission to reprint "On the Generality of Critical Reasons" by Monroe C. Beardsley, *The Journal of Philosophy*, Vol. 59 (1962).

Lawrence & Wishart Ltd. for British Empire rights to reprint from *Illusion and Reality* by Christopher Caudwell, 1947.

iii

Liveright Publishing Corporation for permission to reprint from *Introductory Lectures on Psycho-Analysis* by Sigmund Freud, 1922, Revised Second Edition, 1929.

McGraw-Hill Book Company for permission to reprint from *Early Writings* by Karl Marx, translated and edited by T. B. Bottomore. © T. B. Bottomore, 1963.

The Macmillan Company for permission to reprint from *Science and the Modern World* by Alfred North Whitehead. Copyright 1925 by the Macmillan Company, renewed 1953 by Evelyn Whitehead.

Macmillan & Co., Ltd., for British Empire rights to reprint from *Oxford Lectures on Poetry* by Andrew Cecil Bradley, 1909; and for permission to reprint from *Three Lectures on Aesthetics* by Bernard Bosanquet, 1915.

John Murray Ltd. for British Empire rights to reprint from *The Nude: A Study in Ideal Form* by Kenneth Clark.

Northwestern University Press for permission to reprint "The Film and the New Psychology" by Maurice Merleau-Ponty in *Sense and Non-Sense*, translated by Hubert L. Dreyfus and Patricia Allen Dreyfus, 1964.

Oxford University Press for permission to reprint from *Ways of Knowledge and Experience* by Louis Arnaud Reid. © George Allen & Unwin Ltd., 1961; and from *What is Art?* by Leo Tolstoy, translated by Aylmer Maude, copyright 1930 by the Oxford University Press.

Princeton University Press for permission to reprint from *Art and Illusion* by E. H. Gombrich, No. 5 in the A. W. Mellon Lectures in the Fine Arts, Bollingen Series, XXXV. Copyright © 1960, 1961, and 1969 by the Trustees of the National Gallery of Art, Washington, D. C.; from *The Demands of Art* by Max Raphael, translated by Norbert Guterman, copyright © 1968 by the Bollingen Foundation; and "The Composer and His Message" by Roger Sessions in *The Intent of the Artist*, ed., with an Introduction, by Augusto Centeno (copyright 1941, © 1969 by Princeton University Press), pp. 104–132.

G. P. Putnam's Sons for permission to reprint from *Art* by Clive Bell; and from *Art As Experience* by John Dewey. Copyright © 1934, 1962 by John Dewey.

Mrs. Gladys C. Quinton, owner of the copyright, Edinburgh, Scotland, for permission to reprint from *Aesthetic* by Benedetto Croce, translated by Douglas Ainslee, Second Edition, 1922.

Random House, Inc., for permission to reprint from *The Birth of Tragedy and The Case of Wagner* by Freidrich Nietzsche, translated by Walter Kaufmann. Copyright © 1967 by Random House, Inc.

The Rice Institute for permission to reprint from *The Breviary of Aesthetic* by Benedetto Croce, 1915.

Routledge & Kegan Paul Ltd. for British Empire rights to reprint from *The Hidden God* by Lucien Goldmann, translated by Philip Thody, copyright 1964; from *Problems of Art* by Susanne K. Langer; and from *Technics and Civilization* by Lewis Mumford.

St. Martin's Press, Inc., for permission to reprint from *Oxford Lectures on Poetry* by Andrew Cecil Bradley, 1909.

Charles Scribner's Sons for permission to reprint from *Problems of Art* by Susanne K. Langer. Copyright © 1957 by Susanne K. Langer; from *Art and Scholasticism and The Frontiers of Poetry* by Jacques Maritain. Copyright © 1962 Jacques Maritain; and from *The Sense of Beauty* by George Santayana. Copyright 1896 Charles Scribner's Sons, 1924 George Santayana.

Sheed & Ward Limited for British Empire rights to reprint from *Art and Scholasticism* by Jacques Maritain.

University of California Press for permission to reprint from *Art and Visual Perception* by Rudolf Arnheim, 1954.

University of Chicago Press for permission to reprint "Style" by Meyer Schapiro from *Anthropology Today*, edited by A. L. Kroeber, 1953.

C. A. Watts & Company for British Empire rights to reprint from *Early Writings* by Karl Marx, translated by T. B. Bottomore.

Cole Weston and Nathan Lyons for permission to reprint "Seeing Photographically" by Edward Weston in *Photographers on Photography*, edited by Nathan Lyons.

Yale University Press for permission to reprint from *The Analysis of Art* by DeWitt H. Parker. Copyright © 1926 by Yale University Press.

Preface

In preparing this fourth edition, I have included a considerable number of works that have appeared since 1960, the date of the third edition, and I have expanded some of the old selections or substituted new ones. The readings, new and old, are varied and present supplementary or conflicting points of view. The book is planned and the selections classified to cover, within the necessary limits of space, almost the entire field of esthetics, including the major arts: music, architecture, painting, literature, motion pictures, industrial design, and others.

There are many possible ways of classifying the readings, but no classification can be perfectly neat unless the original essays are arbitrarily selected and distorted to fit it. I have found in teaching that the classification I have adopted is serviceable, but the divisions are not sharp and the selections overlap and interlock in a great variety of ways. Part I discusses the creative process; Part II, the work of art; Part III, the response of the beholder, the critic, and the community; and the Postscript, the nature and value of esthetic theory. In my general Introduction and the introductory note to each chapter, I have tried to clarify and interrelate the selections. Finally, there is a comprehensive bibliography.

Philosophers who complain of the "dreariness" of esthetics either have a narrow, preconceived idea of its limits or have never been confronted with the problem of choosing readings for an anthology such as this. Not the scarcity but the abundance of non-dreary discussions constitutes the problem of what to include or eliminate.

In the interest of saving space, I have omitted certain readings that are easily accessible, such as George Dickie's "The Myth of the Aesthetic Attitude" and Frank Sibley's "Aesthetic Concepts," which have been widely anthologized and are obtainable inexpensively in the Bobbs-Merrill Reprint Series in Philosophy.

In the readings new to this edition, spelling faithful to the original source has been employed. Hence variant spellings, such as "esthetics" and "aesthetics," appear in the present edition, in contrast to the uniform spelling of the three previous editions.

Although it has not always been possible to follow the advice that I have received in preparing this edition, I am nonetheless grateful. Thanks for generous suggestions and criticisms are due Virgil Aldrich, Lee Baxandall, Monroe Beardsley, Teddy Brunius, Donald W. Crawford, William H. Hayes, Daniel O'Connor, Harold Osborne, Harriet Jeffery, Bertram

Jessup, Arthur Lothstein, Stefan Morawski, John Moulton, David Rader, Alexander Sesonske, Willis Truitt, and Kendall Walton. I am deeply indebted to my wife Virginia for many hours of illuminating conversation about the arts.

M. R.

Seattle, Washington
September 1972

Contents

INTRODUCTION
The Meaning of Art

I. THE QUESTION OF DEFINITION

A natural object, such as the song of a meadowlark, has esthetic qualities; and therefore esthetics, which is the theory of esthetic objects and experiences, applies both to natural objects and to works of art. In appreciating the latter, we respond not only to sensuous qualities and forms but also to technical, psychological, and cultural values—to the *human* expressiveness of the works. The writers represented in the present anthology have a great deal to say about natural objects, but their main emphasis is upon art; and it is art that I now wish to discuss.

As we turn the pages of this book, we find that art is interpreted in many ways. Among the primary concepts employed are play, illusion, imitation, beauty, emotional expression, imagination, intuition, wish-fulfillment, pleasure, technique, sensuous surface, meaning, form, function, empathy, abstraction, and esthetic distance. At first glance, these concepts represent a bewildering diversity of opinion; but careful study will reveal that much of this disagreement is merely nominal. Terms such as "imagination," "form," "meaning," and "distance" indicate different facets of a rich and varied subject rather than mutually exclusive definitions. Some of the terms refer primarily to the creation of art, others to the art object, and still others to the act of appreciation. Many unnecessary disputes, as Morris Weitz has suggested, can be avoided if esthetic labels are not pasted in one piece on the whole body of art, but rather are applied separately to the various constituents of the creative process, the esthetic artifact, and the esthetic experience.[1] In his essay "The Role of Theory in Esthetics," Weitz concludes that art is too complex and variable to reduce to a single definition.

Ludwig Wittgenstein's strain of thought, which underlies Weitz's argument, raises issues too complex for discussion in this brief Introduction. The question of definition is best postponed to the Postscript, since it has greater meaning after the reader has reviewed the leading theories of esthetics. At this point we shall touch only lightly on the problem of defining art.

Let us agree with Wittgenstein that art, like religion and science, cannot be reduced to a simple notion, and that it is foolish to try to draw a sharp line between it and other human activities. But there is much

more of a consensus among writers on art than appears on the surface.
In *An Introduction to Aesthetics* (London, 1949), Professor E. F. Carritt
quoted from over forty representative estheticians, ancient and modern,
to illustrate the recognition that art, as a creative process, is the
expression of mood, feeling, or spirit. There are two parts to this
consensus: first, that art is expression, and second, that spirit, feeling, or
mood is expressed.

The prevalence of the concept of expression has been remarked by
Alan Tormey:

> The history of the philosophy of art could, without excessive distortion, be
> written as a study of the significance of a handful of concepts. The successive
> displacement of "imitation" by "representation," and of "representation" by
> "expression," for example, marks one of the more revealing developments in the
> literature of esthetics; and it would be only a slight exaggeration to claim that
> from the close of the eighteenth century to the present "expression" and its
> cognates have dominated both esthetic theorizing and the critical appraisal of
> the arts.[2]

Some writers in this anthology use other words, such as "communication"
(Tolstoy), "objectification" (Santayana), "embodiment" (Bosanquet
and Reid), and "symbolization" (Langer and Arnheim). These are not
alternatives to "expression" but are cognate terms.

A considerable number of estheticians point out that "expression"
does not mean *self*-expression. The artist expresses, as Langer has said,
"not his own actual feelings, but what he knows about human feelings."
Hence, it is not the case, as some critics have supposed, that the expression
theory commits us to treating art works as autobiographical revelations.
Almost all estheticians distinguish between a mere gushing or venting
of emotion, which has nothing to do with art, and artistic expression
of the "quality," "mental image," or "epitome" of emotion. Expressing a
mood or feeling, Collingwood (Chapter 3) points out, is not the same
as *arousing* it in someone's mind. For example, music that expresses
sadness need not make the listener feel sad. Without transmitting the
actual feeling, the music conveys the impression, or as some would
prefer to say, the conception or abstracted pattern, of sadness. As
Carroll C. Pratt remarked, "Music sounds the way emotions feel."[3]
Expressive qualities in objects do not always imply some correlative
act of expression. Sophisticated proponents of the expression theory,
especially those steeped in Gestalt psychology, recognize that many
things have expressive qualities without being *created* with this end in
view, or without being created at all. These qualities abound in the world
quite apart from art, and this is the reason that artists can so often
borrow a motif from actuality. Arnheim, in a selection reproduced in
this anthology (Chapter 9), refers to the soft or threateningly harsh
profile of a mountain, the twisted, sad, tired appearance of a blanket
thrown over a chair, the weariness of slowly floating tar, or the energetic
ringing of a telephone bell. Hence, not all but only some expressiveness
is the product of artistic activity. The sceptic might still contend that art

in no way implies expression, and this is true in some meanings of the word. But if by "expression" one means the intentional making of objects with expressive qualities, it is difficult to deny that art is a kind of expression. We would not call a wholly inexpressive object a work of art. Since the concept of expression, as used in esthetic discourse, is open to alternative statements and misunderstandings, it has been subjected to considerable criticism; but these criticisms can be met by more exact explication of its meaning.

The further statement that art is the expression of mood, emotion, feeling, or spirit may seem to slight the role that Imitation and Form have played in the history of esthetic theory. But if we look beyond the label to the substance of these theories, we find that they do not differ radically from the doctrine of expression. Neither Plato nor Aristotle, for example, favors imitation in the sense of nonexpressive copying. Plato refers to the painters and poets that he condemns as mere imitators; but in many passages, he recognizes the existence and value of artistic inspiration, which is nonimitative in any literal sense. According to the *Laws, Phaedrus, Symposium,* and *Ion,* the highest art is inspired by a direct vision of the pure eternal forms of Beauty, Truth, Goodness, and the like. Plato's conclusion, in the *Republic,* is that "the real artist, who knew what he was imitating, would be interested in realities and not in imitations."[4]

In the *Poetics,* Aristotle maintains that poetry has sprung from the mimetic impulse and the instinct for harmony and rhythm. He thus recognizes form as no less fundamental than imitation—indeed, the importance of unity and design is emphasized throughout his essay. The reality imitated, he indicates, is human life and human nature—acts expressive of spirit. An act viewed merely as an external process is not the true object of esthetic imitation. A work of art imitates its original, not as it is in itself but as it *appears* to the senses and imagination. Accordingly, the poet ought to prefer "probable impossibilities to possible improbabilities"; that is to say, he should aim at convincing semblance. If literal truth is stranger than fiction, then all the worse for truth in the literal sense. Art imitates the *universal*; it expresses the real, rid of irrelevancies and the disturbances of chance; it exhibits the common designs of destiny; it is in this sense more philosophical than history. Tragic characters are "imitated" not as they are but as they "ought to be," displaying a lofty nobility and greatness despite their tragic flaws. In the *Politics* Aristotle contends that music is, in a sense, the *most* imitative of the arts. "Melodies have the power of representing character in themselves," he declares. "There seems to be a sort of kinship of harmonies and rhythms to our souls."[5]

Such ancient doctrines of imitation are not opposed to the expressionist thesis. They recognize, perhaps implicitly, that the artist presents his evaluative interpretation of reality, and thereby is expressing his feeling and sense of values. In the selection presented in Chapter 1, E. H. Gombrich formulates a kind of modern analogue of the ancient theories in which he clearly recognizes that the artistic representation of nature cannot be separated from imaginative expression.

Likewise, formalist doctrines should not be regarded as antithetical to the principle of expression. Plato, again to cite his ideas as illustrative, emphasized form as having a profound affinity to spirit and as thus providing a necessary basis for the expression and cultivation of the human soul. He saw that esthetic experience is shot through with formal characteristics—with rhythm, harmony, design—the collaboration of which constitutes the whole. He believed that esthetic education, especially in the early and most formative years of life, would cultivate the habit of seeing things thus in context, in their unity and inward coherence. Little by little, the mind would develop its power of imaginative sympathy, its intuitive sense of order, until the feeling for likeness and fellowship and harmony would become second nature, almost an instinct. The reason that he wanted to censor art is not that he valued it so little but that he valued it so much. He was wrong, I think, in his desire to censor, but right in his emphasis upon form and his estimate of art and esthetic education. When thoroughly ingrained and integral to the psyche, esthetic culture impresses the sense of interrelatedness upon the deepest levels of the mind. Without such a deep spontaneous appreciation of vivid qualities, in their mutual relevance and interfusion, there could be little feeling for the unity of life or the spiritual integration of a community.

If we turn from Plato to Immanuel Kant, another great formalist, we find less emphasis upon the moral and political uses of art and greater emphasis upon the isolation and disinterestedness of the esthetic experience. Conceiving fine art as the free creation of beauty for beauty's sake, Kant discovered the essence of beauty in design enjoyed simply for itself. There is a harmonious play of our faculties—a dynamic equilibrium of sense, feeling, imagination, and understanding—which corresponds to, and is stimulated by the work of art. This harmonious state must be communicable, for one mark of art is its sharability. Thus, form is both outward and inward—the design of the work and the harmony of the mind—and the sensuous medium is the vehicle for the communication of form, in this twofold sense. Genius, the talent that creates beautiful works of art, is characterized in addition by *Geist*—"soul" or "spirit"—which is the faculty of conceiving and expressing "esthetical ideas." Such ideas, unlike the concepts of science, have a profundity and connotativeness that can not be put into definite meanings. They provide the elusive and inexhaustible significance that characterizes every great work of art and that gives such mysterious depth to form. Now this theory, although it may be called formalist, is no far cry from the doctrine of expression.

Neither imitation nor form, taken as exclusive, could be considered the defining mark of art, whereas expression comes much closer to the required degree of generality. The expressionist theory, when adequately formulated, incorporates the insights involved in the other two theories, treating the representational and formal elements as the means of expression. Not mere imitation but *expressive* imitation, not mere form but *expressive* form, have artistic point and relevance. The recognition of this fact constitutes the central standpoint of modern esthetics.

Of course there is some disagreement about what side or aspect of the human mind is expressed in art. For example, Maritain emphasized the intellect; Santayana, pleasure; Croce, intuition; Nietzsche and Freud, desire and the unconscious; Schiller, the play of imagination; Bosanquet and Dewey, the mind as an organic whole. But even here it is possible to exaggerate the differences. Freud agreed with Santayana that art is surcharged with pleasure, and with Tolstoy that it expresses emotions and not merely desires. Maritain agreed with Santayana in emphasizing beauty and in defining beauty in terms of pleasure; and he met Croce and Collingwood halfway when he declared that esthetics should recognize both intellectual and intuitive factors in art. Schiller stressed the play of imagination, but agreed with Dewey and Bosanquet that art engages and harmonizes the whole mind-body. So, likewise, with other writers in this book—they tend to reach out and embrace the truths represented by the different points of view.

Art, like every creative enterprise, is fluid and "open," and no tight definition will serve. But it is well to try to define what we are concerned with in this book—otherwise our ideas will be too hazy or chaotic. The extent to which estheticians disagree has been exaggerated; their considerable measure of agreement provides a basis for a tentative, working definition. Rather than the advice of Wittgenstein, "Beware of definition," I prefer the guiding principle, "Seek definition *but distrust it.*" This recognizes the virtue of defining while adding the necessary note of caution.

The task of definition in esthetics is incorrectly described when it is characterized as the search for the necessary and sufficient properties of art. In this sense of defining, it is the attempt to find an eternal and exclusive essence that marks off art from every other human activity. So conceived, the definition of art *is* impossible. There is too much overlapping and interpenetration among the various human activities—art, religion, science, technology, economic production, and so on—to permit this kind of demarcation. The question we should seek to answer is not "What can art *alone* do?" but rather "What can art do *best*?"

II. The Expression of Values

We have already mentioned that there is a considerable consensus among estheticians that art can best serve as a mode of expression, and that it can best express the inner life of the psyche, such as mood, feeling, and desire. This sort of definition, although it contains a large measure of truth, puts a too exclusive emphasis upon the subjective side of art, namely, the portrayal of the inner life. A preferable way to characterize art is to say that it is the expression or embodiment of values.

A number of the estheticians represented in this anthology characterize art in this way. Whitehead (Chapter 5) maintains that in art "the concrete facts are so arranged as to elicit attention to the particular values which are realizable through them. . . . The habit of art is the habit of enjoying vivid values." Nietzsche (Chapter 4) is obsessed with the idea that all values may be questioned and that the goal of art, as of life in general, is the transvaluation of values. "What does all art do?" he asks. "Does it not praise? Does it not glorify? Does it not select? Does it not bring things into prominence? In all this it strengthens or weakens certain valuations."[6] Santayana (Chapter 6) declares that esthetics is concerned with the perception of values, and he distinguishes between art, as the expression of values, and science, as the description of facts. But his theory of value, in *The Sense of Beauty*, is hedonistic and subjective. Louis Arnaud Reid (Chapter 6) avoids one-sided subjectivism and defines value in relational terms, as a thing or quality felt and appreciated. I sympathize with these views, especially the theory of Reid, and I think this sort of axiological approach to art is the most illuminating.

As Bertram Jessup and Melvin Rader declared:

> It is only when feeling and quality are . . . united that we can speak of esthetic value. . . . It is possible and even useful for some purposes to abstract quality or feeling from its relational setting and to consider it separately. If we wish to emphasize the objective pole of the relation, we can say that the function of art is clear and vivid realization of quality. Or if we wish to emphasize the subjective pole, we can say that the function of art is the expression and cultivation of feeling. Now these functions are not really separate and independent—they are two sides of the same process. The function of art is to make articulate the whole gamut of human values, and this function embraces and unites the other two.[7]

All the writers represented in this book support, in some measure, this point of view, although some emphasize the subjective pole while others choose the objective. All maintain that a work of art is not the report of a bare matter of fact, but is the projection of the artist's inspiration, his emotions, preferences, appreciations, or sense of values. I do not mean that they all adopt the phrase "expression of values"— other terms are more often employed; but despite the divergences in terminology, there is almost universal agreement that art is a spiritual language, expressing valuations rather than formulating objective descriptions.

The pivot of this doctrine is the distinction between facts and values. Let us therefore carefully examine this distinction. "X is square" is judged a *fact* if a number of competent observers, upon carefully measuring X, find it to be square. Science is the coordination of facts, and the very meaning of a fact, or of a scientific truth as the accurate description of facts, is that it can meet the test of *social* verification. The distinguishing mark of science is its public character, the result of a process of abstraction, generalization, and collective verification; no belief has scientific validity as long as it remains private, the esoteric object of a single individual's perspective. It must be transmitted and interpreted to others and substantiated by them; it must be verified by stubborn and irreducible data, admitted by all qualified observers. It must be consistent with established laws and theories, which in turn have been verified by scientists, living and dead. Science is therefore appropriately characterized by Charles Peirce and Josiah Royce as a "community of interpretation."

A *value*, on the other hand, is a quality that excites appreciation. Art, as value-expressive, springs from attitudes of appraisal. It does not reflect existence as merely neutral and colorless; it selects, distorts, and intensifies. What Francis Bacon wrote about poetry applies to all art: ". . . It doth raise and erect the Mind, by submitting the show of things to the desires of the Mind, whereas reason doth buckle and bow the Mind unto the Nature of things."[8] Thus, a natural landscape is valued esthetically because it has certain qualities, but some other of its qualities will be quite indifferent or unsatisfactory. An artist intent upon expressing the positive values of the landscape would select the qualities he appreciates and would express these and not the indifferent features. The only way he can do so is to remodel the landscape by means of imagination.

Values, in contrast to facts, are often merely imaginary. "Possibility," as Emily Dickinson said, "is a fairer house than Prose."[9] Even when values are not possibilities envisaged by the imagination, they are always related to our appreciative attitudes, which *may* be quite private and peculiar. Whereas facts have a uniform character for a community of observers, values have a variable character depending upon the subjective preferences of the individual appreciator. But, as I shall explain in some detail, this variability can be confined within limits; and through art, values attain a kind of social objectivity that is quite different from the objectivity of science.

Values are expressed in the creative activity of the artist whenever he purposefully creates the objective occasions for appreciations. Usually, he communicates attitudes of valuation by supplying an appropriate object—namely, a work of art—to another mind; but the object may be created for the artist himself to contemplate as the adequate ground for his own appreciative attitudes. The problem of the artist is to find the objective forms and qualities that will induce the person who contemplates them to discover in the object the values that he wishes to embody. If he succeeds in doing this, he has "expressed" the values. This does not mean that the values which the artist expresses need be completely in mind before he starts work. As Croce and Collingwood (Chapter 3) insist, both Beethoven in writing a symphony and Michelangelo in decorating the Sistine Chapel must have elaborated an inward vision in the process of objectifying—and it is this vision that is expressed. To this extent, intuition and expression are identical.

The problem of the contemplator is somewhat different. The work of art that he beholds consists of an array of signs which he must interpret. It is for him, himself, to supply the sense of values to which these signs correspond. It will depend upon him whether the work awakens to life in his imagination or remains dead and inexpressive. He must evoke from within himself the appropriate attitudes—and thereby intensify his qualitative appreciation of the object—in which he thus discovers the values that the artist has embodied. If he succeeds in doing all this, he has "expressed" values in contemplation, since his own activity is, like all interpretative art, essentially creative. From the standpoint of the artist and also from that of the contemplator, art is the expression of values

—though we should distinguish between the free expression of the artist and the interpretative expression of the contemplator. Croce, in particular, insists that contemplation is thus expressive, and I think he is right.

III. THE COMMUNITY OF APPRECIATION

Science describes facts; art expresses values. It would *seem*, therefore, that science has a collective and impersonal character that art lacks. Science, it may be argued, deals with the more permanent, public, and universal elements of experience; art, with the more fleeting, private, and particular elements. Now this contrast has some basis, but I believe that it is a mistake to set up such a sharp dichotomy. Gregory Vlastos pointed out that *both* art and science are essentially communal. "In science," he wrote, "one finds truth only insofar as one recasts one's private insight into its most universally sharable form; thus placing it at the disposal of all. Scientific truth is discovered in a community of inquiry in which there is the minimum of hoarding and the maximum of sharing—where each receives the fruit of the labors of others and gives back to the utmost of his ability." Artistic expression is similarly interpersonal: "Beauty is created only in a process of communication wherein the product of individual originality becomes the common possession of mankind. . . . The creator must lose to find himself, lose a subjective intuition to recover it as objective form."[10] Art is man's supreme means of socializing the world of appreciations. By communicating the "incommunicable," art creates a community of appreciation to supplement the community of scientific interpretation. Just as the objectivity of science implies the recognition of a "common world" of describable objects, so the communicability of art implies a "social ego," a common *inner* world of value-appreciation.

A brief discussion of some of the ideas of Josiah Royce, a writer not generally regarded as an esthetician, will help to make clear what we mean by a community of appreciation. A recurrent theme in his books is the contrast between "the world of description" and "the world of appreciation." The world of description is the realm of science—an abstraction from experience of its most communicable aspects. To be describable, the data of experience must be "public"—the same for all qualified observers; and hence the rich, variegated, subjective, fleeting immediacies of experience must be thinned down to pointer readings, or at least to some order and fixity of type, whereby each person's interpretations can be precisely the same as his neighbor's. Such abstract characteristics as number, shape, weight, and spatial and temporal relations are the most exact and describable. Less so, but still in some measure describable, are such qualities as heat, yellow, or hardness. Comparatively indescribable are the nuances of our inner life. These latter "appreciations," according to Royce, must therefore be excluded from science.

Yet every immediate experience has its appreciative aspect. "That is; it feels to me so or so. I like it or I hate it. Or again, where pleasure and pain aren't marked, still there is an essentially indescribable value that my experience has for me when regarded just as my own feeling. Tastes have one sort of worth for me, colors another. An electric shock from a Leyden jar is appreciated as a peculiar and atrocious interruption of all other trains of feeling, such that its painful value is surely, but inexpressibly, different from that of all other experiences."[11] This appreciative side of life, according to Royce, eludes all our scientific categories and exact measures. Its vivid qualities are too individual, subjective, and personal, too secret and fugitive, too inexpressibly different, to be caught within the web of science. Not the peculiar and private "feel" of things but the observable fact, not the appreciation but the description, give outer truth, and hence a communicable content.

According to Royce, the world of description is, in a sense, real but superficial. If you are describing a friend, you can indicate his height, his weight, the color of his hair and eyes, even his intelligence quotient; but this leaves out what endears him to you. You can "explain" the sunset according to uniform natural laws, but this leaves out its radiance. All that we value most, Royce believes, falls within the world of appreciation, and yet, he sometimes seems to say, there is no language for this world comparable to the exact language of science. Whereas *facts* are publicly observable and hence describable, *appreciations* are not thus public: we are not mind readers—we cannot *observe* the appreciations within another mind. Yet it is precisely in this realm that there is the greatest need of community: the need of sympathy and understanding and spiritual integration without which life is an arid waste.

Royce tried to secure such a community upon the basis of moral and religious activity; above all, through the virtue of loyalty. Believing that the detached individual is a lost soul, he attempted to transcend the incommunicability of appreciative experiences by "the willing and practical and thoroughgoing devotion of a person to a cause." But this is to put the cart before the horse. Loyalty itself must rest upon social sympathy, and it is therefore dependent upon a community of appreciation. It is easy to say as Royce did, "Live as if thine and thy neighbor's life were one to thee." But how can you do so if there is no way to share your appreciations by means of a vivid and effective language? Although in one of his later works, *The Problem of Christianity*, Royce states that art is a mode of social interpretation, he failed to elaborate his meaning. Hence his account of community remains a bit fragmentary and unconvincing.

In his earlier book, *The Spirit of Modern Philosophy*, he makes the problem unnecessarily difficult by exaggerating the dualism between the world of description and the world of appreciation. Within limits, appreciations *are* describable. Psychologists such as William James, Edward Titchener, Sigmund Freud, and Wolfgang Köhler acutely described many aspects of the inner life of feeling and volition. Although such descriptions are less exact than the mathematical formulations of modern physics, they are sometimes very illuminating.

There is, however, a profound difference between the scientific account of mental vagaries by a psychologist and the artistic expression of a neurotic's "appreciations" by a novelist such as Dostoevsky. In the former case we are dealing with abstractions; in the latter, with the immediacies of vivid experience as kindled in the mind by imagination. There can be not only *some* description of our appreciation, but also the imaginative expression of appreciation by means of art.

Following the practice of Royce, I have been using the term "appreciation" to stand for the inner, subjective pole of value. We must not forget that there is also the objective pole, the *quality* that is the object of our appreciation. This quality has a kind of phenomenal objectivity that enables strangers to enjoy it too and to join with us in a community of interpretation.

Let me sum up what I have been saying. Just as there is a community of scientists engaged in the cooperative search for facts and using the language of description, so there is a community of artists engaged in the cooperative search for values and using the "language" of appreciations and vivid qualities. Art is the making of perceptible forms expressive of human values. These values have both subjective and objective poles, and are both individual and social.

IV. THE CREATIVE PROCESS

In the light of the foregoing definition of art, we can characterize art in terms of three standpoints: the creative activity of the artist, the work of art, and the reception of art by the public. Each of these is covered by a Part of the present volume; the divisions are not sharp, each Part throws light on all three standpoints. I shall first characterize the creative process.

The activity of the artist, as already stated, is the expression of values. To illustrate, I cite the following passage from a letter written by Vincent van Gogh to his brother:

> I should like to paint the portrait of an artist friend, a man who dreams great dreams, who works as the nightingale sings, because it is in his nature. He'll be a fair man. I want to put into my picture my appreciation, the love that I have for him. So I paint him as he is, as faithfully as I can. But the picture is not finished yet. To finish it I am now going to be the arbitrary colorist. I exaggerate the fairness of the hair; I come even to orange tones, chromes, and pale lemon-yellow. Beyond the head, instead of painting the ordinary wall of the mean room, I paint infinity, a plain background of the richest, intensest blue that I can contrive, and by this simple combination of the bright head against the rich blue background I get a mysterious effect, like a star in the depths of an azure sky.[12]

What van Gogh sought to communicate through his painting was not a mere factual description; he wished to paint his "appreciation," his "love," the qualities that excited his preference. He did not literally imitate; faithful reproduction, as he said, is only a point of departure. He imagined the colors and shapes, the contrasts and relationships that would express his sense of values—the mood of appreciation that his friend excited within him.

Yet van Gogh did not merely express his admiration for his friend. He created *new* values in the very act of expression. Each color or shape that he painted has a worth of its own. The "rich blue," for example, is beautiful in itself, and it is more beautiful in contrast with the orange shades, the chrome, the pale lemon-yellow. The finished painting can be enjoyed as a pattern of colors and shapes even if it were to be turned upside down so that it is no longer regarded as the representation of a human figure. Many modern pictures, as we all know, do not represent or imitate any natural fact, just as a fugue of Bach does not thus represent or imitate. Since the time of Pythagoras, philosophers have recognized the value-expressiveness of harmonies, rhythms, patterns of color, three-dimensional shapes, and other nonrepresentational elements. One of the merits of certain writers in this anthology, such as Susanne Langer and Rudolf Arnheim, is that they help to explain how such expressiveness occurs.

Many works of art are representational; all works of art have form. Like most artists in Western tradition, van Gogh expresses both representational and formal values. A writer such as Clive Bell (Chapter 8), who minimized representational values, and a writer such as Leo Tolstoy, who minimized formal values, were both one-sided.

The appreciations expressed by an artist are not separate from their mode of expression. The *what* of art is not separable from the *how*. When James Joyce expresses a shaver's disgust at "the clammy slather of the lather in which the brush was stuck," it is a clammy-slathery disgust that he is expressing. When Picasso expresses serenity with the muted colors and voluminous form of his "Woman in White," it is a color-muted and voluminous serenity that is being expressed. The sadness of music is a peculiarly musical sadness; it is impossible, for instance, to give an adequate verbal phrasing to the majestic sadness of Chopin's Sonata in B Flat Minor. Even in poetry, the values cannot truly be formulated in words other than those of the poem itself. There is a real creative synthesis, a fusion of mood with sensory configuration. As sensation blends with sensation to create a new quality (for instance, when notes combine to form a chord), so feeling or desire blends with sensation to create the esthetic effect.

To depict the artist as he is sometimes depicted—a kind of spiritual Robinson Crusoe forever marooned on the island of his own subjectivity —is to forget that in art the duality of subject and object disappears. The artist's inner experiences, his appreciative thoughts and moods, are expressed outwardly in the language of sensory qualities. As in dreams, subjective thought and feeling are embodied in sensory images, but in a form communicable to others. The work of art is objective and yet is dyed with emotion and sensibility. It radiates spiritual expressiveness and is thus a link between mind and mind. Art is the only "language" whereby we can *vividly* transmit our values to others. It breaks down the walls between human beings, and is thus a great solvent of conflict and selfishness. "Love consists in this," the poet Rilke has written, "that two solitudes protect and touch and greet each other."[13] By means of art, the solitudes flow together; love and imaginative understanding become possible.

The artist not only discloses his own moods but also transcends his private feelings. He has the singular ability to draw the outer object into his own being—to sense its qualities and to feel at one with it. John Keats was reporting more than a personal idiosyncrasy when he wrote: "If a Sparrow come before my window, I take part in its existence and pick about the gravel."[14] In another letter, Keats described the nature of a poet and cited himself as an example:

> A poet is the most unpoetical of anything in existence, because he has no Identity—he is continually in for [*sic*] and filling some other body. The Sun,— the Moon,—the Sea, and men and women, who are creatures of impulse, are poetical, and have about them an unchangeable attribute, the poet has none, no identity—he is certainly the most unpoetical of all God's creatures. . . . It is a wretched thing to confess; but it is a very fact, that not one word I ever utter can be taken for granted as an opinion growing out of my identical Nature—how can it, when I have no Nature? When I am in a room with people, if I ever am free from speculating on creations of my own brain, then, not myself goes home to myself, but the identity of everyone in the room begins to press upon me, so that I am in a very little time annihilated—not only among men; it would be the same in a nursery of Children."[15]

Keats is here describing, in rather paradoxical language, the sensibility that is pre-eminently the artist's but which is shared to a degree by everyone. It is thus that we are "in touch" with other people and things. All of the arts—not simply poetry—cultivate this empathic sensitivity. "Empathy," in this broad sense, still retains meaning for art, in characterizing not only the beholder but also the creator of the work of art. The tendency in contemporary esthetics to abandon the theory of Vernon Lee (Chapter 10) and Theodor Lipps has gone too far.

V. The Work of Art

The work of art conveys the sense of a living presence—it is infused with emotion, instinct with a kind of life. Its beholder reaches out and touches another spirit.

For this reason, idealistic writers such as Croce and Collingwood (Chapter 3) maintained that the work of art is spiritual rather than physical. A number of recent writers have attacked this position, contending that the work is, at least in many cases, a physical artifact. Both sides of the dispute are calling attention to important facts. Except in the case of mere imagery, which we would hesitate to call a work of art, there is indeed a physical artifact, such as a canvas covered with pigments. But the more idealistic philosophers say that this artifact is only a means to an end, awakening in the mind an imaginative process that creates the real work of art; conversely, the more materialistic philosophers contend that the physical thing is the work of art itself. I think that, as occasions vary, we choose to mean different things by the phrase "work of art," and sometimes our meaning is more akin to the materialist's and at other times is more like the idealist's. A theory such as that sketched by Stephen Pepper (Chapter 11) in the latter part of his essay on

"Contextualist Criticism" seems more meaningful because it recognizes and gives due credit to both the physical and the mental sides. The insistence of Bernard Bosanquet and Edward Weston (Chapter 7) on the importance of the physical medium is a proper corrective to a purely idealistic theory.

The work of art may be defined as an organic unity of value-expressive constituents. The constituents include representations, connotations, and purely sensuous materials, and there is almost no value that cannot be represented, connoted, or sensuously presented. It is therefore impossible to restrict the content of works of art, as Santayana initially and many other writers tried to do, by limiting it to *beauty*. The content, of course, must be *valued* in concrete terms, and hence must be concretely appreciated. The qualities of the object must be apprehended as, for example, gay, sad, horrible, sublime, or demonic; they must be liked or disliked because of some such concrete value-character; and, I believe, the experience of the work must somehow have intrinsic perceptual worth if it is properly to be called *esthetic*. But no other limitation can be put upon the content of works of art. Not all arts, of course, have the same scope, and it takes all in combination to include, even potentially, every kind of value-content.

Some artists and estheticians agree with Tolstoy and Véron that ugliness may be legitimately introduced into the work of art, not merely as a foil to beauty but also for the sake of its own independent expressiveness. Others agree with Croce that artistic beauty is simply success in art, or in other words, that the beautiful in art is the completely expressive and the ugly is the inexpressive. Croce's theory would not be seriously transformed if every mention of beauty and ugliness in his pages were deleted: the concepts of expressiveness and inexpressiveness would suffice. Most contemporary artists seem to agree with either Croce or Véron and Tolstoy. Works of art, in the modern mode, have a vast range: They embrace whatever is spiritually expressive, even if the expressiveness is achieved by cacophony in poetry, discords in music, harshness in painting, or unsparing realism in literature.

A work of art, whatever its content, is an organic unity—a concrete structure in which the character of the whole influences the *intrinsic* character of the parts. Every chord in a musical composition, every patch of color in a painting, every sound or image in a poem, attains its meaning and value in its *context*: It is infected through and through by its relations to the other elements and to the whole. This implies that the distinction between form and content is relative; the content is the elements in relation, the form is the relation among the elements, and the total work is both in irrefragable unity. One of the considerable merits of A. C. Bradley's fine essay, "Poetry for Poetry's Sake" (Chapter 8), is that it vividly describes the work of art in terms of such organic unity.

One of the lively controversies in recent esthetics is concerned with whether art makes "truth claims" and therefore commands belief. The theory that art is the expression of values provides a basis for answering this question. If by "truth" one means *description*, the positivists are right in maintaining that it falls within the realm of science and not of art.

The statement, "The sky is blue," is true in a descriptive sense if it is objectively the case for all qualified observers. But such a truth is quite different from the sentiment expressed in an old hobo song:

> O, why don't you work like other men do?
> How the hell can I work when the sky's so blue?

The *blue* referred to in this song is esthetic, not scientific. It is a value—it has feeling-tone; it is *not* "neutral" for all observers. It is the kind of blue that makes the heart leap up and kick over the traces. Before "blue," as a concept, can become a descriptive term, it must be disinfected of such subjective coloration. Drawn into the sphere of verifiable fact, it has only those features that all can equally acknowledge. These tend to be quantitative because quantities have a publicly verifiable character. Hence, for exact scientific purposes, "blue" becomes associated with a certain wavelength and frequency. It is scientifically true that an object is blue if it radiates waves of this type. At this level of abstraction, "blue" has lost artistic expressiveness; and, of course, art has nothing to do with "truth" so conceived.

But if by "truth" we mean a value socially communicable, a work of art does indeed contain truths. The "truth" crudely expressed in the hobo song is also social: It has been felt by many hoboes; it appeals to the hobo in all of us. Such a truth can be expressed in a song, a poem, or possibly in a painting. Wordsworth's great sonnet "The world is too much with us" expresses a comparable mood. Such a work of art has a poignancy, a warmth, a vividness, a specificity that withers in a scientific description.

It seems to me that the so-called truths of art can always be so analyzed. They are not abstract formulations; they are concrete evaluations—and consequently no merely prosaic and summary statement can do justice to them. We can say, for example, that Tolstoy's *War and Peace* expresses the deterministic interpretation of history that is abstractly formulated in the appendix to his novel. But surely no one imagines that this appendix, or any similar abstract formulation, can possibly convey the rich, concrete, warmhearted truth of Tolstoy's story. That truth can be expressed only by the intense *appreciative* visions that the novel itself kindles within the reader's imagination. Whereas scientific truth can usually be translated into quite different language, artistic "truth" cannot thus be translated. In art, as I have already said, *what* is expressed is inseparable from *how* it is expressed.

Noting that a work of art is highly individual and that artists shun mere abstract thought, Benedetto Croce defined art as the knowing of particulars, or intuition, as distinguished from the knowing of universals, or conception. A particular, he supposed, was a unique quality apprehended by an individual mind. His emphasis upon the imaginative inwardness and singularity of art makes it difficult to explain the sharability of the esthetic vision. He failed to note, or at least to emphasize, that qualities may be ever so individualized and still be repeated. The high-fidelity recording of a musical masterpiece by a superb orchestra is a very particularized and unique creation, but it may be issued in thousands of identical copies. Even when the record is played, and the music comes to life in the feeling and imagination of the auditor, its qualities may be essentially the same as in the experience of another listener. In Keats' great *Ode*, the song of the nightingale, which symbolizes the work of art, is no abstract universal; yet it remains the same in the most varied times and places:

> Thou wast not born for death, immortal Bird!
> No hungry generations tread thee down;
> The voice I hear this passing night was heard
> In ancient days by emperor and clown:
> Perhaps the self-same song that found a path
> Through the sad heart of Ruth, when, sick for home,
> She stood in tears amid the alien corn;
> The same that oft-times hath
> Charm'd magic casements, opening on the foam
> Of perilous seas, in faery lands forlorn.[16]

The work of art, like the nightingale's song, is vivid and emotionally toned, but it is as communicable as the most abstract scientific description. When two sensitive beholders contemplate the same work of art, their experiences may not be identical, but they are surely quite similar. The contagiousness of art—its capacity to create a community of appreciation—can be explained upon no other assumption. Art thus involves, even in its uniqueness, a social element: The work of art conveys a *repeatable* particularity.

There is another side to art, the generic, that Croce, with his intuitional theory, tended to deny. Art is both specific and general, intuitional and intellectual; it involves both creative imagination and cognitive insight. What distinguishes an artist from an ordinary person is very largely his ability to imagine some new concrete variation of the old abstract theme. About two-thirds of the poems in the *Oxford Book of English Verse*, for example, deal with love or death, but each one is a unique creation.

The artist *knows*—he does not merely feel—but he knows by sympathetic identification and imaginative insight. He knows as the perspicacious lover knows about the nature of love, by "proving it upon his pulses." He knows by feeling at one with the object, as Keats felt at one with the sparrow. He knows the reality that he suffers when the outer object is drawn into his own being, into the mysterious depths of subjectivity. He knows not bare facts or abstract laws but vivid values—he knows things appreciatively, in their immediacy and concreteness. He knows with the totality of his mind and body: with sense, mood, instinct, and intelligence, both conscious and subconscious. He knows by descending to the roots of being, which no abstract idea can encompass—to the obscure spring of man's creative intuition—the source alike of dreams and of art.

There, in the deep recesses of his mind, he is in touch with the instinctively common part of man's nature—with the values that are not peculiar to him as an artist nor to one man or a few, but are basic in

the emotional experiences and secret longings of most human beings. If it
were not so, art could not serve as the language of all humanity—a way
of communicating across all the barriers of time and place. The cave
paintings by men of the reindeer age—the paintings at Lascaux and
Altamira—would not speak so eloquently to us today; nor would the art of
the whole world be a "museum without walls," where any man can find
incomparable treasures. The work of all ages and countries—Gothic
counterpoint, Egyptian sculpture, Chinese landscape, Mayan temple,
Russian ballet, English drama, and American novel—bear alike
the spiritual imprint of humanity. In the realm of art, far more than in
morals, politics, or religion, the whole world is kin.

The positivistic account of valuation as mere subjective attitude is
fraught with insuperable difficulties. One may be truly objective in
apprehending values, and an artist sometimes expresses in his work not
what he subjectively likes or dislikes but what he actually finds to be
characteristic of the spiritual nature of life. (If some of my readers refuse
to call this "truth," I shall not quarrel with them. In many works of art
there is a kind of value-significance that is faithful to the nature of
human existence—call it whatever you will.) A work of art may, in this
sense, be as severely subordinated to reality-thinking as a scientific treatise.
The tendency of Freud to conceive of art as evasion has only a limited
validity. At the same time, the appropriate response to a work of art is
not belief in abstract factual propositions, but rather a kind of imaginative
enactment of value-experience. The imagination must have free play,
which ordinary literal belief does not permit. In creating or appreciating
art—to again quote Keats—the capacity that we need is the "quality
. . . which Shakespeare possessed so enormously—I mean *Negative
Capability*, that is, when a man is capable of being in uncertainties,
mysteries, doubts without any irritable reaching after fact and reason."[17]
Only with this freedom of the imagination can the values expressed in
works of art be realized in their immediacy and vividness.

VI. THE RESPONSE TO THE WORK OF ART

If we turn from the work of art to the audience, we can distinguish
between a contemplative and a critical aspect in the audience's reaction.
Esthetic contemplation, which is described in the present volume in such
terms as "psychical distance," "empathy," and "abstraction," can be
more simply characterized as receptivity to the values expressed by,
or embodied in, the esthetic object. It is, so to speak, a "listening" or
"looking" or "tasting" with our capacity for value-appreciation. The values
are what are to be "tasted" and rolled on one's appreciative "tongue";
and the attitudes of distance, empathy, abstraction, engagement, and
so forth are the means of tasting and savoring the values. Of course
"tasting" is a metaphor, but it suggests the nature of contemplation—the
throwing open of oneself to esthetic values as intrinsically interesting,
the development of keenness and breadth of appreciation.

A fundamental issue in Part III is to be found in the contrast
between the writers who emphasize isolation and *high* distance, and the

writers who emphasize context and *low* distance. This cleavage between
the isolationists and the contextualists appears also in other Parts of
our anthology. Roughly on the side of isolationism are Croce (Chapter 3)
and his fencing off of art from other activities, Worringer (Chapter 10)
and his abstraction from the fleeting and accidental phenomena of organic
life, Kemp (Chapter 11) and his attack on the "intentional fallacy,"
and Bell (Chapter 8) and his exclusive formalism. Typical of isolationism
is Bell's statement that "to create and appreciate the greatest art the most
absolute abstraction from the affairs of life is essential."[18] Aligned on
the other side are such thinkers as Tolstoy (Chapter 2), Dewey (Chapter
5), Goldmann (Chapter 11), and Mumford (Chapter 12), who
emphasize the continuity between esthetic and nonesthetic values and
between art and life rather than their separation.

The isolationist type of theory stresses the uniqueness and immediacy
of "pure" esthetic experience. If we concentrate solely upon this
component, our senses and concrete imagery *do* fence us off from the
world. Insofar as the artist is exclusively absorbed in this phase of art, he
concerns himself not with "the why, the whence, or the whither" of
things, nor with their discursive import or ulterior connections, but
with "the what" as he immediately apprehends them. The experience out
of which a work of art springs stirs the mind because of no merely
ulterior reason, nor because it is the sign or correlate of something absent,
but because it is intrinsically moving. The work of art, as the embodiment
of such experience, is likewise exciting in its own right, and therefore
the beholding of it involves an absorption in certain values as immediately
present to sense and imagination.

Recently the concept of esthetic distance has been sharply criticized by
George Dickie and other estheticians. Even John Hospers (Chapter 10),
in his judicious account of the esthetic attitude, remarked that Bullough's
discussion of "psychical distance" (Chapter 10) is so full of ambiguities
as to "render the use of the term 'distance' more confusing than helpful."
Although these ambiguities need to be eliminated and the word
"distance" clarified, I should not like to see the term discarded. "It is hard
to see in perspective and comprehend what is very close to us," Walter
Kaufmann has written. "Comprehension requires some distance," and
"emotional involvement may blind us."[19] Not the original emotion but the
"emotion recollected in tranquillity" is expressed by the artist, and a
similar measure of detachment is required of the contemplator. There
must be a forcing back of the raw material of art, its removal to a
distance, so that it no longer impinges too violently on the beholder or
tempts him to become practically, rather than contemplatively, involved in
it. In the phrasing of Nietzsche, the Dionysian strain in art needs to be
moderated and transfigured by an infusion of the Apollinian.

Although there is an important measure of truth in theories of distance
and isolation, we may question whether it is the whole truth. The
conception of art as the expression or appreciation of values lends
support to the contextualist view that art is broadly human. Life, in
its very essence, is the experience of values; and hence art, which alone
can express values concretely, is terribly relevant to life, and is limited

in its scope and depth only by its autonomous nature and by the bounds of human life and human genius. Art not only expresses but also creates values; for, as Nietzsche truly declares: "Valuing is creating: hear it, ye creating ones! Valuation itself is the treasure and jewel of the valued things."[20] Art is thus fundamental to the whole enterprise of living as a means of expression, creation, and appreciation. Art is art, and not morality, religion, technology, or social reform; but neither is it an anodyne or a piddling luxury or an esoteric escape from life. Whether we are speaking of the artist or the contemplator, we should try to reconcile the truth in the isolationist type of theory with the truth in the contextualist type. One of the merits of Bullough's essay and of Kenneth Clark's discussion (Chapter 10) of the nude is that they seek a balance between participation and detachment, low and high distances.

The *critical* aspect of esthetic experience consists of *judgment* of the *worth* of the esthetic object. Judgment implies some standard of appraisal, and in Chapter 11 we find various standards proposed: the degree of realism (Goldmann), the uniqueness and originality (Boas), the combination of surprise and expectation (Greenberg), the internal coherence or formal perfection (Greenberg and Beardsley), and the vividness of quality (Pepper). But the basic criterion of art is the richness and the fineness of the value-appreciation that it yields. I am using the word "appreciation" not in the superficial sense of amusement or entertainment, but in the deeper sense, so eloquently stated by Dewey, of a memorable and satisfying experience. We must remember that the worth of any great work of art is not something that can be grasped in a moment. To appreciate and judge an excellent painting, for example, we must do much more than glance at it in a gallery. Ordinarily, we must *live* with it until its sensuous qualities, meanings, and forms sink deep into our conscious and subconscious mind. If then, day after day, it works its magic upon us—if its appeal is deep and varied enough to be lasting—we can realize its excellence because our lives are being substantially enriched. The expert critic is one who can sense this amplitude and fineness of value more quickly and surely than the ordinary man.

One of the persistent questions in esthetics is whether there are any valid general standards of judgment. Boas, with his defense of uniqueness, tends toward a relativistic or pluralist point of view, whereas Beardsley (Chapter 11) counters with a defense of the generality of critical reasons. The question is especially acute in the evaluation of avant-garde art, and in this area the essay by Clement Greenberg (Chapter 11), who sees beyond the novelties of the moment to the deeper meaning of originality, is a model of sanity and critical acumen.

It should not be overlooked that contemplation and criticism, as Dewey points out, are necessary aspects of the artist's activity and not merely of the public's reaction to his works. No artist can create without appreciating the values that he wishes to express; without contemplating the expressive medium, elements, and forms; and without criticizing the work as it takes shape under his hand. The artist himself is a beholder and judge, and the fineness of his art depends largely upon the quality of his appreciation and judgment. The work of art, on the other hand, comes alive only in imagination, and hence the public must share something of the creative capacity of the artist. There is no absolute distinction between creation and contemplation, between artist and beholder.

The whole community as well as the individual experiences and judges art. The public response is often unsympathetic, and the artist or lover of the arts tends to feel estranged. In a predominantly technological and commercial civilization, the mass of people is preoccupied with getting and spending. A "high standard of living"—the goal of almost everybody—has come to mean greater material comfort rather than spiritual enrichment. Even the scientists and technicians, who have so largely created the texture and set the tone of modern life, are much more concerned with their factual and technical problems than with imaginative or spiritual values. The objectives of the artist are in sharp contrast to the main preoccupations of modern man: The artist is bent upon creativeness rather than acquisitiveness; original design rather than standardized and quantitative production; imaginative freedom and human breadth rather than specialization; cultivation of the sensuous and instinctive elements of the personality rather than narrow rationality; the search for a common spiritual center rather than competitive individualism; the principle of form, harmony, and inner coherence rather than the chaotic rush, din, and overstimulation of urban living. Consequently, the works of artists have seemed to have nothing to do with everyday problems. Those artists who put themselves, either as commercial designers or as purveyors of luxury and amusement, at the disposal of organized business are considered good enough to spark sales or wile away leisure hours, but stubbornly independent artists appear to the practical men of affairs little better than fools or idle dreamers.

In Chapter 12, this "practical" reaction to the arts is sharply challenged. Schiller, Marx, Raphael, Mumford, and McHarg, each in his own way, contend that art is not a delicate speciality on the margin of life but a necessity at its very center. They foreshadow that profound transvaluation and radical reconstruction of life which is now the very mandate for human survival. Whether or not one agrees with their daring proposals, they are the harbingers of a great change and efflorescence.

VII. Conclusion

In this Introduction, I have tried to do justice to the diverse standpoints represented in this anthology, while sketching an inclusive and coherent theory of art. It has been one of my contentions that the main diversities and oppositions in esthetic theory find their synthesis in the concept of value-expressive form. There are many important problems that I have not mentioned, but I have suggested some basis for the reconciliation of doctrines that might appear contradictory.

This attempt to resolve conflicts in theory seems to me peculiarly appropriate to esthetics, for art itself is the great reconciler of those opposites in our practical life which ordinarily exclude each other. More than any other form of human experience, art combines such contrasting moments as variety and unity, familiarity and strangeness, repose and stimulation, order and spontaneity, distance and engagement, the Apollinian and Dionysian moods. In great tragedy, for example, the intensification of emotions, far from excluding a sense of repose, produces the dynamic calmness that Aristotle termed "catharsis." Likewise, as Freud and Caudwell (Chapter 4) point out, art involves the harmonious co-working of the conscious and the subconscious: The dream is inserted into the texture of waking life; the "ir-real" and the real are fused. Or, as Schiller (Chapter 12) indicates, art is the reconciliation of law and impulse: The form, the pattern, the "lawfulness" of the experience becomes the expression, not the repression or impulse. Or, as Lipps and Lee (Chapter 10) observe, the images of esthetic experience are seemingly objective and yet are colored by the emotion and sensibility of the beholder: The duality of subject and object disappears: the work of art is, in a sense, myself, and I am the object, since I project myself into it. Or, as Aristotle and Maritain (Chapter 1) say, the universal essence merges into the specific image; the more seamless is the unity, the more perfect is the esthetic moment.

Because art, in combining such opposites, is more inclusive than other modes of experience, Schiller, in his *Letters on the Aesthetic Education of Man*, is justified in his contention that it makes man whole and that man is only whole when he engages in such activity. Likewise, John Dewey (Chapter 5) is right when he declares: "Art is the living and concrete proof that man is capable of restoring consciously, and thus on the plane of meaning, the union of sense, need, impulse, and action characteristic of the live creature."[21]

Art was once at the very center of life's text, but in our scientific and technological age, it tends to be shoved into the margin. No one questions it as a diversion or amusement, but some of us are not satisfied with this conception. We feel that art has a vital function that should be taken seriously in our schools, from the primary level to the university, and even in our city councils and legislative chambers.

Notes

1. Refer to *Philosophy of the Arts* (Harvard University Press, Cambridge, 1950), p. 2.

2. Alan Tormey, *The Concept of Expression* (Princeton University Press, 1971), p. 97.

3. Carroll C. Pratt, "Design of Music," *Journal of Aesthetics and Art Criticism*, Vol. 12 (1954), p. 296.

4. *Republic* (translated by Benjamin Jowett), X, #599. Plato used "artist" in a sense wide enough to include the philosopher-king.

5. Translated by E. F. Carritt, *Philosophies of Beauty* (Oxford University Press, New York, 1931), p. 34.

6. *The Twilight of the Idols* (Macmillan, New York, 1924), p. 79.

7. Bertram Jessup and Melvin Rader, *Art and Human Values* (Appleton-Century-Crofts, New York, 1973), chap. 4. This book is a study of art as value-expressive and of the relation between esthetic and other basic values of life.

8. *The Proficience and Advancement of Learning*, 1605, II, xiii.

9. *The Poems of Emily Dickinson* (Little, Brown, Boston, 1932), p. 289.

10. Gregory Vlastos, "The Religious Foundations of Democracy, Fraternity, and Equality," *Journal of Religion*, Vol. 22 (1942), pp. 152–153.

11. Josiah Royce, *The Spirit of Modern Philosophy* (Houghton Mifflin, Boston, 1892), p. 389.

12. Irving Stone, *Dear Theo: The Autobiography of Vincent Van Gogh* (Houghton Mifflin, Boston, 1937), p. 441.

13. Quoted by Walter de la Mare, *Love* (Morrow, New York, 1946), p. 11.

14. Letter to Benjamin Bailey, Nov. 22, 1817.

15. Letter to Richard Woodhouse, Oct. 27, 1818.

16. In my comment on this passage, I am indebted to Andrew Paul Ushenko, *Dynamics of Art* (Indiana University Press, Bloomington, 1953), pp. 158–159.

17. Letter to George and Thomas Keats, Dec. 21, 1817.

18. *Art* (Frederick A. Stokes Co. [Lippincott], Philadelphia, 1914), p. 266.

19. Walter Kaufmann, Introductory Essay to Richard Schacht, *Alienation* (Doubleday, New York, 1970), p. xxv.

20. *Thus Spake Zarathustra* (Macmillan, New York, 1909), p. 74.

21. *Art as Experience* (Minton, Balch & Co., New York, 1934), p. 25.

PART
I
The
Creative
Process

———————

CHAPTER

1

Imitation
and Imagination

JACQUES MARITAIN: Beauty and Imitation
E. H. GOMBRICH: Truth and the Stereotype

One of the perennial themes of esthetic theory is the relation of art to nature. In the history of Western thought, the two most influential treatments of this theme are the theory of "imitation," enunciated by Plato and Aristotle, and the theory of "imagination," formulated by Coleridge and other romanticists. The theory of imitation emphasizes the cognitive and realistic elements in art; the theory of imagination stresses the emotional and purely imaginative factors. These contrasting points of view are synthesized in the interpretations set forth in this chapter. The work of art is conceived as both imitative and imaginative—a convincing semblance that the imagination creates from the data of perception.

The question of the relation of art to nature is basic in the scholastic tradition—the tradition of Aristotle, Saint Thomas Aquinas, and modern Catholic philosophers. Jacques Maritain (1882–   ), the famous French neo-scholastic philosopher, has written in this current of thought, but he has also drawn upon a wide knowledge of art and artists. His friendships with painters, musicians, and writers include a close association with Rouault, who has greatly inspired and influenced him. He has also learned much from his wife Raïssa, the poet.

His crowning achievement in esthetics is *Creative Intuition in Art and Poetry,* which grew out of his six A. W. Mellon Lectures in the Fine Arts, given at the National Gallery of Art in Washington in the spring of 1952. But I have chosen a selection from his earlier work, *Art and Scholasticism,* because it tersely sets forth his fundamental ideas and his relation to Saint Thomas and Aristotle.

Maritain classifies human activities as follows:

1. *Pure Knowing* (corresponding to Aristotle's theoretical sciences—metaphysics, mathematics, and physics).
2. *Action,* or doing as distinct from knowing.
    (a) *Practice* (corresponding to Aristotle's practical sciences—politics, ethics, economics).

(b) *Making*, or *Art* in the wide sense (corresponding to Aristotle's
    productive sciences—poetics, rhetoric, technology in general).
    (1) *Craftsmanship*, or the making of *useful* things—for
    example, shoemaking, tailoring, carpentry.
    (2) *Fine Art*, or the making of *beautiful* things—for
    example, painting, poetry, music.

As distinguished from pure knowing, art is not to be confused with
science or philosophy, or even with the "intuition" of Croce and Bergson
(that is, the knowing of what is individual). As distinguished from
practice, art is directed toward the making of some artifact. *Fine* art is
closely related to craftsmanship, but it is distinguished by the nature of
its function—to make *beautiful* rather than useful things.

Accepting the definition of Saint Thomas, Maritain maintains that
beauty is desired, but the desire is appeased on sight, for beauty is what
pleases in the mere contemplation. The basis of the enjoyment is not
wholly in the mind or wholly in the object, but in a correspondence
between the two. The object is fitted, as it were, to be joyfully received by
the senses and the intellect; what is intelligible in the object is appreciated
by what is intelligent in the subject. Hence, as Santayana says, beauty
is the result of a "conformity between the soul and nature," and thus is
a sign of "the supremacy of the good."[1]

The main constituent of beauty is "form," which is not bare abstract
design, but a revelation of the specific principle of the thing contemplated
(as when the basic meaning of death seems to be revealed in a tragedy).
The form may be the essence of a type or species, or of an individual,
or of a particular attitude or quality; but in any event it is, in art, a concrete
presentment, a vision, appealing simultaneously to the senses and the
intelligence. The goal of art is thus delightful meaning that shines out
in the unity and design of the sensible constituents. To embody such
meaning, the work of art must exhibit clarity, integrity, and right
proportion.

With its emphasis on order and intelligibility, this theory is akin to
Aristotle's theory of imitation. Maritain explains that art imitates the *forms*
of things, but its function is to delight by making something beautiful
and not to copy servilely. He conceives the work of art as simultaneously
imitative and imaginative—a more-or-less abstract image that reflects the
nature of things and delights in doing so. In this way he extends and
deepens the meaning of representation to cover the ancient spiritual
interpretation of reality and the practices of modern artists.

Without Maritain's background in scholastic philosophy, Ernst H.
Gombrich (1909–   ), formerly Professor of Fine Art at both Oxford and
Cambridge and now Director of the Warburg Institute and Professor
at the University of London, has written a profound study of the role of
representation and illusion in art. The selection from his influential
book, *Art and Illusion*, maintains that there is no "innocent eye" which
perceives the world in its bare actuality. The cultural tradition,
embodied in the artistic style of each historical period, acts as a selective
screen that admits only those features which the prevailing mental set

is prepared to recognize. Hence, the artist tends "to see what he paints rather than to paint what he sees," and we who behold the picture see what the painter has taught us to see. Imagination and imitation are intertwined; the objectification of spirit and the subjectification of nature are two parts of the same creative process.

NOTE

1. George Santayana, *The Sense of Beauty* (Scribner's, New York, 1896), p. 270.

JACQUES MARITAIN

Beauty and Imitation

Editor's Note: To assist the reader in understanding Maritain's discussion, I am prefacing it by the following selections from St. Thomas Aquinas (The *"Summa Theologica"*):

§ 1

Beauty and goodness in a thing are identical fundamentally; for they are based upon the same thing, namely, the form, and consequently goodness is praised as beauty. But they differ logically, for goodness properly relates to the appetite (goodness being what all things desire); and therefore it has the aspect of an end (the appetite being a kind of movement towards a thing). On the other hand, beauty relates to the cognitive faculty; for beautiful things are those which please when seen. Hence beauty consists in due proportion; for the senses delight in things duly proportioned, as in what is after their own kind—because even sense is a sort of reason, just as is every cognitive faculty. Now, since knowledge is by assimilation,[1] and similarity relates to form, beauty properly belongs to the nature of a formal cause.[2] (Part I, question 5, article 4.)

§ 2

For beauty includes three conditions, *integrity* or *perfection*, since those things which are impaired are by the very fact ugly; due *proportion* or *harmony*; and lastly *brightness*, or *clarity*, whence things are called beautiful which have a bright color. . . .

An image is said to be beautiful if it perfectly represents even an ugly thing. (Part I, question 39, article 8.)

§ 3

The beautiful is the same as the good, and they differ in aspect only. For since good is what all seek, the notion of good is that which calms the desire; while the notion of the beautiful is that which calms the desire, by being seen or known. Consequently those senses chiefly regard the beautiful, which are the most cognitive, viz., sight and hearing, as ministering to reason; for we speak of beautiful sights and beautiful sounds. But in reference to the other objects of the other senses, we do not use the expression *beautiful,* for we do not speak of beautiful tastes, and beautiful odors. Thus it is evident that beauty adds to goodness a relation to the cognitive faculty; so that *good* means that which simply pleases the appetite; while the beautiful is something pleasant to apprehend. (Part II, [First Part], question 27, article 1.)

I. ART AND BEAUTY[3]

1. St. Thomas, who was as simple as he was wise, defined the beautiful as what gives pleasure on sight, *id quod visum placet.* The four words say all that is necessary: a vision, that is to say an *intuitive knowledge,* and a *joy.* The beautiful is what gives joy, not all joy, but joy in knowledge; not the joy peculiar to the act of knowing, but a joy superabounding and over-flowing from such an act because of the object known. If a thing exalts and delights the soul by the bare fact of its being given to the intuition of the soul, it is good to apprehend, it is beautiful.

Beauty is essentially the object of *intelligence,* for what *knows* in the full meaning of the word is the mind, which alone is open to the infinity of being. The natural site of beauty is the intelligible world: thence it descends. But it also falls in a way within the grasp of the senses, since the senses in the case of man serve the mind and can themselves rejoice in knowing: "the beautiful relates only to sight and hearing of all the senses, because these two are *maxime cognoscitive.*"[4] The part played by the senses in the perception of beauty becomes in our case enormous and well-nigh indispensable, because our mind is not intuitive like the angelic mind: it can perceive, no doubt, but only on condition of abstracting and discoursing. In man only knowledge derived through the senses possesses fully the intuivity necessary for the perception of the beautiful. So also man can certainly enjoy purely intelligible beauty, but the beautiful which is *connatural* to man is that which comes to delight the mind through the senses and their intuition. Such also is the peculiar beauty of our art, which works upon a sensible matter for the joy of the spirit. It would fain so persuade itself that paradise is not lost. It has the savor of the terrestrial paradise, because it restores for a brief moment the simultaneous peace and delight of the mind and the senses.

If beauty delights the mind, it is because beauty is essentially a certain excellence or perfection in the proportion of things to the mind. Hence the three conditions assigned to it by St. Thomas: integrity, because the mind likes being; proportion, because the mind likes order and likes unity; lastly and above all brightness or clarity, because the mind likes light and intelligibility. A certain splendor is indeed according to all the Ancients the essential character of beauty—*claritas est de ratione pulchritudinis,*[5] *lux pulchrificat, quia sine luce omnia sunt turpia,*[6]—but it is a splendor of intelligibility: *splendor veri,*[7] said the Platonists, *splendor ordinis,*[8] said St. Augustine, adding that "unity is the form of all beauty"[9]; *splendor formæ,*[10] said St. Thomas with a metaphysician's precision of language: for *form*, that is to say the principle determining the peculiar perfection of everything which is, constituting and completing things in their essence and their qualities, the ontological secret, so to speak, of their innermost being, their spiritual essence, their operative mystery, is above all the peculiar principle of intelligibility, the peculiar *clarity* of every thing. Every form, moreover, is a remnant or a ray of the creative Mind impressed upon the heart of the being created. All order and proportion, on the other hand, are the work of the mind. So, to say with the Schoolmen that beauty is the *splendor of form shining on the proportioned parts of matter*[11] is to say that it is a lightning of mind on a matter intelligently arranged. The mind rejoices in the beautiful because in the beautiful it finds itself again: recognizes itself, and comes into contact with its very own light. This is so true that they especially perceive and particularly relish the beauty of things who, like St. Francis of Assisi, for example, know that they emanate from a mind and refer them to their Author.

Every sensible beauty, no doubt, implies a certain delight of the eye or the ear or the imagination: but there can be no beauty unless the mind also is in some way rejoiced. A beautiful color "washes the eye" as a powerful scent dilates the nostrils: but of these two "forms" or qualities only color is called "beautiful," because being received, as opposed to the perfume, in a sense capable of disinterested knowledge, it can be, even through its purely sensible brilliance, an object of joy to the mind. Again, the more highly developed a man's culture becomes, the more spiritual grows the brilliance of the form which ravishes him.

It is important, however, to observe that in the beauty which has been termed connatural to man and is peculiar to human art this brilliance of form, however purely intelligible it may be in itself, is apprehended *in the sensible and by the sensible*, and not separately from it. The intuition of artistic beauty so stands at the opposite pole from the abstraction of scientific truth. For in the former case it is precisely through the apprehension of sense that the light of being penetrates to the mind.

The mind then, spared the least effort of abstraction, rejoices without labor and without discussion. It is excused its customary task, it has not to extricate something intelligible from the matter in which it is buried and then step by step go through its various attributes; like the stag at the spring of running water, it has nothing to do but drink, and it drinks the clarity of being. Firmly fixed in the intuition of sense, it is irradiated by an intelligible light granted to it of a sudden in the very sensible in which it glitters; and it apprehends this light not *sub ratione veri*, but rather *sub ratione delectabilis,*[12] by the happy exercise it procures for it and the succeeding joy in appetite, which leaps out to every good of the soul as its own peculiar object. Only afterwards will it more or less successfully analyze in reflection the causes of such joy.[13]

So, although the beautiful is in close dependence upon what is metaphysically true, in the sense that every splendor of intelligibility in things presupposes some degree of conformity with that Intelligence which is the cause of things, the beautiful nevertheless is not a kind of truth, but a kind of good. The perception of the beautiful is related to knowledge, but by way of addition, "as its bloom is an addition to youth"; it is not so much a kind of knowledge as a kind of delight.

The beautiful is essentially delightful. Therefore by its very nature, by its very beauty, it stirs desire and produces love, whereas truth as such only illuminates. "*Omnibus igitur est pulchrum et bonum desiderabile et amabile et diligibile. . . .*"[14]

2. The speculations of the Ancients concerning the nature of the beautiful must be taken in the most formal sense and their thought should not be materialized in any too narrow specification. The idea of *integrity* or perfection or complete execution can be realized not in one way only but in a thousand or ten thousand different ways. The lack of a head or an arm is a considerable defect in a woman but of much less account in a statue—whatever disappointment M. Ravaisson may have felt at being unable to *complete* the Venus of Melos. The slightest sketch of Leonardo's or even Rodin's is nearer to perfection than the most finished Bouguereau. And if it pleases a futurist to paint a lady with only one eye, or a quarter of an eye, nobody denies him such a right; all one is entitled to require— and here is the whole problem—is that the quarter eye is all the lady needs *in the given case.*

It is the same with proportion, fitness, and harmony. They differ with the object and the end aimed at. Proportions good in a man are not good in a child. Figures constructed according to the Greek or the Egyptian canon are perfectly proportioned in their kind: but Rouault's yokels are also as perfectly proportioned in their kind. Integrity and proportion have no absolute significance and must be understood solely *in relation* to the end of the work, which is to make a form shine on the matter.

Last and most important: this very brilliance of form, the essence of beauty, shines on matter in an infinite variety of ways.[15]

At one time it is the sensible brilliance of color or tone, at another the intelligible clarity of an arabesque, a rhythm or an harmonious balance, an activity or a movement, or again the reflection upon things of some human or divine thought, but above all it is the profound splendor of the soul shining through, of the soul which is the principle of life and animal energy or the principle of spiritual life, of pain and passion. There is also a more exalted splendor, the splendor of Grace, which the Greeks never knew.

II. Imitation in Art

Art, as such, consists not in imitating but in making, in composing or constructing, and that according to the laws of the very thing to be placed in being (ship, house, carpet, colored canvas, or hewn block of stone). This requisite of its generic concept preponderates over everything else in it, and to allot to it for essential end the representation of the real is to destroy it. Plato, with his theory of various degrees of imitation and poetry as an illusion, misconceives, like all extravagant intellectualists, the peculiar nature of art; hence his contempt for poetry. It is clear that if art were a *means of knowledge,* it would be wildly inferior to geometry.

But if art, as such, is far removed from imitation, the Fine Arts, as ordered to Beauty, are related to imitation, in a way difficult enough to define.

"Imitation is natural to mankind from childhood . . ., man is the most imitative of animals; through imitation he acquires his first knowledge and from imitations everyone derives pleasure. Works of art prove this, for the very things it gives us pain to see, we enjoy looking at in exact reproductions, the forms, for example, of the most horrible beasts, and corpses. The reason is that to be learning something is the pleasantest thing in the world not only to philosophers but to the rest of men. . . ."[16] When Aristotle wrote this with reference to the first causes of poetry, he was propounding a specific condition imposed upon the Fine Arts, a condition grasped in their earliest origin. But Aristotle is to be understood here in the most *formal* way. If the Philosopher, pursuing his usual method, goes straight to the primitive elementary case, it would be a complete mistake to stop there and to restrict the word "imitation" to its popularly accepted meaning of *exact reproduction or representation of a given reality.* When the man of the reindeer age scrawled the shapes of animals on the walls of caves he was no doubt principally moved by the pleasure of reproducing something exactly.[17] But the *joy of imitation* has since then become remarkably purified. I will try to sharpen the point of this idea of imitation in art.

The Fine Arts aim at producing, by the object they make, joy or delight in the mind through the intuition of the senses: the object of painting, said Poussin, is delight. Such joy is not the joy of the simple act of knowing, the joy of possessing knowledge, of having truth. It is a joy overflowing from such an act, when the object upon which it is brought to bear is well proportioned to the mind.

Such joy, therefore, presupposes knowledge, and the more knowledge there is, the more things given to the mind, the greater will be the possibility of joy. For this reason art, as ordered to beauty, never stops—at all events when its object permits it—at shapes or colors, or at sounds or words, considered in themselves and *as things* (they must be so considered to begin with, that is the first condition), but considers them *also* as making known something other than themselves, that is to say *as symbols.* And the thing symbolized can be in turn a symbol, and the more charged with symbolism the work of art (but spontaneous symbolism intuitively apprehended, not hieroglyphic symbolism), the more immense, the richer and the higher will be the possibility of joy and beauty. The beauty of a picture or a statue is thus incomparably richer than the beauty of a carpet, a Venetian glass, or an amphora.

In this sense, painting, sculpture, poetry, music, even dancing, are imitative arts, that is to say arts realizing the beauty of the work and procuring the joy of the soul by the use of imitation or by producing through the medium of certain sensible symbols the spontaneous presence in the mind of something over and above such symbols. Painting *imitates* with colors and plane forms given things outside us, music *imitates* with sound and rhythms—and dancing with rhythm alone, "the character and temperament," in Aristotle's phrase,[18] of the personages represented, and the movements of the soul, the invisible world stirring within us. Making allowance for such a difference in regard to the object symbolized, painting is no more imitative than music, and music no less imitative than painting, if "imitation" be understood exactly in the sense just defined.

But the joy procured by the beautiful does not consist formally in the act of knowing reality or in the act of conformity with what is; it does not depend upon the perfection of the imitation as a reproduction of the real, or the fidelity of the representation. Imitation as reproduction or representation of the real—in other words, imitation *materially considered*—is merely a means, not an end; it relates, along with manual dexterity, to the artistic activity, but no more constitutes it. And the things made present to the soul by the sensible symbols of art—by rhythm, sound, line, color, form, volume, words, meter, rhyme and image, the *proximate matter* of art—are themselves merely a material element of the beauty of the work, just like the symbols in question; they are the *remote matter*, so to speak, at the disposal of the artist, on which he must make the brilliance of a form, the light of being, shine. To set up the perfection of imitation materially considered as an end would therefore involve ordering oneself with a view to what is purely material in the work of art; a servile imitation absolutely foreign to art.[19]

What is required is not that the representation shall conform exactly to a given reality, but that through the material elements of the beauty of the work there shall be transmitted, sovereign and entire, the brilliance of a form—of a form, and therefore of *some truth*; in that sense the great phrase of the Platonists, *splendor veri*, abides for ever. But if the joy produced by a work of beauty proceeds from *some truth*, it does not proceed from the truth of *imitation as a reproduction of things*, it proceeds from the perfection with which the work expresses or manifests form, in the metaphysical sense of the word, it proceeds from the truth *of imitation as manifestation of a form*. There is the *formal element* of imitation in art, the expression or manifestation, in a suitably proportioned work, of some secret principle of intelligibility shining forth. There the *joy of imitation* in art is brought to bear. And it is that which gives art its *universal* value. . . .

. . . If "imitation" were to be understood as meaning *exact reproduction or copy of reality*,[20] it would have to be admitted that, apart from the art of the cartographer or the draughtsman of anatomical plates, there is no art of imitation. In that sense, and however deplorable his precepts may be in other respects, Gauguin, in maintaining that painters should give up *painting what they saw*, was formulating an elementary truth which the Masters have never ceased to practice. Cézanne's familiar dictum expressed the same truth: "What we must do is Poussin over again on nature. That's the whole secret."[21] The imitative arts aim neither at copying the appearance of nature nor at depicting "the ideal," but at making something beautiful by the display of a *form* with the help of visible symbols.

The human artist or poet whose mind is not, like the Divine Mind, the cause of things, cannot draw this form complete out of his creative spirit: he goes and gathers it first and foremost in the vast treasure of created things, of sensitive nature as of the world of souls, and of the interior world of his own soul. From this point of view he is first and foremost a man who sees more deeply than other men and discovers in reality spiritual radiations which others are unable to discern. But to make these radiations shine out in his work and so to be truly docile and faithful to the invisible Spirit at play in things, he can, and indeed he must to some extent, deform, reconstruct and transfigure the material appearance of nature. Even in a portrait which is "a speaking likeness" of its subject—in Holbein's drawings, for example—it is always a form conceived in the mind of the artist and truly brought to birth in that mind which is expressed by the work, true portraits being merely the "ideal reconstruction of individuals."[22]

Art, then, is fundamentally constructive and creative. It is the faculty of producing, not of course *ex nihilo*, but out of a pre-existing matter, a new creature, an original being capable in its turn of moving a human soul. The new creature is the fruit of a spiritual marriage uniting the activity of the artist to the passivity of a given matter. . . .

Nature is therefore in the first place a stimulus and a check to artists, not a model to be slavishly copied. Ask real painters how they need her. They stand before her in timidity and awe, but with the timidity of modesty, not of servility. They imitate her, in a truly *filial* spirit, and according to the creative agility of the spirit; but their imitation is not literal and servile. As we were coming back after a walk in winter time, Rouault told me that looking at the countryside under the snow in the sunshine he had realized how to paint the white trees of spring. "The model," said Renoir, "is there only to set me alight, to let me dare things I could never imagine without it . . . and it makes me come a cropper, if ever I go too far."[23] Such freedom do the sons of the Creator enjoy.

—*Art and Scholasticism* (1920; translated 1930 by J. F. Scanlan)

NOTES

1. Assimilation of the knower to the known. Aquinas elsewhere says (I, 27, 1): "It is clear that the more a thing is understood, the more closely is the intellectual conception joined and united to the intelligent agent; since the intellect by the very act of understanding is made one with the object understood."

2. That is to say, beauty results from the grasp of those characteristics of the object that serve to define its essence or type.

3. Maritain added many notes, which I omit or abbreviate. (Editor.)

4. "Most cognoscent." (The translations in these notes are mine.—Editor.)

5. "Clarity is of the nature of beauty." St. Thomas, *Comment. in lib. de Divin. Nomin.*, lect. 6.

6. "Light beautifies, because without light all things are ugly." St. Thomas, *Comment. in Psalm. Ps.* xxv. 5.

7. "Splendor of truth."

8. "Splendor of order."

9. *De Vera Religione*, cap. 41.

10. "Splendor of form."

11. *Opusc. de Pulchro et Bono*, attributed to Albertus Magnus and sometimes to St. Thomas.

12. "Not according to the mode of truth, but rather according to the mode of delight."

13. . . . Artistic contemplation affects the heart with a joy which is *before all intellectual*, and it must be admitted with Aristotle (*Poetics*, ix, 3, 1451 b 6) that "poetry is something more philosophic and of graver import than history, since its statements are of the nature rather of universals, whereas those of history are singulars" (Bywater's translation: Aristotle, *On the Art of Poetry*, Oxford, 1909), and yet the apprehension of the universal or the intelligible takes place there without speech or any effort of abstraction. The capital error in Benedetto Croce's neo-Hegelian Esthetics is the failure to perceive that artistic contemplation, however *intuitive* it may be, is none the less above all *intellectual*. Esthetics ought to be *intellectualist* and *intuitivist* at the same time.

14. "By all, therefore, the beautiful and the good are desired and loved and cherished." Dionysius the Areopagite, *De Divin. Nomin.*, cap. iv.

15. By *brilliance of form* must be understood an *ontological* splendor which happens to be revealed to our minds, not a *conceptual* clarity. There must be no misunderstanding here: the words *clarity, intelligibility* and *light*, used to characterize the part played by *form* in the heart of things, do not necessarily indicate something clear and intelligible *to us*, but rather something which, although clear and luminous *in itself*, intelligible *in itself*, often remains obscure to our eyes either because of the matter in which the form in question is buried or because of the transcendence of the form itself in the things of the spirit. The more substantial and profound this secret significance, the more concealed from us it is. . . .

16. Aristotle, *Poetics*, iv, 1448 b 5–14.

17. Or, more probably, from the desire to signify an object by means of an ideogram, with perhaps a magical intention: for such drawings, being necessarily in the dark, could not have been made to be looked at. . . .

18. *Poetics*, i, 1447 a 28.

19. "[Cézanne] once asked me what collectors thought of Rosa Bonheur. I told him it was generally agreed that the *Laboureur Nivernaise* was stunning.—'Yes,' replied Cézanne, 'it's *horribly like* the real thing' " (Ambroise Vollard, *Paul Cézanne*, Paris, Crès, 1919).

20. The truth is, it is difficult to determine in what precisely this imitation-copy consists, the concept of which seems so clear to minds which have their being among the simplified schemata of the popular imagination.

Is it the imitation or the copy of what the thing in itself *is* and its intelligible *type*? But that is an object of conception, not of sensation, a thing invisible and intangible, which art, consequently, cannot directly reproduce. Is it the imitation or the copy of the *sensations* produced in us by the thing? But the sensations attain the consciousness of each one of us only as refracted by an inner atmosphere of memories and emotions, and are, moreover, eternally changing in a flux in which all things become distorted and are continuously intermingled; so that from the point of view of *pure sensation* it must be admitted with the Futurists that "a galloping horse has not four hoofs but twenty, that our bodies sink into the sofas on which we sit and the sofas sink into us, that the motor-bus rushes into the houses it goes past, and that the houses in turn hurl themselves upon the motor-bus and become one with it. . . ."

The reproduction or exact copy of nature thus appears as the object of an impossible pursuit—a concept which vanishes when an attempt is made to define it. In practice it resolves itself into the idea of such a representation of things as photography or casting would give, or rather—for such mechanical processes themselves produce results which are "false" as far as our perception is concerned—into the idea of a representation of things *capable of giving us an illusion and deceiving our senses* (it is then no longer a copy pure and simple but presupposes, on the contrary, an artificial faking). . . .

21. Ambroise Vollard, *Paul Cézanne*, Paris, Crès, 1919. "On Nature," that is to say, contemplating and deriving inspiration from Nature. If it were to be understood as doing Poussin over again *by painting according to nature*, with nature for a constituent feature, Cézanne's observation would deserve all the criticism it has received. "It is not by sensation you become classical, but by the mind" (Gino Severini, *Du Cubisme au Classicisme*). . . .

22. Baudelaire, *Curiosités esthétiques*, Le Musée Bonne-Nouvelle.

23. Quoted by M. Albert Ondré in his book on *Renoir* (Crès).

E. H. GOMBRICH

Truth and the Stereotype

The schematism by which our understanding deals with the phenomenal world . . . is a skill so deeply hidden in the human soul that we shall hardly guess the secret trick that Nature here employs.

IMMANUEL KANT, *Kritik der reinen Vernunft*

I

In his charming autobiography, the German illustrator Ludwig Richter relates how he and his friends, all young art students in Rome in the 1820's, visited the famous beauty spot of Tivoli and sat down to draw. They looked with surprise, but hardly with approval, at a group of French artists who approached the place with enormous baggage, carrying large quantities of paint which they applied to the canvas with big, coarse brushes. The Germans, perhaps roused by this self-confident artiness, were determined on the opposite approach. They selected the hardest, best-pointed pencils, which could render the motif firmly and minutely to its finest detail, and each bent down over his small piece of paper, trying to transcribe what he saw with the utmost fidelity. "We fell in love with every blade of grass, every tiny twig, and refused to let anything escape us. Everyone tried to render the motif as objectively as possible."

Nevertheless, when they then compared the fruits of their efforts in the evening, their transcripts differed to a surprising extent. The mood, the color, even the outline of the motif had undergone a subtle transformation in each of them. Richter goes on to describe how these different versions reflected the different dispositions of the four friends, for instance, how the melancholy painter had straightened the exuberant contours and emphasized the blue tinges. We might say he gives an illustration of the famous definition by Emile Zola, who called a work of art "a corner of nature seen through a temperament."

It is precisely because we are interested in this definition that we must probe it a little further. The "temperament" or "personality" of the artist, his selective preferences, may be one of the reasons for the transformation which the motif undergoes under the artist's hands, but there must be others—everything, in fact, which we bundle together into the word "style," the style of the period and the style of the artist. When this transformation is very noticeable we say the motif has been greatly "stylized," and the corollary to this observation is that those who happen to be interested in the motif, for one reason or another, must learn to discount the style. This is part of that natural adjustment, the change in what I call "mental set," which we all perform quite automatically when looking at old illustrations. We can "read" the Bayeux tapestry without reflecting on its countless "deviations from reality." We are not tempted for a moment to think the trees at Hastings in 1066 looked like palmettes and the ground at that time consisted of scrolls. It is an extreme example, but it brings out the all-important fact that the word "stylized" somehow tends to beg the question. It implies there was a special activity by which the artist transformed the trees, much as the Victorian designer was taught to study the forms of flowers before he turned them into patterns. It was a practice which chimed in well with ideas of Victorian architecture, when railways and factories were built first and then adorned with the marks of a style. It was not the practice of earlier times.

The very point of Richter's story, after all, is that style rules even where the artist wishes to reproduce nature faithfully, and trying to analyze these limits to objectivity may help us get nearer to the riddle of style. One of these limits . . . is indicated in Richter's story by the contrast between coarse brush and fine pencil. The artist, clearly, can render only what his tool and his medium are capable of rendering. His technique restricts his freedom of choice. The features and relationships the pencil picks out will differ from those the brush can indicate. Sitting in front of his motif, pencil in hand, the artist will, therefore, look out for those aspects which can be rendered in lines—as we say in a pardonable abbreviation, he will tend to see his motif in terms of lines, while, brush in hand, he sees it in terms of masses.

The question of why style should impose similar limitations is less easily answered, least of all when we do not know whether the artist's intentions were the same as those of Richter and his friends.

Historians of art have explored the regions where Cézanne and van Gogh set up their easels and have photographed their motifs. Such comparisons will always retain their fascination since they almost allow us to look over the artist's shoulder—and who does not wish he had this privilege? But however instructive such confrontations may be when handled with care, we must clearly beware of the fallacy of "stylization." Should we believe the photograph represents the "objective truth" while the painting records the artist's subjective vision—the way he transformed "what he saw"? Can we here compare "the image on the retina" with the "image in the mind"? Such speculations easily lead into a morass of unprovables.

Take the image on the artist's retina. It sounds scientific enough, but actually there never was *one* such image which we could single out for comparison with either photograph or painting. What there was was an endless succession of innumerable images as the painter scanned the landscape in front of him, and these images sent a complex pattern of impulses through the optic nerves to his brain. Even the artist knew nothing of these events, and we know even less. How far the picture that formed in his mind corresponded to or deviated from the photograph it is even less profitable to ask. What we do know is that these artists went out into nature to look for material for a picture and their artistic wisdom led them to organize the elements of the landscape into works of art of marvelous complexity that bear as much relationship to a surveyor's record as a poem bears to a police report.

Does this mean, then, that we are altogether on a useless quest? That artistic truth differs so much from prosaic truth that the question of objectivity must never be asked? I do not think so. We must only be a little more circumspect in our formulation of the question.

II

The National Gallery in Washington possesses a landscape painting by a nineteenth-century artist which almost seems made to clarify this issue.

It is an attractive picture by George Inness of "The Lackawanna Valley," which we know from the master's son was commissioned in 1855 as an advertisement for a railroad. At the time there was only one track running into the roundhouse, "but the president insisted on having four or five painted in, easing his conscience by explaining that the road would eventually have them." Inness protested, and we can see that when he finally gave in for the sake of his family, he shamefacedly hid the patch with the nonexistent tracks behind puffs of smoke. To him this patch was a lie, and no aesthetic explanation about mental images or higher truth could have disputed this away.

But, strictly speaking, the lie was not in the painting. It was in the advertisement, if it claimed by caption or implication that the painting gave accurate information about the facilities of the railway's roundhouses. In a different context the same picture might have illustrated a true statement—for instance, if the president had taken it to a shareholders' meeting to demonstrate improvements he was anxious to make. Indeed in that case, Inness' rendering of the nonexistent tracks might conceivably have given the engineer some hints about where to lay them. It would have served as a sketch or blueprint.

Logicians tell us—and they are not people to be easily gainsaid—that the terms "true" and "false" can only be applied to statements, propositions. And whatever may be the usage of critical parlance, a picture is never a statement in that sense of the term. It can no more be true or false than a statement can be blue or green. Much confusion has been caused in aesthetics by disregarding this simple fact. It is an understandable confusion because in our culture pictures are usually labeled, and labels, or captions, can be understood as abbreviated statements. When it is said "the camera cannot lie," this confusion is apparent. Propaganda in wartime often made use of photographs falsely labeled to accuse or exculpate one of the warring parties. Even in scientific illustrations it is the caption which determines the truth of the picture. In a *cause célèbre* of the last century, the embryo of a pig, labeled as a human embryo to prove a theory of evolution, brought about the downfall of a great reputation. Without much reflection, we can all expand into statements the laconic captions we find in museums and books. When we read the name "Ludwig Richter" under a landscape painting, we know we are thus informed that he painted it and can begin arguing whether this information is true or false. When we read "Tivoli," we infer the picture is to be taken as a view of that spot, and we can again agree or disagree with the label. How and when we agree, in such a case, will largely depend on what we want to know about the object represented. The Bayeux tapestry, for instance, tells us there was a battle at Hastings. It does not tell us what Hastings "looked like."

Now the historian knows that the information pictures were expected to provide differed widely in different periods. Not only were images scarce in the past, but so were the public's opportunities to check their captions. How many people ever saw their ruler in the flesh at sufficiently close quarters to recognize his likeness? How many traveled widely enough to tell one city from another? It is hardly surprising, therefore, that pictures of people and places changed their captions with sovereign disregard for truth. The print sold on the market as a portrait of a king would be altered to represent his successor or enemy.

There is a famous example of this indifference to truthful captions in one of the most ambitious publishing projects of the early printing press, Hartmann Schedel's so-called "Nuremberg Chronicle" with woodcuts by Dürer's teacher Wolgemut. What an opportunity such a volume should give the historian to see what the world was like at the time of Columbus! But as we turn the pages of this big folio, we find the same woodcut of a medieval city recurring with different captions as Damascus, Ferrara, Milan, and Mantua. Unless we are prepared to believe these cities were as indistinguishable from one another as their suburbs may be today, we must conclude that neither the publisher nor the public minded whether the captions told the truth. All they were expected to do was to bring home to the reader that these names stood for cities.

These varying standards of illustration and documentation are of interest to the historian of representation precisely because he can soberly test the information supplied by picture and caption without becoming entangled too soon in problems of aesthetics. Where it is a question of information imparted by the image, the comparison with the correctly labeled photograph should be of obvious value. Three topographical prints representing various approaches to the perfect picture post card should suffice to exemplify the results of such an analysis.

The first shows a view of Rome from a German sixteenth-century newssheet reporting a catastrophic flood when the Tiber burst its banks. Where in Rome could the artist have seen such a timber structure, a castle with black-and-white walls, and a steep roof such as might be found in Nuremberg? Is this also a view of a German town with a misleading caption?

Strangely enough, it is not. The artist, whoever he was, must have made some effort to portray the scene, for this curious building turns out to be the Castel Sant' Angelo in Rome, which guards the bridge across the Tiber. A comparison with a photograph shows that it does embody quite a number of features which belong or belonged to the castle: the angel on the roof that gives it its name, the main round bulk, founded on Hadrian's mausoleum, and the outworks with the bastions that we know were there.

I am fond of this coarse woodcut because its very crudeness allows us to study the mechanism of portrayal as in a slow-motion picture. There is no question here of the artist's having deviated from the motif in order to express his mood or his aesthetic preferences. It is doubtful, in fact, whether the designer of the woodcut ever saw Rome. He probably adapted a view of the city in order to illustrate the sensational news. He knew the Castel Sant' Angelo to be a castle, and so he selected from the drawer of his mental stereotypes the appropriate cliché for a castle—a German *Burg* with its timber structure and high-pitched roof. But he did not simply repeat his stereotype—he adapted it to its particular function by embodying certain distinctive features which he knew belonged to that particular building in Rome. He supplies some information over and above the fact that there is a castle by a bridge.

Once we pay attention to this principle of the adapted stereotype, we also find it where we would be less likely to expect it: that is, within the idiom of illustrations, which look much more flexible and therefore plausible.

The example from the seventeenth century, from the views of Paris by that well-known and skillful topographical artist Matthäus Merian, represents Notre Dame and gives, at first, quite a convincing rendering of that famous church. Comparison with the real building, however, demonstrates that Merian has proceeded in exactly the same way as the anonymous German woodcutter. As a child of the seventeenth century, his notion of a church is that of a lofty symmetrical building with large, rounded windows, and that is how he designs Notre Dame. He places the transept in the center with four large, rounded windows on either side, while the actual view shows seven narrow, pointed Gothic windows to the west and six in the choir. Once more portrayal means for Merian the adaptation or adjustment of his formula or scheme for churches to a particular building through the addition of a number of distinctive features—enough to make it recognizable and even acceptable to those who are not in search of architectural information. If this happened to be the only document extant to tell us about the Cathedral of Paris, we would be very much misled.

One last example in this series: a nineteenth-century lithograph of Chartres Cathedral, done in the heyday of English topographical art. Here, surely, we might expect a faithful visual record. By comparison with the previous instances, the artist really gives a good deal of accurate information about that famous building. But he, too, it turns out, cannot escape the limitations which his time and interests impose on him. He is a romantic to whom the French cathedrals are the greatest flowers of the Gothic centuries, the true age of faith. And so he conceives of Chartres as a Gothic structure with pointed arches and fails to record the Romanesque rounded windows of the west façade, which have no place in his universe of form.

I do not want to be misunderstood here. I do not want to prove by these examples that all representation must be inaccurate or that all visual documents before the advent of photography must be misleading. Clearly, if we had pointed out to the artist his mistake, he could have further modified his scheme and rounded the windows. My point is rather that such matching will always be a step-by-step process—how long it takes and how hard it is will depend on the choice of the initial schema to be adapted to the task of serving as a portrait. I believe that in this respect these humble documents do indeed tell us a lot about the procedure of any artist who wants to make a truthful record of an individual form. He begins not with his visual impression but with his idea or concept: the German artist with his concept of a castle that he applies as well as he can to that individual castle, Merian with his idea of a church, and the lithographer with his stereotype of a cathedral. The individual visual information, those distinctive features I have mentioned, are entered, as it were, upon a pre-existing blank or formulary. And, as often happens with blanks, if they have no provisions for certain kinds of information we consider essential, it is just too bad for the information.

The comparison, by the way, between the formularies of administration and the artist's stereotypes is not my invention. In medieval parlance there was one word for both, a *simile*, or pattern, that is applied to individual incidents in law no less than in pictorial art.

And just as the lawyer or the statistician could plead that he could never get hold of the individual case without some sort of framework provided by his forms or blanks, so the artist could argue that it makes no sense to look at a motif unless one has learned how to classify and catch it within the network of a schematic form. This, at least, is the conclusion to which psychologists have come who knew nothing of our historical series but who set out to investigate the procedure anyone adopts when copying what is called a "nonsense figure," an inkblot, let us say, or an irregular patch. By and large, it appears, the procedure is always the same. The draftsman tries first to classify the blot and fit it into some sort of familiar schema—he will say, for instance, that it is triangular or that it looks like a fish. Having selected such a schema to fit the form approximately, he will proceed to adjust it, noticing for instance that the triangle is rounded at the top, or that the fish ends in a pigtail. Copying, we learn from these experiments, proceeds through the rhythms of schema and correction. The schema is not the product of a process of "abstraction," of a tendency to "simplify"; it represents the first approximate, loose category which is gradually tightened to fit the form it is to reproduce.

III

One more important point emerges from these psychological discussions of copying: it is dangerous to confuse the way a figure is drawn with the way it is seen. "Reproducing the simplest figures," writes Professor Zangwill, "constitutes a process itself by no means psychologically simple. This

process typically displays an essentially constructive or reconstructive character, and with the subjects employed, reproduction was mediated pre-
eminently through the agency of verbal and geometrical formulae. . . ."

If a figure is flashed on a screen for a short moment, we cannot retain it
without some appropriate classification. The label given it will influence
the choice of a schema. If we happen to hit on a good description we will
succeed best in the task of reconstruction. In a famous investigation by
F. C. Bartlett, students had to draw such a "nonsense figure" from memory.
Some called it a pickax and consequently drew it with pointed prongs.
Others accepted it as an anchor and subsequently exaggerated the size of
the ring. There was only one person who reproduced the shape correctly.
He was a student who had labeled the shape for himself "a pre-historic
battle axe." Maybe he was trained in classifying such objects and was
therefore able to portray the figure that happened to correspond to a
schema with which he was familiar.

Where such a pre-existing category is lacking, distortion sets in. Its
effects become particularly amusing when the psychologist imitates the
parlor game of "drawing consequences." Thus F. C. Bartlett had an
Egyptian hieroglyph copied and recopied till it gradually assumed the
familiar shape and formula of a pussycat.

To the art historian these experiments are of interest because they help
to clarify certain fundamentals. The student of medieval art, for instance,
is constantly brought up against the problem of tradition through copy.
Thus the copies of classical coins by Celtic and Teutonic tribes have
become fashionable of late as witnesses to the barbaric "will-to-form."
These tribes, it is implied, rejected classical beauty in favor of the abstract
ornament. Maybe they really disapproved of naturalistic shapes, but if
they did we would need other evidence. The fact that in being copied and
recopied the image became assimilated into the schemata of their own
craftsmen demonstrates the same tendency which made the German woodcut transform the Castel Sant' Angelo into a timbered *Burg*. The "will-to-
form" is rather a "will-to-make-conform," the assimilation of any new
shape to the schemata and patterns an artist has learned to handle.

The Northumbrian scribes were marvelously skilled in the weaving of
patterns and the shaping of letters. Confronted with the task of copying the
image of a man, the symbol of St. Matthew, from a very different tradition,
they were quite satisfied to build it up from those units they could handle
so well. The solution in the famous Echternach Gospels is so ingenious as
to arouse our admiration. It is creative, not because it differs from the
presumed prototype—Bartlett's pussycat also differs from the owl—but
because it copes with the challenge of the unfamiliar in a surprising and
successful way. The artist handles the letter forms as he handles his
medium, with complete assurance in creating from it the symbolic image
of a man.

But did the designer of the Bayeux tapestry act very differently? He was
obviously trained in the intricate interlace work of eleventh-century ornament and adjusted these forms as far as he thought necessary to signify
trees. Within his universe of form this procedure was both ingenious and
consistent.

Could he have done otherwise? Could he have inserted naturalistic renderings of beeches or firs if only he had wanted to? The student of art is generally discouraged from asking this question. He is supposed to look for explanations of style in the artist's will rather than in his skill. Moreover, the historian has little use for questions of might-have-been. But is not this reluctance to ask about the degree of freedom that exists for artists to change and modify their idiom one of the reasons why we have made so little progress in the explanation of style?

In the study of art no less than in the study of man, the mysteries of success are frequently best revealed through an investigation of failures. Only a pathology of representation will give us some insight into the mechanisms which enabled the masters to handle this instrument with such assurance.

Not only must we surprise the artist when he is confronted with an unfamiliar task that he cannot easily adjust to his means; we must also know that his aim was in fact portrayal. Given these conditions, we may do without the actual comparison between photograph and representation that was our starting point. For, after all, nature is sufficiently uniform to allow us to judge the information value of a picture even when we have never seen the specimen portrayed. The beginnings of illustrated reportage, therefore, provide another test case where we need have no doubt about the will and can, consequently, concentrate on the skill.

IV

Perhaps the earliest instance of this kind dates back more than three thousand years, to the beginnings of the New Kingdom in Egypt, when the Pharaoh Thutmose included in his picture chronicle of the Syrian campaign a record of plants he had brought back to Egypt. The inscription, though somewhat mutilated, tells us that Pharoah pronounces these pictures to be "the truth." Yet botanists have found it hard to agree on what plants may have been meant by these renderings. The schematic shapes are not sufficiently differentiated to allow secure identification.

An even more famous example comes from the period when medieval art was at its height, from the volume of plans and drawings by the Gothic master builder, Villard de Honnecourt, which tells us so much about the practice and outlook of the men who created the French cathedrals. Among the many architectural, religious, and symbolic drawings of striking skill and beauty to be found in this volume, there is a curiously stiff picture of a lion, seen *en face*. To us, it looks like an ornamental or heraldic image, but Villard's caption tells us that he regarded it in a different light: *"Et sacies bien,"* he says, *"qu'il fu contrefais al vif."* "Know well that it is drawn from life." These words obviously had a very different meaning for Villard than they have for us. He can have meant only that he had drawn his schema in the presence of a real lion. How much of his visual observation he allowed to enter into the formula is a different matter.

Once more the broadsheets of popular art show us to what extent this attitude survived the Renaissance. The letterpress of a German woodcut from the sixteenth century informs us that we here see "the exact counterfeit" of a kind of locust that invaded Europe in menacing swarms. But the zoologist would be rash to infer from this inscription that there existed an entirely different species of creatures that has never been recorded since. The artist had again used a familiar schema, compounded of animals he had learned to portray, and the traditional formula for locusts that he knew from an Apocalypse where the locust plague was illustrated. Perhaps the fact that the German word for a locust is *Heupferd (hay horse)* tempted him to adopt a schema of a horse for the rendering of the insect's prance.

The creation of such a name and the creation of the image have, in fact, much in common. Both proceed by classifying the unfamiliar with the familiar, or more exactly, to remain in the zoological sphere, by creating a subspecies. Since the locust is called a kind of horse it must therefore share some of its distinctive features.

The caption of a Roman print of 1601 is as explicit as that of the German woodcut. It claims the engraving represents a giant whale that had been washed ashore near Ancona the same year and "was drawn accurately from nature." (*"Ritratto qui dal naturale appunto."*) The claim would be more trustworthy if there did not exist an earlier print recording a similar "scoop" from the Dutch coast in 1598. But surely the Dutch artists of the late sixteenth century, those masters of realism, would be able to portray a whale? Not quite, it seems, for the creature looks suspiciously as if it had ears, and whales with ears, I am assured on higher authority, do not exist. The draftsman probably mistook one of the whale's flippers for an ear and therefore placed it far too close to the eye. He, too, was misled by a familiar schema, the schema of the typical head. To draw an unfamiliar sight presents greater difficulties than is usually realized. And this, I suppose, was also the reason why the Italian preferred to copy the whale from another print. We need not doubt the part of the caption that tells the news from Ancona, but to portray it again "from the life" was not worth the trouble.

In this respect, the fate of exotic creatures in the illustrated books of the last few centuries before the advent of photography is as instructive as it is amusing. When Dürer published his famous woodcut of a rhinoceros, he had to rely on secondhand evidence which he filled in from his own imagination, colored, no doubt, by what he had learned of the most famous of exotic beasts, the dragon with its armored body. Yet it has been shown that this half-invented creature served as a model for all renderings of the rhinoceros, even in natural-history books, up to the eighteenth century. When, in 1790, James Bruce published a drawing of the beast in his *Travels to Discover the Source of the Nile,* he proudly showed that he was aware of this fact:

"The animal represented in this drawing is a native of Tcherkin, near Ras el Feel . . . and this is the first drawing of the rhinoceros with a double horn that has ever yet been presented to the public. The first figure of the Asiatic rhinoceros, the species having but one horn, was painted by Albert Dürer, from the life. . . . It was wonderfully ill-executed in all its parts, and was the origin of all the monstrous forms under which that animal has been painted, ever since. . . . Several modern philosophers have made amends for this in our days; Mr. Parsons, Mr. Edwards, and the Count de Buffon, have given good figures of it from life; they have indeed some faults, owing chiefly to preconceived prejudices and inattention. . . . This . . . is the first that has been published with two horns, it is designed from the life, and is an African."

If proof were needed that the difference between the medieval draftsman and his eighteenth-century descendant is only one of degree, it could be found here. For the illustration, presented with such flourishes of trumpets, is surely not free from "preconceived prejudices" and the all-pervading memory of Dürer's woodcut. We do not know exactly what species of rhinoceros the artist saw at Ras el Feel, and the comparison of his picture with a photograph taken in Africa may not, therefore, be quite fair. But I am told that none of the species known to zoologists corresponds to the engraving claimed to be drawn *al vif!*

The story repeats itself whenever a rare specimen is introduced into Europe. Even the elephants that populate the paintings of the sixteenth and seventeenth centuries have been shown to stem from a very few archetypes and to embody all their curious features, despite the fact that information about elephants was not particularly hard to come by.

These examples demonstrate, in somewhat grotesque magnification, a tendency which the student of art has learned to reckon with. The familiar will always remain the likely starting point for the rendering of the unfamiliar; an existing representation will always exert its spell over the artist even while he strives to record the truth. Thus it was remarked by ancient critics that several famous artists of antiquity had made a strange mistake in the portrayal of horses: they had represented them with eyelashes on the lower lid, a feature which belongs to the human eye but not to that of the horse. A German ophthalmologist who studied the eyes of Dürer's portraits, which to the layman appear to be such triumphs of painstaking accuracy, reports somewhat similar mistakes. Apparently not even Dürer knew what eyes "really look like."

This should not give us cause for surprise, for the greatest of all the visual explorers, Leonardo himself, has been shown to have made mistakes in his anatomical drawings. Apparently he drew features of the human heart which Galen made him expect but which he cannot have seen.

The study of pathology is meant to increase our understanding of health. The sway of schemata did not prevent the emergence of an art of scientific illustration that sometimes succeeds in packing more correct visual information into the image than even a photograph contains. But the diagrammatic maps of muscles in our illustrated anatomies are not "transcripts" of things seen but the work of trained observers who build up the picture of a specimen that has been revealed to them in years of patient study.

Now in this sphere of scientific illustration it obviously makes sense to say that Thutmose's artists or Villard himself could not have done what the modern illustrator can do. They lacked the relevant schemata, their starting point was too far removed from their motif, and their style was too rigid to allow a sufficiently supple adjustment. For so much certainly emerges from a study of portrayal in art: you cannot create a faithful image out of nothing. You must have learned the trick if only from other pictures you have seen.

V

In our culture, where pictures exist in such profusion, it is difficult to demonstrate this basic fact. There are freshmen in art schools who have facility in the objective rendering of motifs that would appear to belie this assumption. But those who have given art classes in other cultural settings tell a different story. James Cheng, who taught painting to a group of Chinese trained in different conventions, once told me of a sketching expedition he made with his students to a famous beauty spot, one of Peking's old city gates. The task baffled them. In the end, one of the students asked to be given at least a picture post card of the building so that they would have something to copy. It is stories such as these, stories of breakdowns, that explain why art has a history and artists need a style adapted to a task.

I cannot illustrate this revealing incident. But luck allows us to study the next stage, as it were—the adjustment of the traditional vocabulary of Chinese art to the unfamiliar task of topographical portrayal in the Western sense. For some decades Chiang Yee, a Chinese writer and painter of great gifts and charm, has delighted us with contemplative records of the Silent Traveller, books in which he tells of his encounters with scenes and people of the English and Irish countryside and elsewhere. I take an illustration from the volume on the English Lakeland.

It is a view of Derwentwater. Here we have crossed the line that separates documentation from art. Mr. Chiang Yee certainly enjoys the adaptation of the Chinese idiom to a new purpose; he wants us to see the English scenery for once "through Chinese eyes." But it is precisely for this reason that it is so instructive to compare his view with a typical "picturesque" rendering from the Romantic period. We see how the relatively rigid vocabulary of the Chinese tradition acts as a selective screen which admits only the features for which schemata exist. The artist will be attracted by motifs which can be rendered in his idiom. As he scans the landscape, the sights which can be matched successfully with the schemata he has learned to handle will leap forward as centers of attention. The style, like the medium, creates a mental set which makes the artist look for certain aspects in the scene around him that he can render. Painting is an activity, and the artist will therefore tend to see what he paints rather than to paint what he sees.

It is this interaction between style and preference which Nietzsche summed up in his mordant comment on the claims of realism:

> "All Nature faithfully"—But by what feint
> Can Nature be subdued to art's constraint?
> Her smallest fragment is still infinite!
> And so he paints but what he likes in it.
> What does he like? He likes, what he can paint!

There is more in this observation than just a cool reminder of the limitations of artistic means. We catch a glimpse of the reasons why these limitations will never obtrude themselves within the domain of art itself. Art
presupposes mastery, and the greater the artist the more surely will he
instinctively avoid a task where his mastery would fail to serve him. The
layman may wonder whether Giotto could have painted a view of Fiesole
in sunshine, but the historian will suspect that, lacking the means, he
would not have wanted to, or rather that he could not have wanted to. We
like to assume, somehow, that where there is a will there is also a way, but
in matters of art the maxim should read that only where there is a way is
there also a will. The individual can enrich the ways and means that his
culture offers him; he can hardly wish for something that he has never
known is possible.

The fact that artists tend to look for motifs for which their style and
training equip them explains why the problem of representational skill
looks different to the historian of art and to the historian of visual information. The one is concerned with success, the other must also observe the
failures. But these failures suggest that we sometimes assume a little rashly
that the ability of art to portray the visible world developed, as it were,
along a uniform front. We know of specialists in art—of Claude Lorrain,
the master of landscape whose figure paintings were poor, of Frans Hals
who concentrated almost exclusively on portraits. May not skill as much as
will have dictated this type of preference? Is not all naturalism in the art
of the past selective?

A somewhat Philistine experiment would suggest that it is. Take the
next magazine containing snapshots of crowds and street scenes and walk
with it through any art gallery to see how many gestures and types that
occur in life can be matched from old paintings. Even Dutch genre paintings that appear to mirror life in all its bustle and variety will turn out to
be created from a limited number of types and gestures, much as the apparent realism of the picaresque novel or of Restoration comedy still applies
and modifies stock figures which can be traced back for centuries. There is
no neutral naturalism. The artist, no less than the writer, needs a vocabulary before he can embark on a "copy" of reality.

VI

Everything points to the conclusion that the phrase the "language of art"
is more than a loose metaphor, that even to describe the visible world in
images we need a developed system of schemata. This conclusion rather
clashes with the traditional distinction, often discussed in the eighteenth
century, between spoken words which are conventional signs and painting
which uses "natural" signs to "imitate" reality. It is a plausible distinction,
but it has led to certain difficulties. If we assume, with this tradition, that
natural signs can simply be copied from nature, the history of art represents
a complete puzzle. It has become increasingly clear since the late nineteenth
century that primitive art and child art use a language of symbols rather
than "natural signs." To account for this fact it was postulated that there
must be a special kind of art grounded not on seeing but rather on

knowledge, an art which operates with "conceptual images." The child—
it is argued—does not look at trees; he is satisfied with the "conceptual"
schema of a tree that fails to correspond to any reality since it does not
embody the characteristics of, say, birch or beech, let alone those of individual trees. This reliance on construction rather than on imitation was
attributed to the peculiar mentality of children and primitives who live in
a world of their own.

But we have come to realize that this distinction is unreal. Gustaf Britsch
and Rudolf Arnheim have stressed that there is no opposition between
the crude map of the world made by a child and the richer map presented
in naturalistic images. All art originates in the human mind, in our reactions to the world rather than in the visible world itself, and it is precisely
because all art is "conceptual" that all representations are recognizable by
their style.

Without some starting point, some initial schema, we could never get
hold of the flux of experience. Without categories, we could not sort our
impressions. Paradoxically, it has turned out that it matters relatively little
what these first categories are. We can always adjust them according to
need. Indeed, if the schema remains loose and flexible, such initial vagueness may prove not a hindrance but a help. An entirely fluid system would
no longer serve its purpose; it could not register facts because it would lack
pigeonholes. But how we arrange the first filing system is not very relevant.

The progress of learning, of adjustment through trial and error, can be
compared to the game of "Twenty Questions," where we identify an object
through inclusion or exclusion along any network of classes. The traditional initial scheme of "animal, vegetable, or mineral" is certainly neither
scientific nor very suitable, but it usually serves us well enough to narrow
down our concepts by submitting them to the corrective test of "yes" or
"no." The example of this parlor game has become popular of late as an
illustration of that process of articulation through which we learn to adjust
ourselves to the infinite complexity of this world. It indicates, however
crudely, the way in which not only organisms but even machines may be
said to "learn" by trial and error. Engineers at their thrilling work on
what they call "servo mechanisms," that is, self-adjusting machines, have
recognized the importance of some kind of "initiative" on the part of the
machine. The first move such a machine may make will be, and indeed
must be, a random movement, a shot in the dark. Provided a report of
success or failure, hit or miss, can be fed back into the machine, it will
increasingly avoid the wrong moves and repeat the correct ones. One of the
pioneers in this field has recently described this machine rhythm of schema
and correction in a striking verbal formula: he calls all learning "an
arboriform stratification of guesses about the world." Arboriform, we may
take it, here describes the progressive creation of classes and subclasses
such as might be described in a diagrammatic account of "Twenty Questions."

We seem to have drifted far from the discussion of portrayal. But it is
certainly possible to look at a portrait as a schema of a head modified by
the distinctive features about which we wish to convey information. The
American police sometimes employ draftsmen to aid witnesses in the

identification of criminals. They may draw any vague face, a random schema, and let witnesses guide their modifications of selected features simply by saying "yes" or "no" to various suggested standard alterations until the face is sufficiently individualized for a search in the files to be profitable. This account of portrait drawing by remote control may well be over-tidy, but as a parable it may serve its purpose. It reminds us that the starting point of a visual record is not knowledge but a guess conditioned by habit and tradition.

Need we infer from this fact that there is no such thing as an objective likeness? That it makes no sense to ask, for instance, whether Chiang Yee's view of Derwentwater is more or less correct than the nineteenth-century lithograph in which the formulas of classical landscapes were applied to the same task? It is a tempting conclusion and one which recommends itself to the teacher of art appreciation because it brings home to the layman how much of what we call "seeing" is conditioned by habits and expectations. It is all the more important to clarify how far this relativism will take us. I believe it rests on the confusion between pictures, words, and statements which we saw arising the moment truth was ascribed to paintings rather than to captions.

If all art is conceptual, the issue is rather simple. For concepts, like pictures, cannot be true or false. They can only be more or less useful for the formation of descriptions. The words of a language, like pictorial formulas, pick out from the flux of events a few signposts which allow us to give direction to our fellow speakers in that game of "Twenty Questions" in which we are engaged. Where the needs of users are similar, the signposts will tend to correspond. We can mostly find equivalent terms in English, French, German, and Latin, and hence the idea has taken root that concepts exist independently of language as the constituents of "reality." But the English language erects a signpost on the roadfork between "clock" and "watch" where the German has only *"Uhr."* The sentence from the German primer, *"Meine Tante hat eine Uhr,"* leaves us in doubt whether the aunt has a clock or a watch. Either of the two translations may be wrong as a description of a fact. In Swedish, by the way, there is an additional roadfork to distinguish between aunts who are "father's sisters," those who are "mother's sisters," and those who are just ordinary aunts. If we were to play our game in Swedish we would need additional questions to get at the truth about the timepiece.

This simple example brings out the fact, recently emphasized by Benjamin Lee Whorf, that language does not give name to pre-existing things or concepts so much as it articulates the world of our experience. The images of art, we suspect, do the same. But this difference in styles or languages need not stand in the way of correct answers and descriptions. The world may be approached from a different angle and the information given may yet be the same.

From the point of view of information there is surely no difficulty in discussing portrayal. To say of a drawing that it is a correct view of Tivoli does not mean, of course, that Tivoli is bounded by wiry lines. It means that those who understand the notation will derive *no false information* from the drawing—whether it gives the contour in a few lines or picks out "every blade of grass" as Richter's friends wanted to do. The complete portrayal might be the one which gives as much correct information about the spot as we would obtain if we looked at it from the very spot where the artist stood.

Styles, like languages, differ in the sequence of articulation and in the number of questions they allow the artist to ask; and so complex is the information that reaches us from the visible world that no picture will ever embody it all. This is not due to the subjectivity of vision but to its richness. Where the artist has to copy a human product he can, of course, produce a facsimile which is indistinguishable from the original. The forger of banknotes succeeds only too well in effacing his personality and the limitations of a period style.

But what matters to us is that the correct portrait, like the useful map, is an end product on a long road through schema and correction. It is not a faithful record of a visual experience but the fruitful construction of a relational model.

Neither the subjectivity of vision nor the sway of conventions need lead us to deny that such a model can be constructed to any required degree of accuracy. What is decisive here is clearly the word "required." The form of representation cannot be divorced from its purpose and the requirements of the society in which the given visual language gains currency.

—*Art and Illusion* (1960; second edition revised, 1961)

CHAPTER
2

Expression
of Emotion

EUGENE VÉRON: Art as the Expression of Emotion
LEO TOLSTOY: The Communication of Emotion
CURT J. DUCASSE: Art and the Language of the Emotions

One of the consequences of the Romantic movement was the shift in
emphasis from imitation theories of art to expression and communication
theories. The Romantic exaltation of the artist-genius in conjunction
with the stress on originality led naturally to theories of this latter type.
"Who touches this touches a man," wrote Walt Whitman of his poetry. The
assumption was that the subject of the work of art is the artist, especially
his inner life of feeling and imagination, and that through the art work
the beholder comes into sympathetic communion with a master spirit.
With the passing of the Romantic movement, expression theories
have persisted in a more sober and analytical form. Theorists of this type
contend that the great function of art is to express the whole gamut of
human emotions, even the sad and the terrible, and that ugliness may
be created for its own expressiveness, not merely as a foil to beauty.

   This point of view was formulated by Eugene Véron (1825–1889)
in *L'Esthetique* (1878). Véron defines art as the expression of emotion.
"The merit of a work of art," he declares, "can be finally measured
by the power with which it manifests or interprets the emotion that was
its determining cause, and that, for a like reason, must constitute its
innermost and supreme unity." Some art, he recognizes, is simply
decorative: Its aim is to create beauty. But other art is broadly expressive:
Its aim is to express emotions that may be quite unconnected with
beauty. We should approach expressive art not with the criterion of
beauty or pleasure but with the criterion of expressiveness or significance.
The question is not, Does this please me? but, Out of how deep a life
does this spring? Great art, to paraphrase Longinus, is the echo of a
great soul. But it is the emotional, or subjective, side of the human
personality that is expressed; and art is distinguished from science by the
predominance of subjectivity over objectivity. Whereas the scientist is
one "whose imagination has no modifying influence over the results of his
direct observation," the artist is "one whose imagination, impressionability

—in a word, whose personality, is so lively and excitable that it spontaneously transforms everything, dyeing them in its own colors, and unconsciously exaggerating them in accordance with its own preferences."

The main contentions of Véron reappear with altered emphasis in the influential pages of Leo Tolstoy (1828–1910). In certain respects they disagree. Tolstoy thinks *communication* is indispensable to art: Véron defines art simply as the *expression* of emotion. Also, Tolstoy formulates a more antihedonistic and moral interpretation of art. But both maintain that art is the "language" of emotions.

Defining art as the *deliberate* communication of emotions (thus excluding spontaneous yawning, swearing, laughing, or weeping), Tolstoy distinguishes between the *technical adequacy* of the work as a vehicle of emotional communication, and the value and character of the emotions expressed. He thus recognizes that there are two questions to be asked in evaluating a work of art: First, are the emotions of the artist put into effective communicable form? Second, are the emotions worthwhile?

It makes a great difference, he believes, whether the emotions are beneficial or injurious; for art is the great molder of human attitudes —coequal in importance with science. The only emotions, he thinks, that art should transmit are simple and universal feelings that all men can appreciate, and Christian feelings, particularly of love and human brotherhood. He condemns most of the sophisticated art of Western culture, even such masterpieces as those of Shakespeare and Beethoven and his own *Anna Karenina* and *War and Peace*.

Tolstoy took the extreme stand he did partly because he appreciated so vividly the power of art to mold human character. His book is the most impressive statement in modern esthetics of the view that the value of art lies in its immense social usefulness. The noble ideal to which he wished to dedicate art, the universal brotherhood of man, is the more moving because, in his own life, he tried with such intense conviction to abide by it. There have been others, such as the Marxists, who have insisted upon the social utility of art, but never with a greater compassion or sincerity.

Curt John Ducasse (1881–1969), Professor of Philosophy at the University of Washington and later at Brown University, was the foremost American champion of a theory of art akin to that of Véron and Tolstoy. His analytical and empiricist method eliminated most of the ambiguities found in the emotionalist theories of his predecessors. It should be noted that he sides with Véron and against Tolstoy in declaring that expression, not communication, of emotion is the essence of art, and that when artistic communication does occur, it is not the raw emotion but its abstracted "image" or "quality" that is transmitted, so that the work of art has, for example, the capacity to make its beholder "taste, or sample, sadness without actually making him sad." Ducasse calls this "tasting" of the emotional import "ecpathy" or "ecpathizing," which he defines as "an extracting from [the object] of the feeling it embodies."[1]

NOTE

1. Cf. Curt John Ducasse, *The Philosophy of Art* (Dover Publications, New York, 1966), pp. 173–178.

EUGENE VÉRON

Art as the Expression of Emotion

I. GENERAL DEFINITION OF ART

Art, far from being the blossom and fruit of civilization, is rather its germ. It began to give evidence of its existence as soon as man became self-conscious, and is to be found clearly defined in his very earliest works.

By its psychologic origin it is bound up with the constituent principles of humanity. The salient and essential characteristic of man is his incessant cerebral activity, which is propagated and developed by countless acts and works of varied kind. The aim and rule of this activity is the search after *the best*; that is to say, the more and more complete satisfaction of physical and moral wants. This instinct, common to all animals, is seconded in man by an exceptionally well-developed faculty to adapt the means to the end.

The effort to satisfy physical wants has given birth to all industries that defend, preserve, and smooth the path of life; the effort to satisfy the moral wants—of which one of the most important is the gratification of our cerebral activity itself—has created the arts, long before it could give them power sufficient for the conscious elaboration of ideas. The life of sentiment preceded the manifestations of intellectual life by many centuries.

The gratification, *in esse* or *in posse*, of either real or imaginary wants, is the cause of happiness, joy, pleasure, and of all the feelings connected with them; the contrary is marked by grief, sadness, fear, etc.: but in both cases there is emotion to give more or less lively evidence of its existence by means of exterior signs. When expressed by gesture and rhythmic movement, such emotion produces the dance; when by rhythmic notes, music; when by rhythmic words, poetry.

As in another aspect man is essentially sympathetic and his joy or pain is often caused as much by the good or evil fortunes of others as by his own; as, besides, he possesses in a very high degree the faculty of combining series of fictitious facts, and of representing them in colors even more lively than those of reality: it results that the domain of art is of infinite extent for him. For the causes of emotion are multiplied for every man—not only by the number of similar beings who live around him and are attached to him by the more or less closely knit bonds of affection, alliance, similitude of situation or community of ideas and interests; but also, by the never-ending multitude of beings and events that are able to originate or direct the imaginings of poets.

To these elements of emotion and moral enjoyment must be added the combinations of lines, of forms and of colors, the dispositions and opposition of light and shade, etc. The instinctive search after this kind of emotion or pleasure, the special organ of which is the eye, has given birth to what are called the arts of design—sculpture, painting and architecture.

We may say then, by way of general definition, that art is the manifestation of emotion, obtaining external interpretation, now by expressive arrangements of line, form or color, now by a series of gestures, sounds, or words governed by particular rhythmical cadence.

If our definition is exact, we must conclude, from it, that the merit of a work of art, whatever it may be, can be finally measured by the power with which it manifests or interprets the emotion that was its determining cause, and that, for a like reason, must constitute its innermost and supreme unity. . . .

II. What We Admire in a Work of Art Is the Genius of the Artist. Definition of Esthetics

Imitation is no more the aim of art than a mere collection of letters and syllables is the aim of a writer who wishes to express his thoughts and feelings by the aid of the words which they form. The poet arranging his verses, the musician composing his airs and harmonies, are well aware that their real object lies beyond words and notes. This distinction, as we have here explained it, is perhaps less clear in matters of painting and sculpture. Some artists, and these not the least capable, are quite convinced that when they have a model before them, their one duty is to imitate it. And indeed they do nothing else; and, by virtue of such imitation, they succeed in producing works of incontestable artistic value.

Here we have simply a misunderstanding. If an artist were really able to reduce himself to the condition of a copying machine; if he could so far efface and suppress himself as to confine his work to the servile reproduction of all the features and details of an object or event passing before his eyes: the only value his work would possess would be that of a more or less exact *procès verbal*, and it would perforce remain inferior to reality. Where is the artist who would attempt to depict sunlight without taking refuge in some legerdemain, calling to his aid devices which the true sun would despise? But enough of this. Just because he is endowed with sensibility and imaginative power, the artist, in presence of the facts of nature or the events of history, finds himself, whether he will or not, in a peculiar situation. However thorough a realist he may think himself, he does not leave himself to chance. Now, choice of subject alone is enough to prove that, from the very beginning, some preference has existed, the result of a more or less predeterminate impression, and of a more or less unconscious agreement between the character of the object and that of the artist. This impression and agreement he sets to work to embody in outward form; it is the real aim of his work, and its possession gives him claim to the name of artist. Without wishing or even knowing it, he molds the features of nature to his dominant impression and to the idea that caused him to take pencil in hand. His work has an accidental stamp, in addition to that of the permanent genius which constitutes his individuality. Poet, musician, sculptor and architect, all pay more or less strict obedience to the same law. To it, point all those rules of artistic composition which pedantic academicism has subtly multiplied until they contradict each other.

The more of this personal character that a work possesses; the more harmonious its details and their combined expression; the more clearly each part communicates the impression of the artist, whether of grandeur, of melancholy or of joy; in fine, the more that expression of human sensation and will predominates over mere imitation, the better will be its chance of obtaining sooner or later the admiration of the world—always supposing that the sentiment expressed be a generous one, and that the execution be not of such a kind as to repel or baffle connoisseurs. It is not of course impossible that an artist endowed with an ill-regulated or morbid imagination may place himself outside all normal conditions and condemn himself to the eternal misapprehension of the public. Impressions that are too particular, eccentric feelings, fantastic execution or processes, which do nothing to raise the intrinsic value or power of inspiration of a work, may give it so strange and ultra-individual a character that it may become impossible for us to arrive at its real merit. The best qualities, when exaggerated, become faults; and that very personality or individuality which, when added to imitative power, results in a work of art, produces when pushed to extravagance nothing but an enigma.

We see, then, if we have succeeded in making ourselves understood, that the beautiful in art springs mainly from the intervention of the genius of man when more or less excited by special emotion.

A work is beautiful when it bears strong marks of the individuality of its author, of the permanent personality of the artist, and of the more or less accidental impression produced upon him by the sight of the object or event rendered.

In a word, it is from the worth of the artist that that of his work is derived. It is the manifestation of the faculties and qualities he possesses which attracts and fascinates us. The more sympathetic power and individuality that these faculties and qualities display, the easier is it for them to obtain our love and admiration. On the other hand, we, for a similar reason, reject and contemn bold and vulgar works that by their shortcomings demonstrate the moral and intellectual mediocrity of their authors, and prove the latter to have mistaken their vocation.

Consequently, then, beauty in art is a purely human creation. Imitation may be its means, as in sculpture and painting; or, on the other hand, it may have nothing to do with it, as in poetry and music. This beauty is of so peculiar a nature that it may exist even in ugliness itself; inasmuch as the exact reproduction of an ugly model may be a beautiful work of art, by the ensemble of qualities which the composition of it may prove are possessed by its author.

The very theory of imitation is but the incomplete and superficial statement of the ideas which we are here advocating. What is it that we admire in imitation? The resemblance? We have that much better in the object itself. But how is it that the similitude of an ugly object can be beautiful? It is obvious that between the object and its counterfeit some new element intervenes. This element is the personality, or, at least, the skill of the artist. This latter, indeed, is what they admire who will have it that beauty consists in imitation. What these applaud, in fact, is the talent of the artist. If we look below the surface and analyze their admiration we shall find that it is so; whether they mean it or not, what they praise in a work is the worker.

This was the opinion of Bürger, who, in his *Salon* of 1863, says: "In works which interest us the authors in a way substitute themselves for nature. However common or vulgar the latter may be, they have some rare and peculiar way of looking at it. It is Chardin himself whom we admire in his representation of a glass of water. We admire the genius of Rembrandt in the profound and individual character which he imparted to every head that posed before him. Thus did they seem to him, and this explains everything simple or fantastic in his expression and execution."

After all this, we need not stop to refute the theory which would found artistic beauty upon the imitation of "beautiful nature." In spite of the brilliant reputation that its triumph in three academies has given to M. Ch. Sevêyne's book upon the science of beauty, it does not seem to us to be founded upon arguments worthy of respect; it has not shown us where "beautiful nature" *(la belle nature)* is to be found in *Le Pouilleux*, in the *Raft of the Medusa*, in the *Battlefield of Eylau*, in the character of *Tartuffe*, or of *La Marneffe*.

The only beauty in a work of art is that placed there by the artist. It is both the result of his efforts and the foundation of his success. As often as he is struck by any vivid impression—whether moral, intellectual, or physical—and expresses that impression by some outward process—by poetry, music, sculpture, painting or architecture—in such a way as to cause its communication with the soul of spectator or auditor; so often does he produce a work of art the beauty of which will be in exact proportion to the intelligence and depth of the sentiment displayed, and the power shown in giving it outward form.

The union of all these conditions constitutes artistic beauty in its most complete expression.

With a few reservations, then, we may preserve the definition of esthetics which usage has sanctified—*The Science of Beauty*. For the sake of clearness, however, and to prevent confusion, we prefer to call it the *Science of Beauty in Art*. Had not the tyranny of formulae by custom become too strong, we would willingly refrain from using the word "beauty" at all, for it has the drawback of being too exclusively connected with the sense of seeing, and of calling up too much the idea of visible form. The employment of this word became general when *the* art *par excellence* was sculpture. To make it apply to the other arts, it was necessary to foist upon it a series of extensions which deprived it of all accuracy. Language possesses no word more vague or less precise. This absence of precision has perhaps contributed more than might at first be supposed to that confusion of ideas which can alone explain the multiplicity and absurdity of current esthetic theories.

All these inconveniences and obscurities may be avoided by simply putting it thus:

Esthetics is the science whose object is the study and elucidation of the manifestations of artistic genius. . . .

III. DECORATIVE AND EXPRESSIVE ART

There are two distinct kinds of art. The one, decorative art, we understand to be that whose main object is the gratification of the eye and ear, and whose chief means to perfection of form are harmony and grace of contour, diction, or sound. Such art rests upon the desire for beauty, and has nothing in view beyond the peculiar delight caused by the sight of beautiful objects. It has produced admirable works in the past, and may produce them again now or in the future, on condition that its inspiration be sought in actual and existing life, and not in the imitation of works sanctified by time. We must recognize, however, that modern art has no tendency in this latter direction. Beauty no longer suffices for us. Indeed, for the last two thousand years something more has been required; for even among the *chefs d'œuvre* of the Greeks not a few owe their creation to a different sentiment. Some of the great artists of antiquity were certainly occupied with the interpretation of the moral life; and had not time destroyed their painted works, we should, at the present moment, probably be able to show absolute proofs of this tendency. But we may readily dispense with the confirmation which they would have afforded to our arguments; for we find more than sufficient evidence in the avowed character of the music of the Greeks, in many of the most important works of their sculptors, and in most of their great poems.

The chief characteristic of modern art—of art, that is, left to follow its own inspiration free from academic patronage—is power of expression. Through form this, the second kind of art, traces the moral life, and endeavors to occupy man, body and soul, but with no thought of sacrificing the one to the other. It is ever becoming more imbued with the quite modern idea that the whole being is *one*, metaphysicians notwithstanding, and that its aim can only be complete by refusing to separate the organ from its function. The moral life is but the general result of the conditions of the physical. The one is bound to the other by necessary connections which cannot be broken without destroying both. The first care of the artist should be to seek out and grasp the methods of manifestation so as to comprehend and master their unity.

Art, thus understood, demands from its votary an ensemble of intellectual faculties higher and more robust than if founded solely upon an ideal of beauty. Art founded upon the latter notion would be sufficiently served by one possessing an acute sense of the beautiful—the degree of his sensibility being indicated by the plastic perfection of his work. But expressive art demands a capability of being moved by many varying sentiments, demands the power to penetrate beneath outward appearances and to seize a hidden thought, the power to grasp either the permanent characteristic or the particular and momentary emotion; in a word, it demands that complete eloquence of representation which art might have dispensed with while it confined itself to the investigation or delineation of a single expression, but which became absolutely indispensable from the moment that the interpretation of the entire man became its avowed object.

We may say, too, that modern art is doubly expressive; because, while the artist is indicating by form and sound the sentiments and ideas of the personages whom he introduces, he is also by the power and manner of such manifestation giving an unerring measure of his own sensibility, imagination, and intelligence.

Expressive art is in no way hostile to beauty; it makes use of it as one element in the subjects which require it, but its domain is not enclosed within the narrow bounds of such a conception. It is by no means indifferent to the pleasures of sight and hearing, but it sees something beyond them. Its worth must not be measured only by perfection of form, but also and chiefly, by the double power of expression which we have pointed out, and, as we must not omit to add, by the value of the sentiments and ideas expressed. This latter point is too often and wrongly ignored by artists.

Between two works which give evidence of equal talent—that is to say, of equal facility to grasp the true accents and characteristics of nature, and equal power to bring out both the inner meaning of things and the personality of the artist—we, for our part, would not hesitate to accord the preference to that of which the *Conception* showed the more vigorous intelligence and elevated feeling. The art critics seem to have made it one of their principles to take no account of choice of subject, but only to look at the technical result. Such a principle is plausible rather than true. The individuality of the author can never be excluded from a work, and choice of subject is frequently one of the points by which this individuality is most clearly indicated.

It is true, of course, that elevation of sentiment can never take the place of art talent. On this point we cannot too strongly condemn the practice of academic juries who, on the one hand, reward mere mechanical labor simply because it has been exercised upon what are called classic subjects; and, on the other, persecute more independent artists to punish their obstinacy in deserting the beaten track. Nothing, then, can be further from our thoughts than to require critics to substitute, in every case, consideration of the subject for that of the work itself; or to condemn *a priori* all artists who remain faithful to the traditions, ideas, and sentiments of the past. In these, indeed, some find their only inspiration. We only wish to affirm our conviction that choice of subject is not so indifferent a matter as some say it is, and that it must be taken into account as of considerable weight in determining an opinion of a work of art.

The necessity for this is one consequence of the distinction which we have established between decorative and expressive art. The former, solely devoted to the gratification of eye and ear, affords no measure of its success beyond the pleasure which it gives. The latter, whose chief object is to express the feelings and ideas, and, through them, to manifest the power of conception and expression possessed by the artist, must obviously be estimated, partly at least, by the moral or other value of the ideas and sentiments in question. And, as the value of a work depends directly upon the capability of its author, and as many artists have been about equal in their technical ability, we must be ready to acknowledge that moral and intellectual superiority is a real superiority, and is naturally marked by the possession of an instinctive and spontaneous power of sympathy.

IV. Style and Personality

Style is the man, says Buffon; and he is right. Get some one who *can* read, to read a page of Demosthenes *and* of Cicero, of Bossuet and of Massillon, of Corneille and of Racine, of Lamartine and of Victor Hugo. However slight may be your literary perceptions, you will at once notice that no two of them sound the same. Apart altogether from the subjects or ideas, which may be identical, each one has an air, an accent, which can never either be confounded or replaced. In some of them we find elegance, finesse, grace, the most seductive and soothing harmony; in others, a force and *élan* like the sound of a trumpet, enough to awaken the Seven Sleepers.

Style only exists by virtue of what Bürger calls *the law of separation.* "A being only exists in consequence of his separation from other beings. . . . This law of successive detachment—which alone renders progress possible—may be proved to influence the course of religion, of politics, of literature, and of art. What was the renaissance but a break in the continuity of the middle ages?" It is by style, by the manner of comprehension, of feeling and interpretation, that epochs, races, schools and individuals are separated and distinguished one from the other. In all the arts, analogous differences are to be found; plainly marked, in proportion as a more or less extensive field is offered for the development of artistic personality. Michelangelo and Raphael, Leonardo and Veronese, Titian and Correggio, Rubens and Rembrandt, resembled each other no more and no less than Beethoven resembled Rossini; Weber, Mozart; or Wagner resembles Verdi. Each has his own style, his peculiar mode of thinking and feeling, and of expressing those feelings and thoughts.

Why have mediocre artists no style? For the same reasons that they are mediocrities. The particular characteristic of mediocrity is commonness or vulgarity of thought and feeling. At each moment in the evolution of a social system, there is a general level which marks, for that moment, the average value of the human soul and intellect. Such works as rise above this general level imply an amount of talent or genius in exact proportion to the amount of superior elevation and spontaneity which they display. Mediocrity comes up to the general level, but does not pass it; thus the mediocre artist thinks and feels like the ordinary run of mankind, and has nothing to "separate" him from the crowd. He may have a manner, an ensemble of habits of working peculiar to himself; but he can have no style in the accurate sense of the word. Facility is not style; for the latter is really a product, a reverberation, if we may use the word, from the soul itself, and can no more be artificially acquired than can the sonorousness of bronze or silver be acquired by lead. . . .

Style, which is a simple reflection of the artist's personality, is naturally found in the work of every artist who possesses any personality. The indescribable quality, the *je ne sais quoi* of which Fromentin speaks, is precisely the assemblage of qualities, the condition of being and temperament which caused Rubens to see things differently from Rembrandt. The two extracted from one and the same object or subject emotions widely different though congenial to their respective natures; just as a tightened string in a concert room will vibrate in response to the note which it would itself produce if struck. The one thing needful is the power to vibrate, which is too often wanting.

The question of style has considerable importance. We might even say that it includes the whole of esthetics, which is in fact the question of personality in art. . . .

Truth and personality: these are the alpha and omega of art formulas; *truth* as to facts, and the *personality* of the artist. But, if we look more closely, we shall see that these two terms are in reality but one. Truth as to fact, so far as art is concerned, is above all the truth of our own sensations, of our own sentiments. It is truth as we see it, as it appears modified by our own temperaments, preferences, and physical organs. It is, in fact, our personality itself. Reality, as given by the photographer, reality taken from a point of view without connection with us or our impressions, is the very negation of art. When this kind of truth predominates in a work of art, we cry, "There is realism for you!" Now, realism partakes of the nature of art, only because the most downright of realists must, whether he will or not, put something of his own individuality into his work. When, on the other hand, the dominant quality is what we call human or personal truth, then we at once exclaim, "Here is an artist!"

And the latter is the right meaning of the word. Art consists essentially in the predominance of subjectivity over objectivity; it is the chief distinction between it and science. The man intended for science is he whose imagination has no modifying influence over the results of his direct observation. The artist, on the other hand, is one whose imagination, impressionability—in a word, whose personality is so lively and excitable that it spontaneously transforms everything, dyeing them in its own colors, and unconsciously exaggerating them in accordance with its own preferences.

We think ourselves justified, then, in calling art the direct and spontaneous manifestation of human personality. But we must not omit also to remember the fact that personality—individual and particular as it is from some points of view—is nevertheless exposed to many successive and temporary modifications caused by the various kinds of civilization through which it has had to pass.

—*Æsthetics* (1878; translated 1879 by W. H. Armstrong)

LEO TOLSTOY

The Communication of Emotion

There is no objective definition of beauty. The existing definitions . . . amount only to one and the same subjective definition, which is (strange as it seems to say so), that art is that which makes beauty manifest, and beauty is that which pleases (without exciting desire). Many estheticians have felt the insufficiency and instability of such a definition, and in order to give it a firm basis have asked themselves why a thing pleases. And they have converted the discussion on beauty into a question of taste, as did Hutcheson, Voltaire, Diderot, and others. But all attempts to define what taste is must lead to nothing, as the reader may see both from the history of esthetics and experimentally. There is and can be no explanation of why one thing pleases one man and displeases another, or *vice versa*; so that the whole existing science of esthetics fails to do what we might expect from it as a mental activity calling itself a science, namely, it does not define the qualities and laws of art, or of the beautiful (if that be the content of art), or the nature of taste (if taste decides the question of art and its merit), and then on the basis of such definitions acknowledge as art those productions which correspond to these laws and reject those which do not come under them. But this science of esthetics consists in first acknowledging a certain set of productions to be art (because they please us), and then framing such a theory of art as all these productions which please a certain circle of people can be fitted into. There exists an art-canon according to which certain productions favored by our circle are acknowledged as being art,—the works of Phidias, Sophocles, Homer, Titian, Raphael, Bach, Beethoven, Dante, Shakespeare, Goethe, and others,—and the esthetic laws must be such as to embrace all these productions. In esthetic literature you will constantly meet with opinions on the merit and importance of art, founded not on any certain laws by which this or that is held to be good or bad, but merely on consideration as to whether this art tallies with the art-canon we have drawn up. . . .

So that the theory of art founded on beauty, expounded by esthetics and in dim outline professed by the public, is nothing but the setting up as good of that which has pleased and pleases us, that is, pleases a certain class of people.

In order to define any human activity, it is necessary to understand its sense and importance; and in order to do this it is primarily necessary to examine that activity in itself, in its dependence on its causes and in connection with its effects, and not merely in relation to the pleasure we can get from it.

If we say that the aim of any activity is merely our pleasure and define it solely by that pleasure, our definition will evidently be a false one. But this is precisely what has occurred in the efforts to define art. . . .

What is art if we put aside the conception of beauty, which confuses the whole matter? The latest and most comprehensible definitions of art, apart from the conception of beauty, are the following:—(1) *a*, Art is an activity arising even in the animal kingdom, and springing from sexual desire and the propensity to play (Schiller, Darwin, Spencer), and *b*, accompanied by a pleasurable excitement of the nervous system (Grant Allen). This is the physiological-evolutionary definition. (2) Art is the external manifestation, by means of lines, colors, movements, sounds, or words, of emotions felt by man (Véron). This is the experimental definition. According to the very latest definition (Sully), (3) Art is "the production of some permanent object or passing action which is fitted not only to supply an active enjoyment to the producer, but to convey a pleasurable impression to a number of spectators or listeners, quite apart from any personal advantage to be derived from it."

Notwithstanding the superiority of these definitions to the metaphysical definitions which depended on the conception of beauty, they are yet far from exact. The first, the physiological-evolutionary definition (1), *a*, is inexact, because instead of speaking about the artistic activity itself, which is the real matter in hand, it treats of the derivation of art. The modification of it, *b*, based on the physiological effects on the human organism, is inexact because within the limits of such definition many other human activities can be included, as has occurred in the neo-esthetic theories which reckon as art the preparation of handsome clothes, pleasant scents, and even of victuals.

The experimental definition, (2), which makes art consist in the expression of emotions, is inexact because a man may express his emotions by means of lines, colors, sounds, or words and yet may not act on others by such expression—and then the manifestation of his emotions is not art.

The third definition (that of Sully) is inexact because in the production of objects or actions affording pleasure to the producer and a pleasant emotion to the spectators or hearers apart from personal advantage, may be included the showing of conjuring tricks or gymnastic exercises, and other activities which are not art. And further, many things the production of which does not afford pleasure to the producer and the sensation received from which is unpleasant, such as gloomy, heart-rending scenes in a poetic description or a play, may nevertheless be undoubted works of art.

The inaccuracy of all these definitions arises from the fact that in them all (as also in the metaphysical definitions) the object considered is the pleasure art may give, and not the purpose it may serve in the life of man and of humanity.

In order to define art correctly it is necessary first of all to cease to consider it as a means to pleasure, and to consider it as one of the conditions of human life. Viewing it in this way we cannot fail to observe that art is one of the means of intercourse between man and man.

Every work of art causes the receiver to enter into a certain kind of relationship both with him who produced or is producing the art, and with all those who, simultaneously, previously, or subsequently, receive the same artistic impression.

Speech transmitting the thoughts and experiences of men serves as a means of union among them, and art serves a similar purpose. The peculiarity of this latter means of intercourse, distinguishing it from intercourse by means of words, consists in this, that whereas by words a man transmits his thoughts to another, by art he transmits his feelings.

The activity of art is based on the fact that a man receiving through his sense of hearing or sight another man's expression of feeling, is capable of experiencing the emotion which moved the man who expressed it. To take the simplest example: one man laughs, and another who hears becomes merry, or a man weeps, and another who hears feels sorrow. A man is excited or irritated, and another man seeing him is brought to a similar state of mind. By his movements or by the sounds of his voice a man expresses courage and determination or sadness and calmness, and this state of mind passes on to others. A man suffers, manifesting his suffering by groans and spasms, and this suffering transmits itself to other people; a man expresses his feelings of admiration, devotion, fear, respect, or love, to certain objects, persons, or phenomena, and others are infected by the same feelings of admiration, devotion, fear, respect, or love, to the same objects, persons, or phenomena.

And it is on this capacity of man to receive another man's expression of feeling and to experience those feelings himself, that the activity of art is based.

If a man infects another or others directly, immediately, by his appearance or by the sounds he gives vent to at the very time he experiences the feeling; if he causes another man to yawn when he himself cannot help yawning, or to laugh or cry when he himself is obliged to laugh or cry, or to suffer when he himself is suffering—that does not amount to art.

Art begins when one person with the object of joining another or others to himself in one and the same feeling, expresses that feeling by certain external indications. To take the simplest example: a boy having experienced, let us say, fear on encountering a wolf, relates that encounter, and in order to evoke in others the feeling he has experienced, describes himself, his condition before the encounter, the surroundings, the wood, his own lightheartedness, and then the wolf's appearance, its movements, the distance between himself and the wolf, and so forth. All this, if only the boy when telling the story again experiences the feelings he had lived through, and infects the hearers and compels them to feel what he had experienced—is art. Even if the boy had not seen a wolf but had frequently been afraid of one, and if wishing to evoke in others the fear he had felt, he invented an encounter with a wolf and recounted it so as to make his hearers share the feelings he experienced when he feared the wolf, that also would be art. And just in the same way it is art if a man, having experienced either the fear of suffering or the attraction of enjoyment (whether in reality or in imagination), expresses these feelings on canvas or in marble so that others are infected by them. And it is also art if a man feels, or imagines to himself, feelings of delight, gladness, sorrow, despair, courage, or despondency, and the transition from one to another of these feelings, and expresses them by sounds so that the hearers are infected by them and experience them as they were experienced by the composer.

The feelings with which the artist infects others may be most various—very strong or very weak, very important or very insignificant, very bad or very good: feelings of love of one's country, self-devotion and submission to fate or to God expressed in a drama, raptures of lovers described in a novel, feelings of voluptuousness expressed in a picture, courage expressed in a triumphal march, merriment evoked by a dance, humor evoked by a funny story, the feeling of quietness transmitted by an evening landscape or by a lullaby, or the feeling of admiration evoked by a beautiful arabesque—it is all art.

If only the spectators or auditors are infected by the feelings which the author has felt, it is art.

To evoke in oneself a feeling one has once experienced and having evoked it in oneself then by means of movements, lines, colors, sounds, or forms expressed in words, so to transmit that feeling that others experience the same feeling—this is the activity of art.

Art is a human activity consisting in this, that one man consciously by means of certain external signs, hands on to others feelings he has lived through, and that others are infected by these feelings and also experience them.

Art is not, as the metaphysicians say, the manifestation of some mysterious Idea of beauty or God; it is not, as the esthetic physiologists say, a game in which man lets off his excess of stored-up energy; it is not the expression of man's emotions by external signs; it is not the production of pleasing objects; and, above all, it is not pleasure; but it is a means of union among men joining them together in the same feelings, and indispensable for the life and progress towards well-being of individuals and of humanity.

As every man, thanks to man's capacity to express thoughts by words, may know all that has been done for him in the realms of thought by all humanity before this day, and can in the present, thanks to this capacity to understand the thoughts of others, become a sharer in their activity and also himself hand on to his contemporaries and descendants the thoughts he has assimilated from others as well as those that have arisen in himself; so, thanks to man's capacity to be infected with the feelings of others by means of art, all that is being lived through by his contemporaries is accessible to him, as well as the feelings experienced by men thousands of years ago, and he has also the possibility of transmitting his own feelings to others.

If people lacked the capacity to receive the thoughts conceived by men who preceded them and to pass on to others their own thoughts, men would be like wild beasts, or like Kasper Hauser.[1]

And if men lacked this other capacity of being infected by art, people might be almost more savage still, and above all more separated from, and more hostile to, one another.

And therefore the activity of art is a most important one, as important as the activity of speech itself and as generally diffused.

As speech does not act on us only in sermons, orations, or books, but in all those remarks by which we interchange thoughts and experiences with one another, so also art in the wide sense of the word permeates our whole life, but it is only to some of its manifestations that we apply the term in the limited sense of the word.

We are accustomed to understand art to be only what we hear and see in theaters, concerts, and exhibitions; together with buildings, statues, poems, and novels. . . . But all this is but the smallest part of the art by which we communicate with one another in life. All human life is filled with works of art of every kind—from cradle-song, jest, mimicry, the ornamentation of houses, dress, and utensils, to church services, buildings, monuments, and triumphal processions. It is all artistic activity. So that by art, in the limited sense of the word, we do not mean all human activity transmitting feelings but only that part which we for some reason select from it and to which we attach special importance. . . .

There is one indubitable sign distinguishing real art from its counterfeit —namely, the infectiousness of art. If a man without exercising effort and without altering his standpoint, on reading, hearing, or seeing another man's work experiences a mental condition which unites him with that man and with others who are also affected by that work, then the object evoking that condition is a work of art. And however poetic, realistic, striking, or interesting, a work may be, it is not a work of art if it does not evoke that feeling (quite distinct from all other feelings) of joy and of spiritual union with another (the author) and with others (those who are also infected by it).

It is true that this indication is an *internal* one and that there are people who, having forgotten what the action of real art is, expect something else from art (in our society the great majority are in this state), and that therefore such people may mistake for this esthetic feeling the feeling of diversion and a certain excitement which they receive from counterfeits of art. But though it is impossible to undeceive these people, just as it may be impossible to convince a man suffering from color-blindness that green is not red, yet for all that, this indication remains perfectly definite to those whose feeling for art is neither perverted nor atrophied, and it clearly distinguishes the feeling produced by art from all other feelings.

The chief peculiarity of this feeling is that the recipient of a truly artistic impression is so united to the artist that he feels as if the work were his own and not some one else's—as if what it expresses were just what he had long been wishing to express. A real work of art destroys in the consciousness of the recipient the separation between himself and the artist, and not that alone, but also between himself and all whose minds receive this work of art. In this freeing of our personality from its separation and isolation, in this uniting of it with others, lies the chief characteristic and the great attractive force of art.

If a man is infected by the author's condition of soul, if he feels this emotion and this union with others, then the object which has effected this is art; but if there be no such infection, if there be not this union with the author and with others who are moved by the same work—then it is not art. And not only is infection a sure sign of art, but the degree of infectiousness is also the sole measure of excellence in art.

The stronger the infection the better is the art, as art, speaking of it now apart from its subject-matter—that is, not considering the value of the feelings it transmits.

And the degree of the infectiousness of art depends on three conditions:

(1) On the greater or lesser individuality of the feeling transmitted; (2) on the greater or lesser clearness with which the feeling is transmitted; (3) on the sincerity of the artist, that is, on the greater or lesser force with which the artist himself feels the emotion he transmits.

The more individual the feeling transmitted the more strongly does it act on the recipient; the more individual the state of soul into which he is transferred the more pleasure does the recipient obtain and therefore the more readily and strongly does he join in it.

Clearness of expression assists infection because the recipient who mingles in consciousness with the author is the better satisfied the more clearly that feeling is transmitted which, as it seems to him, he has long known and felt and for which he has only now found expression.

But most of all is the degree of infectiousness of art increased by the degree of sincerity in the artist. As soon as the spectator, hearer, or reader, feels that the artist is infected by his own production and writes, sings, or plays, for himself, and not merely to act on others, this mental condition of the artist infects the recipient; and, on the contrary, as soon as the spectator, reader, or hearer, feels that the author is not writing, singing, or playing, for his own satisfaction—does not himself feel what he wishes to express, but is doing it for him, the recipient—resistance immediately springs up, and the most individual and the newest feelings and the cleverest technique not only fail to produce any infection but actually repel.

I have mentioned three conditions of contagion in art, but they may all be summed up into one, the last, sincerity; that is, that the artist should be impelled by an inner need to express his feeling. That condition includes the first; for if the artist is sincere he will express the feeling as he experienced it. And as each man is different from everyone else, his feeling will be individual for everyone else; and the more individual it is—the more the artist has drawn it from the depths of his nature—the more sympathetic and sincere will it be. And this same sincerity will impel the artist to find clear expression for the feeling which he wishes to transmit.

Therefore this third condition—sincerity—is the most important of the three. It is always complied with in peasant art, and this explains why such art always acts so powerfully; but it is a condition almost entirely absent from our upper-class art, which is continually produced by artists actuated by personal aims of covetousness or vanity.

Such are the three conditions which divide art from its counterfeits, and which also decide the quality of every work of art considered apart from its subject matter.

The absence of any one of these conditions excludes a work from the category of art and relegates it to that of art's counterfeits. If the work does not transmit the artist's peculiarity of feeling and is therefore not individual, if it is unintelligibly expressed, or if it has not proceeded from the author's inner need for expression—it is not a work of art. If all these conditions are present even in the smallest degree, then the work even if a weak one is yet a work of art.

The presence in various degrees of these three conditions: individuality, clearness, and sincerity, decides the merit of a work of art as art, apart from subject matter. All works of art take order of merit according to the degree in which they fulfil the first, the second, and the third, of these conditions. In one the individuality of the feeling transmitted may predominate; in another, clearness of expression; in a third, sincerity; while a fourth may have sincerity and individuality but be deficient in clearness; a fifth, individuality and clearness, but less sincerity; and so forth, in all possible degrees and combinations.

Thus is art divided from what is not art, and thus is the quality of art, as art, decided, independently of its subject matter, that is to say, apart from whether the feelings it transmits are good or bad. . . .

How in the subject matter of art are we to decide what is good and what is bad?

Art like speech is a means of communication and therefore of progress, that is, of the movement of humanity forward towards perfection. Speech renders accessible to men of the latest generation all the knowledge discovered by the experience and reflection both of preceding generations and of the best and foremost men of their own times; art renders accessible to men of the latest generations all the feelings experienced by their predecessors and also those felt by their best and foremost contemporaries. And as the evolution of knowledge proceeds by truer and more necessary knowledge dislodging and replacing what was mistaken and unnecessary, so the evolution of feeling proceeds by means of art—feelings less kind and less necessary for the well-being of mankind being replaced by others kinder and more needful for that end. That is the purpose of art. And speaking now of the feelings which are its subject matter, the more art fulfils that purpose the better the art, and the less it fulfils it the worse the art.

The appraisement of feelings (that is, the recognition of one or other set of feelings as more or less good, more or less necessary for the well-being of mankind) is effected by the religious perception of the age.

In every period of history and in every human society there exists an understanding of the meaning of life, which represents the highest level to which men of that society have attained—an understanding indicating the highest good at which that society aims. This understanding is the religious perception of the given time and society. And this religious perception is always clearly expressed by a few advanced men and more or less vividly perceived by members of the society generally. Such a religious perception and its corresponding expression always exists in every society. If it appears to us that there is no religious perception in our society, this is not because there really is none, but only because we do not wish to see it. And we often wish not to see it because it exposes the fact that our life is inconsistent with that religious perception.

Religious perception in a society is like the direction of a flowing river. If the river flows at all it must have a direction. If a society lives, there must be a religious perception indicating the direction in which, more or less consciously, all its members tend.

And so there always has been, and is, a religious perception in every society. And it is by the standard of this religious perception that the feelings transmitted by art have always been appraised. It has always been only on the basis of this religious perception of their age, that men have chosen from amid the endlessly varied spheres of art that art which transmitted feelings making religious perception operative in actual life. And such art has always been highly valued and encouraged, while art transmitting feelings already outlived, flowing from the antiquated religious perceptions of a former age, has always been condemned and despised. All the rest of art transmitting those most diverse feelings by means of which people commune with one another was not condemned and was tolerated if only it did not transmit feelings contrary to religious perception. Thus for instance among the Greeks, art transmitting feelings of beauty, strength, and courage (Hesiod, Homer, Phidias) was chosen, approved, and encouraged, while art transmitting feelings of rude sensuality, despondency, and effeminacy, was condemned and despised. Among the Jews, art transmitting feelings of devotion and submission to the God of the Hebrews and to His will (the epic of Genesis, the prophets, the Psalms) was chosen and encouraged, while art transmitting feelings of idolatry (the Golden Calf) was condemned and despised. All the rest of art—stories, songs, dances, ornamentation of houses, of utensils, and of clothes—which was not contrary to religious perception, was neither distinguished nor discussed. Thus as regards its subject matter has art always and everywhere been appraised and thus it should be appraised, for this attitude towards art proceeds from the fundamental characteristics of human nature, and those characteristics do not change.

I know that according to an opinion current in our times religion is a superstition humanity has outgrown, and it is therefore assumed that no such thing exists as a religious perception common to us all by which art in our time can be appraised. I know that this is the opinion current in the pseudo-cultured circles of today. People who do not acknowledge Christianity in its true meaning because it undermines their social privileges, and who therefore invent all kinds of philosophic and esthetic theories to hide from themselves the meaninglessness and wrongfulness of their lives, cannot think otherwise. These people intentionally, or sometimes unintentionally, confuse the notion of a religious cult with the notion of religious perception, and think that by denying the cult they get rid of the perception. But even the very attacks on religion and the attempts to establish an idea of life contrary to the religious perception of our times, most clearly demonstrate the existence of a religious perception condemning the lives that are not in harmony with it.

If humanity progresses, that is, moves forward, there must inevitably be a guide to the direction of that movement. And religions have always furnished that guide. All history shows that the progress of humanity is accomplished no otherwise than under the guidance of religion. But if the race cannot progress without the guidance of religion—and progress is always going on, and consequently goes on also in our own times—then there must be a religion of our times. So that whether it pleases or displeases the so-called cultured people of today, they must admit the existence of religion —not of a religious cult, Catholic, Protestant, or another, but of religious perception—which even in our times is the guide always present where there is any progress. And if a religious perception exists amongst us, then the feelings dealt with by our art should be appraised on the basis of that religious perception; and as has been the case always and everywhere, art transmitting feelings flowing from the religious perception of our time should be chosen from amid all the indifferent art, should be acknowledged, highly valued, and encouraged, while art running counter to that perception should be condemned and despised, and all the remaining, indifferent, art should neither be distinguished nor encouraged.

The religious perception of our time in its widest and most practical application is the consciousness that our well-being, both material and spiritual, individual and collective, temporal and eternal, lies in the growth of brotherhood among men—in their loving harmony with one another. This perception is not only expressed by Christ and all the best men of past ages, it is not only repeated in most varied forms and from most diverse sides by the best men of our times, but it already serves as a clue to all the complex labor of humanity, consisting as this labor does on the one hand in the destruction of physical and moral obstacles to the union of men, and on the other hand in establishing the principles common to all men which can and should unite them in one universal brotherhood. And it is on the basis of this perception that we should appraise all the phenomena of our life and among the rest our art also: choosing from all its realms and highly prizing and encouraging whatever transmits feelings flowing from this religious perception, rejecting whatever is contrary to it, and not attributing to the rest of art an importance that does not properly belong to it. . . .

Whatever the work may be and however it may have been extolled, we have first to ask whether this work is one of real art, or a counterfeit. Having acknowledged, on the basis of the indication of its infectiousness even to a small class of people, that a certain production belongs to the realm of art, it is necessary on this basis to decide the next question, Does this work belong to the category of bad exclusive art opposed to religious perception, or of Christian art uniting people? And having acknowledged a work to belong to real Christian art, we must then, according to whether it transmits feelings flowing from love of God and man, or merely the simple feelings uniting all men, assign it a place in the ranks of religious art, or in those of universal art.

Only on the basis of such verification shall we find it possible to select from the whole mass of what in our society claims to be art, those works which form real, important, necessary, spiritual food, and to separate them from all the harmful and useless art and from the counterfeits of art which surround us. Only on the basis of such verification shall we be able to rid ourselves of the pernicious results of harmful art and avail ourselves of that beneficent action which is the purpose of true and good art, and which is indispensable for the spiritual life of man and of humanity.

—*What Is Art?* (1896; translated 1905 by Aylmer Maude)

NOTE

1. "The foundling of Nuremberg," found in the marketplace of that town on 23rd May 1828, apparently some sixteen years old. He spoke little and was almost totally ignorant even of common objects. He subsequently explained that he had been brought up in confinement underground and visited by only one man, whom he saw but seldom.

C. J. DUCASSE

Art and the Language of the Emotions

That art is the language of the emotions has been widely held since Eugène Véron in 1878 declared that art is "the emotional expression of human personality," and Tolstoy in 1898 that "art is a human activity consisting in this, that one man consciously, by means of certain external signs, hands on to others feelings he has lived through, and that other people are infected by these feelings, and also experience them."

1. *Expression? or expression and transmission?* Whether transmission of the emotions expressed occurs or not, however, is largely accidental; for a given work of art may happen never to come to the attention of persons other than the artist himself; and yet it remains a work of art. Moreover, the individual psychological constitution of persons other than the artist who may contemplate his work is one of the variables that determine whether the feelings those persons then experience are or are not the same as the feelings the artist intended the object he has created to express. Evidently the activity of the artist *as artist* terminates with his creation of the work of art. What the word *language* signifies in the phrase *language of the emotions* is therefore essentially *medium of expression*, and only adventitiously means of transmission.

But even after this has been realized, the term *language of the emotions* still remains ambiguous in several respects. The present paper attempts to eliminate its ambiguities and thereby to make clear in precisely what sense the statement that art is the language of the emotions must be taken if it is to constitute a true answer to the two questions, What is art? and What is a work of art?

2. *The arts, and the fine arts.* The first of the facts to which attention must be called is that the word *art* in its generic sense means *skill*; and that the purposes in pursuit of which one employs skill may be more specifically pragmatic, or epistemic, or aesthetic.

Let it therefore be understood that, in what follows, only *aesthetic* art, i.e., what is commonly called *fine art*, will be in view. Indeed, because of the limited space here available, only the visual and the auditory arts, but not the literary arts, will be directly referred to. What will be said about the former arts, however, would in essentials apply also to the latter.

3. *The two central questions.* So much being clear, the two questions mentioned above may now be stated more fully as follows:

a. Just what does the *creative operation* termed *expression of emotion* consist in, which *the artist* is performing at the time he is creating a work of art? b. Just what is meant by saying that *the work of art*, once it has come into existence, then itself "expresses emotions"?

4. *The feelings, and the emotions.* Before the attempt is made to answer these two questions, it is necessary to point out that a fairer statement of what is really contended when art is said to be the language of the emotions would be that art is the language *of the feelings.* For the term *the emotions* ordinarily designates the relatively few feelings—anger, love, fear,

joy, anxiety, jealousy, sadness, etc.—for which names were needed because their typical spontaneous manifestations, and the typical situations that arouse those particular feelings, present themselves again and again in human life. And if, when art is said to be the language of the emotions, "the emotions" were taken to designate only the few dozen varieties of feelings that have names, then that conception of art would apply to only a small proportion of the things that are admittedly works of art. The fact is that human beings experience, and that works of art and indeed works of nature too express, many feelings besides the few ordinarily thought of when the term *the emotions* is used. These other feelings are too rare, or too fleeting, or too unmanifested, or their nuances too subtle, to have pragmatic importance and therefore to have needed names.

5. *Being sad vs. imagining sadness.* Taking it as granted, then, that the emotions of which art is said to be the language include these many nameless feelings as well as the emotions, moods, sentiments, and attitudes that have names, the next important distinction is between *having* a feeling—for instance, *being* sad—and only *imagining* the feeling called sadness; that is, imagining it not in the sense of supposing oneself to be sad, but in the sense of entertaining a *mental image* of sadness.

The essential distinction here as regards feelings, and in the instance as regards the feeling-quality called *sadness* is the same as the distinction in the case of a color, or a tone, or a taste, etc., between actually *sensing* it, and only *imagining* it; for example, between *seeing* some particular shade of red, and only *imagining* that shade, i.e., calling up a mental image of it as one does when perhaps remembering the red one saw the day before.

6. *Venting vs. objectifying sadness.* Next two possible senses of the statement that *a person* is expressing sadness must be clearly distinguished.

If a person who *is* sad manifests the fact at all in his behavior, the behavior that manifests it consists of such things as groans, or sighs, or a dejected posture or countenance; and these behaviors express his sadness in the sense of *venting* it, i.e., of being *effusions* of it. They are not intentional; and the interest of other persons in them is·normally not aesthetic interest, but *diagnostic*—diagnostic of the nature of his emotional state; and possibly also *pragmatic* in that these evidences of his sadness may move other persons to try to cheer him up.

Unlike such venting or effusion, however, which is automatic, the *composing* of sad music—or, comprehensively, the creating of a work of any of the arts—is *a critically controlled purposively creative operation.* If the composer manages to accomplish it, *he* then has expressed sadness. In order to do it, however, he need not at all—and preferably should not—himself *be* sad at the time but rather, and essentially, *intent* and striving to achieve his intent. This is, to compose music that will be sad not in the sense of itself experiencing sadness, since music does not experience feelings, but in the sense of *objectifying* sadness.

And that a particular musical composition objectifies sadness means that it has the *capacity*—the power—to cause an *image* of sadness to arise in the consciousness of a person who attends to the music with aesthetic interest; or, as we might put it, the capacity to make him taste, or sample, sadness without actually making him sad. It is sad in the sense in which quinine is bitter even at times when it is not being tasted; for bitter, as predicated of *quinine*, is the name of the *capacity or power* of quinine, when put on the tongue, to cause experience of bitter taste; whereas bitter, as predicated *of a taste*, is the name not of a capacity or power of that taste, but *of that taste quality itself.*

7. *Aesthetic contemplation.* A listener who is attending to the music with interest in its emotional import is engaged in aesthetic contemplation of the music. He is doing what the present writer has elsewhere proposed to call *ecpathizing* the music—ecpathizing being the analogue in the language of feeling of what reading is in the language of concepts. Reading *acquaints* the reader with, for instance, the opinion which a given sentence formulates but does not necessarily cause him to adopt it himself. Similarly, listening with aesthetic interest to sad music *acquaints* the listener with the taste of sadness, but does not ordinarily make him sad.

8. *The process of objectification of feeling.* The psychological process in the artist, from which a work of art eventually results, is ordinarily gradual. Except in very simple works of art, the artist very seldom imagines precisely from the start either the finished elaborate work he is about to record or the rich complex of feelings it will objectify in the sense stated above. Normally, the creative process has many steps, each of them of the trial and error type. In the case of music, the process may get started by some sounds the composer hears, or more likely by some sound-images that emerge spontaneously out of his subconsciousness and inspire him. That they inspire him means that they move him to add to them some others in some particular temporal pattern. Having done so, he then contemplates aesthetically the bit of music he has just invented and perhaps actually played; and, if need be, he then alters it until its emotional import satisfies the inspiration that generated it. Next, contemplation in turn of the created and now satisfactory musical fragment generates spontaneously some addition to it, the emotional import of which in the temporal context of the previously created fragment is then in its turn contemplated, judged, and either approved or altered until found satisfactory. Each such complex step both inspires a particular next step, and rules out particular others which a different composer might have preferred.

This process—of inspiration-creation-contemplation-judgment and correction or approval—is repeated again and again until the musical composition, or as the case may be the painting, or statue, or work of one of the other arts, is finished; each image that is found satisfactory being ordinarily recorded in musical notation, or in paint on canvas, etc., rather than trusted to memory.

9. *The sources of the emotional import of an object.* The feelings, of which images are caused to arise in a person when he contemplates with aesthetic interest a given work of art, or indeed any object, have several possible sources.

One of them is the *form* of the object; that is, the particular *arrangement of its parts in space, or in time, or both.* Taking as simplest example a tone expressive of sadness, its form would consist of its *loudness-shape,* e.g., diminuendo from moderately loud to nothing.

A second source of feeling would be what might be called the *material* of the tone; that is, its *quality* as made up of its fundamental pitch, of such overtones as may be present, and of the mere noise it may also contain.

And still another source of feeling would be the emotional import of what the presented tone may *represent* whether consciously or subconsciously to a particular hearer; that is, the emotional import which the tone may be *borrowing* from past experiences of his to which it was intrinsic, that happened to be closely associated with experience of that same tone at some time in the history of the person now hearing it again. For instance the tone, although itself rather mournful, might happen to have been the signal of quitting time at the factory where he worked at a tedious job. This would have made the tone *represent* something cheerful—would have given the tone a cheerful *meaning*; the cheerfulness of which henceforth automatically mingles with, or perhaps masks for him, the otherwise mournful feeling-import of the tone's presented quality and loudness shape. This third possible source of the emotional import of an aesthetically contemplated object may be termed the object's *connotation*; so that in the example just used the tone has mournfulness of quality and form, but cheerfulness of *connotation*. . . .

10. *"The language of the emotions" defined.* The effect of the several distinctions, to the indispensability of which attention has been called in what precedes, is, the writer believes, to make it possible now to state precisely the sense in which it is true that art is the language of the emotions. This sense is as follows.

Art is the critically controlled purposive activity which aims to create an object having the capacity to reflect to its creator, when he contemplates it with interest in its emotional import, the feeling-images that had dictated the specific form and content he gave the object; the created object being capable also of generating, in other persons who contemplate it aesthetically, feeling-images similar or dissimilar to those which dictated the specific features given the object by the artist, according as the psychological constitution of these other persons resembles or differs from that of the artist who created the particular work of art.

—*The Journal of Aesthetics and Art Criticism*, Vol. 22 (1964)

CHAPTER
3
Intuition-Expression

BENEDETTO CROCE: Intuition and Expression
R. G. COLLINGWOOD: Art as Expression

Benedetto Croce (1866–1952), the most famous Italian philosopher of this century, was like Véron, Tolstoy, and Ducasse in maintaining that art expresses human feelings, and he was like Gombrich in contending that art combines imagination and knowledge. Unlike intellectualists such as Aristotle, he believed that the objects known through art are particulars, not universals—unique qualities, not general characteristics.

His fundamental doctrine is that art is intuition, which he defines in this selection as the knowing of what is individual. Intuition, he declares somewhat paradoxically, is equivalent to expression.

Clinging to idealism, the view that reality consists of minds and their activities, he is intent upon analyzing the stages of mental activity. Apart from sensation, which is relatively passive, these stages may be schematized as follows:

1. *Knowing*, or theoretic activity.
   (a) *Art*, the knowing of particulars, or intuition.
      Its value is the *beautiful*; its disvalue, the *ugly*.[1]
   (b) *Pure Science and Philosophy*, the knowing of universals, or conception.
      Value: the *true*; disvalue: the *false*.
2. *Doing*, or practical activity.
   (a) *Economic and Prudential Activity*, the pursuit of individual ends.
      Value: the *useful*; disvalue, the *harmful*.
   (b) *Morality*, the pursuit of universal ends.
      Value: the *morally good*; disvalue, the *morally evil*.

These divisions are not sharp. "The forms of the spirit," declares Croce, "are distinct and not separate, and when the spirit is found in one of its forms, or is *explicit* in it, the other forms are also in it, but *implicit*."[2] For example, thinking involves doing, and vice versa. Also, intuition is accompanied by conception and by the two forms of practical activity. But each stage is marked by its fundamental emphasis, whereby it is defined. Esthetic philosophy, for Croce, consists in explaining the nature of art as intuition, and in contrasting art with sensation and the other stages of human activity.

Sensation is passive; art is active. Art is not mere passive perception or daydreaming; it is inner vision formulated in images. Halfway between the passivity of sensation and the activity of art is fancy. It is art only in the making because it lacks the unity of genuine intuition. Fancy is too passive; it allows images and sensations to float lazily through the mind, or combines them arbitrarily. Art is complete only when the spirit works upon the relatively formless materials of experience, converting them into expressive and harmonious images.

What gives unity to this imaginative vision is a *lyrical content*, the pervasive expression of "feeling." "Feeling" does not mean merely *emotion*, but rather any subjective mood, including volitional attitudes. "We do not ask the artist for a philosophical system nor for a relation of facts," Croce declares, "but for a dream of his own, for nothing but the expression of a world desired or abhorred, or partly desired and partly abhorred. If he makes us live again in this dream the rapture of joy or the incubus of terror, in solemnity or in humility, in tragedy, or in laughter, that suffices."[3] In thus including both emotion and desire, Croce in effect synthesizes the voluntaristic theory of Schopenhauer, Nietzsche, and Freud and the emotionalist theory of Véron and Tolstoy.

As an imaginative grasp of the unique, art is not concerned with the true and false, real and unreal, useful or harmful, good or bad. Nothing counts in art but the perfection of the imaginative vision in itself, and by its own standard of "expressiveness," which was for Croce another word for "beauty."

Intuition, so interpreted, is equivalent to expression. Croce doubts the existence of "mute inglorious Miltons," burdened with inspiration but lacking the gift of expression. If a man truly has Miltonic intuitions, he has no difficulty expressing himself. Indeed, he does not know what he wants to express until he has expressed it, imaginatively, if not overtly.

The influence of Croce in the English-speaking world was heightened by the work of Robin George Collingwood (1889–1943), professor at Oxford and author of important books on philosophy and history. In a letter to Croce dated May 29, 1921, he spoke of himself as "a friend and disciple of your philosophy." When he completed *The Principles of Art*, he sent a copy to Croce, remarking in a letter of April 20, 1938: "I hope that you will do me the honor of accepting it in token of the debt (far too great and too complex to be acknowledged in detail) which I owe you in every department of thought and more especially in aesthetic."[4]

In writing the selection contained in this chapter, Collingwood was intent on clarifying the meaning of the artistic expression of emotion, distinguishing it from describing, or communicating, or arousing, or betraying the emotion. He does not deny that these latter activities may accompany artistic expression, but he does deny that they constitute its core. In distinguishing between expression and description,

Collingwood restates Croce's theme that art is the lyrical expression of individual qualities. He is also in accord with Croce in maintaining that expression and intuition go hand in hand.

NOTES

1. For Croce, value is tendency-fulfillment. Value results when the activity unfolds freely; disvalue, when the activity is hindered, impeded.

2. Benedetto Croce, *The Philosophy of the Practical* (Macmillan, London, 1913), pp. 33–34.

3. *Ibid.*, p. 268.

4. Quoted by Alan Donagan, *The Later Philosophy of Collingwood* (Oxford, Clarendon Press, 1962), pp. 314–315.

BENEDETTO CROCE

Intuition and Expression

I. ART AS INTUITION

. . . As to what is art—I will say at once, in the simplest manner, that art is *vision* or *intuition*. The artist produces an image or a phantasm; and he who enjoys art turns his gaze upon the point to which the artist has pointed, looks through the chink which he has opened, and reproduces that image in himself. "Intuition," "vision," "contemplation," "imagination," "fancy," "figurations," "representations," and so on, are words continually recurring, like synonyms, when discoursing upon art, and they all lead the mind to the same conceptual sphere which indicates general agreement.

But this reply, that art is intuition, obtains its force and meaning from all that it implicitly denies and from which it distinguishes art. What negations are implicit in it? I shall indicate the principal, or at least those that are the most important for us at this present moment of our culture.

It denies, above all, that art is a *physical fact*: for example, certain determined colors, or relations of colors; certain definite forms of bodies; certain definite sounds, or relations of sounds; certain phenomena of heat or of electricity—in short, whatsoever be designed as "physical." The inclination toward this error of physicizing art is already present in ordinary thought, and as children who touch the soap-bubble and would wish to touch the rainbow, so the human spirit, admiring beautiful things, hastens spontaneously to trace out the reasons for them in external nature, and proves that it must think, or believes that it should think, certain colors beautiful and certain other colors ugly, certain forms beautiful and certain other forms ugly. But this attempt has been carried out intentionally and with method on several occasions in the history of thought: from the "canons" which the Greek theoreticians and artists fixed for the beauty of bodies, through the speculations as to the geometrical and numerical relations of figures and sounds, down to the researches of the estheticians of the nineteenth century (Fechner, for example), and to the "communications" presented in our day by the inexpert, at philosophical, psychological, and natural science congresses, concerning the relations of physical phenomena with art. And if it be asked why art cannot be a physical fact, we must reply, in the first place, that physical facts *do not possess reality*, and that art, to which so many devote their whole lives and which fills all with a divine joy, is *supremely real*; thus it cannot be a physical fact, which is something unreal. This sounds at first paradoxical, for nothing seems more solid and secure to the ordinary man than the physical world; but we, in the seat of truth, must not abstain from the good reason and substitute for it one less good, solely because the first should have the appearance of a lie; and besides, in order to surpass what of strange and difficult may be contained in that truth, to become at home with it, we may take into consideration the fact that the demonstration of the unreality of the physical world has not only been proved in an indisputable manner and is admitted by all philosophers (who are not crass materialists and are not involved in the strident contradictions of materialism), but is professed by these same physicists in the spontaneous philosophy which they mingle with their physics, when they conceive physical phenomena as products of principles that are beyond experience, of atoms or of ether, or as the manifestation of an Unknowable: besides, the matter itself of the materialists is a super-material principle. Thus physical facts reveal themselves, by their internal logic and by common consent, not as reality, but as a *construction of our intellect for the purposes of science*. Consequently, the question whether art be a physical fact must rationally assume this different signification: that is to say, *whether it be possible to construct art physically*. And this is certainly possible, for we indeed carry it out always, when, turning from the sense of a poem and ceasing to enjoy it, we set ourselves, for example, to count the words of which the poem is composed and to divide them into syllables and letters; or, disregarding the esthetic effect of a statue, we weigh and measure it: a most useful performance for the packers of statues, as is the other for the typographers who have to "compose" pages of poetry; but most useless for the contemplator and student of art, to whom it is neither useful nor licit to allow himself to be "distracted" from his proper object. Thus art is not a physical fact in this second sense, either; which amounts to saying that when we propose to ourselves to penetrate its nature and mode of action, to construct it physically is of no avail.

Another negation is implied in the definition of art as intuition: if it be intuition, and intuition is equivalent to *theory* in the original sense of contemplation, art cannot be a utilitarian act; and since a utilitarian act aims always at obtaining pleasure and therefore at keeping off a pain, art, considered in its own nature, has nothing to do with the *useful* and with *pleasure* and *pain*, as such. It, will be admitted, indeed, without much difficulty, that a pleasure as a pleasure, any sort of pleasure, is not of itself artistic; the pleasure of a drink of water that slakes thirst, or a walk in the open air that stretches our limbs and makes our blood circulate more lightly, or the obtaining of a longed-for post that settles us in practical life, and so on, is not artistic. Finally, the difference between pleasure and art leaps to the eyes in the relations that are developed between ourselves and works of art, because the figure represented may be dear to us and represent the most delightful memories, and at the same time the picture may be ugly; or, on the other hand, the picture may be beautiful and the figure represented hateful to our hearts, or the picture itself, which we approve as beautiful, may also cause us rage and envy, because it is the work of our enemy or rival, for whom it will procure advantage and on whom it will confer new strength: our practical interests, with their relative pleasures and pains, mingle and sometimes become confused with art and disturb, but are never *identified* with, our esthetic interest. At the most it will be affirmed, with a view to maintaining more effectively the definition of art as the pleasurable, that it is not the pleasurable in general, but a *particular* form of the pleasurable. But such a restriction is no longer a defense, it is indeed an abandonment of that thesis; for given that art is a particular form of pleasure, its distinctive character would be supplied, not by the pleasurable, but by what distinguishes that pleasurable from other pleasurables, and it would be desirable to turn the attention to that distinctive element —more than pleasurable or different from pleasurable. Nevertheless, the doctrine that defines art as the pleasurable has a special denomination (hedonistic esthetic), and a long and complicated development in the history of esthetic doctrines: it showed itself in the Greco-Roman world, prevailed in the eighteenth century, reflowered in the second half of the nineteenth, and still enjoys much favor, being especially well received by beginners in esthetic, who are above all struck by the fact that art causes pleasure. The life of this doctrine has consisted of proposing in turn one or another class of pleasures, or several classes together (the pleasure of the superior senses, the pleasure of play, of consciousness of our own strength, of criticism, etc.), or of adding to it elements differing from the pleasurable, the useful for example (when understood as distinct from the pleasurable), the satisfaction of cognoscitive and moral wants, and the like. And its progress has been caused just by this restlessness, and by its allowing foreign elements to ferment in its bosom, which it introduces through the necessity of somehow bringing itself into agreement with the reality of art, thus attaining to its dissolution as hedonistic doctrine and to the promotion of a new doctrine, or at least to drawing attention to its necessity. And since every error has its element of truth (and that of the physical doctrine has been seen to be the possibility of the physical "construction" of art as of any other fact), the hedonistic doctrine has its eternal element of truth in the placing in relief the hedonistic accompaniment, or pleasure, common to the esthetic activity as to every form of spiritual activity, which it has not at all been intended to deny in absolutely denying the identification of art with the pleasurable, and in distinguishing it from the pleasurable by defining it as intuition.

A third negation, effected by means of the theory of art as intuition, is that art is a *moral act*; that is to say, that form of practical act which, although necessarily uniting with the useful and with pleasure and pain, is not immediately utilitarian and hedonistic, and moves in a superior spiritual sphere. But the intuition, in so far as it is a theoretic act, is opposed to the practical of any sort. And in truth, art, as has been remarked from the earliest times, does not arise as an act of the will; good will, which constitutes the honest man, does not constitute the artist. And since it is not the result of an act of will, so it escapes all moral discrimination, not because a privilege of exemption is accorded to it, but simply because moral discrimination cannot be applied to art. An artistic image portrays an act morally praiseworthy or blameworthy; but this image, as image, is neither morally praiseworthy nor blameworthy. Not only is there no penal code that can condemn an image to prison or to death, but no moral judgment, uttered by a rational person, can make of it its object: we might just as well judge the square moral or the triangle immoral as the Francesca of Dante immoral or the Cordelia of Shakespeare moral, for these have a purely artistic function, they are like musical notes in the souls of Dante and of Shakespeare. Further, the moralistic theory of art is also represented in the history of esthetic doctrines, though much discredited in the common opinion of our times, not only on account of its intrinsic demerit, but also, in some measure, owing to the moral demerit of certain tendencies of our times, which render possible, owing to psychological dislike, that refutation of it which should be made—and which we here make—solely for logical reasons. The end attributed to art, of directing the good and inspiring horror of evil, of correcting and ameliorating customs, is a derivation of the moralistic doctrine; and so is the demand addressed to artists to collaborate in the education of the lower classes, in the strengthening of the national or bellicose spirit of a people, in the diffusion of the ideals of a modest and laborious life; and so on. These are all things that art cannot do, any more than geometry, which, however, does not lose anything of its importance on account of its inability to do this; and one does not see why art should do so, either. That it cannot do these things was partially perceived by the moralistic estheticians also; who very readily effected a transaction with it, permitting it to provide pleasures that were not moral, provided they were not openly dishonest, or recommending it to employ to a good end the dominion that, owing to its hedonistic power, it possessed over souls, to gild the pill, to sprinkle sweetness upon the rim of the glass containing the bitter draught—in short, to play the courtesan (since it could not get rid of its old and inborn habits), in the service of holy church or of morality: *meretrix ecclesiæ*. On other occasions they have sought to avail themselves of it for purposes of instruction, since not only virtue but also science is a difficult thing, and art could remove this difficulty and render pleasant and attractive the entrance into the ocean of science—indeed, lead them through it as through a garden of Armida, gayly and voluptuously, without their being conscious of the lofty protection they had obtained, or of the crisis of renovation which they were preparing for themselves. We cannot now refrain from a smile when we talk of these theories, but should not forget that they were once a serious matter corresponding to a serious effort to understand the nature of art and to elevate the conception of it; and that among those who believed in it (to limit ourselves to Italian literature) were Dante and Tasso, Parini and Alfieri, Manzoni and Mazzini. And the moralistic doctrine of art was and is and will be perpetually beneficial by its very contradictions; it was and will be an effort, however unhappy, to separate art from the merely pleasing, with which it is sometimes confused, and to assign to it a more worthy post: and it, too, has its true side, because, if art be beyond morality, the artist is neither this side of it nor that, but under its empire, insofar as he is a man who cannot withdraw himself from the duties of man, and must look upon art itself— art, which is not and never will be moral—as a mission to be exercised as a priestly office.

Again (and this is the last and perhaps the most important of all the general negations that it suits me to recall in relation to this matter), with the definition of art as intuition, we deny that it has the character of *conceptual knowledge*. Conceptual knowledge, in its true form, which is the philosophical, is always realistic, aiming at establishing reality against unreality, or at lowering unreality by including it in reality as a subordinate moment of reality itself. But intuition means, precisely, indistinction of reality and unreality, the image with its value as mere image, the pure ideality of the image; and opposing the intuitive or sensible knowledge to the conceptual or intelligible, the esthetic to the noetic, it aims at claiming the autonomy of this more simple and elementary form of knowledge, which has been compared to the dream (the dream, and not the sleep) of the theoretic life, in respect to which philosophy would be the waking. And indeed, whoever should ask, when examining a work of art, whether what the artist has expressed be metaphysically and historically true or false, asks a question that is without meaning, and commits an error analogous to his who should bring the airy images of the fancy before the tribunal of morality: without meaning, because the discrimination of true and false always concerns an affirmation of reality, or a judgment, but it cannot fall under the head of an image or of a pure subject, which is not the subject of a judgment, since it is without qualification or predicate. It is useless to object that the individuality of the image cannot subsist without reference to the universal, of which that image is the individuation, because we do not here deny that the universal, as the spirit of God, is everywhere and animates all things with itself, but we deny that the universal is rendered logically explicit and is thought in the intuition. Useless also is the appeal to the principle of the unity of the spirit, which is not broken, but, on the contrary, strengthened by the clear distinction of fancy from thought, because from the distinction comes opposition, and from opposition concrete unity.

Ideality (as has also been called this character that distinguishes the intuition from the concept, art from philosophy and from history, from the affirmation of the universal and from the perception or narration of what has happened) is the intimate virtue of art; no sooner are reflection and judgment developed from that ideality, than art is dissipated and dies: it dies in the artist, who becomes a critic; it dies in the contemplator, who changes from an entranced enjoyer of art to a meditative observer of life. . . .

And since this vindication of the alogical character of art is, as I have said, the most difficult and important of the negations included in the formula of art-intuition, the theories that attempt to explain art as philosophy, as religion, as history, or as science, and in a lesser degree as mathematics, occupy the greater part of the history of esthetic science and are adorned with the names of the greatest philosophers. Schelling and Hegel afford examples of the identification or confusion of art with religion and philosophy in the eighteenth century; Taine, of its confusion with the natural sciences; the theories of the French verists, of its confusion with historical and documentary observation; the formalism of the Herbartians, of its confusion with mathematics. But it would be vain to seek pure examples of these errors in any of these authors and in the others that might be mentioned, because error is never pure, for if it were so, it would be truth. . . .

But doubt springs up at the feet of truth, "like a young shoot"—as the *terzina* of father Dante has it—doubt, which is what drives the intellect of man "from mount to mount." The doctrine of art as intuition, as fancy, as form, now gives rise to an ulterior (I have not said an "ultimate") problem, which is no longer one of opposition and distinction toward physics, hedonistic, ethic and logic, but the field of images itself, which sets in doubt the capacity of the image to define the character of art and is in reality occupied with the mode of separating the genuine from the spurious image, and of enriching in this way the concept of the image and of art. What function (it is asked) can a world of pure images possess in the spirit of man, without philosophical, historical, religious, or scientific value, and without even moral or hedonistic value? What is more vain than to dream with open eyes in life, which demands, not only open eyes, but an open mind and a nimble spirit? Pure images! But to nourish oneself upon pure images is called by a name of little honor, "to dream," and there is usually added to this the epithet of "idle." It is a very insipid and inconclusive thing; can it ever be art? Certainly, we sometimes amuse ourselves with the reading of some sensational romance of adventure, where images follow images in the most various and unexpected way; but we thus enjoy ourselves in moments of fatigue, when we are obliged to kill time, and with a full consciousness that such stuff is not art. Such instances are of the nature of a pastime, a game; but were art a game or a pastime, it would fall into the wide arms of hedonistic doctrine, ever open to receive it. And it is a utilitarian and hedonistic need that impels us sometimes to relax the bow of the mind and the bow of the will, and to stretch ourselves, allowing images to follow one another in our memory, or combining them in quaint forms with the aid of the imagination, in a sort of waking sleep, from which we rouse ourselves as soon as we are rested; and we sometimes rouse ourselves just to devote ourselves to the work of art, which cannot be produced by a mind relaxed. Thus either art is not pure intuition, and the claims put forward in the doctrines which we believed we had above confuted, are not satisfied, and so the confutation itself of these doctrines is troubled with doubts; or intuition cannot consist in a simple act of imagination. . . .

The intuition is the product of an image, and not of an incoherent mass of images obtained by recalling former images and allowing them to succeed one another capriciously, by combining one image with another in a like capricious manner, joining a horse's neck to a human head, and thus playing a childish game. Old Poetic availed itself above all of the concept of *unity*, in order to express this distinction between the intuition and imagining, insisting that whatever the artistic work, it should be *simplex et unum*; or of the allied concept of *unity in variety*—that is to say, the multiple images were to find their common center unit of union in a comprehensive image: and the esthetic of the nineteenth century created with the same object the distinction, which appears in not a few of its philosophers, between *fancy* (the peculiar artistic faculty) and *imagination* (the extra-artistic faculty).[1] To amass, select, cut up, combine images, presupposes the possession of particular images in the spirit; and fancy produces, whereas imagination is sterile, adapted to extrinsic combinations and not to the generation of organism and life. . . .

The intuition is truly artistic, it is truly intuition, and not a chaotic mass of images, only when it has a vital principle that animates it, making it all one with itself; but what is this principle?

The answer to such a question may be said to result from the examination of the greatest ideal strife that has ever taken place in the field of art (and is not confined to the epoch that took its name from it and in which it was predominant): the strife between *romanticism* and *classicism*. Giving the general definition, here convenient, and setting aside minor and accidental determinations, romanticism asks of art, above all, the spontaneous and violent effusion of the affections, of love and hate, of anguish and jubilation, of desperation and elevation; and is willingly satisfied and pleased with vaporous and indeterminate images, broken and allusive in style, with vague suggestions, with approximate phrases, with powerful and troubled sketches: while classicism loves the peaceful soul, the wise design, figures studied in their characteristics and precise in outline, ponderation, equilibrium, clarity; and resolutely tends toward *representation*, as the other tends toward feeling. And whoever puts himself at one or the other point of view finds crowds of reasons for maintaining it and for confuting the opposite point of view; because (say the romantics), what is the use of an art, rich in beautiful images, which, nevertheless, does not speak to the heart? And if it do speak to the heart, what is the use if the images be not beautiful? And the others will say, What is the use of the shock of the passions, if the spirit do not rest upon a beautiful image? And if the image be beautiful, if our taste be satisfied, what matters the absence of those emotions which can all of them be obtained outside art, and which life does not fail to provide, sometimes in greater quantity than we desire? But when we begin to feel weary of the fruitless defense of both partial views; above all, when we turn away from the ordinary works of art produced by the romantic and classical schools, from works convulsed with passion or coldly decorous, and fix them on the works, not of the disciples, but of the masters, not of the mediocre, but of the supreme, we see the contest disappear in the distance and find ourselves unable to call the great portions of these works, romantic or classiç or representative, because they are both classic and romantic, feelings and representations, a vigorous feeling which has become all most brilliant representation. Such, for example, are the works of Hellenic art, and such those of Italian poetry and art: the transcendentalism of the Middle Ages became fixed in the bronze of the Dantesque *terzina*; melancholy and suave fancy, in the transparency of the songs and sonnets of Petrarch; sage experience of life and badinage with the fables of the past, in the limpid *ottava rima* of Ariosto; heroism and the thought of death, in the perfect blank-verse hendecasyllabics of Foscolo; the infinite variety of everything, in the sober and austere songs of Giacomo Leopardi. Finally (be it said in parenthesis and without intending comparison with the other examples adduced), the voluptuous refinements and animal sensuality of international decadentism have received their most perfect expression in the prose and verse of an Italian, D'Annunzio. All these souls were profoundly passionate (all, even the serene Lodovico Ariosto, who was so amorous, so tender, and so often repressed his emotion with a smile); their works of art are the eternal flower that springs from their passions.

These expressions and these critical judgments can be theoretically resumed in the formula, that what gives coherence and unity to the intuition is feeling: the intuition is really such because it represents a feeling, and can only appear from and upon that. Not the idea, but the feeling, is what confers upon art the airy lightness of the symbol: an aspiration enclosed in the circle of a representation—that is art; and in it the aspiration alone stands for the representation, and the representation alone for the aspiration. Epic and lyric, or drama and lyric, are scholastic divisions of the indivisible: art is always lyrical—that is, epic and dramatic in feeling. What we admire in genuine works of art is the perfect fanciful form which a state of the soul assumes; and we call this life, unity, solidity of the work of art. What displeases us in the false and imperfect forms is the struggle of several different states of the soul not yet unified, their stratification, or mixture, their vacillating method, which obtains apparent unity from the will of the author, who for this purpose avails himself of an abstract plan or idea, or extra-esthetic, passionate emotion. A series of images which seem to be, each in turn, rich in power of conviction, leaves us nevertheless deluded and diffident, because we do not see them generated from a state of the soul, from a "sketch" (as the painters call it), from a motive; and they follow one another and crowd together without that precise intonation, without that accent, which comes from the heart. And what is the figure cut out from the background of the picture or transported and placed against another background, what is the personage of drama or of romance outside his relation with all the other personages and with the general action? And what is the value of this general action if it be not an action of the spirit of the author? The secular disputes concerning dramatic unity are interesting in this connection; they are first applied to the unity of "action" when they have been obtained from an extrinsic determination of time and place, and this finally applied to the unity of "interest," and the interest would have to be in its turn dissolved in the interest of the spirit of the poet—that is, in his intimate aspiration, in his feeling. The negative issue of the great dispute between classicists and romanticists is interesting, for it resulted in the negation both of the art which strives to distract and illude the soul as to the deficiency of the image with mere feeling, with the practical violence of feeling, with feeling that has not become contemplation, and of the art which, by means of the superficial clearness of the image, of drawing correctly false, of the word falsely correct, seeks to deceive as to its lack of inspiration and its lack of an esthetic reason to justify what it has produced. A celebrated sentence uttered by an English critic,[2] and become one of the commonplaces of journalism, states that "all the arts tend to the condition of music"; but it would have been more accurate to say that all the arts are music, if it be thus intended to emphasize the genesis of esthetic images in feeling, excluding from their number those mechanically constructed or realistically ponderous. And another not less celebrated utterance of a Swiss semi-philosopher, which has had the like good or bad fortune of becoming trivial, discovers that "every landscape is a state of the soul"[3]: which is indisputable, not because the landscape is landscape, but because the landscape is art.

Artistic intuition, then, is always *lyrical* intuition: this latter being a word that is not present as an adjective or definition of the first, but as a synonym, another of the synonyms that can be united to the several that I have mentioned already, and which, all of them, designate the intuition. And if it be sometimes convenient that instead of appearing as a synonym, it should assume the grammatical form of the adjective, that is only to make clear the difference between the intuition-image, or nexus of images (for what is called image is always a nexus of images, since image-atoms do not exist any more than thought-atoms), which constitutes the organism, and, as organism, has its vital principle, which is the organism itself— between this, which is true and proper intuition, and that false intuition which is a heap of images put together in play or intentionally or for some other practical purpose, the connection of which, being practical, shows itself to be not organic, but mechanic, when considered from the esthetic point of view. But the word *lyric* would be redundant save in this explicative or polemical sense; and art is perfectly defined when it is simply defined as intuition.

—*The Breviary of Æsthetic* (1913; translated 1915 by Douglas Ainslee)

NOTES

1. Croce here employs the terms "imagination" and "fancy" in a sense opposite to the modern English usage. The Italian *"fantasia"* corresponds to our word "imagination," and the Italian *"immaginazione"* to our "fancy." The distinction that Croce is making corresponds to Coleridge's contrast between imagination and fancy, except that the terms are interchanged. For Coleridge's account see his *Biographia Literaria*, chapters 4, 12, and 13. Wordsworth has a similar account in his *Preface to the Poems of 1815*. (Editor's note.)

2. Walter Pater, *The Renaissance*, Essay on "The School of Giorgione." (Editor's note.)

3. Amiel. (Editor's note.)

II. INTUITION AND EXPRESSION

Knowledge has two forms: it is either *intuitive* knowledge or *logical* knowledge; knowledge obtained through the *imagination* or knowledge obtained through the *intellect*; knowledge of the *individual* or knowledge of the *universal*; of *individual things* or of the *relations* between them: it is, in fact, productive either of *images* or of *concepts*.

In ordinary life, constant appeal is made to intuitive knowledge. It is said that we cannot give definitions of certain truths; that they are not demonstrable by syllogisms; that they must be learnt intuitively. The politician finds fault with the abstract reasoner, who possesses no lively intuition of actual conditions; the educational theorist insists upon the necessity of developing the intuitive faculty in the pupil before everything else; the critic in judging a work of art makes it a point of honor to set aside theory and abstractions, and to judge it by direct intuition; the practical man professes to live rather by intuition than by reason.

But this ample acknowledgment granted to intuitive knowledge in ordinary life, does not correspond to an equal and adequate acknowledgment in the field of theory and of philosophy. There exists a very ancient science of intellectual knowledge, admitted by all without discussion, namely, Logic; but a science of intuitive knowledge is timidly and with difficulty asserted by but a few. Logical knowledge has appropriated the lion's share; and if she does not slay and devour her companion outright, yet yields to her but grudgingly the humble place of maidservant or door-keeper.—What can intuitive knowledge be without the light of intellectual knowledge? It is a servant without a master; and though a master find a servant useful, the master is a necessity to the servant, since he enables him to gain his livelihood. Intuition is blind; intellect lends her eyes.

Now, the first point to be firmly fixed in the mind is that intuitive knowledge has no need of a master, nor to lean upon any one; she does not need to borrow the eyes of others, for she has excellent eyes of her own. Doubtless it is possible to find concepts mingled with intuitions. But in many other intuitions there is no trace of such a mixture, which proves that it is not necessary. The impression of a moonlight scene by a painter; the outline of a country drawn by a cartographer; a musical motive, tender or energetic; the words of a sighing lyric, or those with which we ask, command and lament in ordinary life, may well all be intuitive facts without a shadow of intellectual relation. But, think what one may of these instances, and admitting further the contention that the greater part of the intuitions of civilized man are impregnated with concepts, there yet remains to be observed something more important and more conclusive. Those concepts which are found mingled and fused with the intuitions are no longer concepts, in so far as they are really mingled and fused, for they have lost all independence and autonomy. They have been concepts, but have now become simple elements of intuition. The philosophical maxims placed in the mouth of a personage of tragedy or of comedy, perform there the function, not of concepts, but of characteristics of such personage; in the same way as the red in a painted face does not there represent the red color of the physicists, but is a characteristic element of the portrait.

The whole is that which determines the quality of the parts. A work of art may be full of philosophical concepts; it may contain them in greater abundance and they may there be even more profound than in a philosophical dissertation, which in its turn may be rich to overflowing with descriptions and intuitions. But notwithstanding all these concepts the total effect of the work of art is an intuition; and notwithstanding all those intuitions, the total effect of the philosophical dissertation is a concept. The *Promessi Sposi* contains copious ethical observations and distinctions, but does not for that reason lose as a whole its character of simple story or intuition. In like manner the anecdotes and satirical effusions to be found in the works of a philosopher like Schopenhauer do not deprive those works of their character of intellectual treatises. The difference between a scientific work and a work of art, that is, between an intellectual fact and an intuitive fact, lies in the difference of the total effect aimed at by their respective authors. This it is that determines and rules over the several parts of each, not these parts separated and considered abstractly in themselves.

But to admit the independence of intuition as regards concept does not suffice to give a true and precise idea of intuition. Another error arises among those who recognize this, or who at any rate do not explicitly make intuition dependent upon the intellect, to obscure and confuse the real nature of intuition. By intuition is frequently understood *perception,* or the knowledge of actual reality, the apprehension of something as *real.*

Certainly perception is intuition: the perceptions of the room in which I am writing, of the ink bottle and paper that are before me, of the pen I am using, of the objects that I touch and make use of as instruments of my person, which, if it write, therefore exists; these are all intuitions. But the image that is now passing through my brain of a me writing in another room, in another town, with different paper, pen and ink, is also an intuition. This means that the distinction between reality and non-reality is extraneous, secondary, to the true nature of intuition. If we imagine a human mind having intuitions for the first time, it would seem that it could have intuitions of actual reality only, that is to say, that it could have perceptions of nothing but the real. But since knowledge of reality is based upon the distinction between real images and unreal images, and since this distinction does not at the first moment exist, these intuitions would in truth not be intuitions either of the real or of the unreal, not perceptions, but pure intuitions. Where all is real, nothing is real. The child, with its difficulty of distinguishing true from false, history from fable, which are all one to childhood, can furnish us with a sort of very vague and only remotely approximate idea of this ingenuous state. Intuition is the undifferentiated unity of the perception of the real and of the simple image of the possible. In our intuitions we do not oppose ourselves as empirical beings to external reality, but we simply objectify our impressions, whatever they be.

Those, therefore, who look upon intuition as sensation formed and arranged simply according to the categories of space and time, would seem to approximate more nearly to the truth. Space and time (they say) are the forms of intuition; to have an intuition is to place it in space and in temporal sequence. Intuitive activity would then consist in this double and concurrent function of spatiality and temporality. But for these two categories must be repeated what was said of intellectual distinctions, when found mingled with intuitions. We have intuitions without space and without time: the color of a sky, the color of a feeling, a cry of pain and an effort of will, objectified in consciousness: these are intuitions which we possess, and with their making space and time have nothing to do. In some intuitions, spatiality may be found without temporality, in others, *vice versa*; and even where both are found, they are perceived by later reflection: they can be fused with the intuition in like manner with all its other elements: that is, they are in it *materialiter* and not *formaliter*, as ingredients and not as arrangement. Who, without an act of reflection which for a moment breaks in upon his contemplation, can think of space while looking at a drawing or a view? Who is conscious of temporal sequence while listening to a story or a piece of music without breaking into it with a similar act of reflection? What intuition reveals in a work of art is not space and time, but *character, individual physiognomy*. The view here maintained is confirmed in several quarters of modern philosophy. Space and time, far from being simple and primitive functions, are nowadays conceived as intellectual constructions of great complexity. And further, even in some of those who do not altogether deny to space and time the quality of formative principles, categories and functions, one observes an effort to unite them and to regard them in a different manner from that in which these categories are generally conceived. Some limit intuition to the sole category of spatiality, maintaining that even time can only be intuited in terms of space. Others abandon the three dimensions of space as not philosophically necessary, and conceive the function of spatiality as void of all particular spatial determination. But what could such a spatial function be, a simple arrangement that should arrange even time? It represents, surely, all that criticism and refutation have left standing—the bare demand for the affirmation of some intuitive activity in general. And is not this activity truly determined, when one single function is attributed to it, not spatializing nor temporalizing, but characterizing? Or rather, when it is conceived as itself a category or function which gives us knowledge of things in their concreteness and individuality?

Having thus freed intuitive knowledge from any suggestion of intellectualism and from every later and external addition, we must now explain it and determine its limits from another side and defend it from a different kind of invasion and confusion. On the hither side of the lower limit is sensation, formless matter, which the spirit can never apprehend in itself as simple matter. This it can only possess with form and in form, but postulates the notion of it as a mere limit. Matter, in its abstraction, is mechanism, passivity; it is what the spirit of man suffers, but does not produce. Without it no human knowledge or activity is possible; but mere matter produces animality, whatever is brutal and impulsive in man, not the spiritual dominion, which is humanity. How often we strive to understand clearly what is passing within us! We do catch a glimpse of something, but this does not appear to the mind as objectified and formed. It is in such moments as these that we best perceive the profound difference between matter and form. These are not two acts of ours, opposed to one another; but the one is outside us and assaults and sweeps us off our feet, while the other inside us tends to absorb and identify itself with that which is outside. Matter, clothed and conquered by form, produces concrete form. It is the matter, the content, which differentiates one of our intuitions from another: the form is constant: it is spiritual activity, while matter is changeable. Without matter spiritual activity would not forsake its abstractness to become concrete and real activity, this or that spiritual content, this or that definite intuition.

It is a curious fact, characteristic of our times, that this very form, this very activity of the spirit, which is essentially ourselves, is so often ignored or denied. Some confound the spiritual activity of man with the metaphorical and mythological activity of what is called nature, which is mechanism and has no resemblance to human activity, save when we imagine, with Æsop, that *"arbores loquuntur non tantum ferae."*[1] Some affirm that they have never observed in themselves this "miraculous" activity, as though there were no difference, or only one of quantity, between sweating and thinking, feeling cold and the energy of the will. Others, certainly with greater reason, would unify activity and mechanism in a more general concept, though they are specifically distinct. Let us, however, refrain for the moment from examining if such a final unification be possible, and in what sense, but admitting that the attempt may be made, it is clear that to unify two concepts in a third implies to begin with the admission of a difference between the two first. Here it is this difference that concerns us and we set it in relief.

Intuition has sometimes been confused with simple sensation. But since this confusion ends by being offensive to common sense, it has more frequently been attenuated or concealed with a phraseology apparently designed at once to confuse and to distinguish them. Thus, it has been asserted that intuition is sensation, but not so much simple sensation as *association* of sensations. Here a double meaning is concealed in the word "association." Association is understood, either as memory, mnemonic association, conscious recollection, and in that case the claim to unite in memory elements which are not intuited, distinguished, possessed in some way by the spirit and produced by consciousness, seems inconceivable: or it is understood as association of unconscious elements, in which case we remain in the world of sensation and of nature. But if with certain associationists we speak of an association which is neither memory nor flux of sensations, but a *productive* association (formative, constructive, distinguishing); then our contention is admitted and only its name is denied to it. For productive association is no longer association in the sense of the sensationalists, but *synthesis*, that is to say, spiritual activity. Synthesis may be called association; but with the concept of productivity is already posited the distinction between passivity and activity, between sensation and intuition.

Other psychologists are disposed to distinguish from sensation something which is sensation no longer, but is not yet intellectual concept: the *representation* or *image*. What is the difference between their representation or image and our intuitive knowledge? Everything and nothing: for "representation" is a very equivocal word. If by representation be understood something cut off and standing out from the psychic basis of the sensations, then representation is intuition. If, on the other hand, it be conceived as complex sensation we are back once more in crude sensation, which does not vary in quality according to its richness or poverty, or according to whether the organism in which it appears is rudimentary or highly developed and full of traces of past sensations. Nor is the ambiguity remedied by defining representation as a psychic product of secondary degree in relation to sensation, defined as occupying the first place. What does secondary degree mean here? Does it mean a qualitative, formal difference? If so, representation is an elaboration of sensation and therefore intuition. Or does it mean greater complexity and complication, a quantitative, material difference? In that case intuition is once more confused with simple sensation.

And yet there is a sure method of distinguishing true intuition, true representation, from that which is inferior to it: the spiritual fact from the mechanical, passive, natural fact. Every true intuition or representation is also *expression*. That which does not objectify itself in expression is not intuition or representation, but sensation and mere natural fact. The spirit only intuits in making, forming, expressing. He who separates intuition from expression never succeeds in reuniting them.

Intuitive activity *possesses intuitions to the extent that it expresses them*. Should this proposition sound paradoxical, that is partly because, as a general rule, a too restricted meaning is given to the word "expression." It is generally restricted to what are called verbal expressions alone. But there exist also non-verbal expressions, such as those of line, color and sound, and to all of these must be extended our affirmation, which embraces therefore every sort of manifestation of the man, as orator, musician, painter, or anything else. But be it pictorial, or verbal, or musical, or in whatever other form it appear, to no intuition can expression in one of its forms be wanting; it is, in fact, an inseparable part of intuition. How can we really possess an intuition of a geometrical figure, unless we possess so accurate an image of it as to be able to trace it immediately upon paper or on the blackboard? How can we really have an intuition of the contour of a region, for example of the island of Sicily, if we are not able to draw it as it is in all its meanderings? Everyone can experience the internal illumination which follows upon his success in formulating to himself his impressions and feelings, but only so far as he is able to formulate them. Feelings or impressions, then, pass by means of words from the obscure region of the soul into the clarity of the contemplative spirit. It is impossible to distinguish intuition from expression in this cognitive process. The one appears with the other at the same instant, because they are not two, but one.

The principal reason which makes our view appear paradoxical as we maintain it, is the illusion or prejudice that we possess a more complete intuition of reality than we really do. One often hears people say that they have many great thoughts in their minds, but that they are not able to express them. But if they really had them, they would have coined them into just so many beautiful, sounding words, and thus have expressed them.

If these thoughts seem to vanish or to become few and meager in the act of expressing them, the reason is that they did not exist or really were few and meager. People think that all of us ordinary men imagine and intuit countries, figures and scenes like painters, and bodies like sculptors; save that painters and sculptors know how to paint and carve such images, while we bear them unexpressed in our souls. They believe that any one could have imagined a Madonna of Raphael; but that Raphael was Raphael owing to his technical ability in putting the Madonna upon canvas. Nothing can be more false than this view. The world which as a rule we intuit is a small thing. It consists of little expressions, which gradually become greater and wider with the increasing spiritual concentration of certain moments. They are the words we say to ourselves, our silent judgments: "Here is a man, here is a horse, this is heavy, this is sharp, this pleases me," etc. It is a medley of light and color, with no greater pictorial value than would be expressed by a haphazard splash of colors, from among which one could barely make out a few special, distinctive traits. This and nothing else is what we possess in our ordinary life; this is the basis of our ordinary action. It is the index of a book. The labels tied to things (it has been said) take the place of the things themselves. This index and these labels (themselves expressions) suffice for small needs and small actions. From time to time we pass from the index to the book, from the label to the thing, or from the slight to the greater intuitions, and from these to the greatest and most lofty. This passage is sometimes far from easy. It has been observed by those who have best studied the psychology of artists that when, after having given a rapid glance at any one, they attempt to obtain a real intuition of him, in order, for example, to paint his portrait, then this ordinary vision, that seemed so precise, so lively, reveals itself as little better than nothing. What remains is found to be at the most some superficial trait, which would not even suffice for a caricature. The person to be painted stands before the artist like a world to discover. Michaelangelo said, "One paints, not with the hands, but with the brain." Leonardo shocked the prior of the Convent of the Graces by standing for days together gazing at the "Last Supper," without touching it with the brush. He remarked of this attitude: "The minds of men of lofty genius are most active in invention when they are doing the least external work." The painter is a painter, because he sees what others only feel or catch a glimpse of, but do not see. We think we see a smile, but in reality we have only a vague impression of it, we do not perceive all the characteristic traits of which it is the sum, as the painter discovers them after he has worked upon them and is thus able to fix them on the canvas. We do not intuitively possess more even of our intimate friend, who is with us every day and at all hours, than at most certain traits of physiognomy which enable us to distinguish him from others. The illusion is less easy as regards musical expression; because it would seem strange to every one to say that the composer had added or attached notes to a motive which was already in the mind of him who is not the composer; as if Beethoven's Ninth Symphony were not his own intuition and his intuition the Ninth Symphony. Now, just as one who is deluded as to the amount of his material wealth is confuted by arithmetic, which states its exact amount, so he who nourishes delusions as to the wealth of his own thoughts and images is brought back to reality, when he is obliged to cross the *Pons Asinorum* of expression. Let us say to the former, count; to the latter, speak; or, here is a pencil, draw, express yourself.

Each of us, as a matter of fact, has in him a little of the poet, of the sculptor, of the musician, of the painter, of the prose writer: but how little, as compared with those who bear those names, just because they possess the most universal dispositions and energies of human nature in so lofty a degree! How little too does a painter possess of the intuitions of a poet! And how little does one painter possess those of another painter! Nevertheless, that little is all our actual patrimony of intuitions or representations. Beyond these are only impressions, sensations, feelings, impulses, emotions, or whatever else one may term what still falls short of the spirit and is not assimilated by man; something postulated for the convenience of exposition, while actually non-existent, since to exist also is a fact of the spirit.

We may thus add this to the various verbal descriptions of intuition, noted at the beginning: intuitive knowledge is expressive knowledge. Independent and autonomous in respect to intellectual function; indifferent to later empirical discriminations, to reality and to unreality, to formations and apperceptions of space and time, which are also later: intuition or representation is distinguished as *form* from what is felt and suffered, from the flux or wave of sensation, or from psychic matter; and this form, this taking possession, is expression. To intuit is to express; and nothing else (nothing more, but nothing less) than *to express*.

—*Æsthetic* 1901; translation of second edition, 1922, by Douglas Ainslee)

NOTE

1. "Talking trees are not so fierce."

R. G. COLLINGWOOD

Art as Expression

1. Expressing Emotion and Arousing Emotion

Our first question is this. Since the artist proper has something to do with emotion, and what he does with it is not to arouse it, what is it that he does? It will be remembered that the kind of answer we expect to this question is an answer derived from what we all know and all habitually say; nothing original or recondite, but something entirely commonplace.

Nothing could be more entirely commonplace than to say he expresses them. The idea is familiar to every artist, and to every one else who has any acquaintance with the arts. To state it is not to state a philosophical theory or definition of art; it is to state a fact or supposed fact about which, when we have sufficiently identified it, we shall have later to theorize philosophically. For the present it does not matter whether the fact that is alleged, when it is said that the artist expresses emotion, is really a fact or only supposed to be one. Whichever it is, we have to identify it, that is, to decide what it is that people are saying when they use the phrase. Later on, we shall have to see whether it will fit into a coherent theory.

They are referring to a situation, real or supposed, of a definite kind. When a man is said to express emotion, what is being said about him comes to this. At first, he is conscious of having an emotion, but not conscious of what this emotion is. All he is conscious of is a perturbation or excitement, which he feels going on within him, but of whose nature he is ignorant. While in this state, all he can say about his emotion is: "I feel . . . I don't know what I feel." From this helpless and oppressed condition he extricates himself by doing something which we call expressing himself. This is an activity which has something to do with the thing we call language: he expresses himself by speaking. It has also something to do with consciousness: the emotion expressed is an emotion of whose nature the person who feels it is no longer unconscious. It has also something to do with the way in which he feels the emotion. As unexpressed, he feels it in what we have called a helpless and oppressed way; as expressed, he feels it in a way from which this sense of oppression has vanished. His mind is somehow lightened and eased.

This lightening of emotions which is somehow connected with the expression of them has a certain resemblance to the "catharsis" by which emotions are earthed through being discharged into a make believe situation; but the two things are not the same. Suppose the emotion is one of anger. If it is effectively earthed, for example by fancying oneself kicking some one down stairs, it is thereafter no longer present in the mind as anger at all: we have worked it off and are rid of it. If it is expressed, for example by putting it into hot and bitter words, it does not disappear from the mind; we remain angry; but instead of the sense of oppression which accompanies an emotion of anger not yet recognized as such, we have that sense of alleviation which comes when we are conscious of our own emotion as anger, instead of being conscious of it only as an unidentified perturbation. This is what we refer to when we say that it "does us good" to express our emotions.

The expression of an emotion by speech may be addressed to some one; but if so it is not done with the intention of arousing a like emotion in him. If there is any effect which we wish to produce in the hearer, it is only the effect which we call making him understand how we feel. But, as we have already seen, this is just the effect which expressing our emotions has on ourselves. It makes us, as well as the people to whom we talk, understand how we feel. A person arousing emotion sets out to affect his audience in a way in which he himself is not necessarily affected. He and his audience stand in quite different relations to the act, very much as physician and patient stand in quite different relations towards a drug administered by the one and taken by the other. A person expressing emotion, on the contrary, is treating himself and his audience in the same kind of way; he is making his emotions clear to his audience, and that is what he is doing to himself.

It follows from this that the expression of emotion, simply as expression, is not addressed to any particular audience. It is addressed primarily to the speaker himself, and secondarily to any one who can understand. Here again, the speaker's attitude towards his audience is quite unlike that of a person desiring to arouse in his audience a certain emotion. If that is what he wishes to do, he must know the audience he is addressing. He must know what type of stimulus will produce the desired kind of reaction in people of that particular sort; and he must adapt his language to his audience in the sense of making sure that it contains stimuli appropriate to their peculiarities. If what he wishes to do is to express his emotions intelligibly, he has to express them in such a way as to be intelligible to himself; his audience is then in the position of persons who overhear[1] him doing this. Thus the stimulus-and-reaction terminology has no applicability to the situation.

The means-and-end, or technique, terminology too is inapplicable. Until a man has expressed his emotion, he does not yet know what emotion it is. The act of expressing it is therefore an exploration of his own emotions. He is trying to find out what these emotions are. There is certainly here a directed process: an effort, that is, directed upon a certain end; but the end is not something foreseen and preconceived, to which appropriate means can be thought out in the light of our knowledge of its special character. Expression is an activity of which there can be no technique.

2. EXPRESSION AND INDIVIDUALIZATION

Expressing an emotion is not the same thing as describing it. To say "I am angry" is to describe one's emotion, not to express it. The words in which it is expressed need not contain any reference to anger as such at all. Indeed, so far as they simply and solely express it, they cannot contain any such reference. The curse of Ernulphus, as invoked by Dr. Slop on the unknown person who tied certain knots, is a classical and supreme expression of anger; but it does not contain a single word descriptive of the emotion it expresses.

This is why, as literary critics well know, the use of epithets in poetry, or even in prose where expressiveness is aimed at, is a danger. If you want to express the terror which something causes, you must not give it an epithet like "dreadful." For that describes the emotion instead of expressing it, and your language becomes frigid, that is inexpressive, at once. A genuine poet, in his moments of genuine poetry, never mentions by name the emotions he is expressing.

Some people have thought that a poet who wishes to express a great variety of subtly differentiated emotions might be hampered by the lack of a vocabulary rich in words referring to the distinctions between them; and that psychology, by working out such a vocabulary, might render a valuable service to poetry. This is the opposite of the truth. The poet needs no such words at all; the existence or non-existence of a scientific terminology describing the emotions he wishes to express is to him a matter of perfect indifference. If such a terminology, where it exists, is allowed to affect his own use of language, it affects it for the worse.

The reason why description, so far from helping expression, actually damages it, is that description generalizes. To describe a thing is to call it a thing of such and such a kind: to bring it under a conception, to classify it. Expression, on the contrary, individualizes. The anger which I feel here and now, with a certain person, for a certain cause, is no doubt an instance of anger, and in describing it as anger one is telling truth about it; but it is much more than mere anger: it is a peculiar anger, not quite like any anger that I ever felt before, and probably not quite like any anger I shall ever feel again. To become fully conscious of it means becoming conscious of it not merely as an instance of anger, but as this quite peculiar anger. Expressing it, we saw, has something to do with becoming conscious of it; therefore, if being fully conscious of it means being conscious of all its peculiarities, fully expressing it means expressing all its peculiarities. The poet, therefore, in proportion as he understands his business, gets as far away as possible from merely labelling his emotions as instances of this or that general kind, and takes enormous pains to individualize them by expressing them in terms which reveal their difference from any other emotion of the same sort.

This is a point in which art proper, as the expression of emotion, differs sharply and obviously from any craft whose aim it is to arouse emotion. The end which a craft sets out to realize is always conceived in general terms, never individualized. However accurately defined it may be, it is always defined as the production of a thing having characteristics that could be shared by other things. A joiner, making a table out of these pieces of wood and no others, makes it to measurements and specifications which, even if actually shared by no other table, might in principle be shared by other tables. A physician treating a patient for a certain complaint is trying to produce in him a condition which might be, and probably has been, often produced in others, namely, the condition of recovering from that complaint. So an "artist" setting out to produce a certain emotion in his audience is setting out to produce not an individual emotion, but an emotion of a certain kind. It follows that the means appropriate to its production will be not individual means but means of a certain kind: that is to say, means which are always in principle replaceable by other similar means. As every good craftsman insists, there is always a "right way" of performing any operation. A "way" of acting is a general pattern to which various individual actions may conform. In order that the "work of art" should produce its intended psychological effect, therefore, whether this effect be magical or merely amusing, what is necessary is that it should satisfy certain conditions, possess certain characteristics: in other words be, not this work and no other, but a work of this kind and of no other.

This explains the meaning of the generalization which Aristotle and others have ascribed to art. We have already seen that Aristotle's *Poetics* is concerned not with art proper but with representative art, and representative art of one definite kind. He is not analysing the religious drama of a hundred years before, he is analysing the amusement literature of the fourth century, and giving rules for its composition. The end being not individual but general (the production of an emotion of a certain kind) the means too are general (the portrayal, not of this individual act, but of an act of this sort; not, as he himself puts it, what Alcibiades did, but what anybody of a certain kind would do). Sir Joshua Reynolds's idea of generalization is in principle the same; he expounds it in connexion with what he calls "the grand style," which means a style intended to produce emotions of a certain type. He is quite right; if you want to produce a typical case of a certain emotion, the way to do it is to put before your audience a representation of the typical features belonging to the kind of thing that produces it: make your kings very royal, your soldiers very soldierly, your women very feminine, your cottages very cottagesque, your oak-trees very oakish, and so on.

Art proper, as expression of emotion, has nothing to do with all this. The artist proper is a person who, grappling with the problem of expressing a certain emotion, says, "I want to get this clear." It is no use to him to get something else clear, however like it this other thing may be. Nothing will serve as a substitute. He does not want a thing of a certain kind, he wants a certain thing. This is why the kind of person who takes his literature as psychology, saying "How admirably this writer depicts the feelings of women, or busdrivers, or homosexuals . . .," necessarily misunderstands every real work of art with which he comes into contact, and takes for good art, with infallible precision, what is not art at all.

3. Selection and Aesthetic Emotion

It has sometimes been asked whether emotions can be divided into those suitable for expression by artists and those unsuitable. If by art one means art proper, and identifies this with expression, the only possible answer is that there can be no such distinction. Whatever is expressible is expressible. There may be ulterior motives in special cases which make it desirable to express some emotions and not others; but only if by "express" one means express publicly, that is, allow people to overhear one expressing oneself. This is because one cannot possibly decide that a certain emotion is one which for some reason it would be undesirable to express thus publicly, unless one first becomes conscious of it; and doing this, as we saw, is somehow bound up with expressing it. If art means the expression of emotion, the artist as such must be absolutely candid; his speech must be absolutely free. This is not a precept, it is a statement. It does not mean that the artist ought to be candid, it means that he is an artist only in so far as he is candid. Any kind of selection, any decision to express this emotion and not that, is inartistic not in the sense that it damages the perfect sincerity which distinguishes good art from bad, but in the sense that it represents a further process of a non-artistic kind, carried out when the work of expression proper is already complete. For until that work is complete one does not know what emotions one feels; and is therefore not in a position to pick and choose, and give one of them preferential treatment.

From these considerations a certain corollary follows about the division of art into distinct arts. Two such divisions are current: one according to the medium in which the artist works, into painting, poetry, music, and the like; the other according to the kind of emotion he expresses, into tragic, comic, and so forth. We are concerned with the second. If the difference between tragedy and comedy is a difference between the emotions they express, it is not a difference that can be present to the artist's mind when he is beginning his work; if it were, he would know what emotion he was going to express before he had expressed it. No artist, therefore, so far as he is an artist proper, can set out to write a comedy, a tragedy, an elegy, or the like. So far as he is an artist proper, he is just as likely to write any one of these as any other; which is the truth that Socrates was heard expounding towards the dawn, among the sleeping figures in Agathon's dining-room.[2] These distinctions, therefore, have only a very limited value. They can be properly used in two ways. (1) When a work of art is complete, it can be labelled *ex post facto* as tragic, comic, or the like, according to the character of the emotions chiefly expressed in it. But understood in that sense the distinction is of no real importance. (2) If we are talking about representational art, the case is very different. Here the so-called artist knows in advance what kind of emotion he wishes to excite, and will construct works of different kinds according to the different kinds of effect they are to produce. In the case of representational art, therefore, distinctions of this kind are not only admissible as an *ex post facto* classification of things to which in their origin it is alien; they are present from the beginning as a determining factor in the so-called artist's plan of work.

The same considerations provide an answer to the question whether there is such a thing as a specific "aesthetic emotion." If it is said that there is such an emotion independently of its expression in art, and that the business of artists is to express it, we must answer that such a view is nonsense. It implies, first, that artists have emotions of various kinds, among which is this peculiar aesthetic emotion; secondly, that they select this aesthetic emotion for expression. If the first proposition were true, the second would have to be false. If artists only find out what their emotions are in the course of finding out how to express them, they cannot begin the work of expression by deciding what emotion to express.

In a different sense, however, it is true that there is a specific aesthetic emotion. As we have seen, an unexpressed emotion is accompanied by a feeling of oppression; when it is expressed and thus comes into consciousness the same emotion is accompanied by a new feeling of alleviation or easement, the sense that this oppression is removed. It resembles the feeling of relief that comes when a burdensome intellectual or moral problem has been solved. We may call it, if we like, the specific feeling of having successfully expressed ourselves; and there is no reason why it should not be called a specific aesthetic emotion. But it is not a specific kind of emotion pre-existing to the expression of it, and having the peculiarity that when it comes to be expressed it is expressed artistically. It is an emotional colouring which attends the expression of any emotion whatever.

4. THE ARTIST AND THE ORDINARY MAN

I have been speaking of "the artist," in the present chapter, as if artists were persons of a special kind, differing somehow either in mental endowment or at least in the way they use their endowment from the ordinary persons who make up their audience. But this segregation of artists from ordinary human beings belongs to the conception of art as craft; it cannot be reconciled with the conception of art as expression. If art were a kind of craft, it would follow as a matter of course. Any craft is a specialized form of skill, and those who possess it are thereby marked out from the rest of mankind. If art is the skill to amuse people, or in general to arouse emotions in them, the amusers and the amused form two different classes, differing in their respectively active and passive relation to the craft of exciting determinate emotions; and this difference will be due, according to whether the artist is "born" or "made," either to a specific mental endowment in the artist, which in theories of this type has gone by the name of "genius," or to a specific training.

If art is not a kind of craft, but the expression of emotion, this distinction of kind between artist and audience disappears. For the artist has an audience only in so far as people hear him expressing himself, and understand what they hear him saying. Now, if one person says something by way of expressing what is in his mind, and another hears and understands him, the hearer who understands him has that same thing in his mind. The question whether he would have had it if the first had not spoken need not here be raised; however it is answered, what has just been said is equally true. If some one says "Twice two is four" in the hearing of some one incapable of carrying out the simplest arithmetical operation, he will be understood by himself, but not by his hearer. The hearer can understand only if he can add two and two in his own mind. Whether he could do it before he heard the speaker say those words makes no difference. What is here said of expressing thoughts is equally true of expressing emotions. If a poet expresses, for example, a certain kind of fear, the only hearers who can understand him are those who are capable of experiencing that kind of fear themselves. Hence, when some one reads and understands a poem, he is not merely understanding the poet's expression of his, the poet's, emotions, he is expressing emotions of his own in the poet's words, which have thus become his own words. As Coleridge put it, we know a man for a poet by the fact that he makes us poets. We know that he is expressing his emotions by the fact that he is enabling us to express ours.

Thus, if art is the activity of expressing emotions, the reader is an artist as well as the writer. There is no distinction of kind between artist and audience. This does not mean that there is no distinction at all. When Pope wrote that the poet's business was to say "what all have felt but none so well express'd," we may interpret his words as meaning (whether or no Pope himself consciously meant this when he wrote them) that the poet's difference from his audience lies in the fact that, though both do exactly the same thing, namely express this particular emotion in these particular words, the poet is a man who can solve for himself the problem of expressing it, whereas the audience can express it only when the poet has shown them how. The poet is not singular either in his having that emotion or in his power of expressing it; he is singular in his ability to take the initiative in expressing what all feel, and all can express.

5. THE CURSE OF THE IVORY TOWER

I have already had occasion to criticize the view that artists can or should form a special order or caste, marked off by special genius or special training from the rest of the community. That view, we have seen, was a by-product of the technical theory of art. This criticism can now be reinforced by pointing out that a segregation of this kind is not only unnecessary but fatal to the artist's real function. If artists are really to express "what all have felt," they must share the emotions of all. Their experiences, the general attitude they express towards life, must be of the same kind as that of the persons among whom they hope to find an audience. If they form themselves into a special clique, the emotions they express will be the emotions of that clique; and the consequence will be that their work becomes intelligible only to their fellow artists. This is in fact what happened to a great extent during the nineteenth century, when the segregation of artists from the rest of mankind reached its culmination.

If art had really been a craft, like medicine or warfare, the effect of this segregation would have been all to the good, for a craft only becomes more efficient if it organizes itself into the shape of a community devoted to serving the interests of the public in a specialized way, and planning its whole life with an eye to the conditions of this service. Because it is not a craft, but the expression of emotions, the effect was the opposite of this. A situation arose in which novelists, for example, found themselves hardly at their ease except in writing novels about novelists, which appealed to nobody except other novelists. This vicious circle was most conspicuous in certain continental writers like Anatole France or D'Annunzio, whose subject-matter often seemed to be limited by the limits of the segregated clique of "intellectuals." The corporate life of the artistic community became a kind of ivory tower whose prisoners could think and talk of nothing except themselves, and had only one another for audience.

Transplanted into the more individualistic atmosphere of England, the result was different. Instead of a single (though no doubt subdivided) clique of artists, all inhabiting the same ivory tower, the tendency was for each artist to construct an ivory tower of his own: to live, that is to say, in a world of his own devising, cut off not only from the ordinary world of common people but even from the corresponding worlds of other artists. Thus Burne-Jones lived in a world whose contents were ungraciously defined by a journalist as "green light and gawky girls"; Leighton in a world of sham Hellenism; and it was the call of practical life that rescued Yeats from the sham world of his youthful Celtic twilight, forced him into the clear air of real Celtic life, and made him a great poet.

In these ivory towers art languished. The reason is not hard to understand. A man might easily have been born and bred within the confines of a society as narrow and specialized as any nineteenth-century artistic coterie, thinking its thoughts and feeling its emotions because his experience contained no others. Such a man, in so far as he expressed these emotions, would be genuinely expressing his own experience. The narrowness or wideness of the experience which an artist expresses has nothing to do with the merits of his art. A Jane Austen, born and bred in an atmosphere of village gossip, can make great art out of the emotions that atmosphere generates. But a person who shuts himself up in the limits of a narrow coterie has an experience which includes the emotions of the larger world in which he was born and bred, as well as those of the little society he has chosen to join. If he decides to express only the emotions that pass current within the limits of that little society, he is selecting certain of his emotions for expression. The reason why this inevitably produces bad art is that, as we have already seen, it can only be done when the person selecting already knows what his emotions are; that is, has already expressed them. His real work as an artist is a work which, as a member of his artistic coterie, he repudiates. Thus the literature of the ivory tower is a literature whose only possible value is an amusement value by which persons imprisoned within that tower, whether by their misfortune or their fault, help themselves and each other to pass their time without dying of boredom or of home-sickness for the world they have left behind; together with a magical value by which they persuade themselves and each other that imprisonment in such a place and in such company is a high privilege. Artistic value it has none.

6. EXPRESSING EMOTION AND BETRAYING EMOTION

Finally, the expressing of emotion must not be confused with what may be called the betraying of it, that is, exhibiting symptoms of it. When it is said that the artist in the proper sense of that word is a person who expresses his emotions, this does not mean that if he is afraid he turns pale and stammers; if he is angry he turns red and bellows; and so forth. These things are no doubt called expressions; but just as we distinguish proper and improper senses of the word "art," so we must distinguish proper and improper senses of the word "expression," and in the context of a discussion about art this sense of expression is an improper sense. The characteristic mark of expression proper is lucidity or intelligibility; a person who expresses something thereby becomes conscious of what it is that he is expressing, and enables others to become conscious of it in himself and in them. Turning pale and stammering is a natural accompaniment of fear, but a person who in addition to being afraid also turns pale and stammers does not thereby become conscious of the precise quality of his emotion. About that he is as much in the dark as he would be if (were that possible) he could feel fear without also exhibiting these symptoms of it.

Confusion between these two senses of the word "expression" may easily lead to false critical estimates, and so to false aesthetic theory. It is sometimes thought a merit in an actress that when she is acting a pathetic scene she can work herself up to such an extent as to weep real tears. There may be some ground for that opinion if acting is not an art but a craft, and if the actress's object in that scene is to produce grief in her audience; and even then the conclusion would follow only if it were true that grief cannot be produced in the audience unless symptoms of grief are exhibited by the performer. And no doubt this is how most people think of the actor's work. But if his business is not amusement but art, the object at which he is aiming is not to produce a preconceived emotional effect on his audience but by means of a system of expressions, or language, composed partly of speech and partly of gesture, to explore his own emotions: to discover emotions in himself of which he was unaware, and, by permitting the audience to witness the discovery, enable them to make a similar discovery about themselves. In that case it is not her ability to weep real tears that would mark out a good actress; it is her ability to make it clear to herself and her audience what the tears are about.

This applies to every kind of art. The artist never rants. A person who writes or paints or the like in order to blow off steam, using the traditional materials of art as means for exhibiting the symptoms of emotion, may deserve praise as an exhibitionist, but loses for the moment all claim to the title of artist. Exhibitionists have their uses; they may serve as an amusement, or they may be doing magic. The second category will contain, for example, those young men who, learning in the torment of their own bodies and minds what war is like, have stammered their indignation in verses, and published them in the hope of infecting others and causing them to abolish it. But these verses have nothing to do with poetry.

Thomas Hardy, at the end of a fine and tragic novel in which he has magnificently expressed his sorrow and indignation for the suffering inflicted by callous sentimentalism on trusting innocence, spoils everything by a last paragraph fastening his accusation upon "the president of the immortals." The note rings false, not because it is blasphemous (it offends no piety worthy of the name), but because it is rant. The case against God, so far as it exists, is complete already. The concluding paragraph adds nothing to it. All it does is to spoil the effect of the indictment by betraying a symptom of the emotion which the whole book has already expressed; as if a prosecuting counsel, at the end of his speech, spat in the prisoner's face.

The same fault is especially common in Beethoven. He was confirmed in it, no doubt, by his deafness; but the cause of it was not his deafness but a temperamental inclination to rant. It shows itself in the way his music screams and mutters instead of speaking, as in the soprano part of the Mass in D, or the layout of the opening page in the *Hammerklavier* Sonata. He must have known his failing and tried to overcome it, or he would never have spent so many of his ripest years among string quartets, where screaming and muttering are almost, one might say, physically impossible. Yet even there, the old Adam struts out in certain passages of the *Grosse Fuge*.

It does not, of course, follow that a dramatic writer may not rant in character. The tremendous rant at the end of *The Ascent of F6*,[3] like the Shakespearian[4] ranting on which it is modelled, is done with tongue in cheek. It is not the author who is ranting, but the unbalanced character he depicts; the emotion the author is expressing is the emotion with which he contemplates that character; or rather, the emotion he has towards that secret and disowned part of himself for which the character stands.

—*The Principles of Art* (1945)

NOTES

1. Further development of the ideas expressed in this paragraph will make it necessary to qualify this word and assert a much more intimate relation between artist and audience; see pp. 311–36 [of Collingwood's book].

2. Plato, *Symposium*, 223 D. But if Aristodemus heard him correctly, Socrates was saying the right thing for the wrong reason. He is reported as arguing, not that a tragic writer as such is also a comic one, but that ὁ τέχνῃ τραγῳδοποιός [one who has skill in writing tragedy] is also a comic writer. Emphasis on the word τέχνῃ [skill] is obviously implied; and this, with a reference to the doctrine (*Republic*, 333 E—334 A) that craft is what Aristotle was to call a potentiality of opposites, i.e. enables its possessor to do not one kind of thing only, but that kind and the opposite kind too, shows that what Socrates was doing was to assume the technical theory of art and draw from it the above conclusion.

3. *Cf.* W. H. Auden and Christopher Isherwood, *The Ascent of F6: A Tragedy in Two Acts* (Random House, New York, 1937).

4. Shakespeare's characters rant (1) when they are characters in which he takes no interest at all, but which he uses simply as pegs on which to hang what the public wants, like Henry V; (2) when they are meant to be despicable, like Pistol; or (3) when they have lost their heads, like Hamlet in the graveyard.

CHAPTER
4

Imaginative
Satisfaction of Desire

FRIEDRICH NIETZSCHE: Apollinian and Dionysian Art
SIGMUND FREUD: Wish-Fulfillment and the Unconscious
CHRISTOPHER CAUDWELL: Poetry's Dream-Work

The intuitionist-expressionists Croce and Collingwood, define art as a
kind of lyrical and disinterested vision. Most of the other writers in this
volume similarly emphasize the nonpractical character of art.
Friedrich Nietzsche (1844–1900), like his great contemporary Leo Tolstoy,
challenged this nonutilitarian interpretation. "What does all art do?" he
asks. "Does it not praise? Does it not glorify? Does it not select? Does it
not bring things into prominence? In all this it *strengthens* or *weakens*
certain valuations."[1] Art is thus fundamental to the whole enterprise of
living. It is sublimely utilitarian.
   Paradoxically combining pessimism and optimism, Nietzsche believes
that the world, if untransformed by the will and imagination, is a
thoroughly nasty place; but that, by means of art and a masterful morality,
existence can be made profoundly satisfactory. There are two artistic
ways of transforming the values of life—the Apollinian and the
Dionysian. Apollinian art is similar to a dream (Apollo is the god of
dreams). Man creates in his waking dreams a world of tranquillity and
formal beauty, embodied especially in sculpture, architecture, painting, and
the more chaste types of literature. The other type of art, symbolized
by Dionysus, the god of wine and fertility, is similar to the state of love or
intoxication, either of which impels us ecstatically to embrace experience.
To explore by means of Dionysian art the depths and agonies of life,
and imaginatively to cry "Yea," is the supreme triumph of the will to
mastery. This type of art is represented above all by music (which for
Nietzsche is the most intense of all the arts), but subordinately by
dancing, lyric poetry, and tragedy. Nietzsche exhibits a keen insight into
the subconscious depths of art, its relation to desire, and its alliance
with dreams and love.
   The esthetic theory of Sigmund Freud (1856–1939) is a continuation
of such voluntaristic esthetics, but deepened and clarified by the knowledge
derived from his general theory of psychoanalysis. Like Schopenhauer
and Nietzsche, he believed that volition is the most fundamental and

dynamic element in the mind. It shows itself in unrest and seeking, leading finally to action that brings the unrest to a close. We might define it broadly as an "impulse toward a goal." If the impulse succeeds, the result is a state of satisfaction. The question arises, Is it possible to separate volition from pleasure and unpleasure? The answer of Freud is *no*. The unrest of desire necessarily involves pain or unpleasure, and the appeasement of desire involves pleasure; these are, in a sense, phases of volition. His theory might be called hedonistic voluntarism.

In his essay, "The Relation of the Poet to Daydreaming," Freud reveals his indebtedness to the play theory of Schiller (see Chapter 12). Both play and art are described as imaginative expressions and fulfillments of wish. When a person grows up, he must put aside childish play, but he substitutes phantasy, in the form either of day or night dreams, and art. But with profound insight and originality, Freud goes far beyond the play theory in interpreting both dreams and art as the disguised expression of wishes—repressed but powerfully operative in "the unconscious." The "libido," the deep instinctive force of life, manifests itself in a continual striving for expression. When it is actively repressed by the more critical faculties, it assumes a multitude of disguises in order to circumvent the repressive forces. Chief among these disguises are the imagery of dreams and phantasies, and the symptoms of neurotic disorders. But the artist has an additional resource. By means of what Freud called "sublimation," he can deflect his psychic energy into channels of creative endeavor. He then learns to control his phantasies, and thus to sublimate his ambition and his sexual impulse in creative art. The dream is consciously inserted into the texture of waking life, and the repressed wishes, which might otherwise lead to neurosis, are fulfilled in imagination.

The shock and disillusionment of the First World War caused Freud to revise his ideas. He thereafter put less emphasis upon "Eros"—the impulse of love—and greater emphasis upon "Thanatos"—the impulse of death and destruction. In addition, he worked out the theory of a threefold structure of human personality. First, there is the *Id* (Latin for "it")—so-called because we tend to regard its manifestations as foreign to ourselves, as when we say, "That was not what I meant." It is governed by "the pleasure principle," and is the bearer of the primal energies of our deepest instinctive nature. Second, there is the *Ego*. It is our wide-awake "social self," governed by "the reality principle," and concerned with the perception of the environment and the self's adjustment to it. Third, there is the *Super-Ego*. It is the seat of our ideals and moral standards, largely unconscious, and built up in the individual in early childhood. The mind as "Censor" acts frequently at the behest of the Super-Ego, whose demands are more archaic and severe than those of the conscious Ego.

As Herbert Read, the English poet and critic, wrote, the work of art derives from all three regions of the mind: "It derives its energy, its irrationality and its mysterious power from the id, which is to be regarded as the source of what we usually call inspiration. It is given formal synthesis and unity by the ego; and finally it may be assimilated to those ideologies or spiritual aspirations which are the peculiar creation of the super-ego."² Unfortunately, Freud himself never wrote a sustained exposition of his more mature esthetic theories.

Toward the end of his essay, "The Relation of the Poet to Day-dreaming," he remarks that the poet may draw upon the "creations of racial psychology" as expressed in myths, legends, and fairy tales; and in our selection from *The Interpretation of Dreams*, he recognizes universal tragic themes that appear in such literary works as *Oedipus Rex* and *Hamlet*. A number of writers, such as Maud Bodkin and Joseph Campbell, explored this lead. They showed that similar symbols, however superficially various, are to be found in the dreams, myths, and imaginative creations of human beings everywhere. This contention has been supported by much data gathered by Frazer and other anthropologists and by the Swiss psychiatrist, Carl Gustav Jung, who, with Freud and Adler, was one of the chief founders of psychoanalysis.

A similar interpretation of art is propounded by Christopher St. John Sprigg, who wrote under the pen name of Christopher Caudwell (1907–1937). An amazingly productive genius (he had published five books on aeronautics, seven detective novels, and both poems and short stories before he reached the age of twenty-five), he attained maturity in the period when fascism and economic crisis were threatening the very existence of civilization; and like many other creative minds—Andre Gide, Pablo Picasso, Stephen Spender, and Ignazio Silone, to mention only a few—he was greatly attracted by the ideas and program of Marxism. Moved to the quick by the Spanish Civil War, he joined the International Brigade, and was killed in action on February 12, 1937. In his brief life, he produced a number of outstanding books: *Illusion and Reality, Studies in a Dying Culture* (two volumes), *Poems*, and *The Crisis in Physics*, all published posthumously.

His esthetic doctrines represent primarily a highly original synthesis of Freudian and Marxian ideas, although he also drew upon his wide knowledge of physical science to define the difference between science and art. He believed that Freud had thought too exclusively in terms of individual psychology, and that the Marxian social emphasis is needed to correct his one-sidedness. The dreams and illusions of the neurotic, he maintained, are just peculiar or aberrant in a personal way; the creations of the artist are more social and general—growing out of the funded experiences and traditions of mankind. The artist draws more fully upon the subconscious than does the ordinary normal person; but he differs from the neurotic in being more social, free, and normal. The artist *uses* his subconscious mind, masters it; the neurotic is *used by* it, enslaved to it. The artist plumbs man's universal instinctive nature (which Caudwell terms "the genotype"), but he socializes the visions that arise from these subconscious depths. With profound insight, Caudwell compares poetry with dreams, contrasts it with prose fiction, and defines the nature and function of art in contradistinction to science.

He declares that the purpose of art is to give external reality an affective organization drawn from the inner heart of life. He thus suggests that not merely the content but the form of the work of art is a sublimation, or imaginative fulfillment, of desire. In Chapter 8, "Form," the selection from DeWitt H. Parker is an elaboration of this theme, and it may be read as a supplement to the present chapter.

NOTES

    1. Friedrich Nietzsche, *The Twilight of the Idols* (Macmillan; New York, 1924), p. 79.
    2. Herbert Read, *Art and Society* (Pantheon Books, New York, 1945), p. 92.

FRIEDRICH NIETZSCHE

Apollinian and Dionysian Art

1

We shall have gained much for the science of aesthetics, once we perceive not merely by logical inference, but with the immediate certainty of vision, that the continuous development of art is bound up with the *Apollinian* and *Dionysian* duality—just as procreation depends on the duality of the sexes, involving perpetual strife with only periodically intervening reconciliations. The terms Dionysian and Apollinian we borrow from the Greeks, who disclose to the discerning mind the profound mysteries of their view of art, not, to be sure, in concepts, but in the intensely clear figures of their gods. Through Apollo and Dionysus, the two art deities of the Greeks, we come to recognize that in the Greek world there existed a tremendous opposition, in origin and aims,[1] between the Apollinian art of sculpture, and the nonimagistic, Dionysian art of music. These two different tendencies run parallel to each other, for the most part openly at variance; and they continually incite each other to new and more powerful births, which perpetuate an antagonism. Only superficially reconciled by the common term "art"; till eventually,[2] by a metaphysical miracle of the Hellenic "will," they appear coupled with each other, and through this coupling ultimately generate an equally Dionysian and Apollinian form of art—Attic tragedy.

    In order to grasp these two tendencies, let us first conceive of them as the separate art worlds of dreams and intoxication. These physiological phenomena present a contrast analogous to that existing between the Apollinian and the Dionysian. It was in dreams, says Lucretius, that the glorious divine figures first appeared to the souls of men; in dreams the great shaper beheld the splendid bodies of superhuman beings; and the Hellenic poet, if questioned about the mysteries of poetic inspiration, would likewise have suggested dreams and he might have given an explanation like that of Hans Sachs in the *Meistersinger:*

The poet's tasks is this, my friend,
to read his dreams and comprehend.
The truest human fancy seems
to be revealed to us in dreams:
all poems and versification
are but true dreams' interpretation.[3]

The beautiful illusion[4] of the dream worlds, in the creation of which every man is truly an artist, is the prerequisite of all plastic art, and, as we shall see, of an important part of poetry also. In our dreams we delight in the immediate understanding of figures; all forms speak to us; there is nothing unimportant or superfluous. But even when this dream reality is most intense, we still have, glimmering through it, the sensation that it is *mere appearance*: at least this is my experience, and for its frequency— indeed, normality—I could adduce many proofs, including the sayings of the poets.

Philosophical men even have a presentiment that the reality in which we live and have our being is also mere appearance and that another, quite different reality lies beneath it. Schopenhauer actually indicates as the criterion of philosophical ability the occasional ability to view men and things as mere phantoms or dream images. Thus the aesthetically sensitive man stands in the same relation to the reality of dreams as the philosopher does to the reality of existence; he is a close and willing observer, for these images afford him an interpretation of life, and by reflecting on these proc- esses he trains himself for life.

It is not only the agreeable and friendly images that he experiences as something universally intelligible: the serious, the troubled, the sad, the gloomy, the sudden restraints, the tricks of accident, anxious expectations, in short, the whole divine comedy of life, including the inferno, also pass before him, not like mere shadows on a wall—for he lives and suffers with these scenes—and yet not without that fleeting sensation of illusion. And perhaps many will, like myself, recall how amid the dangers and terrors of dreams they have occasionally said to themselves in self-encouragement, and not without success: "It is a dream! I will dream on!" I have likewise heard of people who were able to continue one and the same dream for three and even more successive nights—facts which indicate clearly how our innermost being, our common ground, experiences dreams with pro- found delight and a joyous necessity.

This joyous necessity of the dream experience has been embodied by the Greeks in their Apollo: Apollo, the god of all plastic energies, is at the same time the soothsaying god. He, who (as the etymology of the name indicates) is the "shining one,"[5] the deity of light, is also ruler over the beautiful illusion of the inner world of fantasy. The higher truth, the perfection of these states in contrast to the incompletely intelligible every- day world, this deep consciousness of nature, healing and helping in sleep and dreams, is at the same time the symbolical analogue of the soothsaying faculty and of the arts generally, which make life possible and worth living. But we must also include in our image of Apollo that delicate boundary which the dream image must not overstep lest it have a pathological effect (in which case mere appearance would deceive us as if it were crude reality). We must keep in mind that measured restraint, that freedom from the wilder emotions, that calm of the sculptor god. His eye must be "sun-like," as befits his origin; even when it is angry and distempered it is still hallowed by beautiful illusion. And so, in one sense, we might apply to Apollo the words of Schopenhauer when he speaks of the man wrapped in the veil of *maya*[6] (*Welt als Wille und Vorstellung*, I, p. 416[7]): "Just as in a stormy sea that, unbounded in all directions, raises and drops moun-tainous waves, howling, a sailor sits in a boat and trusts in his frail bark: so in the midst of a world of torments the individual human being sits quietly, supported by and trusting in the *principium individuationis*."[8] In fact, we might say of Apollo that in him the unshaken faith in this *princi-pium* and the calm repose of the man wrapped up in it receive their most sublime expression; and we might call Apollo himself the glorious divine image of the *principium individuationis*, through whose gestures and eyes all the joy and wisdom of "illusion," together with its beauty, speak to us.

In the same work Schopenhauer has depicted for us the tremendous *terror* which seizes man when he is suddenly dumfounded by the cognitive form of phenomena because the principle of sufficient reason, in some one of its manifestations, seems to suffer an exception. If we add to this terror the blissful ecstasy that wells from the innermost depths of man, indeed of nature, at this collapse of the *principium individuationis,* we steal a glimpse into the nature of the *Dionysian* which is brought home to us most intimately by the analogy of intoxication.

Either under the influence of the narcotic draught, of which the songs of all primitive men and peoples speak, or with the potent coming of spring that penetrates all nature with joy, these Dionysian emotions awake, and as they grow in intensity everything subjective vanishes into complete self-forgetfulness. In the German Middle Ages, too, singing and dancing crowds, ever increasing in number, whirled themselves from place to place under this same Dionysian impulse. In these dancers of St. John and St. Vitus, we rediscover the Bacchic choruses of the Greeks, with their prehis-tory in Asia Minor, as far back as Babylon and the orgiastic Sacaea.[9] There are some who, from obtuseness or lack of experience, turn away from such phenomena as from "folk-disease," with contempt or pity born of the con-sciousness of their own "healthy-mindedness." But of course such poor wretches have no idea how corpselike and ghostly their so-called "healthy-mindedness" looks when the glowing life of the Dionysian revelers roars past them.

Under the charm of the Dionysian not only is the union between man and man reaffirmed, but nature which has become alienated, hostile, or sub-jugated, celebrates once more her reconciliation with her lost son,[10] man. Freely, earth proffers her gifts, and peacefully the beasts of prey of the rocks and desert approach. The chariot of Dionysus is covered with flowers and garlands; panthers and tigers walk under its yoke. Transform Bee-thoven's "Hymn to Joy" into a painting; let your imagination conceive the multitudes bowing to the dust, awestruck—then you will approach the Dionysian. Now the slave is a free man; now all the rigid, hostile barriers that necessity, caprice, or "impudent convention"[11] have fixed between man and man are broken. Now, with the gospel of universal harmony, each one feels himself not only united, reconciled and fused with his neighbor, but as one with him, as if the veil of *maya* had been torn aside and were now merely fluttering in tatters before the mysterious primordial unity.

In song and in dance man expresses himself as a member of a higher community; he has forgotten how to walk and speak and is on the way toward flying into the air, dancing. His very gestures express enchantment. Just as the animals now talk, and the earth yields milk and honey, supernatural sounds emanate from him, too: he feels himself a god, he himself now walks about enchanted, in ecstasy, like the gods he saw walking in his dreams. He is no longer an artist, he has become a work of art: in these paroxysms of intoxication the artistic power of all nature reveals itself to the highest gratification of the primordial unity. The noblest clay, the most costly marble, man, is here kneaded and cut, and to the sound of the chisel strokes of the Dionysian world-artist rings out the cry of the Eleusinian mysteries: "Do you prostrate yourselves, millions? Do you sense your Maker, world?"[12]

2

Thus far we have considered the Apollinian and its opposite, the Dionysian, as artistic energies which burst forth from nature herself, *without the mediation of the human artist*—energies in which nature's art impulses are satisfied in the most immediate and direct way—first in the image world of dreams, whose completeness is not dependent upon the intellectual attitude or the artistic culture of any single being; and then as intoxicated reality, which likewise does not heed the single unit, but even seeks to destroy the individual and redeem him by a mystic feeling of oneness. With reference to these immediate art-states of nature, every artist is an "imitator," that is to say, either an Apollinian artist in dreams or a Dionysian artist in ecstasies, or finally—as for example in Greek tragedy —at once artist in both dreams and ecstasies; so we may perhaps picture him sinking down in his Dionysian intoxication and mystical self-abnegation, alone and apart from the singing revelers, and we may imagine how, through Apollinian dream-inspiration, his own state, i.e., his oneness with the inmost ground of the world, is revealed to him in a *symbolical dream image*.

So much for these general premises and contrasts. Let us now approach the *Greeks* in order to learn how highly these *art impulses of nature* were developed in them. Thus we shall be in a position to understand and appreciate more deeply that relation of the Greek artist to his archetypes which is, according to the Aristotelian expression, "the imitation of nature." In spite of all the dream literature and the numerous dream anecdotes of the Greeks, we can speak of their *dreams* only conjecturally, though with reasonable assurance. If we consider the incredibly precise and unerring plastic power of their eyes, together with their vivid, frank delight in colors, we can hardly refrain from assuming even for their dreams (to the shame of all those born later) a certain logic of line and contour, colors and groups, a certain pictorial sequence reminding us of their finest bas-reliefs whose perfection would certainly justify us, if a comparison were possible, in designating the dreaming Greeks as Homers and Homer as a dreaming Greek—in a deeper sense than that in which modern man, speaking of his dreams, ventures to compare himself with Shakespeare.

On the other hand, we need not conjecture regarding the immense gap which separates the *Dionysian Greek* from the Dionysian barbarian. From all quarters of the ancient world—to say nothing here of the modern—from Rome to Babylon, we can point to the existence of Dionysian festivals, types which bear, at best, the same relation to the Greek festivals which the bearded satyr, who borrowed his name and attributes from the goat, bears to Dionysus himself. In nearly every case these festivals centered in extravagant sexual licentiousness, whose waves overwhelmed all family life and its venerable traditions; the most savage natural instincts were unleashed, including even that horrible mixture of sensuality and cruelty which has always seemed to me to be the real "witches' brew." For some time, however, the Greeks were apparently perfectly insulated and guarded against the feverish excitements of these festivals, though knowledge of them must have come to Greece on all the routes of land and sea; for the figure of Apollo, rising full of pride, held out the Gorgon's head to this grotesquely uncouth Dionysian power—and really could not have countered any more dangerous force. It is in Doric art that this majestically rejecting attitude of Apollo is immortalized.

The opposition between Apollo and Dionysus became more hazardous and even impossible, when similar impulses finally burst forth from the deepest roots of the Hellenic nature and made a path for themselves: the Delphic god, by a seasonably effected reconciliation, now contented himself with taking the destructive weapons from the hands of his powerful antagonist. This reconciliation is the most important moment in the history of the Greek cult: wherever we turn we note the revolutions resulting from this event. The two antagonists were reconciled; the boundary lines to be observed henceforth by each were sharply defined, and there was to be a periodical exchange of gifts of esteem. At bottom, however, the chasm was not bridged over. But if we observe how, under the pressure of this treaty of peace, the Dionysian power revealed itself, we shall now recognize in the Dionysian orgies of the Greeks, as compared with the Babylonian Sacaea with their reversion of man to the tiger and the ape, the significance of festivals of world redemption and days of tranfiguration. It is with them that nature for the first time attains her artistic jubilee; it is with them that the destruction of the *principium individuationis* for the first time becomes an artistic phenomenon.

The horrible "witches' brew" of sensuality and cruelty becomes ineffective; only the curious blending and duality in the emotions of the Dionysian revelers remind us—as medicines remind us of deadly poisons—of the phenomenon that pain begets joy, that ecstasy may wring sounds of agony from us. At the very climax of joy there sounds a cry of horror or a yearning lamentation for an irretrievable loss. In these Greek festivals, nature seems to reveal a sentimental[13] trait; it is as if she were heaving a sigh at her dismemberment into individuals. The song and pantomime of such dually-minded revelers was something new and unheard-of in the Homeric-Greek world; and the Dionysian *music* in particular excited awe and terror. If music, as it would seem, had been known previously as an Apollinian art, it was so, strictly speaking, only as the wave beat of rhythm whose formative power was developed for the representation of Apollinian states. The music of Apollo was Doric architectonics in tones, but in tones that were merely suggestive, such as those of the cithara. The very element which forms the essence of Dionysian music (and hence of music in general) is carefully excluded as un-Apollinian—namely, the emotional power of the tone, the uniform flow of the melody, and the utterly incomparable world of harmony. In the Dionysian dithyramb man is incited to the greatest exaltation of all his symbolic faculties; something never before experienced struggles for utterance—the annihilation of the veil of *maya,* oneness as the soul of the race and of nature itself. The essence of nature is now to be expressed symbolically; we need a new world of symbols; and the entire symbolism of the body is called into play, not the mere symbolism of the lips, face, and speech but the whole pantomime of dancing, forcing every member into rhythmic movement. Then the other symbolic powers suddenly press forward, particularly those of music, in rhythmics, dynamics, and harmony. To grasp this collective release of all the symbolic powers, man must have already attained that height of self-abnegation which seeks to express itself symbolically through all these powers—and so the dithyrambic votary of Dionysus is understood only by his peers. With what astonishment must the Apollinian Greek have beheld him! With an astonishment that was all the greater the more it was mingled with the shuddering suspicion that all this was actually not so very alien to him after all, in fact, that it was only his Apollinian consciousness which, like a veil, hid this Dionysian world from his vision.

3

To understand this, it becomes necessary to level the artistic structure of the *Apollinian culture,* as it were, stone by stone, till the foundations on which it rests become visible. First of all we see the glorious *Olympian* figures of the gods, standing on the gables of this structure. Their deeds, pictured in brilliant reliefs, adorn its friezes. We must not be misled by the fact that Apollo stands side by side with the others as an individual deity, without any claim to priority of rank. For the same impulse that embodied itself in Apollo gave birth to this entire Olympian world, and in this sense Apollo is its father. What terrific need was it that could produce such an illustrious company of Olympian beings?

Whoever approaches these Olympians with another religion in his heart, searching among them for moral elevation, even for sanctity, for disincarnate spirituality, for charity and benevolence, will soon be forced to turn his back on them, discouraged and disappointed. For there is nothing here that suggests asceticism, spirituality, or duty. We hear nothing but the accents of an exuberant, triumphant life in which all things, whether good or evil, are deified.[14] And so the spectator may stand quite bewildered before this fantastic excess of life, asking himself by virtue of what magic potion these high-spirited men could have found life so enjoyable that, wherever they turned, their eyes beheld the smile of Helen, the ideal picture of their own existence, "floating in sweet sensuality." But to this spectator, who has already turned his back, we must say: "Do not go away, but stay and hear what Greek folk wisdom has to say of this very life, which with such inexplicable gaiety unfolds itself before your eyes.

"There is an ancient story that King Midas hunted in the forest a long time for the wise Silenus, the companion of Dionysus, without capturing him. When Silenus at last fell into his hands, the king asked what was the best and most desirable of all things for man. Fixed and immovable, the demigod said not a word, till at last, urged by the king, he gave a shrill laugh and broke out into these words: 'Oh, wretched ephemeral race, children of chance and misery, why do you compel me to tell you what it would be most expedient for you not to hear? What is best of all is utterly beyond your reach: not to be born, not to *be,* to be *nothing.* But the second best for you is—to die soon.' "[15]

How is the world of the Olympian gods related to this folk wisdom? Even as the rapturous vision of the tortured martyr to his suffering.

Now it is as if the Olympian magic mountain[16] had opened before us and revealed its roots to us. The Greek knew and felt the terror and horror of existence. That he might endure this terror at all, he had to interpose between himself and life the radiant dream-birth of the Olympians. That overwhelming dismay in the face of the titanic powers of nature, the Moira[17] enthroned inexorably over all knowledge, the vulture of the great lover of mankind, Prometheus, the terrible fate of the wise Oedipus, the family curse of the Atridae which drove Orestes to matricide: in short, that entire philosophy of the sylvan god, with its mythical exemplars, which caused the downfall of the melancholy Etruscans—all this was again and again overcome by the Greeks with the aid of the Olympian *middle world* of art; or at any rate it was veiled and withdrawn from sight. It was in order to be able to live that the Greeks had to create these gods from a most profound need. Perhaps we may picture the process to ourselves somewhat as follows: out of the original Titanic divine order of terror, the Olympian divine order of joy gradually evolved through the Apollinian impulse toward beauty, just as roses burst from thorny bushes. How else could this people, so sensitive, so vehement in its desires, so singularly capable of *suffering,* have endured existence, if it had not been revealed to them in their gods, surrounded with a higher glory?

The same impulse which calls art into being, as the complement and consummation of existence, seducing one to a continuation of life, was also the cause of the Olympian world which the Hellenic "will" made use of as a transfiguring mirror. Thus do the gods justify the life of man: they themselves live it—the only satisfactory theodicy! Existence under the bright sunshine of such gods is regarded as desirable in itself, and the real pain of Homeric men is caused by parting from it, especially by early parting: so that now, reversing the wisdom of Silenus, we might say of the Greeks that "to die soon is worst of all for them, the next worst—to die at all." Once heard, it will ring out again; do not forget the lament of the short-lived Achilles, mourning the leaflike change and vicissitudes of the race of men and the decline of the heroic age. It is not unworthy of the greatest hero to long for a continuation of life, even though he live as a day laborer.[18] At the Apollinian stage of development, the 'will' longs so vehemently for this existence, the Homeric man feels himself so completely at one with it, that lamentation itself becomes a song of praise.

Here we should note that this harmony which is contemplated with such longing by modern man, in fact, this oneness of man with nature (for which Schiller introduced the technical term "naïve"), is by no means a simple condition that comes into being naturally and as if inevitably. It is not a condition that, like a terrestrial paradise, *must* necessarily be found at the gate of every culture. Only a romantic age could believe this, an age which conceived of the artist in terms of Rousseau's *Emile* and imagined that in Homer it had found such an artist Emile, reared at the bosom of nature. Where we encounter the "naïve" in art, we should recognize the highest effect of Apollinian culture—which always must first overthrow an empire of Titans and slay monsters, and which must have triumphed over an abysmal and terrifying view of the world and the keenest susceptibility to suffering through recourse to the most forceful and pleasurable illusions. But how rarely is the naïve attained—that consummate immersion in the beauty of mere appearance! How unutterably sublime is *Homer* therefore, who, as an individual being, bears the same relation to this Apollinian folk culture as the individual dream artist does to the dream faculty of the people and of nature in general.

The Homeric "naïveté" can be understood only as the complete victory of Apollinian illusion: this is one of those illusions which nature so frequently employs to achieve her own ends. The true goal is veiled by a phantasm: and while we stretch out our hands for the latter, nature attains the former by means of our illusion. In the Greeks the "will" wished to contemplate itself in the transfiguration of genius and the world of art; in order to glorify themselves, its creatures had to feel themselves worthy of glory; they had to behold themselves again in a higher sphere, without this perfect world of contemplation acting as a command or a reproach. This is the sphere of beauty, in which they saw their mirror images, the Olympians. With this mirroring of beauty the Hellenic will combated its artistically correlative talent for suffering and for the wisdom of suffering—and, as a monument of its victory, we have Homer, the naïve artist.

4

Now the dream analogy may throw some light on the naïve artist. Let us imagine the dreamer: in the midst of the illusion of the dream world and without disturbing it, he calls out to himself: "It is a dream, I will dream on." What must we infer? That he experiences a deep inner joy in dream contemplation; on the other hand, to be at all able to dream with this inner joy in contemplation, he must have completely lost sight of the waking reality and its ominous obtrusiveness. Guided by the dream-reading Apollo, we may interpret all these phenomena in roughly this way. Though it is certain that of the two halves of our existence, the waking and the dreaming states, the former appeals to us as infinitely preferable, more important, excellent, and worthy of being lived, indeed, as that which alone is lived—yet in relation to that mysterious ground of our being of which we are the phenomena, I should, paradoxical as it may seem, maintain the very opposite estimate of the value of dreams. For the more clearly I perceive in nature those omnipotent art impulses, and in them an ardent longing for illusion, for redemption through illusion, the more I feel myself impelled to the metaphysical assumption that the truly existent primal unity, eternally suffering and contradictory, also needs the rapturous vision, the pleasurable illusion, for its continuous redemption. And we, completely wrapped up in this illusion and composed of it, are compelled to consider this illusion as the truly nonexistent—i.e., as a perpetual becoming in time, space, and causality—in other words, as empirical reality. If, for the moment, we do not consider the question of our own "reality," if we conceive of our empirical existence, and of that of the world in general, as a continuously manifested representation of the primal unity, we shall then have to look upon the dream as a *mere appearance of mere appearance*, hence as a still higher appeasement of the primordial desire for mere appearance. And that is why the innermost heart of nature feels that ineffable joy in the naïve artist and the naïve work of art, which is likewise only "mere appearance of mere appearance."

In a symbolic painting, *Raphael*, himself one of these immortal "naïve" ones, has represented for us this demotion of appearance to the level of mere appearance, the primitive process of the naïve artist and of Apollinian culture. In his *Transfiguration*, the lower half of the picture, with the possessed boy, the despairing bearers, the bewildered, terrified disciples, shows us the reflection of suffering, primal and eternal, the sole ground of the world: the "mere appearance" here is the reflection of eternal contradiction, the father of things. From this mere appearance arises, like ambrosial vapor, a new visionary world of mere appearances, invisible to those wrapped in the first appearance—a radiant floating in purest bliss, a serene contemplation beaming from wide-open eyes. Here we have presented, in the most sublime artistic symbolism, that Apollinian world of beauty and its substratum, the terrible wisdom of Silenus; and intuitively we comprehend their necessary interdependence. Apollo, however, again appears to us as the apotheosis of the *principium individuationis,* in which alone is consummated the perpetually attained goal of the primal unity, its redemption through mere appearance. With his sublime gestures, he shows us how necessary is the entire world of suffering, that by means of it the individual may be impelled to realize the redeeming vision, and then, sunk in contemplation of it, sit quietly in his tossing bark, amid the waves.

If we conceive of it at all as imperative and mandatory, this apotheosis of individuation knows but one law—the individual, i.e., the delimiting of the boundaries of the individual, *measure* in the Hellenic sense. Apollo, as ethical deity, exacts measure of his disciples, and, to be able to maintain it, he requires self-knowledge. And so, side by side with the aesthetic necessity for beauty, there occur the demands "know thyself" and "nothing in excess"; consequently overweening pride and excess are regarded as the truly hostile demons of the non-Apollinian sphere, hence as characteristics of the pre-Apollinian age—that of the Titans; and of the extra-Apollinian world—that of the barbarians. Because of his titanic love for man, Prometheus must be torn to pieces by vultures; because of his excessive wisdom, which could solve the riddle of the Sphinx, Oedipus must be plunged into a bewildering vortex of crime. Thus did the Delphic god interpret the Greek past.

The effects wrought by the *Dionysian* also seemed "titanic" and "barbaric" to the Apollinian Greek; while at the same time he could not conceal from himself that he, too, was inwardly related to these overthrown Titans and heroes. Indeed, he had to recognize even more than this: despite all its beauty and moderation, his entire existence rested on a hidden substratum of suffering and of knowledge, revealed to him by the Dionysian. And behold: Apollo could not live without Dionysus! The "titanic" and the "barbaric" were in the last analysis as necessary as the Apollinian.

And now let us imagine how into this world, built on mere appearance and moderation and artificially dammed up, there penetrated, in tones ever more bewitching and alluring, the ecstatic sound of the Dionysian festival; how in these strains all of nature's *excess* in pleasure, grief, and knowledge became audible, even in piercing shrieks; and let us ask ourselves what the psalmodizing artist of Apollo, with his phantom harpsound, could mean in the face of this demonic folk-song! The muses of the arts of "illusion" paled before an art that, in its intoxication, spoke the truth. The wisdom of Silenus cried "Woe! woe!" to the serene Olympians. The individual, with all his restraint and proportion, succumbed to the self-oblivion of the Dionysian states, forgetting the precepts of Apollo. *Excess* revealed itself as truth. Contradiction, the bliss born of pain, spoke out from the very heart of nature. And so, wherever the Dionysian prevailed, the Apollinian was checked and destroyed. But, on the other hand, it is equally certain that, wherever the first Dionysian onslaught was successfully withstood, the authority and majesty of the Delphic god exhibited itself as more rigid and menacing than ever. For to me the *Doric* state[19] and Doric art are explicable only as a permanent military encampment of the Apollinian. Only incessant resistance to the titanic-barbaric nature of the Dionysian could account for the long survival of an art so defiantly prim and so encompassed with bulwarks, a training so warlike and rigorous, and a political structure so cruel and relentless.

Up to this point we have simply enlarged upon the observation made at the beginning of this essay: that the Dionysian and the Apollinian, in new births ever following and mutually augmenting one another, controlled the Hellenic genius; that out of the age of "bronze," with its wars of the Titans and its rigorous folk philosophy, the Homeric world developed under the sway of the Apollinian impulse to beauty; that this "naïve" splendor was again overwhelmed by the influx of the Dionysian; and that against this new power the Apollinian rose to the austere majesty of Doric art and the Doric view of the world. If amid the strife of these two hostile principles, the older Hellenic history thus falls into four great periods of art, we are now impelled to inquire after the final goal of these developments and processes, lest perchance we should regard the last-attained period, the period of Doric art, as the climax and aim of these artistic impulses. And here the sublime and celebrated art of *Attic tragedy* and the dramatic dithyramb presents itself as the common goal of both these tendencies whose mysterious union, after many and long precursory struggles, found glorious consummation in this child—at once Antigone and Cassandra.[20]

5

We now approach the real goal of our investigation, which is directed toward knowledge of the Dionysian-Apollinian genius and its art product, or at least toward some feeling for and understanding of this mystery of union. Here we shall begin by seeking the first evidence in Greece of that new germ which subsequently developed into tragedy and the dramatic dithyramb. The ancients themselves give us a symbolic answer, when they place the faces of *Homer* and *Archilochus*,[21] as the forefathers and torchbearers of Greek poetry, sidy by side on gems, sculptures, etc., with a sure feeling that consideration should be given only to these two, equally completely original, from whom a stream of fire flows over the whole of later Greek history. Homer, the aged self-absorbed dreamer, the type of the Apollinian naïve artist, now beholds with astonishment the passionate head of the warlike votary of the muses, Archilochus, who was hunted savagely through life. Modern aesthetics, by way of interpretation, could only add that here the first "objective" artist confronts the first "subjective" artist. But this interpretation helps us little, because we know the subjective artist only as the poor artist, and throughout the entire range of art we demand first of all the conquest of the subjective, redemption from the "ego," and the silencing of the individual will and desire; indeed, we find it impossible to believe in any truly artistic production, however insignificant, if it is without objectivity, without pure contemplation devoid of interest.[22] Hence our aesthetics must first solve the problem of how the "lyrist" is possible as an artist—he who, according to the experience of all ages, is continually saying "I" and running through the entire chromatic scale of his passions and desires. Compared with Homer, Archilochus appalls us by his cries of hatred and scorn, by his drunken outbursts of desire. Therefore is not he, who has been called the first subjective artist, essentially the non-artist? But, in this case, how explain the reverence which was shown to him—the poet—in very remarkable utterances by the Delphic oracle itself, the center of "objective" art?

Schiller has thrown some light on the poetic process by a psychological observation, inexplicable but unproblematic to his own mind. He confessed that before the act of creation he did not have before him or within him any series of images in a causal arrangement, but rather a *musical mood.* ("With me the perception has at first no clear and definite object; this is formed later. A certain musical mood comes first, and the poetical idea only follows later.") Let us add to this the most important phenomenon of all ancient lyric poetry: they took for granted *the union,* indeed the *identity,* of the *lyrist with the musician.* Compared with this, our modern lyric poetry seems like the statue of a god without a head. With this in mind we may now, on the basis of our aesthetical metaphysics set forth above, explain the lyrist to ourselves in this manner.

In the first place, as a Dionysian artist he has identified himself with the primal unity, its pain and contradiction. Assuming that music has been correctly termed a repetition and a recast of the world, we may say that he produces the copy of this primal unity as music. Now, however, under the Apollinian dream inspiration, this music reveals itself to him again as a *symbolic dream image*. The inchoate, intangible reflection of the primordial pain in music, with its redemption in mere appearance, now produces a second mirroring as a specific symbol or example. The artist has already surrendered his subjectivity in the Dionysian process. The image that now shows him his identity with the heart of the world is a dream scene that embodies the primordial contradiction and primordial pain, together with the primordial pleasure of mere appearance. The "I" of the lyrist therefore sounds from the depth of his being: its "subjectivity," in the sense of modern aestheticians is a fiction. When Archilochus, the first Greek lyrist, proclaims to the daughters of Lycambes both his mad love and his contempt, it is not his passion alone that dances before us in orgiastic frenzy; but we see Dionysus and the Maenads, we see the drunken reveler Archilochus sunk down in slumber—as Euripides depicts it in the *Bacchae*,[23] the sleep on the high mountain pasture, in the noonday sun. And now Apollo approaches and touches him with the laurel. Then the Dionysian-musical enchantment of the sleeper seems to emit image sparks, lyrical poems, which in their highest development are called tragedies and dramatic dithyrambs.

The plastic artist, like the epic poet who is related to him, is absorbed in the pure contemplation of images. The Dionysian musician is, without any images, himself pure primordial pain and its primordial re-echoing. The lyric genius is conscious of a world of images and symbols—growing out of his state of mystical self-abnegation and oneness. This world has a coloring, a causality, and a velocity quite different from those of the world of the plastic artist and the epic poet. For the latter lives in these images, and only in them, with joyous satisfaction. He never grows tired of contemplating lovingly even their minutest traits. Even the image of the angry Achilles is only an image to him whose angry expression he enjoys with the dreamer's pleasure in illusion. Thus, by this mirror of illusion, he is protected against becoming one and fused with his figures. In direct contrast to this, the images of the *lyrist* are nothing but *his very* self and, as it were, only different projections of himself, so he, as the moving center of this world, may say "I": of course, this self is not the same as that of the waking, empirically real man, but the only truly existent and eternal self resting at the basis of things, through whose images the lyric genius sees this very basis.

Now let us suppose that among these images he also beholds *himself* as nongenius, i.e., his subject, the whole throng of subjective passions and agitations of the will directed to a definite object which appears real to him. It might seem as if the lyric genius and the allied non-genius were one, as if the former had of its own accord spoken that little word "I." But this mere appearance will no longer be able to lead us astray, as it certainly led astray those who designated the lyrist as the subjective poet. For, as a matter of fact, Archilochus, the passionately inflamed, loving, and hating man, is but a vision of the genius, who by this time is no longer merely Archilochus, but a world-genius expressing his primordial pain symbolically in the symbol of the man Archilochus—while the subjectively willing and desiring man, Archilochus, can never at any time be a poet. It is by no means necessary, however, that the lyrist should see nothing but the phenomenon of the man Archilochus before him as a reflection of eternal being; and tragedy shows how far the visionary world of the lyrist may be removed from this phenomenon which, to be sure, is closest at hand.[24]

Schopenhauer, who did not conceal from himself the difficulty the lyrist presents in the philosophical contemplation of art, thought he had found a way out on which, however, I cannot follow him. Actually, it was in his profound metaphysics of music that he alone held in his hands the means for a solution. I believe I have removed the difficulty here in his spirit and to his honor. Yet he describes the peculiar nature of song as follows (*Welt als Wille und Vorstellung,* I, p. 295):

"It is the subject of the will, *i.e.,* his own volition, which fills the consciousness of the singer, often as a released and satisfied desire (joy), but still oftener as an inhibited desire (grief), always as an affect, a passion, a moved state of mind. Besides this, however, and along with it, by the sight of surrounding nature, the singer becomes conscious of himself as the subject of pure will-less knowing, whose unbroken blissful peace now appears, in contrast to the stress of desire, which is always restricted and always needy. The feeling of this contrast, this alternation, is really what the song as a whole expresses and what principally constitutes the lyrical state. In it pure knowing comes to us as it were to deliver us from willing and its strain; we follow, but only for moments; willing, the remembrance of our own personal ends, tears us anew from peaceful contemplation; yet ever again the next beautiful environment in which pure will-less knowledge presents itself to us lures us away from willing. Therefore, in the song and the lyrical mood, willing (the personal interest of the ends) and pure perception of the environment are wonderfully mingled; connections between them are sought and imagined; the subjective mood, the affection of the will, imparts its own hue to the perceived environment, and vice versa. Genuine song is the expression of the whole of this mingled and divided state of mind."

Who could fail to recognize in this description that lyric poetry is here characterized as an incompletely attained art that arrives at its goal infrequently and only, as it were, by leaps? Indeed, it is described as a semi-art whose *essence* is said to consist in this, that willing and pure contemplation, i.e., the unaesthetic and the aesthetic condition, are wonderfully mingled with each other. We contend, on the contrary, that the whole opposition between the subjective and objective, which Schopenhauer still uses as a measure of value in classifying the arts, is altogether irrelevant in aesthetics, since the subject, the willing individual that furthers his own egoistic ends, can be conceived of only as the antagonist, not as the origin of art. Insofar as the subject is the artist, however, he has already been released from his individual will, and has become, as it were, the medium through which the one truly existent subject celebrates his release in appearance. For to our humiliation *and* exaltation, one thing above all must be clear to us. The entire comedy of art is neither performed for our betterment or education nor are we the true authors of this art world. On the contrary, we may assume that we are merely images and artistic projections for the true author, and that we have our highest dignity in our significance as works of art—for it is only as an *aesthetic phenomenon* that existence and the world are eternally *justified*[25]—while of course our consciousness of our own significance hardly differs from that which the soldiers painted on canvas have of the battle represented on it. Thus all our knowledge of art is basically quite illusory, because as knowing beings we are not one and identical with that being which, as the sole author and spectator of this comedy of art, prepares a perpetual entertainment for itself. Only insofar as the genius in the act of artistic creation coalesces with this primordial artist of the world, does he know anything of the eternal essence of art; for in this state he is, in a marvelous manner, like the weird image of the fairy tale which can turn its eyes at will and behold itself; he is at once subject and object, at once poet, actor, and spectator.

6

In connection with Archilochus, scholarly research has discovered that he introduced the *folk song* into literature and on account of this deserved, according to the general estimate of the Greeks, his unique position beside Homer. But what is the folk song in contrast to the wholly Apollinian epos? What else but the *perpetuum vestigium* of a union of the Apollinian and the Dionysian? Its enormous diffusion among all people, further reenforced by ever-new births, is testimony to the power of this artistic dual impulse of nature, which leaves its vestiges in the folk song just as the orgiastic movements of a people immortalize themselves in its music. Indeed, it might also be historically demonstrable that every period rich in folk songs has been most violently stirred by Dionysian currents, which we must always consider the substratum and prerequisite of the folk song.

First of all, however, we must conceive the folk song as the musical mirror of the world, as the original melody, now seeking for itself a parallel dream phenomenon and expressing it in poetry. *Melody is therefore primary and universal*, and so may admit of several objectifications in several texts. Likewise, in the naïve estimation of the people, it is regarded as by far the more important and essential element. Melody generates the poem out of itself, ever again: that is what *the strophic form of the folk song* signifies, a phenomenon which I had always beheld with astonishment, until at last I found this explanation. Anyone who in accordance with this theory examines a collection of folk songs, such as *Des Knaben Wunderhorn*,[26] will find innumerable instances of the way the continuously generating melody scatters image sparks all around, which in their variegation, their abrupt change, their mad precipitation, manifest a power quite unknown to the epic and its steady flow. From the standpoint of the epos, this unequal and irregular image world of lyrical poetry is simply to be condemned: and it certainly has been thus condemned by the solemn epic rhapsodists of the Apollinian festivals in the age of Terpander.[27]

Accordingly, we observe that in the poetry of the folk song, language is strained to its utmost that it may *imitate music*; and with Archilochus begins a new world of poetry, basically opposed to the Homeric. And in saying this we have indicated the only possible relation between poetry and music, between word and tone: the word, the image, the concept here seeks an expression analogous to music and now feels in itself the power of music. In this sense we may discriminate between two main currents in the history of the language of the Greek people, according to whether their language imitated the world of image and phenomenon or the world of music. One need only reflect more deeply on the linguistic difference with regard to color, syntactical structure, and vocabulary in Homer and Pindar, in order to understand the significance of this contrast; indeed, it becomes palpably clear that in the period between Homer and Pindar the *orgiastic flute tones of Olympus* must have been sounded, which, even in Aristotle's time, when music was infinitely more developed, transported people to drunken ecstasy, and which, in their primitive state of development, undoubtedly incited to imitation all the poetic means of expression of contemporaneous man.

I here call attention to a familiar phenomenon of our own times, against which our aesthetic raises many objections. Again and again we have occasion to observe that a Beethoven symphony compels its individual auditors to use figurative speech in describing it, no matter how fantastically variegated and even contradictory may be the composition and make-up of the different worlds of images produced by a piece of music. To exercise its poor wit on such compositions, and to overlook a phenomenon which is certainly worth explaining, are quite in keeping with this aesthetic. Indeed, even when the tone-poet expresses his composition in images, when for instance he designates a certain symphony as the "pastoral" symphony, or a passage in it as the "scene by the brook," or another as the "merry gathering of rustics," these two are only symbolical representations born of music—and not the imitated objects of music—representations which can teach us nothing whatsoever concerning the *Dionysian* content of music, and which indeed have no distinctive value of their own beside other images. We have now to transfer this process of a discharge of music in images to some fresh, youthful, linguistically creative people, in order to get some notion of the way in which the strophic folk song originates, and the whole linguistic capacity is excited by this new principle of the imitation of music.

If, therefore, we may regard lyric poetry as the imitative fulguration of music in images and concepts, we should now ask: "As what does music *appear* in the mirror of images and concepts?" It *appears as* will, taking the term in Schopenhauer's sense, i.e., as the opposite of the aesthetic, purely contemplative, and passive frame of mind. Here, however, we must make as sharp a distinction as possible between the concepts of essence and phenomenon; for music, according to its essence, cannot possibly be will. To be will it would have to be wholly banished from the realm of art

—for the will is the unaesthetic-in-itself; but it *appears* as will. For in order to express its appearance in images, the lyrist needs all the agitations of passion, from the whisper of mere inclination to the roar of madness. Impelled to speak of music in Apollinian symbols he conceives of all nature, and himself in it, as willing, as desiring, as eternal longing. But insofar as he interprets music by means of images, he himself rests in the calm sea of Apollinian contemplation, though everything around him that he beholds through the medium of music is in urgent and active motion. Indeed, when he beholds himself through this same medium, his own image appears to him as an unsatisfied feeling: his own willing, longing, moaning, rejoicing, are to him symbols by which he interprets music. This is the phenomenon of the lyrist: as Apollinian genius he interprets music through the image of the will, while he himself, completely released from the greed of the will, is the pure, undimmed eye of the sun.

Our whole discussion insists that lyric poetry is dependent on the spirit of music just as music itself in its absolute sovereignty does not *need* the image and the concept, but merely *endures* them as accompaniments. The poems of the lyrist can express nothing that did not already lie hidden in that vast universality and absoluteness in the music that compelled him to figurative speech. Language can never adequately render the cosmic symbolism of music, because music stands in symbolic relation to the primordial contradiction and primordial pain in the heart of the primal unity, and therefore symbolizes a sphere which is beyond and prior to all phenomena. Rather, all phenomena, compared with it, are merely symbols: hence *language*, as the organ and symbol of phenomena, can never by any means disclose the innermost heart of music; language, in its attempt to imitate it, can only be in superficial contact with music; while all the eloquence of lyric poetry cannot bring the deepest significance of the latter one step nearer to us.

7

We must now avail ourselves of all the principles of art considered so far, in order to find our way through the labyrinth, as we must call it, of *the origin of Greek tragedy*. I do not think I am unreasonable in saying that the problem of this origin has as yet not even been seriously posed, to say nothing of solved, however often the ragged tatters of ancient tradition have been sewn together in various combinations and torn apart again. This tradition tells us quite unequivocally *that tragedy arose from the tragic chorus*, and was originally only chorus and nothing but chorus. Hence we consider it our duty to look into the heart of this tragic chorus as the real proto-drama, without resting satisfied with such arty clichés as that the chorus is the "ideal spectator" or that it represents the people in contrast to the aristocratic region of the scene. This latter explanation has a sublime sound to many a politician—as if the immutable moral law had been embodied by the democratic Athenians in the popular chorus, which always won out over the passionate excesses and extravagances of kings. This theory may be ever so forcibly suggested by one of Aristotle's observations; still, it has no influence on the original formation of tragedy, inasmuch as the whole opposition of prince and people—indeed the whole politico-social sphere—was excluded from the purely religious origins of tragedy. But even regarding the classical form of the chorus in Aeschylus and Sophocles, which is known to us, we should deem it blasphemy to speak here of intimations of "constitutional popular representation." From this blasphemy, however, others have not shrunk. Ancient constitutions knew of no constitutional representation of the people in *praxi,* and it is to be hoped that they did not even "have intimations" of it in tragedy.

Much more famous than this political interpretation of the chorus is the idea of A. W. Schlegel,[28] who advises us to regard the chorus somehow as the essence and extract of the crowd of spectators—as the "ideal spectator." This view, when compared with the historical tradition that originally tragedy was only chorus, reveals itself for what it is—a crude, unscientific, yet brilliant claim that owes its brilliancy only to its concentrated form of expression, to the typically Germanic bias in favor of anything called "ideal," and to our momentary astonishment. For we are certainly astonished the moment we compare our familiar theatrical public with this chorus, and ask ourselves whether it could ever be possible to idealize from such a public something analogous to the Greek tragic chorus. We tacitly deny this, and now wonder as much at the boldness of Schlegel's claim as at the totally different nature of the Greek public. For we had always believed that the right spectator, whoever he might be, must always remain conscious that he was viewing a work of art and not an empirical reality. But the tragic chorus of the Greeks is forced to recognize real beings in the figures on the stage. The chorus of the Oceanides really believes that it sees before it the Titan Prometheus, and it considers itself as real as the god of the scene. But could the highest and purest type of spectator regard Prometheus as bodily present and real, as the Oceanides do? Is it characteristic of the ideal spectator to run onto the stage and free the god from his torments? We had always believed in an aesthetic public and considered the individual spectator the better qualified the more he was capable of viewing a work of art as art, that is, aesthetically. But now Schlegel tells us that the perfect, ideal spectator does not at all allow the world of the drama to act on him aesthetically, but corporally and empirically. Oh, these Greeks! we sigh; they upset all our aesthetics! But once accustomed to this, we repeated Schlegel's saying whenever the chorus came up for discussion.

Now the tradition, which is quite explicit, speaks against Schlegel. The chorus as such, without the stage—the primitive form of tragedy—and the chorus of ideal spectators do not go together. What kind of artistic genre could possibly be extracted from the concept of the spectator, and find its true form in the "spectator as such"? The spectator without the spectacle is an absurd notion. We fear that the birth of tragedy is to be explained neither by any high esteem for the moral intelligence of the masses nor by the concept of the spectator without a spectacle; and we consider the problem too deep to be even touched by such superficial considerations.

An infinitely more valuable insight into the significance of the chorus was displayed by Schiller in the celebrated Preface to his *Bride of Messina,* where he regards the chorus as a living wall that tragedy constructs around itself in order to close itself off from the world of reality and to preserve its ideal domain and its poetical freedom.

With this, his chief weapon, Schiller combats the ordinary conception of the natural, the illusion usually demanded in dramatic poetry. Although the stage day is merely artificial, the architecture only symbolical, and the metrical language ideal in character, nevertheless an erroneous view still prevails in the main, as he points out: it is not sufficient that one merely tolerates as poetic license what is actually the essence of all poetry. The introduction of the chorus, says Schiller, is the decisive step by which war is declared openly and honorably against all naturalism in art.

It would seem that to denigrate this view of the matter our would-be superior age has coined the disdainful catchword "pseudo-idealism." I fear, however, that we, on the other hand, with our present adoration of the natural and the real, have reached the opposite pole of all idealism, namely, the region of wax-work cabinets. There is an art in these, too, as there is in certain novels much in vogue at present; but we really should not be plagued with the claim that such art has overcome the "pseudo-idealism" of Goethe and Schiller.

It is indeed an "ideal" domain, as Schiller correctly perceived, in which the Greek satyr chorus, the chorus of primitive tragedy, was wont to dwell. It is a domain raised high above the actual paths of mortals. For this chorus the Greek built up the scaffolding of a fictitious *natural state* and on it placed fictitious *natural beings*. On this foundation tragedy developed and so, of course, it could dispense from the beginning with a painstaking portrayal of reality. Yet it is no arbitrary world placed by whim between heaven and earth; rather it is a world with the same reality and credibility that Olympus with its inhabitants possessed for the believing Hellene. The satyr, as the Dionysian chorist, lives in a religiously acknowledged reality under the sanction of myth and cult. That tragedy should begin with him, that he should be the voice of the Dionysian wisdom of tragedy, is just as strange a phenomenon for us as the general derivation of tragedy from the chorus.

Perhaps we shall have a point of departure for our inquiry if I put forward the proposition that the satyr, the fictitious natural being, bears the same relation to the man of culture that Dionysian music bears to civilization. Concerning the latter, Richard Wagner says that it is nullified[29] by music just as lamplight is nullified by the light of day. Similarly, I believe, the Greek man of culture felt himself nullified in the presence of the satyric chorus; and this is the most immediate effect of the Dionysian tragedy, that the state and society and, quite generally, the gulfs between man and man give way to an overwhelming feeling of unity leading back to the very heart of nature. The metaphysical comfort—with which, I am suggesting even now, every true tragedy leaves us—that life is at the bottom of things, despite all the changes of appearances indestructibly powerful and pleasurable—this comfort appears in incarnate clarity in the chorus of saytrs, a chorus of natural beings who live ineradicably, as it were, behind all civilization and remain eternally the same, despite the changes of generations and of the history of nations.

With this chorus the profound Hellene, uniquely susceptible to the tenderest and deepest suffering, comforts himself, having looked boldly right into the terrible destructiveness of so-called world history as well as the cruelty of nature, and being in danger of longing for a Buddhistic negation of the will.[30] Art saves him, and through art—life.

For the rapture of the Dionysian state with its annihilation of the ordinary bounds and limits of existence contains, while it lasts, a *lethargic* element in which all personal experiences of the past become immersed. This chasm of oblivion separates the worlds of everyday reality and of Dionysian reality. But as soon as this everyday reality re-enters consciousness, it is experienced as such, with nausea: an ascetic, will-negating mood is the fruit of these states.

In this sense the Dionysian man resembles Hamlet: both have once looked truly into the essence of things, they have *gained knowledge*, and nausea inhibits action; for their action could not change anything in the eternal nature of things; they feel it to be ridiculous or humiliating that they should be asked to set right a world that is out of joint. Knowledge kills action; action requires the veils of illusion: that is the doctrine of Hamlet, not that cheap wisdom of Jack the Dreamer who reflects too much and, as it were, from an excess of possibilities does not get around to action. Not reflection, no—true knowledge, an insight into the horrible truth, outweighs any motive for action, both in Hamlet and in the Dionysian man.

Now no comfort avails any more; longing transcends a world after death, even the gods; existence is negated along with its glittering reflection in the gods or in an immortal beyond. Conscious of the truth he has once seen, man now sees everywhere only the horror or absurdity of existence; now he understands what is symbolic in Ophelia's fate; now he understands the wisdom of the sylvan god, Silenus: he is nauseated.

Here, when the danger to his will is greatest, *art* approaches as a saving sorceress, expert at healing. She alone knows how to turn these nauseous thoughts about the horror or absurdity of existence into notions with which one can live: these are the *sublime* as the artistic taming of the horrible, and the *comic* as the artistic discharge of the nausea of absurdity. The satyr chorus of the dithyramb is the saving deed of Greek art; faced with the intermediary world of these Dionysian companions, the feelings described here exhausted themselves.[31]

—*The Birth of Tragedy* (1872; translated by Walter Kaufmann, 1967)

NOTES

1. In the first edition: ". . . an opposition of style: two different tendencies run parallel in it, for the most part in conflict; and they . . ." Most of the changes in the revision of 1874 are as slight as this (compare the next footnote) and therefore not indicated in the following pages. This translation, like the standard German editions, follows Nietzsche's revision.

2. First edition: "till eventually, at the moment of the flowering of the Hellenic 'will,' they appear fused to generate together the art form of Attic tragedy."

3. Wagner's original text reads:

Mein Freund, das grad' ist Dichters Werk,
dass er sein Träumen deut' und merk'.
Glaubt mir, des Menschen wahrster Wahn
wird ihm im Traume aufgethan:
all' Dichtkunst und Poëterei
ist nichts als Wahrtraum-Deuterei.

4. *Schein* has been rendered in these pages sometimes as "illusion" and sometimes as "mere appearance."

5. *Der "Scheinende."* The German words for illusion and appearance are *Schein* and *Erscheinung.*

6. A Sanskrit word usually translated as illusion. For detailed discussions see, e.g., *A Source Book of Indian Philosophy*, ed. S. Radhakrishnan and Charles Moore (Princeton, N.J., Princeton University Press, 1957); Heinrich Zimmer, *Philosophies of India*, ed. Joseph Campbell (New York, Meridian Books, 1956); and Helmuth von Glasenapp, *Die Philosophie der Inder* (Stuttgart, Kröner, 1949), consulting the indices.

7. This reference, like subsequent references to the same work, is Nietzsche's own and refers to the edition of 1873 edited by Julius Frauenstädt—still one of the standard editions of Schopenhauer's works.

8. Principle of individuation.

9. A Babylonian festival that lasted five days and was marked by general license. During this time slaves are said to have ruled their masters, and a criminal was given all royal rights before he was put to death at the end of the festival. For references, see e.g., *The Oxford Classical Dictionary.*

10. In German, "the prodigal son" is *der verlorene Sohn* (the lost son).

11. An illusion to Friedrich Schiller's hymn *An die Freud* (to joy), used by Beethoven in the final movement of his Ninth Symphony.

12. Quotation from Schiller's hymn.

13. *Sentimentalisch* (not *sentimental*): an illusion to Schiller's influential contrast of *naïve* (Goethean) poetry with his own *sentimentalische Dichtung.*

14. This presage of the later coinage "beyond good and evil" is lost when *base* is mistranslated as "bad" instead of "evil."

15. Cf. Sophocles, *Oedipus at Colonus*, lines 1224ff.

16. *Zauberberg*, as in the title of Thomas Mann's novel.

17. Fate.

18. An allusion to Homer's *Odyssey*, XI, lines 489ff.

19. Sparta.

20. In footnote 32 of his first polemic (1872) Wilamowitz said: "Whoever explains these last words, to which Mephistopheles' remark about the witch's arithmetic [Goethe's *Faust*, lines 2565–66] applies, receives a suitable reward from me." It would seem that Sophocles' Antigone is here seen as representative of the Apollinian, while Aeschylus' Cassandra (in *Agamemnon*) is associated with the Dionysian.

21. An early Greek poet whose dates are disputed. He mentions an eclipse that some believe to be the one of 711 B.C., others that of 648 B.C. *The Oxford Classical Dictionary* considers the earlier date more probable. His mother was a slave, and he was killed in battle.

22. This conception of contemplation devoid of interest, as well as much else that is indebted to Schopenhauer, was later expressly criticized by Nietzsche.

23. Lines 677ff.

24. The poet's ego is closest at hand, but the tragic poet can use Cassandra or Hamlet as a mask no less than his own empirical self.

25. This parenthetical remark, repeated in section 24, is one of the most famous dicta in *The Birth of Tragedy.*

26. An anthology of medieval German folk songs (1806–08), edited by Achim von Arnim (1781–1831) and his brother-in-law, Clemens Brentano (1778–1842). The title means "The Boy's Magic Horn."

27. Middle of the seventh century B.C. Terpander, a poet, was born in Lesbos and lived in Sparta.

28. One of the leading spirits of the early German romantic movement, especially renowned for his translations of about half of Shakespeare's plays; born 1767, died 1845.

29. *Aufgehoben*: one of Hegel's favorite words, which can also mean lifted up or preserved.

30. Here Nietzsche's emancipation from Schopenhauer becomes evident, and their difference from each other concerns the central subject of the whole book: the significance of tragedy. Nietzsche writes about tragedy as the great life-affirming alternative to Schopenhauer's negation of the will. One can be as honest and free of optimistic illusions as Schopenhauer was, and still celebrate life as fundamentally powerful and pleasurable as the Greeks did.

31. Having finally broken loose from Schopenhauer, Nietzsche for the first time shows the brilliancy of his own genius. It is doubtful whether anyone before him had illuminated *Hamlet* so extensively in so few words: the passage invites comparison with Freud's great footnote on *Hamlet* in the first edition of *Die Traümdeutung* (interpretation of dreams), 1900. Even more obviously, the last three paragraphs invite comparison with existentialist literature, notably, but by no means only, Sartre's *La Nausée* (1938).

SIGMUND FREUD

Wish-Fulfillment and the Unconscious

I. Phantasy-making and Art

. . . Consider . . . the origin and meaning of that mental activity called "phantasy-making." In general, as you know, it enjoys high esteem, although its place in mental life has not been clearly understood. I can tell you as much as this about it. You know that the ego in man is gradually trained by the influence of external necessity to appreciate reality and to pursue the reality-principle, and that in so doing it must renounce temporarily or permanently various of the objects and aims—not only sexual—of its desire for pleasure. But renunciation of pleasure has always been very hard for man; he cannot accomplish it without some kind of compensation. Accordingly he has evolved for himself a mental activity in which all these relinquished sources of pleasure and abandoned paths of gratification are permitted to continue their existence, a form of existence in which they are free from the demands of reality and from what we call the exercise of "testing reality." Every longing is soon transformed into the idea of its fulfillment; there is no doubt that dwelling upon a wish-fulfillment in phantasy brings satisfaction, although the knowledge that it is not reality remains thereby unobscured. In phantasy, therefore, man can continue to enjoy a freedom from the grip of the external world, one which he has long relinquished in actuality. He has contrived to be alternately a pleasure-seeking animal and a reasonable being; for the meager satisfaction that he can extract from reality leaves him starving. "There is no doing without accessory constructions," said Fontane. The creation of the mental domain of phantasy has a complete counterpart in the establishment of "reservations" and "nature-parks" in places where the inroads of agriculture, traffic, or industry threaten to change the original face of the earth rapidly into something unrecognizable. The "reservation" is to maintain the old condition of things which has been regretfully sacrificed to necessity everywhere else; there everything may grow and spread as it pleases, including what is useless and even what is harmful. The mental realm of phantasy is also such a reservation reclaimed from the encroachments of the reality-principle.

The best-known productions of phantasy have already been met by us; they are called daydreams, and are imaginary gratifications of ambitious, grandiose, erotic wishes, dilating the more extravagantly the more reality admonishes humility and patience. In them is shown unmistakably the essence of imaginary happiness, the return of gratification to a condition in which it is independent of reality's sanction. We know that these daydreams are the kernels and models of night dreams; fundamentally the night dream is nothing but a daydream distorted by the nocturnal form of mental activity and made possible by the nocturnal freedom of instinctual excitations. We are already familiar with the idea that a daydream is not necessarily conscious, that unconscious daydreams also exist[1]; such unconscious daydreams are therefore just as much the source of night dreams as of neurotic symptoms. . . .

The return of the libido[2] . . . to phantasy is an intermediate step on the way to symptom-formation which well deserves a special designation. C. G. Jung has coined for it the very appropriate name of *Introversion,* but inappropriately he uses it also to describe other things. We will adhere to the position that *introversion* describes the deflection of the libido away from the possibilities of real satisfaction and its excessive accumulation upon phantasies previously tolerated as harmless. An introverted person is not yet neurotic, but he is in an unstable condition; the next disturbance of the shifting forces will cause symptoms to develop, unless he can yet find other outlets for his pent-up libido. The unreal character of neurotic satisfaction and the disregard of the difference between phantasy and reality are already determined by the arrest at this stage of introversion. . . .

Before you leave today I should like to direct your attention for a moment to a side of phantasy-life of very general interest. There is, in fact, a path from phantasy back again to reality, and that is—art. The artist has also an introverted disposition and has not far to go to become neurotic. He is one who is urged on by instinctual needs which are too clamorous; he longs to attain to honor, power, riches, fame, and the love of women; but he lacks the means of achieving these gratifications. So, like any other with an unsatisfied longing, he turns away from reality and transfers all his interest, and all his libido too, on to the creation of his wishes in the life of phantasy, from which the way might readily lead to neurosis. There must be many factors in combination to prevent this becoming the whole outcome of his development; it is well known how often artists in particular suffer from partial inhibition of their capacities through neurosis. Probably their constitution is endowed with a powerful capacity for sublimation and with a certain flexibility in the repressions determining the conflict. But the way back to reality is found by the artist thus: He is not the only one who has a life of phantasy; the intermediate world of phantasy is sanctioned by general human consent, and every hungry soul looks to it for comfort and consolation. But to those who are not artists the gratification that can be drawn from the springs of phantasy is very limited; their inexorable repressions prevent the enjoyment of all but the meager daydreams which can become conscious. A true artist has more at his disposal. First of all he understands how to elaborate his daydreams, so that they lose that personal note which grates upon strange ears and become enjoyable to others; he knows too how to modify them sufficiently so that their origin in prohibited sources is not easily detected. Further, he possesses the mysterious ability to mold his particular material until it expresses the ideas of his phantasy faithfully; and then he knows how to attach to this reflection of his phantasy-life so strong a stream of pleasure that, for a time at least, the repressions are outbalanced and dispelled by it. When he can do all this, he opens out to others the way back to the comfort and consolation of their own unconscious sources of pleasure, and so reaps their gratitude and admiration; then he has won—through his phantasy—what before he could only win in phantasy: honor, power, and the love of women.

> —*Introductory Lectures on Psychoanalysis* (Lectures delivered 1915–17; translated 1922 by Joan Riviere)

NOTES

1. As Freud earlier explains, a latent dream, the realization of a wish-phantasy, is frequently built up in the unconsciousness. The act of repression creates in the unconscious sphere hidden ideas and impulses isolated from the rest of the personality (Editor's note).

2. For the meaning of "libido," and an explanation of its artistic sublimation, see the editor's introductory note to this chapter.

II. THE RELATION OF THE POET TO DAYDREAMING

We laymen have always wondered greatly—like the cardinal who put the question to Ariosto—how that strange being, the poet, comes by his material. What makes him able to carry us with him in such a way and to arouse emotions in us of which we thought ourselves perhaps not even capable? Our interest in the problem is only stimulated by the circumstance that if we ask poets themselves they give us no explanation of the matter, or at least no satisfactory explanation. The knowledge that not even the clearest insight into the factors conditioning the choice of imaginative material, or into the nature of the ability to fashion that material, will ever make writers of us does not in any way detract from our interest.

If we could only find some activity in ourselves, or in people like ourselves, which was in any way akin to the writing of imaginative works! If we could do so, then examination of it would give us a hope of obtaining some insight into the creative powers of imaginative writers. And indeed, there is some prospect of achieving this—writers themselves always try to lessen the distance between their kind and ordinary human beings; they so often assure us that every man is at heart a poet, and that the last poet will not die until the last human being does.

We ought surely to look in the child for the first traces of imaginative activity. The child's best-loved and most absorbing occupation is play. Perhaps we may say that every child at play behaves like an imaginative writer, in that he creates a world of his own or, more truly, he rearranges the things of his world and orders it in a new way that pleases him better. It would be incorrect to think that he does not take this world seriously; on the contrary, he takes his play very seriously and expends a great deal of emotion on it. The opposite of play is not serious occupation but— reality. Notwithstanding the large affective cathexis[1] of his play-world, the child distinguishes it perfectly from reality; only he likes to borrow the objects and circumstances that he imagines from the tangible and visible things of the real world. It is only this linking of it to reality that still distinguishes a child's "play" from "daydreaming."

Now the writer does the same as the child at play; he creates a world of phantasy which he takes very seriously; that is, he invests it with a great deal of affect, while separating it sharply from reality. Language has preserved this relationship between children's play and poetic creation. It designates certain kinds of imaginative creation, concerned with tangible objects and capable of representation, as "plays"; the people who present them are called "players." The unreality of this poetical world of imagination, however, has very important consequences for literary technique; for many things which if they happened in real life could produce no pleasure can nevertheless give enjoyment in a play—many emotions which are essentially painful may become a source of enjoyment to the spectators and hearers of a poet's work.

There is another consideration relating to the contrast between reality and play on which we will dwell for a moment. Long after a child has grown up and stopped playing, after he has for decades attempted to grasp the realities of life with all seriousness, he may one day come to a state of mind in which the contrast between play and reality is again abrogated. The adult can remember with what intense seriousness he carried on his childish play; then by comparing his would-be serious occupations with his childhood's play, he manages to throw off the heavy burden of life and obtain the great pleasure of humor.

As they grow up, people cease to play, and appear to give up the pleasure they derived from play. But anyone who knows anything of the mental life of human beings is aware that hardly anything is more difficult to them than to give up a pleasure they have once tasted. Really we never can relinquish anything; we only exchange one thing for something else. When we appear to give something up, all we really do is to adopt a substitute. So when the human being grows up and ceases to play he only gives up the connection with real objects; instead of playing he then begins to create phantasy. He builds castles in the air and creates what are called daydreams. I believe that the greater number of human beings create phantasies at times as long as they live. This is a fact which has been overlooked for a long time, and its importance has therefore not been properly appreciated.

The phantasies of human beings are less easy to observe than the play of children. Children do, it is true, play alone, or form with other children a closed world in their minds for the purposes of play; but a child does not conceal his play from adults, even though his playing is quite unconcerned with them. The adult, on the other hand, is ashamed of his daydreams and conceals them from other people; he cherishes them as his most intimate possessions and as a rule he would rather confess all his misdeeds than tell his daydreams. For this reason he may believe that he is the only person who makes up such phantasies, without having any idea that everybody else tells themselves stories of the same kind. Daydreaming is a continuation of play, nevertheless, and the motives which lie behind these two activities contain a very good reason for this different behavior in the child at play and in the daydreaming adult.

The play of children is determined by their wishes—really by the child's *one* wish, which is to be grown-up, the wish that helps to "bring him up." He always plays at being grown-up; in play he imitates what is known to him of the lives of adults. Now he has no reason to conceal this wish. With the adult it is otherwise; on the one hand, he knows that he is expected not to play any longer or to daydream, but to be making his way in a real world. On the other hand, some of the wishes from which his phantasies spring are such as to have to be entirely hidden; therefore he is ashamed of his phantasies as being childish and as something prohibited.

If they are concealed with so much secretiveness, you will ask, how do we know so much about the human propensity to create phantasies? Now there is a certain class of human beings upon whom not a god, indeed, but a stern goddess—Necessity—has laid the task of giving an account of what they suffer and what they enjoy. These people are the neurotics; among other things they have to confess their phantasies to the physician to whom they go in the hope of recovering through mental treatment. This is our best source of knowledge, and we have later found good reason to suppose that our patients tell us about themselves nothing that we could not also hear from healthy people.

Let us try to learn some of the characteristics of daydreaming. We can begin by saying that happy people never make phantasies, only unsatisfied ones. Unsatisfied wishes are the driving power behind phantasies; every separate phantasy contains the fulfillment of a wish, and improves on unsatisfactory reality. The impelling wishes vary according to the sex, character, and circumstances of the creator; they may be easily divided, however, into two principal groups. Either they are ambitious wishes, serving to exalt the person creating them, or they are erotic. In young women erotic wishes dominate the phantasies almost exclusively, for their ambition is generally comprised in their erotic longings; in young men egoistic and ambitious wishes assert themselves plainly enough alongside their erotic desires. But we will not lay stress on the distinction between these two trends; we prefer to emphasize the fact that they are often united. In many altarpieces the portrait of the donor is to be found in one corner of the picture; and in the greater number of ambitious day-dreams, too, we can discover a woman in some corner, for whom the dreamer performs all his heroic deeds and at whose feet all his triumphs are to be laid. Here you see we have strong enough motives for conceal-ment; a well-brought-up woman is, indeed, credited with only a minimum of erotic desire, while a young man has to learn to suppress the overween-ing self-regard he acquires in the indulgent atmosphere surrounding his childhood, so that he may find his proper place in a society that is full of other persons making similar claims.

We must not imagine that the various products of this impulse towards phantasy, castles in the air or daydreams, are stereotyped or unchangeable. On the contrary, they fit themselves into the changing impressions of life, alter with the vicissitudes of life; every deep new impression gives them what might be called a "date stamp." The relation of phantasies to time is altogether of great importance. One may say that a phantasy at one and the same moment hovers between three periods of time—the three periods of our ideation. The activity of phantasy in the mind is linked up with some current impression, occasioned by some event in the present, which had the power to rouse an intense desire. From there it wanders back to the memory of an early experience, generally belonging to infancy, in which this wish was fulfilled. Then it creates for itself a situation which is to emerge in the future, representing the fulfillment of the wish—this is the daydream or phantasy, which now carries in it traces both of the occasion which engendered it and of some past memory. So past, present, and future are threaded, as it were, on the string of the wish that runs through them all.

A very ordinary example may serve to make my statement clear. Take the case of a poor orphan lad, to whom you have given the address of some employer where he may perhaps get work. On the way there he falls into a daydream suitable to the situation from which it springs. The content of the phantasy will be somewhat as follows: He is taken on and pleases his new employer, makes himself indispensable in the business, is taken into the family of the employer, and marries the charming daughter of the house. Then he comes to conduct the business, first as a partner, and then as successor to his father-in-law. In this way the dreamer regains what he had in his happy childhood, the protecting house, his loving parents and the first objects of his affection. You will see from such an example how the wish employs some event in the present to plan a future on the pattern of the past.

Much more could be said about phantasies, but I will only allude as briefly as possible to certain points. If phantasies become over-luxuriant and over-powerful, the necessary conditions for an outbreak of neurosis or psychosis are constituted; phantasies are also the first preliminary stage in the mind of the symptoms of illness of which our patients complain. A broad bypath here branches off into pathology.

I cannot pass over the relation of phantasies to dreams. Our nocturnal dreams are nothing but such phantasies, as we can make clear by interpreting them.[2] Language, in its unrivaled wisdom, long ago decided the question of the essential nature of dreams by giving the name of "daydreams" to the airy creations of fantasy. If the meaning of our dreams usually remains obscure in spite of this clue, it is because of the circumstance that at night wishes of which we are ashamed also become active in us, wishes which we have to hide from ourselves, which were consequently repressed and pushed back into the unconscious. Such repressed wishes and their derivatives can therefore achieve expression only when almost completely disguised. When scientific work had succeeded in elucidating the distortion in dreams, it was no longer difficult to recognize that nocturnal dreams are fulfillments of desires in exactly the same way as daydreams are—those phantasies with which we are all so familiar.

So much for daydreaming; now for the poet! Shall we dare really to compare an imaginative writer with "one who dreams in broad daylight," and his creations with daydreams? Here, surely, a first distinction is forced upon us; we must distinguish between poets who, like the bygone creators of epics and tragedies, take over their material ready-made, and those who seem to create their material spontaneously. Let us keep to the latter, and let us also not choose for our comparison those writers who are most highly esteemed by critics. We will choose the less pretentious writers of romances, novels, and stories, who are read all the same by the widest circles of men and women. There is one very marked characteristic in the productions of these writers which must strike us all: they all have a hero who is the center of interest, for whom the author tries to win our sympathy by every possible means, and whom he places under the protection of a special providence. If at the end of one chapter the hero is left unconscious and bleeding from severe wounds, I am sure to find him at the beginning of the next being carefully tended and on the way to recovery; if the first volume ends in the hero being shipwrecked in a storm at sea, I am certain to hear at the beginning of the next of his hair-breadth escape—otherwise, indeed, the story could not continue. The feeling of security with which I follow the hero through his dangerous adventures is the same as that with which a real hero throws himself into the water to save a drowning man, or exposes himself to the fire of the enemy while storming a battery. It is this very feeling of being a hero which one of our best authors has well expressed in the famous phrase, *"Es kann mir nix g'schehen!"*[3] It seems to me, however, that this significant mark of invulnerability very clearly betrays—His Majesty the Ego, the hero of all daydreams and all novels.

The same relationship is hinted at in yet other characteristics of these egocentric stories. When all the women in a novel invariably fall in love with the hero, this can hardly be looked upon as a description of reality, but it is easily understood as an essential constituent of a daydream. The same thing holds good when the other people in the story are sharply divided into good and bad, with complete disregard of the manifold variety in the traits of real human beings; the "good" ones are those who help the ego in its character of hero, while the "bad" are his enemies and rivals.

We do not in any way fail to recognize that many imaginative productions have traveled far from the original naïve daydream, but I cannot suppress the surmise that even the most extreme variations could be brought into relationship with this model by an uninterrupted series of transitions. It has struck me in many so-called psychological novels, too, that only one person—once again the hero—is described from within; the author dwells in his soul and looks upon the other people from outside. The psychological novel in general probably owes its peculiarities to the tendency of modern writers to split up their ego by self-observation into many component-egos, and in this way to personify the conflicting trends in their own mental life in many heroes. There are certain novels, which might be called "eccentric," that seem to stand in marked contradiction to the typical daydream; in these the person introduced as the hero plays the least active part of anyone, and seems instead to let the actions and sufferings of other people pass him by like a spectator. Many of the later novels of Zola belong to this class. But I must say that the psychological analysis of people who are not writers, and who deviate in many things from the so-called norm, has shown us analogous variations in their daydreams in which the ego contents itself with the role of spectator.

If our comparison of the imaginative writer with the daydreamer, and of poetic production with the daydream, is to be of any value, it must show itself fruitful in some way or other. Let us try, for instance, to examine the works of writers in reference to the idea propounded above, the relation of the phantasy to the wish that runs through it and to the three periods of time; and with its help let us study the connection between the life of the writer and his productions. Hitherto it has not been known what preliminary ideas would constitute an approach to this problem; very often this relation has been regarded as much simpler than it is; but the insight gained from phantasies leads us to expect the following state of things. Some actual experience which made a strong impression on the writer had stirred up a memory of an earlier experience, generally belonging to childhood, which then arouses a wish that finds a fulfillment in the work in question, and in which elements of the recent event and the old memory should be discernible.

Do not be alarmed at the complexity of this formula; I myself expect that in reality it will prove itself to be too schematic, but that possibly it may contain a first means of approach to the true state of affairs. From some attempts I have made I think that this way of approaching works of the imagination might not be unfruitful. You will not forget that the stress laid on the writer's memories of his childhood, which perhaps seems so strange, is ultimately derived from the hypothesis that imaginative creation, like daydreaming, is a continuation of and substitute for the play of childhood.

We will not neglect to refer also to that class of imaginative work which must be recognized not as spontaneous production, but as a refashioning of ready-made material. Here, too, the writer retains a certain amount of independence, which can express itself in the choice of material and in changes in the material chosen, which are often considerable. As far as it goes, this material is derived from the racial treasure-house of myths, legends, and fairy tales. The study of these creations of racial psychology is in no way complete, but it seems extremely probable that myths, for example, are distorted vestiges of the wish-phantasies of whole nations— the age-long dreams of young humanity.

You will say that, although writers came first in the title of this paper, I have told you far less about them than about phantasy. I am aware of that, and will try to excuse myself by pointing to the present state of our knowledge. I could only throw out suggestions and bring up interesting points which arise from the study of phantasies, and which pass beyond them to the problem of the choice of literary material. We have not touched on the other problem at all, that is, what are the means which writers use to achieve those emotional reactions in us that are roused by their productions. But I would at least point out to you the path which leads from our discussion of daydreams to the problems of the effect produced on us by imaginative works.

You will remember that we said the daydreamer hid his phantasies carefully from other people because he had reason to be ashamed of them. I may now add that even if he were to communicate them to us, he would give us no pleasure by his disclosures. When we hear such phantasies they repel us, or at least leave us cold. But when a man of literary talent presents his plays, or relates what we take to be his personal daydreams, we experience great pleasure arising probably from many sources. How the writer accomplishes this is his innermost secret; the essential *ars poetica* lies in the technique by which our feeling of repulsion is overcome, and this has certainly to do with those barriers erected between every individual being and all others. We can guess at two methods used in this technique. The writer softens the egotistical character of the daydream by changes and disguises, and he bribes us by the offer of a purely formal, that is esthetic, pleasure in the presentation of his phantasies. The increment of pleasure which is offered us in order to release yet greater pleasure arising from deeper sources in the mind is called an "incitement premium" or technically, "fore-pleasure." I am of the opinion that all the esthetic pleasure we gain from the works of imaginative writers is of the same type as this "fore-pleasure," and that the true enjoyment of literature proceeds from the release of tensions in our minds. Perhaps much that brings about this result consists in the writer's putting us into a position in which we can enjoy our own daydreams without reproach or shame. Here we reach a path leading into novel, interesting, and complicated researches, but we also, at least for the present, arrive at the end of the present discussion.

—*New Revue,* Volume I (1908) ; translation first published in *Collected Papers,* Volume IV (1925) by I. F. Grant Duff

NOTES

1. From a Greek word, *Kathexo*, to occupy. "Cathexis" is used here to signify a state of being charged or invested with emotional energy. (Editor's note.)
2. *Cf.* Freud, *Die Traumdeutung (The Interpretation of Dreams).*
3. Anzengruber. [The phrase means "Nothing can happen to *me!*"—Translator.]

III. TRAGIC THEMES

According to my already extensive experience, parents play a leading part in the infantile psychology of all persons who subsequently become psychoneurotics. Falling in love with one parent and hating the other forms part of the permanent stock of the psychic impulses which arise in early childhood, and are of such importance as the material of the subsequent neurosis. But I do not believe that psychoneurotics are to be sharply distinguished in this respect from other persons who remain normal—that is, I do not believe that they are capable of creating something absolutely new and peculiar to themselves. It is far more probable—and this is confirmed by incidental observations of normal children—that in their amorous or hostile attitude toward their parents, psychoneurotics do no more than reveal to us, by magnification, something that occurs less markedly and intensively in the minds of the majority of children. Antiquity has furnished us with legendary matter which corroborates this belief, and the profound and universal validity of the old legends is explicable only by an equally universal validity of the above-mentioned hypothesis of infantile psychology.

I am referring to the legend of King Oedipus and the *Oedipus Rex* of Sophocles. Oedipus, the son of Laius, king of Thebes, and Jocasta, is exposed as a suckling, because an oracle had informed the father that his son, who was still unborn, would be his murderer. He is rescued, and grows up as a king's son at a foreign court, until, being uncertain of his origin, he, too, consults the oracle, and is warned to avoid his native place, for he is destined to become the murderer of his father and the husband of his mother. On the road leading away from his supposed home he meets King Laius, and in a sudden quarrel strikes him dead. He comes to Thebes, where he solves the riddle of the Sphinx, who is barring the way to the city, whereupon he is elected king by the grateful Thebans, and is rewarded with the hand of Jocasta. He reigns for many years in peace and honor, and begets two sons and two daughters upon his unknown mother, until at last a plague breaks out—which causes the Thebans to consult the oracle anew. Here Sophocles' tragedy begins. The messengers bring the reply that the plague will stop as soon as the murderer of Laius is driven from the country. But where is he?

> "Where shall be found,
> Faint, and hard to be known, the trace of the ancient guilt?"

The action of the play consists simply in the disclosure, approached step by step and artistically delayed (and comparable to the work of a psychoanalysis) that Oedipus himself is the murderer of Laius, and that he is the son of the murdered man and Jocasta. Shocked by the abominable crime which he has unwittingly committed, Oedipus blinds himself, and departs from his native city. The prophecy of the oracle has been fulfilled.

The *Oedipus Rex* is a tragedy of fate; its tragic effect depends on the conflict between the all-powerful will of the gods and the vain efforts of human beings threatened with disaster; resignation to the divine will, and the perception of one's own impotence is the lesson which the deeply moved spectator is supposed to learn from the tragedy. Modern authors have therefore sought to achieve a similar tragic effect by expressing the same conflict in stories of their own invention. But the playgoers have looked on unmoved at the unavailing efforts of guiltless men to avert the fulfillment of curse or oracle; the modern tragedies of destiny have failed of their effect.

If the *Oedipus Rex* is capable of moving a modern reader or play-goer no less powerfully than it moved the contemporary Greeks, the only possible explanation is that the effect of the Greek tragedy does not depend upon the conflict between fate and human will, but upon the peculiar nature of the material by which this conflict is revealed. There must be a voice within us which is prepared to acknowledge the compelling power of fate in the *Oedipus,* while we are able to condemn the situations occurring in *Die Ahnfrau* or other tragedies of fate as arbitrary inventions. And there actually is a motive in the story of King Oedipus which explains the verdict of this inner voice. His fate moves us only because it might have been our own, because the oracle laid upon us before our birth the very curse which rested upon him. It may be that we were all destined to direct our first sexual impulses toward our mothers, and our first impulses of hatred and violence toward our fathers; our dreams convince us that we were. King Oedipus, who slew his father Laius and wedded his mother Jocasta, is nothing more or less than a wish-fulfillment—the fulfillment of the wish of our childhood. But we, more fortunate than he, in so far as we have not become psychoneurotics, have since our childhood succeeded in withdrawing our sexual impulses from our mothers, and in forgetting our jealousy of our fathers. We recoil from the person for whom this primitive wish of our childhood has been fulfilled with all the force of the repression which these wishes have undergone in our minds since childhood. As the poet brings the guilt of Oedipus to light by his investigation, he forces us to become aware of our own inner selves, in which the same impulses are still extant, even though they are suppressed. The antithesis with which the chorus departs:—

> ". . . Behold, this is Oedipus,
> Who unravelled the great riddle, and was first in power,
> Whose fortune all the townsmen praised and envied;
> See in what dread adversity he sank!"

—this admonition touches us and our own pride, us who since the years of our childhood have grown so wise and so powerful in our own estimation. Like Oedipus, we live in ignorance of the desires that offend morality, the desires that nature has forced upon us and after their unveiling we may well prefer to avert our gaze from the scenes of our childhood.

In the very text of Sophocles' tragedy there is an unmistakable reference to the fact that the Oedipus legend had its source in dream-material of immemorial antiquity, the content of which was the painful disturbance of the child's relations to its parents caused by the first impulses of sexuality. Jocasta comforts Oedipus—who is not yet enlightened, but is troubled by the recollection of the oracle—by an allusion to a dream which is often dreamed, though it cannot, in her opinion, mean anything:—

> "For many a man hath seen himself in dreams
> His mother's mate, but he who gives no heed
> To suchlike matters bears the easier life."

The dream of having sexual intercourse with one's mother was as common then as it is today with many people, who tell it with indignation and astonishment. As may well be imagined, it is the key to the tragedy and the complement to the dream of the death of the father. The Oedipus fable is the reaction of phantasy to these two typical dreams, and just as such a dream, when occurring to an adult, is experienced with feelings of aversion, so the content of the fable must include terror and self-chastisement. The form which it subsequently assumed was the result of an uncomprehending secondary elaboration of the material, which sought to make it serve a theological intention. The attempt to reconcile divine omnipotence with human responsibility must, of course, fail with this material as with any other.

Another of the great poetic tragedies, Shakespeare's *Hamlet*, is rooted in the same soil as *Oedipus Rex*. But the whole difference in the psychic life of the two widely separated periods of civilization, and the progress, during the course of time, of repression in the emotional life of humanity, is manifested in the differing treatment of the same material. In *Oedipus Rex* the basic wish-phantasy of the child is brought to light and realized as it is in dreams; in *Hamlet* it remains repressed, and we learn of its existence—as we discover the relevant facts in a neurosis—only through the inhibitory effects which proceed from it. In the more modern drama, the curious fact that it is possible to remain in complete uncertainty as to the character of the hero has proved to be quite consistent with the overpowering effect of the tragedy. The play is based upon Hamlet's hesitation in accomplishing the task of revenge assigned to him; the text does not give the cause or the motive of this hesitation, nor have the manifold attempts at interpretation succeeded in doing so. According to the still prevailing conception, a conception for which Goethe was first responsible, Hamlet represents the type of man whose active energy is paralyzed by excessive intellectual activity: "Sicklied o'er with the pale cast of thought." According to another conception, the poet has endeavored to portray a morbid, irresolute character, on the verge of neurasthenia. The plot of the drama, however, shows us that Hamlet is by no means intended to appear as a character wholly incapable of action. On two separate occasions we see him assert himself: once in a sudden outburst of rage, when he stabs the eavesdropper behind the arras, and on the other occasion when he deliberately, and even craftily, with the complete unscrupulousness of a prince of the Renaissance, sends the two courtiers to the death which was intended for himself. What is it, then, that inhibits him in accomplishing the task which his father's ghost has laid upon him? Here the explanation offers itself that it is the peculiar nature of this task. Hamlet is able to do anything but take vengeance upon the man who did away with his father and has taken his father's place with his mother— the man who shows him in realization the repressed desires of his own childhood. The loathing which should have driven him to revenge is thus replaced by self-reproach, by conscientious scruples, which tell him that he himself is no better than the murderer whom he is required to punish. I have here translated into consciousness what had to remain unconscious in the mind of the hero; if anyone wishes to call Hamlet an hysterical subject I cannot but admit that this is the deduction to be drawn from my interpretation. The sexual aversion which Hamlet expresses in conversation with Ophelia is perfectly consistent with this deduction—the same sexual aversion which during the next fews years was increasingly to take possession of the poet's soul, until it found its supreme utterance in *Timon of Athens*. It can, of course, be only the poet's own psychology with which we are confronted in *Hamlet*; and in a work on Shakespeare by Georg Brandes (1896) I find the statement that the drama was composed immediately after the death of Shakespeare's father (1601)—that is to say, when he was still mourning his loss, and during a revival, as we may fairly assume, of his own childish feelings in respect of his father. It is known, too, that Shakespeare's son, who died in childhood, bore the name of Hamnet (identical with Hamlet). Just as *Hamlet* treats of the relation of the son to his parents, so *Macbeth*, which was written about the same period, is based upon the theme of childlessness. Just as all neurotic symptoms, like dreams themselves, are capable of hyper-interpretation, and even require such hyper-interpretation before they become perfectly intelligible, so every genuine poetical creation must have proceeded from more than one motive, more than one impulse in the mind of the poet, and must admit of more than one interpretation. I have here attempted to interpret only the deepest stratum of impulses in the mind of the creative poet.

—*The Intepretation of Dreams* (1900; translated 1913 by A. A. Brill)

CHRISTOPHER CAUDWELL

Poetry's Dream-Work

§ 1

Dream is neither directed thinking nor directed feeling, but free—that is non-social—association. Hence the associations of dream are personal and can only be understood by reference to the dreamer's personal life. The secret law of dream's structure is the "dream-work."

Poetic irrationality bears this resemblance to dream, that its flow of images is explained by affective laws; but it is not "free" association as in dream. Poetic feeling is directed feeling—feeling controlled by the social ego. Poetic associations are social.

As the dreamer lives entirely in the images of his dream, without reference to another reality, so the reader of poetry lives in the words of the poetry, without reference to the external world. The poet's world is *his* world. As he reads the poem he feels the emotions of the poet. Just as the pythoness or bacchante speaks for the god in the first person, so the reader under the influence of poetic illusion feels for the poet in the first person.

The images of dream, like the ideas of poetry, are concrete. In each dream, and in each poem, the memory-image and the word play a different part, and therefore have different meanings. Dreams and poems are inconsistent among themselves. Each dream and each poem is a world of its own.

Poetry is rhythmical. Rhythm secures the heightening of physiological consciousness so as to shut out sensory perception of the environment. In the rhythm of dance, music or song we become *self*-conscious instead of conscious. The rhythm of heart-beat and breathing and physiological periodicity negates the physical rhythm of the environment. In this sense sleep too is rhythmical. The dreamer retires into the citadel of the body and closes the doors.

Why is "physiological" introversion more necessary in poetry than in story, so that the poet accepts the difficulties of meter and rhyme? The answer is that introversion must be stronger in poetry. By introversion is not meant merely a turning-away from immediate environment—that could be secured by sitting in a quiet study, without disturbance. Such introversion is equally desirable for all kinds of thought, for scientific thinking and novel-reading as well as poetry, and it is not secured by the order of the words but by an effort of concentration. Some people can "concentrate" on a difficult scientific book or a book of poetry in conditions where others cannot. This kind of introversion does not therefore depend upon the order of the words. No one has suggested facilitating scientific writing by making it metrical.

But there is another aspect of introversion. In introversion for scientific phantasy it is true that we turn away from immediate environment, yet none the less we turn towards those parts of external reality of which the words are symbols. Ordinarily we see, hovering behind language, the world of external reality it describes. But in poetry the thoughts are to be directed on to the feeling-tone of the words themselves. Attention must sink below the pieces of external reality symbolized by the poetry, down into the emotional underworld adhering to those pieces. In poetry we must penetrate behind the dome of many-colored glass into the white radiance of the self. Hence the need for a physiological introversion, which is a turning-away not from the immediate environment of the reader *but from the environment (or external reality) depicted in the poem*. Hence poetry in its use of language continually distorts and denies the structure of reality to exalt the structure of the self. By means of rhyme, assonance or alliteration it couples together words which have no rational connection, that is, no nexus through the world of external reality. It breaks the words up into lines of arbitrary length, cutting across their logical construction. It breaks down their associations, derived from the world of external reality, by means of inversion and every variety of artificial stressing and counterpoint.

Thus the world of external reality recedes, and the world of instinct, the affective emotional linkage behind the words, rises to the view and becomes the world of reality. The subject emerges from the object: the social ego from the social world. Wordsworth said correctly: "The tendency of meter is to divest language, in a certain degree, of its reality, and thus to throw a sort of half-consciousness of unsubstantial existence over the whole composition." In the same way Coleridge reached out after a like conception to ours: "Meter is simply a stimulant of attention" —not of any attention but a special kind of attention—attention to the affective associations of the words themselves.

We have here a distinction between poetry and the novel which it is vital to grasp. In the novel too the subjective elements are valued for themselves and rise to view, but in a different way. The novel blots out external reality by substituting a more or less consistent mock reality which has sufficient "stuff" to stand between reader and reality. This means that in the novel the emotional associations attach not to the words but to the moving current of mock reality symbolized by the words. That is why rhythm, "preciousness," and style are alien to the novel; why the novel translates so well; why novels are not composed of words. They are composed of scenes, actions, *stuff*, people, just as plays are. A "jeweled" style is a disadvantage to the novel because it distracts the eye from the things and people to the words—not as words, as black outlines, but as symbols to which a variety of feeling-tone is directly attached. For example when someone exclaims "Brute!" we do not think of animals and then of brutish qualities, but have a powerful subjective reaction suggesting cruelty and clumsiness. This is a poetic reaction to a word; the other is a story reaction.

Because words are few they are what Freud called "over-determined." One word has many affective associations because it has many "meanings" (for example, the word "brute" can mean a foolish person, a cruel person, the order of animals, etc.). In novel-writing the words are arranged so that all other pieces of reality are excluded except the piece required, and the emotional association is to the resulting structure. Poetic writing is concerned with making the emotional associations either exclude or reinforce each other, without a prior reference to a coherent piece of reality; for example, in novel-writing, in the phrase "the Indian Ocean" the word "ocean" has been restricted to a specific geographical ocean, which *then* has emotional associations for the reader. In poetry "the Indian sea" has a different meaning, for the emotional associations are, not to a particular sea but to the word "Indian" and the word "sea," which affect each other and blend to produce a glowing cloudy "feeling" quite different from the novel-writer's phrase.

Of course there may be stretches of poetic writing in a novel (for example in Proust, Malraux, Lawrence, and Melville) or of novel-writing in poetry (the purely explanatory patches in Shakespeare's plays), but this does not affect the general characteristics. The difference is so marked that it explains the strange insensitivity to poetry displayed by so many great novelists, and a similar fondness for bad novels on the part of so many great poets. This difference between the technique of poetry and the novel determines the difference between the spheres of the two arts.

§ 2

What is the basis of literary art? What is the inner contradiction which produces its onward movement? Evidently it can only be a special form of the contradiction which produces the whole movement of society, the contradiction between the instincts and the environment, the endless struggle between man and Nature which is life.

I, the artist, have a certain consciousness, molded by my social world. As artist I am concerned with my artistic consciousness, represented by the direct and indirect effect on me of all the art I have felt, and all the emotional organization which has produced in me a conscious subject. This consciousness is contradicted by my experience—that is, I have a *new* personal experience, something not given in the social world of poetry. Therefore I desire what is called self-expression but is really self-socialization, the casting of my private experience in such a form that it will be incorporated in the social world of art and appear as an art-work. The art-work represents the negation of the negation—the synthesis between the existing world of art (existing consciousness of theory) and my experience (life or practice).[1]

Therefore at the finish the world of art will be changed by the incursion of my art-work. That is the revolutionary aspect of my role as artist. But also my consciousness will be changed because I have, through the medium of the art world, forced my life experience, new, dumb, and unformulated, to become conscious, to enter my conscious sphere. That is the adaptative aspect of my role as artist. In the same way with the appreciator of art, his consciousness will be revolutionized by the incursion into it of a new art-work; but his appreciation of it will only be possible to the extent that he had had some similar experience in life. The former process will be revolutionary; the latter adaptative.

Rather than use the word revolutionary, however, it would be better to use the word evolutionary, restricting the other to cases where the new content of experience is so opposed to the existing consciousness that it requires a wholesale change, a complete revision of existing categories (conventions, traditions, artistic standards) for its inclusion, a revision which is only possible because concrete life itself has undergone a similar change in the period. The Elizabethan age was one of such periods. We are at the beginning of another such now.

It is plain that it is the emotional consciousness—that consciousness which springs directly from the instincts—with which the artist is concerned. Yet exactly the same relation holds between the scientist and his hypothesis (equivalent of the art-work) and the rational consciousness, that consciousness which springs directly from the perception.

Since the mediating factor in art processes is the social ego in its relation to the experience of individuals, it is plain that the integration performed by the art-work can only be achieved on condition that the item of private experience which is integrated *(a) is important,* concerned with deep emotional drives, with the unchanging instincts which, because they remain the same beneath the changing adaptations of culture, act as the skeleton, the main organizing force in the social ego which ages of art have built up; *(b)* is *general,* is not a contradictory item of experience peculiar to the artist or one of two men, but is encountered in a dumb unconscious way in the experiences of most men—otherwise how could the art-work be meaningful to them, how could it integrate and give expression to their hitherto anarchic experience as it gave expression to the artist's?

Condition *(a)* secures that great art—art which performs a wide and deep feat of integration—has something universal, something timeless and enduring from age to age. This timelessness we now see to be the timelessness of the instincts, the unchanging secret face of the genotype which persists beneath all the rich superstructure of civilization. Condition *(b)* explains why contemporary art has a special and striking meaning for us, why we find in even minor contemporary poets something vital and immediate not to be found in Homer, Dante, or Shakespeare. They live in the same world and meet the same bodiless forces whose power they experience.

This also explains why it is correct to have a materialist approach to art, to look in the art-works of any age for a reflection of the social relations of that age. For the experience of men in general is determined in general by the social relations of that age or, to be more accurate, the social relations of that age are simply man's individual experiences averaged out, just as a species is a group of animals' physical peculiarities averaged out. Since art lives in the social world, and can only be of value in integrating experiences general to men, it is plain that the art of any age can only express the general experiences of men in that age. So far from the artist's being a lone wolf, he is the normal man of that age—insofar as he is an artist. Of course normality in consciousness is as rare as normality in vision, and, unlike the latter, it is not a fixed physical standard but one which varies from year to year. Moreover his normality is, so to speak, the norm of abnormal experiences. It is the norm of the queerness and newness and accident in contemporary men's lives: all the incursions of the unexpected which shake their inherited consciousness. Hence the apparent abnormality of the artist.

This, finally, explains why in a class society art is class art. For a class, in the Marxian sense, is simply a group of men whose life-experiences are substantially similar, that is, with less internal differences on the average than they have external differences from the life-experiences of men in other classes. This difference of course has an economic basis, a material cause arising from the inevitable conditions of economic production. Therefore the artist will necessarily integrate the new experience and voice the consciousness of that group whose experience in general resembles his own—his own class. This will be the class which practices art—

the class at whose pole gathers the freedom and consciousness of society, in all ages the ruling class.

This is the most general movement of literary art, reflecting the most general law of society. Because of the different techniques of poetry and the novel—already explained—this movement is expressed in different ways in poetry and in the novel.

Poetry concentrates on the immediate affective associations of the word, instead of going first to the object or entity symbolized by the word and then drawing the affective association from that. Since words are fewer than the objects they symbolize, the affects of poetry are correspondingly condensed, but poetry itself is correspondingly cloudy and ambiguous. This ambiguity, which Empson takes to be the essence of poetry, is in fact a by-product.[2] Now this concentration upon the affective tones of words, instead of going first to the symbolized reality and then to the feeling-tone of that reality, is—because of the nature of language—a concentration on the more dumb and instinctive part of man's consciousness. It is an approach to the more instinctively common part of man's consciousness. It is an approach to the secret unchanging core of the genotype in adapted man. Hence the importance of physiological introversion in poetry.

This genotype is undifferentiated because it is relatively unchanging. Hence the timelessness of poetry as compared to the importance of time sequence in the novel. Poetry speaks timelessly for one common "I" round which all experience is orientated. In poetry all the emotional experiences of men are arranged round the instincts, round the "I." Poetry is a bundle of instinctive perspectives of reality taken from one spot. Precisely because it is cloudly and ambiguous, its view is far-reaching; its horizon seems to open and expand and stretch out to dim infinity. Because it is instinctive, it is enduring. In it the instincts give one loud cry, a cry which expresses what is common in the general relation of every man to contemporary life as a whole.

But the novel goes out first to reality to draw its subjective associations from it. Hence we do not seem to feel the novel "in us," we do not identify our feelings with the feeling-tones of the novel. We stand inside the mock world of the novel and survey it; at the most we identify ourselves with the hero and look round with him at the "otherness" of his environment. The novel does not express the general tension between the instincts and the surroundings, but the changes of tension which take place as a result of change in the surroundings (life-experience). This incursion of the time element (reality as a process) so necessary in a differentiated society where men's time-experiences differ markedly among themselves, means that the novel must particularize and have characters whose actions and feelings are surveyed from without. Poetry is internal—a bundle of "I" perspectives of the world taken from one point, the poet. The story is external—a bundle of perspectives of one "I" (the character) taken from different parts of the world.

Obviously the novel can only evolve in a society where men's experiences do differ so markedly among themselves as to make this objective approach necessary, and this difference of experience is itself the result of rapid change in society, of an increased differentiation of functions, of an increased realization of life as process, as dialectic. Poetry is the product of a tribe, where life flows on without much change between youth and age; the novel belongs to a restless age where things are always happening to people and people therefore are always altering.

§ 3

Yet all art is subjective. All art is emotional and therefore concerned with the instincts whose adaptation to social life produces emotional consciousness. Hence art cannot escape its close relation with the genotype whose secret desires link in one endless series all human culture.

Now this genotype can be considered from two aspects: the timeless and the timeful, the changeless and changeful, the general and the particular.

(a) Timeless, changeless, general in that on the whole the genotype is substantially constant in all societies and all men. There is a substratum of likeness. Man does not change from Athenian to Ancient Briton and then to Londoner by innate differences stamped in by natural selection, but by acquired changes derived from social evolution. Poetry expresses this constant instinctive factor.

(b) Yet beneath this likeness the genotypes, because they are bundles of genes, reveal individual differences. These genes are perpetually shuffled to reveal new personalities. Because men differ in this way among themselves they cannot be satisfied with the simple tribal life of collective civilization. They demand "luxuries," freedom, special products which cannot be satisfied within the ambit of such a primitive economy. This leads to an economic differentiation of society which . . . is not the means of suppressing individuality but of realizing it. Hence these individual genetic differences produce change in time and also the realization of *characters*, of man's deviation from the social "norm." Thus the very technique of the novel makes it interested in the way characters strive to realize in existing society their individual differences.

Poetry expresses the freedom which inheres in man's general timeless unity in society; it is interested in society as the sum and guardian of common instinctive tendencies; it speaks of death, love, hope, sorrow, and despair as all men experience them. The novel is the expression of that freedom which men seek, not in their unity in society but in their differences, of their search for freedom in the pores of society, and therefore of their repulsions from, clashes with, and concrete motions against *other* individuals different from themselves.

The novel was bound to develop therefore under capitalism, whose increase in the productive forces brought about by the division of labor not only vastly increased the differentiation of society but also, by continually revolutionizing its own basis, produced an endless flux and change in life. Equally, as capitalism decayed, the novel was bound to voice the experience of men that economic differentiation had changed from a means of freedom to a rubber-stamp crushing individuality (the ossification of classes), and that the productive forces, by being held back from developing further, had choked the free movement of life (the general economic crisis). Necessarily therefore in such a period the decay of the novel occurs together with a general revolutionary turmoil.

Thus we see in the technical differences of poetry and the novel the difference between changelessness and change, space and time, and it is clear that these are not mutually exclusive opposites but are opposites which interpenetrate, and, as they fly apart, continually generate an enrichening reality.

This was the same kind of difference as that between the evolutionary and classificatory sciences.[3] And just as the technique of poetry demands an immediate concentration on the word, so the classificatory sciences, such as geometry and mathematics, demand an immediate concentration on the symbol. The novel demands that we pass from the symbol to reality, and only then to the affective organization; biology demands that we go first to the concrete objects, and only then to their rational organization. Poetry passes straight from the word to the affective organization, careless of the reality whose relation it accepts as already given in the word. Mathematics passes straight from the symbol to the perceptual organization, careless of the concrete object, whose important qualities (to it) are already accepted as crystallized in the symbol. Hence the vital importance of precise speech—of the absolutely correct word or correct symbol—both to poet and mathematician, contrasted with the looser speech permitted to the biologist or novelist.

We have seen that music is an extreme kind of poetry, that just as mathematics escapes almost altogether from the subjective qualities of matter, so music (unlike poetry) escapes almost altogether from the objective references of sounds. Therefore the musician is even preciser in his language than the poet, and the affective laws of music's symbols are as careful and minute as are the perceptual laws of mathematical symbols.

We can now understand more clearly why poetry resembles dream in its technique. The characteristic of dreams is that the dreamer always plays the leading part in it. He is always present in it, sometimes (as analysis shows) in many disguises. The same egocentricity is characteristic of poetry. Quite naïvely the poet records directly all his impressions, experiences, thought, images. Hence the apparent egoism of poetry, for everything is seen and experienced directly. Poetry is a relationship of memory-images mediated by only two words—"I" and "like."

But this is not the egoism of dream; it is a social egoism. The particular emotional organization of the poet is condensed into words, and the words are read, and the psyche of the reader experiences the same emotional reorganization. The reader puts himself, for the duration of the poem, in the place of the poet, and sees with his eyes. He *is* the poet.

In a poem by Shelley, we are Shelley. As we read Shakespeare, we see with his profound shimmering vision. Hence the unexpected individuality of the poet. Though it is the common human creature, the genotype, and not the "character" who looks out in poetry on the common contemporary scene, she looks at it through the eyes of one man, through the windows of the poet's psyche.

How is this done? That is the peculiar secret of poetic technique. Just as poetry can be equated with dream, poetic technique is similar to dream technique. The nature of dream technique has been explored by analysts under the general name of "the dream-work."

A dream consists of two layers. Obvious is the *manifest* content. We are walking by the seaside, a ship comes alongside, we step on it, we land in France, certain adventures befall us, and so on. This is the manifest content of the dream as we tell it at breakfast next morning to our bored family, who cannot understand our interest in it. But our interest in it was due to the fact that the illusion was perfect. While they lasted, these things really seemed to be happening to us. And this vividness must spring from some affective cause. But we felt little real emotion in the dream, however surprising the adventures that befell us. If we felt emotion, it was out of all real proportion to our adventures. Surprising things happened and we were not surprised. Trifling things happened and we were appalled. The affects were displaced in relation to reality. If we are asked to give our associations to these various component images just as they spring to our mind, a whole undergrowth of displaced affective life is revealed. Each symbol is associated with memories in our life, not by association of ideas but by affective associations.

The characteristic of "dream-work" is that every dream-symbol is over-determined and has a multitude of different emotional significances. This we also saw was the characteristic of poetic words, and springs from the same cause, that dream-symbols are valued directly for their affective content and not as symbols of a consistent mock world in which we first orientate ourselves. Hence the inconsequence of dream matches the "illogical" rhythm and assonance of poetry.

The organization of the psyche is such that in sleep all the conscious wishes, hopes, fears and love of the instinctive are replaced by apparently arbitrary memory-images, but which really are associated by the affective ties of simple unconscious wishes. They are organized by the appetitive activity of the instinctive and therefore unsleeping part of the psyche which, because it is archaic phylogenetically, is unmodified and therefore anti-social, or rather non-social. This affective substratum does not normally appear in dream. It is "repressed." Only the arbitrary symbols, apparently unconnected, appear in the consciousness. But this affective basis is the "reasoning" of the dream, and directs its course. It is the latent content. . . . Dreams, then, contain a manifest and a latent content. The manifest content is imagic phantasy, the latent content is affective reality. . . .

§ 4

. . . Poetry, like dream, contains *manifest* and *latent* contents. The manifest content can be roughly arrived at by paraphrasing the poem. It is the imagery or the "ideas." In a paraphrase the latent content, that is, the emotional content, has almost entirely vanished. It was contained, then, not in the external reality symbolized by the words (for this has been preserved) but in the words themselves. The manifest content is the poetry interpreted "rationally." It is the external reality in the poem. It can be expressed in other ways and other languages. But the latent content of poetry is in that particular form of wording, and in no other.

How is the latent content contained in the original words and not contained in the *sense* of the words—that is, in the portions of external reality which the words symbolize? The emotions are not associated affectively with the portion of external reality symbolized by the manifest content, for another language can be made to symbolize the same portion of external reality, and still it is not the poem. How then did the original words contain the emotional content "in themselves" and not in the things they symbolized? Dream analysis gives us the answer, by *affective* association of ideas. In any association of ideas two images are tied to each other by something different, like sticks by a cord. In poetry they are tied by affects.

If a word is abstracted from its surroundings and concentrated on in the same way as an analyst asked his patient to concentrate on any particular image of a dream, a number of associations will rise vaguely to the mind. In a simple word like "spring" there are hundreds of them; of greenness, of youth, of fountains, of jumping; every word drags behind it a vast bag and baggage of emotional associations, picked up in the thousands of different circumstances in which the word was used. It is these associations that provided the latent content of affect which is the poem. Not the ideas of "greenness," "youth," but the affective cord linking the ideas of "greenness" and "youth" to the word "spring," constitutes the raw material of poetry.

Of course the *thing* "spring" (the season) denoted by the word "spring" also has many affective associations. These are used by the novel. Poetry is concerned with the more general, subtle and instinctive affects which are immediately associated with the word "spring" and therefore include such almost punning associations as those connected with spring (a fountain) and spring (to jump). Hence the tendency of poetry to play with words, to pun openly or secretly, to delight in the texture of words. This is part of the technique of poetry which treats words anti-grammatically to realize their immediate and even contradictory affective tones. The novel uses words grammatically so as sharply to exclude all meanings and therefore all affective tones, except one clear piece of reality, and then derives the emotional content from this piece of reality and its active relation with the other pieces of reality in the story as part of a perceptual life-experience.

When we read a line of poetry these other ideas to which the affects are associated do not rise to the mind. We get the leaping and gushiness of "spring" in poetry's use of it as a word for the idea "season," but we do not get the fountain or the jump except in an open poetic pun. They remain unconscious. *Poetry is a kind of inverted dream.* Whereas in dream the real affects are partly suppressed and the blended images rise into the conscious, in poetry the associated images are partly suppressed and it is the blended affects that are present in the consciousness, in the form of affective organization.

Why is there a manifest content at all? Why are not all images suppressed? Why is not great poetry like the poetry of the extreme symbolists, a mere collection of words, meaning nothing, but words themselves full of affective association? Why should poetry state, explain, narrate, obey grammar, have syntax, be capable of paraphrase, since if paraphrased it loses its affective value?

The answer is, because poetry is an adaptation to external reality. It is an emotional attitude towards the world. It is made of language and language was created to signify otherness, to indicate portions of objective reality shared socially. It lives in the same language as scientific thought. The manifest content represents a statement of external reality. The manifest content is symbolic of a certain *piece* of external reality—be it scene, problem, thought, event. And the emotional content is *attached* to this statement of reality, not in actual experience but in the poem. The emotional content sweats out of the piece of external reality. In life this piece of external reality is devoid of emotional tone, but described in those particular words, and no others, it suddenly and magically shimmers with affective coloring. That affective coloring represents an emotional organization similar to that which the poet himself felt when faced (in phantasy or actuality) with that piece of external reality. When the poet says,

> Sleep, that knits up the ravelled sleave of care,

he is making a manifest statement. The paraphrase

> Slumber, that unties worry, which is like a piece of tangled knitting,

carries over most of the manifest content, but the affective tones which lurked in the associations of the words used have vanished. It is like a conjuring trick. The poet holds up a piece of the world and we see it glowing with a strange emotional fire. If we analyze it "rationally," we find no fire. Yet none the less, for ever afterwards, that piece of reality still keeps an after glow about it, is still fragrant with emotional life. So poetry enriches external reality for us.

The affective associations used by poetry are of many forms. Sometimes they are sound associations, and then we call the line "musical"—not that the language is specially harmonious; to a foreigner it would probably have no particular verbal melody:

> Thick as autumnal leaves that strow the brooks
> In Vallambrosa

is not musical to someone who knows no English. But to an English ear the emotive associations wakened are aroused through sound rather than sense linkages, and hence we call the line musical. So, too, with Verlaine's line, musical only to ears attuned to the emotive associations of French nasals:

> *Et O—ces voix d'enfants chantant dans la coupole,*

or the old fairy-tale title, "La Belle aux bois dormant."

It is impossible to have affects in poetry without their adherence to symbols of external reality, for poetry's affects (insofar as they are poetic) are social, and it is impossible for different subjects to be linked except by a common object (by "matter"). The logical conclusion of symbolism is not poetry but music. And here it may be objected—music consists of sounds which refer to no external reality and yet music is an art and has a social content. Exactly—because in music the symbols have ceased to "re- fer" to external reality and have become portions of external reality themselves and, in doing so, have necessarily generated a formal structure (the scale, "rules" of harmony, etc.) which gives them the rigidity and social status of external reality. The notes of music themselves are the manifest content of music, and they therefore obey not grammatical (sub- jective) but pseudo-mathematical (objective) laws: of course they are necessarily distorted or organized within the compass of those rules. In the same way architecture becomes external reality and is distorted or orga- nized within the compass of the rules of use-function.

The technique of the poet consists in this, that not all the affects asso- ciated with any particular words rise up into the consciousness, but only those that are required. This is done by the arrangement of the words in such a way that their clusters of associations, impinging on each other heighten some affective associations and inhibit the others, and so form an organized mass of emotion. The affective coloring of one word takes reflected shadow and light from the colors of the other words. It does this partly through their contiguity, particularly in synthetic languages (Latin and Greek), and partly through their grammatical connection, particu- larly in analytic languages (English, Chinese); but chiefly through the "meaning" as a whole. The manifest content, the literal meaning, the paraphrasable sense, is a kind of bridge, or electrical conductor which puts all the affective currents of each word into contact. It is like a switch- board; some of the affective associations fade away directly they enter it, others run down into other words and alter their color; others blend to- gether and heighten a particular word. The whole forms the specific fused glow which is that poem's affective organization or emotional attitude to its meaning. Hence the same word has a different affective coloration in one poem from what it has in another, and it is for this reason that a poem is concrete. It is affectively concrete; each word has a special affective significance in that poem different from what it has in another. In this way the emotional content does not float about fluidly in the mind; it is firmly attached, by a hundred interweaving strands, to the manifest con- tent—a piece of external reality. A poem's content is not just emotion, it is *organized* emotion, an organized emotional attitude to a piece of external reality. Hence its value—and difficulty—as compared with other emotions, however strong, but unorganized—a sudden inexplicable fit of sorrow, a gust of blind rage, a blank despair. Such emotions are unesthetic because unorganized. They are unorganized socially because they are not orga- nized in relation to a socially accepted external reality. They are uncon- scious of outer necessity. The emotions of poetry are *part* of the manifest content. They seem to be in the external reality as it appears in the poem. We do not appear to take up an emotional attitude to a piece of reality; it is there, given in the reality: that is the way of emotional cogni- tion. In poetic cognition, objects are presented already stamped with feeling-judgments. Hence the adaptive value of poetry. It is like a real emotional experience.

It is plain that poetry may be judged in different ways; either by the importance of the manifest content, or by the vividness of the affective coloring. To a poet who brings a new portion of external reality into the ambit of poetry, we feel more gratitude than to one who brings the old stale manifest contents. But the first poet may be poor in the affective coloring with which he soaks his piece of reality. It may be the old stale coloring, whereas our other poet, in spite of his conventional piece of reality, may achieve a new affective tone. Old poets we shall judge almost entirely by their affective tone; their manifest contents have long belonged to our world of thought. Hence the apparent triteness of old poetry which yet is a *great* triteness. From new poets we demand new manifest contents and new affective coloring, for it is their function to give us new emotional attitudes to a new social environment. A poet who provides both to a high degree will be a good poet. A poet who brings into his net a vast amount of new reality to which he attaches a wide-ranging affective coloring we shall call a *great* poet, giving Shakespeare as an instance. Hence great poems are always long poems, just because of the quantity of reality they must include as manifest content. But the manifest content, whatever it is, is not the *purpose* of the poem. The purpose is the specific emotional organization directed towards the manifest content and provided by the released affects. The affects are not "latent," as in dream; it is the associated ideas which are suppressed to form the latent content. Just as the key to dream is a series of instinctive attitudes which provide the mechanism of dream-work, so the key to poetry is a cluster of suppressed pieces of external reality—a vague unconscious world of life-experience.

Poetry colors the world of reality with affective tones. These affective colors are not "pretty-pretty," for it is still the real world of necessity, and great poetry will not disguise the nakedness of outer necessity, only cause it to shine with the glow of interest. Poetry soaks external reality—nature and society—with emotional significance. This significance, because it gives the organism an appetitive interest in external reality, enables the organism to deal with it more resolutely, whether in the world of reality or of phantasy. The primitive who would lose interest in the exhausting labor necessary to plow an arid abstract collection of soil, will find heart when the earth is charged with the affective coloring of "Mother Nature," for now, by the magic of poetry, it glows with the appetitive tints of sexuality or filial love. These affective colors are not unreal because they are not scientific, for they are the coloring of the genotype's own instincts, and these instincts are as real as the earth is real. The significant expression projected by poetry on to the face of external reality is simply this, a prophecy of the endless attempt of the genotype to mold necessity to its own likeness, in which it obtains a continually increasing success. "Matter, surrounded by a sensuous poetic glamour, seems to attract man's whole entity by winning smiles." So said Marx and Engels of materialism before it became one-sided mechanical materialism, when it was still bathed in the artistic splendor of the Renaissance. That sensuous glamour is given by poetry; and materialism became one-sided when, afraid of feeling the self, it became aridly scientific, and matter vanishes in a logical but empty wave-system. Poetry restores life and value to matter and puts back the genotype into the world from which it was banished. . . .

§ 5

If we are asked the purpose of art, we can make an answer—the precise nature of it depending on what we mean by *purpose*. Art has "survived"; cultures containing art have outlived and replaced those that have not, because art adapts the psyche to the environment, and is therefore one of the conditions of the development of society. But we get another answer if we ask *how* art performs its task, for it does this by taking a piece of environment and distorting it, giving it a non-likeness to external reality which is also a likeness to the genotype. It remolds external reality nearer to the likeness of the genotype's instincts, but since the instinctive genotype is nothing but an unconscious and dynamic desire it remolds external reality nearer to the heart's desire. Art becomes more socially and biologically valuable and greater art the more that remolding is comprehensive and true to the nature of reality, using as its material the sadness, the catastrophes, the blind necessities, as well as the delights and pleasures of life. An organism which thinks life is all "for the best in the best possible of worlds" will have little survival value. Great art can thus be great tragedy, for here, reality at its bitterest—death, despair, eternal failure—is yet given an organization, a shape, an affective arrangement which expresses a deeper and more social view of fate. By giving external reality an affective organization drawn from its heart, the genotype makes all reality, even death, more interesting because more true. The world glows with interest; our hearts go out to it with appetite to encounter it, to live in it, to get to grips with it. A great novel is how we should like our own lives to be, not petty or dull, but full of great issues, turning even death to a noble sound:

> *Notre vie est noble et tragique*
> *Comme le masque d'un tyran*
> *Nul drame hazardeux et magique*
> *Aucun détail indifférent*
> *Ne rend notre amour pathetique.*[4]

A great picture is how we should like the world to look to us—brighter, full of affective color. Great music is how we should like our emotions to run on, full of strenuous purpose and deep aims. And because, for a moment, we saw how it might be, were given the remade object into our hands, forever after we tend to make our lives less petty, tend to look around us with a more-seeing eye, tend to feel richly and strenuously.

If we ask why art, by making the environment wear the expression of the genotype, comes to us with the nearness and significance it does, we must say still more about art's essence. In making external reality glow with our expression, art tells us about ourselves. No man can look directly at himself, but art makes of the Universe a mirror in which we catch glimpses of ourselves, not as we are, but as we are in active potentiality of becoming in relation to reality through society. The genotype we see is the genotype stamped with all the possibilities and grandeur of man-kind—an elaboration which in its turn is extracted by society from the rest of reality. Art gives us so many glimpses of the inner heart of life; and that is its significance, different from and yet arising out of its purpose. It is like a magic lantern which projects our real selves on the Universe and promises us that we, as we desire, can alter the Universe, alter it to the measure of our needs. But to do so, we must know more deeply our real needs, must make ourselves yet more conscious of ourselves. The more we grip external reality, the more our art develops and grows increasingly subtle, the more the magic lantern show takes on new subtleties and fresh richnesses. Art tells us what science cannot tell us, and what religion only feigns to tell us—what we are and why we are, why we hope and suffer and love and die. It does not tell us this in the language of science, as theology and dogma attempt to do, but in the only language that can express these truths, the language of inner reality itself, the language of affect and emotion. And its message is generated by our attempt to realize its essence in an active struggle with Nature, the struggle called life.

—*Illusion and Reality* (1937)

NOTES

1. According to Hegel and Marx, development generally takes the form of a threefold movement: first, an active force or tendency (the thesis); second, a coun-terforce or conflicting tendency (the antithesis, or *negation*); and third, a recon-ciliation of the conflicting forces or tendencies in a new synthesis (the synthesis, or *negation of the negation*). Caudwell is here maintaining that the art-work represents a creative synthesis which reconciles the *personal* consciousness and self-expression of the artist with the *social* traditions and demands of art. (Editor's note.)
2. *Cf.* William Empson's discussion of poetic ambiguity in his *Seven Types of Ambiguity* (Chatto and Windus, London, 1930). (Editor's note.)
3. Caudwell refers to this distinction in an earlier passage (pp. 184–5): "The classificatory sciences, of which mathematics is the queen and physics an important sphere, deal with space-like orderings which are independent of time. . . . The evolutionary sciences . . . are historical in their approach. They deal with reality as a process, as the emergence of new qualities. Sociology, biology, geology, psy-chology, astronomy, and physiology are all sciences which are interested in time. . . . The same division in the field of art gives rise to a similar distinction. In literary art the novel is evolutionary and the poem is classificatory." Music, archi-tecture, and the static plastic arts are "classificatory" like poetry; prose drama, film, and ballet are "evolutionary" like the novel. (Editor's note.)
4. Apollinaire.

CHAPTER

5

Enhancement
of Experience

Siding with writers such as Nietzsche and Caudwell in opposing an
isolationist interpretation of art, the great American pragmatist, John
Dewey (1859–1952), reacts strongly against the idea that esthetic and
practical activity are quite separate. Instead of emphasizing the difference
between art and nature or between art and actual experience, he
maintains that the function of art is to organize experience more
meaningfully, more coherently, more vividly, than ordinary life permits.
Art is experience in its most articulate and adequate form: "the union
of sense, mood, impulse, and action characteristic of the live creature." It is
not differentiated by the predominance of any one mental faculty, such
as emotion or imagination, but by a greater inclusiveness of psychological
factors. It has no highly restricted subject matter: anything vividly and
imaginatively realized, indeed, may be the source of "an experience that is
an experience"—the kind of experience that is art.

Underlying this doctrine of the oneness of art and life is the conviction
that means and ends should not be sharply separated. Experience is most
satisfactory when means and ends interpenetrate, and art is experience
when it reaches this peak. For art is not a mere anodyne, an escape, an
isolated pastime, nor is it a grim discipline undertaken simply for the sake
of its consequences. It is full of enjoyed meanings, and yet it is instrumental
to new satisfying events. The frequent tendency to separate means and
ends leads to some of the worst evils of our civilization. As Irwin
Edman, a follower of Dewey, says, "It produces, on the one hand, a
practical civilization in which there is no interest in sensuous charm or
imaginative grace, the Land of Smoke-Over celebrated in the legends of
L. P. Jacks. It produces, on the other hand, the soft luxuriance of the
esthete whose dainty creations and enjoyments have no connection with
the rest of life."[1] Against such dualism, Dewey's philosophy is a
powerful protest.

We must not exaggerate this insistence on the continuity of art and life.
The esthetician Andrew Paul Ushenko expressed to Dewey his opinion
that the emphasis on this continuity "does not do justice to the fact

that an esthetic experience is disinterested, that is, indifferent to matters of practical concern. Dewey answered that the conception of 'an esthetic experience, as defined in *Arts as Experience,* is intended to recognize both the basic continuity between life and art and the distinctive quality of being completed in itself, which makes a work of art stand apart from the field of practical transaction."[2] A careful reading of the following selection will confirm Dewey's answer.

The effort to re-integrate art and life found another contemporary spokesman in Alfred North Whitehead (1861–1947). When his *Science and the Modern World* was published, John Dewey greeted the book with the exclamation, "There is news in the realm of the mind. The intellectual climate, the mentality, which has prevailed for three centuries is changing."[3] As a leader in this fundamental intellectual reorientation, Whitehead maintains that reality is organic in structure, and interprets the laws of the mechanical sciences as expressing certain abstract relations between organisms—not as summing up mechanistically the whole content and limits of nature. He endeavors to bridge the chasm between external nature and concrete experience, and interprets the values of the latter as not irrelevant to the former. He thinks the opposite tendency of science, to emphasize *things* to the exclusion of *values*, often plays a mischievous role. For example, the abstractions of economics have "been disastrous in their influence on modern mentality." The remedy is partly to cultivate the esthetic capacity to perceive vivid values and to foster the initiative toward the practice and appreciation of art, broadly interpreted. "The habit of art," he declares, "is the habit of enjoying vivid values."

NOTES

1. Irwin Edman, *The World, The Arts, and the Artist* (Norton, New York, 1928), pp. 34–35.
2. Andrew Paul Ushenko, *Dynamics of Art* (Indiana University Press, 1953), pp. 11–12.
3. *The New Republic,* Feb. 17, 1926, p. 360.

JOHN DEWEY

Having an Experience

Experience occurs continuously, because the interaction of live creature and environing conditions is involved in the very process of living. Under conditions of resistance and conflict, aspects and elements of the self and the world that are implicated in this interaction qualify experience with emotions and ideas so that conscious intent emerges. Oftentimes, however, the experience had is inchoate. Things are experienced but not in such a way that they are composed into *an* experience. There is distraction and dispersion; what we observe and what we think, what we desire and what we get, are at odds with each other. We put our hands to the plow and turn back; we start and then we stop, not because the experience has reached the end for the sake of which it was initiated but because of extraneous interruptions or of inner lethargy.

In contrast with such experience, we have *an* experience when the material experienced runs its course to fulfillment. Then and then only is it integrated within and demarcated in the general stream of experience from other experiences. A piece of work is finished in a way that is satisfactory; a problem receives its solution; a game is played through; a situation, whether that of eating a meal, playing a game of chess, carrying on a conversation, writing a book, or taking part in a political campaign, is so rounded out that its close is a consummation and not a cessation. Such an experience is a whole and carries with it its own individualizing quality and self-sufficiency. It is *an* experience.

Philosophers, even empirical philosophers, have spoken for the most part of experience at large. Idiomatic speech, however, refers to experiences each of which is singular, having its own beginning and end. For life is no uniform uninterrupted march or flow. It is a thing of histories, each with its own plot, its own inception and movement toward its close, each having its own particular rhythmic movement; each with its own unrepeated quality pervading it throughout. A flight of stairs, mechanical as it is, proceeds by individualized steps, not by undifferentiated progression, and an inclined plane is at least marked off from other things by abrupt discreteness.

Experience in this vital sense is defined by those situations and episodes that we spontaneously refer to as being "real experiences"; those things of which we say in reading them, "that *was* an experience." It may have been something of tremendous importance—a quarrel with one who was once an intimate, a catastrophe finally averted by a hair's breadth. Or it may have been something that in comparison was slight—and which perhaps because of its very slightness illustrates all the better what it is to be an experience. There is that meal in a Paris restaurant of which one says "that *was* an experience." It stands out as an enduring memorial of what food may be. Then there is that storm one went through in crossing the Atlantic—the storm that seemed in its fury, as it was experienced, to sum up in itself all that a storm can be, complete in itself, standing out because marked out from what went before and what came after.

In such experiences, every successive part flows freely, without seam and without unfilled blanks, into what ensues. At the same time there is no sacrifice of the self-identity of the parts. A river, as distinct from a pond, flows. But its flow gives a definiteness and interest to its successive portions greater than exist in the homogenous portions of a pond. In an experience, flow is from something to something. As one part leads into another and as one part carries on what went before, each gains distinctness in itself. The enduring whole is diversified by successive phases that are emphases of its varied colors.

Because of continuous merging, there are no holes, mechanical junctions, and dead centers when we have *an* experience. There are pauses, places of rest, but they punctuate and define the quality of movement. They sum up what has been undergone and prevent its dissipation and idle evaporation. Continued acceleration is breathless and prevents parts from gaining distinction. In a work of art, different acts, episodes, occurrences melt and fuse into unity, and yet do not disappear and lose their own character as they do so—just as in a genial conversation there is a continuous interchange and blending, and yet each speaker not only retains his own character but manifests it more clearly than is his wont.

An experience has a unity that gives it its name, that meal, that storm, that rupture of friendship. The existence of this unity is constituted by a single *quality* that pervades the entire experience in spite of the variation of its constituent parts. This unity is neither emotional, practical, nor intellectual, for these terms name distinctions that reflection can make within it. In discourse *about* an experience, we must make use of these adjectives of interpretation. In going over an experience in mind *after* its occurrence, we may find that one property rather than another was sufficiently dominant so that it characterizes the experience as a whole. There are absorbing inquiries and speculations which a scientific man and philosopher will recall as "experiences" in the emphatic sense. In final import they are intellectual. But in their actual occurrence they were emotional as well; they were purposive and volitional. Yet the experience was not a sum of these different characters; they were lost in it as distinctive· traits. No thinker can ply his occupation save as he is lured and rewarded by total integral experiences that are intrinsically worthwhile. Without them he would never know what it is really to think and would be completely at a loss in distinguishing real thought from the spurious article. Thinking goes on in trains of ideas, but the ideas form a train only because they are much more than what an analytic psychology calls ideas. They are phases, emotionally and practically distinguished, of a developing underlying quality; they are its moving variations, not separate and independent like Locke's and Hume's so-called ideas and impressions, but are subtle shadings of a pervading and developing hue.

We say of an experience of thinking that we reach or draw a conclusion. Theoretical formulation of the process is often made in such terms as to conceal effectually the similarity of "conclusion" to the consummating phase of every developing integral experience. These formulations apparently take their cue from the separate propositions that are premises and the proposition that is the conclusion as they appear on the printed page. The impression is derived that there are first two independent and ready-made entities that are then manipulated so as to give rise to a third. In fact, in an experience of thinking, premises emerge only as a conclusion becomes manifest. The experience, like that of watching a storm reach its height and gradually subside, is one of continuous movement of subject-matters. Like the ocean in the storm, there are a series of waves; suggestions reaching out and being broken in a clash, or being carried onwards by a cooperative wave. If a conclusion is reached, it is that of a movement of anticipation and cumulation, one that finally comes to completion. A "conclusion" is no separate and independent thing; it is the consummation of a movement.

Hence *an* experience of thinking has its own esthetic quality. It differs from those experiences that are acknowledged to be esthetic, but only in its materials. The material of the fine arts consists of qualities; that of experience having intellectual conclusion are signs or symbols having no intrinsic quality of their own, but standing for things that may in another experience be qualitatively experienced. The difference is enormous. It is one reason why the strictly intellectual art will never be popular as music is popular. Nevertheless, the experience itself has a satisfying emotional quality because it possesses internal integration and fulfillment reached through ordered and organized movement. This artistic structure may be immediately felt. Insofar, it is esthetic. What is even more important is that not only is this quality a significant motive in undertaking intellectual inquiry and in keeping it honest, but that no intellectual activity is an integral event (is *an* experience), unless it is rounded out with this quality. Without it, thinking is inconclusive. In short, esthetic cannot be sharply marked off from intellectual experience since the latter must bear an esthetic stamp to be itself complete.

The same statement holds good of a course of action that is dominantly practical, that is, one that consists of overt doings. It is possible to be efficient in action and yet not have a conscious experience. The activity is too automatic to permit of a sense of what it is about and where it is going. It comes to an end but not to a close or consummation in consciousness. Obstacles are overcome by shrewd skill, but they do not feed experience. There are also those who are wavering in action, uncertain, and inconclusive like the shades in classic literature. Between the poles of aimlessness and mechanical efficiency, there lie those courses of action in which through successive deeds there runs a sense of growing meaning conserved and accumulating toward an end that is felt as accomplishment of a process. Successful politicians and generals who turn statesmen like Caesar and Napoleon have something of the showman about them. This of itself is not art, but it is, I think, a sign that interest is not exclusively, perhaps not mainly, held by the result taken by itself (as it is in the case of mere efficiency), but by it as the outcome of a process. There is interest in completing an experience. The experience may be one that is harmful to the world and its consummation undesirable. But it has esthetic quality.

The Greek identification of good conduct with conduct having proportion, grace, and harmony, the *kalon-agathon*, is a more obvious example of distinctive esthetic quality in moral action. One great defect in what passes as morality is its anesthetic quality. Instead of exemplifying wholehearted action, it takes the form of grudging piecemeal concessions to the demands of duty. But illustrations may only obscure the fact that any practical activity will, provided that it is integrated and moves by its own urge to fulfillment, have esthetic quality.

A generalized illustration may be had if we imagine a stone, which is rolling downhill, to have an experience. The activity is surely sufficiently "practical." The stone starts from somewhere, and moves, as consistently as conditions permit, toward a place and state where it will be at rest— toward an end. Let us add, by imagination, to these external facts, the ideas that it looks forward with desire to the final outcome; that it is interested in the things it meets on its way, conditions that accelerate and retard its movement with respect to their bearing on the end; that it acts and feels toward them according to the hindering or helping function it attributes to them; and that the final coming to rest is related to all that went before as the culmination of a continuous movement. Then the stone would have an experience, and one with esthetic quality.

If we turn from this imaginary case to our own experience we shall find much of it is nearer to what happens to the actual stone than it is to anything that fulfills the conditions fancy just laid down. For in much of our experience we are not concerned with the connection of one incident with what went before and what comes after. There is no interest that controls attentive rejection or selection of what shall be organized into the developing experience. Things happen, but they are neither definitely included nor decisively excluded; we drift. We yield according to external pressure, or evade and compromise. There are beginnings and cessations, but no genuine initiations and concludings. One thing replaces another, but does not absorb it and carry it on. There is experience, but so slack and discursive that it is not *an* experience. Needless to say, such experiences are anesthetic.

Thus the non-esthetic lies within two limits. At one pole is the loose succession that does not begin at any particular place and that ends—in the sense of ceasing—at no particular place. At the other pole is arrest, constriction, proceeding from parts having only a mechanical connection with one another. There exists so much of one and the other of these two kinds of experience that unconsciously they come to be taken as norms of all experience. Then, when the esthetic appears, it so sharply contrasts with the picture that has been formed of experience, that it is impossible to combine its special qualities with the features of the picture and the esthetic is given an outside place and status. The account that has been given of experience dominantly intellectual and practical is intended to show that there is no such contrast involved in having an experience; that, on the contrary, no experience of whatever sort is a unity unless it has esthetic quality.

The enemies of the esthetic are neither the practical nor the intellectual. They are the humdrum; slackness of loose ends; submission to convention in practice and intellectual procedure. Rigid abstinence, coerced submission, tightness on one side and dissipation, incoherence and aimless indulgence on the other, are deviations in opposite directions from the unity of an experience. Some such considerations perhaps induced Aristotle to invoke the "mean proportional" as the proper designation of what is distinctive of both virtue and the esthetic. He was formally correct. "Mean" and "proportion" are, however, not self-explanatory, nor to be taken over in a prior mathematical sense, but are properties belonging to an experience that has a developing movement toward its own consummation.

I have emphasized the fact that every integral experience moves toward a close, an ending, since it ceases only when the energies active in it have done their proper work. This closure of a circuit of energy is the opposite of arrest, of *stasis*. Maturation and fixation are polar opposites. Struggle and conflict may be themselves enjoyed, although they are painful, when they are experienced as means of developing an experience; members in that they carry it forward, not just because they are there. There is, as will appear later, an element of undergoing, of suffering in its large sense, in every experience. Otherwise there would be no taking in of what preceded. For "taking in" in any vital experience is something more than placing something on the top of consciousness over what was previously known. It involves reconstruction which may be painful. Whether the necessary undergoing phase is by itself pleasurable or painful is a matter of particular conditions. It is indifferent to the total esthetic quality save that there are few intense esthetic experiences that are wholly gleeful. They are certainly not to be characterized as amusing, and as they bear down upon us they involve a suffering that is none the less consistent with, indeed a part of, the complete perception that is enjoyed.

I have spoken of the esthetic quality that rounds out an experience into completeness and unity as emotional. The reference may cause difficulty. We are given to thinking of emotions as things as simple and compact as are the words by which we name them. Joy, sorrow, hope, fear, anger, curiosity, are treated as if each in itself were a sort of entity that enters full-made upon the scene, an entity that may last a long time or a short time, but whose duration, whose growth and career, is irrelevant to its nature. In fact emotions are qualities, when they are significant, of a complex experience that moves and changes. I say, when they are *significant*, for otherwise they are but the outbreaks and eruptions of a disturbed infant. All emotions are qualifications of a drama and they change as the drama develops. Persons are sometimes said to fall in love at first sight. But what they fall into is not a thing of that instant. What would love be were it compressed into a moment in which there is no room for cherishing and for solicitude? The intimate nature of emotion is manifested in the experience of one watching a play on the stage or reading a novel. It attends the development of a plot; and a plot requires a stage, a space, wherein to develop and time in which to unfold. Experience is emotional but there are no separate things called emotions in it.

By the same token, emotions are attached to events and objects in their movement. They are not, save in pathological instances, private. And even an "objectless" emotion demands something beyond itself to which to attach itself, and thus it soon generates a delusion in lack of something real. Emotion belongs of a certainty to the self. But it belongs to the self that is concerned in the movement of events toward an issue that is desired or disliked. We jump instantaneously when we are scared, as we blush on the instant when we are ashamed. But fright and shamed modesty are not in this case emotional states. Of themselves they are but automatic reflexes. In order to become emotional they must become parts of an inclusive and enduring situation that involves concern for objects and their issues. The jump of fright becomes emotional fear when there is found or thought to exist a threatening object that must be dealt with or escaped from. The blush becomes the emotion of shame when a person connects, in thought, an action he has performed with an unfavorable reaction to himself of some other person.

Physical things from far ends of the earth are physically transported and physically caused to act and react upon one another in the construction of a new object. The miracle of mind is that something similar takes place in experience without physical transport and assembling. Emotion is the moving and cementing force. It selects what is congruous and dyes what is selected with its color, thereby giving qualitative unity to materials externally disparate and dissimilar. It thus provides unity in and through the varied parts of an experience. When the unity is of the sort already described, the experience has esthetic character even though it is not, dominantly, an esthetic experience.

Two men meet; one is the applicant for a position, while the other has the disposition of the matter in his hands. The interview may be mechanical, consisting of set questions, the replies to which perfunctorily settle the matter. There is no experience in which the two men meet, nothing that is not a repetition, by way of acceptance or dismissal, of something which has happened a score of times. The situation is disposed of as if it were an exercise in bookkeeping. But an interplay may take place in which a new experience develops. Where should we look for an account of such an experience? Not to ledger-entries nor yet to a treatise on economics or sociology or personnel-psychology, but to drama or fiction. Its nature and import can be expressed only by art, because there is a unity of experience that can be expressed only as an experience. The *experience* is of material fraught with suspense and moving toward its own consummation through a connected series of varied incidents. The primary emotions on the part of the applicant may be at the beginning hope or despair, and elation or disappointment at the close. These emotions qualify the experience as a unity. But as the interview proceeds, secondary emotions are evolved as variations of the primary underlying one. It is even possible for each attitude and gesture, each sentence, almost every word, to produce more than a fluctuation in the intensity of the basic emotion; to produce, that is, a change of shade and tint in its quality. The employer sees by means of his own emotional reactions the character of the one applying. He projects him imaginatively into the work to be done and judges his fitness by the way in which the elements of the scene assemble and either clash or fit together. The presence and behavior of the applicant either harmonize with his own attitudes and desires or they conflict and jar. Such factors as these, inherently esthetic in quality, are the forces that carry the varied elements of the interview to a decisive issue. They enter into the settlement of every situation, whatever its dominant nature, in which there are uncertainty and suspense.

There are, therefore, common patterns in various experiences, no matter how unlike they are to one another in the details of their subject matter. There are conditions to be met without which an experience cannot come to be. The outline of the common pattern is set by the fact that every experience is the result of interaction between a live creature and some aspect of the world in which he lives. A man does something; he lifts, let us say, a stone. In consequence he undergoes, suffers, something: the weight, strain, texture of the surface of the thing lifted. The properties thus undergone determine further doing. The stone is too heavy or too angular, not solid enough; or else the properties undergone show it is fit for the use for which it is intended. The process continues until a mutual adaptation of the self and the object emerges and that particular experience comes to a close. What is true of this simple instance is true, as to form, of every experience. The creature operating may be a thinker in his study and the environment with which he interacts may consist of ideas instead of a stone. But interaction of the two constitutes the total experience that is had, and the close which completes it is the institution of a felt harmony.

An experience has pattern and structure, because it is not just doing and undergoing in alternation, but consists of them in relationship. To put one's hand in the fire that consumes it is not necessarily to have an experience. The action and its consequence must be joined in perception. This relationship is what gives meaning; to grasp it is the objective of all intelligence. The scope and content of the relations measure the significant content of an experience. A child's experience may be intense, but, because of lack of background from past experience, relations between undergoing and doing are slightly grasped, and the experience does not have great depth or breadth. No one ever arrives at such maturity that he perceives all the connections that are involved. There was once written (by Mr. Hinton) a romance called "The Unlearner." It portrayed the whole endless duration of life after death as a living over the incidents that happened in a short life on earth, in continued discovery of the relationships involved among them.

Experience is limited by all the causes which interfere with perception of the relations between undergoing and doing. There may be interference because of excess on the side of doing or of excess on the side of receptivity, of undergoing. Unbalance on either side blurs the perception of relations and leaves the experience partial and distorted, with scant or false meaning. Zeal for doing, lust for action, leaves many a person, especially in this hurried and impatient human environment in which we live, with experience of an almost incredible paucity, all on the surface. No one experience has a chance to complete itself because something else is entered upon so speedily. What is called experience becomes so dispersed and miscellaneous as hardly to deserve the name. Resistance is treated as an obstruction to be beaten down, not as an invitation to reflection. An individual comes to seek, unconsciously even more than by deliberate choice, situations in which he can do the most things in the shortest time.

Experiences are also cut short from maturing by excess of receptivity.

What is prized is then the mere undergoing of this and that, irrespective of perception of any meaning. The crowding together of as many impressions as possible is thought to be "life," even though no one of them is more than a flitting and a sipping. The sentimentalist and the daydreamer may have more fancies and impressions pass through their consciousness than has the man who is animated by lust for action. But his experience is equally distorted, because nothing takes root in mind when there is no balance between doing and receiving. Some decisive action is needed in order to establish contact with the realities of the world and in order that impressions may be so related to facts that their value is tested and organized.

Because perception of relationship between what is done and what is undergone constitutes the work of intelligence, and because the artist is controlled in the process of his work by his grasp of the connection between what he has already done and what he is to do next, the idea that the artist does not think as intently and penetratingly as a scientific inquirer is absurd. A painter must consciously undergo the effect of his every brush stroke or he will not be aware of what he is doing and where his work is going. Moreover, he has to see each particular connection of doing and undergoing in relation to the whole that he desires to produce. To apprehend such relations is to think, and is one of the most exacting modes of thought. The difference between the pictures of different painters is due quite as much to differences of capacity to carry on this thought as it is to differences of sensitivity to bare color and to differences in dexterity of execution. As respects the basic quality of pictures, difference depends, indeed, more upon the quality of intelligence brought to bear upon perception of relations than upon anything else—though of course intelligence cannot be separated from direct sensitivity and is connected, though in a more external manner, with skill.

Any idea that ignores the necessary role of intelligence in production of works of art is based upon identification of thinking with use of one special kind of material, verbal signs and words. To think effectively in terms of relations of qualities is as severe a demand upon thought as to think in terms of symbols, verbal and mathematical. Indeed, since words are easily manipulated in mechanical ways, the production of a work of genuine art probably demands more intelligence than does most of the so-called thinking that goes on among those who pride themselves on being "intellectuals."

I have tried to show . . . that the esthetic is no intruder in experience from without, whether by way of idle luxury or transcendent ideality, but that it is the clarified and intensified development of traits that belong to every normally complete experience. This fact I take to be the only secure basis upon which esthetic theory can build. It remains to suggest some of the implications of the underlying fact.

We have no word in the English language that unambiguously includes what is signified by the two words "artistic" and "esthetic." Since "artistic" refers primarily to the act of production and "esthetic" to that of perception and enjoyment, the absence of a term designating the two processes taken together is unfortunate. Sometimes, the effect is to separate the two from each other, to regard art as something superimposed upon esthetic material, or, upon the other side, to an assumption that, since art is a process of creation, perception and enjoyment of it have nothing in common with the creative act. In any case, there is a certain verbal awkwardness in that we are compelled sometimes to use the term "esthetic" to cover the entire field and sometimes to limit it to the receiving perceptual aspect of the whole operation. I refer to these obvious facts as preliminary to an attempt to show how the conception of conscious experience as a perceived relation between doing and undergoing enables us to understand the connection that art as production and perception and appreciation as enjoyment sustain to each other.

Art denotes a process of doing or making. This is as true of fine as of technological art. Art involves molding of clay, chipping of marble, casting of bronze, laying on of pigments, construction of buildings, singing of songs, playing of instruments, enacting roles on the stage, going through rhythmic movements in the dance. Every art does something with some physical material, the body or something outside the body, with or without the use of intervening tools, and with a view to production of something visible, audible, or tangible. So marked is the active or "doing" phase of art, that the dictionaries usually define it in terms of skilled action, ability in execution. The Oxford Dictionary illustrates by a quotation from John Stuart Mill: "Art is an endeavor after perfection in execution" while Matthew Arnold calls it "pure and flawless workmanship."

The word "esthetic" refers, as we have already noted, to experience as appreciative, perceiving, and enjoying. It denotes the consumer's rather than the producer's standpoint. It is Gusto, taste; and, as with cooking, overt skillful action is on the side of the cook who prepares, while taste is on the side of the consumer, as in gardening there is a distinction between the gardener who plants and tills and the householder who enjoys the finished product.

These very illustrations, however, as well as the relation that exists in having an experience between doing and undergoing, indicate that the distinction between esthetic and artistic cannot be pressed so far as to become a separation. Perfection in execution cannot be measured or defined in terms of execution; it implies those who perceive and enjoy the product that is executed. The cook prepares food for the consumer and the measure of the value of what is prepared is found in consumption. Mere perfection in execution, judged in its own terms in isolation, can probably be attained better by a machine than by human art. By itself, it is at most technique, and there are great artists who are not in the first ranks as technicians (witness Cézanne), just as there are great performers on the piano who are not great esthetically, and as Sargent is not a great painter.

Craftsmanship to be artistic in the final sense must be "loving"; it must care deeply for the subject matter upon which skill is exercised. A sculptor comes to mind whose busts are marvelously exact. It might be difficult to tell in the presence of a photograph of one of them and of a photograph of the original which was of the person himself. For virtuosity they are remarkable. But one doubts whether the maker of the busts had an experience of his own that he was concerned to have those share who look at his products. To be truly artistic, a work must also be esthetic—that is, framed for enjoyed receptive perception. Constant observation is, of course, necessary for the maker while he is producing. But if his perception is not also esthetic in nature, it is a colorless and cold recognition of what has been done, used as a stimulus to the next step in a process that is essentially mechanical.

In short, art, in its form, unites the very same relation of doing and undergoing, outgoing and incoming energy, that makes an experience to be an experience. Because of elimination of all that does not contribute to mutual organization of the factors of both action and reception into one another, and because of selection of just the aspects and traits that contribute to their interpenetration of each other, the product is a work of esthetic art. Man whittles, carves, sings, dances, gestures, molds, draws and paints. The doing or making is artistic when the perceived result is of such a nature that *its* qualities *as perceived* have controlled the question of production. The act of producing that is directed by intent to produce something that is enjoyed in the immediate experience of perceiving has qualities that a spontaneous or uncontrolled activity does not have. The artist embodies in himself the attitude of the perceiver while he works.

Suppose, for the sake of illustration, that a finely wrought object, one whose texture and proportions are highly pleasing in perception, has been believed to be a product of some primitive people. Then there is discovered evidence that proves it to be an accidental natural product. As an external thing, it is now precisely what it was before. Yet at once it ceases to be a work of art and becomes a natural "curiosity." It now belongs in a museum of natural history, not in a museum of art. And the extraordinary thing is that the difference that is thus made is not one of just intellectual classification. A difference is made in appreciative perception and in a direct way. The esthetic experience—in its limited sense—is thus seen to be inherently connected with the experience of making.

The sensory satisfaction of eye and ear, when esthetic, is so because it does not stand by itself but is linked to the activity of which it is the consequence. Even the pleasures of the palate are different in quality to an epicure than in one who merely "likes" his food as he eats it. The difference is not of mere intensity. The epicure is conscious of much more than the taste of the food. Rather, there enter into the taste, as directly experienced, qualities that depend upon reference to its source and its manner of production in connection with criteria of excellence. As production must absorb into itself qualities of the product as perceived and be regulated by them, so, on the other side, seeing, hearing, tasting, become esthetic when relation to a distinct manner of activity qualifies what is perceived.

There is an element of passion in all esthetic perception. Yet when we are overwhelmed by passion, as in extreme rage, fear, jealousy, the experience is definitely non-esthetic. There is no relationship felt to the qualities of the activity that has generated the passion. Consequently, the material of the experience lacks elements of balance and proportion. For these can be present only when, as in the conduct that has grace or dignity, the act is controlled by an exquisite sense of the relations which the act sustains— its fitness to the occasion and to the situation.

The process of art in production is related to the esthetic in perception organically—as the Lord God in creation surveyed his work and found it good. Until the artist is satisfied in perception with what he is doing, he continues shaping and reshaping. The making comes to an end when its result is experienced as good—and that experience comes not by mere intellectual and outside judgment but in direct perception. An artist, in comparison with his fellows, is one who is not only especially gifted in powers of execution but in unusual sensitivity to the qualities of things. This sensitivity also directs his doings and makings.

As we manipulate, we touch and feel, as we look, we see; as we listen, we hear. The hand moves with etching needle or with brush. The eye attends and reports the consequence of what is done. Because of this intimate connection, subsequent doing is cumulative and not a matter of caprice nor yet of routine. In an emphatic artistic-esthetic experience, the relation is so close that it controls simultaneously both the doing and the perception. Such vital intimacy of connection cannot be had if only hand and eye are engaged. When they do not, both of them, act as organs of the whole being, there is but a mechanical sequence of sense and movement, as in walking that is automatic. Hand and eye, when the experience is esthetic, are but instruments through which the entire live creature, moved and active throughout, operates. Hence the expression is emotional and guided by purpose.

Because of the relation between what is done and what is undergone, there is an immediate sense of things in perception as belonging together or as jarring; as reinforcing or as interfering. The consequences of the act of making as reported in sense show whether what is done carries forward the idea being executed or marks a deviation and break. In as far as the development of an experience is *controlled* through reference to these immediately felt relations of order and fulfillment, that experience becomes dominantly esthetic in nature. The urge to action becomes an urge to that kind of action which will result in an object satisfying in direct perception. The potter shapes his clay to make a bowl useful for holding grain; but he makes it in a way so regulated by the series of perceptions that sum up the serial acts of making, that the bowl is marked by enduring grace and charm. The general situation remains the same in painting a picture or molding a bust. Moreover, at each stage there is anticipation of what is to come. This anticipation is the connecting link between the next doing and its outcome for sense. What is done and what is undergone are thus reciprocally, cumulatively, and continuously instrumental to each other.

The doing may be energetic, and the undergoing may be acute and intense. But unless they are related to each other to form a whole in perception, the thing done is not fully esthetic. The making, for example, may be a display of technical virtuosity, and the undergoing a gush of sentiment or a revery. If the artist does not perfect a new vision in his process of doing, he acts mechanically and repeats some old model fixed like a blueprint in his mind. An incredible amount of observation and of the kind of intelligence that is exercised in perception of qualitative relations characterizes creative work in art. The relations must be noted not only with respect to one another, two by two, but in connection with the whole under construction; they are exercised in imagination as well as in observation. Irrelevancies arise that are tempting distractions; digressions suggest themselves in the guise of enrichments. There are occasions when the grasp of the dominant idea grows faint, and then the artist is moved unconsciously to fill in until his thought grows strong again. The real work of an artist is to build up an experience that is coherent in perception while moving with constant change in its development.

When an author puts on paper ideas that are already clearly conceived and consistently ordered, the real work has been previously done. Or, he may depend upon the greater perceptibility induced by the activity and its sensible report to direct his completion of the work. The mere act of transcription is esthetically irrelevant save as it enters integrally into the formation of an experience moving to completeness. Even the composition conceived in the head and, therefore, physically private, is public in its significant content, since it is conceived with reference to execution in a product that is perceptible and hence belongs to the common world. Otherwise it would be an aberration or a passing dream. The urge to express through painting the perceived qualities of a landscape is continuous with demand for pencil or brush. Without external embodiment, an experience remains incomplete; physiologically and functionally, sense organs are motor organs and are connected, by means of distribution of energies in the human body and not merely anatomically, with other motor organs. It is no linguistic accident that "building," "construction," "work," designate both a process and its finished product. Without the meaning of the verb that of the noun remains blank.

Writer, composer of music, sculptor, or painter can retrace, during the process of production, what they have previously done. When it is not satisfactory in the undergoing or perceptual phase of experience, they can to some degree start afresh. This retracing is not readily accomplished in the case of architecture—which is perhaps one reason why there are so many ugly buildings. Architects are obliged to complete their idea before its translation into a complete object of perception takes place. Inability to build up simultaneously the idea and its objective embodiment imposes a handicap. Nevertheless, they too are obliged to think out their ideas in terms of the medium of embodiment and the object of ultimate perception unless they work mechanically and by rote. Probably the esthetic quality of medieval cathedrals is due in some measure to the fact that their constructions were not so much controlled by plans and specifications made in advance as is now the case. Plans grew as the building grew. But even a Minerva-like product, if it is artistic, presupposes a prior period of gestation in which doings and perceptions projected in imagination interact and mutually modify one another. Every work of art follows the plan of, and pattern of, a complete experience, rendering it more intensely and concentratedly felt.

It is not so easy in the case of the perceiver and appreciator to understand the intimate union of doing and undergoing as it is in the case of the maker. We are given to supposing that the former merely takes in what is there in finished form, instead of realizing that this taking in involves activities that are comparable to those of the creator. But receptivity is not passivity. It, too, is a process consisting of a series of responsive acts that accumulate toward objective fulfillment. Otherwise, there is not perception but recognition. The difference between the two is immense. Recognition is perception arrested before it has a chance to develop freely. In recognition there is a beginning of an act of perception. But this beginning is not allowed to serve the development of a full perception of the thing recognized. It is arrested at the point where it will serve some *other* purpose, as we recognize a man on the street in order to greet or to avoid him, not so as to see him for the sake of seeing what is there.

In recognition we fall back, as upon a stereotype, upon some previously formed scheme. Some detail or arrangement of details serves as cue for bare identification. It suffices in recognition to apply this bare outline as a stencil to the present object. Sometimes in contact with a human being we are struck with traits, perhaps of only physical characteristics, of which we were not previously aware. We realize that we never knew the person before; we had not seen him in any pregnant sense. We now begin to study and to "take in." Perception replaces bare recognition. There is an act of reconstructive doing, and consciousness becomes fresh and alive. *This* act of seeing involves the cooperation of motor elements even though they remain implicit and do not become overt, as well as cooperation of all funded ideas that may serve to complete the new picture that is forming. Recognition is too easy to arouse vivid consciousness. There is not enough resistance between new and old to secure consciousness of the experience that is had. Even a dog that barks and wags his tail joyously on seeing his master return is more fully alive in his reception of his friend than is a human being who is content with mere recognition.

Bare recognition is satisfied when a proper tag or label is attached, "proper" signifying one that serves a purpose outside the act of recognition —as a salesman identifies wares by a sample. It involves no stir of the organism, no inner commotion. But an act of perception proceeds by waves that extend serially throughout the entire organism. There is, therefore no such thing in perception as seing or hearing *plus* emotion. The perceived object or scene is emotionally pervaded throughout. When an aroused emotion does not permeate the material that is perceived or thought of, it is either preliminary or pathological.

The esthetic or undergoing phase of experience is receptive. It involves surrender. But adequate yielding of the self is possible only through a controlled activity that may well be intense. In much of our intercourse with our surroundings we withdraw; sometimes from fear, if only of expending unduly our store of energy; sometimes from preoccupation with other matters, as in the case of recognition. Perception is an act of the going-out of energy in order to receive, not a withholding of energy. To steep ourselves in a subject matter we have first to plunge into it. When we are only passive to a scene, it overwhelms us and, for lack of answering activity, we do not perceive that which bears us down. We must summon energy and pitch it at a responsive key in order to *take* in.

Every one knows that it requires apprenticeship to see through a microscope or telescope, and to see a landscape as the geologist sees it. The idea that esthetic perception is an affair for odd moments is one reason for the backwardness of the arts among us. The eye and the visual apparatus may be intact; the object may be physically there, the cathedral of Notre Dame, or Rubens' portrait of Hendrik Stoeffel. In some bald sense, the latter may be "seen." They may be looked at, possibly recognized, and have their correct names attached. But for lack of continuous interaction between the total organism and the objects, they are not perceived, certainly not esthetically. A crowd of visitors steered through a picture-gallery, by a guide, with attention called here and there to some high point, does not perceive; only by accident is there even interest in seeing a picture for the sake of subject matter vividly realized.

For to perceive, a beholder must *create* his own experience. And his creation must include relations comparable to those which the original producer underwent. They are not the same in any literal sense. But with the perceiver, as with the artist, there must be an ordering of the elements of the whole that is in form, although not in details, the same as the process of organization the creator of the work consciously experienced. Without an act of re-creation the object is not perceived as a work of art. The artist selected, simplified, clarified, abridged and condensed according to his interest. The beholder must go through these operations according to his point of view and interest. In both, an act of abstraction, that is of extraction of what is significant, takes place. In both there is comprehension in its literal signification—that is, a gathering together of details and particulars physically scattered into an experienced whole. There is work done on the part of the percipient as there is on the part of the artist. The one who is too lazy, idle, or indurated in convention to perform his work will not see or hear. His "appreciation" will be a mixture of scraps of learning with conformity to norms of conventional admiration and with a confused, even if genuine, emotional excitation.

The considerations that have been presented imply both the community and the unlikeness, because of specific emphasis, of *an* experience, in its pregnant sense, and esthetic experience. The former has esthetic quality; otherwise its materials would not be rounded out into a single coherent experience. It is not possible to divide in a vital experience the practical, emotional, and intellectual from one another and to set the properties of one over against the characteristics of the others. The emotional phase binds parts together into a single whole; "intellectual" simply names the fact that the experience has meaning; "practical" indicates that the organism is interacting with events and objects which surround it. The most elaborate philosophic or scientific inquiry and the most ambitious industrial or political enterprise has, when its different ingredients constitute an integral experience, esthetic quality. For then its varied parts are linked to one another, and do not merely succeed one another. And the parts through their experienced linkage move toward a consummation and close, not merely to cessation in time. This consummation, moreover, does not wait in consciousness for the whole undertaking to be finished. It is anticipated throughout and is recurrently savored with special intensity.

Nevertheless, the experiences in question are dominantly intellectual or practical, rather than *distinctly* esthetic, because of the interest and purpose that initiate and control them. In an intellectual experience, the conclusion has value on its own account. It can be extracted as a formula or as a "truth," and can be used in its independent entirety as factor and guide in other inquiries. In a work of art there is not such single self-sufficient deposit. The end, the terminus, is significant not by itself but as the integration of the parts. It has no other existence. A drama or novel is not the final sentence, even if the characters are disposed of as living happily ever after. In a distinctly esthetic experience, characteristics that are subdued in other experiences are dominant; those that are subordinate are controlling—namely, the characteristics in virtue of which the experience is an integrated complete experience on its own account.

In every integral experience there is form because there is dynamic organization. I call the organization dynamic because it takes time to complete it, because it is a growth. There are inception, development, fulfillment. Material is ingested and digested through interaction with that vital organization of the results of prior experience that constitutes the mind of the worker. Incubation goes on until what is conceived is brought forth and is rendered perceptible as part of the common world. An esthetic experience can be crowded into a moment only in the sense that a climax of prior long enduring processes may arrive in an outstanding movement which so sweeps everything else into it that all else is forgotten. That which distinguishes an experience as esthetic is conversion of resistance and tensions, of excitations that in themselves are temptations to diversion, into a movement toward an inclusive and fulfilling close.

Experiencing like breathing is a rhythm of intakings and outgivings. Their succession is punctuated and made a rhythm by the existence of intervals, periods in which one phase is ceasing and the other is inchoat and preparing. William James aptly compared the course of a conscious experience to the alternate flights and perchings of a bird. The flights and perchings are intimately connected with one another; they are not so many unrelated lightings succeeded by a number of equally unrelated hoppings. Each resting place in experience is an undergoing in which is absorbed and taken home the consequences of prior doing, and, unless the doing is that of utter caprice or sheer routine, each doing carries in itself meaning that has been extracted and conserved. As with the advance of an army, all gains from what has been already effected are periodically consolidated, and always with a view to what is to be done next. If we move too rapidly, we get away from the base of supplies—of accrued meanings —and the experience is flustered, thin, and confused. If we dawdle too long after having extracted a net value, experience perishes of inanition.

The *form* of the whole is therefore present in every member. Fulfilling, consummating, are continuous functions, not mere ends, located at one place only. An engraver, painter, or writer is in process of completing at every stage of his work. He must at each point retain and sum up what has gone before as a whole and with reference to a whole to come. Otherwise there is no consistency and no security in his successive acts. The series of doings in the rhythm of experience give variety and movement; they save the work from monotony and useless repetitions. The undergoings are the corresponding elements in the rhythm, and they supply unity; they save the work from the aimlessness of a mere succession of excitations. An object is peculiarly and dominantly esthetic, yielding the enjoyment characteristic of esthetic perception, when the factors that determine anything which can be called *an* experience are lifted high above the threshold of perception and are made manifest for their own sake.

—*Art as Experience* (1934)

ALFRED NORTH WHITEHEAD

The Experience of Vivid Values

There is no easy single solution of the practical difficulties of education. We can, however, guide ourselves by a certain simplicity in its general theory. The student should concentrate within a limited field. Such concentration should include all practical and intellectual acquirements requisite for that concentration. This is the ordinary procedure; and, in respect to it, I should be inclined even to increase the facilities for concentration rather than to diminish them. With the concentration there are associated certain subsidiary studies, such as languages for science. Such a scheme of professional training should be directed to a clear end congenial to the student. It is not necessary to elaborate the qualifications of these statements. Such a training must, of course, have the width requisite for its end. But its design should not be complicated by the consideration of other ends. This professional training can only touch one side of education. Its center of gravity lies in the intellect, and its chief tool is the printed book. The center of gravity of the other side of training should lie in intuition without an analytical divorce from the total environment. Its object is immediate apprehension with the minimum of eviscerating analysis. The type of generality, which above all is wanted, is the appreciation of variety of value. I mean an esthetic growth. There is something between the gross specialized values of the mere practical man, and the thin specialized values of the mere scholar. Both types have missed something; and if you add together the two sets of values, you do not obtain the missing elements. What is wanted is an appreciation of the infinite variety of vivid values achieved by an organism in its proper environment. When you understand all about the sun and all about the atmosphere and all about the rotation of the earth, you may still miss the radiance of the sunset. There is no substitute for the direct perception of the concrete fact with a high light thrown on what is relevant to its preciousness.

What I mean is art (and esthetic education). It is, however, art in such a general sense of the term that I hardly like to call it by that name. Art is a special example. What we want is to draw out habits of esthetic apprehension. According to the metaphysical doctrine which I have been developing, to do so is to increase the depth of individuality. The analysis of reality indicates the two factors, activity emerging into individualized esthetic value. Also the emergent value is the measure of the individualization of the activity. We must foster the creative initiative towards the maintenance of objective values. You will not obtain the apprehension without the initiative, or the initiative without the apprehension. As soon as you get towards the concrete, you cannot exclude action. Sensitiveness without impulse spells decadence, and impulse without sensitiveness spells brutality. I am using the word "sensitiveness" in its most general significance, so as to include apprehension of what lies beyond oneself; that is to say sensitiveness to all the facts of the case. Thus "art" in the general sense which I require is any selection by which the concrete facts are so arranged as to elicit attention to particular values which are realizable by them. For example, the mere disposing of the human body and the eyesight so as to get a good view of a sunset is a simple form of artistic selection. The habit of art is the habit of enjoying vivid values.

But, in this sense, art concerns more than sunsets. A factory, with its machinery, its community of operatives, its social service to the general population, its dependence upon organizing and designing genius, its potentialities as a source of wealth to the holders of its stock is an organism exhibiting a variety of vivid values. What we want to train is the habit of apprehending such an organism in its completeness. It is very arguable that the science of political economy, as studied in its first period after the death of Adam Smith (1790), did more harm than good. It destroyed many economic fallacies, and taught how to think about the economic revolution then in progress. But it riveted on men a certain set of abstractions which were disastrous in their influence on modern mentality. It de-humanized industry. This is only one example of a general danger inherent in modern science. Its methodological procedure is exclusive and intolerant, and rightly so. It fixes attention on a definite group of abstractions, neglects everything else and elicits every scrap of information and theory which is relevant to what it has retained. This method is triumphant, provided that the abstractions are judicious. But, however triumphant, the triumph is within limits. The neglect of these limits leads to disastrous oversights. The anti-rationalism of science is partly justified, as a preservation of its useful methodology; it is partly mere irrational prejudice. Modern professionalism is the training of minds to conform to the methodology. The historical revolt of the seventeenth century, and the earlier reaction towards naturalism, were examples of transcending the abstractions which fascinated educated society in the Middle Ages. These early ages had an ideal of rationalism, but they failed in its pursuit. For they neglected to note that the methodology of reasoning requires the limitations involved in the abstract. Accordingly, the true rationalism must always transcend itself by recurrence to the concrete in search of inspiration. A self-satisfied rationalism is in effect a form of anti-rationalism. It means an arbitrary halt at a particular set of abstractions. This was the case with science.

There are two principles inherent in the very nature of things, recurring in some particular embodiments whatever field we explore—the spirit of change, and the spirit of conservation. There can be nothing real without both. Mere change without conservation is a passage from nothing to nothing. Its final integration yields mere transient nonentity. Mere conservation without change cannot conserve. For after all, there is a flux of circumstance, and the freshness of being evaporates under mere repetition. The character of existent reality is composed of organisms enduring through the flux of things. The low type of organisms have achieved a self-identity dominating their whole physical life. Electrons, molecules, crystals, belong to this type. They exhibit a massive and complete sameness. In the higher types, where life appears, there is greater complexity. Thus, though there is a complex, enduring pattern, it has retreated into deeper recesses of the total fact. In a sense, the self-identity of a human being is more abstract than that of a crystal. It is the life of the spirit. It relates rather to the individualization of the creative activity; so that the changing circumstances received from the environment, are differentiated from the living personality, and are thought of as forming its perceived field. In truth, the field of perception and the perceiving mind are abstractions which, in the concrete, combine into the successive bodily events. The psychological field, as restricted to sense-objects and passing emotions, is the minor permanence, barely rescued from the non-entity of mere change; and the mind is the major permanence, permeating that complete field, whose endurance is the living soul. But the soul would wither without fertilization from its transient experiences. The secret of the higher organisms lies in their two grades of permanences. By this means the freshness of the environment is absorbed into the permanence of the soul. The changing environment is no longer, by reason of its variety, an enemy to the endurance of the organism. The pattern of the higher organism has retreated into the recesses of the individualized activity. It has become a uniform way of dealing with circumstances; and this way is only strengthened by having a proper variety of circumstances to deal with.

This fertilization of the soul is the reason for the necessity of art. A static value, however serious and important, becomes unendurable by its appalling monotony of endurance. The soul cries aloud for release into change. It suffers the agonies of claustrophobia. The transitions of humor, wit, irreverence, play, sleep, and—above all—of art are necessary for it. Great art is the arrangement of the environment so as to provide for the soul vivid, but transient, values. Human beings require something which absorbs them for a time, something out of the routine which they can stare at. But you cannot subdivide life, except in the abstract analysis of thought. Accordingly, the great art is more than a transient refreshment. It is something which adds to the permanent richness of the soul's self-attainment. It justifies itself both by its immediate enjoyment, and also by its discipline of the inmost being. Its discipline is not distinct from enjoyment, but by reason of it. It transforms the soul into the permanent realization of values extending beyond its former self. This element of transition in art is shown by the restlessness exhibited in its history. An epoch gets saturated by the masterpieces of any one style. Something new must be discovered. The human being wanders on. Yet there is a balance in things. Mere change before the attainment of adequacy of achievement, either in quality or output, is destructive of greatness. But the importance of a living art, which moves on and yet leaves its permanent mark, can hardly be exaggerated.

In regard to the esthetic needs of civilized society the reactions of science have so far been unfortunate. Its materialistic basis has directed attention to *things*, as opposed to *values*. The antithesis is a false one, if taken in a concrete sense. But it is valid at the abstract level of ordinary thought. This misplaced emphasis coalesced with the abstractions of political economy, which are in fact the abstractions in terms of which commercial affairs are carried on. Thus all thought concerned with social organization expressed itself in terms of material things and of capital. Ultimate values were excluded. They were politely bowed to, and then handed over to the clergy to be kept for Sundays. A creed of competitive business morality was evolved, in some respects curiously high; but entirely devoid of consideration for the value of human life. The workmen were conceived as mere hands, drawn from the pool of labor. To God's question, men gave the answer of Cain—"Am I my brother's keeper?"; and they incurred Cain's guilt. This was the atmosphere in which the industrial revolution was accomplished in England, and to a large extent elsewhere. The internal history of England during the last half century has been an endeavor slowly and painfully to undo the evils wrought in the first stage of the new epoch. It may be that civilization will never recover from the bad climate which enveloped the introduction of machinery. This climate pervaded the whole commercial system of the progressive northern European races. It was partly the result of the esthetic errors of Protestantism and partly the result of scientific materialism, and partly the result of the abstractions of political economy. An illustration of my point is to be found in Macaulay's essay criticizing Southey's *Colloquies on Society*. It was written in 1830. Now Macaulay was a very favorable example of men living at that date, or at any date. He had genius; he was kind-hearted, honorable, and a reformer. This is the extract: "We are told, that our age has invented artrocities beyond the imagination of our fathers; that society has been brought into a state compared with which extermination would be a blessing; and all because the dwellings of cotton-spinners are naked and rectangular. Mr. Southey has found out a way he tells us, in which the effects of manufacturers and agriculture may be compared. And what is this way? To stand on a hill, to look at a cottage and a factory, and to see which is the prettier."

Southey seems to have said many silly things in his book; but, so far as this extract is concerned, he could make a good case for himself if he returned to earth after the lapse of nearly a century. The evils of the early industrial system are now a commonplace of knowledge. The point which I am insisting on is the stone-blind eye with which even the best men of that time regarded the importance of esthetics in a nation's life. I do not believe that we have as yet nearly achieved the right estimate.

—*Science and the Modern World* (1925)

CHAPTER
6
Embodiment
of Values

GEORGE SANTAYANA: *The Nature of Beauty*
LOUIS ARNAUD REID: *Values, Feeling and Embodiment*

The contention of Whitehead (Chapter 5) that "the habit of art is the habit of enjoying vivid values" is a foretaste of the theories that we shall now review. They are alike in regarding art as the objectification or embodiment of values.

Traditionally, it has been thought that the value embodied in the work of art is beauty—the third of the classical trilogy of the Good, the True, and the Beautiful. Art, it is said, is the incarnation of beauty in human artifacts. There was no more eloquent representative of this doctrine than George Santayana (1863–1952). Born in Madrid of Spanish parents, but educated largely in America, he was steeped in the Greek and Catholic tradition. Nevertheless, he was a naturalist by conviction and drew his inspiration from diverse sources. While a young professor of philosophy at Harvard, he wrote his first book, *The Sense of Beauty* (1896), in which he defines beauty in terms of pleasure and conceives art as the making of beautiful things.

In his penetrating analysis, he delimits beauty by a series of exclusions. Since beauty is a value and there is no value apart from conscious preference, the beautiful cannot be the unconscious or the merely indifferent. The purely rational must also be excluded, since value in general and beauty in particular involve feeling rather than reason or knowledge. Moral values, which are mainly negative and extrinsic, must also be distinguished from esthetic values, which are positive and intrinsic. Next, Santayana contrasts esthetic and physical pleasures: The former give us the illusion of being relatively free of our bodies; the latter do not. He finally defines beauty as *objectified pleasure.*

By "objectification" he means the process of imputing some subjective quality to an object, as when we speak of a *nasty* snow storm or a *lonely* place. Nothing is more natural and primitive than thus to project our mental states into phenomenal objects. Pleasure is transformed into beauty whenever the value is unconsciously imputed to the object contemplated and not to the body or mind of the person contemplating.

Santayana recognizes three kinds of beauty: the sensuous beauty of the physical stuff; the formal beauty of the design; and the expressive beauty of the meaning and connotations ultimately derived from past experience. This is a narrower meaning of "expression" than in the writings of most estheticians, and I have included an excerpt to elucidate its meaning.

To the division of expressive beauty belongs the effect of sublimity. The "Stoic sublime" consists of a lofty feeling of self-integrity and detachment. This reaction arises especially in the contemplation of evil, as in tragedy. We purge the self of pity and fear by eliminating from consciousness all the elements that are personal and self-regarding.

> . . . to envisage circumstance, all calm,
> That is the top of sovereignty.

Santayana points out that that there is another kind of sublimity—"the Epicurean sublime." Just as Epicurus, the Greek philosopher, recoiled from the immensity of the material universe into the equipoise of the detached spirit, so the beholder of stellar spaces, or of any other object immeasurably great, may achieve an exalted feeling of detachment by inwardly bracing himself against so overwhelming a prospect. This reaction is not the opposite of the beautiful, in the wide sense of that term, but it is rather "the supremely, the intoxicatingly beautiful," so intense "that it begins to lose its objectivity, and to declare itself, what it always fundamentally was, an inward passion of the soul."

In his later works, Santayana suggested, as an alternative to his theory of objectified pleasure, the view that beauty is "a vital harmony felt and fused into an image under the form of eternity." This characterization of beauty (it is not a definition, he said, for beauty is undefinable) cannot be wholly understood without a knowledge of his metaphysics. But we can at least say that beauty involves "a synthesis of distinct terms," notably an image and a pleasure. As a result of the synthesis, a glory is felt to reside in the object or to radiate from it. The object is regarded as an "essence"; that is to say, it is contemplated merely for its intrinsic qualities, and belief or disbelief does not arise. An essence thus intuited is felt to be independent of the act of apprehension; "it visits time, but belongs to eternity."

A wider and less subjective conception of esthetic value than that of the youthful Santayana has been formulated by Louis Arnaud Reid (1895–   ), Professor Emeritus of Philosophy in the University of London. Value, as he conceives it, is a relational property, the quality of an object related to a human interest. Far from being a mere subjective phantom, or at the other extreme, a thing-in-itself sundered from human attitudes, a value is always something felt and appreciated. The stuff of art is the felt qualities of things—"not the things alone, nor the feelings alone, but the things-as-experienced-with feeling." In art, value is concrete and individuated—not detached and free-floating but intrinsic to the work. From this point of view, art is in its very nature the embodiment of values.

GEORGE SANTAYANA

The Nature of Beauty

I. BEAUTY DEFINED

The Philosophy of Beauty Is a Theory of Values

It would be easy to find a definition of beauty that should give in a few words a telling paraphrase of the word. We know on excellent authority that beauty is truth, that it is the expression of the ideal, the symbol of divine perfection, and the sensible manifestation of the good. A litany of these titles of honor might easily be compiled, and repeated in praise of our divinity. Such phrases stimulate thought and give us a momentary pleasure, but they hardly bring any permanent enlightenment. A definition that should really define must be nothing less than the exposition of the origin, place, and elements of beauty as an object of human experience. We must learn from it, as far as possible, why, when, and how beauty appears, what conditions an object must fulfill to be beautiful, what elements of our nature make us sensible of beauty, and what the relation is between the constitution of the object and the excitement of our susceptibility. Nothing less will really define beauty or make us understand what esthetic appreciation is. The definition of beauty in this sense will be the task of this whole book, a task that can be only very imperfectly accomplished within its limits.

The historical titles of our subject may give us a hint towards the beginning of such a definition. Many writers of the last century called the philosophy of beauty *Criticism*, and the word is still retained as the title for the reasoned appreciation of works of art. We could hardly speak, however, of delight in nature as criticism. A sunset is not criticized; it is felt and enjoyed. The word "criticism," used on such an occasion, would emphasize too much the element of deliberate judgment and of comparison with standards. Beauty, although often so described, is seldom so perceived, and all the greatest excellences of nature and art are so far from being approved of by a rule that they themselves furnish the standard and ideal by which critics measure inferior effects.

This age of science and of nomenclature has accordingly adopted a more learned word, *Esthetics*, that is, the theory of perception or of susceptibility. If criticism is too narrow a word, pointing exclusively to our more artificial judgments, esthetics seems to be too broad and to include within its sphere all pleasures and pains, if not all perceptions whatsoever. Kant used it, as we know, for his theory of time and space as forms of all perception; and it has at times been narrowed into an equivalent for the philosophy of art.

If we combine, however, the etymological meaning of criticism with that of esthetics, we shall unite two essential qualities of the theory of beauty. Criticism implies judgment, and esthetics perception. To get the common ground, that of perceptions which are critical, or judgments which are perceptions, we must widen our notion of deliberate criticism so as to include those judgments of value which are instinctive and immediate, that is, to include pleasures and pains; and at the same time we must narrow our notion of esthetics so as to exclude all perceptions which are not appreciations, which do not find a value in their objects. We thus reach the sphere of critical or appreciative perception, which is, roughly speaking, what we mean to deal with. And retaining the word "esthetics," which is now current, we may therefore say that esthetics is concerned with the perception of values. The meaning and conditions of value are, then, what we must first consider.

Since the days of Descartes it has been a conception familiar to philosophers that every visible event in nature might be explained by previous visible events, and that all the motions, for instance, of the tongue in speech, or of the hand in painting, might have merely physical causes. If consciousness is thus accessory to life and not essential to it, the race of man might have existed upon the earth and acquired all the arts necessary for its subsistence without possessing a single sensation, idea, or emotion. Natural selection might have secured the survival of those automata which made useful reactions upon their environment. An instinct of self-preservation would have been developed, dangers would have been shunned without being feared, and injuries revenged without being felt.

In such a world there might have come to be the most perfect organization. There would have been what we should call the expression of the deepest interests and the apparent pursuit of conceived goods. For there would have been spontaneous and ingrained tendencies to avoid certain contingencies and to produce others; all the dumb show and evidence of thinking would have been patent to the observer. Yet there would surely have been no thinking, no expectation, and no conscious achievement in the whole process.

The onlooker might have feigned ends and objects of forethought, as we do in the case of the water that seeks its own level, or in that of the vacuum which nature abhors. But the particles of matter would have remained unconscious of their collocation, and all nature would have been insensible of their changing arrangement. We only, the possible spectators of that process, by virtue of our own interests and habits, could see any progress or culmination in it. We should see culmination where the result attained satisfied our practical or esthetic demands, and progress wherever such a satisfaction was approached. But apart from ourselves, and our human bias, we can see in such a mechanical world no element of value whatever. In removing consciousness, we have removed the possibility of worth.

But it is not only in the absence of all consciousness that value would be removed from the world; by a less violent abstraction from the totality of human experience, we might conceive beings of a purely intellectual cast, minds in which the transformations of nature were mirrored without any emotion. Every event would then be noted, its relations would be observed, its recurrence might even be expected; but all this would happen without a shadow of desire, of pleasure, or of regret. No event would be repulsive, no situation terrible. We might, in a word, have a world of idea without a world of will. In this case, as completely as if consciousness were absent altogether, all value and excellence would be gone. So that for the existence of good in any form it is not merely consciousness but emotional consciousness that is needed. Observation will not do, appreciation is required.

Preference Is Ultimately Irrational

We may therefore at once assert this axiom, important for all moral philosophy and fatal to certain stubborn incoherences of thought, that there is no value apart from some appreciation of it, and no good apart from some preference of it before its absence or its opposite. In appreciation, in preference, lie the root and essence of all excellence. Or, as Spinoza clearly expresses it, we desire nothing because it is good, but it is good only because we desire it.

It is true that in the absence of an instinctive reaction we can still apply these epithets by an appeal to usage. We may agree that an action is bad or a building good, because we recognize in them a character which we have learned to designate by that adjective; but unless there is in us some trace of passionate reprobation or of sensible delight, there is no moral or esthetic judgment. It is all a question of propriety of speech, and of the empty titles of things. The verbal and mechanical proposition, that passes for judgment of worth, is the great cloak of ineptitude in these matters. Insensibility is very quick in the conventional use of words. If we appealed more often to actual feelings, our judgments would be more diverse, but they would be more legitimate and instructive. Verbal judgments are often useful instruments of thought, but it is not by them that worth can ultimately be determined.

Values spring from the immediate and inexplicable reaction of vital impulse, and from the irrational part of our nature. The rational part is by its essence relative; it leads us from data to conclusions, or from parts to wholes; it never furnishes the data with which it works. If any preference or precept were declared to be ultimate and primitive, it would thereby be declared to be irrational, since mediation, inference, and synthesis are the essence of rationality. The idea of rationality is itself as arbitrary, as much dependent on the needs of a finite organization, as any other ideal. Only as ultimately securing tranquillity of mind, which the philosopher instinctively pursues, has it for him any necessity. In spite of the verbal propriety of saying that reason demands rationality, what really demands rationality, what makes it a good and indispensable thing and gives it all its authority, is not its own nature, but our need of it both in safe and economical action and in the pleasures of comprehension.

It is evident that beauty is a species of value, and what we have said of value in general applies to this particular kind. A first approach to a definition of beauty has therefore been made by the exclusion of all intellectual judgments, all judgments of matter of fact or of relation. To substitute judgments of fact for judgments of value, is a sign of a pedantic and borrowed criticism. If we approach a work of art or nature scientifically, for the sake of its historical connections or proper classification, we do not approach it esthetically. The discovery of its date or of its author may be otherwise interesting; it only remotely affects our esthetic appreciation by adding to the direct effect certain associations. If the direct effect were absent, and the object in itself uninteresting, the circumstances would be immaterial. Molière's *Misanthrope* says to the court poet who commends his sonnet as written in a quarter of an hour,

Voyons, monsieur, le temps ne fait rien à l'affaire,

and so we might say to the critic that sinks into the archaeologist, show us the work, and let the date alone.

In an opposite direction the same substitution of facts for values makes its appearance, whenever the reproduction of fact is made the sole standard of artistic excellence. Many half-trained observers condemn the work of some naïve or fanciful masters with a sneer, because, as they truly say, it is out of drawing. The implication is that to be correctly copied from a model is the prerequisite of all beauty. Correctness is, indeed, an element of effect and one which, in respect to familiar objects, is almost indispensable, because its absence would casue a disappointment and dissatisfaction incompatible with enjoyment. We learn to value truth more and more as our love and knowledge of nature increase. But fidelity is a merit only because it is in this way a factor in our pleasure. It stands on a level with all other ingredients of effect. When a man raises it to a solitary pre-eminence and becomes incapable of appreciating anything else, he betrays the decay of esthetic capacity. The scientific habit in him inhibits the artistic.

That facts have a value of their own, at once complicates and explains this question. We are naturally pleased by every perception, and recognition and surprise are particularly acute sensations. When we see a striking truth in any imitation we are therefore delighted, and this kind of pleasure is very legitimate, and enters into the best effects of all the representative arts. Truth and realism are therefore esthetically good, but they are not all-sufficient, since the representation of everything is not equally pleasing and effective. The fact that resemblance is a source of satisfaction justifies the critic in demanding it, while the esthetic insufficiency of such veracity shows the different value of truth in science and in art. Science is the response to the demand for information, and in it we ask for the whole truth and nothing but the truth. Art is the response to the demand for entertainment, for the stimulation of our senses and imagination, and truth enters into it only as it subserves these ends.

Even the scientific value of truth is not, however, ultimate or absolute. It rests partly on practical, partly on esthetic interests. As our ideas are gradually brought into conformity with the facts by the painful process of selection—for intuition runs equally into truth and into error, and can settle nothing if not controlled by experience—we gain vastly in our command over our environment. This is the fundamental value of natural science, and the fruit it is yielding in our day. We have no better vision of nature and life than some of our predecessors, but we have greater material resources. To know the truth about the composition and history of things is good for this reason. It is also good because of the enlarged horizon it gives us, because the spectacle of nature is a marvelous and fascinating one, full of a serious sadness and large peace, which gives us back our birthright as children of the planet and naturalizes us upon the earth. This is the poetic value of the scientific *Weltanschauung.* From these two benefits, the practical and the imaginative, all the value of truth is derived.

Esthetic and moral judgments are accordingly to be classed together in contrast to judgments intellectual; they are both judgments of value, while intellectual judgments are judgments of fact. If the latter have any value, it is only derivative, and our whole intellectual life has its only justification in its connection with our pleasures and pains.

Contrast between Moral and Esthetic Values

The relation between esthetic and moral judgments, between the spheres of the beautiful and the good, is close, but the distinction between them is important. One factor of this distinction is that while esthetic judgments are mainly positive, that is, perceptions of good, moral judgments are mainly and fundamentally negative, or perceptions of evil. Another factor of the distinction is that whereas, in the perception of beauty, our judgment is necessarily intrinsic and based on the character of the immediate experience, and never consciously on the idea of an eventual utility in the object, judgments about moral worth, on the contrary, are always based, when they are positive, upon the consciousness of benefits probably involved. Both these distinctions need some elucidations.

Hedonistic ethics have always had to struggle against the moral sense of mankind. Earnest minds, that feel the weight and dignity of life, rebel against the assertion that the aim of right conduct is enjoyment. Pleasure usually appears to them as a temptation, and they sometimes go so far as to make avoidance of it a virtue. The truth is that morality is not mainly concerned with the attainment of pleasure; it is rather concerned, in all its deeper and more authoritative maxims, with the prevention of suffering. There is something artificial in the deliberate pursuit of pleasure; there is something absurd in the obligation to enjoy oneself. We feel no duty in that direction; we take to enjoyment naturally enough after the work of life is done, and the freedom and spontaneity of our pleasures are what is most essential to them.

The sad business of life is rather to escape certain dreadful evils to which our nature exposes us—death, hunger, disease, weariness, isolation, and contempt. By the awful authority' of these things which stand like specters behind every moral injunction, conscience in reality speaks, and a mind which they have duly impressed cannot but feel, by contrast, the hopeless triviality of the search for pleasure. It cannot but feel that a life abandoned to amusement and to changing impulses must run unawares into fatal dangers. The moment, however, that society emerges from the early pressure of the environment and is tolerably secure against primary evils, morality grows lax. The forms that life will further assume are not to be imposed by moral authority, but are determined by the genius of the race, the opportunities of the moment, and the tastes and resources of individual minds. The reign of duty gives place to the reign of freedom, and the law and the covenant to the dispensation of grace.

The appreciation of beauty and its embodiment in the arts are activities which belong to our holiday life, when we are redeemed for the moment from the shadow of evil and the slavery to fear, and are following the bent of our nature where it chooses to lead us. The values, then, with which we here deal are positive; they were negative in the sphere of morality. The ugly is hardly an exception, because it is not the cause of any real pain. In itself it is rather a source of amusement. If its suggestions are vitally repulsive, its presence becomes a real evil towards which we assume a practical and moral attitude. And, correspondingly, the pleasant is never, as we have seen, the object of a truly moral injunction.

Work and Play

We have here, then, an important element of the distinction between esthetic and moral values. It is the same that has been pointed to in the famous contrast between work and play. These terms may be used in different senses and their importance in moral classification differs with the meaning attached to them. We may call everything play which is useless activity, exercise that springs from the physiological impulse to discharge the energy which the exigencies of life have not called out. Work will then be all action that is necessary or useful for life. Evidently if work and play are thus objectively distinguished as useful and useless action, work is a eulogistic term and play a disparaging one. It would be better for us that all our energy should be turned to account, that none of it should be wasted in aimless motion. Play, in this sense, is a sign of imperfect adaptation. It is proper to childhood, when the body and mind are not yet fit to cope with the environment, but it is unseemly in manhood and pitiable in old age, because it marks an atrophy of human nature, and a failure to take hold of the opportunities of life.

Play is thus essentially frivolous. Some persons, understanding the term in this sense, have felt an aversion, which every liberal mind will share, to classifying social pleasures, art, and religion under the head of play, and by that epithet condemning them, as a certain school seems to do, to gradual extinction as the race approaches maturity. But if all the useless ornaments of our life are to be cut off in the process of adaptation, evolution would impoverish instead of enriching our nature. Perhaps that is the tendency of evolution, and our barbarous ancestors amid their toils and wars, with their flaming passions and mythologies, lived better lives than are reserved to our well-adapted descendants.

We may be allowed to hope, however, that some imagination may survive parasitically even in the most serviceable brain. Whatever course history may take—and we are not here concerned with prophecy—the question of what is desirable is not affected. To condemn spontaneous and delightful occupations because they are useless for self-preservation shows an uncritical prizing of life irrespective of its content. For such a system the worthiest function of the universe should be to establish perpetual motion. Uselessness is a fatal accusation to bring against any act which is done for its presumed utility, but those which are done for their own sake are their own justification.

At the same time there is an undeniable propriety in calling all the liberal and imaginative activities of man play, because they are spontaneous, and not carried on under pressure of external necessity or danger. Their utility for self-preservation may be very indirect and accidental, but they are not worthless for that reason. On the contrary, we may measure the degree of happiness and civilization which any race has attained by the proportion of its energy which is devoted to free and generous pursuits, to the adornment of life and the culture of the imagination. For it is in the spontaneous play of his faculties that man finds himself and his happiness. Slavery is the most degrading condition of which he is capable, and he is as often a slave to the niggardliness of the earth and the inclemency of heaven, as to a master or an institution. He is a slave when all his energy is spent in avoiding suffering and death, when all his action is imposed from without, and no breath or strength is left him for free enjoyment.

Work and play here take on a different meaning, and become equivalent to servitude and freedom. The change consists in the subjective point of view from which the distinction is now made. We no longer mean by work all that is done usefully, but only what is done unwillingly and by the spur of necessity. By play we are designating, no longer what is done fruitlessly, but whatever is done spontaneously and for its own sake, whether it have or not an ulterior utility. Play, in this sense, may be our most useful occupation. So far would a gradual adaptation to the environment be from making this play obsolete, that it would tend to abolish work, and to make play universal. For with the elimination of all the conflicts and errors of instinct, the race would do spontaneously whatever conduced to its welfare and we should live safely and prosperously without external stimulus or restraint. . . .

In this second and subjective sense, then, work is the disparaging term and play the eulogistic one. All who feel the dignity and importance of the things of the imagination, need not hesitate to adopt the classification which designates them as play. We point out thereby, not that they have no value, but that their value is intrinsic, that in them is one of the sources of all wotth. Evidently all values must be ultimately intrinsic. The useful is good because of the excellence of its consequences; but these must somewhere cease to be merely useful in their turn, or only excellent as means; somewhere we must reach the good that is good in itself and for its own sake, else the whole process is futile, and the utility of our first object illusory. We here reach the second factor in our distinction, between esthetic and moral values, which regards their immediacy. . . .

Esthetic and Physical Pleasure

We have now separated with some care intellectual and moral judgments from the sphere of our subject, and found that we are to deal only with perceptions of value, and with these only when they are positive and immediate. But even with these distinctions the most remarkable characteristic of the sense of beauty remains undefined. All pleasures are intrinsic and positive values, but all pleasures are not perceptions of beauty. Pleasure is indeed the essence of that perception, but there is evidently in this particular pleasure a complication which is not present in others and which is the basis of the distinction made by consciousness and language between it and the rest. It will be instructive to notice the degrees of this difference.

The bodily pleasures are those least resembling perceptions of beauty. By bodily pleasures we mean, of course, more than pleasures with a bodily seat; for that class would include them all, as well as all forms and elements of consciousness. Esthetic pleasures have physical conditions, they depend on the activity of the eye and the ear, of the memory and the other ideational functions of the brain. But we do not connect those pleasures with their seats except in physiological studies; the ideas with which esthetic pleasures are associated are not the ideas of their bodily causes. The pleasures we call physical, and regard as low, on the contrary, are those which call our attention to some part of our own body, and which make no object so conspicuous to us as the organ in which they arise.

There is here, then, a very marked distinction between physical and esthetic pleasure; the organs of the latter must be transparent, they must not intercept our attention, but carry it directly to some external object. The greater dignity and range of esthetic pleasure is thus made very intelligible The soul is glad, as it were, to forget its connection with the body and to fancy that it can travel over the world with the liberty with which it changes the objects of its thought. The mind passes from China to Peru without any conscious change in the local tensions of the body. This illusion of disembodiment is very exhilarating, while immersion in the flesh and confinement to some organ gives a tone of grossness and selfishness to our consciousness. The generally meaner associations of physical pleasures also help to explain their comparative crudity. . . .

The Differentia of Esthetic Pleasure: Its Objectification

There is, however, something more in the claim to universality in esthetic judgments than the desire to generalize our own opinions. There is the expression of a curious but well-known psychological phenomenon, namely, the transformation of an element of sensation into the quality of a thing. If we say that other men should see the beauties we see, it is because we think those beauties *are in the object*, like its color, proportion, or size. Our judgment appears to us merely the perception and discovery of an external existence, of the real excellence that is without. But this notion is radically absurd and contradictory. Beauty, as we have seen, is a value; it cannot be conceived as an independent existence which affects our senses and which we consequently perceive. It exists in perception, and cannot exist otherwise. A beauty not perceived is a pleasure not felt, and a contradiction. But modern philosophy has taught us to say the same thing of every element of the perceived world; all are sensations; and their grouping into objects imagined to be permanent and external is the work of certain habits of our intelligence. We should be incapable of surveying or retaining the diffused experiences of life, unless we organize and classified them, and out of the chaos of impressions framed the world of conventional and recognizable objects.

How this is done is explained by the current theories of perception. External objects usually affect various senses at once, the impressions of which are thereby associated. Repeated experiences of one object are also associated on account of their similarity; hence a double tendency to merge and unify into a single percept, to which a name is attached, the group of those memories and reactions which in fact had one external thing for their cause. But this percept, once formed, is clearly different from those particular experiences out of which it grew. It is permanent, they are variable. They are but partial views and glimpses of it. The constituted notion therefore comes to be the reality, and the materials of it merely the appearance. The distinction between substance and quality, reality and appearance, matter and mind, has no other origin.

The objects thus conceived and distinguished from our ideas of them, are at first compacted of all the impressions, feelings, and memories, which offer themselves for association and fall within the vortex of the amalgamating imagination. Every sensation we get from a thing is originally treated as one of its qualities. Experiment, however, and the practical need of a simpler conception of the structure of objects lead us gradually to reduce the qualities of the object to a minimum, and to regard most perceptions as an effect of those few qualities upon us. These few primary qualities, like extension which we persist in treating as independently real and as the quality of a substance, are those which suffice to explain the order of our experiences. All the rest, like color, are relegated to the subjective sphere, as merely effects upon our minds, and apparent or secondary qualities of the object.

But this distinction has only a practical justification. Convenience and economy of thought alone determine what combination of our sensations we shall continue to objectify and treat as the cause of the rest. The right and tendency to be objective is equal in all, since they are all prior to the artifice of thought by which we separate the concept from its materials, the thing from our experiences.

The qualities which we now conceive to belong to real objects are for the most part images of sight and touch. One of the first classes of effects to be treated as secondary were naturally pleasures and pains, since it could commonly conduce very little to intelligent and successful action to conceive our pleasures and pains as resident in objects. But emotions are essentially capable of objectification, as well as impressions of sense; and one may well believe that a primitive and inexperienced consciousness would rather people the world with ghosts of its own terrors and passions than with projections of those luminous and mathematical concepts which as yet it could hardly have formed.

This animistic and mythological habit of thought still holds its own at the confines of knowledge, where mechanical explanations are not found. In ourselves, where nearness makes observation difficult, in the intricate chaos of animal and human life, we still appeal to the efficacy of will and ideas, as also in the remote night of cosmic and religious problems. But in all the intermediate realm of vulgar day, where mechanical science has made progress, the inclusion of emotional or passionate elements in the concept of the reality would be now an extravagance. Here our idea of things is composed exclusively of perceptual elements, of the ideas of form and of motion.

The beauty of objects, however, forms an exception to this rule. Beauty is an emotional element, a pleasure of ours, which nevertheless we regard as a quality of things. But we are now prepared to understand the nature of this exception. It is the survival of a tendency originally universal to make every effect of a thing upon us a constituent of its conceived nature. The scientific idea of a thing is a great abstraction from the mass of perceptions and reactions which that thing produces; the esthetic idea is less abstract, since it retains the emotional reaction, the pleasure of the perception, as an integral part of the conceived thing.

Nor is it hard to find the ground of this survival in the sense of beauty of an objectification of feeling elsewhere extinct. Most of the pleasures which objects cause are easily distinguished and separated from the perception of the object: the object has to be applied to a particular organ, like the palate, or swallowed like wine, or used and operated upon in some way before the pleasure arises. The cohesion is therefore slight between the pleasure and the other associated elements of sense; the pleasure is separated in time from the perception, or it is localized in a different organ, and consequently is at once recognized as an effect and not as a quality of the object. But when the process of perception itself is pleasant, as it may easily be, when the intellectual operation, by which the elements of sense are associated and projected, and the concept of the form and substance of the thing produced, is naturally delightful, then we have a pleasure intimately bound up in the thing, inseparable from its character and constitution, the seat of which in us is the same as the seat of the perception. We naturally fail, under these circumstances, to separate the pleasure from the other objectified feelings. It becomes, like them, a quality of the object, which we distinguish from pleasures not so incorporated in the perception of things, by giving it the name of beauty.

The Definition of Beauty

We have now reached our definition of beauty, which, in the terms of our successive analysis and narrowing of the conception, is value positive, intrinsic, and objectified. Or, in less technical language, Beauty is pleasure regarded as the quality of a thing.

This definition is intended to sum up a variety of distinctions and identifications which should perhaps be here more explicitly set down. Beauty is a value, that is, it is not a perception of a matter of fact or of a relation: it is an emotion, an affection of our volitional and appreciative nature. An object cannot be beautiful if it can give pleasure to nobody: a beauty to which all men were forever indifferent is a contradiction in terms.

In the second place, this value is positive, it is the sense of the presence of something good, or (in the case of ugliness) of its absence. It is never the perception of a positive evil, it is never a negative value. That we are endowed with the sense of beauty is a pure gain which brings no evil with it. When the ugly ceases to be amusing or merely uninteresting and becomes disgusting, it becomes indeed a positive evil: but a moral and practical, not an esthetic, one. In esthetics that saying is true—often so disingenuous in ethics—that evil is nothing but the absence of good: for even the tedium and vulgarity of an existence without beauty is not itself ugly so much as lamentable and degrading. The absence of esthetic goods is a moral evil: the esthetic evil is merely relative, and means less of esthetic good than was expected at the place and time. No form in itself gives pain, although some forms give pain by causing a shock of surprise even when they are really beautiful: as if a mother found a fine bull pup in her child's cradle, when her pain would not be esthetic in its nature.

Further, this pleasure must not be in the consequence of the utility of the object or event, but in its immediate perception; in other words, beauty is an ultimate good, something that gives satisfaction to a natural function, to some fundamental need or capacity of our minds. Beauty is therefore a positive value that is intrinsic; it is a pleasure. These two circumstances sufficiently separate the sphere of esthetics from that of ethics. Moral values are generally negative, and always remote. Morality has to do with the avoidance of evil and the pursuit of good: esthetics only with enjoyment.

Finally, the pleasures of sense are distinguished from the perception of beauty, as sensation in general is distinguished from perception; by the objectification of the elements and their appearance as qualities rather of things than of consciousness. The passage from sensation to perception is gradual, and the path may be sometimes retraced: so it is with beauty and the pleasures of sensation. There is no sharp line between them, but it depends upon the degree of objectivity my feeling has attained at the moment whether I say "It pleases me," or "It is beautiful." If I am self-conscious and critical, I shall probably use one phrase; if I am impulsive and susceptible, the other. The more remote, interwoven, and inextricable the pleasure is, the more objective it will appear; and the union of two pleasures often makes one beauty. In Shakespeare's LIVth sonnet are these words:

> O how much more doth beauty beauteous seem
> By that sweet ornament which truth doth give!
> The rose looks fair, but fairer we it deem
> For that sweet odor which doth in it live.
> The canker-blooms have full as deep a dye
> As the perfumèd tincture of the roses,
> Hang on such thorns, and play as wantonly
> When summer's breath their maskèd buds discloses.
> But, for their beauty only is their show,
> They live unwooed and unrespected fade;
> Die to themselves. Sweet roses do not so:
> Of their sweet deaths are sweetest odors made.

One added ornament, we see, turns the deep dye, which was but show and mere sensation before, into an element of beauty and reality; and as truth is here the cooperation of perceptions, so beauty is the cooperation of pleasures. If color, form, and motion are hardly beautiful without the sweetness of the odor, how much more necessary would they be for the sweetness itself to become a beauty! If we had the perfume in a flask, no one would think of calling it beautiful: it would give us too detached and controllable a sensation. There would be no object in which it could be easily incorporated. But let it float from the garden, and it will add another sensuous charm to objects simultaneously recognized, and help to make them beautiful. Thus beauty is constituted by the objectification of pleasure. It is pleasure objectified.

II. BEAUTY AS EXPRESSION

Expression Defined

We have found in the beauty of material and form the objectification of certain pleasures connected with the process of direct perception, with the formation, in the one case of a sensation, or quality, in the other of a synthesis of sensations or qualities. But the human consciousness is not a perfectly clear mirror, with distinct boundaries and clear-cut images, determinate in number and exhaustively perceived. Our ideas half emerge for a moment from the dim continuum of vital feeling and diffused sense, and are hardly fixed before they are changed and transformed, by the shifting of attention and the perception of new relations, into ideas of really different objects. This fluidity of the mind would make reflection impossible, did we not fix in words and other symbols certain abstract contents; we thus become capable of recognizing in one perception the repetition of another, and of recognizing in certain recurrences of impressions a persistent object. This discrimination and classification of the contents of consciousness is the work of perception and understanding, and the pleasures that accompany these activities make the beauty of the sensible world.

But our hold upon our thoughts extends even further. We not only construct visible unities and recognizable types, but remain aware of their affinities to what is not at the time perceived; that is, we find in them a certain tendency and quality, not original to them, a meaning and a tone, which upon investigation we shall see to have been the proper characteristics of other objects and feelings, associated with them once in our experience. The hushed reverberations of these associated feelings continue in the brain, and by modifying our present reaction, color the image upon which our attention is fixed. The quality thus acquired by objects through association is what we call their expression. Whereas in form or material there is one object with its emotional effect, in expression there are two, and the emotional effect belongs to the character of the second or suggested one. Expression may thus make beautiful by suggestion things in themselves indifferent, or it may come to heighten the beauty which they already possess.

Expression is not always distinguishable in consciousness from the value of material or form, because we do not always have a distinguishable memory of the related idea which the expressiveness implies. When we have such a memory, as at the sight of some once frequented garden, we clearly and spontaneously attribute our emotion to the memory and not to the present fact which it beautifies. The revival of a pleasure and its embodiment in a present object which in itself might have been indifferent, is here patent and acknowledged.

The distinctness of the analysis may indeed be so great as to prevent the synthesis; we may so entirely pass to the suggested object, that our pleasure will be embodied in the memory of that, while the suggestive sensation will be overlooked, and the expressiveness of the present object will fail to make it beautiful. Thus the mementos of a lost friend do not become beautiful by virtue of the sentimental associations which may make them precious. The value is confined to the images of the memory; they are too clear to let any of that value escape and diffuse itself over the rest of our consciousness, and beautify the objects which we actually behold. We say explicitly: I value this trifle for its associations. And so long as this division continues, the worth of the thing is not for us esthetic.

But a little dimming of our memory will often make it so. Let the images of the past fade, let them remain simply as a halo and suggestion of happiness hanging about a scene; then this scene, however empty and uninteresting in itself, will have a deep and intimate charm; we shall be pleased by its very vulgarity. We shall not confess so readily that we value the place for its associations; we shall rather say: I am fond of this landscape; it has for me an ineffable attraction. The treasures of the memory have been melted and dissolved, and are now gilding the object that supplants them; they are giving this object expression. . . .

In all expression we may thus distinguish two terms: the first is the object actually presented, the word, the image, the expressive thing; the second is the object suggested, the further thought, emotion, or image evoked, the thing expressed.

These lie together in the mind, and their union constitutes expression. If the value lies wholly in the first term, we have no beauty of expression. The decorative inscriptions in Saracenic monuments can have no beauty of expression for one who does not read Arabic; their charm is wholly one of material and form. Or if they have any expression, it is by virtue of such thoughts as they might suggest, as, for instance, of the piety and oriental sententiousness of the builders and of the aloofness from us of all their world. And even these suggestions, being a wandering of our fancy rather than a study of the object, would fail to arouse a pleasure which would be incorporated in the present image. The scroll would remain without expression, although its presence might have suggested to us interesting visions of other things. The two terms would be too independent, and the intrinsic values of each would remain distinct from that of the other. There would be no visible expressiveness, although there might have been discursive suggestions.

Indeed, if expression were constituted by the external relation of object with object, everything would be expressive equally, indeterminately, and universally. The flower in the crannied wall would express the same thing as the bust of Cæsar or the *Critique of Pure Reason*. What constitutes the individual expressiveness of these things is the circle of thoughts allied to each in a given mind; my words, for instance, express the thoughts which they actually arouse in the reader; they may express more to one man than to another, and to me they may have expressed more or less than to you. My thoughts remain unexpressed, if my words do not arouse them in you, and very likely your greater wisdom will find in what I say the manifestation of a thousand principles of which I never dreamed. Expression depends upon the union of two terms, one of which must be furnished by the imagination; and a mind cannot furnish what it does not possess. The expressiveness of everything accordingly increases with the intelligence of the observer.

But for expression to be an element of beauty, it must, of course, fulfil another condition. I may see the relations of an object, I may understand it perfectly, and may nevertheless regard it with entire indifference. If the pleasure fails, the very substance and protoplasm of beauty is wanting. Nor, as we have seen, is even the pleasure enough; for I may receive a letter full of the most joyous news, but neither the paper, nor the writing, nor the style, need seem beautiful to me. Not until I confound the impressions, and suffuse the symbols themselves with the emotions they arouse, and find joy and sweetness in the very words I hear, will the expressiveness constitute a beauty; as when they sing, *Gloria in excelsis Deo.*

The value of the second term must be incorporated in the first; for the beauty of expression is as inherent in the object as that of material or form, only it accrues to that object not from the bare act of perception, but from the association with it of further processes, due to the existence of former impressions. We may conveniently use the word "expressiveness" to mean all the capacity of suggestion possessed by a thing, and the word "expression" for the esthetic modification which that expressiveness may cause in it. Expressiveness is thus the power given by experience to any image to call up others in the mind; and this expressiveness becomes an esthetic value, that is, becomes expression, when the value involved in the associations thus awakened are incorporated in the present object.

Esthetic Value in the Second Term

That the noble associations of any object should embellish that object is very comprehensible. Homer furnishes us with a good illustration of the constant employment of this effect. The first term, one need hardly say, leaves with him little to be desired. The verse is beautiful. Sounds, images, and composition conspire to stimulate and delight. This immediate beauty is sometimes used to clothe things terrible and sad; there is no dearth of the tragic in Homer. But the tendency of his poetry is nevertheless to fill the outskirts of our consciousness with the trooping images of things no less fair and noble than the verse itself. The heroes are virtuous. There is none of importance who is not admirable in his way. The palaces, the arms, the horses, the sacrifices, are always excellent. The women are always stately and beautiful. The ancestry and the history of every one are honorable and good. The whole Homeric world is clean, clear, beautiful, and providential, and no small part of the perennial charm of the poet is that he thus immerses us in an atmosphere of beauty; a beauty not concentrated and reserved for some extraordinary sentiment, action, or person, but permeating the whole and coloring the common world of soldiers and sailors, war and craft, with a marvellous freshness and inward glow. There is nothing in the associations of life in this world or in another to contradict or disturb our delight. All is beautiful, and beautiful through and through.

Something of this quality meets us in all simple and idyllic compositions. There is, for instance, a popular demand that stories and comedies should "end well." The hero and heroine must be young and handsome; unless they die,—which is another matter,—they must not in the end be poor. The landscape in the play must be beautiful; the dresses pretty; the plot without serious mishap. A pervasive presentation of pleasure must give warmth and ideality to the whole. In the proprieties of social life we find the same principle; we study to make our surroundings, manner, and conversation suggest nothing but what is pleasing. We hide the ugly and disagreeable portion of our lives, and do not allow the least hint of it to come to light upon festive and public occasions. Whenever, in a word, a thoroughly pleasing effect is found, it is found by the expression, as well as presentation, of what is in itself pleasing—and when this effect is to be produced artificially, we attain it by the suppression of all expression that is not suggestive of something good.

If our consciousness were exclusively esthetic, this kind of expression would be the only one allowed in art or prized in nature. We should avoid as a shock or an insipidity, the suggestion of anything not intrinsically beautiful. As there would be no values not esthetic, our pleasure could never be heightened by any other kind of interest. But as contemplation is actually a luxury in our lives, and things interest us chiefly on passionate and practical grounds, the accumulation of values too exclusively esthetic produces in our minds an effect of closeness and artificiality. So selective a diet cloys, and our palate, accustomed to much daily vinegar and salt, is surfeited by such unmixed sweet.

Instead we prefer to see through the medium of art—through the beautiful first term of our expression—the miscellaneous world which is so well known to us—perhaps so dear, and at any rate so inevitable, an object. We are more thankful for this presentation of the unlovely truth in a lovely form, than for the like presentation of an abstract beauty; what is lost in the purity of the pleasure is gained in the stimulation of our attention, and in the relief of viewing with esthetic detachment the same things that in practical life hold tyrannous dominion over our souls. The beauty that is associated only with other beauty is therefore a sort of esthetic dainty; it leads the fancy through a fairyland of lovely forms, where we must forget the common objects of our interest. The charm of such an idealization is undeniable; but the other important elements of our memory and will cannot long be banished. Thoughts of labor, ambition, lust, anger, confusion, sorrow, and death must needs mix with our contemplation and lend their various expressions to the objects with which in experience they are so closely allied. Hence the incorporation in the beautiful of values of other sorts, and the comparative rareness in nature or art of expressions the second term of which has only esthetic value. . . .

The Liberation of Self

The esthetic effect of objects is always due to the total emotional value of the consciousness in which they exist. We merely attribute this value to the object by a projection which is the ground of the apparent objectivity of beauty. Sometimes this value may be inherent in the process by which the object itself is perceived; then we have sensuous and formal beauty; sometimes the value may be due to the incipient formation of other ideas, which the perception of this object evokes; then we have beauty of expression. But among the ideas with which every object has relation there is one vaguest, most comprehensive, and most powerful one, namely, the idea of self. The impulses, memories, principles, and energies which we designate by that word baffle enumeration; indeed, they constantly fade and change into one another; and whether the self is anything, everything, or nothing depends on the aspect of it which we momentarily fix, and especially on the definite object with which we contrast it.

Now, it is the essential privilege of beauty so to synthesize and bring to a focus the various impulses of the self, so to suspend them to a single image, that a great peace falls upon that perturbed kingdom. In the experience of these momentary harmonies we have the basis of the enjoyment of beauty, and of all its mystical meanings. But there are always two methods of securing harmony: one is to unify all the given elements, and another is to reject and expunge all the elements that refuse to be unified. Unity by inclusion gives us the beautiful; unity by exclusion, opposition, and isolation gives us the sublime. Both are pleasures: but the pleasure of the one is warm, passive, pervasive; that of the other, cold, imperious, and keen. The one identifies us with the world, the other raises us above it.

There can be no difficulty in understanding how the expression of evil in the object may be the occasion of this heroic reaction of the soul. In the first place, the evil may be felt; but at the same time the sense that, great as it may be in itself, it cannot touch us, may stimulate extraordinarily the consciousness of our own wholeness. This is the sublimity which Lucretius calls "sweet" in the famous lines in which he so justly analyzes it. We are not pleased because another suffers an evil, but because, seeing it is an evil, we see at the same time our own immunity from it. We might soften the picture a little, and perhaps make the principle even clearer by so doing. The shipwreck observed from the shore does not leave us wholly unmoved; we suffer, also, and if possible, would help. So, too, the spectacle of the erring world must sadden the philosopher even in the Acropolis of his wisdom; he would, if it might be, descend from his meditation and teach. But those movements of sympathy are quickly inhibited by despair of success; impossibility of action is a great condition of the sublime. If we could count the stars, we should not weep before them. While we think we can change the drama of history, and of our own lives, we are not awed by our destiny. But when the evil is irreparable, when our life is lived, a strong spirit has the sublime resource of standing at bay and of surveying almost from the other world the vicissitudes of this.

The more intimate to himself the tragedy he is able to look back upon with calmness, the more sublime that calmness is, and the more divine the ecstasy in which he achieves it. For the more of the accidental vesture of life we are able to strip ourselves of, the more naked and simple is the surviving spirit; the more complete its superiority and unity, and, consequently, the more unqualified its joy. There remains little in us, then, but that intellectual essence, which several great philosophers have called eternal and identified with the Divinity.

A single illustration may help to fix these principles in the mind. When Othello has discovered his fatal error, and is resolved to take his own life, he stops his groaning, and addresses the ambassadors of Venice thus:

> Speak of me as I am: nothing extenuate,
> Nor set down aught in malice: then, must you speak
> Of one that loved, not wisely, but too well;
> Of one not easily jealous, but, being wrought,
> Perplexed in the extreme; of one whose hand,
> Like the base Indian, threw a pearl away
> Richer than all his tribe; of one whose subdued eyes,
> Albeit unusèd to the melting mood,
> Drop tears as fast as the Arabian trees
> Their medicinal gum. Set you down this:
> And say, besides, that in Aleppo once
> When a malignant and a turbaned Turk
> Beat a Venetian, and traduced the state,
> I took by the throat the circumcisèd dog,
> And smote him, thus.

There is a kind of criticism that would see in all these allusions, figures of speech, and wandering reflections, an unnatural rendering of suicide. The man, we might be told, should have muttered a few broken phrases, and killed himself without this pomp of declamation, like the jealous husbands in the daily papers. But the conventions of the tragic stage are more favorable to psychological truth than the conventions of real life. If we may trust the imagination (and in imagination lies, as we have seen, the test of propriety), this is what Othello would have felt. If he had not expressed it, his dumbness would have been due to external hindrances, not to the failure in his mind of just such complex and rhetorical thoughts as the poet has put into his mouth. The height of passion is naturally complex and rhetorical. Love makes us poets, and the approach of death should make us philosophers. When a man knows that his life is over, he can look back upon it from a universal standpoint. He has nothing more to live for, but if the energy of his mind remains unimpaired, he will still wish to live, and, being cut off from his personal ambitions, he will impute to himself a kind of vicarious immortality by identifying himself with what is eternal. He speaks of himself as he is, or rather as he was. He sums himself up, and points to his achievement. This I have been, says he, this I have done.

This comprehensive and impartial view, this synthesis and objectification of experience, constitutes the liberation of the soul and the essence of sublimity. That the hero attains it at the end consoles us, as it consoles him, for his hideous misfortunes. Our pity and terror are indeed purged; we go away knowing that, however tangled the net may be in which we feel ourselves caught, there is liberation beyond, and an ultimate peace.

The Sublime Independent of the Expression of Evil

So natural is the relation between the vivid conception of great evils, and that self-assertion of the soul which gives the emotion of the sublime, that the sublime is often thought to depend upon the terror which these conceived evils inspire. To be sure, that terror would have to be inhibited and subdued, otherwise we should have a passion too acute to be incorporated in any object; the sublime would not appear as an esthetic quality in things, but remain merely an emotional state in the subject. But this subdued and objectified terror is what is commonly regarded as the essence of the sublime, and so great an authority as Aristotle would seem to countenance some such definition. The usual cause of the sublime is here confused, however, with the sublime itself. The suggestion of terror makes us withdraw into ourselves: there with the supervening consciousness of safety or indifference comes a rebound, and we have that emotion of detachment and liberation in which the sublime really consists.

Thoughts and actions are properly sublime, and visible things only by analogy and suggestion when they induce a certain moral emotion; whereas beauty belongs properly to sensible things, and can be predicated of moral facts only by a figure of rhetoric. What we objectify in beauty is a sensation. What we objectify in the sublime is an act. This act is necessarily pleasant, for if it were not the sublime would be a bad quality and one we should rather never encounter in the world. The glorious joy of self-assertion in the face of an uncontrollable world is indeed so deep and entire, that it furnishes just that transcendent element of worth for which we were looking when we tried to understand how the expression of pain could sometimes please. It can please, not in itself, but because it is balanced and annulled by positive pleasures, especially by this final and victorious one of detachment. If the expression of evil seems necessary to the sublime, it is so only as a condition of this moral reaction.

We are commonly too much engrossed in objects and too little centered in ourselves and our inalienable will, to see the sublimity of a pleasing prospect. We are then enticed and flattered, and won over to a commerce with these external goods, and the consummation of our happiness would lie in the perfect comprehension and enjoyment of their nature. This is the office of art and of love; and its partial fulfilment is seen in every perception of beauty. But when we are checked in this sympathetic endeavor after unity and comprehension; when we come upon a great evil or an irreconcilable power, we are driven to seek our happiness by the shorter and heroic road; then we recognize the hopeless foreignness of what lies before us, and stiffen ourselves against it. We thus for the first time reach the sense of our possible separation from our world, and of our abstract stability; and with this comes the sublime.

But although experience of evil is the commonest approach to this attitude of mind, and we commonly become philosophers only after despairing of instinctive happiness, yet there is nothing impossible in the attainment of detachment by other channels. The immense is sublime as well as the terrible; and mere infinity of the object, like its hostile nature, can have the effect of making the mind recoil upon itself. Infinity, like hostility, removes us from things, and makes us conscious of our independence. The simultaneous view of many things, innumerable attractions felt together, produce equilibrium and indifference, as effectually as the exclusion of all. If we may call the liberation of the self by the consciousness of evil in the world, the Stoic sublime, we may assert that there is also an Epicurean sublime, which consists in liberation by equipoise. Any wide survey is sublime in that fashion. Each detail may be beautiful. We may even be ready with a passionate response to its appeal. We may think we covet every sort of pleasure, and lean to every kind of vigorous, impulsive life. But let an infinite panorama be suddenly unfolded; the will is instantly paralyzed, and the heart choked. It is impossible to desire everything at once, and when all is offered and approved, it is impossible to choose everything. In this suspense, the mind soars into a kind of heaven, benevolent but unmoved. . . .

The sense of the sublime is essentially mystical: it is the transcending of distinct perception in favor of a feeling of unity and volume. So in the moral sphere, we have the mutual cancelling of the passions in the breast that includes them all, and their final subsidence beneath the glance that comprehends them. This is the Epicurean approach to detachment and perfection; it leads by systematic acceptance of instinct to the same goal which the stoic and the ascetic reach by systematic rejection of instinct. It is thus possible to be moved to that self-enfranchisement which constitutes the sublime, even when the object contains no expression of evil.

This conclusion supports that part of our definition of beauty which declares that the values beauty contains are all positive; a definition which we should have had to change if we had found that the sublime depended upon the suggestion of evil for its effect. But the sublime is not the ugly, as some descriptions of it might lead us to suppose; it is the supremely, the intoxicatingly beautiful. It is the pleasure of contemplation reaching such an intensity that it begins to lose its objectivity, and to declare itself, what it always fundamentally was, an inward passion of the soul. For while in the beautiful we find the perfection of life by sinking into the object, in the sublime we find a purer and more inalienable perfection by defying the object altogether. The surprised enlargement of the vision, the sudden escape from our ordinary interests and the identification of ourselves with something permanent and superhuman, something much more abstract and inalienable than our changing personality, all this carries us away from the blurred objects before us, and raises us into a sort of ecstasy.

In the trite examples of the sublime, where we speak of the vast mass, strength, and durability of objects, or of their sinister aspect, as if we were moved by them on account of our own danger, we seem to miss the point. For the suggestion of our own danger would produce a touch of fear; it would be a practical passion, or if it could by chance be objectified enough to become esthetic, it would merely make the object hateful and repulsive, like a mangled corpse. The object is sublime when we forget our danger, when we escape from ourselves altogether, and live as it were in the object itself, energizing in imitation of its movement, and saying, "Be thou me, impetuous one!" This passage into the object, to live its life, is indeed a characteristic of all perfect contemplation. But when in thus translating ourselves we rise and play a higher personage, feeling the exhilaration of a life freer and wilder than our own, then the experience is one of sublimity. The emotion comes not from the situation we observe, but from the powers we conceive; we fail tó sympathize with the struggling sailors because we sympathize too much with the wind and waves. And this mystical cruelty can extend even to ourselves; we can so feel the fascination of the cosmic forces that engulf us as to take a fierce joy in the thought of our own destruction. We can identify ourselves with the abstractest essence of reality, and, raised to that height, despise the human accidents of our own nature. Lord, we say, though thou slay me, yet will I trust in thee. The sense of suffering disappears in the sense of life and the imagination overwhelms the understanding.

—*The Sense of Beauty* (1896)

LOUIS ARNAUD REID

Values, Feeling and Embodiment

1. THE EMBODIMENT OF VALUES

In the light of all that has been said, the question "What does art embody?" must be put carefully and the answer must be a complex one. There are on the one hand the sources of art in life-experiences. On the other, there are meanings which arise directly out of the use of the various materials of the arts, with their symbolic import. These latter meanings are also related to ordinary life, are attached to it by a sort of umbilical cord. Sounds, shapes, colours, the sounds of words . . . and their significances, are all part of our sensitive ordinary experiences.

Aesthetic meaning may be found, upon analytic examination, to be *derived* in part from sources in life outside art. Viewed from *inside* the experience of art, it may well seem that the question "What does art embody?" is the wrong question. Looked at from within, the short answer is that what art embodies, what it means, cannot be stated in words at all. Even if the art is an art of words, as poetry is, a paraphrase will not do; the meaning of the poem is what the poem as read, says. Likewise, the "meaning" of a picture or a piece of music cannot be put into words; if it could, the art would be superfluous. Experience-knowledge of aesthetic meaning is a unique way of knowing, is *sui generis*. On the other hand, if we think not of the meaning as actually known in aesthetic experience, of the history, of the genesis of the work, of what "inspired" it, we can often, though not always, discover some relation of meaning in art to life-experiences. This is more often true of "representative" arts like literature, drama, and a good deal of painting. (It is much less apparent in music.) And further, there is a quite *general* sense in which we can ask the question, "What is embodied?" It is the sense in which we may be asking, not about the particular origins of what is embodied here and now in this individual work, but about the *kind* of thing which is embodied, and its ontological status. Is it, for instance, matter of *fact* which is embodied? Is it *emotion*? Is it *"values"*? I will speak first of this last question, returning to the others.

Thinking for the time being of the partial derivation of art meanings from life-experiences (always a one-sided kind of thinking)—from what *sort* of life-experiences are they derived? Crudely put, What is it that is trying to get "expressed"?[1] Is it "facts" apprehended—the facts of the structure of a landscape or a face or the details of a person's character, acts, life? Is it "ideas" about love, or duty, or suffering, or mortality, or God . . . freedom, immortality? Or can it be "feelings" or "emotions"?

None of these answers seem to me to be adequate, though all of them may enter as elements into the true answer. The true answer, I venture to think, is that it is not facts or ideas as such, nor feelings nor emotions as such that try "to get expressed," but feelings-about-things, or things (facts, ideas, anything)—as-felt. Things-we-are-interested in, things-experienced-as-interesting, exciting, as in some very broad sense of the term, good, evil, attractive, repulsive, etc. The life-resources of art are events or facts or concepts or images as experienced, and as experienced with feeling. They are not the things alone, nor the feelings alone, but the things-as-experienced-with feeling.

Another way, and a short way of saying the same thing is to affirm that what "tries to get expressed" are *values*. Professor R. B. Perry once defined "value" as "object of interest."[2] Without necessarily accepting this as a final definition of value, I take it to be a fair account of what we ordinarily mean. The much used word "value" is also much abused; it is a dangerous world because it is a substantive, and it is all too easy to think of "values" as vaguely floating about somewhere. But taken as standing for a relationship between things and our interested selves ("interest" involving some degree of "feeling") it is a useful word, particularly in aesthetics, because it avoids a one-sided emphasis on object, or on subject. To avoid one-sided emphasis I have used hyphens above. It is, then, "values" which "try to get expressed," or things-as-felt (or experienced, with interest and feeling), feelings-about-things. . . .

It is not bare facts (or "knowledge that") which "get expressed." When Tennyson wrote, "Into the valley of death rode the six hundred," he was not merely affirming the fact, but was concerned with it as an event moving the feelings. If a painter paints trees or cows, he is not, *qua* artist, depicting the bare literal facts; he attends to what interests and excites him. He is moved by colours and shapes and dynamic relationships in such a way that the form of a painted tree may reveal, perhaps, as ordinary matter-of-fact seeing will not do, the fascinating way it springs up, spreads its branches and leaves, and supports its weight. If, again, we think of art as partially arising from the "unconscious," it is no exception to the statement that events . . . experienced as exciting are the causes or subject-matter of some arts. Art may express unconscious wishes or fantasies, and some—perhaps all—art is "symbolic" in one or more of the several psychoanalytic senses. And these contents of course are very highly charged with "value";

the artist must have felt strongly about them or they would not have been repressed or expressed.

An example of the fallacy that it is facts which "get expressed" is a confused belief among architects and writers on architecture, that architecture should "express function or structure." "Express" is not defined. It may mean little more than "show up." A modern building ought, some think to "show up" its engineering structure unashamedly (though much engineering structure is too complex to be shown up in a building and for various reasons must be hidden). Why? Because architecture is nothing but engineering? But if engineering, why "ought" it to show its structure? There must be aesthetic premises somewhere concealed. The concealed premises are that architecture is not only engineering but art and ought to show structure because structure is beautiful. Structure and function, however, as independent facts and in themselves, are neither beautiful nor ugly. To a percipient who sees them as embodying the "values" of function and structure, they may appear as beautiful (though it is a doubtful assumption that *any* structure may be so perceived). Sheer structure often delights and may be aesthetically perceived (with the inward selectiveness which aesthetic perception always involves) and in some cases it may be enough for an architect to let the structure show. But this is a *deliberate* and aesthetic choice. Often, however, the architect shows up the aesthetic quality by selective treatment, emphasis, simplification, elaboration. This takes many different forms. There is the freedom and variety of the essential Gothic structure, with aesthetic treatment of vaulting or buttress, or the modern deliberate emphasis of the glass-and-steel structural grid, or the use in various ways of organic or geometrical *motifs*. In all cases architecture as art is more than engineering, and more than the mere factual presentation of structure and function to the eye. It is a deliberate creation of something new, arising out of delight in the *value* of these things.

Nor is it bare *ideas* which "get expressed." If by "ideas" we mean concepts, then philosophy or science are the proper media for the expression of concepts and their relations. Concepts are abstractions, they are structures or forms which can best be expressed in language which is quite cold and impersonal. Such language is simply a means to clearer conception, and a means to the communication of ideas. If scientists and philosophers are talking about mathematical propositions, or electrons, or duty, freedom, the status of secondary qualities . . . they rightly use this "cold" impersonal abstract language in the endeavour to clarify, express and convey the truths they are claiming. The language is a means to this end, and there are often equally good alternative ways of saying exactly the same thing—as in art there are not. (Two philosophers may entirely agree on a point, but they seldom use *exactly* the same language.) And the ideas of philosophy and science can be adequately translated into, or re-expressed in, various languages.

Of course scientists and philosophers sometimes get excited about their ideas and about the clarity of thought. If a philosopher is moved to enthusiasm by these, and happens also to be a master of prose and an artist, his feeling may "get into" his writing and make art of it. As well as clear and efficient exposition (which can also be inelegantly expressed[3]) one gets in his style the sense of the *joy* of ideas, the joy of clarity, which may show itself in choice and placing of words, rhythms, emphasis, balance, even in punctuation. A philosopher may be a prose artist in his writing of philosophy. English and French philosophy are fortunately plentiful in examples of clear joyous philosophical writing elegantly done. But the *first*, and the *essential*, aim of philosophical (and scientific) language is efficiency in conveying, not feeling of ideas, but ideas themselves. "Well said" in philosophy primarily means conveying an abstract idea clearly. "Well said" in art means more than this.

Consider now a poem "about" ideas. Suppose a poet is writing—like Shelley, for example—about "scientific" or "philosophical" ideas. He is not a philosopher (or a scientist); his first loyalty is not to ideas as such. He is a poet, and it is his excitement-in-ideas which moves him to write. He has a freedom in the selection and manipulation of his subject-matter (in exactly the same way as the painter freely selects from the features of a landscape) to which the philosopher has no right. It is ideas-as-he-feels-them (ideas as "values"), that "get into" the poem. As with the painter, his emphasis, his style, is affected by the rhythm and pulsings of his feeling. Whereas in the writing of philosophy and science the quality of style is primarily subordinate to the clarity of ideas, now it embodies the *values* of ideas.

2. VALUE, FEELING AND EMOTION

What of the place of feeling and emotion? After the Romantic Revival it became an almost unexamined assumption that the artist "expresses" in art his feelings or emotions. Temporarily letting the term "expression" pass, can it be feeling or emotion which is expressed in works of art? Mrs Susanne Langer, who herself strongly inclines to the view that in some sense feelings inhere in art objects, points out the difficulties of this language. She refers to Otto Baensch who believes that we can objectify and hold and handle feelings by "creating objects wherein the feelings we seek to hold are so definitely embodied that any subject confronted with these objects, and emphatically disposed towards them, cannot but experience a non-sensuous apperception of the feelings in question. Such objects are called 'Works of Art.' "[4] About this Mrs Langer remarks[5] that "feeling that is not subjective presents a . . . paradox," and (p. 22) "the status of the unfelt feelings that inhere in art objects is ontologically obscure. . . ." Mrs Langer's distinguished book, *Feeling and Form*, is in a way a systematic attempt to make sense of this idea of objectified feelings embodied in a work of art. Here I can only observe that it seems to me that she gets into difficulties about feeling which she would not have encountered had she, alternatively, conceived of art as embodying *values*. Feeling, and sometimes emotion, is very intimately bound up with the creation, the enjoyment, and the interpretation of works of art. But, since the terms "feeling" and "emotion" are so irreducibly associated with subjective states and processes, it does not seem possible to conceive of feelings or emotions as being sufficiently "objectified" to inhere in perceived works of art.

"Value," on the other hand, is a subjective-objective idea. Feeling by itself belongs to the subjective side. But our feelings-about-an-event, a fact, an idea, can be expressed by the way, the manner, the mode in which the event, fact, idea is represented. Tennyson felt about the event of the charge of the Light Brigade. He "expressed" not his own strictly incommunicable private subjective feelings, but the idea of the Charge-of-the-Light-Brigade-as-he-felt-it, and he did it by representing the Charge in a particular rhythmical *form*. The painter, excited by the springing tree, does not "objectify" sheer subjective excitement. (He cannot.) He paints the *tree* he sees in a certain way, so that when he, and we, see the painting, our experience in part derives from his delight in the springing tree. "Value," since it is a two-sided notion, objective as well as subjective, can be "expressed" objectively in art. Feeling alone cannot. The mistakes of theories which stress only the objective side ("Mirror to Nature theories"), which say that art represents facts or ideas only, is that they can condone dull uninspired-literalism which is not art but poor photography. The mistakes of traditional theories which say "the function of art is to 'express' the artist's feeling or emotion" are that they are describing the aesthetically impossible, and that the stress on feelings and emotions leads to unbalance, sentimentality and emotionalism and too much emphasis upon what goes on inside the artist's "personality."

We have been discussing for the last few pages what *kind* of thing it is which is embodied in the work of art, and have, simply for convenience sake, considered life-sources for art—facts, ideas, emotions—which may "try to get expressed." The phrase, however, "try to get expressed" was deliberately crude, and it needs now to be corrected.

3. Art, "Expression" and Embodiment

The view that art is "expression" is capable of many different interpretations. Some of them are, I have urged, inadmissible, as that the artist has an experience, "expresses" this experience in a work, so that others can in turn have the same experience. There are various subtler versions of the expression view—in Croce, Carritt, Collingwood, Langer. And "expression" may be used as a synonym for "embodiment", in the sense in which I have expounded it here.[6] (But "embodiment" in my sense stresses the importance of the actual *material* medium in a way these thinkers do not consistently do.[7])

It is not necessary to say much more about "expression" as expression of life-experience, or of facts, ideas, feelings, in art. The process of making a work of art may certainly include "expression" in various senses. It may relieve the tension of gestation: to put something "into" words or action or paint ("express" it) is easing. To discover meaning through embodiment is satisfying; satisfaction follows the restless and often vague desire to discover through doing one hardly knows what; this can be called a satisfaction of "expression." But the "expression" which is relief need not be aesthetic. It may mean only the relief which John Dewey calls vulgarly "spewing forth".[8] Any action may "express" a pent-up emotion even if it is stamping with rage or jumping for joy. Further, such actions may "express" in the sense of *exhibiting* to others. These "expressions" *exhibit* the kind of feeling it was: stamping or jumping are crudely appropriate to the feeling. There is, too, the partially valid sense in which one can say that a life-experience, idea, value . . . is *represented* in a poem or a play or a picture. "The artist is expressing the idea that. . . ." And there is what is called, vaguely, "self-expression" or "expression of one's personality." Perhaps other kinds of "expression" may enter, in complex and overlapping ways, into the making and completion of works of art. They are in their own way interesting and important, sometimes psychologically and educationally very important indeed. The practice of art can be cathartic, therapeutic, or nourishing to the growth of personality. It can bring a person out of himself into the external world and the world of other people, establishing communication with them. Although its educational potency is often considerably overdrawn, artistic "expression" can be a kind of conversion and a beginning of new life.

All this can be said confidently, and without implying that the nature of art *is* expression of "life" outside art. Artistic activity, when it comes to its fruition, is never just expression in art of anything that existed completely before it, but is (to repeat) discovery of new embodied meaning, of meaning in embodiment. If, therefore, we say, as we have been saying, that it is *values* which art "embodies," and if we have taken "life"-values as examples, this crude picture must now be corrected by asserting all over again that the values which art embodies are the values to be discovered *in* the art, and never, completely, anywhere else. All aesthetic expression is consummated and transformed in the new creation of embodiment.

Not all arts have their source or genesis—at least in any obvious sense—in life-experiences. Pure music may start with musical ideas and with experiment in musical material. However that be, once the work of art is made, its meaning and its embodiment, its "content" or "matter," and its "form," are of a single piece, one spirit and one body. Collingwood writes:[9] "When the poem is written, there is nothing in it of which we can say 'this is a matter which might have taken a different form' or 'this is a form which might have been realized in a different matter.'" Or as Mrs Langer has it;[10] "in a 'presentational symbol [e.g. art] the symbolic import permeates the whole structure, because every articulation of that structure is an articulation of the idea it conveys; the meaning . . . is the content of the symbolic form, given with it, as it were, to perception." Again, criticizing the distinction between form and content, she says (p. 520), "An artistic symbol is a much more intricate thing than what we usually think of as a 'form,' because it involves *all* the relationships of its elements to one another, all similarities and differences of quality, not only geometric or other familiar relations. That is why qualities enter directly into the form itself, not as its contents, but as constitutive elements in it. . . . A work of art is a structure whose interrelated elements are often qualities, or properties of qualities such as their degrees of intensity; qualities enter into the form and in this way are as much one with it as the relations which they, and they only, have; and to speak of them as 'content,' from which the form could be abstracted logically, is nonsense."

The same kind of thing "goes" for all the other "life" subject-matters of art. Psychoanalysis, no doubt, can throw light upon the genesis of at least some art. But it is impossible to discover embodied meaning directly by psychoanalysis. Unconscious events may be the genesis of artistic creation; the embodied meaning can only be found in the full and living appreciation of the completed work of art itself.

—Ways of Knowledge and Experience (1961)

NOTES

1. For a brief criticism of "expression," see below, pp. 70–2. In the meantime I deliberately use an awkward phrase to indicate that the idea, provisionally used, *is* an awkward one.

2. R. B. Perry, *The General Theory of Value* (New York, Longmans).

3. This is debatable. I incline to believe that the philosopher who writes clearly with economic elegance is the better thinker for it.

4. Otto Baensch: 'Kunst unt Gefuhl', *Logos*, Vol. II, p. 14.

5. *Feeling and Form* (Routledge & Kegan Paul, 1953), p. 18.

6. Mr. H. Osborne (*Aesthetics and Criticism*, Routledge & Kegan Paul, pp. 142–3) accuses me, along with Carritt, Collingwood and Stace, of having come under the "spell" of Croce. I do not think that was ever true. And, though I formerly used the word "expressive" a good deal, perhaps sometimes loosely, it was intended very much as an equivalent for embodiment in the present sense. The main thesis of my *A Study in Aesthetics* was a *protest* against the idea that art is a translation of life-experience into the medium of art. See *A Study in Aesthetics* (Allen & Unwin), e.g., pp. 196–201.

7. For a fuller treatment, see my *Aesthetics and Education* (Bretton Hall, Wakefield).

8. Quoted by John Hospers, "Expression," *Proceedings of the Aristotelian Society*, Vol. LV. See this paper for a good discussion of expression.

9. R. G. Collingwood, *The Principles of Art* (Oxford: Oxford University Press, 1938), p. 24.

10. Susanne K. Langer, "The Principles of Creation in Art," *Hudson Review*, Vol. 2 (1949–1950), p. 521.

PART

II

The Work of Art

CHAPTER

7

The Medium
and Sensory Constituents

BERNARD BOSANQUET: The Esthetic Attitude in Its Embodiments
EDWARD WESTON: Seeing Photographically
DAVID W. PRALL: Sensuous Elements and Esthetic Orders

Part II is devoted to the work of art—its materials, form, and expressiveness. According to the idealistic interpretation, the work of art is not physical but spiritual. For example, Croce maintained that the physical objects—the statue, the building, the printed poem, and so forth—are not to be confused with art. They are simply "memoranda," physical stimulants for imaginative activity. The work of art, which is an apparition, lives in the imagination and there alone. Croce quite agrees with Walt Whitman:

All architecture is what you do to it when you look upon it.
(Did you think it was in the white or gray stone? or the lines of the arches and cornices?)
All music is what awakens from you when you are reminded by the instruments,
It is not the violins and the cornets, it is not the oboe nor the beating drums, nor the score of the baritone singing his sweet romanza, nor that of the men's chorus, nor that of the women's chorus,
It is nearer and farther than they.

The physical object is esthetically important only because it stimulates imagination, and the object in nature is important for the same reason. This point of view is implied by Croce in his identification of intuition and expression, and it has been explicitly developed by R. G. Collingwood in *The Principles of Art* and by Jean-Paul Sartre in *The Psychology of Imagination*.

A less idealistic interpretation of the work of art is contained in Stephen C. Pepper's "Contextualistic Criticism," Chapter 11. Pepper distinguishes between the physical work of art—for example, the stone or bronze of a statue—and the esthetic work of art, "which rolls up all that is relevant in the line of preceding perceptions and intuits the whole potentiality of the physical work of art in a total vivid seizure." The physical work of art acts as a continuous substratum and control object, but apart from the spectator, the esthetic qualities of the perceived work would not be actualized.

A somewhat similar interpretation, although written from a very different philosophical standpoint, is advanced by Bernard Bosanquet (1848–1923), a distinguished British philosopher. Art, he maintains, evokes an integrated response of the whole "body-and-mind." He calls this response "feeling," and the feeling, he says, is always embodied in an object. "It is a *relevant* feeling," he explains. "I mean it is attached, annexed, to the quality of some object—to all its detail. . . . My feeling in its special quality is evoked by the special quality of which it is the feeling, and in fact is one with it."[1] Thus emphasizing the *embodiment* of feeling, he opposes the tendency of Benedetto Croce to minimize the esthetic importance of the sensuous medium and the physical objects of nature. Although Bosanquet was an idealist, he believed that Croce's was a "false idealism" because it neglected the yearning of the creative imagination toward externalization and the influence of the external medium upon the imagination. As he says elsewhere, "To reject the function of the body—our own and nature's—is not to honor but to bereave the spirit."[2]

His emphasis upon the importance of the medium is no new principle: It is at least as old as Aristotle and received its classic expression in Lessing's *Laocoön*. But in a sense, it has been rediscovered by modern artists and estheticians, and it has had an extraordinary cleansing and renovating effect upon the arts. For example, the work of an architect such as Frank Lloyd Wright, of a designer such as Moholy-Nagy, of a sculptor such as Henry Moore, or of a painter such as Henri Matisse has been profoundly influenced by this principle. "Respect your medium" has been a principal imperative of modern art.

The importance of the medium is illustrated in the discussion of camera art by Edward Weston (1886–1958), one of America's great photographers. He denounces the folly of using a camera to imitate the work of the painter, and emphasizes the importance of "learning to *see* photographically." One must develop a keen sense of the capacities of photographic tools and processes, such as the color filter, the camera angle, the length of exposure, and the method of developing. Directed by an understanding of his medium, the photographer learns to see things in terms of their potentialities for photographic treatment. He can then use the camera eye "to produce a heightened sense of reality—a kind of super-realism that reveals the vital essences of things."[3] Not only the photographer but also the beholder of his work needs to "see photographically," since his enjoyment depends on an appreciation of what the camera can do best.

Whereas the medium is the *particular* natural stuff out of which the work of art is made, the more abstract sensuous qualities, such as line, shape, and color in the visual arts, or pitch, timbre, and degree of loudness in the auditory arts, may be considered apart from the particular medium and form of art (color, for example, is common to many mediums and various arts).

These abstract sensuous elements were perspicaciously discussed by David Wight Prall (1886–1940), Professor of Philosophy at the University of California and later at Harvard, in his important books *Aesthetic Analysis* and *Aesthetic Judgment*. He begins with an analysis of the sensuous materials, then describes the composition of these materials in orders or forms, and finally discusses the expressive features that result from reference to the surrounding world. Although he thus deals with referential expression, his books are characterized by their emphasis upon immediate sensuous surface and form. "It is characteristic of esthetic apprehension," he declares, "that the surface fully presented to sense is the total object of apprehension. . . . As we leave this surface in our attention, to go deeper into meanings or more broadly into connections and relations, we depart from the typically esthetic attitude."[4]

Although he thus tends to abstract from relations *external* to the work of art, he emphasizes relations that are internal and native to the materials. The pitch, timbre, and intensity (degree of loudness) of sound; the hue, saturation, and "brightness" (lightness or darkness) of color; the geometrical properties of lines, surfaces, and masses; and the spatial or temporal extension common to various arts, all afford a natural basis for formal composition or order. The order, in each case, is intrinsic to the elements as such; and one reason that odors, tastes, and tactile qualities are artistically less important than tones and colors is that they lack any intrinsic principle of order, such as pitch or hue.

NOTES

1. Bernard Bosanquet, *Three Lectures on Aesthetic* (Macmillan, London, 1915), pp. 3, 5.
2. Bernard Bosanquet, "Croce's Aesthetic," *Proceedings of the British Academy*, Vol. 9 (1919–1920), p. 272.
3. Edward Weston, "What is Photographic Beauty?" *Camera Craft*, Vol. 46 (1939), p. 254.
4. David W. Prall, *Aesthetic Judgment* (Crowell, New York, 1929), p. 20.

BERNARD BOSANQUET

The Esthetic Attitude in Its Embodiments

Why are there different arts? The simple answer to this question takes us, I believe, to the precise root and source of the whole principle of esthetic expressiveness. . . .

We should begin, I am convinced, from the very simplest facts. Why do artists make different patterns, or treat the same pattern differently, in wood-carving, say, and clay-modeling, and wrought-iron work? If you can answer this question thoroughly, then, I am convinced, you have the secret of the classification of the arts and of the passage of feeling[1] into its esthetic embodiment; that is, in a word, the secret of beauty.

Why, then, in general does a worker in clay make different decorative patterns from a worker in wrought-iron? I wish I could go into this question with illustrations and details, but I will admit at once that I am not really competent to do so, though I have taken very great interest in the problem. But in general there can surely be no doubt of the answer. You cannot make the same things in clay as you can in wrought-iron, except by a *tour de force*. The feeling of the work is, I suppose, altogether different. The metal challenges you, coaxes you, as William Morris said of the molten glass, to do a particular kind of thing with it, where its tenacity and ductility make themselves felt. The clay, again, is delightful, I take it, to handle, to those who have a talent for it; but it is delightful of course in quite different manipulations from those of the wrought-iron. I suppose its facility of surface, how it lends itself to modeling or to throwing on the wheel, must be its great charm. Now the decorative patterns which are carried out in one way or the other may, of course, be suggested *ab extra* by a draughtsman, and have all sorts of properties and interests in themselves as mere lines on paper. But when you come to carry them out in the medium, then, if they are appropriate, or if you succeed in adapting them, they become each a special phase of the embodiment of your whole delight and interest of "body-and-mind" in handling the clay or metal or wood or molten glass. It is alive in your hands, and its life grows or rather magically springs into shapes which it, and you in it, seem to desire and feel inevitable. The feeling for the medium, the sense of what can rightly be done in it only or better than in anything else, and the charm and fascination of doing it so—these, I take it, are the real clue to the fundamental question of esthetics, which is "how feeling and its body are created adequate to one another." It is parallel to the question in general philosophy, "Why the soul has a body." It is the same sort of thing as the theory of the rising mountain,[2] but it is much less open to caprice, being absolute fact all through, and it explains not merely the interpretation of lines and shapes, but the whole range and working of the esthetic imagination in the province of fine art, which is its special province.

To this doctrine belongs the very fruitful modern topic of the relation of beautiful handicraft with the workman's life, as the outcome and expression of his body-and-mind, and amid all the disparagement which the most recent views of art are apt to throw upon Ruskin, we must remember that it was first and foremost to his inspired advocacy that this point of view owes its recognition today, and William Morris, for instance, recognized him, in this respect at least, as his master.

The differences of the great arts then are simply such differences as those between clay-modeling, wood-carving, and wrought-iron work, developed on an enormous scale, and with their inevitable consequences for whole provinces of esthetic imagination.

For this is a fact of the highest importance. Every craftsman, we saw, feels the peculiar delight and enjoys the peculiar capacity of his own medium. This delight and sense of capacity are of course not confined to the moments when he is actually manipulating his work. His fascinated imagination lives in the powers of his medium; he thinks and feels in terms of it; it is the peculiar body of which *his* esthetic imagination and no other is the peculiar soul.

Thus there grow up the distinct traditions, the whole distinctive worlds of imaginative thought and feeling, in which the great imaginative arts have their life and being. . . .

The ideal of every art must be revealed, I take it, in terms of the art itself; and it must be what underlies the whole series of efforts which the artist's imagination has made and is making, to create, in his own medium, an embodied feeling in which he can rest satisfied. It is the world as he has access to it through his art. It may seem to him more than any of his works; but it only has existence in them and in the effort which they imply when taken all together. The danger is to try and make a picture of this effort, apart from any of its achievements, which is really nothing. Then you get the enfeebled ideal, which means the omission of all character and individuality.

Now let us take a particular case. If our view of the distinction and connection of the arts is right, and it is simply a question of the medium adopted by each, and the capacities of that medium as proved by experience, what is to be said of the distinctive character of *poetry?* It seems in a sense to have almost no material element, to work directly with significant ideas in which the objects of the imagination are conveyed. Language is so transparent, that it disappears, so to speak, into its own meaning, and we are left with no characteristic medium at all.

I do not think there can be any doubt about the true attitude here. Poetry, like the other arts, has a physical or at least a sensuous medium, and this medium is sound. It is, however, significant sound, uniting inseparably in itself the factors of formal expression through an immediate pattern, and of representation through the meanings of language, exactly as sculpture and painting deal at once and in the same vision both with formal patterns and with significant shapes. That language is a physical fact with its own properties and qualities is easily seen by comparing different tongues, and noting the form which different patterns, such as sapphic or hexameter verse, necessarily receive in different languages, such as Greek and Latin. To make poetry in different languages, for example, in French and German, is as different a task as to make decorative work in clay and iron. The sound, meter, and meaning are the same inseparable product in a poem as much as the color, form, and embodied feeling in a picture. And it is only an illusion to suppose that because you have significant sentences in poetry, therefore you are dealing with meanings which remain the same outside the poem, any more than a tree or a person whom you think you recognize in a picture, is, as you know them at home so to speak, *the* tree or *the* person *of* the picture. Poetry no more keeps its meaning when turned into corresponding prose, than a picture or a sonata keeps its meaning in the little analyses they print in the catalogues or programs.

Shelley, according to Professor Bradley, had a feeling of the kind referred to. Poetry seemed to him to deal with a perfectly apt and transparent medium, with no qualities of its own, and therefore approaching to being no medium at all, but created out of nothing by the imagination for the use of the imagination. While the media employed by the other arts, being gross and physical and having independent qualities of their own, seemed to him rather obstacles in the way of expression than apt instruments of it. The answer to such a view is what we have just given.

It is the qualities of the media which give them the capacity to serve as embodiments of feeling; and sonorous language, the medium of poetry, has its peculiarities and definite capacities precisely like the others.

Here, I cannot but think, we are obliged to part company, with some regret, from Benedetto Croce. He is possessed, as so often is the case with him, by a fundamental truth, so intensely that he seems incapable of apprehending what more is absolutely necessary to its realization. Beauty, he sees, is for the mind and in the mind. A physical thing, supposed unperceived and unfelt, cannot be said in the full sense to possess beauty. But he forgets throughout, I must think, that though feeling is necessary to its embodiment, yet also the embodiment is necessary to feeling. To say that because beauty implies a mind, therefore it is an internal state, and its physical embodiment is something secondary and incidental, and merely brought into being for the sake of permanence and communication —this seems to me a profound error of principle, a false idealism. It meets us, however, throughout Croce's system, according to which "intuition"— the inward vision of the artist—is the only true expression. External media, he holds, are, strictly speaking, superfluous, so that there is no meaning in distinguishing between one mode of expression and another (as between paint and musical sound and language). Therefore there can be no classification of the arts, and no fruitful discussion of what can better be done by one art than by another. And esthetic—the philosophy of expression—is set down as all one with linguistic—the philosophy of speech. For there is no meaning in distinguishing between language in the sense of speech, and other modes of expression. Of course, if he had said that speech is not the only form of language, but that every art speaks to us in a language of its own, that would have had much to be said for it. But I do not gather that that is his intention.

His notion is not a new one among theorists. It really is deeply rooted in a philosophical blunder. No doubt it seems obvious, when once pointed out, that things are not all there, not complete in all qualities, except when they are appreciated in a mind. And then, having rightly observed that this is so, we are apt to go on and say that you have them complete, and have all you want of them, if you have them before your mind and have not the things in bodily presence at all. But the blunder is, to think that you can have them completely before your mind without having their bodily presence at all. And because of this blunder, it seems fine and "ideal" to say that the artist operates in the bodiless medium of pure thought or fancy, and that the things of the bodily world are merely physical causes of sensation, which do not themselves enter into the effects he uses. It is rather a natural thing to say about poetry, because we discount the physical side of language. We glance at its words and do not sound them. And Shelley, as we saw, says something very like that.

But at the very beginning of all this notion, as we said, there is a blunder. Things, it is true, are not complete without minds, but minds, again, are not complete without things; not any more, we might say, than minds are complete without bodies. Our resources in the way of sensation, and our experiences in the way of satisfactory and unsatisfactory feeling, are all of them won out of our intercourse with things, and are thought and imagined by us as qualities and properties of the things. Especially we see this in music. Here we have an art entirely made up of a material—musical tone—which one may say does not exist at all in the natural world, and is altogether originated by our inventive and imaginative manipulation of physical things, pressing on in the line of creative discovery which something very like accident must at first have opened up to us.[3] Apart from this imaginative operation upon physical things, our fancy in the realm of music could have done as good as nothing.

And in principle it is the same with all the arts. All the material and the physical process which the artist uses—take our English language as used in poetry for an example—has been elaborated and refined, and, so to speak, consecrated by ages of adaptation and application in which it has been fused and blended with feeling—and it carries the life-blood of all this endeavor in its veins; and that is how, as we have said over and over again, feelings get their embodiment, and embodiments get their feeling. If you try to cut the thought and fancy loose from the body of the stuff in which it molds its pictures and poetic ideas and musical constructions, you impoverish your fancy, and arrest its growth, and reduce it to a bloodless shade. When I pronounce even a phrase so commonplace in itself as "rule, Britannia!" the actual vibrations of the sound, the bodily experience I am aware of in saying it, is alive with the history of England which passed into the words in the usage and formation of the language. Up to a certain point, language is poetry ready-made for us.

And I suppose that a great painter, in his actual handling of his brush, has present with him a sense of meaning and fitness which is one with the joy of execution, both of which the experience of a lifetime has engrained in the co-operation of his hand and eye. I take it, there is a pleasure in the brush stroke, which *is also* a sense of success in the use of the medium, and of meaning in hitting the exact effect which he wants to get. We common people have something analogous to all this, when we enjoy the too-rare sensation of having found the right word. In such "finding" there is a creative element. A word is, quite strictly speaking, not used twice in the same sense.

Croce says, indeed, that the artist has every stroke of the brush in his mind as complete before he executes it as after. The suggestion is that using the brush adds nothing to his inward or mental work of art. I think that this is false idealism. The bodily thing adds immensely to the mere idea and fancy, in wealth of qualities and connections. If we try to cut out the bodily side of our world, we shall find that we have reduced the mental side to a mere nothing.

And so, when we said that you can carry away the soul of a thing and leave its body behind, we always added that you must in doing so confer its soul upon a new and spiritualized body.[4] Your imagination must be an imagination of something, and if you refuse to give that something a definate structure, you pass from the esthetic semblance to the region of abstract thought. I have spoken of sound as physical; if this is a difficulty it is enough to call it sensuous, and sensuous in immediate connection with other physical properties and experiences. This applies both to music and to language.

All this later argument of ours, starting from the importance of medium and technique, has aimed at exhibiting in detail the double process of creation and contemplation which is implied in the esthetic attitude, and the impossibility of separating one factor of it from another. And it is the same question as that stated in other words, how a feeling can be got into an object. This is the central problem of the esthetic attitude; and, as we have seen, the best material for solving it for us who are not great artists comes from any minor experience we may have at command in which we have been aware of the outgoing of feeling into expression. We must think not merely of the picture in the gallery or the statue in the museum, but of the song and the dance, the dramatic reading, the entering into music, or the feel of the material in the minor arts, or simply, of the creative discovery of the right word.

The festal or social view of art will help us here. Suppose a tribe or a nation has won a great victory; "they are feeling big, and they want to make something big," as I have heard an expert say. That, I take it, is the rough account of the beginning of the esthetic attitude. And according to their capacity and their stage of culture, they may make a pile of their enemies' skulls, or they may build the Parthenon. The point of the esthetic attitude lies in the adequate fusion of body and soul, where the soul is a feeling, and the body its expression, without residue on either side.

—Three Lectures on Æsthetic (1915)

NOTES

1. What Bosanquet means by "feeling" and by "body-and-mind," terms which appear several times in the pages here reproduced, is made clear by the following quotation from the Preface to his book: "I must appear unfortunate in having laid so much stress on 'feeling,' just when high authorities are expressing a doubt whether the word has any meaning at all. . . . I can only say here that the first and main thing which the word suggests to me is the concernment of the whole 'body-and-mind,' as Plato puts it in building up his account of psychical unity on the single sentence, 'The man has a pain in his finger' [*Republic*, 462 D]. It is the whole man, the 'body-and-mind,' who has the pain, and in it is one, though it is referred to the finger and localized there. When a 'body-and-mind' is, as a whole, in any experience, that is the chief feature, I believe, of what we mean by feeling. Think of him as he sings, or loves, or fights. When he is one, I believe it is always through feeling, whatever distinctions may supervene upon it. That unity, at all events, is the main thing the word conveys to me."

2. See the account of Empathy, by Vernon Lee, reproduced in this volume. (Editor.)

3. This applies even to the development of song, so far as that involves a musical system.

4. This sentence refers back to an idea developed in a preceding part of Bosanquet's lecture, namely, that "the real sting of even the crudest glorification of copying is this wonder that you can carry off with you a thing's soul, and leave its body behind."

EDWARD WESTON
Seeing Photographically

Each medium of expression imposes its own limitations on the artist—limitations inherent in the tools, materials, or processes he employs. In the older art forms these natural confines are so well established they are taken for granted. We select music or dancing, sculpture or writing because we feel that within the *frame* of that particular medium we can best express whatever it is we have to say.

THE PHOTO-PAINTING STANDARD

Photography, although it has passed its hundredth birthday, has yet to attain such familiarization. In order to understand why this is so, we must examine briefly the historical background of this youngest of the graphic arts. Because the early photographers who sought to produce creative work had no tradition to guide them, they soon began to borrow a ready-made one from the painters. The conviction grew that photography was just a new kind of painting, and its exponents attempted by every means possible to make the camera produce painter-like results. This misconception was responsible for a great many horrors perpetrated in the name of art, from allegorical costume pieces to dizzying out of focus blurs.

But these alone would not have sufficed to set back the photographic clock. The real harm lay in the fact that the false standard became firmly established, so that the goal of artistic endeavor became photo-painting rather than photography. The approach adopted was so at variance with the real nature of the medium employed that each basic improvement in the process became just one more obstacle for the photo-painters to overcome. Thus the influence of the painters' tradition delayed recognition of the real creative field photography had provided. Those who should have been most concerned with discovering and exploiting the new pictorial resources were ignoring them entirely, and in their preoccupation with producing pseudo-paintings, departing more and more radically from all photographic values.

As a consequence, when we attempt to assemble the best work of the past, we most often choose examples from the work of those who were not primarily concerned with aesthetics. It is in commercial portraits from the daguerreotype era, records of the Civil War, documents of the American frontier, the work of amateurs and professionals who practiced photography for its own sake without troubling over whether or not it was art, that we find photographs that will still stand with the best of contemporary work.

But in spite of such evidence that can now be appraised with a calm, historical eye, the approach to creative work in photography today is frequently just as muddled as it was eighty years ago, and the painters' tradition still persists, as witness the use of texture screens, handwork on negatives, and ready-made rules of composition. People who wouldn't think of taking a sieve to the well to draw water fail to see the folly in taking a camera to make a painting.

Behind the photo-painter's approach lay the fixed idea that a straight photograph was purely the product of a machine and therefore not art. He developed special techniques to combat the mechanical nature of his process. In his system the negative was taken as a point of departure—a first rough impression to be "improved" by hand until the last traces of its unartistic origin had disappeared.

Perhaps if singers banded together in sufficient numbers, they could convince musicians that the sounds they produced through *their machines* could not be art because of the essentially mechanical nature of their instruments. Then the musician, profiting by the example of the photo-painter, would have his playing recorded on special discs so that he could unscramble and rescramble the sounds until he had transformed the product of a good musical instrument into a poor imitation of the human voice!

To understand why such an approach is incompatible with the logic of the medium, we must recognize the two basic factors in the photographic process that set it apart from the other graphic arts: the nature of the recording process and the nature of the image.

NATURE OF THE RECORDING PROCESS

Among all the arts photography is unique by reason of its instantaneous recording process. The sculptor, the architect, the composer all have the possibility of making changes in, or additions to, their original plans while their work is in the process of execution. A composer may build up a symphony over a long period of time; a painter may spend a lifetime working on one picture and still not consider it finished. But the photographer's recording process cannot be drawn out. Within its brief duration, no stopping or changing or reconsidering is possible. When he uncovers his lens every detail within its field of vision is registered in far less time than it takes for his own eyes to transmit a similar copy of the scene to his brain.

NATURE OF THE IMAGE

The image that is thus swiftly recorded possesses certain qualities that at once distinguish it as photographic. First there is the amazing precision of definition, especially in the recording of fine detail; and second, there is the unbroken sequence of infinitely subtle gradations from black to white. These two characteristics constitute the trade-mark of the photograph; they pertain to the mechanics of the process and cannot be duplicated by any work of the human hand.

The photographic image partakes more of the nature of a mosaic than of a drawing or painting. It contains no *lines* in the painter's sense, but is entirely made up of tiny particles. The extreme fineness of these particles gives a special tension to the image, and when that tension is destroyed— by the intrusion of handwork, by too great enlargement, by printing on a rough surface, etc.—the integrity of the photograph is destroyed.

Finally, the image is characterized by lucidity and brilliance of tone, qualities which cannot be retained if prints are made on dull-surface papers. Only a smooth, light-giving surface can reproduce satisfactorily the brilliant clarity of the photographic image.

RECORDING THE IMAGE

It is these two properties that determine the basic procedure in the photographer's approach. Since the recording process is instantaneous, and the nature of the image such that it cannot survive corrective handwork, it is obvious that *the finished print must be created in full before the film is exposed.* Until the photographer has learned to visualize his final result in advance, and to predetermine the procedures necessary to carry out that visualization, his finished work (if it be photography at all) will represent a series of lucky—or unlucky—mechanical accidents.

Hence the photographer's most important and likewise most difficult task is not learning to manage his camera, or to develop, or to print. It is learning to *see photographically*—that is, learning to see his subject matter in terms of the capacities of his tools and processes, so that he can instantaneously translate the elements and values in a scene before him into the photograph he wants to make. The photo-painters used to contend that photography could never be an art because there was in the process no means for controlling the result. Actually, the problem of learning to see photographically would be simplified if there were fewer means of control than there are.

By varying the position of his camera, his camera angle, or the focal length of his lens, the photographer can achieve an infinite number of varied compositions with a single, stationary subject. By changing the light on the subject, or by using a color filter, any or all of the values in the subject can be altered. By varying the length of exposure, the kind of emulsion, the method of developing, the photographer can vary the registering of relative values in the negative. And the relative values as registered in the negative can be further modified by allowing more or less light to affect certain parts of the image in printing. Thus, within the limits of his medium, without resorting to any method of control that is not photographic (i.e., of an optical or chemical nature), the photographer can depart from literal recording to whatever extent he chooses.

This very richness of control facilities often acts as a barrier to creative work. The fact is that relatively few photographers ever master their medium. Instead they allow the medium to master them and go on an endless squirrel cage chase from new lengths to new paper to new developer to new gadget, never staying with one piece of equipment long enough to learn its full capacities, becoming lost in a maze of technical information that is of little or no use since they don't know what to do with it.

Only long experience will enable the photographer to subordinate technical considerations to pictorial aims, but the task can be made immeasurably easier by selecting the simplest possible equipment and procedures and staying with them. Learning to see in terms of the field of one lens, the scale of one film and one paper, will accomplish a good deal more than gathering a smattering of knowledge about several different sets of tools.

The photographer must learn from the outset to regard his process as a whole. He should not be concerned with the "right exposure," the "perfect negative," etc. Such notions are mere products of advertising mythology. Rather he must learn the kind of negative necessary to produce a given kind of print, and then the kind of exposure and development necessary to produce that negative. When he knows how these needs are fulfilled for one kind of print, he must learn how to vary the process to produce other kinds of prints. Further he must learn to translate colors into their monochrome values, and learn to judge the strength and quality of light. With practice this kind of knowledge becomes intuitive; the photographer learns to see a scene or object in terms of his finished print without having to give conscious thought to the steps that will be necessary to carry it out.

SUBJECT MATTER AND COMPOSITION

So far we have been considering the mechanics of photographic seeing. Now let us see how this camera-vision applies to the fields of subject matter and composition. No sharp line can be drawn between the subject matter appropriate to photography and that more suitable to the other graphic arts. However, it is possible, on the basis of an examination of past work and our knowledge of the special properties of the medium, to suggest certain fields of endeavor that will most reward the photographer, and to indicate others that he will do well to avoid.

Even if produced with the finest photographic technique, the work of the photo-painters referred to could not have been successful. Photography is basically too honest a medium for recording superficial aspects of a subject. It searches out the actor behind the make-up and exposes the contrived, the trivial, the artificial, for what they really are. But the camera's innate honesty can hardly be considered a limitation of the medium, since it bars only that kind of subject matter that properly belongs to the painter. On the other hand it provides the photographer with a means of looking deeply into the nature of things, and presenting his subjects in terms of their basic reality. It enables him to reveal the essence of what lies before his lens with such clear insight that the beholder may find the recreated image more real and comprehensible than the actual object.

It is unfortunate, to say the least, that the tremendous capacity photography has for revealing new things in new ways should be overlooked or ignored by the majority of its exponents—but such is the case. Today the waning influence of the painter's tradition, has been replaced by what we may call *Salon Psychology*, a force that is exercising the same restraint over photographic progress by establishing false standards and discouraging any symptoms of original creative vision.

Today's photographer need not necessarily make his picture resemble a wash drawing in order to have it admitted as art, but he must abide by "the rules of composition." That is the contemporary nostrum. Now to consult rules of composition before making a picture is a little like consulting the law of gravitation before going for a walk. Such rules and laws are deduced from the accomplished fact; they are the products of reflection and after-examination, and are in no way a part of the creative impetus. When subject matter is forced to fit into preconceived patterns, there can be no freshness of vision. Following rules of composition can only lead to a tedious repetition of pictorial clichés.

Good composition is only the strongest way of seeing the subject. It cannot be taught because, like all creative effort, it is a matter of personal growth. In common with other artists the photographer wants his finished print to convey to others his own response to his subject. In the fulfillment of this aim, his greatest asset is the directness of the process he employs. But this advantage can only be retained if he simplifies his equipment and technique to the minimum necessary, and keeps his approach free from all formula, art-dogma, rules, and taboos. Only then can he be free to put his photographic sight to use in discovering and revealing the nature of the world he lives in.

—*The Complete Photographer*, Vol. 9 (1943)

DAVID WIGHT PRALL

Sensuous Elements and Esthetic Orders

What is the language of esthetics? What are its nouns or terms? What are their adjectives or relations? If it is admitted that nature and the arts give us concrete structural complexes, and that esthetic understanding is grasping the nature of these, as constituted of sensory elements in relation, then we must abstract such aspects of quality as are clearly relational, and survey the elements in the orders constituted by such relations. And since . . .

these relations are peculiar to certain qualitative aspects of sensuous material, we shall not expect to find them limited to the spatial or the temporal merely. What is characteristic of color contrasts is not only that they are spatially exhibited, but that the colors as such really do contrast, really are far apart in some aspect of color as such. And since this is not so obviously the case with tastes and smells and other sorts of sensory content like the feeling of muscular strain or of rhythmic pulse, we shall turn our attention at first to sound and color to see what we can discover in them that will explain, namely, make intelligible, the structures of music and painting.

What we do find are non-numerical, non-spatial, non-temporal serial relations constituting serial orders. But the situation is complicated by the fact that these serial orders are not of the concrete sounds, not of hearable notes nor of concrete visible colors as such, but of aspects of these which are conveniently called dimensions on the analogy to spatial dimensions. As a geometrical structure may vary in length while it remains the same in breadth, so sound can vary in pitch while it remains the same in loudness, or *vice versa*. It is such independent variation that establishes the grouping of elements or terms in all analysis, and in our case a grouping in serial orders.

A relation constituting a serial order has certain properties. If it applies to a group of elements, then every one of these elements is related to every other by this same relation. This is called the connexity of the relation. A relation is said to have connexity when between any two elements of the field whatever this relation holds. Now all sounds have pitch, and every distinct pitch is either above or below any other pitch that we may choose. Thus all sounds are related in a single order, every sound to every other sound. We might simply say that sounds are pitch-related. But the point of a serial relation is that the sense of the relation, its direction, is part of what gives it its special character. Instead of being reversible or symmetrical, above-in-pitch is asymmetrical. A relation is called asymmetrical when, if it is the relation of, say, x to y, it cannot be the relation of y to x. Thus if it is the fact that x is taller than y, this involves the fact that y is not taller than x, but shorter. If B is higher in pitch than A, A cannot be higher in pitch than B. If this seems too obvious to notice, we need only call attention to such a series as that of selected points on the surface of the earth. Chicago is related to New York by the relation west-of. And it seems at first obvious that New York cannot be related to Chicago by this same relation, but only by its converse, east-of. But if we go east from New York to Southampton and Gibraltar and Singapore and San Francisco, and keep on going east through Omaha, we shall get to Chicago by a route on which New York is west and not east of Chicago. The series of pitches is not like this. It runs out in both directions instead of coming back upon itself.

The relation higher-in-pitch-than has a further property, called transitiveness. If B is higher in pitch than A, and C is higher in pitch than B, then C is higher in pitch than A. It is clear then that every sound (and we distinguish sounds from noises by just this criterion that they have clearly perceptible pitch) lies in this single linear series of pitches, each at its own fixed point. The order is one-dimensional, to use a convenient term, and it is also not cyclical. And no sound can be removed from this given pitch order. Nor can anything enter this order except sounds. By virtue of being what we call a single sound, a note has to be at a particular pitch; and to be at a particular pitch is to be at a point fixed in the single series of all the pitches that there are.

The important fact for esthetics is not merely that a musical sound has its particular place in the single order of all pitches, but that we cannot help hearing it at this place, not too exactly always, but necessarily as relatively high or relatively low, and always as higher or lower than any other note whose pitch we can distinguish from its. The serial order is thus native to sound as such. It is intrinsic to sounds in the sense that every sound is in this serial order and that nothing that is not a sound can possibly be in this order. It is this orderliness, as we have seen, that makes concrete pitch patterns in successive notes a possibility. Sounds differing in pitch always lie near-in-pitch-to, and far-in-pitch-from, other sounds. In any given set of notes we can therefore speak of the pitch distance or interval between them, once we have established a measure for such distances. . . . We have here a basic structural possibility, the necessary condition of melody, for example, insofar as melody is pitch pattern made up of a succession of notes at distinguishable intervals from one another, and heard as at these intervals. And this quite regardless of any special set of intervals chosen, or of our having technical musical names for the intervals.

That this is more significant than the mere fact that sounds vary is plain, if we think of smells or tastes. Loudness and softness in sounds, the dimension called their intensity, may be said to be paralleled by intensity in smells or tastes; but only very roughly even for our perception. And our control over the production of smells, for example, for direct patterned presentation, is so far behind our control of sound intensities, as with our own voices or by means of instruments, as to be almost negligible. Of pitch, our control, far from being thus negligible, is both accurate and of the wide range defined by many instruments. And what in smell or taste corresponds to pitch in sound? That aspect of an odor or a taste, no doubt, that is specifically characteristic; what defines it as resinous or fragrant or putrid, or salty or sour. Even so we have rather a complex of dimensions than a relatively simple line of variation, a somewhat confusing or confused quality, more comparable to the complexity of timbre, perhaps, than to pitch. And what could be said to lie exactly, or even very roughly, as far from the odor of pine needles in one direction and some other given odor lies in another? The directions of variation here are not plain to ordinary perception. As our systematic knowledge of smells and tastes grows, we can discern order in them, and even without this they themselves furnish esthetic content as elements more or less alike, more or less contrasting. But just as there is no clear, complete order in them directly apprehended by us, which is intrinsic to their nature as pitch order is to the nature of sounds, so in composition with them we have no adequate control of structural forms or distinctly perceptible intelligible patterns.

It is plainly enough the felt pitch relations, depending upon the intrinsic order of sounds in pitch, that give to music the possibility of melody, so far, we must repeat, as melody depends on pitch for its heard character. That it does so depend characteristically will hardly be denied. A pattern of noises or of sounds of unvarying pitch, or of sounds not at recognizable intervals in pitch, we do not even call melody; and if we did, it must be granted that this would be a melody lacking the distinctive character that melodies in the more usual application of the word are defined by.

Sounds then do not merely vary; they vary systematically. They vary in the two directions of a serial order, along the line of a single dimension. . . . This allows us to select a limited number of points on the line at recognized intervals, those relations of pitch distance out of which all of our western musical compositions have been made.

But in this emphasis on pitch, we must not neglect the other dimensions of variation in sound. For these are equally conditions, though less strikingly characteristic conditions, of musical structure. The relation louder-than, with its converse, softer-than, is a relation establishing for all sounds—and for all noises, too, so that noise can enter strictly into structure—another one-dimensional serial order intrinsic to sounds and noises, found, that is, in nothing else and always present when sound or noise is present. It is the fact that noises, even with no distinguishable pitch, have their fixed places in this dimension of loudness-softness that makes them possible as integral elements in genuine musical composition. And here again there is not mere variation or mere contrast or similarity, but distinguishable degrees of similarity and contrast, distances in loudness-softness as measured along a single dimension, at one fixed point of which every noise and every sound lies by virtue of its degree of loudness, where also it is heard to lie, if we hear it at all.

For color variation the serially ordered aspects are not quite so easy to exhibit. But at least we have an adequate scheme of them, in which every aspect of variation appears to be systematically included. While the distances between variations differ according as we use one or another of the various color diagrams—the color cones of psychology or the color body of Ostwald's theoretically more regular and systematically more easily intelligible scheme—still the fact of serial orders or dimensions dictated by the intrinsic nature of color variation remains the same. There are the hues from yellow through orange and red, and on through purple and violet to blue and blue-green and green and green-yellow back to yellow. There are the lighter tints for each hue, running up into white in all of them, and the darker shades running down into black. And there are the variations for hues at all degrees of lightness and darkness from maximum saturation to the neutral grays. This gives us three convenient main dimensions of color variation, all compactly illustrated in the familiar diagram of a double cone. The neutral variations, white to black through the grays, are represented along the vertical axis from upper to lower apex; the saturated hues lie on the circumference of the double base; the pure light variations (which may be thought of as mixtures of pure saturated hues with white) run upward to white itself on the surface of the upper cone; and the pure dark variations (which may be thought of as saturated hues mixed with increasing amounts of black) correspondingly run downward on the outer lower surface to black. The points beneath the surface, inside the cone, would represent all the rest of the possibilities of color variation. In general, the downward direction is from light to dark, the direction inward to the axis is from saturation to neutral, and the variations along the circles with centers on the axis, in planes parallel to the base of the double cone, are variations in hue, at all the various intensities and various saturations. To fix convenient points on the circumference of the base of the cone, the complementaries red and green, and yellow and blue, may be placed at the extremities of diameters of this base circle, the two diameters lying at right angles to each other. Thus the circumference is quartered red to yellow, yellow to green, green to blue, and blue back to red.

The scheme fails to represent accurately some of the relative distances as measured in terms of felt degrees of similarity and contrast. Full saturated yellow is not for our vision so far from white as any of the other full hues; and the hues on the red-yellow sector are brighter and warmer than those on the blue-green sector. Moreover, it is obvious that any line through the cone at any angle will give a set of variations along a dimension that constitutes a series just as clearly as the sets of variations along the traditionally selected three lines. But these three are those that have been conventionally named, and they serve our purposes well enough. For all that we wish to establish is that every color variation is to be found somewhere in the scheme, and that therefore every color variation lies at a determinately felt distance from others along any single dimension chosen.

But it will be clear at once that the selection of scales of color variation is guided by relations peculiar to color and not strictly parallel to the relations that make up musical scales. For in color, although hue is perhaps fundamentally characteristic, variations in hue are no more significant for color composition, no more characteristic of color design, than variations of saturation or of brightness. The order of the hues is cyclical, too, while the orders of the variations in saturation and brightness are not. In sound the two serial orders, that of pitch and that of loudness, are like these latter in being non-cyclical. But while notes are regularly named by their pitch—an indication of the greater significance of pitch than of loudness to musical pattern—colors are named sometimes for their hue, sometimes for their other aspects, or for at least two of their aspects in combination. A name like brown is nowhere applicable on the main lines of variation that we have indicated. Nor is brown a "hue." Its "hue" is orange, and yet the name orange does not fit it at all. In fact, of course, it is a name covering a range in the sector about orange, which depends for its characteristic concrete quality largely on being not a saturated color. The fact that we so often speak of browns and grays together as contrasted with reds and greens and yellows and blues, shows how the feeling of its lack of saturation has been taken as its distinguishing characteristic without reference explicitly to any scheme. But the ordinary scheme definitely includes it, and its name, instead of removing it from the scheme, fairly indicates its place there, provided we attend to its characteristic meaning and not merely to the name itself, which might lead us to think of it as one among the other hues.

But another point occurs at once. A pitch pattern is easily recognizable as an aspect of melodic structure and hence of music. But pictures are not so regularly or so readily apprehended as being color patterns. In fact, in much of what we think of under the term painting, it is spatial design not color design that is the characteristic distinction. The parallel with music is still clear, though obviously not at all adequate. As colors are spread over surfaces, so notes are extended through time, and rhythm may enter into melody as distinctly as pitch itself, though a definite rhythmic beat may be entirely absent, as in plain song. At any rate, it is perfectly clear that painting has not traditionally been sheer color design to any such degree as that in which musical composition has been pitch pattern; and although temporal spread is as necessary a condition of music as spatial spread is of painting, it seems at least fair to say that the relative emphasis on the intrinsic nature of sound in music as distinguished from its one-dimensional extension in time, is greater than the relative emphasis on color as such as distinguished from spatial design in painting.

In both cases, however, it is clear not only that the qualitative orders require either spatial or temporal extension of their elements in order to be concretely present to an organism, but also that the spatial and temporal aspects of the concrete content are themselves structural.

Like pitch, time, whatever else it may be, is an order. That space is an order we all realize from an elementary acquaintance with geometry. Two lines on a surface cannot remain merely separate lines. They are necessarily related as parallel to each other or at an angle, and at a determinate angle. And these intrinsic properties of all spatial elements lend themselves to structure, carry structure in their very nature. But without visually perceptible, that is to say colored, area, no spatial pattern can be sensuously present. Even figures in geometry must be black against white or gray if they are to be seen. So that the qualitative elements of our intrinsic qualitative orders are as necessary to the sensuous presentation of spatial character as spatial character is to the presentation of elements of color, or duration and succession in a time order to the presentation of elements of sound.

Two different orders must combine, so to speak, if we are to have any concrete pattern at all. Philosophically this was recognized by Plato in the notion of the communication of the categories. Since every sound in order to be heard, and every color in order to be seen, must be more than pitch and loudness in the one case, more than hue and saturation and brightness in the other, spatial and temporal structure and the orders intrinsic to space and time are as essential to concrete esthetic surface as what we usually call sensuous content as *distinguished* from spatio-temporal structure. Since, however, we can conceive color and sound abstractly in qualitative orders neither spatial nor temporal, this distinction between so-called content and formal structure lies within concrete content. In fact the distinction of form from matter or of structure from content is entirely relative. We never have the one without the other in actuality. They are both abstractions. And just as this is nothing derogatory to them, since it is true of all the aspects of concretely experienced data, so it is fairly absurd to speak as if qualitative elements and orders were less fundamentally significant in composition than spatial and temporal elements and forms.

Our vastly greater systematization of what we have distinguished by abstraction of the features of the spatial and temporal aspects of our world in mathematics and science inclines us to neglect the significance, even for the arts, of the serial qualitative orders intrinsic to color and sound. We have used mathematical and geometrical abstractions so much that the elements among which these abstract relations subsist have literally vanished, as points have become by definition the vanishing points of lines, and lines the vanishing points or disappearing boundaries between intersecting planes. Space and time have become purely formal as we have realized their abstractness in systematic analysis. There are no real but only nominal elements of space and time. But it takes very little meditation on the nature of pitch and hue to see that once we abstract their formal nature in the same way from sound and color, these latter become purely formal too. It is the lack of full attention to what we mean by color contrast itself, as distinguished from the spatial presentation of such contrast, that makes us unwilling to admit that color as such has no extension, but is only an abstract formal scheme, just as pitch is a purely formal continuum, which is one of the analytical aspects of sound. And adequate analysis would resolve sound totally into such formal aspects, if we treated sound as we do space, and dropped out of our account of it its feeling in concrete presentation.

Thus our scheme of esthetic analysis may be accused indifferently of formalizing esthetics, or of reducing all the formal aspects of art and nature to sensuous content. The point is that any content concretely presented, anything experienced directly, is qualitative; that no concrete quality is absolutely simple, that all the surface of the experienced world as clearly apprehended consists, upon analysis, of elements intrinsically ordered and also ordered spatially and temporally. The temporal cannot be present except as it attaches itself to what is qualitatively and spatially extended any more than the qualitative can be altogether unenduring. What is extended in no way at all is nothing. Our purest spiritual longings are the longings of an organism, and they are inconceivable as concretely existent in separation from it. Only in abstraction are they clearly conceivable and at all intelligible, just as color contrast or pitch pattern is conceivable in abstraction from the concrete. Thinking about things in order to know them involves just such abstracting; and it appears to be our good fortune to live in a time when men have penetrated far enough into the nature of logic to allow analysis to be clearly discerned as constituted of the forms which such abstracting makes out. All science involves the discriminating of elements and relations necessary to generality and systematization. The established sciences are the fields where this process has developed sufficiently to give us confidence in the usefulness and validity of the method.

One further point seems required here if we are to be sure that we have not misplaced our emphasis on qualitative orders. We have spoken of these orders as intrinsic to sound and intrinsic to color. We have spoken of spatial and temporal orders as intrinsic to elements that are spatial and temporal. And we have noticed that for actual concretely apparent surfaces for ear and eye we require spatio-temporal structure as well as qualitative structure. A note must have duration just as truly as it must have pitch or timbre; and spatial and temporal structures can appear only as qualitied. We keep "quality" as a term for the very purpose of distinguishing such aspects of color and sound from extensional aspects whether spatial or temporal.

Why, then, are the qualitative orders any more intrinsic to sound and color than spatial or temporal order? And why, if we are to be rigorous, are temporal and spatial order any more intrinsic to spatial and temporal elements than the qualitative orders, since only as qualitied and hence as involving qualitative orders, can either spatial or temporal elements appear concretely? That the answer is in the end a matter of definition must be plain. But good definitions serve honest purposes, and we do not distinguish and define usefully where there is no significant difference. The difference in our case is, however, easy to indicate. Every sound has a pitch and lies in the pitch order, as every color has brightness and saturation and hue and lies in these orders. Also every sound has temporal duration and every color, spatial extension. But everything in the world has duration, while nothing but sound has pitch, as nothing in the world but sound has loudness in the specific use of the word as here applied. Vast numbers of things in the world have spatial extension, while nothing in the world but color has hue or what is meant by brightness or darkness as these terms apply to color. What we are doing is simply to limit the application of the terms that we use to abstract aspects of experience in a way that appears at once to be unambiguous and to serve the purposes of the sort of knowledge that we seek by indicating relevant distinctions for esthetics. . . .

Thus our analytical base is outlined. The elements in it are elements of sensuous content intrinsically ordered, elements that are found by means of discrimination in the concrete, but ordered and conceived in abstract series. The serial orders are of at least two sorts, qualitative and spatio-temporal, the former intrinsic to certain qualities, the latter to space-time configurations. And from their intrinsic orders elements cannot be removed. A note carries with it its position in the pitch series into any composition, and maintains its determinate distance in pitch from notes of other pitch placed near or far from it in any temporal succession of notes. In the same way any configuration in space or time simply exhibits selected parts out of the ordered manifolds that constitute the nature of space and time. And as qualities cannot appear concretely except within spatio-temporal structure, so spatial and temporal configurations require for concrete exhibition qualitative content. The qualitative orders and the spatio-temporal orders are equally abstract, but they are clearly distinct in nature, and while they are dependent reciprocally for concrete exhibition, they are independently variable.

The possibilities for structure are thus infinite; and the arts have selected out of these infinite possibilities a relatively limited number of determinate modes or fundamental patterns on the basis of which works of art have been constructed. Moreover, artists have had to consider many non-esthetic aspects of the physical media that are the bearers of esthetic form and quality. And esthetics is forced into considering such media, and various non-esthetic purposes, if for no other reason than to distinguish practical technique and practical knowledge of structural materials from what is strictly esthetic knowledge of esthetic structures and their constituents as esthetic surface. The relatively simple analytical basis just outlined is no doubt fundamental and even necessary to esthetic comprehension. But we shall have to account on non-esthetic grounds for a great deal that would otherwise remain inexplicable. Our present need is to exhibit those natural conditions that have set up for us ordered and limited selections of elements and basic patterns for composition with these elements.

—Aesthetic Analysis (1936)

CHAPTER
8
Form

CLIVE BELL: *Significant Form*
A. C. BRADLEY: *Poetry for Poetry's Sake*
DE WITT H. PARKER: *The Problem of Esthetic Form*
HORATIO GREENOUGH: *Structure and Organization*
MEYER SCHAPIRO: *Style*

The work of art is an organized complex of sensuous and expressive elements, and its organization is its form. Recent art and esthetics have tended to emphasize formal values, but estheticians have disagreed as to the meaning of form. A number of writers have interpreted form as sheer abstract design, minimizing or excluding connotations and representations. A similar interpretation, with particular reference to the visual arts, was formulated by the famous English critics Roger Fry (1886–1934) and Clive Bell (1881–1964).

Their ideas were greatly influenced by "the Bloomsbury circle," a group of intimate friends, including the philosopher G. E. Moore, the economist John Maynard Keynes, and the novelist Virginia Woolf. A close study will reveal the indebtedness of Fry and Bell to the ideas of Moore, especially to the remarks about esthetic emotion and formal beauty in his *Principia Ethica* (1903) and the contention that goodness or beauty is a unique and "non-natural" quality (refer to Moore's remarks *Principia Ethica* about the "naturalistic fallacy"). It is not surprising that Bell and Fry, thus linked together, came to much the same conclusions. Although Fry had the more subtle and complex theory of art, Bell was the more uncompromising in his espousal of formalism. I shall quote the latter as the more challenging of the two.

Bell agrees with Véron and Tolstoy that art is emotional, but he thinks that there is a peculiarly esthetic emotion, quite different from the emotions of ordinary life, that is directed to "significant form." By significant form he means a unique quality resulting from certain combinations of lines, colors, and spatial elements. The representation of space is necessary to achieve certain kinds of visual form, but any other kind of representation is esthetically irrelevant. Like Hanslick and Gurney in musical esthetics, Bell insists upon the "isolated" character of esthetic experience and works of art.

What, then, does he mean by the word "significant"? The significance in question, it would appear, consists of the expression of the artist's emotion, but the only emotion that Bell considers legitimate in art—the peculiarly "esthetic" emotion—is aroused by the vision of significant form. He suggests, however, a possible escape from the circularity of this definition. Art may be a revelation, he says, of the universal "rhythm of reality." But since he insists that the significance of art "is unrelated to the significance of life," this so-called "metaphysical hypothesis" remains extremely vague. Perhaps we may interpret it as meaning that the artist emulates, without definitely imitating, the structural harmonies of his natural environment, such as the pattern of a sea shell or the floret of a sunflower.

The question naturally arises whether Bell extended his formalist theory to the nonvisual arts. He indicates that his doctrine is applicable to nonprogrammatic music, and indeed he finds in pure music the very ideal of art. But in a later essay he declares that literature is an exception:

> I can see no formal beauty worth speaking of in Balzac or Dickens. . . . Now a picture is quite valueless without formal beauty, . . . and he who has no sense of this sort of beauty will get nothing worth having from visual art. The fact is, subject and the overtones emanating from it, wit, pathos, drama, criticism, didacticism even—qualities which in painting count for little or nothing—do seem to be the essence of literature. . . . A reasonable explanation seems to be that literature is one thing, painting and music another.[1]

This statement was not Bell's final word. In a little book on *Proust* (1928), he declared that "the supreme masterpieces" of literature "derive their splendor, their supernatural power, not from flashes of insight, nor yet from characterization, nor from an understanding of the human heart even, but from *form*—I use the word in its richest sense, I mean the thing that artists create, their expression. Whether you call it "significant form or something else, the supreme quality in art is formal; it has to do with order, sequence, movement and shape."[2]

A less isolationist theory was expressed by Andrew Cecil Bradley (1851–1935), a distinguished critic and professor of poetry at Oxford University. Although he primarily discussed form and content in poetry, his conception of form can be extended to all the arts.

He agrees with Bell that works of art have their own *intrinsic* value and significance, and that art neither *is* life nor a copy of it. But he does not discount the importance of subject matter. He admits that the subject as such, apart from artistic treatment, has no esthetic value, but he thinks that a great subject may be the focus that brings to the artist's imagination a great artistic vision. He also rejects the antithesis between form and content. In the well-composed poem or work of art, content and form are not two separate things, but one thing regarded from two different points of view. The content is the elements-in-relation; the form is the relations-among-the-elements; and the total work is the organic unity of relational elements. Content and form, *separately* conceived, are not in the poem. It follows that the content cannot be paraphrased—that a poem, for example, cannot *really* be translated. For we have in the poem a form-meaning or a meaning-in-form, and to separate the meaning from the form is to mutilate it.

A substantially similar point of view is expressed by DeWitt Henry Parker (1885–1949), professor of philosophy at the University of Michigan, who contends that the all-embracing principle of form—its very essence and meaning—is organic unity. This consists of completeness without redundancy, harmony without the sacrifice of richness, achieved in an experience isolated and self-sufficient. All other principles of form—theme, thematic variation, balance, rhythm, hierarchy, and evolution—serve this one master principle. Form thus conceived is not limited to mere design or pattern, such as the abstract relation of colors or sounds apart from their suggestiveness or dramatic import. On the contrary, it is the organization of all its elements—pure sensuous materials, representations, and connotations—into a single and inclusive experience. Thus, form is no independent thing, imposed as from the outside upon an independent subject matter, but is the perfectly natural and inevitable development of expression.

The latter part of Parker's discussion is an amplification of his theory that art is a kind of wish-fulfillment. He advances beyond Freud, who said little about the formal side of art, in demonstrating that the design of a beautiful work of art embodies the same principles as the organization of a happy life and that, consequently, the form of the good and the form of the beautiful are the same.

It is not the formal identity of the good and the beautiful but of the beautiful and the useful that is the leading principle of the "functionalist esthetics" of modern architecture and industrial design. This principle is no recent discovery; it was enunciated by Vitruvius in ancient Rome and it was practiced by primitive man long before any esthetic theory was formulated. But it has often been violated or forgotten; and it has been, in a sense, rediscovered by such modern architects and designers as Le Corbusier (1887–1965) and Moholy-Nagy (1895–1946).

The great prophet in this revival of functionalism was Horatio Greenough (1805–1852)—a worthy contemporary of Emerson and Thoreau. Leaving the United States before he received his Harvard diploma, Greenough set up a studio in Florence and practiced the art of sculpture for the next twenty-two years. Then he returned and surprised the people of Boston by praising the clipper ship as a work of art. "*There* is something," he exclaimed, "I should not be ashamed to show Phidias!" In shipbuilding the form is determined by the function: The adaptation to wind and wave results in harmony and grace. So should it be in architecture. The rule must be "to plant a building firmly on the ground," that is, to adapt its design to the site; then, "instead of forcing the functions of every sort of building into one general form, without reference to the inner distribution, let us begin from the heart as a nucleus, and *work outward*," achieving "the *external expression* of the *inward functions* of the building." All meaningless, inorganic decoration should be stripped away: There must be "the entire and immediate banishment of all makeshift and make-believe."

To his countrymen, Greenough, a lover of Greek architecture, gives this advice:

The fundamental laws of building found at the basis of every style of architecture must be the basis of ours. The adaptation of the forms and magnitude of structures to the climate they are exposed to, and the offices for which they are intended, teaches us to study our own varied wants in these respects. The harmony of their ornaments with the nature that they embellished, and the institutions from which they sprang, calls on us to do the like justice to our country, our government, and our faith. . . . So the American builder by a truly philosophic investigation of ancient art will learn of the Greeks to be American. . . . I contend for Greek principles, not Greek things. . . . The men who have reduced locomotion to its simplest elements, in the trotting wagon and the yacht *America*, are nearer to Athens at this moment than they who would bend the Greek temple to every use.

In other words, we should respect the eternal laws of building but plagiarize nothing from the past.

Greenough breaks down any sharp distinction between the applied and the fine arts, and insists that a machine should be a thing of beauty: "If we compare the form of a newly invented machine with the perfected type of the same instrument, we observe, as we trace it through the phases of improvement, how weight is shaken off where strength is less needed, how functions are made to approach without impeding each other, how straight becomes curved, and the curve is straightened, till the straggling and cumbersome machine becomes the compact, effective, and beautiful engine." Thus the fundamental principle of sound design, according to Greenough, whether it be in architecture or in the industrial arts, is a stripping down to essentials and an adaptation of form to function.

The concept of style applies to all the arts, functionalist and nonfunctionalist alike, and is the historical adaptation of the idea of form, marking off periods and phases in the development of the arts. Hence, it is of particular concern to the art historian. The meaning of style is elucidated in the following selection from Meyer Schapiro (1904–   ), professor of fine arts and archeology at Columbia University and author of such important works as *Van Gogh* (1950) and *Cézanne* (1952). Style, as a persistent form and manner of expression, may be exhibited by an individual, group, civilization, or historical period. Although such an inclusive term suffers from vagueness, Schapiro's discussion is admirably clear and precise. I have reproduced less than half of his essay; the remaining part is devoted to an erudite interpretation of the causes and morphology of styles, reviewing the theories of Wölfflin, Riegl, and others. I know of no better intoduction to the subject of style.

NOTES

1. "The 'Difference' of Literature," *New Republic*, Vol. 33 (Nov. 29, 1922), pp. 18–19.

2. *Proust*, London. 1928, p. 67.

CLIVE BELL

Significant Form

I THE ESTHETIC HYPOTHESIS

The starting-point for all systems of esthetics must be the personal experience of a peculiar emotion. The objects that provoke this emotion we call works of art. All sensitive people agree that there is a peculiar emotion provoked by works of art. I do not mean, of course, that all works provoke the same emotion. On the contrary, every work produces a different emotion. But all these emotions are recognizably the same in kind; so far, at any rate, the best opinion is on my side. That there is a particular kind of emotion provoked by works of visual art, and that this emotion is provoked by every kind of visual art, by pictures, sculptures, buildings, pots, carvings, textiles, etc., is not disputed, I think, by any one capable of feeling it. This emotion is called the esthetic emotion; and if we can discover some quality common and peculiar to all the objects that provoke it, we shall have solved what I take to be the central problem of esthetics. We shall have discovered the essential quality in a work of art, the quality that distinguishes works of art from all other classes of objects.

For either all works of visual art have some common quality, or when we speak of "works of art" we gibber. Every one speaks of "art," making a mental classification by which he distinguishes the class "works of art" from all other classes. What is the justification of this classification? What is the quality common and peculiar to all members of this class? Whatever it be, no doubt it is often found in company with other qualities; but they are adventitious—it is essential. There must be some one quality without which a work of art cannot exist; possessing which, in the least degree, no work is altogether worthless. What is this quality? What quality is shared by all objects that provoke our esthetic emotions? What quality is common to Sta. Sophia and the windows at Chartres, Mexican sculpture, a Persian bowl, Chinese carpets, Giotto's frescoes at Padua, and the masterpieces of Poussin, Piero della Francesca, and Cézanne? Only one answer seems possible—significant form. In each, lines and colors combined in a particular way, certain forms and relations of forms, stir our esthetic emotions. These relations and combinations of lines and colors, these esthetically moving forms, I call "Significant Form"; and "Significant Form" is the one quality common to all works of visual art.

At this point it may be objected that I am making esthetics a purely subjective business, since my only data are personal experiences of a particular emotion. It will be said that the objects that provoke this emotion vary with each individual, and that therefore a system of esthetics can have no objective validity. It must be replied that any system of esthetics which pretends to be based on some objective truth is so palpably ridiculous as not to be worth discussing. We have no other means of recognizing a work of art than our feeling for it. The objects that provoke esthetic emotion vary with each individual. Esthetic judgments are, as the saying goes, matters of taste; and about tastes, as every one is proud to admit, there is no disputing.

A good critic may be able to make me see in a picture that had left me cold things that I had overlooked, till at last, receiving the esthetic emotion, I recognize it as a work of art. To be continually pointing out those parts, the sum, or rather the combination, of which unite to produce significant form, is the function of criticism. But it is useless for a critic to tell me that something is a work of art; he must make me feel it for myself. This he can do only by making me see; he must get at my emotions through my eyes. Unless he can make me see something that moves me, he cannot force my emotions. I have no right to consider anything a work of art to which I cannot react emotionally; and I have no right to look for the essential quality in anything that I have not *felt* to be a work of art. The critic can affect my esthetic theories only by affecting my esthetic experience. All systems of esthetics must be based on personal experience—that is to say, they must be subjective.

Yet, though all esthetic theories must be based on esthetic judgments, and ultimately all esthetic judgments must be matters of personal taste, it would be rash to assert that no theory of esthetics can have general validity. For, though A, B, C, D are the works that move me, and A, D, E, F the works that move you, it may well be that x is the only quality believed by either of us to be common to all the works in his list. We may all agree about esthetics, and yet differ about particular works of art. We may differ as to the presence or absence of the quality x. My immediate object will be to show that significant form is the only quality common and peculiar to all the works of visual art that move me; and I will ask those whose esthetic experience does not tally with mine to see whether this quality is not also, in their judgment, common to all works that move them, and whether they can discover any other quality of which the same can be said. . . .

"Are you forgetting about color?" some one inquires. Certainly not; my term "significant form" included combinations of lines and of colors. The distinction between form and color is an unreal one; you cannot conceive a colorless line or a colorless space; neither can you conceive a formless relation of colors. In a black and white drawing the spaces are all white and all are bounded by black lines; in most oil paintings the spaces are multi-colored and so are the boundaries; you cannot imagine a boundary line without any content, or a content without a boundary line. Therefore, when I speak of significant form, I mean a combination of lines and colors (counting white and black as colors) that moves me esthetically.

Some people may be surprised at my not having called this "beauty." Of course, to those who define beauty as "combinations of lines and colors that provoke esthetic emotion," I willingly concede the right of substituting their word for mine. But most of us, however strict we may be, are apt to apply the epithet "beautiful" to objects that do not provoke that peculiar emotion produced by works of art. Every one, I suspect, has called a butterfly or a flower beautiful. Does any one feel the same kind of emotion for a butterfly or a flower that he feels for a cathedral or a picture? Surely, it is not what I call an esthetic emotion that most of us feel, generally, for natural beauty. I shall suggest, later, that some people may, occasionally, see in nature what we see in art, and feel for her an esthetic emotion; but I am satisfied that, as a rule, most people feel a very different kind of emotion for birds and flowers and the wings of butterflies from that which they feel for pictures, pots, temples, and statues. Why these beautiful things do not move us as works of art move is another, and not an esthetic, question. For our immediate purpose we have to discover only what quality is common to objects that do move us as works of art. In the last part of this chapter, when I try to answer the question—"Why are we so profoundly moved by some combinations of lines and colors?" I shall hope to offer an acceptable explanation of why we are less profoundly moved by others.

Since we call a quality that does not raise the characteristic esthetic emotion "Beauty," it would be misleading to call by the same name the quality that does. To make "beauty" the object of the esthetic emotion, we must give to the word an over-strict and unfamiliar definition. Every one sometimes uses "beauty" in an unesthetic sense; most people habitually do so. To every one, except perhaps here and there an occasional esthete, the commonest sense of the word is unesthetic. Of its grosser abuse, patent in our chatter about "beautiful huntin' " and "beautiful shootin'," I need not take account; it would be open to the precious to reply that they never do so abuse it. Besides, here there is no danger of confusion between the esthetic and the non-esthetic use; but when we speak of a beautiful woman there is. When a ordinary man speaks of a beautiful woman he certainly does not mean only that she moves him esthetically; but when an artist calls a withered old hag beautiful he may sometimes mean what he means when he calls a battered torso beautiful. The ordinary man, if he be also a man of taste, will call the battered torso beautiful, but he will not call a withered hag beautiful because, in the matter of women, it is not to the esthetic quality that the hag may possess, but to some other quality that he assigns the epithet. Indeed, most of us never dream of going for esthetic emotions to human beings, from whom we ask something very different. This "something," when we find it in a young woman, we are apt to call "beauty." We live in a nice age. With the man-in-the-street "beautiful" is more often than not synonymous with "desirable"; the word does not necessarily connote any esthetic reaction whatever, and I am tempted to believe that in the minds of many the sexual flavor of the word is stronger than the esthetic. I have noticed a consistency in those to whom the most beautiful thing in the world is a beautiful woman, and the next most beautiful thing a picture of one. The confusion between esthetic and sensual beauty is not in their case so great as might be supposed. Perhaps there is none; for perhaps they have never had an esthetic emotion to confuse with their other emotions. The art that they call "beautiful" is generally closely related to the women. A beautiful picture is a photograph of a pretty girl; beautiful music, the music that provokes emotions similar to those provoked by young ladies in musical farces; and beautiful poetry, the poetry that recalls the same emotions felt, twenty years earlier, for the rector's daughter. Clearly the word "beauty" is used to connote the objects of quite distinguishable emotions, and that is a reason for not employing a term which would land me inevitably in confusions and misunderstandings with my readers.

On the other hand, with those who judge it more exact to call these combinations and arrangements of form that provoke our esthetic emotions, not "significant form," but "significant relations of form," and then try to make the best of two worlds, the esthetic and the metaphysical, by calling these relations "rhythm," I have no quarrel whatever. Having made it clear that by "significant form" I mean arrangements and combinations that move us in a particular way, I willingly join hands with those who prefer to give a different name to the same thing.

The hypothesis that significant form is the essential quality in a work of art has at least one merit denied to many more famous and more striking—it does help to explain things. We are all familiar with pictures that interest us and excite our admiration, but do not move us as works of art. To this class belongs what I call "Descriptive Painting"—that is, painting in which forms are used not as objects of emotion, but as means of suggesting emotion or conveying information. Portraits of psychological and historical value, topographical works, pictures that tell stories and suggest situations, illustrations of all sorts, belong to this class. That we all recognize the distinction is clear, for who has not said that such and such a drawing was excellent as illustration, but as a work of art worthless? Of course many descriptive pictures possess, amongst other qualities, formal significance, and are therefore works of art: but many more do not. They interest us; they may move us too in a hundred different ways, but they do not move us esthetically. According to my hypothesis they are not works of art. They leave untouched our esthetic emotions because it is not their forms but the ideas or information suggested or conveyed by their forms that affect us. . . .

Let no one imagine that representation is bad in itself; a realistic form may be as significant, in its place as part of the design, as an abstract. But if a representative form has value, it is as form, not as representation. The representative element in a work of art may or may not be harmful; always it is irrelevant. For, to appreciate a work of art we need bring with us nothing from life, no knowledge of its ideas and affairs, no familiarity with its emotions. Art transports us from the world of man's activity to a world of esthetic exaltation. For a moment we are shut off from human interests; our anticipations and memories are arrested; we are lifted above the stream of life. The pure mathematician rapt in his studies knows a state of mind which I take to be similar, if not identical. He feels an emotion for his speculations which arises from no perceived relation between them and the lives of men, but springs, inhuman or super-human, from the heart of an abstract science. I wonder, sometimes, whether the appreciators of art and of mathematical solutions are not even more closely allied. Before we feel an esthetic emotion for a combination of forms, do we not perceive intellectually the rightness and necessity of the combination? If we do, it would explain the fact that passing rapidly through a room we recognize a picture to be good, although we cannot say that it has provoked much emotion. We seem to have recognized intellectually the rightness of its forms without staying to fix our attention, and collect, as it were, their emotional significance. If this were so, it would be permissible to inquire whether it was the forms themselves or our perception of their rightness and necessity that caused esthetic emotion. But I do not think I need linger to discuss the matter here. I have been inquiring why certain combinations of forms move us; I should not have traveled by other roads had I enquired, instead, why certain combinations are perceived to be right and necessary, and why our perception of their rightness and necessity is moving. What I have to say is this: the rapt philosopher, and he who contemplates a work of art, inhabit a world with an intense and peculiar significance of its own; that significance is unrelated to the significance of life. In this world the emotions of life find no place. It is a world with emotions of its own.

To appreciate a work of art we need bring with us nothing but a sense of form and color and a knowledge of three-dimensional space. That bit of knowledge, I admit, is essential to the appreciation of many great works, since many of the most moving forms ever created are in three dimensions. To see a cube or a rhomboid as a flat pattern is to lower its significance, and a sense of three-dimensional space is essential to the full appreciation of most architectural forms. Pictures which would be insignificant if we saw them as flat patterns are profoundly moving because, in fact, we see them as related planes. If the representation of three-dimensional space is to be called "representation," then I agree that there is one kind of representation which is not irrelevant. Also, I agree that along with our feeling for line and color we must bring with us our knowledge of space if we are to make the most of every kind of form. Nevertheless, there are mangificent designs to an appreciation of which this knowledge is not necessary: so, though it is not irrelevant to the appreciation of some works of art it is not essential to the appreciation of all. What we must say is that the representation of three-dimensional space is neither irrelevant nor essential to all art, and that every other sort of representation is irrelevant.

That there is an irrelevant representative or descriptive element in many great works of art is not in the least surprising. Why it is not surprising I shall try to show elsewhere. Representation is not of necessity baneful, and highly realistic forms may be extremely significant. Very often, however, representation is a sign of weakness in an artist. A painter too feeble to create forms that provoke more than a little esthetic emotion will try to eke that little out by suggesting the emotions of life. To evoke the emotions of life he must use representation. Thus a man will paint an execution, and, fearing to miss with his first barrel of significant form, will try to hit with his second by raising an emotion of fear or pity. But if in the artist an inclination to play upon the emotions of life is often the sign of a flickering inspiration, in the spectator a tendency to seek, behind form, the emotions of life is a sign of defective sensibility always. It means that his esthetic emotions are weak or, at any rate, imperfect. Before a work of art people who feel little or no emotion for pure form find themselves at a loss. They are deaf men at a concert. They know that they are in the presence of something great, but they lack the power of apprehending it. They know that they ought to feel for it a tremendous emotion, but it happens that the particular kind of emotion it can raise is one that they can feel hardly or not at all. And so they read into the forms of the work those facts and ideas for which they are capable of feeling emotion, and feel for them the emotions that they can feel—the ordinary emotions of life. When confronted by a picture, instinctively they refer back its forms to the world from which they came. They treat created form as though it were imitated form, a picture as though it were a photograph. Instead of going out on the stream of art into a new world of esthetic experience, they turn a sharp corner and come straight home to the world of human interests. For them the significance of a work of art depends on what they bring to it; no new thing is added to their lives, only the old material is stirred. A good work of visual art carries a person who is capable of appreciating it out of life into ecstasy: to use art as a means to the emotions of life is to use a telescope for reading the news. You will notice that people who cannot feel pure esthetic emotions remember pictures by their subjects; whereas people who can, as often as not, have no idea what the subject of a picture is. They have never noticed the representative element, and so when they discuss pictures they talk about the shapes of forms and the relations and quantities of colors. Often they can tell by the quality of a single line whether or no a man is a good artist. They are concerned only with lines and colors, their relations and quantities and qualities; but from these they win an emotion more profound and far more sublime than any that can be given by the description of facts and ideas.

This last sentence has a very confident ring—over-confident, some may think. Perhaps I shall be able to justify it, and make my meaning clearer too, if I give an account of my own feelings about music. I am not really musical. I do not understand music well. I find musical form exceedingly difficult to apprehend, and I am sure that the profounder subtleties of harmony and rhythm more often than not escape me. The form of a musical composition must be simple indeed if I am to grasp it honestly. My opinion about music is not worth having. Yet, sometimes, at a concert, though my appreciation of the music is limited and humble, it is pure. Sometimes, though I have a poor understanding, I have a clean palate. Consequently, when I am feeling bright and clear and intent, at the beginning of a concert for instance, when something that I can grasp is being played, I get from music that pure esthetic emotion that I get from visual art. It is less intense, and the rapture is evanescent; I understand music too ill for music to transport me far into the world of pure esthetic ecstasy. But at moments I do appreciate music as pure musical form, as sounds combined according to the laws of a mysterious necessity, as pure art with a tremendous significance of its own and no relation whatever to the significance of life; and in those moments I lose myself in that infinitely sublime state of mind to which pure visual form transports me. How inferior is my normal state of mind at a concert. Tired or perplexed, I let slip my sense of form, my esthetic emotion collapses, and I begin weaving into the harmonies, that I cannot grasp, the ideas of life. Incapable of feeling the austere emotions of art, I begin to read into the musical forms human emotions of terror and mystery, love and hate, and spend the minutes, pleasantly enough, in a world of turbid and inferior feeling. At such times, were the grossest pieces of onomatopoeic representation—the song of a bird, the galloping of horses, the cries of children, or the laughing of demons—to be introduced into the symphony, I should not be offended. Very likely I should be pleased; they would afford new points of departure for new trains of romantic feeling or heroic thought. I know very well what has happened. I have been using art as a means to the emotions of life and reading into it the ideas of life. I have been cutting blocks with a razor. I have tumbled from the superb peaks of esthetic exaltation to the snug foothills of warm humanity. It is a jolly country. No one need be ashamed of enjoying himself there. Only no one who has ever been on the heights can help feeling a little crestfallen in the cozy valleys. And let no one imagine, because he has made merry in the warm tilth and quaint nooks of romance, that he can even guess at the austere and thrilling raptures of those who have climbed the cold, white peaks of art.

About music most people are as willing to be humble as I am. If they cannot grasp musical form and win from it a pure esthetic emotion, they confess that they understand music imperfectly or not at all. They recognize quite clearly that there is a difference between the feeling of the musician for pure music and that of the cheerful concert-goer for what music suggests. The latter enjoys his own emotions, as he has every right to do, and recognizes their inferiority. Unfortunately, people are apt to be less modest about their powers of appreciating visual art. Every one is inclined to believe that out of pictures, at any rate, he can get all that there is to be got; every one is ready to cry "humbug" and "impostor" at those who say that more can be had. The good faith of people who feel pure esthetic emotions is called in question by those who have never felt anything of the sort. It is the prevalence of the representative element, I suppose, that makes the man in the street so sure that he knows a good picture when he sees one. For I have noticed that in matters of architecture, pottery, textiles, etc., ignorance and ineptitude are more willing to defer to the opinions of those who have been blest with peculiar sensibility. It is a pity that cultivated and intelligent men and women cannot be induced to believe that a great gift of esthetic appreciation is at least as rare in visual as in musical art. A comparison of my own experience in both has enabled me to discriminate very clearly between pure and impure appreciation. Is it too much to ask that others should be as honest about their feelings for pictures as I have been about mine for music? For I am certain that most of those who visit galleries do feel very much what I feel at concerts. They have their moments of pure ecstasy; but the moments are short and unsure. Soon they fall back into the world of human interests and feel emotions, good no doubt, but inferior. I do not dream of saying that what they get from art is bad or nugatory; I say that they do not get the best that art can give. I do not say that they cannot understand art; rather I say that they cannot understand the state of mind of those who understand it best. I do not say that art means nothing or little to them; I say they miss its full significance. I do not suggest for one moment that their appreciation of art is a thing to be ashamed of; the majority of the charming and intelligent people with whom I am acquainted appreciate visual art impurely; and, by the way, the appreciation of almost all great writers has been impure. But provided that there be some fraction of pure esthetic emotion, even a mixed and minor appreciation of art is, I am sure, one of the most valuable things in the world—so valuable, indeed, that in my giddier moments I have been tempted to believe that art might prove the world's salvation.

Yet, though the echoes and shadows of art enrich the life of the plains, her spirit dwells on the mountains. To him who woos, but woos impurely, she returns enriched what is brought. Like the sun, she warms the good seed in good soil and causes it to bring forth good fruit. But only to the perfect lover does she give a new strange gift—a gift beyond all price. Imperfect lovers bring to art and take away the ideas and emotions of their own age and civilization. In twelfth-century Europe a man might have been greatly moved by a Romanesque church and found nothing in a T'ang picture. To a man of later age, Greek sculpture meant much and Mexican nothing, for only to the former could he bring a crowd of associated ideas to be the objects of familiar emotions. But the perfect lover, he who can feel the profound significance of form, is raised above the accidents of time and place. To him the problems of archaeology, history, and hagiography are impertinent. If the forms of a work are significant its provenance is irrelevant. Before the grandeur of those Sumerian figures in the Louvre he is carried on the same flood of emotion to the same esthetic ecstasy as, more than four thousand years ago, the Chaldean lover was carried. It is the mark of great art that its appeal is universal and eternal.[1] Significant form stands charged with the power to provoke esthetic emotion in any one capable of feeling it. The ideas of men go buzz and die like gnats; men change their institutions and their customs as they change their coats; the intellectual triumphs of one age are the follies of another; only great art remains stable and unobscure. Great art remains stable and unobscure because the feelings that it awakens are independent of time and place, because its kingdom is not of this world. To those who have and hold a sense of the significance of form what does it matter whether the forms that move them were created in Paris the day before yesterday or in Babylon fifty centuries ago? The forms of art are inexhaustible; but all lead by the same road of esthetic emotion to the same world of esthetic ecstasy.

II THE METAPHYSICAL HYPOTHESIS

It seems to me possible, though by no means certain, that created form moves us so profoundly because it expresses the emotion of its creator. . . . If this be so, it will explain that curious but undeniable fact, to which I have already referred, that what I call material beauty (*e.g.,* the wing of a butterfly) does not move most of us in at all the same way as a work of art moves us. It is beautiful form, but it is not significant form. It moves us, but it does not move us esthetically. It is tempting to explain the difference between "significant form" and "beauty"—that is to say, the difference between form that provokes our esthetic emotions and form that does not—by saying that significant form conveys to us an emotion felt by its creator and that beauty conveys nothing.

For what, then, does the artist feel the emotion that he is supposed to express? Sometimes it certainly comes to him through material beauty. The contemplation of natural objects is often the immediate cause of the artist's emotion. Are we to suppose, then, that the artist feels, or sometimes feels, for material beauty what we feel for a work of art? Can it be that sometimes for the artist material beauty is somehow significant—that is, capable of provoking esthetic emotion? And if the form that provokes esthetic emotion be form that expresses something, can it be that material beauty is to him expressive? Does he feel something behind it as we imagine that we feel something behind the forms of a work of art? . . .

The emotion that the artist felt in his moment of inspiration he did not feel for objects seen as means, but for objects seen as pure forms—that is, as ends in themselves. He did not feel emotion for a chair as a means to phys-ical well-being, nor as an object associated with the intimate life of a family, nor as the place where some one sat saying things unforgettable, nor yet as a thing bound to the lives of hundreds of men and women, dead or alive, by a hundred subtle ties; doubtless an artist does often feel emotions such as these for the things that he sees, but in the moment of esthetic vision he sees ob-jects, not as means shrouded in associations, but as pure forms. It is for, or at any rate through, pure form that he feels his inspired emotion.

Now to see objects as pure forms is to see them as ends in themselves. For though, of course, forms are related to each other as parts of a whole, they are related on terms of equality; they are not a means to anything ex-cept emotion. But for objects seen as ends in themselves, do we not feel a profounder and a more thrilling emotion than ever we felt for them as means? All of us, I imagine, do, from time to time, get a vision of material objects as pure forms. We see things as ends in themselves, that is to say; and at such moments is seems possible, and even probable, that we see them with the eye of an artist. Who has not, once at least in his life, had a sudden vision of landscape as pure form? For once, instead of seeing it as fields and cottages, he has felt it as lines and colors. In that moment has he not won from material beauty a thrill indistinguishable from that which art gives? And, if this be so, is it not clear that he has won from material beauty the thrill that, generally, art alone can give, because he has contrived to see it as a pure formal combination of lines and colors? May we go on to say that, having seen it as pure form, having freed it from all casual and adventitious interest, from all that it may have acquired from its commerce with human beings, from all its significance as a means, he has felt its significance as an end in itself? . . .

But if an object considered as an end in itself moves us more profoundly (*i.e.,* has greater significance) than the same object considered as a means to practical ends or as a thing related to human interests—and this undoubtedly is the case—we can only suppose that when we consider anything as an end in itself we become aware of that in it which is of greater moment than any qualities it may have acquired from keeping company with human beings. Instead of recognizing its accidental and conditioned importance, we become aware of its essential reality, of the God in everything, of the universal in the particular, of the all-pervading rhythm. Call it by what name you will, the thing that I am talking about is that which lies behind the appearance of all things—that which gives to all things their individual significance. . . . And if a more or less unconscious apprehension of this latent reality of material things be, indeed, the cause of that strange emotion, a passion to express which is the inspiration of many artists, it seems reasonable to sup-pose that those who, unaided by material objects, experience the same emo-tion have come by another road to the same country.

That is the metaphysical hypothesis. Are we to swallow it whole, accept a part of it, or reject it altogether? Each must decide for himself. I insist only on the rightness of my esthetic hypothesis. And of one other thing am I sure. Be they artists or lovers of art, mystics or mathematicians, those who achieve ecstasy are those who have freed themselves from the arrogance of humanity. He who would feel the significance of art must make himself humble before it. Those who find the chief importance of art or of philosophy in its rela-tion to conduct or its practical utility—those who cannot value things as ends in themselves or, at any rate, as direct means to emotion—will never get from anything the best that it can give. Whatever the world of esthetic contemplation may be, it is not the world of human business and passion; in it the chatter and tumult of material existence is unheard, or heard only as the echo of some more ultimate harmony.

—Art (1913)

NOTE

1. Mr. Roger Fry permits me to make use of an interesting story that will illustrate my view. When Mr. Okakura, the Government editor of *The Temple Treasures of Japan,* first came to Europe, he found no difficulty in appreciating the pictures of those who from want of will or want of skill did not create illusions but concentrated their energies on the creation of form. He understood immediately the Byzantine masters and the French and Italian Primitives. In the Renaissance painters, on the other hand, with their descriptive pre-occupations, their literary and anecdotic interests, he could see nothing but vulgarity and muddle. The uni-versal and essential quality of art, significant form, was missing, or rather had dwindled to a shallow stream, overlaid and hidden beneath weeds, so the uni-versal response, esthetic emotion, was not evoked. It was not till he came on to Henri-Matisse that he again found himself in the familiar world of pure art. Similarly, sensitive Europeans who respond immediately to the significant forms of great Oriental art, are left cold by the trivial pieces of anecdote and social criticism so lovingly cherished by Chinese dilettanti. It would be easy to multiply instances did not decency forbid the laboring of so obvious a truth.

ANDREW CECIL BRADLEY

Poetry for Poetry's Sake

The words "Poetry for poetry's sake" recall the famous phrase "Art for Art." It is far from my purpose to examine the possible meanings of that phrase, or all the questions it involves. I propose to state briefly what I understand by "Poetry for poetry's sake," and then, after guarding against one or two misapprehensions of the formula, to consider more fully a single problem connected with it. And I must premise, without attempting to justify them, certain explanations. We are to consider poetry in its essence, and apart from the flaws which in most poems accompany their poetry. We are to include in the idea of poetry the metrical form, and not to regard this as a mere accident or a mere vehicle. And, finally, poetry being poems, we are to think of a poem as it actually exists; and, without aiming here at accuracy, we may say that an actual poem is the succession of experiences—sounds, images, thoughts, emotions—through which we pass when we are reading as poetically as we can. Of course this imaginative experience—if I may use the phrase for brevity—differs with every reader and every time of reading: a poem exists in innumerable degrees. But that insurmountable fact lies in the nature of things and does not concern us now.

What then does the formula "Poetry for poetry's sake" tell us about this experience? It says, as I understand it, these things. First, this experience is an end in itself, is worth having on its own account, has an intrinsic value. Next, its *poetic* value is this intrinsic worth alone. Poetry may have also an ulterior value as a means to culture or religion; because it conveys instructions, or softens the passions, or furthers a good cause; because it brings the poet fame or money or a quiet conscience. So much the better: let it be valued for these reasons too. But its ulterior worth neither is nor can directly determine its poetic worth as a satisfying imaginative experience; and this is to be judged entirely from within. And to these two positions the formula would add, though not of necessity, a third. The consideration of ulterior ends, whether by the poet in the act of composing or by the reader in the act of experiencing, tends to lower poetic value. It does so because it tends to change the nature of poetry by taking it out of its own atmosphere. For its nature is to be not a part, nor yet a copy, of the real world (as we commonly understand that phrase), but to be a world by itself, independent, complete, autonomous; and to possess it fully you must enter the world, conform to its laws, and ignore for the time the beliefs, aims, and particular conditions which belong to you in the other world of reality.

Of the more serious misapprehensions to which these statements may give rise I will glance only at one or two. The offensive consequences often drawn from the formula "Art for Art" will be found to attach not to the doctrine that Art is an end in itself, but to the doctrine that Art is the whole or supreme end of human life. And as this latter doctrine, which seems to me absurd, is in any case quite different from the former, its consequences fall outside my subject. The formula "Poetry is an end in itself" has nothing to say on the various questions of moral judgment which arise from the fact that poetry has its place in a many-sided life. For anything it says, the intrinsic value of poetry might be so small, and its ulterior effects so mischievous, that it had better not exist. The formula only tells us that we must not place in antithesis poetry and human good, for poetry is one kind of human good; and that we must not determine the intrinsic value of this kind of good by direct reference to another. If we do, we shall find ourselves maintaining what we did not expect. If poetic value lies in the stimulation of religious feelings, *Lead, Kindly Light*[1] is no better a poem than many a tasteless version of a Psalm: if in the excitement of patriotism, why is *Scots, Wha Hae*[2] superior to *We Don't Want to Fight?* if in the mitigation of the passions, the Odes of Sappho will win but little praise: if in instruction, Armstrong's *Art of Preserving Health* should win much.

Again, our formula may be accused of cutting poetry away from its connection with life. And this accusation raises so huge a problem that I must ask leave to be dogmatic as well as brief. There is plenty of connection between life and poetry, but it is, so to say, a connection underground. The two may be called different forms of the same thing: one of them having (in the usual sense) reality, but seldom fully satisfying imagination; while the other offers something which satisfies imagination but has not full "reality." They are parallel developments which nowhere meet, or, if I may use loosely a word which will be serviceable later, they are analogous. Hence we understand one by help of the other, and even, in a sense, care for one because of the other; but hence also, poetry neither is life, nor, strictly speaking, a copy of it. They differ not only because one has more mass and the other a more perfect shape, but because they have different *kinds* of existence. The one touches us as beings occupying a given position in space and time, and having feelings, desires, and purposes due to that position: it appeals to imagination, but appeals to much besides. What meets us in poetry has not a position in the same series of time and space, or, if it has or had such a position, it is taken apart from much that belonged to it there; and therefore it makes no direct appeal to those feelings, desires, and purposes, but speaks only to contemplative imagination—imagination the reverse of empty or emotionless, imagination saturated with the results of "real" experience, but still contemplative. Thus, no doubt, one main reason why poetry has poetic value for us is that it presents to us in its own way something which we meet in another form in nature or life; and yet the test of its poetic value for us lies simply in the question whether it satisfies our imagination; the rest of us, our knowledge or conscience, for example, judging it only so far as they appear transmuted in our imagination. So also Shakespeare's knowledge or his moral insight, Milton's greatness of soul, Shelley's "hate of hate" and "love of love," and that desire to help men or make them happier which may have influenced a poet in hours of meditation—all these have, as such, no poetical worth: they have that worth only when, passing through the unity of the poet's being, they reappear as qualities of imagination, and then are indeed mighty powers in the world of poetry.

I come to a third misapprehension, and so to my main subject. This formula, it is said, empties poetry of its meaning: it is really a doctrine of form for form's sake. "It is of no consequence what a poet says, so long as he says the thing well. The *what* is poetically indifferent: it is the *how* that counts. Matter, subject, content, substance, determines nothing; there is no subject with which poetry may not deal: the form, the treatment, is everything. Nay, more: not only is the matter indifferent, but it is the secret of Art to 'eradicate the matter by means of the form,' "—phrases and statements like these meet us everywhere in current criticism of literature and the other arts. They are the stock-in-trade of writers who understand of them little more than the fact that somehow or other they are not "bourgeois." But we find them also seriously used by writers whom we must respect, whether they are anonymous or not; something like one or another of them might be quoted, for example, from Professor Saintsbury, the late R. A. M. Stevenson, Schiller, Goethe himself; and they are the watchwords of a school in the one country where esthetics has flourished. They come, as a rule, from men who either practice one of the arts, or, from study of it, are interested in its methods. The general reader—a being so general that I may say what I will of him—is outraged by them. He feels that he is being robbed of almost all that he cares for in a work of art. "You are asking me," he says, "to look at the Dresden Madonna as if it were a Persian rug. You are telling me that the poetic value of *Hamlet* lies solely in its style and versification, and that my interest in the man and his fate is only an intellectual or moral interest. You allege that, if I want to enjoy the poetry of *Crossing the Bar*, I must not mind what Tennyson says there, but must consider solely his way of saying it. But in that case I can care no more for a poem than I do for a set of nonsense verses; and I do not believe that the authors of *Hamlet* and *Crossing the Bar* regarded their poems thus."

These antitheses of subject, matter, substance on the one side, form, treatment, handling on the other, are the field through which I especially want, in this lecture, to indicate a way. It is a field of battle; and the battle is waged for no trivial cause; but the cries of the combatants are terribly ambiguous. Those phrases of the so-called formalist may each mean five or six different things. Taken in one sense they seem to me chiefly true; taken as the general reader not unnaturally takes them, they seem to me false and mischievous. It would be absurd to pretend that I can end in a few minutes a controversy which concerns the ultimate nature of Art, and leads perhaps to problems not yet soluble; but we can at least draw some plain distinctions which, in this controversy, are too often confused.

In the first place, then, let us take "subject" in one particular sense; let us understand by it that which we have in view when, looking at the title of an unread poem, we say that the poet has chosen this or that for his subject. The subject, in this sense, so far as I can discover, is generally something, real or imaginary, as it exists in the minds of fairly cultivated people. The subject of *Paradise Lost* would be the story of the Fall as that story exists in the general imagination of a Bible-reading people. The subject of Shelley's stanzas *To a Skylark* would be the ideas which arise in the mind of an educated person when, without knowing the poem, he hears the word "skylark." If the title of a poem conveys little or nothing to us, the "subject" appears to be either what we should gather by investigating the title in a dictionary or other book of the kind, or else such a brief suggestion as might be offered by a person who had read the poem, and who said, for example, that the subject of *The Ancient Mariner* was a sailor who killed an albatross and suffered for his deed.

Now the subject, in this sense (and I intend to use the word in no other), is not, as such, inside the poem, but outside it. The contents of the stanzas *To a Skylark* are not the ideas suggested by the word "skylark" to the average man; they belong to Shelley just as much as the language does. The subject, therefore, is not the matter *of* the poem at all; and its opposite is not the *form* of the poem, but the whole poem. The subject is one thing; the poem, matter and form alike, another thing. This being so, it is surely obvious that the poetic value cannot lie in the subject, but lies entirely in its opposite, the poem. How can the subject determine the value when on one and the same subject poems may be written of all degrees of merit and demerit; or when a perfect poem may be composed on a subject so slight as a pet sparrow,[3] and, if Macaulay[4] may be trusted, a nearly worthless poem on a subject so stupendous as the omnipresence of the Deity? The "formalist" is here perfectly right. Nor is he insisting on something unimportant. He is fighting against our tendency to take the work of art as a mere copy or reminder of something already in our heads, or at the best as a suggestion of some idea as little removed as possible from the familiar. The sightseer who promenades a picture-gallery, remarking that this portrait is so like his cousin, or that landscape the very image of his birthplace, or who, after satisfying himself that one picture is about Elijah, passes on rejoicing to discover the subject, and nothing but the subject, of the next—what is he but an extreme example of this tendency? Well, but the very same tendency vitiates much of our criticism, much criticism of Shakespeare, for example, which, with all its cleverness and partial truth, still shows that the critic never passed from his own mind into Shakespeare's; and it may be traced even in so fine a critic as Coleridge, as when he dwarfs the sublime struggle of Hamlet into the image of his own unhappy weakness. Hazlitt by no means escaped its influence. Only the third of that great trio, Lamb, appears almost always to have rendered the conception of the composer.

Again, it is surely true that we cannot determine before hand what subjects are fit for Art, or name any subject on which a good poem might not possibly be written. To divide subjects into two groups, the beautiful or elevating, and the ugly or vicious, and to judge poems according as their subjects belong to one of these groups or the other, is to fall into the same pit, to confuse with our preconceptions the meaning of the poet. What the thing is in the poem he is to be judged by, not by the thing as it was before he touched it; and how can we venture to say beforehand that he cannot make a true poem out of something which to us was merely alluring or dull or revolting? The question whether, having done so, he ought to publish his poem; whether the thing in the poet's work will not be still confused by the incompetent Puritan or the incompetent sensualist with the thing in *his* mind, does not touch this point; it is a further question, one of ethics, not of art. No doubt the upholders of "Art for Art's sake" will generally be in favor of the courageous course, of refusing to sacrifice the better or stronger part of the public to the weaker or worse; but their maxim in no way binds them to this view. Rossetti suppressed one of the best of his sonnets, a sonnet chosen for admiration by Tennyson, himself extremely sensitive about the moral effect of poetry; suppressed it, I believe, because it was called fleshly. One may regret Rossetti's judgment and at the same time respect his scrupulousness; but in any case he judged in his capacity of citizen, not in his capacity of artist.

So far then the "formalist" appears to be right. But he goes too far, I think, if he maintains that the subject is indifferent and that all subjects are the same to poetry. And he does not prove his point by observing that a good poem might be written on a pin's head, and a bad one on the Fall of Man. That truth shows that the subject *settles* nothing, but not that it counts for nothing. The Fall of Man is really a more favorable subject than a pin's head. The Fall of Man, that is to say, offers opportunities of poetic effects wider in range and more penetrating in appeal. And the fact is that such a subject, as it exists in the general imagination, has some esthetic value before the poet touches it. It is, as you may choose to call it, an inchoate poem or the debris of a poem. It is not an abstract idea or a bare isolated fact, but an assemblage of figures, scenes, actions, and events, which already appeal to emotional imagination; and it is already in some degree organized and formed. In spite of this a bad poet would make a bad poem on it; but then we should say he was unworthy of the subject. And we should not say this if he wrote a bad poem on a pin's head. Conversely, a good poem on a pin's head would almost certainly transform its subject far more than a good poem on the Fall of Man. It might revolutionize its subject so completely that we should say, "The subject may be a pin's head, but the substance of the poem has very little to do with it."

This brings us to another and a different antithesis. Those figures, scenes, events, that form part of the subject called the Fall of Man, are not the substance of *Paradise Lost*; but in *Paradise Lost* there are figures, scenes, and events resembling them in some degree. These, with much more of the same kind, may be described as its substance, and may then be contrasted with the measured language of the poem, which will be called its form. Subject is the opposite not of form but of the whole poem. Substance is within the poem, and its opposite, form, is also within the poem. I am not criticizing this antithesis at present, but evidently it is quite different from the other. It is practically the distinction used in the old-fashioned criticism of epic and drama, and it flows down, not unsullied, from Aristotle. Addison,[5] for example, in examing *Paradise Lost* considers in order the fable, the characters, and the sentiments; these will be the substance: then he considers the language, that is, the style and numbers; this will be the form. In like manner, the substance or meaning of a lyric may be distinguished from the form.

Now I believe it will be found that a large part of the controversy we are dealing with arises from a confusion between these two distinctions of substance and form, and of subject and poem. The extreme formalist lays his whole weight on the form because he thinks its opposite is the mere subject. The general reader is angry, but makes the same mistake, and gives to the subject praises that rightly belong to the substance.[6] I will give an example of what I mean. I can only explain the following words of a good critic[7] by supposing that for the moment he has fallen into this confusion: "The mere matter of all poetry—to wit, the appearances of nature and the thoughts and feelings of men—being unalterable, it follows that the difference between poet and poet will depend upon the manner of each in applying language, meter, rhyme, cadence, and what not, to this invariable material." What has become here of the substance of *Paradise Lost*—the story, scenery, characters, sentiments as they are in the poem? They have vanished clean away. Nothing is left but the form on one side, and on the other not even the subject, but a supposed invariable material, the appearances of nature and the thoughts and feelings of men. Is it surprising that the whole value should then be found in the form?

So far we have assumed that this antithesis of substance and form is valid, and that it always has one meaning. In reality it has several, but we will leave it in its present shape, and pass to the question of its validity. And this question we are compelled to raise, because we have to deal with the two contentions that the poetic value lies wholly or mainly in the substance, and that it lies wholly or mainly in the form. Now these contentions, whether false or true, may seem at least to be clear; but we shall find, I think, that they are both of them false, or both of them nonsense: false if they concern anything outside the poem, nonsense if they apply to something in it. For what do they evidently imply? They imply that there are in a poem two parts, factors, or components, a substance and a form; and that you can conceive them distinctly and separately, so that when you are speaking of the one you are not speaking of the other. Otherwise how can you ask the question, In which of them does the value lie? But really in a poem, apart from defects, there are no such factors or components; and therefore it is strictly nonsense to ask in which of them the value lies. And on the other hand, if the substance and the form referred to are not in the poem, then both the contentions are false, for its poetic value lies in itself.

What I mean is neither new nor mysterious; and it will be clear, I believe, to any one who reads poetry poetically and who closely examines his experience. When you are reading a poem, I would ask—not analyzing it, and much less criticizing it, but allowing it, as it proceeds, to make its full impression on you through the exertion of your re-creating imagination—do you then apprehend and enjoy as one thing a certain meaning or substance, and as another thing certain articulate sounds, and do you somehow compound these two? Surely you do not, any more than you apprehend apart, when you see someone smile, those lines in the face which express a feeling, and the feeling that the lines express. Just as there the lines and their meaning are to you one thing, not two, so in poetry the meaning and the sounds are one: there is, if I may put it so, a resonant meaning, or a meaning resonance. If you read the line, "The sun is warm, the sky is clear,"[8] you do not experience separately the image of a warm sun and clear sky, on the one side, and certain unintelligible rhythmical sounds on the other; nor yet do you experience them together, side by side; but you experience the one *in* the other. And in like manner when you are really reading *Hamlet,* the action and the characters are not something which you conceive apart from the words; you apprehend them from point to point *in* the words, and the words as expressions of them. Afterwards, no doubt, when you are out of the poetic experience but remember it, you may by analysis decompose this unity, and attend to a substance more or less isolated, and a form more or less isolated. But these are things in your analytic head, not in the poem, which is *poetic* experience. And if you want to have the poem again, you cannot find it by adding together these two products of decomposition; you can only find it by passing back into poetic experience. And then what you recover is no aggregate of factors, it is a unity in which you can no more separate a substance and a form than you can separate living blood and the life in the blood. This unity has, if you like, various "aspects" or "sides," but they are not factors or parts; if you try to examine one, you find it is also the other. Call them substance and form if you please, but these are not the reciprocally exclusive substance and form to which the two contentions *must* refer. They do not "agree," for they are not apart: they are one thing from different points of view, and in that sense identical. And this identity of content and form, you will say, is no accident; it is of the essence of poetry insofar as it is poetry, and of all art insofar as it is art. Just as there is in music not sound on one side and a meaning on the other, but expressive sound, and if you ask what is the meaning you can only answer by pointing to the sounds; just as in painting there is not a meaning *plus* paint, but a meaning *in* paint, or significant paint, and no man can really express the meaning in any other way than in paint and in *this* paint; so in a poem the true content and the true form neither exist nor can be imagined apart. When then you are asked whether the value of a poem lies in a substance got by decomposing the poem, and present, as such, only in reflective analysis, or whether the value lies in a form arrived at and existing in the same way, you will answer, "It lies neither in one, nor in the other, nor in any addition of them, but in the poem, where they are not."

We have then, first, an antithesis of subject and poem. This is clear and valid; and the question in which of them does the value lie is intelligible; and its answer is, *In the poem.* We have next a distinction of substance and form. If the subtance means ideas, images, and the like taken alone, and the form means the measured language taken by itself, this is a possible distinction, but it is a distinction of things not in the poem, and the value lies *in neither of them.* If substance and form mean anything *in* the poem, then each is involved in the other, and the question in which of them the value lies has no sense. No doubt you may say, speaking loosely, that in this poet or poem the aspect of substance is the more noticeable, and in that the aspect of form; and you may pursue interesting discussions on this basis, though no principle or ultimate question of value is touched by them. And apart from that question, of course, I am not denying the usefulness and necessity of the distinction. We cannot dispense with it. To consider separately the action or the characters of a play, and separately its style or versification, is both legitimate and valuable, so long as we remember what we are doing. But the true critic in speaking of these apart does not really think of them apart; the whole, the poetic experience, of which they are but aspects, is always in his mind; and he is always aiming at a richer, truer, more intense repetition of that experience. On the other hand, when the question of principle, of poetic value, is raised, these aspects *must* fall apart into components, separately inconceivable; and then there arise two heresies, equally false, that the value lies in one of two things, both of which are outside the poem, and therefore where its value cannot lie.

On the heresy of the separable substance a few additional words will suffice. This heresy is seldom formulated, but perhaps some unconscious holder of it may object: "Surely the action and the characters of *Hamlet* are in the play; and surely I can retain these, though I have forgotten all the words. I admit that I do not possess the whole poem, but I possess a part, and the most important part." And I would answer: "If we are not concerned with any question of principle, I accept all that you say except the last words, which do raise such a question. Speaking loosely, I agree that the action and characters, as you perhaps conceive them, together with a great deal more, are in the poem. Even then, however, you must not claim to possess all of this kind that is in the poem; for in forgetting the words you must have lost innumerable details of the action and the characters. And, when the question of value is raised, I must insist that the action and characters, as you conceive them, are not in *Hamlet* at all. If they are, point them out. You cannot do it. What you find at any moment of that succession of experiences called *Hamlet* is words. In these words, to speak loosely again, the action and characters (more of them than you can conceive apart) are focused; but your experience is not a combination of them, as ideas, on the one side, with certain sounds on the other; it is an experience of something in which the two are indissolubly fused. If you deny this, to be sure I can make no answer, or can only answer that I have reason to believe that you cannot read poetically, or else are misinterpreting your experience. But if you do not deny this, then you will admit that the action and characters of the poem, as you separately imagine them, are no part of it, but a product of it in your reflective imagination, a faint analogue of one aspect of it taken in detachment from the whole. Well, I do not dispute, I would even insist, that, in the case of so long a poem as *Hamlet*, it may be necessary from time to time to interrupt the poetic experience, in order to enrich it by forming such a product and dwelling on it. Nor, in a wide sense of 'poetic,' do I question the poetic value of this product, as you think of it apart from the poem. It resembles our recollections of the heroes of history or legend, who move about in our imaginations, 'forms more real than living man,' and are worth much to us though we do not remember anything they said. Our ideas and images of the 'substance' of a poem have this poetic value, and more, if they are at all adequate. But they cannot determine the poetic value of the poem, for (not to speak of the competing claims of the 'form') nothing that is outside the poem can do that, and they, as such, are outside it."[9]

Let us turn to the so-called form—style and versification. There is no such thing as mere form in poetry. All form is expression. Style may have indeed a certain esthetic worth in partial abstraction from the particular matter it conveys, as in a well-built sentence you may take pleasure in the build almost apart from the meaning. Even so, style is expressive—presents to sense, for example, the order, ease, and rapidity with which ideas move in the writer's mind—but it is not expressive of the meaning of that particular sentence. And it is possible, interrupting poetic experience, to decompose it and abstract for comparatively separate consideration this nearly formal element of style. But the esthetic value of style so taken is not considerable[10]; you could not read with pleasure for an hour a composition which had no other merit. And in poetic experience you never apprehend this value by itself; the style is here expressive also of a particular meaning, or rather is one aspect of that unity whose other aspect is meaning. So that what you apprehend may be called indifferently an expressed meaning or a significant form. Perhaps on this point I may in Oxford appeal to authority, that of Matthew Arnold and Walter Pater, the latter at any rate an authority whom the formalist will not despise. What is the gist of Pater's teaching about style, if it is not that in the end the one virtue of style is truth or adequacy; that the word, phrase, sentence, should express perfectly the writer's perception, feeling, image or thought; so that, as we read a descriptive phrase of Keats's, we exclaim, "That is the thing itself"; so that, to quote Arnold, the words are "symbols equivalent with the thing symbolized," or, in our technical language, a form identical with its content? Hence in true poetry it is, in strictness, impossible to express the meaning in any but its own words, or to change the words without changing the meaning. A translation of such poetry is not really the old meaning in a fresh dress; it is a new product, something like the poem, though, if one chooses to say so, more like it in the aspect of meaning than in the aspect of form.

No one who understands poetry, it seems to me, would dispute this, were it not that, falling away from his experience, or misled by theory, he takes the word "meaning" in a sense almost ludicrously inapplicable to poetry. People say, for instance, "steed" and "horse" have the same meaning; and in bad poetry they have, but not in poetry that *is* poetry.

> "Bring forth the horse!" The horse was brought:
> In truth he was a noble steed!

says Byron in *Mazeppa*. If the two words mean the same here, transpose them:

> "Bring forth the steed!" The steed was brought:
> In truth he was a noble horse!

and ask again if they mean the same. Or let me take a line certainly very free from "poetic diction":

> To be or not to be, that is the question.

You may say that this means the same as "What is just now occupying my attention is the comparative disadvantages of continuing to live or putting an end to myself." And for practical purposes—the purpose, for example, of a coroner—it does. But as the second version altogether misrepresents the speaker at that moment of his existence, while the first does represent him, how can they for any but a practical or logical purpose be said to have the same sense? Hamlet was well able to "unpack his heart with words," but he will not unpack it with our paraphrases.

These considerations apply equally to versification. If I take the famous line which describes how the souls of the dead stood waiting by the river, imploring a passage from Charon:

> *Tendebantque manus ripae ulterioris amore,*[11]

and if I translate it, "and were stretching forth their hands in longing for the further bank," the charm of the original has fled. Why has it fled? Partly (but we have dealt with that) because I have substituted for five words, and those the words of Virgil, twelve words, and those my own. In some measure because I have turned into rhythmless prose a line of verse which, as mere sound, has unusual beauty. But much more because in doing so I have also changed the *meaning* of Virgil's line. What that meaning is *I* cannot say: Virgil has said it. But I can see this much, that the translation conveys a far less vivid picture of the outstretched hands and of their remaining outstretched, and a far less poignant sense of the distance of the shore and the longing of the souls. And it does so partly because this picture and this sense are conveyed not only by the obvious meaning of the words, but through the long-drawn sound of "tende-bantque," through the time occupied by the five syllables and therefore by the idea of "ulterioris," and through the identity of the long sound "or" in the penultimate syllables of "ulterioris amore"—all this, and much more, apprehended not in this analytical fashion, nor as *added* to the beauty of mere sound and to the obvious meaning, but in unity with them and so as expressive of the poetic meaning of the whole.

It is always so in fine poetry. The value of versification, when it is indissolubly fused with meaning, can hardly be exaggerated. The gift for feeling it, even more perhaps than the gift for feeling the value of style, is the *specific* gift for poetry, as distinguished from other arts. But versification, taken, as far as possible, all by itself, has a very different worth. Some esthetic worth it has; how much, you may experience by reading poetry in a language of which you do not understand a syllable. The pleasure is quite appreciable, but it is not great; nor in actual poetic experience do you meet with it, as such, at all. For, I repeat, it is not *added* to the pleasure of the meaning when you read poetry that you do understand: by some mystery the music is then the music *of* the meaning, and the two are one. However fond of versification you might be, you would tire very soon of reading verses in Chinese; and before long of reading Virgil and Dante if you were ignorant of their languages. But take the music as it is *in* the poem, and there is a marvelous change. Now

> It gives a very echo to the seat
> Where Love is throned,[12]

or "carries far into your heart," almost like music itself, the sound

> Of old, unhappy, far-off things
> And battles long ago.[13]

What then is to be said of the following sentence of the critic quoted before[14]: "But when anyone who knows what poetry is reads—

> Our noisy years seem moments in the being
> Of the eternal silence,[15]

he sees that, quite independently of the meaning, . . . there is one note added to the articulate music of the world—a note that never will leave off resounding till the eternal silence itself gulfs it"? I must think that the writer is deceiving himself. For I could quite understand his enthusiasm, if it were an enthusiasm for the music of the meaning; but as for the music, "quite independently of the meaning," so far as I can hear it thus (and I doubt if any one who knows English can quite do so), I find it gives some pleasure, but only a trifling pleasure. And indeed I venture to doubt whether, considered as mere sound, the words are at all exceptionally beautiful, as Virgil's line certainly is. . . .

Pure poetry is not the decoration of a preconceived and clearly defined matter: it springs from the creative impulse of a vague imaginative mass pressing for development and definition. If the poet already knew exactly what he meant to say, why should he write the poem? The poem would in fact already be written. For only its completion can reveal, even to him, exactly what he wanted. When he began and while he was at work, he did not possess his meaning; it possessed him. It was not a fully formed soul asking for a body: it was an inchoate soul in the inchoate body of perhaps two or three vague ideas and a few scattered phrases. The growing of this body into its full stature and perfect shape was the same thing as the gradual self-definition of the meaning. And this is the reason why such poems strike us as creations, not manufactures, and have the magical effect which mere decoration cannot produce. This is also the reason why, if we insist on asking for the meaning of such a poem, we can only be answered, "It means itself."

And so at last I may explain why I have troubled myself and you with what may seem an arid controversy about mere words. It is not so. These heresies which would make poetry a compound of two factors—a matter common to it with the merest prose, *plus* a poetic form, as the one heresy says: a poetical substance *plus* a negligible form, as the other says—are not only untrue, they are injurious to the dignity of poetry. In an age already inclined to shrink from those higher realms where poetry touches religion and philosophy, the formalist heresy encourages men to taste poetry as they would a fine wine, which has indeed an esthetic value, but a small one. And then the natural man, finding an empty form, hurls into it the matter of cheap pathos, rancid sentiment, vulgar humor, bare lust, ravenous vanity—everything which, in Schiller's phrase,[16] the form should extirpate, but which no mere form can extirpate. And the other heresy— which is indeed rather a practice than a creed—encourages us in the habit so dear to us of putting our own thoughts or fancies into the place of the poet's creation. What he meant by *Hamlet,* or the *Ode to a Nightingale,* or *Abt Vogler,* we say, is this or that which we knew already; and so we lose what he had to tell us. But he meant what he said, and said what he meant.

Poetry in this matter is not, as good critics of painting and music often affirm, different from the other arts; in all of them the content is one thing with the form. What Beethoven meant by his symphony, or Turner by his picture, was not something which you can name, but the picture and the symphony. Meaning they have, but *what* meaning can be said in no language but their own: and we know this, though some strange delusion makes us think the meaning has less worth because we cannot put it into words. Well, it is just the same with poetry. But because poetry is words, we vainly fancy that some other words than its own will express its meaning. And they will do so no more—or, if you like to speak loosely, only a little more—than words will express the meaning of the Dresden Madonna. Something a little like it they may indeed express. And we may find analogues of the meaning of poetry outside it, which may help us to appropriate it. The other arts, the best ideas of philosophy or religion, much that nature and life offer us or force upon us, are akin to it. But they are only akin. Nor is it the expression of them. Poetry does not present to imagination our highest knowledge or belief, and much less our dreams and opinions; but it, content and form in unity, embodies in its own irreplaceable way something which embodies itself also in other irreplaceable ways, such as philosophy or religion. And just as each of these gives a satisfaction which the other cannot possibly give, so we find in poetry, which cannot satisfy the needs they meet, that which by their natures they cannot afford us. But we shall not find it fully if we look for something else.

And now, when all is said, the question will still recur, though now in quite another sense, What does poetry mean? This unique expression, which cannot be replaced by any other, still seems to be trying to express something beyond itself. And this, we feel, is also what the other arts, and religion, and philosophy are trying to express: and that is what impels us to seek in vain to translate the one into the other. About the best poetry, and not only the best, there floats an atmosphere of infinite suggestion. The poet speaks to us of one thing, but in this one thing there seems to lurk the secret of all. He said what he meant, but his meaning seems to beckon away beyond itself, or rather to expand into something boundless which is only focused in it; something also which, we feel, would satisfy not only the imagination, but the whole of us; that something within us, and without, which everywhere

> makes us seem
> To patch up fragments of a dream,
> Part of which comes true, and part
> Beats and trembles in the heart.[17]

Those who are susceptible to this effect of poetry find it not only, perhaps not most, in the ideals which she has sometimes described, but in a child's song by Christina Rossetti about a mere crown of wind-flowers, and in tragedies like *Lear*, where the sun seems to have set forever. They hear this spirit murmuring its undertone through the *Aeneid*, and catch its voice in the song of Keats's nightingale, and its light upon the figures on the Urn, and it pierces them no less in Shelley's hopeless lament, *O world, O life, O time*, than in the rapturous ecstasy of his *Life of Life*. This all-embracing perfection cannot be expressed in poetic words or words of any kind, nor yet in music or in color, but the suggestion of it is in much poetry, if not all, and poetry has in this suggestion, this "meaning," a great part of its value. We do it wrong, and we defeat our own purposes when we try to bend it to them:

> We do it wrong, being so majestical,
> To offer it the show of violence;
> For it is as the air invulnerable,
> And our vain blows malicious mockery.[18]

It is a spirit. It comes we know not whence. It will not speak at our bidding, nor answer in our language. It is not our servant; it is our master.
—*Oxford Lectures on Poetry* (1909)

NOTES

1. Newman.
2. Burns.
3. Catullus.
4. *Robert Mongomery.*
5. *Spectator,* 267, &c.
6. What is here called "substance" is what people generally mean when they use the word "subject" and insist on the value of the subject. I am not arguing against this usage, or in favor of the usage which I have adopted for the sake of clearness. It does not matter which we employ, so long as we and others know what we mean. (I use "substance" and "content" indifferently.)
7. George Saintsbury.
8. Shelley, "Lines Written in Dejection Near the Bay of Naples."
9. These remarks will hold good, *mutatis mutandis,* if by "substance" is understood the "moral" or the "idea" of a poem, although perhaps in one instance out of five thousand this may be found in so many words in the poem.
10. On the other hand, the absence, or worse than absence, of style, in this sense, is a serious matter.
11. *Aeneid,* VI, 314.
12. *Twelfth Night,* II. iv.
13. Wordsworth, "The Solitary Reaper."
14. Saintsbury, *History of English Prosody,* iii. pp. 74–75.
15. Wordsworth, "Ode on the Intimations of Immortality."
16. Not that to Schiller "form" meant mere style and versification.
17. Shelley, "Is it that in some brighter sphere?"
18. Hamlet, I. 1.

DeWITT H. PARKER

The Problem of Esthetic Form

I shall try to reduce the general characteristics of esthetic form to their simplest principles, hoping to provide the elements of what might be called a logic of esthetic form. These principles are, I think, very few; as few, indeed, as six: the principle of organic unity, or unity in variety, as it has been called; the principle of the theme; the principle of thematic variation; balance; the principle of hierarchy; and evolution. I do not assert that there are no more principles, but I at least have been unable to find any of equal generality. Others that have been suggested can be shown either to be identical with the six mentioned or to be special cases of them. I shall consider each at some length.

First, the long-established principle of organic unity. By this is meant the fact that each element in a work of art is necessary to its value, that it contains no elements that are not thus necessary, and that all that are needful are there. The beautiful object is organized all through, "baked all through like a cake." Since everything that is necessary is there, we are not led to go beyond it to seek something to complete it; and since there are no unnecessary elements, there is nothing present to disturb its value. Moreover, the value of the work as a whole depends upon the reciprocal relations of its elements: each needs, responds to, demands, every other element. For example, in the Young Woman with a Water Jug (by Johannes Vermeer: Metropolitan Museum), the cool green needs the warm yellow and both need the red; the casement demands the table, the map requires the dark shadow under the casement, to balance it. In a melody, each tone requires its successor to continue the trend that is being established. In short, the meaning of the whole is not something additional to the elements of the work of art, but their cooperative deed.

This principle cannot, however, be described in so external a fashion. For the unity of a work of art is the counterpart of a unity within the experience of the beholder. Since the work of art becomes an embodiment not only of the imagination of the artist, but of the imagination of the spectator as well, his own experience is, for the moment, concentrated there. He is potentially as completely absorbed in it as he is in a dream; it is for the moment, in fact, his dream. And he can and does remain in the dream because the artist has so fashioned his work that everything there tends to continue and deepen it, and nothing to disturb and interrupt it. Art is the expression of the whole man, because it momentarily makes of man a whole. The "isolation" of the esthetic experience of Hugo Münsterberg[1] and the "repose in the object" of Ethel Puffer[2] are descriptions of the fact to which I am calling attention. This does not mean, of course, that the work of art is not related to other things or that it is actually isolated; but only that its relations are irrelevant to its value, and that it cuts itself off from the rest of the world during appreciation; and this it does, first, because it embodies my dream and, second, because it is so constructed as to make me dream on. The marble of which the statue is made comes from a certain quarry and has an interesting geological history there; it stands in a certain part of space, and hence is related to other parts of space; but all such facts are of no account to its beauty. By placing the statue on a pedestal, we indicate its isolation from the space of the room, as by putting a frame around a picture we isolate it, too, from everything else in the world. It is true that, in order to understand a work of art in its historical relations, I must connect it with the artist's personality, with other works of his, with the "moral temperature" of the age, with the development of artistic styles, and the full appreciation of its beauty depends upon acquaintance with its spiritual background. Who, for example, can appreciate the whole meaning of Signorelli's Pan without some knowledge of classical antiquity and the Italian renaissance? Yet at the moment of appreciation, all such knowledge becomes focused in the work of art, gathered and contained there like rays in a prism, and does not divert us from it.

The ancient law of organic unity is the master principle of esthetic form; all the other principles serve it. First among them is what I would call the principle of the theme. This corresponds to the "dominant character" or *idee mère* of Taine.[3] In every complex work of art there is some one (or there may be several) pre-eminent shape, color, line, melodic pattern or meaning, in which is concentrated the characteristic value of the whole. It contains the work of art in little; represents it; provides the key to our appreciation and understanding of it. Thus every good pattern is built up of one or more shapes, the disposition of which constitutes the design. When there is color as well as shape, there is some dominant color that appears again and again or in related degrees of saturation, or else there is a color chord that is similarly repeated or is analyzed. In architecture, each style has its characteristic shape, line, or volume, as the pointed arch of the Gothic, the round arch of the Roman, the ellipse of the baroque. In music, there are the one or more themes that express the essential significance of each composition. Likewise, every sculptor, every draughtsman, has his unique and inimitable line. In every poem, there is a peculiar inflection and a regnant idea which constitute the basis of the design. In the drama or the novel, there is someone, or there may be several persons, whose character and fate create the plot.

The third principle is thematic variation. It is not sufficient to state the theme of a work of art; it must be elaborated and embroidered. One of the prominent ways of doing this is to make it echo and re-echo in our minds. Usually, if the theme can be repeated once only we are better pleased than with a single appearance. Yet to find the same thing barely repeated is monotonous; hence what we want is the same, to be sure, but the same with a difference: thematic variation. The simplest type of thematic variation is recurrence of the theme, as in any pattern built upon a repeat. Here is the maximum of sameness with the minimum of difference: mere difference of spatial or temporal position. A slight acquaintance with primitive art is sufficient to convince one of the overwhelming importance of recurrence there. Yet it is needless to say that recurrence is not confined to primitive art. We find it in all civilized art: the recurrence of the same shape and proportions in architecture and sculpture; the recurrence of the theme in music; the recurrence of the same type of foot in meter; repetition of the same color in painting; recurrence of lines and directions of lines (parallelism) in painting and sculpture and architecture; the refrain in poetry; the reappearance of the hero in different scenes in the drama and novel. However, because of the monotony of mere repetition, recurrence gives place to what may be called, in a generalized sense, transposition of theme, as when a melody is transposed to another key or tempo; or when in a design the same shape appears in a different color, or a color appears in different degrees of saturation or brightness; or in architecture, where a shape occurs in different sizes or members—in doors, windows, gables, choir-stalls, and the like. Still another kind of thematic variation is alternation, which requires, of course, more than one theme, or at least two different transpositions of the same theme. Of this, again, the illustrations are legion. Finally, there is inversion of theme, as when melody is inverted or, in painting or sculpture, a curve is reversed. These are not all the possible types of thematic variation, but they are, I think, the most important and usual.

Another principle of esthetic form is balance. Balance is equality of opposing or contrasting elements. Balance is one kind of esthetic unity, for despite the opposition of the elements in balance, each needs the other and together they create a whole. Thus the blue demands the gold and the gold the blue, and together they make a new whole, gold-and-blue. Opposition or contrast is never absent from balance, for even in symmetry, where the balancing elements are alike, the directions of these elements are opposed, right and left. But contrast is never by itself esthetically satisfactory, for the contrasting elements must offset each other, they must balance. In color, the warm offsets the cold; in a picture, the small object, properly placed, offsets the large one. Hence, just as only equal weights will balance in a scale pan, so only elements that are somehow equal in value, despite their opposition, will balance esthetically. Not every tint of blue will balance every shade of yellow; that depth of blue must reappear in a corresponding depth of yellow; a light, superficial blue would never balance a deep yellow. But the identity of the opposites is even greater than this. For, as has been remarked, the elements of a balanced unity demand each other; the blue demands the yellow; the line which falls in one direction demands the line that falls in the opposite direction. Now the demand which the color or line makes for its opposite is itself a foreshadowing of the latter; in its demand it already contains the prophecy of its opposite. And even when, as may occur in painting, there is balance between elements of unlike quality—balance, say, of brightness of color against distance or size—the attention value of each must be the same, though opposed in direction. The essential thing about balance is equality of opposed values, however unlike be the things that embody or carry the values.

The pervasiveness of the principle of balance is too generally recognized to need much illustration or agrument. In painting we expect, with a reservation that I shall consider in a moment, a threefold balance: horizontal, perpendicular, and radial or diagonal—between the right and left sides, the upper and lower portions, and between what may roughly be called the corners. This last has not received the attention which it deserves; but in many pictures, as for example, Tintoretto's "Mercury" and the "Three Graces," the diagonal axis is the main axis; and in all cases of circular composition, radial balance is fundamental. In architecture, we find balance between right and left, and often between upper and lower parts. In music, there is not seldom a balance between earlier and later parts of a composition, or between opposing themes. In sculpture, there is the balance characteristic of the human body made more perfect by the artist.

Pervasive as balance is, its universality has not stood unquestioned. Nevertheless, many apparent exceptions can be explained away, as is well known, as cases of disguised or subtle balance. The older interpretation of balance after the analogy of symmetry—the balance of like parts—is only a special kind of balance, and has to be supplemented by the wider conception of balance of unlike parts.[4] With this richer conception in mind, we can understand the balance—as in Bruegel's "Harvesters"—between prominent objects in the right-hand part and little except a vista on the left. Similarly, there is a balance—as in the same picture—between the upper and lower halves of a painting, even when the horizon line is high, and the upper part seems therefore to be relatively empty of masses; for the distance values in the sky balance the heavier lower part. No more difficult of explanation are some cases where asymmetry appears to be definitely sought, as when a girl will put a patch on one cheek but not on another, or will tie the lock of hair on the right with a ribbon, but not the lock on the left. For the piquancy of this procedure comes from the fact that there is a background of decisive symmetry, against which the asymmetrical element stands out. This is quite different from absolute lack of balance. One finds similar eccentric elements in all complex patterns; but always with a background of emphatic balance. And if it is true that such elements disturb symmetry, it is equally true that they serve to emphasize it. The triangle of passion is another illustration; for there also a balanced relationship is the background against which the unbalanced derives its interest.

There are, however, more difficult cases to consider. Many works of art, of the temporal arts in particular, are superficially considered rhythmical rather than balanced, and rhythm may seem to be opposed to balance. Yet an analysis of rhythm shows it to be built upon the two fundamental esthetic forms, thematic repetition and balance. For what are the typical characteristics of rhythm? Every rhythm is a motion of waves, all of a relatively constant or lawfully varying shape and temporal and spatial span, with balancing crests and troughs. The crest may be an accent or the swing up of a line; the trough may be one or more unaccented syllables, a pause, or the swing back of a line in the opposite direction. The rhythm may begin with the trough, as in iambic meter. The swing up and the swing back may both be very complex, as in free verse, yet the fundamental pattern, as it has just been described, is maintained: in every case there is the recurrence of a certain type of wave form, and the opposition—and balance —between the rising and falling swings. The simplest repeat, if you take its elements in succession, is a rhythm. In the diaper pattern, for example, there is the recurrence of the rising and falling lines, and their opposition and balance, two by two. Or a colonnade, as you apprehend the columns in succession, is a rhythm of identical and balancing filled and empty spaces, the columns corresponding to the arsis, and the spatial interval to the thesis.

Hence when balance seems to be replaced by rhythm, balance is still present, only it is not the simple type of balance so easily recognized, but balance as an element in the complex structure we call rhythm. This more subtle type of balance exists oftentimes in pictorial composition—in "open" as opposed to "closed" forms—where the ordinary mode of balance is rejected. I remember one of Monet's "Lily Ponds," in which I searched vainly for the usual type of balance with reference to some axis, only to find that the elements of the picture were arranged in a clear-cut rhythm.

Rhythm often replaces right-and-left balance in wall paintings, as in those of Puvis de Chavannes. In the Metropolitan Museum he has two paintings, both decorative sketches, which illustrate this: "Inter Artes et Naturam" and "The River." In the former, notice how we do not view the picture from a vertical central axis, but rather from left or right, taking each group of figures in turn as an element in a rhythmically disposed sequence of filled and empty spaces. In "The River," the rhythmical arrangement is in deep space.

Another and, last type of unity I call evolution. By this I mean the unity of a process when the earlier parts determine the later, and all together create a total meaning. For illustrations, one naturally turns first to the temporal arts. The course of a well-fashioned story is a good example, for each incident determines its follower and all the incidents determine the destiny of the characters involved. The drama offers similar illustrations: the form is the same, only transposed to theatrical presentation. In the older, orthodox story or play there were three stages in the development, an initial one of introduction of characters, a second stage of complication, ending in the climax, and then the unraveling. But these stages may be compressed. The story may begin with the complication already there; the play may begin with the climax and proceed to the unraveling, and go back, as in Ibsen, to the preparation. But in every case, there is necessary relation between means and consequences, causes and effects, and a total resulting meaning. Illustrations of this type of unity abound also in the static arts. Any line which we appreciate as having a beginning, middle, and end, and any composition of figures where we are led on from one figure or group of figures to another, is an illustration; for there, too, although the figures be physically static, our appreciation of them is a process in time, and through the process the meaning of the whole is evolved. Of all painters, I think El Greco offers the best illustrations of evolution, as in the "Crucifixion" (Prado museum), where we follow an intensely dramatic movement from the lower to the upper part of the picture.

Is evolution a genuinely distinct type of esthetic unity? Can it be reduced to one or more of the preceding forms? The most closely allied form is rhythm; yet that evolution is distinct from rhythm can easily be seen. For in rhythm, unless combined with evolution, there is no obvious development, no tendency toward a goal. Rhythm is recurrence and balance of systole and diastole, with no growth from one phase to another. It is true that we sometimes speak of any movement of growth as a rhythm, as when we talk of the rhythm of life, but in such cases rhythm exists in combination with evolution. For there is, of course, a rhythm in all life— birth and death, sleep and waking, activity and repose. And if life be taken generically or historically, there are other equally well-known rhythms, as in the history of art, with the alternation of the opposed directions from realism to romanticism. In melody also, except in the most eccentric types of music, harmonic evolution is joined with an accentual or time rhythm. Moreover, even in the most mechanical types of rhythm, like the simple repeat, provided they be esthetic, there is some felt growth of value through the recurrence and balance of parts, and some, however slight, looking forward to the end term as a goal. Only in purely natural rhythms, as of the tides, is there no growth at all, but these, unless they enter into the mind and emotion of man, are not esthetic in character. Nevertheless, although there is always some evolution in every esthetic rhythm, evolution is not itself necessarily rhythmical. In literature, the rhythm of prose and poetry overlies a development of meanings which does not itself have a quasi-mechanical character of rhythm; the rhythm of time and accent is united with the melodic development of the musical theme, but does not constitute it. The essential character of evolution is, as Bergson has shown, growth or accumulation of meaning, which need not be rhythmical.

Two different types of evolutionary unity must be discriminated, the dramatic and the non-dramatic. In the dramatic type there is an element of overshadowing importance, the climax or goal; in the other type, this element is lacking. To be sure, every process must have an end, and the end has a distinctive importance as such, but it is not always true that the end has a greater importance than some other element or elements. The consummation of the meaning may occur through the agency of all parts evenly, rather than through a particular one. Many stories are of this character; there is an unfolding, a working out of something, with no obvious high points. Here and there the meaning rises, but there is no place where it becomes so central that we feel that the whole story depends upon it. And, if I mistake not, there is much music of this character; there is a definite drift or unfolding, but no climax or finale.

Closeness of connection, yet ultimate difference, marks the relation between evolution and the other types of esthetic unity, balance and thematic variation. The static character of balance is opposed to the dynamic character of evolution; indeed, all movement depends upon the upsetting of an established equilibrium. Yet seldom, even in the static arts, is balance found without movement; for there exists a tendency to proceed from one to another of the balanced elements. In a simple color contrast, for example, there is ever so slight a movement from the cold to the warm color. And, on the other hand, there is often a balance within evolution, between the complication and the unraveling of the plot, or the earlier and later parts of a musical theme. But the union of evolution and balance does not militate against the uniqueness of either. There remains for comparison, thematic variation. This form, too, might seem at first sight to be opposed to evolution, yet not so. for there is probably no case of variation in which the evolutionary element is not present. For the series of variations is not fruitless; each contributes something to a meaning which accumulates and is complete when the variations are over. So many, and no more, exist as are necessary to this end. Insofar as, in this way, a meaning is worked out, evolution and thematic variation approach and meet. Yet a difference remains. For the mode of the creation of the meaning is different. In the one case, it occurs through the recurrence of the central meaning in new shapes; in the other, through the realization of some single dominant idea, which extends over the entire work and is expressed once and once only. In the one case, we start with an idea already given, and work it out by repetition; in the other, we have no definite, but only a very vague idea to start with, and construct it step by step. The one method may be called analytic, the other synthetic. For example, we do not know what a musical theme is like until we have heard it entire; building it up is one thing; then, having got it, it is another thing to modulate, invert, and vary it. The same is true of a line.

Nevertheless, in the construction of a theme, both thematic variation and balance may be employed. For example, in building a melody, we may proceed from tone to tone consonant with a given tone, thus repeating the fundamental psychophysical rhythm of the two tones which is the basis of their harmony; or we may proceed through opposition by introducing dissonances. Again, in constructing a linear theme, it is possible to proceed either by repeating or continuing the curve with which we start, or else by introducing opposing and balancing lines. Or for the elucidation of a story it may be expedient to place the persons in various situations, in order that they may manifest their characters—the method of thematic variation —or to balance them against unlike characters. Yet by themselves neither mere variation of theme nor balance of opposites will create evolution. Thematic variation, balance, and evolution remain, therefore, the fundamental and irreducible types of esthetic unity. I personally have been unable to find other types. Types which seem to be different, like rhythm or circular composition, can easily be shown to be species of one or another of these pre-eminent forms. The reduction of rhythm has already been effected. As for circular composition, it is evidently a case of evolution; for there is always a beginning and an end; but evolution is combined with repetition, for the beginning and the end are the same. A melody that begins and ends on the tonic is a simple illustration. I have shown that all three forms are intermingled; and most works of art contain all three; yet they remain, nevertheless, distinct.[5]

The principle of hierarchy is not so much a mode of organic unity, like thematic variation, balance, and evolution, as rather a species of organization of elements in each of these modes. Sometimes, although not always, there is some one element, or there may be more, of a complex work of art which occupies a position of commanding importance there. These elements always embody the theme in an emphatic way, and have a significance far greater than any of the other elements. Thus, in a portrait, the figure is more important than the background, and the face is more significant than anything else. In a novel or drama there may be a scene of unusual significance for the development of the plot, or in a musical composition a single passage, like the Liebestod in Tristan, which overshadows the remainder of the composition or is the climax of its movement. Every dramatic species of evolution illustrates this, as we have seen. In balance also, as again we have already observed, one or the other of the elements may dominate, though slightly. However, dominance is a relative matter, and an element, not itself of unusual importance in the whole, may nevertheless overshadow another element, relatively. Thus, in the "Young Woman with a Water Jug" of Vermeer, the pitcher is more prominent than the box. Any quality whatever—large size, unusual brightness, richness of elaboration, central position, fullness of meaning—that attracts the attention to itself more strongly than the attention is attracted to other elements, creates relative dominance. However, there may be no elements of outstanding importance in the whole, as is the case in many a landscape painting and in the non-dramatic types of evolution, but only varying degrees of importance among all the elements.

What is the explanation of aesthetic design? The hypothesis which I shall present is closely connected, as I have indicated, with the general theory of art which I accept. A work of art—such has been the thesis—is the imaginative embodiment of a wish, expressed in a sensuous shape, through which both imagination and the wish acquire clarity, objectivity, and communicability. Or to put the same thing in a different way, a work of art is a reconstruction of sensuous reality into an image of desire. Art is expression, a language, but what it expresses is a dream. Now what I hope to show is that aesthetic form is precisely the form which a thing should have if it is to be in fact the imaginative satisfaction of desire. If the content of a work of art is the symbol of a wish, so is the form. Aesthetic form is desirable form. This form is, moreover, not peculiar to art, but is, as Plato divined, merely the perfection of that form which all experience has when it is happiest.

In a world which fulfilled my wish everything would be as I wanted it to be in terms of the wish. Everything would be both means and end; means as furthering satisfaction, and end as the material or terminus of satisfaction. Not only the eventual meanings, but the present qualities of my world would satisfy me. And such a world would contain no elements that were not expressions of desire. For obviously if any such elements existed, they would disturb the completeness of my satisfaction. They would either hinder or divert me from my purpose. They might satisfy some rival interest, but in so far as they did, my original purpose would be impaired. It might be necessary for satisfaction that there be obstacles to desire, to give it zest, but at least there would not be irrelevance or rivalry of interest. The wish would still command and pervade every element. For the achievement of this end, two conditions are necessary: first, the utter plasticity of the materials, and, second, the isolation of the experience in which the wish is fulfilled. These conditions are perfectly realized only in the dream and in those voluntary constructions of the imagination which, embodying dreams, we call works of art. The materials of the dream are images, things freed from the laws and conditions of reality, perfectly plastic to the dreamer's desires. The restrictions of time, place, and matter are removed; everything can be as the dreamer wishes it to be—in his dream. Wrapt in himself, nothing from the outside world can enter to disturb him, no duties, no demands. It is true that as he sleeps lightly sensations may now and then reach the sleeper, but they do not disturb or divert; for they are quickly woven into the fabric of his dream. In the day-dream also the same conditions obtain. The rigid attitude of body and absent-minded expression of face indicate the isolation of the dreamer from the rest of reality and his absorption in the dream.

It is clear that the conditions of complete wish fulfilment as we have described them are the exact counterpart of the principle of organic unity. The inference is unavoidable that the principle itself is a derivative of the wish. It was only gradually, however, that the full implications of this principle were worked out. At first it was applied to the meanings or content of the work of art only. When paleolithic man first drew the image of the bison or reindeer in his cave, he was creating a rudimentary work of art, an image of his desire. Those red or black marks meant the animal, the possession of which he so urgently needed. But it was only the animal that he was interested in—and he drew it with a poignant and consummate realism; he was not interested in the black or red marks themselves. Yet they, too, were his own work and subject potentially to his will. And eventually they claimed his attention. Gradually, we notice an interest in the colors or lines as such. The colors become pleasing and expressive; so too the lines; the wish has mastered the medium also. So that now we scarcely regard anything as a work of art unless it has this character of complete expressiveness. And where the form is most plastic to desire, there we agree that a work of art is most artistic, most nearly art—as with music and painting and sculpture, and occasionally with poetry (for language is rarely utterly responsive, even to a poet's will); and less often with architecture and the other industrial arts. The fineness of art depends upon this.

In passing from imagination to reality the conditions of perfect wish fulfilment are only partially satisfied; and therefore the principle of organic unity is only approximately realized; yet it is important to observe that there is partial fulfilment. The nearest approaches to the perfect realization of the wish are the so-called beauties of nature and machines. There is something seemingly miraculous about the former, for they come to man, without any effort of his own, already embodiments of his wish. It is as if some purpose were at work there favorable to man, moulding the aspect of things in accordance with his heart's desire. Thus to a man a woman is given, not created, beautiful—the visible expression of his amorous dream for play, for companionship, for comfort. She is just as he would have her be, as if he himself had designed and created her, and in contemplation of her his instincts find a rapt and total imaginative fulfilment. Yet ever not quite. There is always some detail that does not go with the rest, some element of structure or line or color. When he paints her or sculptures her, he will change something. So a sunset on a summer's sea, or a moonrise over dark hills, without any effort of his own, will cause him to dream, and keep him in his dream, and thus will be beautiful. But to his critical eye there will be something there also, too much or too little, something to add or something to exclude (hence the artistic superiority of still life over nature), unless through some stupendous vision, like the Grand Cañon of Arizona, he is overwhelmed and his power of criticism shattered.

For any one who has used or known of the use of a machine, it too expresses a wish. There, too, as in a work of art, we observe the coöperation of parts to a single end; there, also, nothing is superfluous and everything needful is provided. Moreover, despite the fact that, in order to be used, a machine must be placed in contact with the object upon which it is to function—as a reaper must be placed in contact with the sheaves—its efficient working depends upon a certain isolation and enclosure of energies within a limited field. In all these respects, a machine is analogous to a work of art; but there are fatal defects from the point of view of the imagination. For, in the first place, the wish is never fulfilled in the machine itself as an object to be contemplated, as the wish is satisfied with art, but only through the use of the machine. To be sure, if well fashioned, a machine offers to the imagination a prophecy and premonition of the values in use, which is itself a delight, but, after all, its purpose is not realized except in actual use. And in use, every machine reveals itself as imperfect and inefficient, magnificently functioning for a time, but soon needing repair and eventually out-of-date, and superseded—never a joy forever. Moreover, although a machine may be relatively good from a practical point of view, certain of its aspects need not be just as one would wish them to be. The lines, for example, although as bearers of mechanical energies they be precisely what we should want them to be in terms of the purpose of the machine, are not necessarily pleasing in themselves. Neither are the colors. Mechanically considered, the lines of a Ford car may be right, but as mere lines they are not. A machine, therefore, although it approximates organization in terms of a wish, is not organized all through; it may satisfy the user, but it does not always satisfy the spectator.

It is thus through the whole of a man's practical world. He is forever striving to reconstruct his environment in terms of his wishes; he succeeds here, he fails there, but never does he win a complete success. In his office he tries to arrange everything—chairs, table, desk, filing case, the routine of his business—so that each item will express his desire, so that nothing shall interfere or divert; but these things, although they may be partly, are never wholly, as he would have them. He comes home; he seeks there an environment that shall express his more intimate, affectionate, playful self; and if fortunate, he will find much that will satisfy, but never all.

To restate my argument. The organic structure of works of art is not unique—except in its perfection. For in his relations with his world, man is trying to do exactly what the artist does—to transform it into an image of his desire. And he would so transform it all through; he would make it utterly his, the embodiment of his dream. But however skilful and fortunate, he cannot succeed. The materials with which he works are not sufficiently plastic to his purpose; he has to rely on other wills which offer him only partial service and coöperation; his own will is faltering and unclear. Some things there are that come to him already satisfactory, for the most part—his own and other organisms, where a will sympathetic with and similar to his own seems to be operative,[6] and institutions which are themselves partially products of desire; yet even these, as we have seen, are imperfect. There remains a realm where man can succeed, the realm of the imagination, dream, play, and art. There he can do perfectly, because there and there alone he is master and creator.

The next two principles, those of the theme and of thematic variation, can well be considered together. The explanation is contained, I think, in the following reflections.

The growth of experience is marked by the gradual emergence of clarity and definiteness, the passage of the mind from vague, diffuse interests to consolidated habits. On the reflective level, these habits become plans of action and expectations of recurrent kinds of satisfaction. Types of activity and value are distinguished: business, recreation, home life, love, study, and the like. And these types are not mere classifications of unrelated experiences that happen to be alike, but highly systematic wholes. In time, as man becomes fully self-conscious, he interprets his life in terms of them. This fact could be accurately expressed by saying that, as experience develops into ripeness, it knows itself as the working out of a number of definitely conceived 'themes,' which recur again and again, are embroidered and varied, like the themes of an arabesque or a musical composition. And, as in music, experience tends, following its own law, to an increasing subordination of its elements to the major themes, few or many, upon which it is built. In proportion as it is masterful, these themes become clear and dominating. Yet in real life they never do become quite clear and dominating; man retains to the end, even when most powerful and self-conscious, a certain vagueness and shiftiness. He does not know just what his purposes are; he does not know just what to expect and plan for; but he always wishes that he did.

Now in art what I have called the principle of the theme is, I believe, the realization of precisely this wish. In the imagination, life can have the clarity and consistency which it seeks, but never quite finds. There it can state its plans, its expectations, its purposes. The theme is such a statement. Knowing a linear or coloristic or musical theme is like knowing a friend's character or plans, or like knowing one's own mind: you know what to expect; you know what the characteristic quality of your experience will be; and that everything will be composed with reference to this quality as a focus. The theme will contain the central meaning of the whole and will serve as the summary and essence of it. Knowing it, you can largely divine and understand the rest. Thus the theme is no new thing; it is not anything peculiar to art. It is the theme which gives to life, as well as to art, what we call style, distinctive pattern, and clarity. Once more we find that aesthetic form is the form of all satisfactory life, only a form perfectly realized because embodied in a material of indefinitely great plasticity.

Important as the theme is in life, no less important is the variation of it. In order that life be satisfactory, it is necessary that a valuable activity be both constantly repeated and constantly varied. Few wishes can be satisfied with a single, instant fulfilment. At the first exercise of an activity the organs are not fully prepared; adaptation comes only by repetition. As I can better attend to a thing when—*ceteris paribus*—I have attended to it before, so I can the better enjoy what I have before enjoyed. Moreover, every valuable experience leaves a delightful memory of itself which becomes a wish for its renewal. When therefore the new experience comes, it comes not merely as a fulfilment of the desire itself, but of the expectation of it, also; it thus acquires a double value. The basis of life's happiness is the recurrence of habitual, expected satisfactions. And yet, although repetition increases value, mere repetition kills it. Too great habituation brings mechanism and the loss of conscious interest. Hence the need for change, for variation, to pique the value into vividness. Throughout life we demand the type, the theme, yet some variation from it.

I can illustrate the need for each as follows. Let us suppose that our friends had new faces each day, how disconcerting! We should have the trouble of getting acquainted with them anew each morning, and there would be no opportunity for the sweet joy of recognition, no anchor for affection. They could not grow in meaning for us, as they do now. Suppose, on the other hand, that our friends' faces were invariable, that they were worn like masks. Once more, how disconcerting! How monotonous, how unresponsive! Our values are best attached to familiar objects which at the same time offer us the spice of novelty. Through the typical, value receives perfectly adjusted realization; through its variation, intensity. "The union of the hazardous and the stable," writes John Dewey, "of the incomplete and the recurrent, is the condition of all experienced satisfaction as truly as of our predicaments and problems. While it is the source of ignorance, error, and the failure of expectation, it is the source of the delights which fulfilment brings. For if there were nothing in the way, if there were no deviations and resistances, fulfilment would be at once and in so being would fulfil nothing, but merely be. It would not be in connection with desire and satisfaction."[7] Such familiar considerations as these suffice, I think, to show that the principle of thematic variation belongs to life as well as to art.

That the demand for balance in art has its analogue in life and that this demand springs from the emotional side of our nature, I shall now proceed to show. Balance depends upon contrast, as we have seen. One might think perhaps that contrast was opposed to the conditions underlying wish fulfilment as expounded so far; for, as we have observed it, the wish demands renewal, repetition of the like, while now we suggest that it demands the unlike. And yet it remains a fact that a wish requires both: both sameness and difference, and that extreme of difference which is contrast. There are several reasons for this. First, as has often been suggested, the contrasting thing, being totally unlike the original, occupies a different set of elements of the mind from those which are brought into play by the former, and thus offers them rest; when therefore the original object reappears, it comes with its value refreshed and enhanced. Each contrasting element therefore increases the value of the other. But this would explain only the value of alternating opposites; it would not explain simultaneous contrast. Hence there must be another reason, a reason far more fundamental, I think.

That reason is this: our entire emotional life is constructed on the principle of polarity: stimulation, repose; joy, sadness; love, hate; tension, relaxation. Not only is the organism bilaterally symmetrical and the muscles built in pairs of balancing antagonists; the inner life has a similar plan. Furthermore, each polar element *demands* its antagonist; it contains within itself already a desire and a premonition of its opposite. Joy contains an impulse to sorrow, and vice versa; hate to love; love to hate. Strange as this fact may seem, it is nevertheless a commonplace among acute observers of human nature. The most striking illustrations of it are to be found among pathological phenomena, but the pathological are only exaggerations, caricatures of the normal. Things which express opposing states of mind come, therefore, not only with their own native values, but with values enhanced through the fulfilment of demands which their very opposites have created. The blue demands the gold; the high tone, the low tone; the curve to the right, a curve to the left; light, darkness; because each of these pairs possesses an emotional significance which craves its opposite. This same principle may be stated in still another form, which is the most fundamental of all: man's entire nature demands expression; this is better fulfilled through contrast, which brings opposing elements into play, than through the mere variation of a single identical theme. A palette of warm colors contains only half a world of color values; a palette that contains also the cold holds the entire world of color value in its compass. Hence the richest works of art are constructed through the variation and embellishment of opposed, yet balanced themes.[8] This principle is of the greatest value in explaining the presence of evil and pain in art; for in the long run man prefers a world in which there is the night side as well as the daylight side of life.

Next we have to prove that the evolutionary type of unity exemplified in works of art is present in the structure of satisfactory life everywhere. Now, independent of the special character of its incidents, the course of life is interesting when, first, there is some major plan or expectation which is worked out through its entire span. The existence of an ambition, purpose, or expectation, as giving meaning and interest to life, would illustrate this. This demand is fulfilled in art through the theme, as we have observed. However, zest in life depends, second, upon the realization of the expectation in such a way that curiosity as to how and when it is to be fulfilled is constantly aroused and satisfied, satisfied and aroused, from moment to moment. A life in which expectation is fulfilled too easily, in which therefore suspense and curiosity are lacking, is boring; on the other hand, a life in which expectation was always balked, a life therefore which was so uncertain that no expectations could arise, would be intolerable. That both these conditions are fulfilled, and in the best possible fashion, in the aesthetic structure which we have called evolution, can be proved by the analysis of one or two concrete examples.

What happens when we listen to a story? It is a fact—is it not?—that, knowing the general plan of human life, there are created in us, through the characters and situations presented to us, certain expectations from point to point in the story which at later points are fulfilled or denied. At the outset our expectations are very general indeed; we know that we are to hear something about human life; hence there will be men and women in the story, and something of love and ambition, with the successful or unsuccessful issue of each. But when the story has fairly opened and the characters and their situation are before us, our expectations become more definite. They do not, however, take us far; they do not enable us to predict the outcome of the story with certainty. They carry us only to the next events, and then only to their general character. Thus, in Chekov's story, *Expensive Lessons,* as soon as the teacher of French enters the scholar's room we know he will fall in love with her, but we are in doubt as to what will be her feeling toward him. At each step in the story a double attitude of mind, part curiosity, part expectation, is created in us, and every time that our curiosity is satisfied, a new curiosity is aroused; every time our expectations are fulfilled, a surprise awaits us. A story that defeated all of our expectations would have no unity; one that allowed us to foretell everything and so aroused no curiosity and suspense, would not interest us. And when our expectations are disappointed, it should seem right—that is, logical—on retrospect, that events should have happened as they did; the story should seem right and we wrong; everything in the story should appear to be necessary, as we review it. In this respect also art should be the image of life, only more perspicuous than life; for as we live forward, looking to an unknown future, events occur which seem at the moment to be fortuitous, and we protest against them as things that might have been otherwise; yet when they are past and we review them in the light of our own natures, which are our fates, and in relation to our history hitherto, we see that they could not have happened otherwise than as they did.

An analysis of melody reveals a similar psychological tissue. As we set ourselves in the attitude of listening, we have certain very vague expectations as to what we shall hear; it will be music, of course, and in a certain key and from a certain instrument. But our expectations become definite only after we have heard the first few tones. The succeeding tones must lie within the tonality of the melody; they must belong to the principal chords of the key. Yet we cannot predict beforehand just what is coming; we are curious to see. Sometimes, as when a dissonance is introduced, our expectations are defeated and we are surprised. But on the resolution of the dissonance, it comes to seem to have been right, in retrospect; and so does every other tone. Step by step there are built up expectations and curiosities which the music satisfies and arouses as it proceeds.[9]

But this account is still not quite adequate. For in emphasizing the step by step character of the development, we have failed to do justice to the dominating unity of the whole. This is very apparent when there is a climax. For in that case it is clear that there is aroused a major expectation and curiosity that pervades the entire story, with reference to which other expectations are as smaller designs in a larger pattern. But the same thing holds when there is no overshadowing element. There is still some main problem that has to be solved, some knot that has to be untied. The facts are the same in melody; the melody arouses a single sweeping wave of expectation which is satisfied when the return to the tonic or to some other tone of the tonic chord is effected, even when its course is even. In rhythm, as opposed to evolution, there is a sequence of expectations and fulfilments; but unless the rhythm is part of an evolution, there is no embracing one. There, there is a series of pulsations, all on a level; here, there is a single one, made up of partial ones. In rhythm there is, moreover, a regularity in the pulsations and a balance among them, two by two, while in evolution, although there may be a regular or irregular ground-rhythm, the minor pulsations are not necessarily balanced. The facts noted here correspond to the differences between rhythm and evolution already recorded. Yet in the dramatic type of evolution, there is probably, as

Langfeld has observed,[10] a balance between the strain of complication and the belief of unraveling.

That, finally, the principle of hierarchy has its analogue in life and its basis in human nature, is not difficult to see. The concerns of life fall naturally into focus and fringe, vocation and avocation, important and less important. Matters of high interest are salient against a background of things of less moment. There is never a dead level of value in life. No life is satisfactory without its hours of intense significance, which give it luster, yet man cannot always 'burn with a gemlike flame'; he must fall back, for rest and refreshment, on the little things. These latter are just as necessary in their way as the great moments. Some of them function as recreation, others as a stage or preparation for the high moments. Yet when life is most satisfactory, these moments of preparation or repose are never merely means to ends; they possess charm of their own as well. When life is so lived it becomes an art, and when a work of art is so constructed, it is an image of life at its best.

What I have tried to prove in this chapter may be summarized briefly as follows: Aesthetic design is the perfect realization of that design which gives value to experience everywhere. When experience is organic, when it has clarity of aim, when that aim finds itself fulfilled in ever new experiences; when the opposing elements of our complex nature receive a balanced realization; when the career of life has plot, embodying suspense and fulfilment, curiosity and expectation; when there is due subordination of its elements to its major interests, yet some value in each on its own account as well; then experience is satisfactory, then it has desirable form. It was inevitable, therefore, that man in his effort to embody his dreams in permanent shape, and make them available for the appreciation of his fellows, should give to them this same form. The design of art, like its content, is the image of desire.

—*The Analysis of Art* (1924)

NOTES

1. *The Eternal Values*, chap. IX.
2. *The Psychology of Beauty*, chap. III.
3. *Philosophie de l'art* part, I, p. 5.
4. Compare Ethel Puffer, "Studies in Symmetry," *Harvard Psychological Studies*, vol. I, 1902.
5. I am reminded by my friend, Miss Shio Sakanishi, that in many forms of Japanese art symmetry and repetition are carefully avoided, yet balance is scrupulously observed.
6. Compare the argument of Kant's *Kritik of Judgment*, part II.
7. John Dewey, *Experience and Nature*, p. 62.
8. This concept of totality through balance of opposites was Goethe's. See E. A. Boucke, *Goethe's Weltanschauung*, p. 263.
9. This analysis applies only to classical music. 'Modernist' music is at the point of dispensing with scales and tonality altogether.
10. Sidney Langfeld, *The Æsthetic Attitude*, p. 241.

HORATIO GREENOUGH

Structure and Organization

The developments of structure in the animal kingdom are worthy of all our attention if we would arrive at sound principles in building. The most striking feature in the higher animal organizations is the adherence to one abstract type. The forms of the fish and the lizard, the shape of the horse, and the lion, and the camelopard, are so nearly framed after one type that the adherence thereto seems carried to the verge of risk. The next most striking feature is the modification of the parts, which, if contemplated independently of the exposure and functions whose demands are thus met, seems carried to the verge of caprice. I believe few persons not conversant with natural history ever looked through a collection of birds, or fish, or insects, without feeling that they were the result of Omnipotence at play for mere variety's sake.

If there be any principle of structure more plainly inculcated in the works of the Creator than all others, it is the principle of unflinching adaptation of forms to functions. I believe that colors also, so far as we have discovered their chemical causes and affinities, are not less organic in relation to the forms they invest than are those forms themselves.

If I find the length of the vertebrae of the neck in grazing quadrupeds increased, so as to bring the incisors to the grass; if I find the vertebrae shortened in beasts of prey, in order to enable the brute to bear away his victims; if I find the wading birds on stilts, the strictly aquatic birds with paddles; if, in pushing still further the investigation, I find color arrayed either for disguise or aggression, I feel justified in taking the ground that organization is the primal law of structure, and I suppose it, even where my imperfect light cannot trace it, unless embellishment can be demonstrated. Since the tints as well as the forms of plants and flowers are shown to have an organic significance and value, I take it for granted that tints have a like character in the mysteriously clouded and pearly shell, where they mock my ken. I cannot believe that the myriads are furnished, at the depths of the ocean, with the complicated glands and absorbents to nourish those dyes, in order that the hundreds may charm my idle eye as they are tossed in disorganized ruin upon the beach.

Let us dwell for a moment upon the forms of several of the higher types of animal structure. Behold the eagle as he sits on the lonely cliff, towering high in the air; carry in your mind the proportions and lines of the dove and mark how the finger of God has, by the mere variation of diameters, converted the type of meekness into the most expressive symbol of majesty. His eye, instead of rushing as it were out of his head, to see the danger behind him, looks steadfastly forward from its deep cavern, knowing no danger but that which it pilots. The structure of his brow allows him to fly upward with his eyes in shade. In his beak and his talons we see at once the belligerent, in the vast expanse of his sailing pinions the patent of his prerogative. *Dei Gratia Raptor!* Whence the beauty and majesty of the bird? It is the oneness of his function that gives him his grandeur, it is transcendental mechanism alone that begets his beauty. Observe the lion as he stands! Mark the ponderous predominance of his anterior extremities, his lithe loins, the lever of his hock, the awful breadth of his jaws, and the depth of his chest. His mane is a curiass, and when the thunder of his voice is added to the glitter of his snarling jaws, man alone with all his means of defense stands self-possessed before him. In his structure again are beheld, as in that of the eagle, the most terrible expression of power and dominion, and we find that it is here also the result of transcendental mechanism. The form of the hare might well be the type of swiftness for him who never saw the greyhound. The greyhound overtakes him, and it is not possible in organization that this result should obtain, without the promise and announcement of it, in the lengths and diameters of this breed of dogs.

Let us now turn to the human frame, the most beautiful organization of earth, the exponent and minister of the highest being we immediately know. This stupendous form, towering as a lighthouse, commanding by its posture a wide horizon, standing in relation to the brutes where the spire stands in relation to the lowly colonnades of Greece and Egypt, touching earth with only one-half the soles of its feet—it tells of majesty and dominion by that upreared spine, of duty by those unencumbered hands. Where is the ornament of this frame? It is all beauty, its motion is grace, no combination of harmony ever equaled, for expression and variety, its poised and stately gait; its voice is music, no cunning mixture of wood and metal ever did more than feebly imitate its tone of command or its warble of love. The savage who envies or admires the special attributes of beasts maims unconsciously his own perfection to assume their tints, their feathers, or their claws; we turn from him with horror, and gaze with joy on the naked Apollo.

I have dwelt a moment on these examples of expression and of beauty that I may draw from them a principle in art, a principle which, if it has been often illustrated by brilliant results, we constantly see neglected, overlooked, forgotten—a principle which I hope the examples I have given have prepared you to accept at once and unhesitatingly. It is this: in art, as in nature, the soul, the purpose of a work will never fail to be proclaimed in that work in proportion to the subordination of the parts to the whole, of the whole to the function. If you will trace the ship through its various stages of improvement, from the dugout canoe and the old galley to the latest type of the sloop-of-war, you will remark that every advance in performance has been an advance in expression, in grace, in beauty, or grandeur, according to the functions of the craft. This artistic gain, effected by pure science in some respects, in others by mere empirical watching of functions where the elements of the structure were put to severe tests, calls loudly upon the artist to keenly watch traditional dogmas and to see how far analogous rules may guide his own operations. You will remark, also, that after mechanical power had triumphed over the earlier obstacles, embellishment began to encumber and hamper ships, and that their actual approximation to beauty has been effected, first, by strict adaptation of forms to functions, second, by the gradual elimination of all that is irrelevant and impertinent. The old chairs were formidable by their weight, puzzled you by their carving, and often contained too much else to contain convenience and comfort. The most beautiful chairs invite you by a promise of ease, and they keep that promise; they bear neither flowers nor dragons, nor idle displays of the turner's caprice. By keeping within their province they are able to fill it well. Organization has a language of its own, and so expressive is that language that a makeshift or make-believe can scarce fail of detection. The swan, the goose, the duck, when they walk toward the water are awkward, when they hasten toward it are ludicrous. Their feet are paddles, and their legs are organized mainly to move those paddles in the water; they, therefore, paddle on land, or as we say, waddle. It is only when their breasts are launched into the pond that their necks assume the expression of ease and grace. A serpent upon a smooth hard road has a similar awkward expression of impotence; the grass, or pebbles, or water, as he meets either, afford him his *sine quâ non,* and he is instantly confident, alert, effective.

If I err not, we should learn from these and the like examples, which will meet us wherever we look for them, that God's world has a distinct formula for every function, and that we shall seek in vain to borrow shapes; we must make the shapes, and can only effect this by mastering the principles.

It is a confirmation of the doctrine of strict adaptation that I find in the purer Doric temple. The sculptures which adorned certain spaces in those temples had an organic relation to the functions of the edifice; they took possession of the worshiper as he approached, lifted him out of everyday life, and prepared him for the presence of the divinity within. The world has never seen plastic art developed so highly as by the men who translated into marble, in the tympanum and the metope, the theogony and the exploits of the heroes. Why, then, those columns uncarved? Why, then, those lines of cornice unbroken by foliages, unadorned by flowers? Why that matchless symmetry of every member, that music of gradation, without the tracery of the Gothic detail, without the endless caprices of arabesque? Because those sculptures *spake,* and speech asks a groundwork of silence and not of babble, though it were of green fields.

I am not about to deny the special beauties and value of any of the great types of building. Each has its meaning and expression. I am desirous now of analyzing that majestic and eloquent simplicity of the Greek temple, because, though I truly believe that it is hopeless to transplant its forms with any other result than an expression of impotent dilettantism, still I believe that its principles will be found to be those of all structures of the highest order.

When I gaze upon the stately and beautiful Parthenon, I do not wonder at the greediness of the moderns to appropriate it. I do wonder at the obtuseness which allowed them to persevere in trying to make it work in the towns. It seems like the enthusiasm of him who should squander much money to transfer an Arabian stallion from his desert home, that, as a blindfolded gelding, he might turn his mill. The lines in which Byron paints the fate of the butterfly that has fallen into the clutches of its childish admirer[1] would apply not inaptly to the Greek temple at the mercy of a sensible building committee, wisely determined to have their money's worth.

When high art declined, carving and embellishment invaded the simple organization. As the South Sea Islanders have added a variety to the human form by tattooing, so the cunning artisans of Greece undertook to go beyond perfection. Many rhetoricians and skilled grammarians refined upon the elements of the language of structure. They all spake: and demigods, and heroes, and the gods themselves, went away and were silent.

If we compare the simpler form of the Greek temple with the ornate and carved specimens which followed it, we shall be convinced, whatever the subtlety, however exquisite the taste that long presided over those refinements, that they were the beginning of the end, and that the turning-point was the first introduction of a fanciful, not demonstrable, embellishment, and for this simple reason, that, embellishment being arbitrary, there is no check upon it; you begin with acanthus leaves, but the appetite for sauces, or rather the need of them, increases as the palate gets jaded. You want jasper, and porphyry, and serpentine, and giallo antico, at last. Nay, you are tired of Aristides the Just, and of straight columns; they must be spiral, and by degrees you find yourself in the midst of a barbaric pomp whose means must be slavery—nothing less will supply its waste,—whose enjoyment is satiety, whose result is corruption.

It was a day of danger for the development of taste in this land, the day when Englishmen perceived that France was laying them under contribution by her artistic skill in manufacture. They organized reprisals upon ourselves, and, in lieu of truly artistic combinations, they have overwhelmed us with embellishment, arbitrary, capricious, setting at defiance all principle, meretricious dyes and tints, catchpenny novelties of form, steam-woven fineries and plastic ornaments, struck with the die or pressed into molds. In even an ordinary house we look around in vain for a quiet and sober resting-place for the eye; we see naught but flowers, flourishes—the renaissance of Louis Quatorze gingerbread embellishment. We seek in vain for aught else. Our own manufacturers have caught the furor, and our foundries pour forth a mass of ill-digested and crowded embellishment which one would suppose addressed to the sympathies of savages or of the colored population, if the utter absence of all else in the market were not too striking to allow such a conclusion.

I do not suppose it is possible to check such a tide as that which sets all this corruption toward our shores. I am aware of the economical sagacity of the English, and how fully they understand the market; but I hope that we are not so thoroughly asphyxiated by the atmosphere they have created as to follow their lead in our own creation of a higher order. I remark with joy that almost all the more important efforts of this land tend, with an instinct and a vigor born of the institutions, toward simple and effective organization; and they never fail whenever they toss overboard the English dictum and work from their own inspirations to surpass the British, and there, too, where the world thought them safe from competition.

I would fain beg any architect who allows fashions to invade the domain of principles to compare the American vehicles and ships with those of England, and he will see that the mechanics of the United States have already outstripped the artists, and have, by the results of their bold and unflinching adaptation, entered the true track, and hold up the light for all who operate for American wants, be they what they will.

In the American trotting wagon I see the old-fashioned and pompous coach dealt with as the old-fashioned palatial display must yet be dealt with in this land. In vain shall we endeavor to hug the associations connected with the old form. The redundant must be pared down, the superfluous dropped, the necessary itself reduced to its simplest expression, and then we shall find, whatever the organization may be, that beauty was waiting for us, though perhaps veiled, until our task was fully accomplished.

—Memorial of Horatio Greenough (1853)

NOTES

1. In *The Giaour*, the passage (lines 388–421) including:
   "For every touch that wooed its stay
   Hath brushed its brightest hues away."

MEYER SCHAPIRO

Style

I

By style is meant the constant form—and sometimes the constant elements, qualities, and expression—in the art of an individual or a group. The term is also applied to the whole activity of an individual or society, as in speaking of a "life-style" or the "style of civilization."

For the archeologist, style is exemplified in a motive or pattern, or in some directly grasped quality of the work of art, which helps him to localize and date the work and to establish connections between groups of works or between cultures. Style here is a symptomatic trait, like the nonesthetic features of an artifact. It is studied more often as a diagnostic means than for its own sake as an important constituent of culture. For dealing with style, the archeologist has relatively few esthetic and physiognomic terms.

To the historian of art, style is an essential object of investigation. He studies its inner correspondences, its life-history, and the problems of its formation and change. He, too, uses style as a criterion of the date and place of origin of works, and as a means of tracing relationships between schools of art. But the style is, above all, a system of forms with a quality and a meaningful expression through which the personality of the artist and the broad outlook of a group are visible. It is also a vehicle of expression within the group, communicating and fixing certain values of religious, social, and moral life through the emotional suggestiveness of forms. It is, besides, a common ground against which innovations and the individuality of particular works may be measured. By considering the succession of works in time and space and by matching the variations of style with historical events and with the varying features of other fields of culture, the historian of art attempts, with the help of common-sense psychology and social theory, to account for the changes of style or specific traits. The historical study of individual and group styles also discloses typical stages and processes in the development of forms.

For the synthesizing historian of culture or the philosopher of history, the style is a manifestation of the culture as a whole, the visible sign of its unity. The style reflects or projects the "inner form" of collective thinking and feeling. What is important here is not the style of an individual or of a single art, but forms and qualities shared by all the arts of a culture during a significant span of time. In this sense one speaks of Classical or Medieval or Renaissance Man with respect to common traits discovered in the art styles of these epochs and documented also in religious and philosophical writings.

The critic, like the artist, tends to conceive of style as a value term; style as such is a quality and the critic can say of a painter that he has "style" or of a writer that he is a "stylist." Although "style" in this normative sense, which is applied mainly to individual artists, seems to be outside the scope of historical and ethnological studies of art, it often occurs here, too, and should be considered seriously. It is a measure of accomplishment and therefore is relevant to understanding of both art and culture as a whole. Even a period style, which for most historians is a collective taste evident in both good and poor works, may be regarded by critics as a great positive achievement. So the Greek classic style was, for Winckelmann and Goethe, not simply a convention of form but a culminating conception with valued qualities not possible in other styles and apparent even in Roman copies of lost Greek originals. Some period styles impress us by their deeply pervasive, complete character, their special adequacy to their content; the collective creation of such a style, like the conscious shaping of a norm of language, is a true achievement. Correspondingly, the presence of the same style in a wide range of arts is often considered a sign of the integration of a culture and the intensity of a high creative moment. Arts that lack a particular distinction or nobility of style are often said to be styleless, and the culture is judged to be weak or decadent. A similar view is held by philosophers of culture and history and by some historians of art.

Common to all these approaches are the assumptions that every style is peculiar to a period of a culture and that, in a given culture or epoch of culture, there is only one style or a limited range of styles. Works in the style of one time could not have been produced in another. These postulates are supported by the fact that the connection between a style and a period, inferred from a few examples, is confirmed by objects discovered later. Whenever it is possible to locate a work through nonstylistic evidence, this evidence points to the same time and place as do the formal traits, or to a culturally associated region. The unexpected appearance of the style in another region is explained by migration or trade. The style is therefore used with confidence as an independent clue to the time and place of origin of a work of art. Building upon these assumptions, scholars have constructed a systematic, although not complete, picture of the temporal and spatial distribution of styles throughout large regions of the globe. If works of art are grouped in an order corresponding to their original positions in time and space, their styles will show significant relationships which can be coordinated with the relationships of the works of art to still other features of the cultural points in time and space.

II

Styles are not usually defined in a strictly logical way. As with languages, the definition indicates the time and place of a style or its author, or the historical relation to other styles, rather than its peculiar features. The characteristics of styles vary continuously and resist a systematic classification into perfectly distinct groups. It is meaningless to ask exactly when ancient art ends and medieval begins. There are, of course, abrupt breaks and reactions in art, but study shows that here, too, there is often anticipation, blending, and continuity. Precise limits are sometimes fixed by convention for simplicity in dealing with historical problems or in isolating a type. In a stream of development the artificial divisions may even be designated by numbers—Styles I, II, III. But the single name given to the style of a period rarely corresponds to a clear and universally accepted characterization of a type. Yet direct acquaintance with an unanalyzed work of art will often permit us to recognize another object of the same origin, just as we recognize a face to be native or foreign. This fact points to a degree of constancy in art that is the basis of all investigation of style. Through careful description and comparison and through formation of a richer, more refined typology adapted to the continuities in development, it has been possible to reduce the areas of vagueness and to advance our knowledge of styles.

Although there is no established system of analysis and writers will stress one or another aspect according to their viewpoint or problem, in general the description of a style refers to three aspects of art: form elements or motives, form relationships, and qualities (including an all-over quality which we may call the "expression").

This conception of style is not arbitrary but has arisen from the experience of investigation. In correlating works of art with an individual or culture, these three aspects provide the broadest, most stable, and therefore most reliable criteria. They are also the most pertinent to modern theory of art, although not in the same degree for all viewpoints. Technique, subject matter, and material may be characteristic of certain groups of works and will sometimes be included in definitions; but more often these features are not so peculiar to the art of a period as the formal and qualitative ones. It is easy to imagine a decided change in material, technique, or subject matter accompanied by little change in the basic form. Or, where these are constant, we often observe that they are less responsive to new artistic aims. A method of stone-cutting will change less rapidly than the sculptor's or architect's forms. Where a technique does coincide with the extension of a style, it is the formal traces of the technique rather than the operations as such that are important for description of the style. The materials are significant mainly for the textural quality and color, although they may affect the conception of the forms. For the subject matter, we observe that quite different themes—portraits, still lifes, and landscapes—will appear in the same style.

It must be said, too, that form elements or motives, although very striking and essential for the expression, are not sufficient for characterizing a style. The pointed arch is common to Gothic and Islamic architecture, and the round arch to Roman, Byzantine, Romanesque, and Renaissance buildings. In order to distinguish these styles, one must also look for features of another order and, above all, for different ways of combining the elements.

Although some writers conceive of style as a kind of syntax or compositional pattern, which can be analyzed mathematically, in practice one has been unable to do without the vague language of qualities in describing styles. Certain features of light and color in painting are most conveniently specified in qualitative terms and even as tertiary (intersensory) or physiognomic qualities, like cool and warm, gay and sad. The habitual span of light and dark, the intervals between colors in a particular palette—very important for the structure of a work—are distinct relationships between elements, yet are not comprised in a compositional schema of the whole. The complexity of a work of art is such that the description of forms is often incomplete on essential points, limiting itself to a rough account of a few relationships. It is still simpler, as well as more relevant to esthetic experience, to distinguish lines as hard and soft than to give measurements of their substance. For precision in characterizing a style, these qualities are graded with respect to intensity by comparing different examples directly or by reference to a standard work. Where quantitative measurements have been made, they tend to confirm the conclusions reached through direct qualitative description. Nevertheless, we have no doubt that, in dealing with qualities, much greater precision can be reached.

Analysis applies esthetic concepts current in the teaching, practice, and criticism of contemporary art; the development of new viewpoints and problems in the latter directs the attention of students to unnoticed features of older styles. But the study of works of other times also influences modern concepts through discovery of esthetic variants unknown in our own art. As in criticism, so in historical research, the problem of distinguishing or relating two styles discloses unsuspected, subtle characteristics and suggests new concepts of form. The postulate of continuity in culture —a kind of inertia in the physical sense—leads to a search for common features in successive styles that are ordinarily contrasted as opposite poles of form; the resemblances will sometimes be found not so much in obvious aspects as in fairly hidden ones—the line patterns of Renaissance compositions recall features of the older Gothic style, and in contemporary abstract art one observes form relationships like those of Impressionist painting.

The refinement of style analysis has come about in part through problems in which small differences had to be disengaged and described precisely. Examples are the regional variations within the same culture; the process of historical development from year to year; the growth of individual artists and the discrimination of the works of master and pupil, originals and copies. In these studies the criteria for dating and attribution are often physical or external—matters of small symptomatic detail—but here, too, the general trend of research has been to look for features that can be formulated in both structural and expressive-physiognomic terms. It is assumed by many students that the expression terms are all translatable into form and quality terms, since the expression depends on particular shapes and colors and will be modified by a small change in the latter. The forms are correspondingly regarded as vehicles of a particular effect (apart from the subject matter). But the relationship here is not altogether clear. In general, the study of style tends toward an ever stronger correlation of form and expression. Some descriptions are purely morphological, as of natural objects—indeed, ornament has been characterized, like crystals, in the mathematical language of group theory. But terms like "stylized," "archaistic," "naturalistic," "mannerist," "baroque," are specifically human, referring to artistic processes, and imply some expressive effect. It is only by analogy that mathematical figures have been characterized as "classic" and "romantic."

III

The analysis and characterization of the styles of primitive and early historical cultures have been strongly influenced by the standard of recent Western art. Nevertheless, it may be said that the values of modern art have led to a more sympathetic and objective approach to exotic arts than was possible fifty or a hundred years ago.

In the past, a great deal of primitive work, especially representation, was regarded as artless even by sensitive people; what was valued were mainly the ornamentation and the skills of primitive industry. It was believed that primitive arts were childlike attempts to represent nature—attempts distorted by ignorance and by an irrational content of the monstrous and grotesque. True art was admitted only in the high cultures, where knowledge of natural forms was combined with a rational ideal which brought beauty and decorum to the image of man. Greek art and the art of the Italian High Renaissance were the norms for judging all art, although in time the classic phase of Gothic art was accepted. Ruskin, who admired Byzantine works, could write that in Christian Europe alone "pure and precious ancient art exists, for there is none in America, none in Asia, none in Africa." From such a viewpoint careful discrimination of primitive styles or a penetrating study of their structure and expression was hardly possible.

With the change in Western art during the last seventy years, naturalistic representation has lost its superior status. Basic for contemporary practice and for knowledge of past art is the theoretical view that what counts in' all art are the elementary esthetic components, the qualities and relationships

of the fabricated lines, spots, colors, and surfaces. These have two characteristics: they are intrinsically expressive, and they tend to constitute a
coherent whole. The same tendencies to coherent and expressive structure
are found in the arts of all cultures. There is no privileged content or
mode of representation (although the greatest works may, for reasons
obscure to us, occur only in certain styles). Perfect art is possible in any
subject matter or style. A style is like a language, with an internal order
and expressiveness, admitting a varied intensity or delicacy of statement.
This approach is a relativism that does not exclude absolute judgments of
value; it makes these judgments possible within every framework by aban-
doning a fixed norm of style. Such ideas are accepted by most students of
art today, although not applied with uniform conviction.

As a result of this new approach, all the arts of the world, even the
drawings of children and psychotics, have become accessible on a common
plane of expressive and form-creating activity. Art is now one of the strongest evidences of the basic unity of mankind.

This radical change in attitude depends partly on the development of
modern styles, in which the raw material and distinctive units of operation
—the plane of the canvas, the trunk of wood, tool marks, brush strokes,
connecting forms, schemas, particles and areas of pure color—are as pronounced as the elements of representation. Even before nonrepresentative
styles were created, artists had become more deeply conscious of the
esthetic-constructive components of the work apart from denoted meanings.

Much in the new styles recalls primitive art. Modern artists were, in
fact, among the first to appreciate the works of natives as true art. The
development of Cubism and Abstraction made the form problem exciting
and helped to refine the perception of the creative in primitive work.
Expressionism, with its high pathos, disposed our eyes to the simpler, more
intense modes of expression, and together with Surrealism, which valued,
above all, the irrational and instinctive in the imagination, gave a fresh
interest to the products of primitive fantasy. But, with all the obvious
resemblances, modern paintings and sculptures differ from the primitive
in structure and content. What in primitive art belongs to an established
world of collective beliefs and symbols arises in modern art as an individual expression, bearing the marks of a free, experimental attitude to
forms. Modern artists feel, nevertheless, a spiritual kinship with the primitive, who is now closer to them than in the past because of their ideal of
frankness and intensity of expression and their desire for a simpler life,
with more effective participation of the artist in collective occasions than
modern society allows.

One result of the modern development has been a tendency to slight the
content of past art; the most realistic representations are contemplated as
pure constructions of lines and colors. The observer is often indifferent to
the original meanings of works, although he may enjoy through them a
vague sentiment of the poetic and religious. The form and expressiveness
of older works are regarded, then, in isolation, and the history of an art is
written as an immanent development of forms. Parallel to this trend, other
scholars have carried on fruitful research into the meanings, symbols, and
iconographic types of Western art, relying on the literature of mythology

and religion; through these studies the knowledge of the content of art has been considerably deepened, and analogies to the character of the styles have been discovered in the content. This has strengthened the view that the development of forms is not autonomous but is connected with changing attitudes and interests that appear more or less clearly in the subject matter of the art.

IV

Students observed early that the traits which make up a style have a quality in common. They all seem to be marked by the expression of the whole, or there is a dominant feature to which the elements have been adapted. The parts of a Greek temple have the air of a family of forms. In Baroque art, a taste for movement determines the loosening of boundaries, the instability of masses, and the multiplication of large contrasts. For many writers a style, whether of an individual or a group, is a pervasive, rigorous unity. Investigation of style is often a search for hidden correspondences explained by an organizing principle which determines both the character of the parts and the patterning of the whole.

This approach is supported by the experience of the student in identifying a style from a small random fragment. A bit of carved stone, the profile of a molding, a few drawn lines, or a single letter from a piece of writing often possesses for the observer the quality of the complete work and can be dated precisely; before these fragments, we have the conviction of insight into the original whole. In a similar way, we recognize by its intrusiveness an added or repaired detail in an old work. The feel of the whole is found in the small parts.

I do not know how far experiments in matching parts from works in different styles would confirm this view. We may be dealing, in some of these observations, with a microstructural level in which similarity of parts only points to the homogeneity of a style or a technique, rather than to a complex unity in the esthetic sense. Although personal, the painter's touch, described by constants of pressure, rhythm, and size of strokes, may have no obvious relation to other unique characteristics of the larger forms. There are styles in which large parts of a work are conceived and executed differently, without destroying the harmony of the whole. In African sculpture an exceedingly naturalistic, smoothly carved head rises from a rough, almost shapeless body. A normative esthetic might regard this as imperfect work, but it would be hard to justify this view. In Western paintings of the fifteenth century, realistic figures and landscapes are set against a gold background, which in the Middle Ages had a spiritualistic sense. In Islamic art, as in certain African and Oceanic styles, forms of great clarity and simplicity in three dimensions—metal vessels and animals or the domes of buildings—have surfaces spun with rich mazy patterns; in Gothic and Baroque art, on the contrary, a complex surface treatment is associated with a correspondingly complicated silhouette of the whole. In Romanesque art the proportions of figures are not submitted to a single canon, as in Greek art, but two or three distinct systems of proportioning exist even within the same sculpture, varying with the size of the figure.

Such variation within a style is also known in literature, sometimes in great works, like Shakespeare's plays, where verse and prose of different texture occur together. French readers of Shakespeare, with the model of their own classical drama before them, were disturbed by the elements of comedy in Shakespeare's tragedies. We understand this contrast as a necessity of the content and the poet's conception of man—the different modes of expression pertain to contrasted types of humanity—but a purist classical taste condemned this as inartistic. In modern literature both kinds of style, the rigorous and the free, coexist and express different viewpoints. It is possible to see the opposed parts as contributing elements in a whole that owes its character to the interplay and balance of contrasted qualities. But the notion of style has lost in that case the crystalline uniformity and simple correspondence of part to whole with which we began. The integration may be of a looser, more complex kind, operating with unlike parts.

Another interesting exception to the homogeneous in style is the difference between the marginal and the dominant fields in certain arts. In early Byzantine works, rulers are represented in statuesque, rigid forms, while the smaller accompanying figures, by the same artist, retain the liveliness of an older episodic, naturalistic style. In Romanesque art this difference can be so marked that scholars have mistakenly supposed that certain Spanish works were done partly by a Christian and partly by a Moslem artist. In some instances the forms in the margin or in the background are more advanced in style than the central parts, anticipating a later stage of the art. In medieval work the unframed figures on the borders of illuminated manuscripts or on cornices, capitals, and pedestals are often freer and more naturalistic than the main figures. This is surprising, since we would expect to find the most advanced forms in the dominant content. But in medieval art the sculptor or painter is often bolder where he is less bound to an external requirement; he even seeks out and appropriates the regions of freedom. In a similar way an artist's drawings or sketches are more advanced than the finished paintings and suggest another side of his personality. The execution of the landscape backgrounds behind the religious figures in paintings of the fifteenth century is sometimes amazingly modern and in great contrast to the precise forms of the large figures. Such observations teach us the importance of considering in the description and explanation of a style the unhomogeneous, unstable aspect, the obscure tendencies toward new forms.

If in all periods artists strive to create unified works, the strict ideal of consistency is essentially modern. We often observe in civilized as well as primitive art the combination of works of different style into a single whole. Classical gems were frequently incorporated into medieval reliquaries. Few great medieval buildings are homogeneous, since they are the work of many generations of artists. This is widely recognized by historians, although theoreticians of culture have innocently pointed to the conglomerate cathedral of Chartres as a model of stylistic unity, in contrast to the heterogeneous character of stylelessness of the arts of modern society. In the past it was not felt necessary to restore a damaged work or to complete an unfinished one in the style of the original. Hence the strange juxtapositions of styles within some medieval objects. It should be said, however, that some styles, by virtue of their open, irregular forms, can tolerate the unfinished and heterogeneous better than others.

Just as the single work may possess parts that we would judge to belong to different styles, if we found them in separate contexts, so an individual may produce during the same short period works in what are regarded as two styles. An obvious example is the writing of bilingual authors or the work of the same man in different arts or even in different genres of the same art—monumental and easel painting, dramatic and lyric poetry. A large work by an artist who works mainly in the small, or a small work by a master of large forms, can deceive an expert in styles. Not only will the touch change, but also the expression and method of grouping. An artist is not present in the same degree in everything he does, although some traits may be constant. In the twentieth century, some artists have changed their styles so radically during a few years that it would be difficult, if not impossible, to identify these as works of the same hand, should their authorship be forgotten. In the case of Picasso, two styles—Cubism and a kind of classicizing naturalism—were practiced at the same time. One might discover common characters in small features of the two styles—in qualities of the brushstroke, the span of intensity, or in subtle constancies of the spacing and tones—but these are not the elements through which either style would ordinarily be characterized. Even then, as in a statistical account small and large samples of a population give different results, so in works of different scale of parts by one artist the scale may influence the frequency of the tiniest elements or the form of the small units. The modern experience of stylistic variability and of the unhomogeneous within an art style will perhaps lead to a more refined conception of style. It is evident, at any rate, that the conception of style as a visibly unified constant rests upon a particular norm of stability of style and shifts from the large to the small forms, as the whole becomes more complex.

What has been said here of the limits of uniformity of structure in the single work and in the works of an individual also applies to the style of a group. The group style, like a language, often contains elements that belong to different historical strata. While research looks for criteria permitting one to distinguish accurately the works of different groups and to correlate a style with other characteristics of a group, there are cultures with two or more collective styles of art at the same moment. This phenomenon is often associated with arts of different function or with different classes of artists. The arts practiced by women are of another style than those of the men; religious art differs from profane, and civic from domestic; and in higher cultures the stratification of social classes often entails a variety of styles, not only with respect to the rural and urban, but within the same urban community. This diversity is clear enough today in the coexistence of an official-academic, a mass-commercial, and a free avant-garde art. But more striking still is the enormous range of styles within the latter—although a common denominator will undoubtedly be found by future historians.

While some critics judge this heterogeneity to be a sign of an unstable, unintegrated culture, it may be regarded as a necessary and valuable consequence of the individual's freedom of choice and of the world scope of modern culture, which permits a greater interaction of styles than was ever possible before. The present diversity continues and intensifies a diversity already noticed in the preceding stages of our culture, including the Middle Ages and the Renaissance, which are held up as models of close integration. The unity of style that is contrasted with the present diversity is one type of style formation, appropriate to particular aims and conditions; to achieve it today would be impossible without destroying the most cherished values of our culture.

If we pass to the relation of group styles of different visual arts in the same period, we observe that, while the Baroque is remarkably similar in architecture, sculpture, and painting, in other periods, for example, the Carolingian, the early Romanesque, and the modern, these arts differ in essential respects. In England, the drawing and painting of the tenth and eleventh centuries—a time of great accomplishment, when England was a leader in European art—are characterized by an enthusiastic linear style of energetic, ecstatic movement, while the architecture of the same period is inert, massive, and closed and is organized on other principles. Such variety has been explained as a sign of immaturity; but one can point to similar contrasts between two arts in later times, for example, in Holland in the seventeenth century where Rembrandt and his school were contemporary with classicistic Renaissance buildings.

When we compare the styles of arts of the same period in different media —literature, music, painting—the differences are no less striking. But there are epochs with a far-reaching unity, and these have engaged the attention of students more than the examples of diversity. The concept of the Baroque has been applied to architecture, sculpture, painting, music, poetry, drama, gardening, script, and even philosophy and science. The Baroque style has given its name to the entire culture of the seventeenth century, although it does not exclude contrary tendencies within the same country, as well as a great individuality of national arts. Such styles are the most fascinating to historians and philosophers, who admire in this great spectacle of unity the power of a guiding idea or attitude to impose a common form upon the most varied contexts. The dominant style-giving force is identified by some historians with a world outlook common to the whole society; by others with a particular institution, like the church or the absolute monarchy, which under certain conditions becomes the source of a universal viewpoint and the organizer of all cultural life. This unity is not necessarily organic; it may be likened also, perhaps, to that of a machine with limited freedom of motion; in a complex organism the parts are unlike and the integration is more a matter of functional interdependence than of the repetition of the same pattern in all the organs.

Although so vast a unity of style is an impressive accomplishment and seems to point to a special consciousness of style—the forms of art being felt as a necessary universal language—there are moments of great achievement in a single art with characteristics more or less isolated from those of the other arts. We look in vain in England for a style of painting that corresponds to Elizabethan poetry and drama; just as in Russia in the nineteenth century there was no true parallel in painting to the great movement of literature. In these instances we recognize that the various arts have different roles in the culture and social life of a time and express in their content as well as style different interests and values. The dominant outlook of a time—if it can be isolated—does not affect all the arts in the same degree, nor are all the arts equally capable of expressing the same outlook. Special conditions within an art are often strong enough to determine a deviant expression.

—*Anthropology Today*, edited by A. L. Kroeber (1953)

CHAPTER
9
Expressiveness

SUSANNE K. LANGER: *Expressiveness and Symbolism*
ROGER SESSIONS: *The Composer and His Message*
RUDOLF ARNHEIM: *The Expressiveness of Visual Forms*
MAURICE MERLEAU-PONTY: *The Film and the New Psychology*
HAROLD OSBORNE: *The Quality of Feeling in Art*

During the second and third decades of this century, estheticians were especially preoccupied with the problem of form. This was the period when such "formalists" as Clive Bell and Roger Fry exercised their greatest influence. They challenged the esthetic relevance of sentimental associations and directed attention to the great importance of plastic organization. It was a movement toward purification in esthetic theory and was paralleled by "abstract" or "nonobjective" trends in the arts (for example, in the works of Kandinsky, Mondrian, and Brancusi). But, as the century wore on, the interest in meaning and symbolism became ever more pronounced. A brilliant generation of thinkers—Whitehead, Russell, Wittgenstein, Freud, Cassirer, Carnap, to name the more prominent—established the new "keynote" of philosophical thought. Esthetics has reflected this general trend. The writers represented in the present chapter are typical of the predominant interest in expressiveness that has characterized esthetics in the past two decades.

Among these authors, Susanne Knauth Langer (1895–   ), professor emeritus of philosophy at Connecticut College, began her philosophical career by exploring logic and the whole field of signs, symbols, languages, and meanings. In her most popular book, *Philosophy in a New Key* (1942), she expounded the fundamental notion of symbolization as the connective link between fields as disparate as music, science, and religion (here following the lead of Ernst Cassirer in his monumental *Philosophy of Symbolic Forms*). Then in *Feeling and Form* (1953) she generalized the theory of music to cover all the arts, and in her *Problems of Art* (1957), *Philosophical Sketches* (1962), and *Mind* Vol. I, (1967), she responded to her critics by reformulating some of her basic ideas.

Her theory is based upon a distinction between two types of "symbolism," the *discursive*, which we find in pure science, and the *presentational*, which confronts us in art. Discursive symbolism is language in its literal use. It employs conventional meaningful units (the "dictionary" meanings) according to rules of grammar and syntax. Each

word has relatively fixed meaning, and the total meaning of the
discourse is built up stepwise by using the words successively. The import
can be paraphrased by using synonyms and logically equivalent sentences,
and it refers to the neutral aspects of our world of observation and
thought—the ideas and facts that are *least* tinged by subjective feeling.
Presentational symbolism, in contrast, employs no fixed constituents to be
combined according to rules; it therefore cannot be broken up into units
with independent and conventional meanings; its meaning inheres in the
total form, and cannot be paraphrased; it expresses, in its total range,
the whole subjective side of existence that discourse is incapable of
expressing—our moods, emotions, desires, the sense of movement, growth,
felt tensions and resolutions, even sensations and thoughts in their
characteristic passage. It does this not by a gushing forth of emotion but
by an articulation of the "logical forms" of subjectivity.

This articulation is made possible by a congruence between the
patterns of art and the patterns of sentience. At this point Professor
Langer invokes a well-known theory of *Gestalt* psychology—that there
may be a similarity of form between different fields of experience. It will be
helpful to cite a concrete example from an essay by Carroll C. Pratt: "In
the space below are two meaningless forms. The reader will be able to
decide without any trouble which of the meaningless sounds, *uloomu* and
takete, applies to each form. The demonstration shows that impressions

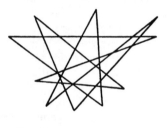

from different sense departments may be very similar with respect to
form. Each of the sounds, *takete* and *uloomu*, fits perfectly one of the
visual designs, but not the other. The impressions are different in content
—one is visual and the other auditory—but similar in form."[1] Dr. Langer
points out that such congruence of form holds not only between one
sense department and another but between a pattern of sense and a
pattern of feeling. "The tonal structures we call 'music,'" for example,
"bear a close logical similarity to the forms of human feeling—forms of
growth and of attenuation, flowing and stowing, conflict and resolution,
speed, arrest, terrific excitement, calm, or subtle activation and dreamy
lapses."[2] Thus subjective experience has a structure that can be
abstracted and articulated by the congruent form of a work of art. But
resemblance is not reference, and in the moment of esthetic vision, any
sense of reference is superseded by the immediate reality of the esthetic
apparition. Since the word "symbol" is almost always used to denote

reference, the work of art is a "symbol" in a somewhat unusual meaning of the word. Symbols, in the ordinary sense, may occur within the work of art, but they function at a different level from the work that contains them.

In explaining the nature of musical expressiveness, Langer cites[3] the "remarkably discerning" essay by Roger Sessions (1896–), of which the Sessions selection in the present chapter is an excerpt. Both Langer and Sessions find a correspondence between the dynamics of musical form and the deep organic rhythms of life and breath.

Educated at Harvard and Yale, Sessions was later a student and assistant under Ernest Bloch, one of the great modern composers, at the Cleveland Institute of Music. It was during this period that he began to compose music of his own, but not until after several years of study in Europe did he become one of America's foremost composers in a variety of musical modes, such as the string quartet, the symphony, and the opera. He has also won fame as a lecturer in musical theory in Princeton University and as a writer of lucid essays and books about music.

Sessions points out that *time* is the principal basis of musical expressiveness. He thinks there is a profound correspondence between the dynamic structure of musical time and the instinctive dynamism of the human organism, such as the beating of the heart, the movements of breathing, the involuntary tensions and relaxations of our nervous system. He recognizes a connotative element in musical expressiveness, for example, the similarity between an agitated musical movement and a storm; but he thinks that music goes deeper than to arouse such associations in the mind—it stirs up and sets pulsating the primal energies of our psychic life. The expressiveness of music, of course, is immeasurably heightened by its formal aspects—the infinite possibilities in harmonic combinations of sounds, and the use of premonition, recognition, progression, and contrast in the elaboration of musical motifs. "Form in music," he concludes, "is identical with content."

Although Sessions never refers by name to *Gestalt* psychology, his recognition of the similarity between tonal structures and psychological patterns is akin to the insights of the *Gestalt* psychologists. A more explicit appeal to Gestalt principles occurs in the writings of Rudolf Arnheim (1904–), Professor of Psychology at Sarah Lawrence College and author of important books and articles on the psychology of art. In the Preface to his *Art and Visual Perception,* he states: "As long as I can remember I have concerned myself with art, studied its nature and history, tried my eyes and hands at it, and sought the company of artists, art theorists, art educators. This interest has been enhanced by my psychological studies." His initial studies were made in Germany, the land of his birth, where he became familiar with the writings of Von Ehrenfels, Max Wertheimer, Wolfgang Köhler, Kurt Koffka, and other *Gestalt* theorists. The combination of this theoretical background with intensive experience of the arts has lent solidity and concreteness to Arnheim's esthetics.

In the selection included in this chapter, he takes issue with the traditional theory of the relation of sensory perception to expression. According to this theory, you perceive pure sense-data and then associate feelings and ideas with these original data. The expressiveness is due to this association. For example, what you perceive when you watch the flames in a fireplace would simply be bright reddish shapes in rapid movement. But you know from past experience "that fire hurts and destroys. It may remind you of violence. Perhaps you associate red with blood, which will reinforce the element of violence. The flames may seem to be moving like snakes. Also, your cultural environment has accustomed you to thinking of red as a color of passion. In consequence of all this, you not only see colors and shapes in motion, but are also struck by the expression of something frightening, violent, passionate."[4] In other words, you *perceive* only sensory data such as color, shape, sound; and expression is a superadded and secondary response due to the association of ideas. Arnheim opposes this theory of expression, which is represented in the present volume by Santayana's account.

As Arnheim explains in this chapter, expression is original and primary. In the case of the fire, one sees "the graceful play of aggressive tongues, flexible striving, lively color." The expressiveness appears in the visible pattern itself and strikes our attention immediately. An expressive whole is not attained by adding up isolated parts, thus combining associated ideas and feelings with sensory data. The expressiveness is intrinsic to the integrated structure of the whole, and this is cognized *en bloc*. The important consequences of this *Gestalt* theory for art and esthetic education are discussed by Arnheim.

In an approach like that of Arnheim, Maurice Merleau-Ponty (1908–1961) extends the principles of the "new psychology" to the film. As a professional philosopher and co-editor of *Les Temps Modernes*, a publication that he founded conjointly with Jean-Paul Sartre and Simone de Beauvoir, he took a very active part—philosophical, political, literary, and esthetic—in the intellectual life of his time. He was especially interested in the phenomenology of perception, and the essay reproduced in this chapter is a reflection of this major concern.

Merleau-Ponty includes under the "new psychology" three fundamental principles: (1) the role of configurations in our grasp of things, (2) the oneness of body-mind, and (3) the unity of the embodied-person with his surroundings. The first principle, that of Gestaltism, leads him to think in terms of configurations and to reject an atomistic theory of perception, according to which we see or hear isolated "sense data" and then artificially combine them into objects. The second principle, that of mind-body unity, makes him turn away from an *exclusive* behaviorism and an *exclusive* introspectionism, and to insist on the involvement of the whole body-mind organism in all its functions. The third principle, that of being-in-the-world, makes him realize that we organize and interpret our world from *within* it, as active participants. Experience, when characterized by these three principles, is movie material par excellence, the film being an art form in which the configurational nature of perception and the twofold unity of mind-body and being-in-the-world are clearly manifest.

All four writers cited so far—Langer, Sessions, Arnheim, and Merleau-Ponty—emphasize the role of configurations in artistic expressiveness, and find a congruence of form between the changing patterns of human feeling, or their behavioral manifestations, and the internal patterns of works of art. This congruence, they believe, largely explains the emotional expressiveness of esthetic objects.

Harold Osborne (1905–   ), editor of *The British Journal of Aesthetics* and distinguished esthetician, prefers a different explanation of expressiveness in art. He points out that we paradoxically attribute feelings to works of art, calling a musical composition "sad" or a painting "gay," and that the paradox is heightened by the fact that we often attribute sadness to the music without feeling sad ourselves, or gayety to the painting without feeling gay. How can we explain the fact that there are perceived properties of things which are expressive of emotion without provoking emotion in the percipient? Not by supposing that the music itself experiences sadness, since an object, such as a pattern of sounds, does not experience feelings. Nor by accepting the explanation of Langer and Arnheim, namely, that the tonal or visual structure is isomorphic with a pattern of feeling. Osborne questions whether our moods really have such complicated patterns and whether these patterns, if they do exist, can be observed and compared with the patterns of esthetic objects. Instead, he seeks explanation in the inadequacies and peculiarities of emotional language. The latter part of his article is an ingenious sketch of of the way in which such an explanation might proceed.

NOTES

1. Carroll G. Pratt, *Music as the Language of Emotion* (Library of Congress, Washington, D.C., 1952), p. 18.
2. Susanne K. Langer, *Feeling and Form* (Scribner's, New York, 1953), p. 27.
3. Langer, p. 67.
4. Rudolf Arnheim, "The Priority of Expression," *Journal of Aesthetics and Art Criticism*, Vol. VIII, December 1949, p. 106,

SUSANNE K. LANGER
Expressiveness and Symbolism

I. EXPRESSIVENESS

When we talk about "Art" with a capital "A"—that is, about any or all of the arts: painting, sculpture, architecture, the potter's and goldsmith's and other designers' arts, music, dance, poetry, and prose fiction, drama and film—it is a constant temptation to say things about "Art" in this general sense that are true only in one special domain, or to assume that what holds for one art must hold for another. For instance, the fact that music is made for performance, for presentation to the ear, and is simply not the same thing when it is given only to the tonal imagination of a reader silently perusing the score, has made some estheticians pass straight to the conclusion that literature, too, must be physically heard to be fully experienced, because words are originally spoken, not written; an obvious parallel, but a careless and, I think, invalid one. It is dangerous to set up principles by analogy, and generalize from a single consideration.

But it is natural, and safe enough, to ask analogous questions: "What is the function of sound in music? What is the function of sound in poetry? What is the function of sound in prose composition? What is the function of sound in drama?" The answers may be quite heterogeneous; and that is itself an important fact, a guide to something more than a simple and sweeping theory. Such findings guide us to exact relations and abstract, variously exemplified basic principles.

At present, however, we are dealing with principles that have proven to be the same in all the arts, when each kind of art—plastic, musical, balletic, poetic, and each major mode, such as literary and dramatic writing, or painting, sculpturing, building plastic shapes—has been studied in its own terms. Such candid study is more rewarding than the usual passionate declaration that all the arts are alike, only their materials differ, their principles are all the same, their techniques all analogous, etc. That is not only unsafe, but untrue. It is in pursuing the differences among them that one arrives, finally, at a point where no more differences appear; then one has found, not postulated, their unity. At that deep level there is only one concept exemplified in all the different arts, and that is the concept of Art.

The principles that obtain wholly and fundamentally in every kind of art are few, but decisive; they determine what is art, and what is not. Expressiveness, in one definite and appropriate sense, is the same in all art works of any kind. What is created is not the same in any two distinct arts —this is, in fact, what makes them distinct—but the principle of creation is the same. And "living form" means the same in all of them.

A work of art is an expressive form created for our perception through sense or imagination, and what it expresses is human feeling. The word "feeling" must be taken here in its broadest sense, meaning *everything that can be felt,* from physical sensation, pain and comfort, excitement and repose, to the most complex emotions, intellectual tensions, or the steady feeling-tones of a conscious human life. In stating what a work of art is, I have just used the words "form," "expressive," and "created"; these are key words. One at a time, they will keep us engaged.

Let us consider first what is meant, in this context, by a *form.* The word has many meanings, all equally legitimate for various purposes; even in connection with art it has several. It may, for instance—and often does— denote the familiar, characteristic structures known as the sonnet form, the sestina, or the ballad form in poetry, the sonata form, the madrigal, or the symphony in music, the contredance or the classical ballet in choreography, and so on. This is not what I mean; or rather, it is only a very small part of what I mean. There is another sense in which artists speak of "form" when they say, for instance, "form follows function," or declare that the one quality shared by all good works of art is "significant form," or entitle a book *The Problem of Form in Painting and Sculpture*, or *The Life of Forms in Art*, or *Search for Form*. They are using "form" in a wider sense, which on the one hand is close to the commonest, popular meaning, namely just the *shape* of a thing, and on the other hand to the quite unpopular meaning it has in science and philosophy, where it designates something more abstract; "form" in its most abstract sense means structure, articulation, a whole resulting from the relation of mutually dependent factors, or more precisely, the way that whole is put together.

The abstract sense, which is sometimes called "logical form," is involved in the notion of expression, at least the kind of expression that characterizes art. That is why artists, when they speak of achieving "form," use the word with something of an abstract connotation, even when they are talking about a visible and tangible art object in which that form is embodied.

The more recondite concept of form is derived, of course, from the naive one, that is, material shape. Perhaps the easiest way to grasp the idea of "logical form" is to trace its derivation.

Let us consider the most obvious sort of form, the shape of an object, say a lampshade. In any department store you will find a wide choice of lampshades, mostly monstrosities, and what is monstrous is usually their shape. You select the least offensive one, maybe even a good one, but realize that the color, say violet, will not fit into your room; so you look about for another shade of the same shape but a different color, perhaps green. In recognizing this same shape in another object, possibly of another material as well as another color, you have quite naturally and easily abstracted the concept of this shape from your actual impression of the first lampshade. Presently it may occur to you that this shade is too big for your lamp; you ask whether they have *this same shade* (meaning another one of this shape) in a smaller size. The clerk understands you.

But what is *the same* in the big violet shade and the little green one? Nothing but the interrelations among their respective various dimensions. They are not "the same" even in their spatial properties, for none of their actual measures are alike; but their shapes are congruent. Their respective spatial factors are put together in the same way, so they exemplify the same form.

It is really astounding what complicated abstractions we make in our ordinary dealing with forms—that is to say, through what twists and transformations we recognize the same logical form. Consider the similarity of your two hands. Put one on the table, palm down, superimpose the other, palm down, as you may have superimposed cut-out geometric shapes in school—they are not alike at all. But their shapes are *exact opposites*. Their respective shapes fit the same description, provided that the description is modified by a principle of application whereby the measures are read one way for one hand and the other way for the other—like a timetable in which the list of stations is marked: "Eastbound, read down; Westbound, read up."

As the two hands exemplify the same form with a principle of reversal understood, so the list of stations describes two ways of moving, indicated by the advice to "read down" for one and "read up" for the other. We can all abstract the common element in these two respective trips, which is called the *route*. With a return ticket we may return only by the same route. The same principle relates a mold to the form of the thing that is cast in it, and establishes their formal correspondence, or common logical form.

So far we have considered only objects—lampshades, hands, or regions of the earth—as having forms. These have fixed shapes; their parts remain in fairly stable relations to each other. But there are also substances that have no definite shapes, such as gases, mists, and water, which take the shape of any bounded space that contains them. The interesting thing about such amorphous fluids is that when they are put into violent motion they do exhibit visible forms, not bounded by any container. Think of the momentary efflorescence of a bursting rocket, the mushroom cloud of an atomic bomb, the funnel of water or dust screwing upward in a whirlwind. The instant the motion stops, or even slows beyond a certain degree, those shapes collapse and the apparent "thing" disappears. They are not shapes of things at all, but forms of motions, or dynamic forms.

Some dynamic forms, however, have more permanent manifestations, because the stuff that moves and makes them visible is constantly replenished. A waterfall seems to hang from the cliff, waving streamers of foam. Actually, of course, nothing stays there in mid-air; the water is always passing; but there is more and more water taking the same paths, so we have a lasting shape made and maintained by its passage—permanent dynamic form. A quiet river, too, has dynamic form; if it stopped flowing it would either go dry or become a lake. Some twenty-five hundred years ago, Heracleitos was struck by the fact that you cannot step twice into the same river at the same place—at least, if the river means the water, not its dynamic form, the flow.

When a river ceases to flow because the water is deflected or dried up, there remains the river bed, sometimes cut deeply in solid stone. That bed is shaped by the flow, and records as graven lines the currents that have ceased to exist. Its shape is static, but it *expresses* the dynamic form of the river. Again, we have two congruent forms, like a cast and its mold, but this time the congruence is more remarkable because it holds between a dynamic form and a static one. That relation is important; we shall be dealing with it again when we come to consider the meaning of "living form" in art.

The congruence of two given perceptible forms is not always evident upon simple inspection. The common *logical* form they both exhibit may become apparent only when you know the principle whereby to relate them, as you compare the shapes of your hands not by direct correspondence, but by correspondence of opposite parts. Where the two exemplifications of the single logical form are unlike in most other respects one needs a rule for matching up the relevant factors of one with the relevant factors of the other; that is to say, a *rule of translation*, whereby one instance of the logical form is shown to correspond formally to the other.

The logical form itself is not another thing, but an abstract concept, or better an *abstractable* concept. We usually don't abstract it deliberately, but only use it, as we use our vocal cords in speech without first learning all about their operation and then applying our knowledge. Most people perceive intuitively the similarity of their two hands without thinking of them as conversely related; they can guess at the shape of the hollow inside a wooden shoe from the shape of a human foot, without any abstract study of topology. But the first time they see a map in the Mercator projection—with parallel lines of longitude, not meeting at the poles—they find it hard to believe that this corresponds logically to the circular map they used in school, where the meridians bulged apart toward the equator and met at both poles. The visible shapes of the continents are different on the two maps, and it takes abstract thinking to match up the two representations of the same earth. If, however, they have grown up with both maps, they will probably see the geographical relationships either way with equal ease, because these relationships are not *copied* by either map, but *expressed*, and expressed equally well by both; for the two maps are different *projections* of the same logical form, which the spherical earth exhibits in still another—that is, a spherical—projection.

An expressive form is any perceptible or imaginable whole that exhibits relationships of parts, or points, or even qualities or aspects within the whole, so that it may be taken to represent some other whole whose elements have analogous relations. The reason for using such a form as a symbol is usually that the thing it represents is not perceivable or readily imaginable. We cannot see the earth as an object. We let a map or a little globe express the relationships of places on the earth, and think about the earth by means of it. The understanding of one thing through another seems to be a deeply intuitive process in the human brain; it is so natural that we often have difficulty in distinguishing the symbolic expressive form from what it conveys. The symbol seems to be the thing itself, or contain it, or be contained in it. A child interested in a globe will not say, "This means the earth," but "Look, this is the earth." A similar identification of symbol and meaning underlies the widespread conception of holy names, of the physical efficacy of rites, and many other primitive but culturally persistent phenomena. It has a bearing on our perception of artistic import; that is why I mention it here.

The most astounding and developed symbolic device humanity has evolved is language. By means of language we can conceive the intangible, incorporeal things we call our *ideas*, and the equally inostensible elements of our perceptual world that we call *facts*. It is by virtue of language that we can think, remember, imagine, and finally conceive a universe of facts. We can describe things and represent their relations, express rules of their interactions, speculate and predict and carry on a long symbolizing process known as reasoning. And above all, we can communicate, by producing a serried array of audible or visible words, in a pattern commonly known, and readily understood to reflect our multifarious concepts and percepts and their interconnections. This use of language is *discourse*; and the pattern of discourse is known as *discursive form*. It is a highly versatile, amazingly powerful pattern. It has impressed itself on our tacit thinking, so that we call all systematic reflection "discursive thought." It has made, far more than most people know, the very frame of our sensory experience —the frame of objective facts in which we carry on the practical business of life.

Yet even the discursive pattern has its limits of usefulness. An expressive form can express any complex of conceptions that, via some rule of projection, appears congruent with it, that is, appears to be of that form. Whatever there is in experience that will not take the impress—directly or indirectly—of discursive form, is not discursively communicable or, in the strictest sense, logically thinkable. It is unspeakable, ineffable; according to practically all serious philosophical theories today, it is unknowable.

Yet there is a great deal of experience that is knowable, not only as immediate, formless, meaningless impact, but as one aspect of the intricate web of life, yet defies discursive formulation, and therefore verbal expression: that is what we sometimes call the *subjective aspect* of experience, the direct feeling of it—what it is like to be waking and moving, to be drowsy, slowing down, or to be sociable, or to feel self-sufficient but alone; what it feels like to pursue an elusive thought or to have a big idea. All such directly felt experiences usually have no names—they are named, if at all, for the outward conditions that normally accompany their occurrence. Only the most striking ones have names like "anger," "hate," "love," "fear," and are collectively called "emotion." But we feel many things that never develop into any designable emotion. The ways we are moved are as various as the lights in a forest; and they may intersect, sometimes without cancelling each other, take shape and dissolve, conflict, explode into passion, or be transfigured. All these inseparable elements of subjective reality compose what we call the "inward life" of human beings. The usual factoring of that life-stream into mental, emotional, and sensory units is an arbitrary scheme of simplification that makes scientific treatment possible to a considerable extent; but we may already be close to the limit of its usefulness, that is, close to the point where its simplicity becomes an obstacle to further questioning and discovery instead of the revealing, eversuitable logical projection it was expected to be.

Whatever resists projection into the discursive form of language is, indeed, hard to hold in conception, and perhaps impossible to communicate, in the proper and strict sense of the word "communicate." But fortunately our logical intuition, or form-perception, is really much more powerful than we commonly believe, and our knowledge—genuine knowledge, understanding—is considerably wider than our discourse. Even in the use of language, if we want to name something that is too new to have a name (for example, a newly invented gadget or a newly discovered creature), or want to express a relationship for which there is no verb or other connective word, we resort to metaphor; we mention it or describe it as something else, something analogous. The principle of metaphor is simply the principle of saying one thing and meaning another, and expecting to be understood to mean the other. A metaphor is not language, it is an idea expressed by language, an idea that in its turn functions as a symbol to express something. It is not discursive and therefore does not really make a statement of the idea it conveys; but it formulates a new conception for our direct imaginative grasp.

Sometimes our comprehension of a total experience is mediated by a metaphorical symbol because the experience is new, and language has words and phrases only for familiar notions. Then an extension of language will gradually follow the wordless insight, and discursive expression will supersede the non-discursive pristine symbol. This is, I think, the normal advance of human thought and language in that whole realm of knowledge where discourse is possible at all.

But the symbolic presentation of subjective reality for contemplation is not only tentatively beyond the reach of language—that is, not merely beyond the words we have; it is impossible in the essential frame of language. That is why those semanticists who recognize only discourse as a symbolic form must regard the whole life of feeling as formless, chaotic, capable only of symptomatic expression, typified in exclamations like "Ah!" "Ouch!" "My sainted aunt!" They usually do believe that art is an expression of feeling, but that "expression" in art is of this sort, indicating that the speaker has an emotion, a pain, or other personal experience, perhaps also giving us a clue to the general kind of experience it is—pleasant or unpleasant, violent or mild—but not setting that piece of inward life objectively before us so we may understand its intricacy, its rhythms and shifts of total appearance. The differences in feeling-tones or other elements of subjective experience are regarded as differences in quality, which must be felt to be appreciated. Furthermore, since we have no intellectual access to pure subjectivity, the only way to study it is to study the symptoms of the person who is having subjective experiences. This leads to physiological psychology—a very important and interesting field. But it tells us nothing about the phenomena of subjective life, and sometimes simplifies the problem by saying they don't exist.

Now, I believe the expression of feeling in a work of art—the function that makes the work an expressive form—is not symptomatic at all. An artist working on a tragedy need not be in personal despair or violent upheaval; nobody, indeed, could work in such a state of mind. His mind would be occupied with the causes of his emotional upset. Self-expression does not require composition and lucidity; a screaming baby gives his feeling far more release than any musician, but we don't go into a concert hall to hear a baby scream; in fact, if that baby is brought in we are likely to go out. We don't want self-expression.

A work of art presents feeling (in the broad sense I mentioned before, as everything that can be felt) for our contemplation, making it visible or audible or in some way perceivable through a symbol, not inferable from a symptom. Artistic form is congruent with the dynamic forms of our direct sensuous, mental, and emotional life; works of art are projections of "felt life," as Henry James called it, into spatial, temporal, and poetic structures. They are images of feeling, that formulate it for our cognition. What is artistically good is whatever articulates and presents feeling to our understanding.

Artistic forms are more complex than any other symbolic forms we know. They are, indeed, not abstractable from the works that exhibit them. We may abstract a shape from an object that has this shape, by disregarding color, weight and texture, even size; but to the total effect that is an artistic form, the color matters, the thickness of lines matters, and the appearance of texture and weight. A given triangle is the same in any position, but to an artistic form its location, balance, and surroundings are not indifferent. Form, in the sense in which we artists speak of "significant form" or "expressive form," is not an abstracted structure, but an apparition; and the vital processes of sense and emotion that a good work of art expresses seem to the beholder to be directly contained in it, not symbolized but really presented. The congruence is so striking that symbol and meaning appear as one reality. Actually, as one psychologist who is also a musician has written, "Music sounds as feelings feel." And likewise, in good painting, sculpture, or building, balanced shapes and colors, lines and masses look as emotions, vital tensions and their resolutions feel.

An artist, then, expresses feeling, but not in the way a politician blows off steam or a baby laughs and cries. He formulates that elusive aspect of reality that is commonly taken to be amorphous and chaotic; that is, he objectifies the subjective realm. What he expresses is, therefore, not his own actual feelings, but what he knows about human feeling. Once he is in possession of a rich symbolism, that knowledge may actually exceed his entire personal experience. A work of art expresses a conception of life, emotion, inward reality. But it is neither a confessional nor a frozen tantrum; it is a developed metaphor, a non-discursive symbol that articulates what is verbally ineffable—the logic of consciousness itself.

II. The Art Symbol and the Symbol in Art[1]

The problems of semantics and logic seem to fit into one frame, those of feeling into another. But somewhere, of course, mentality has arisen from more primitive vital processes. Somehow they belong into one and the same scientific frame. I am scouting the possibility that *rationality arises as an elaboration of feeling*.

Such a hypothesis leads one, of course, to the possible forms of feeling, and raises the problem of how they can be conceived and abstractly handled. Every theoretical construction requires a model. Especially if you want to get into elaborate structures you have to have a model—not an instance, but a symbolic form that can be manipulated, to convey, or perhaps to hold, your conceptions.

Language is the symbolic form of rational thought. It is more than that, but at least it can be fairly well pared down to abstract the elements of such thought and cognition. The structure of discourse expresses the forms of rational cogitation; that is why we call such thinking "discursive."

But discursive symbols offer no apt model of primitive forms of feeling. There has been a radical change—a special organization—in the making of rationality, perhaps under the influence of very specialized perception, perhaps under some other controlling condition. To express the forms of what might be called "unlogicized" mental life (a term we owe to Professor Henry M. Sheffer of Harvard), or what is usually called the "life of feeling," requires a different symbolic form.

This form, I think, is characteristic of art and is, indeed, the essence and measure of art. If this be so, then a work of art is a symbolic form in another way than the one (or ones) usually conceded to it. We commonly think of a work of art as representing something, and of its symbolic function, therefore, as representation. But this is not what I mean; not even secret or disguised representation. Many works represent nothing whatever. A building, a pot, a tune is usually beautiful without intentionally representing anything; and its unintentional representation may be found in bad and ugly pieces too. But if it is beautiful it is expressive; what it expresses is not an idea of some other thing, but an idea of a feeling. Representational works, if they are good art, are so for the same reason as non-representational ones. They have more than one symbolic function —representation, perhaps after two kinds, and also artistic expression, which is presentation of ideas of feeling.

There are many difficulties connected with the thesis that a work of art is primarily an expression of feeling—an "expression" in the logical sense, presenting the fabric of sensibility, emotion, and the strains of more concerted cerebration, for our impersonal cognition—that is, *in abstracto*. This sort of symbolization is the prime office of works of art, by virtue of which I call a work of art an *expressive form*.

In *Feeling and Form* I called it "the art symbol." This aroused a flood of criticism from two kinds of critics—those who misunderstood the alleged symbolic function and assimilated everything I wrote about it to some previous, familiar theory, either treating art as a genuine language or *symbolism*, or else confusing the art symbol with *the symbol of art* as known to iconologists or to modern psychologists; and, secondly, those critics who understood what I said but resented the use of the word "symbol" that differed from accepted usage in current semantical writings. Naturally the critics who understood what I said were the more influential ones; and their objections brought home the nature and extent of the difference between the function of a genuine symbol and a work of art. The difference is greater than I had realized before. Yet the function of what I called "the art symbol"—which is, in every case, the work of art as a whole, and purely as such—is more *like* a symbolic function than like anything else. A work of art is expressive in the way a proposition is expressive—as the formulation of an idea for conception. An idea may be well expressed or badly expressed. Similarly, in a work of art, feeling is well expressed or badly, and the work accordingly is good, or poor, or even bad—note that in the last case an artist would condemn it as *false*. The "significance" of a work, by virtue of which some early twentieth-century writers called it "significant form," is what is expressed. Since, however, *signification* is not its semantic function—it is quite particularly *not* a signal—I prefer Professor Melvin Rader's phrase, which he proposed in a review of *Feeling and Form*: "expressive form." This, he said, would be a better term than "the art symbol." I have used it ever since. Similarly, Professor Ernest Nagel objected to calling that which it expresses its "meaning," since it is not "meaning" in any of the precise senses known to semanticists; since then I have spoken of the *import* of an expressive form. This is the more convenient as the work may have *meanings* besides.

As a work of art is an expressive form somewhat like a symbol, and has import which is something like meaning, so it makes a logical abstraction, but not in the familiar way of genuine symbols—perhaps, indeed, a pseudo-abstraction. The best way to understand all these pseudo-semantics is to consider what a work of art is and does, and then compare it with language, and its doings with what language (or any genuine symbolism) does.

The expressive form, or art symbol, is, as I said before, the work of art itself, as it meets the eye (let us, for simplicity's sake, stay in the realm of pictorial art). It is the visible form, the apparition created out of paint deployed on a ground. The paint and the ground themselves disappear. One does not see a picture as a piece of spotted canvas, any more than one sees a screen with shadows on it in a movie. Whether there be things and persons in the picture or not, it presents volumes in a purely created space. These volumes define and organize the pictorial space which they are, in fact, creating; the purely visual space seems to be alive with their balanced or strained interactions. The lines that divide them (which may be physically drawn, or implied) create a rhythmic unity, for what they divide they also relate, to the point of complete integration. If a picture is successful it presents us with something quite properly, even though metaphorically, called "living form."

The word "form" connotes to many people the idea of a dead, empty shell, a senseless formality, lip-service, and sometimes an imposed rule to which actions, speeches, and works must *conform*. Many people think of form as a set of prescriptions when they speak of art forms, such as the sonata form or the rondo in music, the French ballade in poetry, etc. In all these uses the word "form" denotes something general, an abstracted concept that may be exemplified in various instances. This is a legitimate and widespread meaning of "form." But it is not the meaning Bell and Fry had in mind, and which I propose here. When they spoke of "significant form" (or, as now I would say, "expressive form") they meant a visible, individual form produced by the interaction of colors, lines, surfaces, lights and shadows, or whatever entered into a specific work. They used the word in the sense of something *formed*, as sometimes wonderful figures of soft color and melting contours are formed by clouds, or a spiral like a coiled spring is formed by the growth of a fern shoot; as a pot is formed out of clay, and a landscape out of paint spots. It may be a solid material form like the pot, or an illusory object like Hamlet's cloudy weasel. But it is a form for perception.

A work of art is such an individual form given directly to perception. But it is a special kind of form, since it seems to be more than a visual phenomenon—seems, indeed, to have a sort of life, or be imbued with feeling, or somehow, without being a genuine practical object, yet present the beholder with more than an arrangement of sense data. It carries with it something that people have sometimes called a quality (Clive Bell called "significant form" a quality), sometimes an emotional content, or the emotional tone of the work, or simply its life. This is what I mean by *artistic import*. It is not one of the qualities to be distinguished in the work, though our perception of it has the immediacy of qualitative experience; artistic import is *expressed*, somewhat as meaning is expressed in a genuine symbol, yet not exactly so. The analogy is strong enough to make it legitimate, even though easily misleading, to call the work of art the art symbol.

The difference, however, between an art symbol and a genuine symbol are of great interest and importance, for they illuminate the relations that obtain between many kinds of symbols, or things that have been so called, and show up the many levels on which symbolic and pseudo-symbolic functions may lie. I think a study of artistic expressiveness shows up a need of a more adaptable, that is to say more general, definition of "symbol" than the one accepted in current semantics and analytical philosophy. But we had better defer this problem to a later point. Let us, for the time being, call a *genuine symbol* whatever meets the strictest definition. Here is a definition offered by Ernest Nagel, in an article called "Symbolism and Science": "By a symbol I understand any occurrence (or type of occurrence), usually linguistic in status, which is taken to signify something else by way of tacit or explicit conventions or rules of language."

A word, say a familiar common noun, is a symbol of this sort. I would say that it conveys a concept, and refers to, or denotes, whatever exemplifies that concept. The word "man" conveys what we call the concept of "man," and denotes any being that exemplifies the concept—i.e., any man.

Now, words—our most familiar and useful symbols—are habitually used not in isolation, but in complex concepts of states of affairs, rather than isolated things, and refer to facts or possibilities or even impossibilities: those bigger units are descriptions and statements and other forms of *discourse*.

In discourse, another function of symbols comes into play, that is present but not very evident in the use of words simply to name things. This further function is the expression of ideas *about* things. A thing cannot be asserted by a name, only mentioned. As soon as you make an assertion you are symbolizing some sort of relation between concepts of things, or maybe things and properties, such as: "The grapes are sour." "All men are born equal." "I hate logic." Assertions, of course, need not be true—that is, they need not refer us to facts.

That brings us to the second great office of symbols, which is not to refer to things and communicate facts, but to express ideas; and this, in turn, involves a deeper psychological process, the formulation of ideas, or conception itself. Conception—giving form and connection, clarity and proportion to our impressions, memories, and objects of judgment—is the beginning of all rationality. Conception itself contains the elementary principles of knowledge: that an object of thought keeps its identity (as Aristotle put it, "A = A"), that it may stand in many relations to other things, that alternative possibilities exclude each other, and one decision entails another. Conception is the first requirement for thought.

This basic intellectual process of conceiving things in connection belongs, I think, to the same deep level of the mind as symbolization itself.

That is the level where imagination is born. Animal intelligence or response to signs, of course, goes further back than that. The process of symbolic presentation is the beginning of human mentality, "mind" in a strict sense. Perhaps that beginning occurs at the stage of neural development where speech originates, and with speech the supreme talent of *envisagement*.

Response to stimuli, adaptation to conditions may occur without any envisagement of anything. Thought arises only where ideas have taken shape, and actual or possible conditions imagined. The word "imagined" contains the key to a new world: the image. I think the popular notion of an image as a replica of a sense impression has made epistemologists generally miss the most important character of images, which is that they are symbolic. That is why, in point of sensuous character, they may be almost indescribably vague, fleeting, fragmentary, or distorted; they may be sensuously altogether unlike what they represent. We think of mathematical relations in images that are just arbitrarily posited symbols; but these symbols are our mathematical images. They may be visual or auditory or what not, but functionally they are images, that articulate the logical relations we contemplate by means of them.

The great importance of reference and communication by means of symbols has led semanticists to regard these uses as the defining properties of symbols—that is, to think of a symbol as essentially a sign which stands for something else and is used to represent that thing in discourse. This preoccupation has led them to neglect, or even miss entirely, the more primitive function of symbols, which is to formulate experience as something imaginable in the first place—to fix entities, and formulate facts and the fact-like elements of thought called "fantasies." This function is *articulation*. Symbols articulate ideas. Even such arbitrarily assigned symbols as mere names serve this purpose, for whatever is named becomes an entity in thought. Its unitary symbol automatically carves it out as a unit in the world pattern.

Now let us return to the Art Symbol. I said before that it is a symbol in a somewhat special sense, because it performs some symbolic functions, but not all; especially, it does not stand for something else, nor refer to anything that exists apart from it. According to the usual definition of "symbol," a work of art should not be classed as a symbol at all. But that usual definition overlooks the greatest intellectual value and, I think, the prime office of symbols—their power of formulating experience, and presenting it objectively for contemplation, logical intuition, recognition, understanding. That is articulation, or logical expression. And this function every good work of art does perform. It formulates the appearance of feeling, of subjective experience, the character of so-called "inner life," which discourse—the normal use of words—is peculiarly unable to articulate, and which therefore we can only refer to in a general and quite superficial way. The actual felt process of life, the tensions interwoven and shifting from moment to moment, the flowing and slowing, the drive and directedness of desires, and above all the rhythmic continuity of our selfhood, defies the expressive power of discursive symbolism. The myriad forms of subjectivity, the infinitely complex sense of life, cannot be rendered linguistically, that is, stated. But they are precisely what comes to light in a good work of art (not necessarily a "masterpiece"; there are thousands of works that are good art without being exalted achievements). A work of art is an expressive form, and vitality, in all its manifestations from sheer sensibility to the most elaborate phases of awareness and emotion, is what it may express.

But what is meant by saying it does not connote a concept or denote its instances? What I mean is that a genuine symbol, such as a word, is only a sign; in appreciating its meaning our interest reaches beyond it to the concept. The word is just an instrument. Its meaning lies elsewhere, and once we have grasped its connotation or identified something as its denotation we do not need the word any more. But a work of art does not point us to a meaning beyond its own presence. What is expressed cannot be grasped apart from the sensuous or poetic form that expresses it. In a work of art we have the direct presentation of a feeling, not a sign that points to it. That is why "significant form" is a misleading and confusing term: an Art Symbol does not signify, but only articulate and present its emotive content; hence the peculiar impression one always gets that feeling is in a beautiful and integral form. The work seems to be imbued with the emotion or mood or other vital experience that it expresses. That is why I call it an "expressive form," and call that which it formulates for us not its meaning, but its *import*. The import of art is perceived as something in the work, articulated by it but not further abstracted; as the import of a myth or a true metaphor does not exist apart from its imaginative expression.

The work as a whole is the image of feeling, which may be called the Art Symbol. It is a single organic composition, which means that its elements are not independent constituents, expressive, in their own right, of various emotional ingredients, as words are constituents of discourse, and have meanings in their own right, which go to compose the total meaning of the discourse. Language is a *symbolism*, a system of symbols with definable though fairly elastic meanings, and rules of combination whereby larger units—phrases, sentences, whole speeches—may be compounded, expressing similarly built-up ideas; Art, contrariwise, is not a symbolism. The elements in a work are always newly created with the total image, and although it is possible to . . . analyze what they contribute to the image, it is not possible to assign them any of its import apart from the whole. That is characteristic of organic form. The import of a work of art is its "life," which, like actual life, is an indivisible phenomenon. Who could say how much of a natural organism's life is in the lungs, how much in the legs, or how much more life would be added to us if we were given a lively tail to wave? The Art Symbol is a single symbol, and its import is not compounded of partial symbolic values. It is, I think, what Cecil Day Lewis means by "the poetic image," and what some painters, valiantly battling against popular misconceptions, call "the absolute image." It is the objective form of life-feeling in terms of space, or musical passage, or other fictive and plastic medium.

At last we come to the issue proposed in the title of this lecture. If the Art Symbol is a single, indivisible symbol, and its import is never compounded of contributive cargoes of import, what shall we make of the fact that many artists incorporate symbols in their works? Is it a mistake to interpret certain elements in poems or pictures, novels or dances, as symbols? Are the symbolists, imagists, surrealists, and the countless religious painters and poets before them all mistaken—everybody out of step except Johnnie?

Symbols certainly do occur in art, and in many, if not most, cases contribute notably to the work that incorporates them. Some artists work with a veritable riot of symbols; from the familiar halo of sacrosanct personages to the terrible figures of the *uernica*, from the obvious rose of womanhood or the lily of chastity to the personal symbols of T. S. Eliot, sometimes concentric as a nest of tables, painters and poets have used symbols. Iconography is a fertile field of research; and where no influence-hunting historian has found any symbols, the literary critics find Bloom as a symbol of Moses, and the more psychological critics find Moses a symbol of birth.

They may all be right. One age revels in the use of symbolism in pictures, drama, and dance, another all but dispenses with it; but the fact that symbols and even whole systems of symbols (like the gesture-symbolism in Hindu dances) may occur in works of art is certainly patent.

All such elements, however, are genuine symbols; they have meanings, and the meanings may be stated. Symbols in art connote holiness, or sin, or rebirth, womanhood, love, tyranny, and so forth. These meanings enter into the work of art as elements, creating and articulating its organic form, just as its subject-matter—fruit in a platter, horses on a beach, a slaughtered ox, or a weeping Magdalen—enter into its construction. Symbols used in art lie on a different semantic level from the work that contains them. Their meanings are not part of its import, but elements in the form that has import, the expressive form. The meanings of incorporated symbols may lend richness, intensity, repetition or reflection or a transcendent unrealism, perhaps an entirely new balance to the work itself. But they function in the normal manner of symbols: they mean something beyond what they present in themselves. It makes sense to ask what a Hound of Heaven or brown sea-girls or Yeat's Byzantium may stand for, though in a poem where symbols are perfectly used it is usually unnecessary. Whether the interpretation has to be carried out or is skipped in reception of the total poetic image depends largely on the reader. The important point for us is that there is a literal meaning (sometimes more than one) connoted by the symbol that occurs in art.

The use of symbols in art is, in fine, a principle of construction—a device, in the most general sense of that word, "device." But there is a difference, often missed by theorists, between principles of construction and principles of art. The principles of art are few: the creation of what might be termed "an apparition" (this term would bear much discussion, but we have no time for it, and I think any one conversant with the arts knows what I mean), the achievement of organic unity or "livingness," the articulation of feeling. These principles of art are wholly exemplified in every work that merits the name of "art" at all, even though it be not great or in the current sense "original" (the anonymous works of ancient potters, for instance, were rarely original designs). Principles of construction, on the other hand, are very many; the most important have furnished our basic devices, and given rise to the Great Traditions of art. Representation in painting, diatonic harmony in music, metrical versification in poetry are examples of such major devices of composition. They are exemplified in thousands of works; yet they are not indispensable. Painting can eschew representation, music can be atonal, poetry can be poetry without any metrical scaffold.

The excited recognition and exploitation of a new constructive device— usually in protest against the traditional devices that have been used to a point of exhaustion, or even the point of corruption—is an artistic revolution. Art in our own day is full of revolutionary principles. Symbols, crowding metaphorical images, indirect subject-matter, dream elements instead of sights or events of waking life, often the one presented through the other, have furnished us lately with a new treasure-trove of motifs that command their own treatments, and the result is a new dawning day in art. The whole old way of seeing and hearing and word-thinking is sloughed off as the possibilities inherent in the modern devices of creation and expression unfold. In that excitement it is natural for the young—the young spirits, I mean, who are not necessarily the people of military or marriageable age—to feel that they are the generation that has discovered, at last, the principles of art, and that heretofore art labored under an incubus, the false principles they repudiate, so there never really was a pure and perfectable art before. They are mistaken, of course; but what of it? So were their predecessors—the Italian Camerata, the English Lake Poets, the early Renaissance painters—who discovered new principles of artistic organization and thought they had discovered how to paint, or how to make real music, or genuine poetry, for the first time. It is we, who philosophize about art and seek to understand its mission, that must keep distinctions clear.

In summary, then, it may be said that the difference between the Art Symbol and the symbol used in art is a difference not only of function but of kind. Symbols occurring in art are symbols in the usual sense, though of all degrees of complexity, from simplest directness to extreme indirectness, from singleness to deep interpenetration, from perfect lucidity to the densest over-determination. They have meanings, in the full sense that any semanticist would accept. And those meanings, as well as the images that convey them, enter into the work of art as elements in its composition. They serve to create the work, the expressive form.

The art symbol, on the other hand, *is* the expressive form. It is not a symbol in the full familiar sense, for it does not convey something beyond itself. Therefore it cannot strictly be said to have a meaning; what it does have is import. It is a symbol in a special and derivative sense, because it does not fulfill all the functions of a true symbol: it formulates and objectifies experience for direct intellectual perception, or intuition, but it does not abstract a concept for discursive thought. Its import is seen in it; not, like the meaning of a genuine symbol, by means of it but separable from the sign. The symbol in art is a metaphor, an image with overt or covert literal signification; the art symbol is the absolute image—the image of what otherwise would be irrational, as it is literally ineffable: direct awareness, emotion, vitality, personal identity—life lived and felt, the matrix of mentality.

—*Problems of Art* (1957)

NOTE

1. The remainder of this selection from Dr. Langer's *Problems of Art* composed an informal talk at the Austin Riggs Psychiatric Centre, 1956.

ROGER SESSIONS

The Composer and His Message

It seems to me that the essential medium of music, the basis of its expressive powers and the element which gives it its unique quality among the arts, is *time,* made living for us through its expressive essence, *movement.*

Music is apprehended through the ear; the visual arts, painting, sculpture, and architecture through the eye. Is there not, more than a difference in function, a genuine and essential contrast in content, between what the eye sees and what the ear hears? I am speaking, of course, not in terms of science, but of ordinary experience. The visual arts govern a world of space, and it seems to me that perhaps the profoundest sensation which we derive from space is not so much that of extension as of permanence. On the most primitive level we feel space to be something permanent, fundamentally unchangeable; when movement is apprehended through the eye it takes place, so to speak, within a static framework, and the psychological impact of this framework is much more powerful than that of the vibrations which occur within its limits. For our experience the visual arts are undifferentiated in time. When we cease to look at a painting or a statue, it nevertheless continues to exist; it undergoes no perceptible change while we are looking at it, and we find it unchanged when we return to it after absence. We may contemplate it as long as we like, and though continued or repeated contemplation will make us familiar with more and more of its details or characteristics, these features have been present from the start, even to our eyes; it is our consciousness, following its own laws and not those of the object itself, which has developed. And when through these or other visual arts movement is suggested, it is through energy implied but not expressed.

Literature, to be sure, takes place in time, and in poetry and the drama time is, in a sense, not wholly unlike music, controlled. But even in poetry time is only a part, and a relatively small part, of the total expression; to a far greater extent than in music it is variable according to the will of the interpreter; its subtle rhythms, moreover, are subject to the laws of speech and of concrete literary sense. The real medium of literature is language, as shaped by the literary imagination. One of the expressive elements of language is rhythm, which is employed by the poet as an active, controlled medium in order to heighten its effect. I venture to say, however, that only in rare and fleeting instances does movement assume the whole or even the principal expressive burden.

In speaking of musical movement, on the other hand, we do not refer to rhythm alone, but rather to music as a complete and essentially indivisible whole. In this connection it is relevant to compare our ordinary experience of sound, the medium of musical movement, with the experience of space as I have described it above. If our visual experience is primarily of the permanent and static, sound, as we are ordinarily aware of it, is essentially of limited duration, fleeting and elusive—and the very essence of our adjustment to it is closely bound up with this fact. We cannot escape from it without fleeing its presence; and if it assumes anything like unchanging permanence this is such an exceptional occurrence that either we become quickly unaware of it, or it becomes intolerable. Sound for us, in other words, is naturally and inextricably associated with our sensation of time.

Time becomes real to us primarily through movement, which I have called its expressive essence; and it is easy to trace our primary musical responses to the most primitive movement of our being—to those movements which are indeed at the very basis of animate existence. The feeling for tempo, so often derived from the dance, has in reality a much more primitive basis in the involuntary movements of the nervous system and the body in the beating of the heart, and more consciously in breathing, later in walking. Accelerated movement is, from these very obvious causes, inevitably associated with excitement, retarded movement with a lessening of dynamic tension. The experience of meter has the most obvious and essential of its origins in the movements of breathing, with its alternation of upward and downward movements. The sense of effort, preparation, suspense, which is the psychological equivalent of the up-beat, finds its prototype in the act of inhalation, and the sense of weight, release, and finality produced by the down-beat corresponds most intimately to the act of exhalation. "In the beginning was rhythm," remarked Hans von Bülow; another distinguished musician remarked later that life begins, according to this above analogy, with an up-beat, the first breath of the new born child corresponding to the preparatory anacrusis of a musical statement, and ends, like the most natural and satisfying rhythm, with a down-beat.

The other primary elements of music—melody and rhythm—derive from more complicated but only slightly less essential muscular movements, which, it has been fairly well demonstrated, are reproduced in miniature by the human nervous system in response to musical impressions. If we instinctively respond to a rising melodic pitch by a feeling of increased tension and hence of heightened expression, or a falling pitch by the opposite sensation; if an increase in intensity of sound intensifies our dynamic response to the music, and vice versa, it is because we have already in our vocal experiences—the earliest and most primitive as well as later and more complicated ones—lived intimately through exactly the same effects. A raising of pitch or an increase in volume is the result of an intensification of effort, energy, and emotional power in the crying child just as truly as in the highly-evolved artistry of a Chaliapin or an Anderson.

Similarly, our feeling for rhythm, in the stricter sense, derives from the subtle and more expressive nervous and muscular movements, such as occur in speech, song, gesture, and the dance. A melodic phrase, for instance, is analogous psychologically to a vocal phrase, even though, because of its range, its length, or its specific technical demands, it may be realizable only on instruments; it must be thought, by the interpreter as well as the listener, "in one breath"—that is to say, with a psychological energy and control, precisely analogous to that with which the singer or orator husbands his vocal resources and controls his breathing, according to the expressive curve of melody or rhetorical declamation. The association between music and dancing is probably even older than that between music and words, and needs no further illustration here; the point I wish to make is that the basic elements of our musical sense, of musical expression, hence of music itself, have their sources in the most primitive regions of our being. In this sense music is the oldest, just as in a quite other sense it is the youngest, of the arts; the primary sensations on which it is based antedate in human experience those of visual perception and, to a greater extent, those of language.

On a still less primitive level than melody or rhythm as such, we meet with the one basic element of music which is not derived directly from movement. This element, harmony, has its origins in the nature of musical sound itself rather than in the impulses of the human organism. Already in speaking of *musical* sound we have moved far from the primitive elements to which I have drawn attention; we have in fact taken note of a stage in the process of their *organization*. When the ear has learned to discriminate between musical "tone" and undifferentiated sound, it has already achieved a high degree of refinement and begun to shape its raw materials into something approaching a controlled medium of expression. The musical tone, however, is not a simple sound but a complex of sounds. It is this fact which, apprehended by the musical ear at an advanced stage in its development, leads to the elaboration of an always more complex set of relationships between sounds, and thereby opens up still further and more decisive possibilities of organization. Speaking for the moment in historical terms, it was only about 1600 that the harmonic sense reached maturity: it was at approximately the same period that music loosed itself from exclusive association with words and gesture, and achieved complete autonomy. From the purely technical standpoint, it was the development of the harmonic sense which made this possible. For this enriched the composer's vocabulary by revealing to him new possibilities in the combination of sounds; through these possibilities, derived from the physical nature of the tone itself, it provided him with a point of departure which enables the ear to find its way through the intricacies of a much vaster tonal design than had ever been dreamed of before. In other words, it added incalculable resources to musical expression, by making possible an infinitely more complex, more supple, and more finely differentiated musical movement.

Harmony, then, more than any other musical element, brings to music the possibility of extension, of larger design, by reason of the well-nigh inexhaustible wealth and variety of tonal relationships which it embraces —and these relationships, as I have said before, have their origin in the unity of the tone itself. I have no intention of entering at this point on a detailed discussion of what musicians call "tonality." It is one of the most intricate and elusive of technical questions, and today so problematical that the term itself must needs be exactly and carefully defined before any fruitful or illuminating discussion could take place. What is not problematical is the psychological need which the principle of tonality, or key, fulfills; the necessity for a unifying organization in the sphere of sound, just as tempo and meter constitute a unifying principle in that of rhythm. Movement becomes expressive only if its directions are clear. To this end points of reference are necessary; suffice it to say that each new development in music has created, on a convincing psychological basis, its own points of reference. Without them, music would hardly be possible. One of the most vivid and effective means by which this is accomplished in music is harmony, with all that this implies.

If the above be true, it will be seen that harmony brings into music its only inherently static element. I have stated that it rests in principle on relationships implicit in the nature of a single tone. The extension and elaboration of these relationships gives musical movement an endless variety and nuance. The unity from which they are derived, however, and their constant implicit reference to that unity, gives them a psychologically compulsive power, an inherent sense of direction which is one of the most compelling expressive means at the composer's disposal. The tensions which it creates in the minds of the hearer are of the very essence of musical expression, and serve admirably to illustrate the real psychological character of what I have called "movement" in music.

Let me take as an illustration the opening bars of the Tristan Prelude—an admirable illustration, because the composer has told us so clearly what the music intends to convey—hopeless, unsatisfied longing. Please observe these points: First, the expression is attained by raising the tensions of which I have spoken to the highest degree of vividness and force. Secondly, the tension is achieved not by purely harmonic means, but rather by the interplay of several other musical means, of which I have mentioned only the most essential. Finally, in their entirety, they constitute a coherent musical design, achieved through the cumulative growth of a harmonic impression, and through the association of musical ideas in the repetition of a musical pattern. . . .

I have brought forward this illustration in order to show certain aspects of what I have called "movement" in music, and in doing so, I have touched upon the question of musical expression. What is it, actually, that music expresses?

Let us consider for a moment the music to which I have just referred. It is associated in Wagner's drama with a definite situation, with definite characters—hence we are accustomed to say it "expresses" the tragic love of Tristan and Isolde. Is it, however, the music that tells us this? Does it tell us anything, in any definite and inevitable sense, of love and tragedy? How much of what is implied in this definition of its content is there by virtue of its association with the drama? Is this association an inevitable one, or is it in the last analysis arbitrary?

The music certainly tells us nothing specifically about Tristan and Isolde, as concrete individuals; in no sense does it identify them or enlighten us regarding the concrete situation in which they find themselves. Does it tell us, then, specifically, anything about love and tragedy which we could identify as such without the aid of the dramatic and poetic images with which Wagner so richly supplies us?

It seems to me that the answer in each case is, inevitably, a negative one. There is, in any specific sense, neither love nor tragedy in the music.

I have attempted a description of . . . music in terms of movement. I have tried to point out how intimately our musical impulses are connected with those primitive movements which are among the very conditions of our existence. I have tried to show, too, how vivid is our response to the primitive elements of musical movement.

Is not this the key both to the content of music and to its extraordinary power? These bars from the Prelude to Tristan do not express for us love or frustration or even longing: but they reproduce for us, both qualitatively and dynamically, certain gestures of the spirit which are to be sure less specifically definable than any of these emotions, but which energize them and make them vital to us.

So it seems to me that this is the essence of musical expression. "Emotion" is specific, individual and conscious; music goes deeper than this, to the energies which animate our psychic life, and out of these creates a pattern which has an existence, laws, and human significance of its own. It reproduces for us the most intimate essence, the tempo and the energy, of our spiritual being; our tranquility and our restlessness, our animation and our discouragement, our vitality and our weakness—all, in fact, of the fine shades of dynamic variation of our inner life. It reproduces these far more directly and more specifically than is possible through any other medium of human communication.

In saying this I do not wish to deny that there is also an associative element in musical expression, or that this has its very definite place in certain types of music. It must be remembered that the emergence of music as an entirely separate art has been, as I have pointed out, of very recent origin; that until the last three hundred years it was always connected with more concrete symbols, whether of the word or the dance. It is but natural, therefore, that this associative element should form a part of the composer's medium. It is, however, I believe, not an essential part, especially since it consists so largely in associations which have their basis in movement. Quiet, lightly contrasted movement, for instance, may be associated with outer as well as inner tranquility—the light rustling of leaves in the wind, or the movement of a tranquil sea—just as agitated movement may be employed to suggest the storms in nature, as well as the perturbations of the spirit. On the other hand, we meet with associations of a far less essential nature—the tone of the trumpet, for instance, suggesting martial ideas, or certain localisms—folk songs, exotic scales, bizarre instrumental combinations, etc., which are used for the purposes of specific and literal coloring. But one would hardly attach more than a very superficial musical significance to associations of this type. They belong definitely in the sphere of applied art, and when they occur in works of serious import they serve, in conformity with an expressed intention of the composer, in a decidedly subordinate capacity, to direct the listener to more concrete associations than the music, in its essential content, can convey.

The above considerations indicate why a certain type of literary rhapsody seems to the musician quite amateurish and beside the point, in spite of the fact that musicians themselves—even great ones—have occasionally indulged in it. At best it is a literary production, bearing no real relationship to the music and throwing no real light on its content, but expressing the literary impulses of the author with more or less significance, according to his personality. Thus it is that of three distinguished commentators on Beethoven's Seventh Symphony—all three of them composers, and two of them composers of genius—one finds it a second Eroica, another a second Pastorale, and the third "the apotheosis of the dance." It must not be forgotten that, for the composer, notes, chords, melodic intervals—all the musical materials—are far more real, far more expressive, than words; that, let us say, a "leading tone" or a chord of the subdominant are for him not only notes, but sensations, full of meaning and capable of infinite nuances of modification; and that when he speaks or thinks in terms of them he is using words which, however obscure and dry they may sound to the uninitiated, are for him fraught with dynamic sense.

So, in trying to understand the work of the composer, one must first think of him as living in a world of sounds, which in response to his creative impulse become animated with movement. The first stage in his work is that of what is generally known by the somewhat shopworn and certainly unscientific term "inspiration." The composer, to use popular language again, "has an idea"—an idea, let me make clear, consisting of definite musical notes and rhythms, which will engender for him the momentum with which his musical thought proceeds. The inspiration may come in a flash, or as sometimes happens, it may grow and develop gradually. I have in my possession photostatic copies of several pages of Beethoven's sketches for the last movement of his "Hammerklavier Sonata"; the sketches show him carefully modelling, then testing in systematic and apparently cold-blooded fashion, the theme of the fugue. Where, one might ask, is the inspiration here? Yet if the word has any meaning at all, it is certainly appropriate to this movement, with its irresistible and titanic energy of expression, already present in the theme. The inspiration takes the form, however, not of a sudden flash of music, but a clearly-envisaged impulse toward a certain goal for which the composer was obliged to strive. When this perfect realization was attained, however, there could have been no hesitation—rather a flash of recognition that this was exactly what he wanted.

Inspiration, then, is the impulse which sets creation in movement: it is also the energy which keeps it going. The composer's principal problem is that of recapturing it in every phase of his work; of bringing, in other words, the requisite amount of energy to bear on every detail, as well as, constantly, on his vision of the whole.

This vision of the whole I should call the conception. For the musician this too takes the form of concrete musical materials—perceived, however, not in detail but in foreshortened form. The experience, I believe, is quite different for the mature and experienced composer from what it is for the young beginner. As he grows in practice and imagination it assumes an ever more preponderant rôle, and appears more and more to be the essential act of creation. It differs from what I have described as "inspiration" only in works of large dimensions which cannot be realized in a short space of time. It arises out of the original inspiration, and is, so to speak, an extension of its logic.

What I have described as inspiration, embodies itself in what is the only true sense of the word "style"; conception, in the only true sense of the word "form." Neither style nor form, in their essence, are derived from convention; they always must be, and are, created anew, and establish and follow their own laws. It is undeniable that certain periods—and the most fortunate ones—have established clearly defined patterns or standards which give the artist a basis on which to create freely. Our own is not one of these; today the individual is obliged to discover his own language before he has completed the mastery of it. Where such standards exist, however, they retain their vitality only as long as they are in the process of development. After this process has stopped, they wither and die, and can be re-created only by a conscious and essentially artificial effort, since they are produced by a unique and unrecoverable impulse, and are suited only to the content which has grown with them.

After inspiration and conception comes execution. The process of execution is first of all that of listening inwardly to the music as it shapes itself; of allowing the music to grow; of following both inspiration and conception wherever they may lead. A phrase, a motif, a rhythm, even a chord, may contain within itself, in the composer's imagination, the energy which produces movement. It will lead the composer on, through the force of its own momentum or tension, to other phrases, other motifs, other chords.

The principles underlying what is generally called musical structure are not briefly or easily formulated. We may, however, easily observe certain general characteristics which are always present in music and which seem inseparable from its nature as an art of movement.

Primary among these is the principle of *association*. I use the term here in a purely musical sense; certain features of the music must recur, and they gain their significance through the fact of their recurrence. The famous first four notes of Beethoven's Fifth Symphony, in spite of the various literary interpretations attached to them, have no possible significance by themselves. To be sure they remind us, who are familiar with musical literature, inevitably of Beethoven—but in the absence of all association they would have no meaning whatever. Musically, they begin to have significance only when they are followed by four other notes, similar in tempo, accent, and interval, but differing slightly in pitch and by this fact becoming, so to speak, the vehicle of movement. The accented E flat, in the second measure, is carried through this associative means downward to the D in the fourth measure. The sense of this motion is the direct result of the association of measures three and four with a parallel passage in the first two measures.

Obviously, such an example is rudimentary in the extreme and serves only to illustrate the principle in its simplest form; to show in some slight measure how association brings to music significance and coherence, and how, through its means, musical movement may be organized on a vaster basis than is possible within the limits of a single phrase. It would be possible of course to proceed with an analysis of the whole first movement of the Symphony and to show how, later, certain variations or transformations of the motif play an important and fateful rôle in introducing contrasts or in intensifying the dynamic outlines.

It is necessary, I feel, to draw a careful distinction between the *psycho-logical* principles of association and the purely material one of repetition, even though the former so often takes shape as the latter in its most literal sense. The classic composers had the finest of instincts in this respect and their art is incredibly rich in resource and variety of associative means. Some of their successors, unfortunately, are more literal minded, often substituting a materialistic principle of repetition for the creative principle of association, and later music finds itself in this respect as in others frequently caught in the toils of a sterile academicism. Artistic form has vitality and coherence only as long as its vitalizing principle is the imagination and impulse of the composer; it withers and dies as soon as the "materials" of music assume an independent existence—a condition which is possible only when the genuine creative impulse is weak.

Closely allied to the principle of association is that of *progression*. This is so obvious, in an art which has its basis in time, as scarcely to need mention. To say that in such an art each individual moment must be, generally speaking, of greater intensity and significance than the one which precedes it, is perhaps a truism. Less obvious and more difficult to describe are the infinitely various means through which progression is achieved. The two examples already given, however, the Tristan Prelude and the opening bars of the Fifth Symphony—each illustrate the principle as clearly as possible; and, indeed, the analysis of each, even from quite different points of view, was largely concerned precisely with the gradual and progressive movement towards a clearly envisaged goal, and, especially in the case of the Tristan Prelude, the steady intensification of effect until this goal is reached.

In music of large design, the various elements group themselves into larger patterns. In the passage from the Tristan Prelude, . . . four short phrases contribute to the unfolding of a sort of superphrase, as clear and expressive in its highly organized outline as the simple primitive vocalization which is the origin and the basis of music. Such organization is, of course, indispensable to music of large dimensions.

I will mention, finally, a third principle, that of *contrast*. In the sense in which I use the word it denotes something quite other than what I have called progression. The latter term applies, obviously, to the development of a single impulse and is the process by which the impulse takes extended shape. When the impulse is complete, however, other necessities appear, and the need for contrast arises. What form the contrast shall take—whether the same materials shall be presented under different aspects, or whether a quite new departure is needed—such questions and the infinite degrees of difference which they include, depend upon the conception, the context, and the scope of the work in question. The large contrasts contained in a work of music, however, reveal its essential outlines and give it its largest rhythm, through the alternation of musical ideas with their contrasting movement, emphasis, and dynamic intensity.

From these remarks it may be inferred quite clearly that conception and execution are inseparable and in the last analysis identical. "Form" in music is identical with "content," regardless of whether the latter be significant or the former coherent. The actual process of composition remains mysterious—the composer is following, as best he can and with all the means at his disposal, the demands of his conception, listening for the sounds and rhythms which embody it, and giving them the shape which his creative vision prescribes.

—*The Intent of the Artist*, edited by Augusto Centeno (1941)

RUDOLF ARNHEIM

The Expressiveness of Visual Forms

1. EXPRESSION

Every work of art must express something. This means, first of all, that the content of the work must go beyond the presentation of the individual objects of which it consists. But such a definition is too large for our purpose. It broadens the notion of "expression" to include any kind of communication. True, we commonly say, for example, that a man "expresses his opinion." Yet artistic expression seems to be something more specific. It requires that the communication of the data produce an "experience," the active presence of the forces that make up the perceived pattern. How is such an experience achieved?

Inside Linked to Outside

In a limited sense of the term, expression refers to features of a person's external appearance and behavior that permit us to find out what the person is feeling, thinking, striving for. Such information may be gathered from a man's face and gestures, the way he talks, dresses, keeps his room, handles a pen or a brush, as well as from the opinions he holds, the interpretation he gives to events. This is less and also more than what I mean here by expression: less, because expression must be considered even when no reference is made to a mind manifesting itself in appearance; more, because much importance cannot be attributed to what is merely inferred intellectually and indirectly from external clues. Nevertheless this more familiar meaning of the term must be discussed briefly here.

We look at a friend's face, and two things may happen: we understand what his mind is up to; and we find in ourselves a duplicate of his experiences. The traditional explanation of this accomplishment may be gathered from a playful review of Lavater's *Physiognomic Fragments for the Advancement of the Knowledge and Love of Our Fellow Man* written by the poet Matthias Claudius around 1775. "Physiognomics is a science of faces. Faces are *concreta* for they are related *generaliter* to natural reality and *specialiter* are firmly attached to people. Therefore the question arises whether the famous trick of the 'abstractio' and the 'methodus analytica' should not be applied here, in the sense of watching out whether the letter *i*, whenever it appears, is furnished with a dot and whether the dot is never found on top of another letter; in which case we should be sure that the dot and the letter are twin brothers so that when we run into Castor we can expect Pollux not to be far away. For an example we posit that there be one hundred gentlemen, all of whom are very quick on their feet, and they had given sample and proof of this, and all of these hundred gentlemen had a wart on their noses. I am not saying that gentlemen with a wart on their noses are cowards but am merely assuming it for the sake of the example. . . . Now *ponamus* there comes to my house a fellow who calls me a wretched scribbler and spits me into the face. Suppose I am reluctant to get into a fist fight and also cannot tell what the outcome would be, and I am standing there and considering the issue. At that moment I discover a wart on his nose, and now I cannot refrain myself any longer, I go after him courageously and, without any doubt, get away unbeaten. This procedure would represent, as it were, the royal road in this field. The progress might be slow but just as safe as that on other royal roads."

In a more serious vein, the theory was stated early in the eighteenth century by the philosopher Berkeley. In his essay on vision he speaks about the way in which the observer sees shame or anger in the looks of a man. "Those passions are themselves invisible: they are nevertheless let in by the eye along with colors and alterations of countenance, which are the immediate object of vision, and which signify them for no other reason than barely because they have been observed to accompany them: without which experience, we should no more have taken blushing for a sign of shame than gladness." Charles Darwin, in his book on the expression of emotions, devoted a few pages to the same problem. He believed that external manifestations and their physical counterparts are connected by the observer either on the basis of an inborn instinct or of learning. "Moreover, when a child cries or laughs, he knows in a general manner what he is doing and what he feels; so that a very small exertion of reason would tell him what crying or laughing meant in others. But the question is, do our children acquire their knowledge of expression solely by experience through the power of association and reason? As most of the movements of expression must have been gradually acquired, afterwards becoming instinctive, there seems to be some degree of *a priori* probability that their recognition would likewise have become instinctive."

Recently a new version of the traditional theory has developed from a curious tendency on the part of many social scientists to assume that when people agree on some fact it is probably based on an unfounded convention. According to this view, judgments of expression rely on "stereotypes," which individuals adopt ready-made from their social group. For example, we have been told that aquiline noses indicate courage and that protruding lips betray sensuality. The promoters of the theory generally imply that such judgments are wrong, as though information not drawn from the individual's firsthand experience could never be trusted. The real danger does not lie in the social origin of the information, but rather in the fact that people have a tendency to acquire simply structured concepts on the basis of insufficient evidence, which may have been gathered firsthand or secondhand, and to preserve these concepts unchanged in the face of contrary experience. Whereas this may make for many one-sided or entirely wrong evaluations of individuals and groups of people, the existence of stereotypes does not explain the origin of physiognomic judgments. If these judgments stem from tradition, what is the tradition's source? Are they right or wrong? Even though often misapplied, traditional interpretations of physique and behavior may still be based on sound observation. In fact, perhaps they are so hardy because they are so true.

Within the framework of associationist thinking, a step forward was made by Lipps, who pointed out that the perception of expression involves the activity of forces. His theory of "empathy" was designed to explain why we find expression even in inanimate objects, such as the columns of a temple. The reasoning was as follows. When I look at the columns, I know from past experience the kind of mechanical pressure and counterpressure that occurs in them. Equally from past experience, I know how I should feel myself if I were in the place of the columns and if those physical forces acted upon and within my own body. I project my own kinesthetic feelings into the columns. Furthermore, the pressures and pulls called up from the stores of memory by the sight tend to provoke responses also in other areas of the mind. "When I project my strivings and forces into nature I do so also as to the way my strivings and forces make me feel, that is, I project my pride, my courage, my stubbornness, my lightness, my playful assuredness, my tranquil complacence. Only thus my empathy with regard to nature becomes truly esthetic empathy."

The characteristic feature of traditional theorizing in all its varieties is the belief that the expression of an object is not inherent in the visual pattern itself. What we see provides only clues for whatever knowledge and feelings we may mobilize from memory and project upon the object. The visual pattern has as little to do with the expression we confer upon it as words have to do with the content they transmit. The letters "pain" mean "suffering" in English and "bread" in French. Nothing in them suggests the one rather than the other meaning. They transmit a message only because of what we have learned about them.

Expression Embedded in Structure

William James was not so sure that body and mind have nothing intrinsically in common. "I cannot help remarking that the disparity between motions and feelings, on which these authors lay so much stress, is somewhat less absolute than at first sight it seems. Not only temporal succession, but such attributes as intensity, volume, simplicity or complication, smooth or impeded change, rest or agitation, are habitually predicated of both physical facts and mental facts." Evidently James reasoned that although body and mind are different media—the one being material, the other not—they might still resemble each other in certain structural properties.

This point was greatly stressed by *gestalt* psychologists. Particularly Wertheimer asserted that the perception of expression is much too immediate and compelling to be explainable merely as a product of learning. When we watch a dancer, the sadness or happiness of the mood seems to be directly inherent in the movements themselves. Wertheimer concluded that this was true because formal factors of the dance reproduced identical factors of the mood. The meaning of this theory may be illustrated by reference to an experiment by Binney in which members of a college dance group were asked individually to give improvisations of such subjects as sadness, strength, or night. The performances of the dancers showed much agreement. For example, in the representation of sadness the movement was slow and confined to a narrow range. It was mostly curved in shape and showed little tension. The direction was indefinite, changing, wavering, and the body seemed to yield passively to the force of gravitation rather than being propelled by its own initiative. It will be admitted that the physical mood of sadness has a similar pattern. In a depressed person the mental processes are slow and rarely go beyond matters closely related to immediate experiences and interests of the moment. In all his thinking and striving are softness and a lack of energy. There is little determination, and activity is often controlled by outside forces.

Naturally there is a traditional way of representing sadness in a dance, and the performances of the students may have been influenced by it. What counts, however, is that the movements, whether spontaneously invented or copied from other dancers, exhibited a formal structure so strikingly similar to that of the intended mood. And since such visual qualities as speed, shape, or direction are immediately accessible to the eye, it seems legitimate to assume that they are the carriers of an expression directly comprehensible to the eye.

If we examine the facts more closely, we find that expression is conveyed not so much by the "geometric-technical" properties of the percept as such, but by the forces they can be assumed to arouse in the nervous system of the observer. Regardless of whether the object moves (dancer, actor) or is immobile (painting, sculpture), it is the kind of directed tension or "movement"—its strength, place, and distribution—transmitted by the visible patterns that is perceived as expression. . . .

The Priority of Expression

The impact of the forces transmitted by a visual pattern is an intrinsic part of the percept, just as shape or color. In fact, expression can be described as the primary content of vision. We have been trained to think of perception as the recording of shapes, distances, hues, motions. The awareness of these measurable characteristics is really a fairly late accomplishment of the human mind. Even in the Western man of the twentieth century it presupposes special conditions. It is the attitude of the scientist and the engineer or of the salesman who estimates the size of a customer's waist, the shade of a lipstick, the weight of a suitcase. But if I sit in front of a fireplace and watch the flames, I do not normally register certain shades of red, various degrees of brightness, geometrically defined shapes moving at such and such a speed. I see the graceful play of aggressive tongues, flexible striving, lively color. The face of a person is more readily perceived and remembered as being alert, tense, concentrated rather than as being triangularly shaped, having slanted eyebrows, straight lips, and so on. This priority of expression, although somewhat modified in adults by a scientifically oriented education, is striking in children and primitives, as has been shown by Werner and Köhler. The profile of a mountain is soft or threateningly harsh; a blanket thrown over a chair is twisted, sad, tired.

The priority of physiognomic properties should not come as a surprise. Our senses are not self-contained recording devices operating for their own sake. They have been developed by the organism as an aid in properly reacting to the environment. The organism is primarily interested in the forces that are active around it—their place, strength, direction. Hostility and friendliness are attributes of forces. And the perceived impact of forces makes for what we call expression.

If expression is the primary content of vision in daily life, the same should be all the more true for the way the artist looks at the world. The expressive qualities are his means of communication. They capture his attention, through them he understands and interprets his experiences, and they determine the form patterns he creates. Therefore the training of art students should be expected to consist basically in sharpening their sense of these qualities and in teaching them to look to expression as the guiding criteria for every stroke of the pencil, brush, or chisel. In fact many good art teachers do precisely this. But there are also plenty of times when the spontaneous sensitivity of the student to expression not only is not developed further, but is even disturbed and suppressed. There is, for example, an old-fashioned but not extinct way of teaching students to draw from the model by asking them to establish the exact length and direction of contour lines, the relative position of points, the shape of masses. In other words, students are to concentrate on the geometric-technical qualities of what they see. In its modern version this method consists in urging the young artist to think of the model or of a freely invented design as a configuration of masses, planes, directions. Again interest is focussed on geometric-technical qualities.

This method of teaching follows the principles of scientific definition rather than those of spontaneous vision. There are, however, other teachers who will proceed differently. With a model sitting on the floor in a hunched-up position, they will not begin by making the students notice that the whole figure can be inscribed in a triangle. Instead they will ask about the expression of the figure; they may be told, for example, that the person on the floor looks tense, tied together, full of potential energy. They will suggest, then, that the student try to render this quality. In doing so the student will watch proportions and directions, but not as geometric properties in themselves. These formal properties will be perceived as being functionally dependent upon the primarily observed expression, and the correctness and incorrectness of each stroke will be judged on the basis of whether or not it captures the dynamic "mood" of the subject. Equally, in a lesson of design, it will be made clear that to the artist, just as to any unspoiled human being, a circle is not a line of constant curvature, whose points are all equally distant from a center, but first of all a compact, hard, restful thing. Once the student has understood that roundness is not identical with circularity, he may try for a design whose structural logic will be controlled by the primary concept of something to be expressed.

For whereas the artificial concentration on formal qualities will leave the student at a loss as to which pattern to select among innumerable and equally acceptable ones, an expressive theme will serve as a natural guide to forms that fit the purpose.

It will be evident that what is advocated here is not the so-called "self-expression." The method of self-expression plays down, or even annihilates, the function of the theme to be represented. It recommends a passive, "projective" pouring-out of what is felt inside. On the contrary, the method discussed here requires active, disciplined concentration of all organizing powers upon the expression that is localized in the object of representation.

It might be argued that an artist must practice the purely formal technique before he may hope to render expression successfully. But that is exactly the notion that reverses the natural order of the artistic process. In fact all good practicing is highly expressive. This first occurred to me many years ago when I watched the dancer Gret Palucca perform one of her most popular pieces, which she called "Technical Improvisations." This number was nothing but the systematic exercise that the dancer practiced every day in her studio in order to loosen up the joints of her body. She would start out by doing turns of her head, then move her neck, then shrug her shoulders, until she ended up wriggling her toes. This purely technical practice was a success with the audience because it was thoroughly expressive. Forcefully precise and rhythmical movements presented, quite naturally, the entire catalogue of human pantomime. They passed through all the moods from lazy happiness to impertinent satire.

In order to achieve technically precise movements, a capable dance teacher may not ask students to perform "geometrically" defined positions, but to strive for the muscular experience of uplift, or attack, or yielding, that will be created by correctly executed movements. (Comparable methods are nowadays applied therapeutically in physical rehabilitation work. For example, the patient is not asked to concentrate on the meaningless, purely formal exercise of flexing and stretching his arm, but on a game or piece of work that involves suitable motions of the limbs as a means to a sensible end.)

The Physiognomics of Nature

The perception of expression does not therefore necessarily—and not even primarily—serve to determine the state of mind of another person by way of externally observable manifestations. Köhler has pointed out that people normally deal with and react to expressive physical behavior in itself rather than being conscious of the psychical experiences reflected by such behavior. We perceive the slow, listless, "droopy" movements of one person as contrasted to the brisk, straight, vigorous movements of another, but do not necessarily go beyond the meaning of such appearance by thinking explicitly of the physical weariness or alertness behind it. Weariness and alertness are already contained in the physical behavior itself; they are not distinguished in any essential way from the weariness of slowly floating tar or the energetic ringing of the telephone bell. It is true, of course, that during a business conversation one person may be greatly concerned with trying to read the other's thoughts and feelings through what can be seen in his face and gestures. "What is he up to? How is he taking it?" But in such circumstances we clearly go beyond what is apparent in the perception of expression itself, and secondarily apply what we have seen to the mental processes that may be hidden "behind" the outer image.

Particularly the content of the work of art does not consist in states of mind that the dancer may pretend to be experiencing in himself or that our imagination may bestow on a painted Mary Magdalen or Sebastian. The substance of the work consists in what appears in the visible pattern itself. Evidently, then, expression is not limited to living organisms that we assume to possess consciousness. A steep rock, a willow tree, the colors of a sunset, the cracks in a wall, a tumbling leaf, a flowing fountain, and in fact a mere line or color or the dance of an abstract shape on the movie screen have as much expression as the human body, and serve the artist equally well. In some ways they serve him even better, for the human body is a particularly complex pattern, not easily reduced to the simplicity of shape and motion that transmits compelling expression. Also it is over-loaded with nonvisual associations. The human figure is not the easiest, but the most difficult, vehicle of artistic expression.

The fact that nonhuman objects have genuine physiognomic properties has been concealed by the popular assumption that they are merely dressed up with human expression by an illusory "pathetic fallacy," by empathy, anthropomorphism, primitive animism. But if expression is an inherent characteristic of perceptual patterns, its manifestations in the human figure are but a special case of a more general phenomenon. The comparison of an object's expression with a human state of mind is a secondary process. A weeping willow does not look sad because it looks like a sad person. It is more adequate to say that since the shape, direction, and flexibility of willow branches convey the expression of passive hanging, a comparison with the structurally similar state of mind and body that we call sadness imposes itself secondarily. The columns of a temple do not strive upward and carry the weight of the roof so dramatically because we put ourselves in their place, but because their location, proportion, and shape are carefully chosen in such a way that their image contains the desired expression. Only because and when this is so, are we enabled to "sympathize" with the columns, if we so desire. An inappropriately designed temple resists all empathy.

To define visual expression as a reflection of human feelings would seem to be misleading on two counts: first, because it makes us ignore the fact that expression has its origin in the perceived pattern and in the reaction of the brain field of vision to this pattern; second, because such a description unduly limits the range of what is being expressed. We found as the basis of expression a configuration of forces. Such a configuration interests us because it is significant not only for the object in whose image it appears, but for the physical and mental world in general. Motifs like rising and falling, dominance and submission, weakness and strength, harmony and discord, struggle and conformance, underlie all existence. We find them within our own mind and in our relations to other people, in the human community and in the events of nature. Perception of expression fulfills its spiritual mission only if we experience in it more than the resonance of our own feelings. It permits us to realize that the forces stirring in ourselves are only individual examples of the same forces acting throughout the universe. We are thus enabled to sense our place in the whole and in the inner unity of that whole.

Some objects and events resemble each other with regard to the underlying patterns of forces; others do not. Therefore, on the basis of their expressive appearance, our eye spontaneously creates a kind of Linnean classification of all things existing. This perceptual classification cuts across the order suggested by other kinds of categories. Particularly in our modern Western civilization we are accustomed to distinguishing between animate and inanimate things, human and nonhuman creatures, the mental and the physical. But in terms of expressive qualities, the character of a given person may resemble that of a particular tree more closely than that of another person. The state of affairs in a human society may be similar to the tension in the skies just before the outbreak of a thunderstorm. Further, our kind of scientific and economic thinking makes us define things by measurements rather than by the dynamics of their appearance. Our criteria for what is useful or useless, friendly or hostile, have tended to sever the connections with outer expression, which they possess in the minds of children or primitives. If a house or a chair suits our practical purposes, we may not stop to find out whether its appearance expresses our style of living. In business relations we define a man by his census data, his income, age, position, nationality, or race—that is, by categories that ignore the inner nature of the man as it is manifest in his outer expression.

Primitive languages give us an idea of the kind of world that derives from a classification based on perception. Instead of restricting itself to the verb "to walk," which rather abstractly refers to locomotion, the language of the African Ewe takes care to specify in every kind of walking the particular expressive qualities of the movement. There are expressions for "the gait of a little man whose limbs shake very much, to walk with a dragging step like a feeble person, the gait of a long-legged man who throws his legs forward, of a corpulent man who walks heavily, to walk in a dazed fashion without looking ahead, an energetic and firm step," and many others. These distinctions are not made out of sheer esthetic sensitivity, but because the expressive properties of the gait are believed to reveal important practical information on what kind of man is walking and what is his intent at the moment.

Although primitive languages often surprise us by their wealth of subdivisions for which we see no need, they also reveal generalizations that to us may seem unimportant or absurd. For example, the language of the Klamath Indians has prefixes for words referring to objects of similar shape or movement. Such a prefix may describe "the outside of a round or spheroidal, cylindrical, discoid or bulbed object, or a ring; also voluminous; or again, an act accomplished with an object which bears such a form; or a circular or semi-circular or waving movement of the body, arms, hands, or other parts. Therefore this prefix is to be found connected with clouds, celestial bodies, rounded slopes on the earth's surface, fruits rounded or bulbed in shape, stones and dwellings (these last being usually circular in form.) It is employed too, for a crowd of animals, for enclosures, social gatherings (since an assembly usually adopts the form of a circle), and so forth."

Such a classification groups things together that to our way of thinking belong in very different categories and have little or nothing in common. At the same time, these features of primitive language remind us that the poetical habit of uniting practically disparate objects by metaphor is not a sophisticated invention of artists, but derives from and relies on the universal and spontaneous way of approaching the world of experience.

George Braque advises the artist to seek the common in the dissimilar. "Thus the poet can say, The swallow knifes the sky, and thereby makes a knife out of a swallow." It is the function of the metaphor to make the reader penetrate the concrete shell of the world of things by combinations of objects that have little in common but the underlying pattern. Such a device, however, would not work unless the reader of poetry was still alive, in his own daily experience, to the symbolic or metaphoric connotation of all appearance and activity. For example, hitting or breaking things normally evokes, if ever so slightly, the overtone of attack and destruction. There is a tinge of conquest and achievement to all rising—even the climbing of a staircase. If the shades are pulled in the morning and the room is flooded with light, more is experienced than a simple change of illumination. One aspect of the wisdom that belongs to a genuine culture is the constant awareness of the symbolic meaning expressed in concrete happening, the sensing of the universal in the particular. This gives significance and dignity to all daily pursuits, and prepares the ground on which the arts can grow. In its pathological extreme this spontaneous symbolism manifests itself in what is known to the psychiatrist as the "organ speech" of psychosomatic and other neurotic symptoms. There are people who cannot swallow because there is something in their lives they "cannot swallow" or whom an unconscious sense of guilt compels to spend hours every day on washing and cleaning. . . .

All Art is Symbolic

If art could do nothing better than reproduce the things of nature, either directly or by analogy, or to delight the senses, there would be little justification for the honorable place reserved to it in every known society. Art's reputation must be due to the fact that it helps man to understand the world and himself, and presents to his eyes what he has understood and believes to be true. Now everything in this world is a unique individual; no two things can be equal. But anything can be understood only because it is made up of ingredients not reserved to itself but common to many or all other things. In science, greatest knowledge is achieved when all existing phenomena are reduced to a common law. This is true for art also. The mature work of art succeeds in subjecting everything to a dominant law of structure. In doing so, it does not distort the variety of existing things into uniformity. On the contrary, it clarifies their differences by making them all comparable. Braque has said, "By putting a lemon next to an orange they cease to be a lemon and an orange and become fruit. The mathematicians follow this law. So do we." He fails to remember that the virtue of such correlation is two-fold. It shows the way in which things are similar and, by doing so, defines their individuality. By establishing a common "style" for all objects, the artist creates a whole, in which the place and function of every one of them are lucidly defined. Goethe said: "The beautiful is a manifestation of secret laws of nature, which would have remained hidden to us forever without its appearance."

Every element of a work of art is indispensable for the one purpose of pointing out the theme, which embodies the nature of existence for the artist. In this sense we find symbolism even in works that, at first sight, seem to be little more than arrangements of fairly neutral objects. We need only glance at the bare outlines of the two still lifes sketched in Figures *a* and *b* to experience two different conceptions of reality. Cézanne's picture (*a*) is dominated by the stable framework of verticals and horizontals in the background, the table, and the axes of bottles and glass. This skeleton

is strong enough to give support even to the sweeping folds of the fabric. A simple order is conveyed by the upright symmetry of each bottle and that of the glass. There is abundance in the swelling volumes and emphasis on roundness and softness even in the inorganic matter. Compare this image of prosperous peace with the catastrophic turmoil in Picasso's work (*b*). Here we find little stability. The vertical and horizontal orientations are avoided. The room is slanted, the right angles of the table, which is turned over, are either hidden by oblique position or distorted. The four legs do not run parallel, the bottle topples, the desperately sprawling corpse of the bird is about to fall off the table. The contours tend to be hard, sharp, lifeless, even in the body of the animal.

Since the basic perceptual pattern carries the theme, we must not be surprised to find that art continues to fulfill its function even when it ceases to represent objects of nature. "Abstract" art does in its own way what art has always done. It is not better than representational art, which also does not hide but reveals the meaningful skeleton of forces. It is no less good, for it contains the essentials. It is not "pure form," because even the simplest line expresses visible meaning and is therefore symbolic. It does not offer intellectual abstractions, because there is nothing more concrete than color, shape, and motion. It does not limit itself to the inner life of man, or to the unconscious, because for art the distinctions between the outer and the inner world and the conscious and the unconscious mind are artificial. The human mind receives, shapes, and interprets its image of the outer world with all its conscious and unconscious powers, and the realm of the unconscious could never enter our experience without the reflection of perceivable things. There is no way of presenting the one without the other. But the nature of the outer and the inner world can be reduced to a play of forces, and this "musical" approach is attempted by the misnamed abstract artists.

We do not know what the art of the future will look like. But we know that "abstraction" is not art's final climax. No style will ever be that. It is one valid way of looking at the world, one view of the holy mountain, which offers a different image from every place but can be seen as the same everywhere.

—*Art and Visual Perception* (1954)

2. Gestalt Psychology and Artistic Form

The French speak of Gestalt psychology as *la psychologie de la forme*. This translation is meant to indicate that the Gestalt principle is only indirectly concerned with the "subject-matter" of natural things. To call a football team or a painting or an electric circuit a Gestalt is to describe a property of their organisation. Gestalten function as wholes, which determine their parts. Four musicians who form a string quartet will create a unified style of performance. This style is a delicate crystallisation of affinities and conflicts of temper. It is the balance of convergent and divergent social forces and, in turn, modifies the behaviour of each player. Change the arm of the left boy in the Laocoon group, and the entire piece of sculpture assumes a different composition. Such internal play of influences obeys rules that are largely independent of the particular medium in which they are observed. In a sense, they refer to "formal" properties.

If, however, we mean by "form" the outer appearance of things—as we do when speaking of the arts—it is necessary to see that the Gestalt theory deals with form only as the manifestation of forces, which are the true object of its interest. Physical and psychical forces can be studied only by their perceivable effects. Thus the overall direction of energy in a given system may appear as a visible axis in the observed pattern. The degree of balance in the distribution of forces may be reflected in the degree of observable symmetry. The direction and strength of water power shows in the "form" of the flow. In the star shape of a flower we recognise the even spread of undisturbed growth. The flaws of a crippled tree or a hunched back tell of interferences with lawful development. Anxiety may express itself in the muscle tension of the body or the broken curve of a gesture.

In all these cases, form is strongly determined by forces inherent in the object itself. This is not always so. It is hardly true at all for the work of art. In the visual arts, except for the effect of such inherent qualities of the medium as the weight of stone, the grain of wood, or the viscosity of oil paint, form is imposed on matter by external force. Neither can a work of art be grown, nor does the artist often use highly organised materials such as crystals or plants. Dancers and actors, who use their own bodies, and to some extent photography, which uses the direct registration of physical objects, are the outstanding exceptions; but it is precisely for this reason that they are suspected of being hybrids of art and nature. The artist prefers the submissiveness of amorphous matter.

Physically, then, the work of art is a "weak Gestalt," an object of low organisation. It makes little difference to the marble of the Laocoon group that an arm is broken off, nor does the paint of a landscape revolt when a busy restorer adds a glaring blue to its faded sky. But, as Benedetto Croce would point out to us, we are now not speaking of art at all. Art cannot be a physical fact because "physical facts have no reality, whereas art, to which so many devote their entire lives and which fills everybody with divine joy, is eminently real". This means that art exists only as a psychological experience; and the forces which generate such experience are the proper object of our attention.

The work of art defined as an experience turns out to be a Gestalt of the highest degree. In fact, from the beginning, Gestalt theorists looked to art for the most convincing examples of sensitively organised wholes. Christian von Ehrenfels, whose essay "Ueber Gestaltqualitäten" gave the theory its name, speaks of a melody as being different from the sum of the tones which constitute it. And we discover with delight such testimony as Cézanne's answer to Vollard, who had pointed out to him two tiny spots of uncovered canvas in his portrait: "You understand, Monsieur Vollard, if I should put there something haphazard, I should be compelled to do my whole picture over, starting from that place!"

The psychological forces that determine artistic form operate essentially in the perceptual process of vision and in the area of motivation and "personality". For the purpose of analysis these factors can be discussed separately. Actually, they interact all the time. Also a more complete presentation would require consideration of further psychological levels, notably thinking and memory.

Vision cannot be explained merely by the properties of the observed object but is dependent on what goes on in the brain. Think of a red triangle in the centre of a rectangular grey ground. "Objectively" we have nothing but two areas of different colour, situated in the same plane, independent of each other, and at perfect rest. If we scrutinise the observer's experience and consider at the same time what is going on in the neural mechanism of vision, we realise first of all that we are dealing with a highly dynamic process. The triangle has broken up the unity of the grey constantly defending itself against the tendency of the plane to regain its homogeneity and to expel the invader. This is successful to the extent that the triangle appears suspended in front of the grey plane thus permitting the ground to continue "behind" the triangle and to maintain its wholeness. The triangle also is far from static. It is dense, compared with the looser texture of the ground. Its pointed corners stab outward in directed, centrifugal movement. Also the red, being a more active colour than grey, shows the property of long wave-length hues to appear closer to the observer. It attacks him. Were it blue, it would withdraw from him. Red is warm and irradiates across the ground. Were it blue, it would be cold and contract toward its centre. Furthermore, the triangle is held in balance by its central location. If it were placed eccentrically, we could actually experience the pushes and pulls that would tend to displace it—for instance, by drawing it toward the centre of the ground. Even in its central position our triangle is no more "at rest" than a rope that does not move because two men of equal strength are pulling it in opposite directions. The antagonistic forces happen to balance each other. Nevertheless, their power remains perceivable to the sensitive eye.

This is not all. Shape and size of the two units constantly define each other. The smallness of the triangle determines the largeness of the ground. The stable verticals and horizontals of the rectangle are enhanced and challenged by the obliqueness of the triangle, and vice versa. The brightness and colour values also interact. The lightness of the ground darkens the triangle. The red evokes in the grey the complementary green.

A simple example has been analysed with some detail in order to show that any description of form in the static terms of sheer geometry, quantity, or location will fatally impoverish the facts. Only if one realises that all visual form is constantly endowed with striving and yielding, contraction and expansion, contrast and adaptation, attack and retreat, can one understand the elementary impact of a painting, statue, or building and its capacity to symbolise the action of life by means of physically motionless objects.

Since visual dynamics is not inherent in the physical object—where are the forces which constitute it? Gestalt psychologists refuse to describe them as an effect of empathy, that is, as a mere projection of previously acquired knowledge upon the percept. They assume that the sensations of push and pull are the conscious counterpart of the physiological processes which organise the percept in the neural field of the optical sector, that is, the cerebral cortex, the optic nerve, and possibly the retinæ of the eyes. According to this theory, visual dynamics is not a secondary attachment of the stimulus, due to accidental, subjective associations, but rather precedes the "geometric" pattern of shape and colour in that this pattern is the result of the organising forces, of whose activity the observer is partially aware. The theory would seem to explain why in actual experience the dynamic, or expressive, qualities are the most powerful and immediate qualities of the percept. In comparison, the static attributes of shape, size, line, or location, on which scientists have concentrated their attention, would seem to be relatively indirect and late products of vision. The detached, measuring gaze of the investigator in the laboratory preserves little of the spontaneous excitement which the child, the primitive, the artist find in the world of sight.

Once this point is strongly made, one may turn to the principles of articulation, to which Gestalt psychologists have devoted most of their investigations of visual form. What makes the visual field split up into segregated objects—trees, houses, cars, people? What makes the "abstract" painter confident that all observers will see roughly the same units of form in his composition? Experiments have shown that articulation is controlled essentially by the nature of the stimulus configuration itself. Thirty years ago, Max Wertheimer established some "rules of visual grouping." It seems now probable that these rules can be reduced to one, namely, the principle of similarity. The relative degree of similarity in a given perceptual pattern makes for a corresponding degree of connection or fusion. Units which resemble each other in shape, size, direction, colour, brightness, or location will be seen together. [See Fig. 1.]

The principle of similarity organises stimulus elements in time as well as in space. The form pattern of a painting, which impinges upon the observer's mind, is not his first visual experience. It is the most recent phase of a prolonged process, within which memory traces interact according to the principle of similarity. The relative strength of the factors which make up the temporal and the spatial contexts will determine what the observer sees at any given moment. Due to its high degree of unity and precision, good artistic form is capable of imposing its own articulation upon different observers in spite of the different "visual history" which each individual brings to the present experience.

It is possible and necessary to interpret the principle of similarity as a special case of a more general law, according to which the forces which constitute a psychological or physiological field tend toward the simplest, most regular, most symmetrical distribution available under the given conditions. This means that of the many possible groupings of elements in a visual pattern the one which makes for the simplest organisation of the whole context will spontaneously occur to the observer.

Described in this way, the organisational processes, which take place in the creation of visual form, are shown to obey a law which governs the functioning of the mind as a whole. In addition, we thus discover a similarity between the behaviour of psychological and physical processes. In

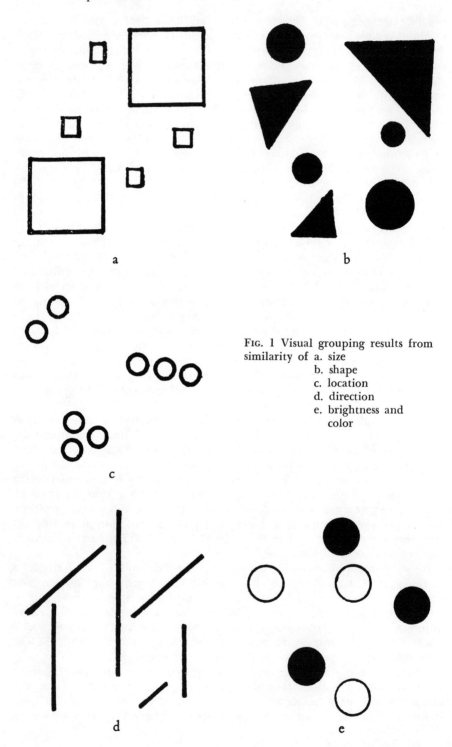

Fig. 1 Visual grouping results from
similarity of a. size
          b. shape
          c. location
          d. direction
          e. brightness and
            color

fact, in 1920, Wolfgang Köhler in his book on "Die physischen Gestalten" pointed to the second law of thermodynamics as a manifestation of the basic Gestalt principle. Physicists assume that the world tends to pass from less probable to more probable configurations or states. There is no reason why the physiological forces in the nervous system should make an exception to this rule. In other words, the mental processes which create visual form can be understood as a reflection of the tendency to simplest structure assumed to exist in the corresponding brain field. [See Fig. 2.]

Psychologists and physicists have arrived at similar conclusions independently of each other. As a curiosity it may be mentioned that while Gestalt theorists recognise a tendency to "good form" or "well organised structure," the physicists see a development from order to disorder. Presumably the contradiction is partly terminological; but the necessary unification of these views is likely to lead to considerations that will be of interest for both parties.

If the human mind in general and the mechanism of vision in particular are governed by a tendency to simplest structure, we may ask why we see any objects at all. Obviously, the simplest possible field of sight would be totally homogeneous like a whitewashed wall—inarticulate, plain, motionless, a foretaste of the dismal state in which, according to the physicists, the chilled universe will find itself at the end of time. Our eyes are saved from such boredom by the fact that the organism is not a "closed system." The influx of external energy constantly upsets and delays the striving toward final rest. In vision, the disturber of the peace is light energy, which,

FIG. 2. The principle of simple form.
a. Circle and cross are seen instead of four independent patterns.
b. Complex figure breaks up into triangle and rectangle.

through the action of the eye-lenses, comes to us in the form of information about objects. Now information, according to Norbert Wiener, is negative entropy; that is, it imports order or form. For our purposes, "objects" can be defined as processes that have been temporarily arrested on their way to final equilibrium. The images of all objects show the partial success of that process, namely, some regularity, some symmetry, some simplicity of form. But they also show the marks of striving and growing, of segregation and independence. Thus the form of objects allows us symbolically to envisage the nature of life in its restless striving towards rest.

Far from being a passive mechanism of registration like the photographic camera, our visual apparatus copes with the incoming images in active struggle. It is upset by the intrusion and animated by the stimulation. It seizes upon the regularities of form, which allow comprehension, and tries to subject the bewilderingly accidental agglomeration of objects in space to whatever order is obtainable. Every-day vision initiates and anticipates the duel of the artist with the image.

So far we have "bracketed out" the activity of the eye, as though it were a self-contained organism, minding its own business and forming pictures for the pictures' sake. This makes for a short-sighted psychology of perception. If applied to aesthetics, it leads to a narrow conception of art as a purely formal manipulation of images. But vision, in daily life as well as in art, functions as a part of the total mind. As such it is an instrument of observation at the service of vital needs. It also reflects symbolically the entire state of mental affairs which constitute "personality." Consequently, pictorial form can be expected to be determined essentially by four factors: (1) the structure of the images of external objects projected on the eyes; (2) the formative powers of the visual apparatus; (3) the need of the organism for observing, selecting, and understanding; (4) attitudes, mood, temperament, tensions, inner conflicts, etc.

The first factor would bear on the realistic truthfulness of pictorial representation. The second accounts for the exploration of shape, for "composition" as a pleasing arrangement of balanced form, for decorative ornament. The third and fourth require more detailed discussion.

The function of artistic form remains incomprehensible as long as one fails to remember that vision does not primarily serve to satisfy detached curiosity and enjoyment. By means of the eyes the organism scans the environment beyond the limits of its own body in order to discover useful or dangerous things. Needs make for perceptual selection. For instance, any movement in the environment automatically attracts attention because movement means a change of conditions, which may call for a reaction. Uninteresting things cast their images on the retina, but as a rule are not perceived.

This selective factor manifests itself in pictorial representation. It determines subject matter and form. It tells what the artist—or his patron—considers important or safe. The psychologist notices that some historical periods or individual artists concentrate on the human figure, others on objects connected with utility and consumption, others again on nature. He finds that under certain conditions art withdraws from subject matter altogether. Form is influenced by concern with, or neglect of, detail. Needs and mores make for distortion. Pictures of the human figure may show large breasts but no genitals. In children's drawings much more space may be devoted to the face than to the body. Arms or clothes may be left out entirely. The dependence of form factors such as size, proportion, location, shape, shading, direction, on the inner needs of the draftsman, are being studied in a recently developed psychological test, which requires patients to draw the picture of a man and a woman. In a more passive way, an observer's interpretation of the perceptual qualities of inkblots (whole vs. part, shape vs. colour, shading, movement, etc.) is found to be significant in the Rorschach test. With certain precautions, it may be possible to apply these findings fruitfully to the analysis of artistic form.

Visual form must also be considered as a basic means of understanding the environment. Man's notions of what things are, how they act, and how they are related to each other, rely greatly on appearance. Particularly the young mind of children and primitives derives most of its judgments from the direct interpretation of perceptual form. Thus a latch-key may look lazy or aggressive, or magic power may be attributed to an object of disturbing shape. In a more general sense the child by gradually conquering the basic geometric forms and applying them to trees, houses, people, or animals grasps something of the nature of these objects. The towering size of a father, the generous spreading of a tree, the flimsiness of smoke are captured by means of comprehensible form and thus acquired for the child's conception of the world.

The child conquers form by observing the objects around him, but also by freely exploring the products of his pencil and crayon on paper. There is no reason to assume that the early drawings and paintings of children are all representations of the environment and that the basic geometric forms evolve from copying the shape of objects. A Gestalt psychologist would expect that the tendency to simple structure would increasingly direct the child's first scribbles. The clear, balanced, comprehensible shape of a circle, a straight line, or a rectangular relationship will be a source of great pleasure. In fact, unless parental pressure hampers free development, non-representational forms—which look like "abstractions" to an art critic but are eminently concrete to the child—will be created for their own sake. Increasingly often, they will also be related to objects of the environment. There is constant interplay between the growing complexity of the forms that can be mastered and the subtler observation of reality, to which richer forms can do better justice.

The clarification of visual forms and their organization in integrated patterns as well as the attribution of such forms to suitable objects is one of the most effective training grounds of the young mind. Educators and psychologists are beginning to see that intelligence does not only operate in verbal abstractions. Visual thinking manifests and develops general intelligence, and the stepwise progress of visual order reflects the development of the person as a whole.

Visual order as a tool of insight has been stressed by the late Gustaf Britsch and his disciples, Kornmann and Schaefer-Simmern. Their findings in the field of art education are in striking agreement with Gestalt principles. It is true that these educators have concentrated on the "formal" aspects of art, but they have also stressed the fact that mechanical copying or imitation leads to the neglect of visual organisation, that is, to ugliness. An image can only be valid if it transmits the artist's conception of his subject by means of the spontaneous symbolism of orderly form. Beauty can be defined as the correspondence of meaning and perceptual symbolism. In the true work of art, the deepest meaning is conveyed by the elementary properties of size, shape, distance, location, or colour. The power of this visual language lies in its spontaneous evidence, its almost childlike simplicity. Darkness means darkness, things that belong together are shown together, and what is great and high appears in large size in high location.

Beauty is lost when meaning and form are split asunder. This results, on the one hand, in playing with formal relationships or pure "composition," which carries no message or contradicts meaning. On the other hand, it leads to the misnamed "literary" approach, which limits meaning to what the observer knows about the subject-matter and therefore offers chaotic, visually incomprehensible form. The tragic consequence of this split in our time has been that so many people have become blind to the meaning of form and that they believe they "see" when they absorb meaning without form.

Point Four of our programme remains to be considered. The symbolism of form is not only a means of interpreting the environment visually, it also reflects the person of its creator. A human body means one thing to Lucas Cranach and another thing to Giorgione, because two different people are looking. Systematic attempts to understand pictorial representations as "projections" of the human personality are being made by therapeutically oriented psychologists. They deal with visual symbolism in two ways.

One of them is used by the psycho-analysts. Whereas Freud himself had cautioned his students that for a correct analysis of symbols one must rely on the comments of the individual who produced them; other analysts, in their discussions of art, do not hesitate to use easy standard interpretations of the dream-book type. This makes for an embarrassingly shallow approach to art. Visual form becomes a code language used by the artist to refer, with monotonous insistence, to the basic physiology of sex. The suspicion that most analyses of this kind are arbitrary is not only based on their disappointing results but also on their method. They use what we may term metaphoric symbolism. One concrete thing is said to stand for another concrete thing, a mandolin for a woman, a man for the artist's father, a bird or a cave for the male or the female genitals. Now interpretations of this kind are safe when metaphors have become institutionalised, that is, when they have been consciously established by cultural convention. For instance, in Christian art the dove stands for the holy ghost and the lily for virginity. But it is in the nature of the psycho-analytic symbols that much of the time their meaning is not permitted to reach consciousness. Only the avowed practice of some surrealists, who have institutionalised

Freud, permits us to be sure that they do what the analyst says they are doing. In other cases no such proof exists, unless a reliable depth analysis of the particular artist is available.

Art can also be interpreted psychologically by means of what may be called isomorphic symbolism. This method does not depend on alleged associations of one object with another object but on perceptual qualities inherent in visual form itself. As an example the investigation of Rose H. Alschuler and La Berta Weiss Hattwick, "Painting and Personality," may be cited. These authors analysed a large number of "designs" done by nursery school children and compared them statistically with what was known about the children themselves. They assert, for example, that children who prefer warm colours show "warmer" relationships to other people while cold colours go with more controlled behaviour. The practice of overlaying one colour with another is found in highly "repressed" children. Children who use heavy strokes and squares, rectangles, or verticals are more assertive than the self-centred children, who like circles in their pictures.

In order to interpret these results one must assume that structural characteristics of visual form are spontaneously related to similar characteristics in human behaviour. We have called this type of symbolism "isomorphic" because this is the term used by gestalt psychologists to describe identity of structure in different media. For instance, a person's mood may be structurally identical with the bodily behaviour which accompanies that mood. This isomorphic correspondence has been used to explain the fact that the "expression" of physical behaviour seems to be directly comprehensible to the onlooker. The gesture of a dancer, but also the motions of a towel on the clothes-line or the shape of a cloud, contain structural features whose kinship with similarly structured mental features is immediately felt. If it is true that structural similarities transcend the difference between body and mind and make for unified total behaviour and experience, then we should expect the child to choose, for the pictures he makes, forms that match his own attitudes. Thus here again the findings of Gestalt theory and work in the arts seem to confirm each other.

The four determinants of visual form which we have discussed have been variously considered in the theory and practice of the arts, often in a one-sided way. There are those who hold that art is merely a faithful recording of whatever percept, memory, image, or phantasy besets the artist's mind. Others, on the contrary, concentrate on the organising powers of the eye without considering that all creation of form involves a coping with the world of experience. Again, the gradual progress of visual order is studied with little reference to the manifestations of the total personality in every stroke or shape. Or the picture is viewed as nothing but a kind of clinical map without sufficient awareness of the developmental steps in visual and motor organisation.

If we wish to understand the relationship between visual form and the total organism, we must consider the complex interaction of the many forces that make up a person.

—*Aspects of Form*, edited by Lancelot Law Whyte (1951)

MAURICE MERLEAU-PONTY

The Film and the New Psychology[1]

Classical psychology considers our visual field to be a sum or mosaic of sensations, each of which is strictly dependent on the local retinal stimulus which corresponds to it. The new psychology reveals, first of all, that such a parallelism between sensations and the nervous phenomenon conditioning them is unacceptable, even for our simplest and most immediate sensations. Our retina is far from homogeneous: certain parts, for example, are blind to blue or red, yet I do not see any discolored areas when looking at a blue or red surface. This is because, starting at the level of simply seeing colors, my perception is not limited to registering what the retinal stimuli prescribe but reorganizes these stimuli so as to re-establish the field's homogeneity. Broadly speaking, we should think of it not as a mosaic but as a system of configurations. Groups rather than juxtaposed elements are principal and primary in our perception. We group the stars into the same constellations as the ancients, yet it is *a priori* possible to draw the heavenly map many other ways. Given the series:

ab cd ef gh ij

we will always pair the dots according to the formula a-b, c-d, e-f, etc., although the grouping b-c, d-e, f-g, etc. is equally probable in principle. A sick person contemplating the wallpaper in his room will suddenly see it transformed if the pattern and figure become the ground while what is usually seen as ground becomes the figure. The idea we have of the world would be overturned if we could succeed in seeing the intervals between things (for example, the space between the trees on the boulevard) as *objects* and, inversely, if we saw the things themselves—the trees—as the ground. This is what happens in puzzles: we cannot see the rabbit or the hunter because the elements of these figures are dislocated and are integrated into other forms: for example, what is to be the rabbit's ear is still just the empty interval between two trees in the forest. The rabbit and the hunter become apparent through a new partition of the field, a new organization of the whole. Camouflage is the art of masking a form by blending its principal defining lines into other, more commanding forms.

The same type of analysis can be applied to hearing: it will simply be a matter of temporal forms rather than spatial ones. A melody, for example, is a figure of sound and does not mingle with the background noises (such as the siren one hears in the distance during a concert) which may accompany it. The melody is not a sum of notes, since each note only counts by virtue of the function it serves in the whole, which is why the melody does not perceptibly change when transposed, that is, when all its notes are changed while their interrelationships and the structure of the whole remain the same. On the other hand, just one single change in these interrelationships will be enough to modify the entire make-up of the melody. Such a perception of the whole is more natural and more primary than the perception of isolated elements; it has been seen from conditioned-reflex experiments, where, through the frequent association of a piece of meat with a light or a sound, dogs are trained to respond to that light or sound by salivating, that the training acquired in response to a certain series of notes is simultaneously acquired for any melody with the same structure. Therefore analytical perception, through which we arrive at absolute value of the separate elements, is a belated and rare attitude— that of the scientist who observes or of the philosopher who reflects. The perception of forms, understood very broadly as structure, grouping, or configuration should be considered our spontaneous way of seeing.

There is still another point on which modern psychology overthrows the prejudices of classical physiology and psychology. It is a commonplace to say that we have five senses, and it would seem, at first glance, that each of them is like a world out of touch with the others. The light or colors which act upon the eye do not affect the ears or the sense of touch. Nevertheless it has been known for a long time that certain blind people manage to represent the colors they cannot see by means of the sounds which they hear: for example, a blind man said that red ought to be something like a trumpet peal. For a long time it was thought that such phenomena were exceptional, whereas they are, in fact, general. For people under mescaline, sounds are regularly accompanied by spots of color whose hue, form, and vividness vary with the tonal quality, intensity, and pitch of the sounds. Even normal subjects speak of hot, cold, shrill, or hard colors, of sounds that are clear, sharp, brilliant, rough, or mellow, of soft noises and of penetrating fragrances. Cézanne said that one could see the velvetiness, the hardness, the softness, and even the odor of objects. My perception is therefore not a sum of visual, tactile, and audible givens: I perceive in a total way with my whole being; I grasp a unique structure of the thing, a unique way of being, which speaks to all my senses at once.

Naturally, classical psychology was well aware that relationships exist between the different parts of my visual field just as between the data of my different senses—but it held this unity to be a construction and referred it to intelligence and memory. In a famous passage from the *Méditations* Descartes wrote: I say that I see men going by in the street, but what exactly do I really see? All I see are hats and coats which might equally well be covering dolls that only move by springs, and if I say that I see men, it is because I apprehend "through an inspection of the mind what I thought I beheld with my eyes." I am convinced that objects continue to exist when I no longer see them (behind my back, for example). But it is obvious that, for classical thought, these invisible objects subsist for me only because my judgment keeps them present. Even the objects right in front of me are not truly seen but merely thought. Thus I cannot see a cube, that is, a solid with six surfaces and twelve edges; all I ever see is a perspective figure of which the lateral surfaces are distorted and the back surface completely hidden. If I am able to speak of cubes, it is because my mind sets these appearances to rights and restores the hidden surface. I cannot see a cube as its geometrical definition presents it: I can only think it. The perception of movement shows even more clearly the extent to which intelligence intervenes in what claims to be vision. When my train starts, after it has been standing in the station, I often "see" the train next to mine begin to move. Sensory data are therefore neutral in themselves and can be differently interpreted according to the hypothesis on which my mind comes to rest. Broadly speaking, classical psychology made perception a real deciphering of sense data by the intelligence, a beginning of science, as it were. I am given certain signs from which I must dig out the meaning; I am presented with a text which I must read or interpret. Even when it takes the unity of the perceptual field into account, classical psychology remains loyal to the notion of sensation which was the starting point of the analysis. Its original conception of visual data as a mosaic of sensations forces it to base the unity of the perceptual field on an operation of the intelligence. What does *gestalt* theory tell us on this point? By resolutely rejecting the notion of sensation it teaches us to stop distinguishing between signs and their significance, between what is sensed and what is judged. How could we define the exact color of an object without mentioning the substance of which it is made, without saying, of this blue rug, for example, that it is a "woolly blue"? Cézanne asked how one is to distinguish the color of things from their shape. It is impossible to understand perception as the imputation of a certain significance to certain sensible signs, since the most immediate sensible texture of these signs cannot be described without referring to the object they signify.

Our ability to recognize an object defined by certain constant properties despite changes of lighting stems, not from some process by which our intellect takes the nature of the incident light into account and deduces the object's real color from it, but from the fact that the light which dominates the environment acts as *lighting* and immediately assigns the object its true color. If we look at two plates under unequal lighting, they will appear equally white and unequally lighted as long as the beam of light from the window figures in our visual field. On the other hand, if we observe the same plates through a whole in a screen, one will immediately appear gray and the other white; and even if we *know* that it is nothing but an effect of the lighting, no intellectual analysis of the way they appear will make us see the true color of the two plates. When we turn on the lights at dusk, the electric light seems yellow at first but a moment later tends to lose all definite color; correlatively, the objects, whose color was at first perceptibly modified, resume an appearance comparable to the one they have during the day. Objects and lighting form a system which tends toward a certain constancy and a certain level of stability—not through the operation of intelligence but through the very configuration of the field. I do not think the world in the act of perception: it organizes itself in front of me. When I perceive a cube, it is not because my reason sets the perspectival appearances straight and thinks the geometrical definition of a cube with respect to them. I do not even notice the distortions of perspective, much less correct them; I am at the cube itself in its manifestness through what I see. The objects behind my back are likewise not represented to me by some operation of memory or judgment; they are present, they *count* for me, just as the ground which I do not see continues nonetheless to be present beneath the figure which partially hides it. Even the perception of movement, which at first seems to depend directly on the point of reference chosen by the intellect is in turn only one element in the global organization of the field. For, although it is true that, when either my train or the one next to it starts, first one, then the other may appear to be moving, one should note that the illusion is not arbitrary and that I cannot willfully induce it by the completely intellectual choice of a point of reference. If I am playing cards in my compartment, the other train will start moving; if, on the other hand, I am looking for someone in the adjacent train, then mine will begin to roll. In each instance the one which seems stationary is the one we have chosen as our abode and which, for the time being, is our environment. Movement and rest distribute themselves in our surroundings not according to the hypotheses which our intelligence is pleased to construct but according to the way we settle ourselves in the world and the position our bodies assume in it. Sometimes I see the steeple motionless against the sky with clouds floating above it, and sometimes the clouds appear still and the steeple falls through space. But here again the choice of the fixed point is not made by the intelligence: the looked-at object in which I anchor myself will always seem fixed, and I cannot take this meaning away from it except by looking elsewhere. Nor do I give it this meaning through thought. Perception is not a sort of beginning science, an elementary exercise of the intelligence; we must rediscover a commerce with the world and a presence to the world which is older than intelligence.

Finally, the new psychology also brings a new concept of the perception of others. Classical psychology unquestioningly accepted the distinction between inner observation, or introspection, and outer observation. "Psychic facts"—anger or fear, for example—could be directly known only from the inside and by the person experiencing them. It was thought to be self-evident that I can grasp only the corporal *signs* of anger or fear from the outside and that I have to resort to the anger or fear I know in myself through introspection in order to interpret these signs. Today's psychologists have made us notice that in reality introspection gives me almost nothing. If I try to study love or hate purely from inner observation, I will find very little to describe: a few pangs, a few heart-throbs—in short, trite agitations which do not reveal the essence of love or hate. Each time I find something worth saying, it is because I have not been satisfied to coincide with my feeling, because I have succeeded in studying it as a way of behaving, as a modification of my relations with others and with the world, because I have managed to think about it as I would think about the behavior of another person whom I happened to witness. In fact, young children understand gestures and facial expressions long before they can reproduce them on their own; the meaning must, so to speak, adhere to the behavior. We must reject that prejudice which makes "inner realities" out of love, hate, or anger, leaving them accessible to one single witness: the person who feels them. Anger, shame, hate, and love are not psychic facts hidden at the bottom of another's consciousness: they are types of behavior or styles of conduct which are visible from the outside. They exist *on* this face or *in* those gestures, not hidden behind them. Psychology did not begin to develop until the day it gave up the distinction between mind and body, when it abandoned the two correlative methods of interior observation and physiological psychology. We learned nothing about emotion as long as we limited ourselves to measuring the rate of respiration or heartbeat in an angry person, and we didn't learn anything more when we tried to express the qualitative and inexpressible nuances of lived anger. To create a psychology of anger is to try to ascertain the *meaning* of anger, to ask oneself how it functions in human life and what purpose it serves. So we find that emotion is, as Janet said, a disorganizing reaction which comes into play whenever we are stuck. On a deeper level, as Sartre has shown, we find that anger is a magical way of acting by which we afford ourselves a completely symbolic satisfaction in the imagination after renouncing effective action in the world, just as, in a conversation, a person who cannot convince his partner will start hurling insults at him which prove nothing or as a man who does not dare strike his opponent will shake his fist at him from a distance. Since emotion is not a psychic, internal fact but rather a variation in our relations with others and the world which is expressed in our bodily attitude, we cannot say that only the signs of love or anger are given to the outside observer and that we understand others indirectly by interpreting these signs: we have to say that others are directly manifest to us as behavior. Our behavioral science goes much farther than we think. When unbiased subjects are confronted with photographs of several faces, copies of several kinds of handwriting, and recordings of several voices and are asked to put together a face, a silhouette, a voice, and a handwriting, it has been shown that the elements are usually put together correctly or that, in any event, the correct matchings greatly outnumber the incorrect ones. Michelangelo's handwriting is attributed to Raphael in 36 cases, but in 221 instances it is correctly identified, which means that we recognize a certain common structure in each person's voice, face, gestures and bearing and that each person is nothing more nor less to us than this structure or way of being in the world. One can see how these remarks might be applied to the psychology of language: just as a man's body and "soul" are but two aspects of his way of being in the world, so the word and the thought it indicates should not be considered two externally related terms: the word bears its meaning in the same way that the body incarnates a manner of behavior.

The new psychology has, generally speaking, revealed man to us not as an understanding which constructs the world but as a being thrown into the world and attached to it by a natural bond. As a result it re-educates us in how to see this world which we touch at every point of our being, whereas classical psychology abandoned the lived world for the one which scientific intelligence succeeded in constructing.

If we now consider the film as a perceptual object, we can apply what we have just said about perception in general to the perception of a film. We will see that this point of view illuminates the nature and significance of the movies and that the new psychology leads us straight to the best observations of the aestheticians of the cinema.

Let us say right off that a film is not a sum total of images but a temporal *gestalt*. This is the moment to recall Pudovkin's famous experiment which clearly shows the melodic unity of films. One day Pudovkin took a close-up of Mosjoukin with a completely impassive expression and projected it after showing: first, a bowl of soup, then, a young woman lying dead in her coffin, and, last, a child playing with a teddy-bear. The first thing noticed was that Mosjoukin seemed to be looking at the bowl, the young woman, and the child, and next one noted that he was looking pensively at the dish, that he wore an expression of sorrow when looking at the woman, and that he had a glowing smile for the child. The audience was amazed at his variety of expression although the same shot had actually been used all three times and was, if anything, remarkably inexpressive. The meaning of a shot therefore depends on what precedes it in the movie, and this succession of scenes creates a new reality which is not merely the sum of its parts. In an excellent article in *Esprit*, R. Leenhardt added that one still has to bring in the time-factor for each shot: a short duration is suitable for an amused smile, one of intermediate length for an indifferent face, and an extended one for a sorrowful expression.[2] Leenhardt drew from this the following definition of cinematographic rhythm: "A certain order of shots and a certain duration for each of these shots or views, so that taken together they produce the desired impression with maximum effectiveness." There really is, then, a cinematographic system of measurements with very precise and very imperious requirements. "When you see a movie, try to guess the moment when a shot has given its all and must move on, and, be replaced either by changing the angle, the distance, or the field. You will get to know that constriction of the chest produced by an overlong shot which brakes the movement and that deliciously intimate acquiescence when a shot fades at the right moment." Since a film consists not only of montage (the selection of shots or views, their order and length) but also of cutting (the selection of scenes or sequences, and their order and length), it seems to be an extremely complex form inside of which a very great number of actions and reactions are taking place at every moment. The laws of this form, moreover, are yet to be discovered, having until now only been sensed by the flair or tact of the director, who handles cinematographic language as a man manipulates syntax: without explicitly thinking about it and without always being in a position to formulate the rules which he spontaneously obeys.

What we have just said about visual films also applies to sound movies, which are not a sum total of words or noises but are likewise a *gestalt*. A rhythm exists for sounds just as for images. There is a montage of noises and sounds, as Leenhardt's example of the old sound movie *Broadway Melody* shows. "Two actors are on stage. We are in the balcony listening to them speak their parts. Then immediately there is a close-up, whispering, and we are aware of something they are saying to each other under their breath. . . ." The expressive force of this montage lies in its ability to make us sense the coexistence, the simultaneity of lives in the same world, the actors as they are for us and for themselves, just as, previously, we saw Pudovkin's visual montage linking the man and his gaze to the sights which surround him. Just as a film is not merely a play photographed in motion and the choice and grouping of the shots constitutes an original means of expression for the motion picture, so, equally, the soundtrack is not a simple phonographic reproduction of noises and words but requires a certain internal organization which the film's creator must invent. The real ancestor of the movie soundtrack is not the phonograph but the radio play.

Nor is that all. We have been considering sight and sound by turns, but in reality the way they are put together makes another new whole, which cannot be reduced to its component parts. A sound movie is not a silent film embellished with words and sounds whose only function is to complete the cinematographic illusion. The bond between sound and image is much closer, and the image is transformed by the proximity of sound. This is readily apparent in the case of dubbed films, where thin people are made to speak with the voices of fat people, the young have the voices of the old, and tall people the voices of tiny ones—all of which is absurd if what we have said is true—namely, that voice, profile, and character form an indivisible unit. And the union of sound and image occurs not only in each character but in the film as a whole. It is not by accident that characters are silent at one moment and speak at another. The alternation of words and silence is manipulated to create the most effective image. There are three sorts of dialogue, as Malraux said in *Verve* (1940). First may be noted expository dialogue, whose purpose is to make the circumstances of the dramatic action known. The novel and the film both avoid this sort of dialogue. Then there is *tonal* dialogue, which gives us each character's particular accent and which dominates, for example, in Proust where the characters are very hard to visualize but are admirably recognizable as soon as they start to talk. The extravagant or sparing use of words, their richness or emptiness, their precision or affectation reveal the essence of a character more surely than many descriptions. Tonal dialogue rarely occurs in movies, since the visible presence of the actor with his own particular manner of behaving rarely lends itself to it. Finally we have dramatic dialogue which presents the discussion and confrontation of the characters and which is the movies' principal form of dialogue. But it is far from continuous. One speaks ceaselessly in the theater but not in the film. "Directors of recent movies," said Malraux, "*break into* dialogue after long stretches of silence, just as a novelist breaks into dialogue after long narrative passages." Thus the distribution of silences and dialogue constitutes a metrics above and beyond the metrics of vision and sound, and the pattern of words and silence, more complex than the other two, superimposes its requirements upon them. To complete the analysis one would still have to study the role of music in this ensemble: let us only say that music should be incorporated into it, not juxtaposed to it. Music should not be used as a stopgap for sonic holes or as a completely exterior commentary on the sentiments or the scenes as so often happens in movies: the storm of wrath unleashes the storm of brass, or the music laboriously imitates a footstep or the sound of a coin falling to the ground. It should intervene to mark a change in a film's style: for example, the passage from an action scene to the "inside" of the character, to the recollection of earlier scenes, or to the description of a landscape. Generally speaking, it should accompany and help bring about a "rupture in the sensory balance," as Jaubert said.[3] Lastly, it must not be another means of expression juxtaposed to the visual expression. "By the use of strictly musical means (rhythm, form, instrumentation) and by a mysterious alchemy of correspondences which ought to be the very foundation of the film composer's profession, it should recreate a sonorous substance beneath the plastic substance of the image, should, finally, make the internal rhythm of the scene physically palpable without thereby striving to translate its sentimental, dramatic, or poetic content" (Jaubert). It is not the job of words in a movie to add ideas to the images, nor is it the job of music to add sentiments. The ensemble tells us something very precise which is neither a thought nor a reminder of sentiments we have felt in our own lives.

What, then, does the film *signify:* what does it mean? Each film tells a *story:* that is, it relates a certain number of events which involve certain characters and which could, it seems, also be told in prose, as, in effect, they are in the scenario on which the film is based. The talking film, frequently overwhelmed by dialogue, completes this illusion. Therefore motion pictures are often conceived as the visual and sonic representation, the closest possible reproduction of a drama which literature could evoke only in words and which the movie is lucky enough to be able to photograph. What supports this ambiguity is the fact that movies do have a basic realism: the actors should be natural, the set should be as realistic as possible; for "the power of reality released on the screen is such that the least stylization will cause it to go flat" (Leenhardt). That does not mean, however, that the movies are fated to let us see and hear what we would see and hear if we were present at the events being related; nor should films suggest some general view of life in the manner of an edifying tale. Aesthetics has already encountered this problem in connection with the novel or with poetry. A novel always has an idea that can be summed up in a few words, a scenario which a few lines can express. A poem always refers to things or ideas. And yet the function of the pure novel or pure poetry is not simply to tell us these facts. If it were, the poem could be exactly transposed into prose and the novel would lose nothing in summary. Ideas and facts are just the raw materials of art: the art of the novel lies in the choice of what one says and what one does not say, in the choice of perspectives (this chapter will be written from the point of view of this character, that chapter from another's point of view), in the varying tempo of the narrative; the essence of the art of poetry is not the didactic description of things or the exposition of ideas but the creation of a machine of language which almost without fail puts the reader in a certain poetic state. Movies, likewise, always have a story and often an idea (for example, in *l'Etrange sursis* the idea that death is terrible only for the man who has not consented to it), but the function of the film is not to make these facts or ideas known to us. Kant's remark that, in knowledge imagination serves the understanding, whereas in art the understanding serves the imagination, is a profound one. In other words, ideas or prosaic facts are only there to give the creator an opportunity to seek out their palpable symbols and to trace their visible and sonorous monogram. The meaning of a film is incorporated into its rhythm just as the meaning of a gesture may immediately be read in that gesture: the film does not mean anything but itself. The idea is presented in a nascent state and emerges from the temporal structure of the film as it does from the coexistence of the parts of a painting. The joy of art lies in its showing how something takes on meaning—not by referring to already established and acquired ideas but by the temporal or spatial arrangement of elements. As we saw above, a movie has meaning in the same way that a thing does: neither of them speaks to an isolated understanding; rather, both appeal to our power tacitly to decipher the world or men and to coexist with them. It is true that in our ordinary lives we lose sight of this aesthetic value of the tiniest perceived thing. It is also true that the perceived form is never perfect in real life, that it always has blurs, smudges, and superfluous matter, as it were. Cinematographic drama is, so to speak, finer-grained than real-life dramas: it takes place in a world that is more exact than the real world. But in the last analysis perception permits us to understand the meaning of the cinema. A movie is not thought; it is perceived.

This is why the movies can be so gripping in their presentation of man: they do not give us his *thoughts,* as novels have done for so long, but his conduct or behavior. They directly present to us that special way of being in the world, of dealing with things and other people, which we can see in the sign language of gesture and gaze and which clearly defines each person we know. If a movie wants to show us someone who is dizzy, it should not attempt to portray the interior landscape of dizziness, as Daquin in *Premier de cordée* and Malraux in *Sierra de Terruel* wished to do. We will get a much better sense of dizziness if we see it from the outside, if we contemplate that unbalanced body contorted on a rock or that unsteady step trying to adapt itself to who knows what upheaval of space. For the movies as for modern psychology dizziness, pleasure, grief, love, and hate are ways of behaving.

This psychology shares with contemporary philosophies the common feature of presenting consciousness thrown into the world, subject to the gaze of others and learning from them what it is: it does not, in the manner of the classical philosophies, present mind *and* world, each particular consciousness *and* the others. Phenomenological or existential philosophy is largely an expression of surprise at this inherence of the self in the world and in others, a description of this paradox and permeation, and an attempt to make us *see* the bond between subject and world, between subject and others, rather than to *explain* it as the classical philosophies did by resorting to absolute spirit. Well, the movies are peculiarly suited to make manifest the union of mind and body, mind and world, and the expression of one in the other. That is why it is not surprising that a critic should evoke philosophy in connection with a film. Astruc in his review of *Défunt récalcitrant* uses Sartrian terms to recount the film, in which a dead man lives after his body and is obliged to inhabit another. The man remains the same for *himself* but is different *for others,* and he cannot rest until through love a girl recognizes him despite his new exterior and the harmony between the *for itself* and the *for others* is re-established. The editors of *Le Canard enchaîné* are annoyed at this and would like to send Astruc back to his philosophical investigations. But the truth is that both parties are right: one because art is not meant to be a showcase for ideas, and the other because contemporary philosophy consists not in stringing concepts together but in describing the mingling of consciousness with the world, its involvement in a body, and its coexistence with others; and because this is movie material *par excellence.*

Finally, if we ask ourselves why it is precisely in the film era that this philosophy has developed, we obviously should not say that the movies grew out of the philosophy. Motion pictures are first and foremost a technical invention in which philosophy counts for nothing. But neither do we have the right to say that this philosophy has grown out of the cinema which it transposes to the level of ideas, for one can make bad movies; after the technical instrument has been invented, it must be taken up by an artistic will and, as it were, re-invented before one can succeed in making real films. Therefore, if philosophy is in harmony with the cinema, if thought and technical effort are heading in the same direction, it is because the philosopher and the moviemaker share a certain way of being, a certain view of the world which belongs to a generation. It offers us yet another chance to confirm that modes of thought correspond to technical methods and that, to use Goethe's phrase, "What is inside is also outside."

    —*Sense and Non-Sense* (1948; translated by Hubert L. Dreyfus and Patricia Allen Dreyfus, 1964)

NOTES

1. Lecture delivered March 13, 1945, at l'Institut des Hautes Études Cinémato-graphiques.
2. *Espirit*, 1936.
3. *Ibid.*

HAROLD OSBORNE
The Quality of Feeling in Art

In this paper I propose to discuss the view that qualities of emotion and feeling may be ascribed to works of art without implied metaphor, so that when I call a piece of music cheerful my words may sometimes mean what they seem to mean and will not always need to be reinterpreted by the philosopher as if I were saying for example that I, or others, feel cheerful when listening to the music or that I regard the music as a sign that the composer was cheerful when he invented it. This theory of straightforward emotional realism about works of art has been advocated in two papers which have recently appeared in *The British Journal of Aesthetics*. In an article entitled "Emotions and Emotional Qualities" Professor R. W. Hepburn argued in favour of the account "which claims that emotional qualities can be described, with perfect propriety, as *in* works of art." And in "The

Language of Feelings" Mr. Huw Morris-Jones wrote: "The connexion between a work of art and feeling must be described in such a way that one can locate the feeling in the work of art itself, in such a way that one can legitimately talk of discovering and discriminating the feelings appropriate and relevant to it. So that when we say that a play or music or sculpture is tragic or happy or sombre, we are not describing what the artist felt like nor are we describing how we feel when we look at or listen to them. It is not I who am tragic or happy or sombre, but the play, the poem, the song, the painting or whatever it is. What I do in saying they are such is to *recognize* the sadness or happiness, and I implicitly claim that others should recognize them too, if they have undergone those perceptual and imaginative experiences which constitute an exhaustive appreciation of those works of art."[1]

To avoid talking at cross purposes the point should be made at the outset that this theory is not concerned to assert merely that emotions and feelings may be objectively present in works of art in the same sort of way that thoughts and ideas are sometimes present in them, as part of their representational content. It is not in dispute that emotional situations are described or depicted by some works of art just as they are described or depicted in newspaper reportage, amusement novels, comic strips, advertisement posters and musical reviews. What the theory alleges is that a work of art itself, or some part of it, may be apprehended as characterized by emotion or feeling. Emotional epithets are applied in this way to nonfigurative art which reflects no images of a reality other than the work itself. Where a work of art is representational it is a common thing for critics to pronounce whether the emotional character of the work itself, or some part or aspect of it, is congruent or at variance with the emotional situations depicted or described in it. The theory to be discussed is a theory about the attribution of emotional qualities to works of art themselves, not a theory about the mechanisms by which information can be communicated about emotional situations real or imaginary.[2]

I do not propose to dispute the factual basis upon which the theory rests. It seems to me to be sufficiently attested that our experience of works of art does sometimes carry with it apprehension of apparently objective qualities such as cheerfulness, melancholy, boisterousness, restlessness, severity and so on. Even with very simple stimuli such as uncombined colours and sounds some experimental psychologists, following Bullough, classify subjects who tend to report the emotional effect of the stimulus upon themselves apart from those who ascribe to it an emotional character objectively. In *The Experimental Psychology of Beauty* (1962) Professor C. W. Valentine records that in certain experiments by Bullough and C. S. Myers in order to clarify whether the comment "cheerful" meant that a colour itself was cheerful or that it made the observer feel cheerful subjects were asked for an explanation "and generally they were very decided, some emphatically asserting that it was the colour itself that appeared cheerful, not that it made them feel cheerful, while to others it appeared absurd to speak of a colour being itself cheerful" (p. 56). There are indeed many people to whom upon reflection it seems absurd to speak of a work of art or a sense impression as having feelings and who nevertheless find it the aptest description of their experience in contact with aesthetic objects. It is undoubtedly a very odd way of talking unless you assume that sentences attributing emotional qualities to works of art are to be understood in a figurative sense. We have not direct awareness of the feelings of other people but infer them from observed demeanour, and we verify our inferences by their subsequent behaviour and their verbal reports of their own introspective observations. Yet the theory seems to be claiming that we directly apprehend affective states in aesthetic objects which are not sentient beings. Nor would matters be helped by assuming that we are indulging in the ancient practice of animism and employing the language of personification, as when the poet speaks of "the remorseless stone."[3] For always of a sentient being or an object personified as if it were a sentient being it makes sense to ask whether it is really cheerful or only seems cheerful. Despair may lurk concealed beneath the antics of the clown. But of a piece of music it makes no sense to ask whether it is really sad or only sounds sad; for the music is the sound. The picture is the visual appearance: it makes no sense to ask whether that appearance is really sombre or whether it only appears so.[4] And in its modern form at any rate this theory of straightforward emotional realism in aesthetics does not invoke personification. Professor Hepburn says explicitly: "People experience emotions: works of art do not." Yet on the next page he can say: "A piece of music may be in despair, but I who listen enjoyably need by no means be in despair."

I do not wish to repudiate but rather to accept that our experience of works of art brings with it *prima facie* apprehension of "phenomenally objective" emotional qualities. But I am puzzled to know what import attaches to such statements as "the music is cheerful" after you have said that the cheerfulness to which the statement refers is not something experienced by the work of art (for works of art do not experience emotions) nor something experienced by the listeners nor something experienced by the composer. There is something there which is apprehended; but in what sense is it "there" and in what sense is it apprehended? I do not believe that the solution lies in a theory that aesthetic experience involves the cognition by direct acquaintance of non-experienced mental states. Professor Hepburn himself says that: "To claim that the emotional quality can be in the work of art is not of course to say that the word 'in' is used in precisely the same sense as when an emotion is said to be 'in' you or 'in' me." I want to carry on from that point and ask in what way this apprehended but unexperienced emotion is "in" the work of art, if indeed it is in fact there.

Theories of the sort we are discussing, which maintain the objective presence of feeling quality in experienced objects other than sentient beings, are not entirely new. An article by Virgil C. Aldrich which appeared in *The Kenyon Review* in 1939 proffered an account of how feeling "may become objective and thereby be converted into aesthetic quality," and the author opined that the lack of such an account hitherto had been "the cardinal weakness of current aesthetics." His argument, which proceeds by analogy, starts with the premise that visual and aural sensation are modes of feeling by which we put out as it were sensory tentacles and so become cognizant of objective qualities—colours and sounds—located in an external environment. When we attend to colours and sounds for their own sake, neither as qualities of physical things in external space nor as "subjective qualities in and of the native organism of the subject" (he calls this passing from the practical to the aesthetic attitude), we experience secondary (emotional) feelings towards these primary (sensation) feelings and similarly become cognizant of emotional qualities which objectively characterize the visual or aural complexes on which our attention is directed. Aldrich held that objective emotional qualities belong only to constellations of colours and sounds and not to works of art regarded as physical objects; for, he says, "no physical object as *physical* is ever an object of aesthetic enjoyment." But in a much discussed article on "Art and Feeling," published in 1924, Otto Baensch had maintained a still more radical view.[5] He denied that feelings exist only as internal states of sentient beings and claimed on the contrary that they exist "quite objectively and apart from us" and are directly cognized as non-sensory qualities of perceived objects. "The landscape does not express the mood but *has* it." In opposition to the then popular theory of empathic projection he maintained that direct apprehension of emotional qualities is integral to all our awareness of external reality and their separation from sensory qualities results only from later theoretical abstraction. But affective states, he thought, are little susceptible of conceptual scientific study and are not easy of access by attentive contemplation. It is the special function of art to capture and fix the fleeting feelings so that their content may be presented to non-conceptual awareness and be apprehended with precision. "According to this view," he says, "the function of art is not to give the percipient any kind of pleasure, however noble, but to acquaint him with something which he has not known before." Baensch also foreshadowed the view later developed by Collingwood, and hinted more recently by Professor J. M. Cameron in his Inaugural Lecture *Poetry and Dialectic*, that by the articulation of feeling in the construction of works of art we have an instrument of emotional cultivation and of self-knowledge. "The separation, the selective condensation, and the internal grouping of the feeling complex to be shaped can only be accomplished," he wrote, "by simultaneously creating and forming the object in which the complex of feelings achieves its existence. In practice, the shaping of the feeling and the shaping of the object into which it will be embedded coincide in one and the same activity."

Both Aldrich and Baensch assume that the emotional quality apprehended as objectively present in a work of art will be identical with an emotion evoked in the percipient. (Aldrich believed that it is the feeling experienced by the percipient in response to a work of art which reveals the corresponding feeling-quality objectively inhering in the work just as the sensation-feeling of yellow reveals the presence of an objective colour-quality yellow in the object. Baensch states: "We become aware of objective feelings only when we feel them ourselves.") For this reason, besides the rather wild nature of their attribution of feelings to non-sentient things, their theories were open to many of the objections brought against the doctrine of empathy. This defect is absent from the formulations of

Morris-Jones and Hepburn, both of whom allow or indeed insist that the percipient need not always himself experience the feeling which he apprehends objectively in the work of art.

Once we have made up our minds to the initial shockingness of language which speaks of feeling qualities inhering in things which do not feel, it is possible to hold with Aldrich that they belong only to aesthetic objects or one may go the whole hog with Baensch and say that although works of art excel other things as repositories of objective feelings, objective feeling qualities permeate all our experience of reality. A modified form of the latter view has recently gained the ascendant among psychologists of the Gestalt school who under the influence of Wertheimer's criticisms have become dissatisfied with the explanations offered by empathy and in place of empathic projection and association have advanced a theory of tertiary qualities. In the context of this theory tertiary qualities are perceptual "regional" properties which are "emergent" and not summative (or in the language of C. D. Broad, "collective" properties which are not "reducible"). They are held to permeate and suffuse all perception but are thought to be most prominent in works of art, where their apprehension is a large part of what is understood by "appreciation." According to C. C. Pratt writers who have adopted this new outlook "tend to agree on at least three points: (*a*) Tertiary qualities can only be described by words which also connote subjective moods, but they themselves are not subjective; (*b*) they are intrinsic properties of visual and auditory perception, not borrowed from any other modality;. and (*c*) they are probably correlated with higher-order stimulus variables."[6]

The notion that constellations of visual and auditory perceptions display regional, non-summative properties emergent at various levels is by now well established. What is new, and indeed strange, is the idea that emotional qualities are objective in this way, that there are perceived properties of things which are expressive of emotion without provoking emotion in the percipient or being interpreted as the sign of emotion in some other sentient being. The advocates of this new way of looking at things do not, I believe, intend to cut across commonsense notions to the extent that Baensch is supposed to have done. I shall therefore assume in the discussion which follows that the following propositions will be common ground between us. When I speak of feelings I shall mean states of consciousness such as some of those with which I have acquaintance in myself by introspection. I have no acquaintance with feelings of any being except myself. I have grounds for believing nevertheless that some other sentient beings at any rate have feelings, and I do so believe. I do not believe that anything which is not a sentient being has feelings: and in particular I do not believe that constellations of my own or other people's sense impressions have feelings other than the feelings which I have when attending to my own sense impressions or which I believe other people have when they attend to theirs. On the basis of these assumptions the question before us is still what meaning attaches to the statement that emotional qualities are objective properties of appearances or, to put it the other way round, why we think that tertiary qualities, being objective "regional" properties, are appropriately describable in words which connote feelings and emotions.

How do these qualities "express feeling" if they are neither stimulus nor sign of actual experienced feelings?

The simplest of the answers given alleges that constellations of visual or auditory impressions are said to express an emotion or to have an emotional quality when their configuration is identical with, or very similar to, the pattern of configuration which we often see in the posture and demeanour of persons whom we believe to be under the sway of that emotion. We do not call the swan proud because it makes us feel proud (proud persons do not make us feel proud either), nor yet because we believe that the swan feels proud. We call it proud because the tense grace of the curving neck and smooth stately sweep of its motion through the water make a pattern identical with a pattern we have observed in the demeanour of proud persons. When Milton calls the nightingale "most musical, most melancholy," he does not necessarily mean to suggest either that the bird is unhappy or that he is unhappy when he hears its voice. He is rather suggesting an objective pattern of melancholy in the nightingale's song—as, indeed, Christina Georgina Rossetti makes explicit in the lines:

> I shall not hear the nightingale
> Sing on, as if in pain.

According to this explanation experienced feeling is the ultimate term of reference for all talk about emotional expression. I say that I am dejected when I am aware of a feeling of dejection in myself. I call a whole group of visual patterns "dejected-looking" because they have a certain drooping, listless pattern of appearance which many people (including myself) often display in their posture and gesture when I believe them to be feeling dejected. As Kant and afterwards Herbert Spencer believed, the expressive character of music is according to this theory attributable to structural identities with the patterns of sound in ordinary language when spoken under the influence of emotion.[7]

This explanation breaks down in face of the greater potentialities for the expression of feeling in art and the relative crudeness of our abilities to communicate or diagnose emotion from facial expression and bodily gesture alone unless one is also given a clue from the situation and context.[8] It would, for example, not seem plausible to reduce the expressive power of the dance to our familiarity with the quotidian use of gesture. Rudolf Arnheim expressly rejects the explanation which derives the expressive character of tertiary qualities from any similarity to the actual physical manifestations of emotion in human beings. On the contrary, he holds that "expression is an inherent characteristic of perceptual patterns" and that "its manifestations in the human figure are but a special case of a more general phenomenon. The comparison of an object's expression with a human state of mind is a secondary process. . . ."[9] He gets over the difficulty by making feeling irrelevant to the expression of feeling. Music which is sad sounds like a sad man looks. But the look of a man who is sad is not sad because it is the look of a man who feels sad. The appearance of the sad man and the sound of the sad music are intrinsically sad irrespective of any reference to an experience of sadness. And once again we must ask, granted that the sad appearance and the sad music have a similar con-figurational pattern, what is the significance of calling that pattern "sad" rather than "jolly" or "rude" or any other name at all unless there is an inherent connection between tertiary qualities and experienced feelings? Some Gestalt psychologists and some aestheticians have sought to find a bridge in a doctrine of psychophysical parallelism which postulates struc-tural identity between "expressive" perceptual configuration qualities and patterns of experienced feeling. According to this view, an observed con-figurational quality expresses an emotion not because it arouses the emo-tion in us which we unconsciously project upon it, and not because it is structurally similar to the visual pattern of a human being expressing the emotion by bodily demeanour and gesture: it does so because its structure is identical with the structure of the experienced feeling. As was said by Paul Guillaume: "If the two aspects (inner and outer) are expressions of one and the same psychophysical dynamism, profound analogies should be encountered between them. . . . The mental or central part of the emotion obeys the same dynamic law as the peripheral part; the same rhythms can be detected in the conscious feeling of a man during emotion as in his muscular reactions; the hidden movements of the psyche and the visible or invisible movements of the body image one another; in the language applied to emotions there is often no difference between the terms applied to the internal feeling and those applied to the external symptom."[10] The pattern-qualities which we observe in the deportment and gestures of other people and the more refined pattern-qualities which we perceive in works of art are therefore expressive because they are identical with the patterns of our own feelings. The music sounds the way an emotion feels.[11] This, if I have understood her correctly, is the sort of thing which Mrs. Susanne Langer was saying when she has spoken of "symbolic presentation."

I am myself profoundly sceptical of the notion that a tonal or a visual structure can be isomorphic with the pattern of an affective state. Besides specific emotions (fury over the loss of a penny) we know in introspection unattached, "objectless" feelings or moods which while they last colour the whole content of conscious experience like a floating charge on the furni-ture of the mind. Moods of sadness or joy, elation, depression, serenity, restlessness (Locke's "uneasiness"), apathy, vivacity, irritability and so on are not directed upon any particular stimulus in awareness or tied up with any impulse to particular action. Their causes are often obscure. The feel-ing fills the whole mind and tinges our attitude to whatever our experience is. When we are sad even joyful news gladdens us the less and we welcome sorrow almost with sympathy. These vague moods of feeling become qualitatively articulated and more precise when they enter into this or that concrete emotion as its affective element, when they are linked to a specific stimulus involving a tendency to action (as sadness becomes grief when linked to the news of a death) or tied in with some situation appraisal (as despondency becomes contrition when joined with a belief that one has committed a sin). But when we use emotional language about works of art we attribute to them the qualities of moods, not the feeling tones of concrete emotions. We say that a tune is merry or gay, lively, languorous, melancholy or serene. We do not hear in the music the emotions of regret, remorse, shame, disappointment, jealousy, fear or amazement. Music may express yearning but not home-sickness, amorousness but not love. But the moods are not highly structured as works of art are structured. So far as I can observe, my feeling of sadness or elation is as nearly structureless as anything I know. While it lasts it is here and everywhere, like an atmosphere or an odour, or a diffused toning of colour, lending a special flavour of melancholy or joy to anything that comes into my mind. It has duration, but it has no internal structure. And the word "rhythm" seems inappropriate to describe the fluctuations and interplay of the various moods in experience. I can find nothing useful in postulating that the higher-level emergent configuration properties of works of art resemble the patterns or rhythms of feeling. It is a statement hard to refute but incapable of proof. It may seem prematurely plausible but takes us nowhere.

I do not believe that we can solve the problem posed by the phenomenal objectivity of feeling qualities except after examining more closely the ways in which emotion-epithets are applied to aesthetic objects. In order to show one way in which such an examination might proceed I propose in the remainder of this article to distinguish three points at which emotional language breaks in upon descriptive accounts of perceptible objects.

1. Speech is fashioned for practical needs and recognizable perceptual qualities exist far in excess of the words available to name them in any language. We draw upon a rich stock of epithets descriptive of visible shape: we describe the things we see as short, long, slender, straight, bent, crooked, bulbous, bloated, pinched, spare, tapering, undulant, crimped, angular, pointed, blunt. . . . We use another group of epithets which belong primarily to descriptions of the human body but are applied by metonymy to other things: obese, lank, gaunt, svelte, plump, chubby, snub, squat, dumpy. . . . Some few shapes have names such as squares, circles, cubes, triangles. . . . But even so we soon run out of words. Specialists who habitually attend to the shapes of natural objects or artifacts for other than the practical purposes of living know a multiplicity—indeed perhaps a very great multiplicity—of shapes for which they have no names even in the esoteric languages which they often invent. But shapes do not become subjective when language is no longer productive of names by which to give them a label. They are apprehended in perception as objective shape-qualities of things perceived. Yet when we need to talk about unnamed shape-qualities we are at a loss and begin to use the language of metaphor, analogy and emotion. Our vocabulary for naming three-dimensional shape-qualities is far more jejune. The epithets available for describing configurations of colours are poorer still. And there are no words for naming the shapes which are used in building up structures of musical sound. In exchanging ideas about music, sculpture and colour the scope for descriptive talking, lying between technical language on the one side and metaphorical-emotional language on the other, is very narrow indeed.

It is further to be observed that apprehension of unnamed perceptual qualities is with many people inclined to be charged with feeling and indeed most people sometimes achieve awareness of recondite qualities, recognize and pinpoint them, in the first instance at any rate by means of feeling. At this point in the inquiry it becomes necessary to admit the existence of cognitive feelings.[12] It is the experience of many people who have habitual commerce with the fine arts or who otherwise attend to the perceptual qualities of things beyond the ordinary needs of daily living that the more recondite perceptual qualities, those which transcend the ingenuity of descriptive linguistic devices, obtrude into awareness first as feeling tone; only as they become more familiar, or clearer to cognition, the feeling fades and the quality which was first intimated through feeling is later apprehended without affective tone in a more penetrating and lucid perceptual act. Feeling seems as it were to grope ahead of perception and to put out cognitive tentacles in advance of clear apprehension. At this level of apprehension competent appreciation cognizes perceptually without the misting haze of feeling.

2. In aesthetic cognition perceptual qualities which are common to more than one mode of perception—sometimes called "intersensory qualities"—come into prominence. They are mostly if not entirely emergent regional properties of more or less high-level configurations. Examples of epithets corresponding to intersensory qualities are: pretty, decorative, delicate, stately, majestic, turgid, bombastic, flamboyant, jejune, simple, austere. . . . These are descriptive terms denoting perceptual qualities which are none the less objective because a certain degree of vagueness or imprecision attaches to the language by which we speak of them. It is by reference to characteristics of this sort that critics describe and demonstrate artistic styles and make stylistic comparisons between the various arts. Groups of intersensory qualities form the basis of those definitions of style upon which many art historians rely. Such general characterizations of style as were proposed, for example, by Wölfflin in his *Principles of Art History* and applied more systematically by Wylie Sypher in *Four Stages of Renaissance Style* over the arts of poetry, painting, architecture, sculpture and theatre are justified only in so far as there are high-level configurational properties common to more than one perceptual mode.

But in this sphere also the intersensory qualities which we discern outstrip the fertility of language to name or discriminate them and where language falls short we communicate perforce by metaphor and analogy. Though "poignant" is an epithet applicable to emotion, it may well be applied in the reaching for exactness to an intersensory quality of perception. Furthermore although intersensory qualities are objective characteristics of perceptual appearances, our awareness of them is often achieved by means of feelings which are cognitive in character. We *feel* that a work of art is dainty, austere, florid, compact. But the feeling is not awareness of an emotional response in ourselves, deflecting attention inwards; it is an outward directed, cognitive feeling. The extent to which apprehension of complex intersensory qualities depends upon feeling, varies from person to person; but in general as appreciation becomes more competent and sure, reliance on feeling diminishes and perceptive cognition is cleared of feeling tone. In this sphere also feeling seems to probe ahead of perceptual awareness and as our sensitivity expands our reliance upon feeling recedes. The choice is not, as is sometimes represented, between emotional response to an art object and technical or intellectual analysis. People of greatest talent and experience appreciate for the most part by lucid and comprehensive perceptual apprehension of high-level emergent qualities.

3. The recondite sensory qualities merge without any sharp dividing line into the intersensory qualities, and there is no fixed boundary between the latter and emotional qualities.[13] Whether such terms as serene, pompous, majestic, stately, solemn, lugubrious, sprightly, comic, express perceptual or emotional qualities, or a combination of the two, can only be decided—with difficulty—from the context in which they occur. The emotional or "expressive" characteristics *are* intersensory and *are* configurational or emergent and often impinge directly upon awareness in the act of perception.

Much of the confusion which attends emotional qualities and their attribution to aesthetic objects derives from a failure to segregate two categories of emotional qualities. They are too often all lumped together wrongly as "physiognomic properties"—a term introduced into psychology by Heinz Werner and adopted generally without sufficiently careful analysis.[14] Physiognomic perception refers primarily to perceiving expressions of anger, joy, fear, sorrow or any other emotion in the object perceived. When a man is described as tall or short, contorted or suffused, we are mentioning his perceptual qualities. When we say that he is angry or merry we are speaking of physiognomic properties. But since we do not believe that feelings are experienced except by sentient beings, we cannot sensibly ascribe physiognomic properties (in this primary meaning of the term) to anything which is not a sentient being or for the time being regarded as such. If we perceive something as joyful, sad, friendly, etc., we assume it to be the appearance of a person who is experiencing (or simulating) these emotions or we more or less deliberately personify what we see. With children and primitives the separation between sentient and insentient is less sharp than with sophisticated adults. But in so far as the distinction is there we do not attribute emotions to insentient things except by analogy or phantasy. Artists, and particularly poets, personify natural objects and speak of "angry sunsets," "weeping willows," and the rest. Children, to whom personification comes easily, tend to project their own emotions upon the inanimate, and it would be idle to deny that empathic projection plays an important part in many people's appreciation of literary art. Since we do not personify musical compositions as such—nor indeed pictures or buildings or poems—it is not meaningful to describe them as joyful or sad, merry or morose, any more than we should refer to them as friendly or hostile, angry or afraid, rancorous, hilarious, jealous or contrite. It is a manner of speaking in which the words do not say what they seem to say.

It is necessary on the other hand to recognize that there is a more elementary, less differentiated manner of perceiving, sometimes called "perceiving emotionally," in which the thing perceived is not held aloof from the percipient but is apprehended in terms of the significance it bears for him. When I become aware of something as awesome, ominous, sinister, menacing, reassuring, stimulating, charming, soothing, interesting, I am *perceiving emotionally*. The qualities apprehended in the object stand in polar relation to the attitude of the percipient and the one is complementary to the other. The anger of the angry man and the repentance of the penitent belong to them whether or not I perceive it or interpret correctly what I perceive. But when a man perceives emotionally the perceived qualities of the object and his attitude towards it are correlative and complementary. In his genetic study of value judgement W. M. Urban spoke of "affective-volitional meaning" in this connexion. Heinz Werner used the term "signal things"—things "whose characteristics are determined by the condition of the perceiver, not by their physical properties or relationships to other objects." And it was with this mode of experiencing the world in mind that J.-P. Sartre, in an essay written in 1939 under the influence of Husserl, said: "L'émotion est une certaine manière d'appréhender le monde." A recent study by Sylvia Honkavaara explicitly distinguishes this type of perception by the name "dynamic-affective attitude" from physiognomic perception.[15]

In practical and scientific perception the emotion of the percipient is separated from the perception and attention fastened on those aspects of the appearance which serve as signs of the properties which an object has independently of the relation in which it stands to the subject. In aesthetic perception the attitude of the subject changes and attention fastens upon the appearance itself without ulterior motive but with the sole purpose of apprehension. Or, still within the aesthetic, non-practical attitude, one may attend rather to the emotional qualities of the presentation: one may perceive the object as menacing, louring, exhilarating, comic or sombre.[16] (Some works of art make a point of emphasizing such emotional qualities while blurring or suppressing the objective perceptual qualities of what they depict.) But because in the aesthetic attitude one is not only detached from practical interest and concern but also from normal emotional involvement, the emotional qualities themselves appear as detached in perception and enter into awareness as it were cut off and anchored in the object, as if presented for observation and savouring rather than as the polar obverse of the observer's own emotional response. For in aesthetic perceiving I cut adrift from emotional involvement just as I cut adrift from practical involvement: when I perceive a design as sinister or mysterious I do not respond as if to the implication that I am in danger from it or with curiosity to discover the secret. I savour and enjoy the quality it has of being sinister or mysterious. When spontaneous practical concern is held in abeyance the close fusion of mood and object which is characteristic of emotional perceiving is disrupted and the mood-implications of the object are enjoyed without the vicissitudes of the mood-experience.

Language is very but not quite consistently defective of terms by which to discriminate moods and their complementary mood-qualities at this level of experience. Most but not all mood-words have to do double duty to indicate both the felt mood and the objective counterpart. We do not indeed have an inclination to apply the word "merry" to the object of merriment: we call it "comic" or "funny." We do not say that a person confronted with a ghost is in a "sinister" mood: we have in this case no word for the emotion, though "awe" comes nearest to it. On the other hand we apply the words "gay" and "cheerful" to that quality of a landscape or a colour ensemble which is the correlate of a mood of gaiety and it is difficult to find any alternative way of saying what we want to say. But we do not want to say that the landscape is experiencing a cheerful mood. Nor do we intend to imply that we can only perceive cheerfulness or gaiety by being ourselves in a gay or cheerful mood. We condemn gay colours as incongruous to our mood at a funeral. Like most mood-words "sad" (and still more clearly the French *triste*) has a dual connotation which is readily apparent to those who are at all sensitive to the uses of language. In its primary signification of mood we cannot say that music is sad, for nobody really wishes to imply or pretend that a constellation of sounds can feel the mood we call sadness. We can say the music is sombre, dismal, depressing, lugubrious, mournful, grim. But "sad" has not only this primary sense. When we call the pudding sad we do not mean that the pudding feels sad. We can say that music or other art objects are sad, cheerful, gay in the secondary senses of these words, when they connote a mood-correlate (as "funny" is—nearly—the correlate of "merry") for which there is no separate term.

It is therefore the contention of this paper that a more careful examination of the language in which we describe our emotional experience of works of art would safeguard us from the bizarre theory that unfelt feelings are perceived "in" aesthetic objects and would release us from the temptation to postulate an implausible isomorphism between the structures of works of art and the unobserved patterns and rhythms of our moods.

—*The British Journal of Aesthetics*, Vol. 3 (1963)

NOTES

1. *B.J.A.*, Vol. 1, No. 4 and Vol. 2, No. 1.

2. In the language of criticism different categories of emotion statements are habitually mingled in a way which makes them difficult to disentangle. For example on a single page (p. 223) of Erwin Christensen's *The History of Western Art* one may find three short descriptive statements about paintings by Raphael. Of the National Gallery *St. George and the Dragon* he writes: "The mood is reposeful, hardly what one might expect in a life and death battle." The *Cowper Madonna*, also in the National Gallery, is "calm and serene . . . Mother and Child are emotionally united, their minds fixed on the future, the Passion. A meditative, serious spirit and a sweet, subdued melancholy underlie the peaceful scene." And thirdly, in the *Sistine Madonna*, where the Queen of Heaven descends from the clouds as the curtains are drawn back, we are told: "Though a heavenly vision, she appears simple and unaffected; the unassuming quality is perhaps the secret of her appeal. The Christ Child's serious expression seems to reveal his divinity, as his unchildlike gaze is contrasted with *putti* below. The Virgin, slightly embarrassed at presenting a divine Child, remains floating above the clouds. St. Barbara sinks into the clouds with eyes modestly removed from the Virgin." The last of these quotations offers the critic's interpretation of the attitudes and demeanour of the depicted figures exactly as though he were describing a scene from real life or a photograph or *tableau vivant*; he says nothing about the emotional qualities of the picture. The second passage combines characterization of the painting, attributing to it serenity and calm, seriousness, sweetness and melancholy, with physiognomic interpretation of the emotions displayed by the depicted figures of the Mother and Child. The first passage attributes an emotional quality to the painting and notes that it is oddly at variance with the theme depicted. In a description of a painting by Domenico Ghirlandaio. Thomas Bodkin has noted that the emotional quality of the picture (which he assumes to be a sign of an emotion felt by the artist when

he painted the picture and to be capable of evoking similar emotion in observers) is at variance with the subject depicted. "The artist has depicted an old man, clad in the scarlet fur-trimmed robe of a Florentine senator and hideously afflicted with elephantiasis, who caresses his grandson. Most of us would be repelled by the appearance of the living man. But the emotion of the artist, reflected through the pictorial harmony he has devised, recreates in us a mood of unruffled serenity and allows us, as well, to recognize in his presentment the unquenchable nobility of the human spirit shackled in decay." (*The Approach to Painting*, p. 63.)

When Fra Pietro da Novellara wrote of the lamb in Leonardo's cartoon of the *The Madonna and Child with St. Anne and St. John Baptist* "that sacrificial animal, which signifies the Passion," he was referring to ideas contained representationally in the picture. So was Vasari when he wrote: "She (The Virgin) looks down sweetly on a little St. John, who plays with a lamb, while St. Anne looks on smiling and overcome with joy at the sight of her earthly progeny become divine—ideas which were truly worthy of Leonardo's intellect and imagination." But Peter Murray was referring to the emotional character of the picture itself when he said that it is "one of the few great masterpieces which stand at the beginning of a formal evolution but have never been equalled in depth of feeling." (*B.J.A.*, Vol. 2, No. 3.) It is in this sense that Yrjö Hirn writes of "the melancholy which can be expressed, without any anthropomorphic element, by a mere relation between light and shadow" (*Origins of Art*, p. 138). And it is in this sense that Van Gogh said: "J'ai voulu représenter par les couleurs les terribles passions humaines."

3. *Odyssey*, xi, 598. Cited by Aristotle as an example of "vividness" (*enargia*) in Homer, along with *Iliad*, xi, 574: "the spears stood upright in the ground anxious to devour their fill of flesh."

4. Professor Hepburn has pointed out to me that the distinction between "seems" and "is" does have an application in art-works, as when I say "All modal music may seem melancholy to you at first: but it isn't really." He adds that this comment does not conflict with the arguments I am here deploying. I believe that I would seek to explain the phenomenon to which he alludes in terms of more and less complete "actualization" of the music by the hearer. Could his "but it isn't really" be rewritten: "but if you successfully apprehend modal music as organic patterns of sound, you will not always hear it as melancholy"?

5. Both this article and that by Aldrich are reprinted in Mrs. Susanne Langer's compilation *Reflections on Art* (1958). In her Introduction she confesses that Baensch's theory strikes her as "slightly mad."

6. *Annual Review of Psychology*, Vol. 12, 1961, p. 76.

7. Herbert Spencer believed himself to have shown that "what we regard as the distinctive traits of song are simply the traits of emotional speech intensified and systematized" and that "vocal music and by consequence all music, is an idealization of the natural language of passion." *The Origin and Function of Music* (1857). The theory was the subject of a brilliant attack by Ernest Newman in *Musical Studies* (1905). Kant attributed the charm of music to the following facts: "Every expression in language has an associated tone suited to its sense. This tone indicates, more or less, a mode in which the speaker is affected, and in turn evokes it in the hearer also, in whom conversely it also excites the idea which in language is expressed with such a tone." (Kant's own attitude to music was, however, somewhat ambivalent. He thought that: "If we estimate the worth of the fine arts by the culture they supply to the mind, and adopt for our standard the expansion of the faculties whose confluence, in judgment, is necessary for cognition, music, since it plays merely with sensations, has the lowest place among the fine arts—just as it has perhaps the highest among those valued at the same time for their agreeableness." None the less, he opines, "music has a certain lack of urbanity about it. For owing chiefly to the character of the instruments, it scatters its influence abroad

to an uncalled-for extent (through the neighbourhood) and thus, as it were, becomes obtrusive and deprives others, outside the musical circle, of their freedom.") Kant was happy to have lived before the days of public broadcasting.

8. We need not go all the way with psychologists like Carney Landis or Samuel Fernberger who in opposition to Charles Darwin claimed that it is impossible ever to diagnose emotion from facial expression and bodily gesture alone unless one is given also a clue from the situation and context. Darwin himself admitted in *The Expression of the Emotions in Man and the Animals* (1872) that the possibilities of external expression are not adequate to differentiate the varieties of emotion known to popular wisdom and enshrined in the common language.

9. *Art and Visual Perception* (1956), pp. 367–8.

10. *La Psychologie de la Forme* (1935).

11. C. C. Pratt, "Structural vs. Expressive Form in Music," *The Journal of Psychology* (1938), 5.

12. Whether one speaks of a vague perception strongly charged with feeling or a feeling which is cognitive in that it carries awareness of a presented quality in the way that perception is cognitive, is a matter of convenience. I propose to use the latter way of talking, if only to counter a too sharp distinction between feeling and perception which has been encouraged by the terminology of classical psychology. It is a way of speaking which seems natural to many who have examined this sector of experience carefully but without linguistic preconceptions. Thus, for example, in *Poetry and Experience* Archibald MacLeish says of the word-structure of a poem: "There is an enhancement of their meanings or perhaps, more precisely, of the significance of their meanings. It is not an enhancement which can be defined by abstract analysis and measurement. But the inability to define in abstract terms does not mean, contrary to notions now in vogue, that an experience is fanciful. It is still possible, even under the new vocabulary, to feel as well as to define. And what is present here is *felt.*" And again: "Emotion *knows* the difference even though mind is defeated in its busy effort to pinch the difference between the thumb and finger of reason and so dispose of it. Emotion—and this is perhaps the point precisely—cannot dispose of it. Emotion stands there staring." And: "And the shape of total meaning when it begins to appear is a shape not in the understanding mind but in the recognizing perceptions—those fingers which can *feel.*"

13. Heinz Werner says that we may speak "in a very real sense not only of the softness of velvet, but also of a colour or a voice." But it is easy to be led astray by linguistic habits and ingrained metaphor. In this case the opposite of tactile softness is hardness; the opposite of soft sound is loudness; and the opposite of a soft colour is vivid or contrasty colour. The only common feature of these three "softs" seems to be a low degree of obtrusiveness.

14. *Comparative Psychology of Mental Development* (1948).

15. W. M. Urban, *Valuation. Its Nature and Laws* (1909). J.-P. Sartre, *Esquisse d'une théorie des émotions* (1939). Sylvia Honkavaara, *The Psychology of Expression* (*The British Journal of Psychology*, Monograph Supplements XXXII, 1961).

16. Aesthetic perceiving has been described as "living in the immediate present." In practical life present experience is subordinated to the future and the past. Whenever we are expectant, anxious or apprehensive, when we are hopeful, confident or exultant, these attitudes shape the present experience in the light of its implications for the future. When we are surprised, disappointed, filled with self-congratulation or regret, soothed with the comfortable feeling of familiarity and recognition, we are experiencing the present in the context and colouring of a selected past. All these attitudes are inhibited in aesthetic contemplation: but we may still become aware of "polar" emotional qualities adhering in the object.

PART
III
The Response to the Esthetic Object

10

The Experience
of the Beholder

VERNON LEE: Empathy
WILHELM WORRINGER: Abstraction and Empathy
EDWARD BULLOUGH: Psychical Distance
KENNETH CLARK: The Naked and the Nude
JOHN HOSPERS: The Esthetic Attitude

In Part III we consider the response of the beholder, the critic, and the community to the work of art. Most of the theories presented in earlier chapters have thrown light on the beholder's response. The characterization of esthetic experience by Croce, Dewey, Santayana, Bosanquet, and Arnheim—to mention only a few names—illuminates not only the creative activity of the artist but also the contemplative activity of the spectator. Although no sharp line can be drawn between the contemplative and the creative phases of art, we turn now to selections that focus on the experience of the beholder and which also shed further light on the nature of the work of art. As I remarked in the preface, the divisions are not sharp and the readings in this book overlap and interlock in a great variety of ways.

An interesting interpretation of form, the subject of Chapter 8, has been advanced by the proponents of "empathy." (The term "empathy" was coined by the psychologist Edward Titchener, in his *Experimental Psychology of the Thought Processes* (1909), as an English rendering of *"einfühlung,"* which means literally "feeling into.") According to this interpretation, the formal elements acquire meaning for the imagination only because we project our activities and feelings into them. Thus, form as an esthetic value is not an objective fact. It is a free creation of the imagination and belongs to the realm of appearances. It is inseparable from expression, since all its spiritual content is derived from the mind.

The most original proponent of empathy writing in English was Violet Paget, whose pen-name was Vernon Lee (1856–1935). Lipps' *Raumaesthetik*, which contained the first detailed exposition of the theory of empathy, was published in 1893–1897, but did not become known to Lee until 1899. Her own account, published two years before she discovered Lipps, appeared in an article "Beauty and Ugliness" in the *Contemporary Review*.

She believes that many aims operate to create art (for example, the making of useful objects, the transmission of knowledge, the expression of emotions), but that there is always a regulative principle, an "esthetic imperative," namely, the attainment of beauty and the avoidance of ugliness. Objects found to be beautiful are essentially formal; they are *configurations* of sounds, colors, lines, words, and so forth. The main question of esthetics becomes, then, what makes certain forms beautiful and other forms ugly. Her answer is: Forms are beautiful when we project into them our own activities, and when this projection arouses pleasure by facilitating our sense of vitality. In the case of ugliness, we feel an opposite sense of obstruction and displeasure.

The main feature of her theory in its earlier formulations was the great stress upon the importance of organic sensations and bodily postures. "We cannot satisfactorily focus a stooping figure like the Medicean Venus," she pointed out, "if we stand before it bolt upright and with tense muscles, nor a very erect and braced figure like the Apoxyomenos if we stand before it humped up and with slackened muscles. In such cases the statue seems to evade our eye, and it is impossible to realize its form thoroughly; whereas, when we adjust our muscles in imitation of the tenseness or slackness of the statue's attitude, the statue immediately becomes a reality to us."[1] But, under the influence of Lipps, she later modified her position, being convinced that she had laid too much stress upon kinesthetic sensations and muscular adjustments. What we project into the object, she realized, are mainly the emotions and ideas of which the organic mimicry and bodily accommodations are the symptoms.

In the account reprinted here, she differs from Lipps in one important respect. She objects to the conception of empathy "as a metaphysical and quasi-mythological *projection of the ego* into the object or shape under consideration." This is in opposition to the tendency of Lipps to speak of the ego as at one with the object. Empathy, according to his view, is based partly upon a feeling of "self-value"; the unity and worth of personality are projected into the object of appreciation.

For reasons of space, I omit a selection from Lipps, but I shall briefly summarize his theory, since it is helpful in understanding Worringer. The work of art, or esthetic object, Lipps maintains, consists of the "sensuous appearance," not the bare physical object, but the image as remodeled by imagination and charged with vital meaning. It is the beautiful thing contemplated, and is therefore to be distinguished from the act of contemplation. Attention is not aware of itself; it is directed outward to the object and absorbed therein. Nevertheless, what gives esthetic import to the object, and what constitutes the *ground* of its enjoyment, is this very act of contemplation. The mind unconsciously enlivens the outward form by fusing into it the modes of its own activity—its striving and willing, its sense of freedom and power, and so forth. The moods thus transported into the object do not spring from the real or practical ego, but only from the ego insofar as it is contemplative.

We are now prepared to define more precisely the nature of the esthetic object. It may be analyzed into two factors: First, there is the inner activity, the emotion of pride, the feeling of vigor or freedom, and so forth; second, there is the external sensuous content as bare physical stimulus. The *esthetic* object springs into existence as a result of the fusion of these two factors. The ego unconsciously supposes itself at one with the object, and there is no longer any duality. Empathy simply means the disappearance of the twofold consciousness of self and object, and the enrichment of experience that results from this interpenetration. So completely is the self transported into the object that the contemplator of a statue, for example, may unconsciously imitate its posture and implied movement by definite muscular adjustments.

Although Lipps recognized the existence of such spontaneous mimicry, he insisted that empathy does not consist in the bodily feelings thus aroused. In fact, we forget all about our bodies and attend simply to the object. Our bodily behavior is a symptom of what we are feeling rather than the object of our awareness. We do not, in fact, attribute kinesthetic feelings even to the object, but attribute to it only the total emotional state that is appropriate to the representation at hand.

Wilhelm Worringer (1881–1965), a famous German art historian, takes as his point of departure the theory of Lipps. His essay draws an interesting contrast between empathy and "abstraction." Whereas in empathy the mind lends to the object its own spirit and feels itself at one with it, in abstraction the mind feels the inviolable and separate integrity of the object. Empathy involves a transference of vital feelings from the subject *into* the object; abstraction involves the withdrawal of subjective feelings *from* the object. When engaged in such abstraction, the mind creates or contemplates abstract geometrical forms—stiff lines, flat surfaces, cubical shapes, and so forth—which, appearing durable and permanent, afford a refuge from the flux and impermanence of sensuous phenomena.

Empathy is the result of a happy sympathetic relation between man and the outside world, whereas abstraction occurs mainly among peoples who feel no such delight in nature and life. "It expresses no joyful affirmation of sensuous vitality," declares Worringer, "but belongs rather to the other domain, which through all the transitoriness and chances of life strives for a higher world, freed from all illusions of the senses, from all false impressions, a domain in which inevitableness and permanency reign."[2] On the whole, abstraction is characteristic of Primitive, Egyptian, Byzantine, Gothic, and Oriental art, and also the "dehumanized" contemporary art discussed by Ortega y Gasset. On the other hand, empathy is more characteristic of late Greco-Roman, Renaissance, and "naturalistic" Western art.

Despite the antithesis between empathy and abstraction, Worringer finds the two esthetic processes alike in being modes of "self-privation"— escapes from the limitations of man's ordinary circumscribed being. In empathy, man "loses himself" in the object; in abstraction, he imaginatively transcends his "human, all too-human" nature through the contemplation of "eternal" forms.

Quite different from the theory of empathy, with its emphasis upon a close rapport between the mind and its object, and more like Worringer's theory of abstraction, are the theories of esthetic disinterestedness or detachment. Since the publication of Kant's *Critique of Judgment,* *disinterestedness* (which, of course, is not *un*interestedness) has been commonly recognized as characteristic of the esthetic attitude. The object of an *"entirely disinterested . . .* satisfaction," declared Kant, "is called beautiful." Such detachment from practical interests is emphasized by Edward Bullough (1880–1934), a distinguished British psychologist, in his concept of "psychical distance." Esthetic distance, he explains, has two aspects: First, there is a negative, inhibitory side—which consists of "a putting of the object out of gear with our practical needs and ends." Second, there is a positive side—"the elaboration of the experience on the new basis created by the inhibitory action of distance." This positive aspect consists in the objectification of one's mental states. The contemplator's feelings are interpreted not as modes of his being but as characteristics of the object.

Distance, being a matter of degree, varies according to two different sets of conditions: the characteristics of the object, and the attitudes of the subject. As the object becomes more stylized, unrealistic, and isolated, the distance correspondingly increases. As the contemplator independently adopts a more impersonal attitude, the distance again increases proportionately. The right mean consists of "the utmost decrease of distance without its disappearance," that is, the maximum personal appeal compatible with distance—a rule that Bullough calls the "antinomy of distance."

Bullough's rule, with its avoidance of high distance, was challenged by the famous Spanish philosopher José Ortega y Gasset, who defended the extreme increase of detachment in recent art. The tendency of modern artists, he declares in *The Dehumanization of Art* (1925), is to return to the "royal road of art," which is "the Will to Style"; and stylistic art is highly distanced art. The result of high distancing is a rejection of the "human, all too human" in art. Since Ortega espoused this position, the pendulum has swung the other way, and more recently the emphasis has been upon low distance. The intent has been to break down the distance between artist and public, actor and audience, the work of art and the beholder. In the performances called "happenings" or constructions called "environments," the stress has been upon participation and engagement—the very opposite of dehumanization.

Mediating between the extremes of high distance and low distance, Sir Kenneth Clark (1903–   ), formerly professor of fine arts at Oxford and eminent art historian, rejects the idea of dehumanization but retains a modicum of distance. In his remarkable study of the nude as an art form (originally presented as the A. W. Mellon Lectures at the National Art Gallery in Washington, D. C.), Clark maintains that the idea of the inhumanity of the work of art is false and enervating. No man can divest himself of his essential humanity, and he should not try. If he should attempt to cut himself off from his body, or divorce himself from his deepest instincts, he will only divide his own nature and destroy the vitality of his art. But the esthetic impulse is no mere attempt to grasp things as they are. "We do not wish to imitate, we wish to perfect." The *ideal* of the oneness of the spirit and body stimulated the Greeks to their highest artistic achievements. The esthetic attitude, so interpreted, is neither an intense participation nor an absolute detachment—it is neither low nor high distance—it is a balance between the two, a synthesis of contraries.

John Hospers (1918–   ), professor of philosophy at the University of Southern California and author of *Meaning and Truth in the Arts* (1946), supplements these interpretations of esthetic experience with a succinct discussion of the question, "Is there an esthetic way of looking at things, and if so, what distinguishes it from other ways of experiencing these things?" He reviews the various answers to this question, ranging from Bullough's theory of "psychical distance" to the skeptical theories of J. O. Urmson and George Dickie. This synoptic account of "the esthetic attitude" is enriched by Hosper's penetrating comments and criticisms.

NOTES

1. Vernon Lee and C. Anstruther-Thomson, *Beauty and Ugliness and other Studies in Psychological Aesthetics* (John Lane, London, 1912), p. 218.
2. Wilhelm Worringer, *Form in Gothic* (G. P. Putnam's Sons, London, 1927), p. 37.

VERNON LEE
Empathy

The mountain rises. What do we mean when we employ this form of words? Some mountains, we are told, have originated in an *upheaval.* But even if this particular mountain did, we never saw it and geologists are still disputing about HOW and WHETHER. So the *rising* we are talking about is evidently not that probable or improbable *upheaval.* On the other hand all geologists tell us that every mountain is undergoing a steady *lowering* through its particles being weathered away and washed down; and our knowledge of landslips and avalanches shows us that the mountain, so far from rising, is *descending.* Of course we all know that, objects the Reader, and of course nobody imagines that the rock and the earth of the mountain is rising, or that the mountain is getting up or growing taller! All we mean is that the mountain *looks* as if it were rising.

The mountain *looks!* Surely here is a case of putting the cart before the horse. No; we cannot explain the mountain *rising* by the mountain *looking,* for the only *looking* in the business is *our* looking *at* the mountain. And if the Reader objects again that these are all *figures of speech,* I shall answer that *Empathy* is what explains why we employ figures of speech at all, and occasionally employ them, as in the case of this rising mountain, when we know perfectly well that the figure we have chosen expresses the exact reverse of the objective truth. Very well; then, (says the Reader) we will avoid all figures of speech and say merely: when we look at the mountain *we somehow or other think of the action of rising.* Is that sufficiently literal and indisputable?

So literal and indisputable a statement of the case, I answer, that it explains, when we come to examine it, why we should have a thought of rising when we look at the mountain, since we cannot look at the mountain, nor at a tree, a tower or anything of which we similarly say that it *rises*, without lifting our glance, raising our eye and probably raising our head and neck, all of which raising and lifting unites into a general awareness of something *rising.* The rising of which we are aware is going on in us. But, as the Reader will remember also, when we are engrossed by something outside ourselves, as we are engrossed in looking at the shape (for we can *look* at only the shape, not the *substance*) of that mountain we cease thinking about ourselves, and cease thinking about ourselves exactly in proportion as we are thinking of the mountain's shape. What becomes therefore of our awareness of raising or lifting or *rising?* What can become of it (so long as it continues to be there!) except that it coalesces with the shape we are looking at; in short that the *rising* continuing to be thought, but no longer to be thought of with reference to ourselves (since we aren't thinking of ourselves), is thought of in reference to what we *are* thinking about, namely, the mountain, or rather the mountain's shape, which is, so to speak, responsible for any thought of rising, since it obliges us to lift, raise or rise ourselves in order to take stock of it. It is a case exactly analogous to our transferring the measuring done by our eye to the line of which we say that it *extends* from A to B, when in reality the only *extending* has been the extending of our glance. It is a case of what I have called the tendency to merge the *activities* of the perceiving subject with the qualities of the perceived object. Indeed if I insisted so much upon this tendency of our mind, I did so largely because of its being at the bottom of the phenomenon of *Empathy,* as we have just seen it exemplified in the *mountain which rises.*

If this is Empathy, says the Reader (relieved and reassured), am I to understand that Empathy is nothing beyond *attributing what goes on in us when we look at a shape to the shape itself?*

I am sorry that the matter is by no means so simple! If what we attributed to each single shape was only the precise action which we happen to be accomplishing in the process of looking at it, Empathy would indeed be a simple business, but it would also be a comparatively poor one. No. The *rising* of the mountain is an idea started by the awareness of our own lifting or raising of our eyes, head or neck, and it is an idea containing the awareness of that lifting or raising. But it is far more than the idea merely of that lifting or raising which we are doing at this particular present moment and in connection with this particular mountain. That present and particular raising and lifting is merely the nucleus to which gravitates our remembrance of all similar acts of raising, or *rising* which we have ever accomplished or seen accomplished, *raising* or *rising* not only of our eyes and head, but of every other part of our body, and of every part of every other body which we ever perceived to be rising. And not merely the thought of past *rising* but the thought also of future rising. All these risings, done by ourselves or watched in others, actually experienced or merely imagined, have long since united together in our mind, constituting a sort of composite photograph whence all differences are eliminated and wherein all similarities are fused and intensified: the general idea of *rising*, not "I rise, rose, will rise, it rises, has risen or will rise" but merely *rising* as such, *rising* as it is expressed not in any particular tense or person of the verb *to rise*, but in that verb's infinitive. It is this universally applicable notion of rising, which is started in our mind by the awareness of the particular present acts of raising or rising involved in our looking at that mountain, and it is this general idea of rising, that is, of *upward movement*, which gets transferred to the mountain along with our own particular present activity of raising some part of us, and which thickens and enriches and marks that poor little thought of a definite raising with the interest, the emotional fullness gathered and stored up in its long manifold existence. In other words: what we are transferring (owing to that tendency to merge the activities of the perceiving subject with the qualities of the perceived object) from ourselves to the looked at shape of the mountain, is not merely the thought of the rising which is really being done by us at that moment, but the thought and emotion, the *idea of rising as such* which had been accumulating in our mind long before we ever came into the presence of that particular mountain. And it is this complex mental process, by which we (all unsuspectingly) invest that inert mountain, that bodiless shape, with the stored up and averaged and essential modes of our activity—it is this process whereby we make the mountain *raise itself*, which constitutes what, accepting Professor Titchener's translation of the German word *Einfühlung*, I have called Empathy.

The German word *Einfühlung*, "feeling into"—derived from a *verb to feel oneself into something* ("sich in Etwas einfühlen") was in current use even before Lotze and Vischer applied it to esthetics, and some years before Lipps (1897) and Wundt (1903) adopted it into psychological terminology; and as it is not consecrated, and no better occurs to me, I have had to adopt it, although the literal connotations of the German word have surrounded its central meaning (as I have just defined it) with several mischievous misinterpretations. Against two of these I think it worth while to warn the Reader, especially as, while so doing, I can, in showing what it is not, make it even clearer what Empathy really is. The first of these two main misinterpretations is based upon the reflexive form of the German verb *"sich einfühlen"* (to feel *oneself* into) and it defines, or rather does not define, Empathy as a metaphysical and quasi-mythological *projection of the ego* into the object or shape under observation; a notion incompatible with the fact that Empathy, being only another of those various mergings of the activities of the perceiving subject with the qualities of the perceived object wherewith we have already dealt, depends upon a comparative or momentary abeyance of all thought of an ego; if we became aware that it is *we* who are thinking the rising, we who are *feeling* the rising, we should not think or feel that the mountain did the rising. The other (and as we shall later see) more justifiable misinterpretation of the word Empathy is based on its analogy with *sympathy*, and turns it into a kind of sympathetic, or as it has been called, *inner*, that is, merely *felt*, *mimicry* of, for instance, the mountain's *rising*. Such mimicry, not only *inner* and *felt*, but outwardly manifold, does undoubtedly often result from very lively *empathic* imagination. But as it is the mimicking, inner or outer, of movements and actions which, like the *rising* of the mountain, take place only in our imagination, it presupposes such previous animation of the inanimate, and cannot therefore be taken either as constituting or explaining Empathy itself.

Such as I have defined and exemplified it in our Rising Mountain, Empathy is, together with mere Sensation, probably the chief factor of preference, that is of an alternative of satisfaction and dissatisfaction, in esthetic contemplation, the muscular adjustments and the measuring, comparing and coordinating activities by which Empathy is started, being indeed occasionally difficult and distressing, but giving in themselves little more than a negative satisfaction, at the most that of difficulty overcome and suspense relieved. But although nowhere so fostered as in the contemplation of shapes, Empathy exists or tends to exist throughout our mental life. It is, indeed, one of our simpler, though far from absolutely elementary, psychological processes, entering into what is called imagination, sympathy, and also into that inference from our own inner experience which has shaped all our conceptions of an outer world, and given to the intermittent and heterogeneous sensations received from without the framework of our constant and highly unified inner experience, that is to say, of our own activities and aims. Empathy can be traced in all modes of speech and thought, particularly in the universal attribution of *doing* and *having* and *tending* where all we can really assert is successive and varied *being*. Science has indeed explained away the anthropomorphic implications of *Force* and *Energy, Attraction* and *Repulsion;* and philosophy had reduced *Cause* and *Effect* from implying intention and effort to meaning mere constant succession. But Empathy still helps us to many valuable analogies; and it is possible that without its constantly checked but constantly renewed action, human thought would be without logical cogency, as it certainly would be without poetical charm. Indeed if Empathy is so recent a discovery, this may be due to its being part and parcel of our thinking; so that we are surprised to learn its existence, as Molière's good man was to hear that he talked prose.

—The Beautiful (1913)

WILHELM WORRINGER

Abstraction and Empathy

The aim of the following discussion is to disprove the assumption that [the] process of empathy has been at all times and places the basis of artistic creation. With the theory of empathy in mind, we stand helpless in face of the artistic creations of many ages and nations. For the understanding of that vast complex of works of art which were produced outside the narrow limits of Greco-Roman and modern occidental art, it offers us no clue. Here we are forced to discern a quite different psychological process, which explains the peculiar quality of that style which is only negatively appreciated by us. Before we seek to characterize this process we must devote a few words to certain basic ideas of esthetics, because it is only by an agreement on these basic ideas that an understanding of what follows is possible.

Since the flowering-time of art history fell in the nineteenth century, the theories of the origin of the work of art were obviously based on a materialistic outlook. It need not be mentioned how healthy and rational was the effect of this attempt to penetrate into the essential nature of art, as a reaction against the speculative esthetics and esthetic beautiful-soulism of the eighteenth century. In this way an extremely valuable foundation was assured for the young science. A work like Semper's *Stil* remains an achievement of art history which, like every structure of thought built on a grand scale and fully elaborated, stands beyond the historical valuations of "true" and "false."[1]

Nevertheless this book with its materialistic theory of the origin of the work of art, which made its way into all circles and for decades until our own time was taken as the tacit presupposition of most researches in art history, is for us today an obstacle to progress and thought. All deeper penetration into the innermost nature of the work of art is obstructed by the excessive estimation of subordinate elements. And besides, not everyone who appeals to Semper has Semper's genius.

Everywhere there is a reaction against this flat and easy artistic materialism. The greatest breach in this system indeed was made by the Vienna scholar who died young, Alois Riegl, whose profound and masterly work on the late Roman art-industry—partly because of the difficulty of access to the publication—unfortunately did not gain the attention which, with its epoch-making importance, it deserved.[2]

Riegl for the first time introduced into the method of art-historical research the concept of the "artistic purpose." By the "absolute purpose of art" must be understood that latent inner demand which, totally independent of the object and the mode of creation, exists for itself and acts as the will to form. It is the primary element of all artistic creation and every work of art is in its innermost essence but an objectification of this absolute art-purpose present *a priori*. The materialistic method of art, which, as must be expressly emphasized, is not to be simply identified with Gottfried Semper, but is based partly on a pedantic misinterpretation of his work, saw in the primitive work of art a product of three factors: utilitarian purpose, raw material, and technique. The history of art was for it in the last resort a history of skill. The new view on the other hand regards the history of art as a history of artistic purpose, starting from the psychological presupposition that skill is only a phenomenon secondary to purpose. The peculiarities of style of past epochs are thus not to be traced to a deficiency of skill, but to a differently directed purpose. Thus what is decisive is what Riegl calls "the absolute purpose of art," which is only modified by those three factors, utilitarian purpose, raw material, and technique. "These three factors no longer have that positive creative role which the materialistic theory has attributed to them, but a hindering, negative role: they form, as it were, the coefficient of friction within the total product." (*Spätrömischen Kunstindustrie.*[3])

In general we shall not understand why the concept of artistic purpose is given such an exclusive importance so long as we start with the naïve deep-rooted presupposition that the artistic purpose—that is, the impulse from which the work of art springs—has been the same at all times, subject only to certain variations which we call stylistic peculiarities, and that, so far as the plastic arts are concerned, the impulse has always been to approximate the natural prototype. . . .

Every code of regarding the history of art which consistently breaks with this one-sidedness is decried as artificial, as an affront to the "healthy human understanding." But what is this healthy human understanding if not the laziness of our minds, which will hardly go beyond the small and limited range of our ideas and recognize the possibilities of other presuppositions. . . .

Before we go farther, let us clarify the relation of the imitation of nature to esthetics. It is necessary to agree on this, that the instinct of imitation, this elementary need of man, stands outside of esthetics in the proper sense and that its satisfaction has in principle nothing to do with art.

But at this point it is well to distinguish between the instinct of imitation and naturalism as a type of art. . . . They are by no means identical and must be sharply distinguished, however difficult this may seem. Every confusion of ideas is in this regard of the most crucial importance. . . .

The primitive instinct of imitation has prevailed in all ages and its history is a history of manual skill without esthetic significance. In the very earliest ages this instinct was quite separate from the artistic impulse in the true sense; it satisfied itself especially in miniature art, as in those small idols and symbolic trifles which we know from all early art-epochs, and which often enough stand in direct contrast to the creations in which the purely artistic impulse of the peoples in question manifested itself. We remember how for example in Egypt the imitative instinct and the artistic impulse developed side by side, simultaneously but separately. While the so-called folk-art with startling realism created such well-known statues as the "Scribe" or the "Country Judge," the true art, falsely called "court art," showed a strict style which departed from all realism. That here there can be no question either of crudity or of stiffness, and that a certain psychological instinct demanded satisfaction, will be maintained in the further course of our discussions. True art has at all times satisfied a deep psychological need, but not the pure instinct of imitation, the petty pleasure of copying the natural prototype. The glory which crowns the concept of art, all the admiring devotion which it has enjoyed in all ages, can be psychologically explained only as we think of an art which, arising from psychological needs, satisfies psychological needs. . . .

The worth of an art-work, which we call its beauty, lies generally speaking in its values as a means to happiness. These values stand naturally in a causal relation to the psychological needs which they satisfy. The "absolute purpose of art" is thus the index to the quality of those psychological needs.

A psychology of the need of art—that is to say, from our modern standpoint, the need of style—has not yet been written. It would be a history of world-feeling (*Weltgefühl*) and as such would have an equal rank by the side of the history of religion. By world-feeling I understand the psychological state with which humanity confronts the cosmos, the phenomena of the external world. This state betrays itself in the quality of psychological needs, that is, in the nature of the absolute purpose of art and finds its external precipitate in the work of art, namely, in the style itself, whose peculiarity is just the peculiarity of the psychological need. Thus in the evolution of artistic style the various gradations of the so-called world-feeling may be read off just as in the theogony of peoples.

Every style represents for mankind, who created it out of its psychological needs, the highest happiness. This must become the prime article of belief for all objective consideration of the history of art. What from our standpoint appears as the grossest distortion must have been for its producer the highest beauty and the fulfillment of his artistic purpose. Thus from our standpoint, that of our modern esthetics, which gives its judgments exclusively in the sense of Greco-Roman antiquity or of the Renaissance, all valuations from a higher standpoint are inanities and platitudes.

After this necessary digression we return to the starting-point, namely, to the thesis of the limited applicability of the theory of empathy.

The need of empathy may be regarded as the presupposition of the artistic purpose only where this purpose inclines to the truth of organic life, that is, to naturalism in the higher sense. The feeling of happiness, which is revived in us by the expression of organic vitality, what modern man calls beauty, is a satisfaction of that inner need of self-exercise, in which Lipps sees the presupposition of the process of empathy. We enjoy ourselves in the forms of a work of art. Esthetic enjoyment is objectified self-enjoyment. The value of a line, of a form, consists for us in the value of the life which it contains for us. It keeps its beauty only through our vital feeling, which we obscurely project into it.

The recollection of the inorganic form of a pyramid, or of the suppression of life exemplified in Byzantine mosaics, tells us at once that the need of empathy, which for obvious reasons always inclines to the organic, cannot possibly have determined the artistic purpose. Indeed we are compelled to think that here there is an impulse which is directly opposed to the impulse of empathy and which seeks to suppress just that in which the need of empathy finds its satisfaction.[4]

The tendency to abstraction appears to us as the polar opposite of the need of empathy. To analyze it and to establish the significance which it assumes in the development of art, is the primary task of the present work. . . .

We find that the artistic purpose of uncivilized peoples, so far as they have such a thing at all, the artistic purpose of all primitive art-epochs, and finally the artistic purpose of certain peoples of Oriental culture, exhibits this abstract tendency. The tendency to abstraction is thus dominant in the initial stage of all art, and remains so with certain peoples at higher levels of culture, while, for example, among the Greeks and other Occidentals it gradually expires to make way for the tendency to empathy.

Now what are the psychological presuppositions of the tendency to abstraction? We have to seek them in the world-feeling of those peoples, in their psychological relation to the cosmos. While the tendency of empathy has as its condition a happy pantheistic relation of confidence between man and the phenomena of the external world, the tendency to abstraction is the result of a great inner conflict between man and his surroundings, and corresponds in religion to a strongly transcendental coloring of all ideas. This state we might call a prodigious mental fear of space. Tibullus says: "First in the world God made fear"; this same feeling of anxiety can be considered the root of artistic creation.

A comparison with that physical dread of open spaces, which as a disease afflicts certain persons, will perhaps explain more fully what we understand by the psychological fear of space. This physical dread may be popularly regarded as a vestige of a normal stage of human evolution, in which man, trying to become accustomed to surrounding space, could not rely on visual impressions alone, but still needed to be reassured by his sense of touch. As soon as he became a biped and thus for the first time appeared in human form, a slight feeling of insecurity must have remained. But in his further evolution he freed himself, by habit and intellectual reflection, from this primitive anxiety toward immense space.[5]

With the psychological fear of space before the vast, incoherent, bewildering world of phenomena, the case is similar. The rationalistic development of mankind repressed that instinctive anxiety which results from the lost state of man within the world-whole. Only the civilized Oriental peoples, whose deeper world-instinct opposed such a rationalistic development, and who always saw in the phenomenal world only the glistening veil of Maya, remained conscious of the inextricable confusion of all the phenomena of life, and thus were not under the illusion of any intellectual external domination over the cosmos. . . .

Vexed by the confused connection and interplay of external phenomena, such peoples were dominated by a great need of rest. The possibility of happiness, which they sought in art, did not consist in immersing themselves in the things of the external world, to enjoy themselves in them, but in freeing the particular thing in the outer world from its arbitrariness and apparent contingency, immortalizing it by approximation to abstract forms, and in this way finding a resting-place in the flight of phenomena. Their strongest impulse was, as it were, to tear the external object out of the context of nature, out of the endless interplay of existence, to purify it of all dependence on life, all arbitrariness, to make it necessary and stable, to make it approximate to its absolute value. Where they attained this, they felt that happiness and satisfaction which the beauty of the form full of organic vitality imparts to us; indeed they knew only one kind of beauty and thus we must call it their beauty.

Riegl says in his *Stilfragen:* "The geometrical style, strictly constructed according to the primary laws of symmetry and rhythm, is from the standpoint of regularity the most perfect. But in our estimation it stands the lowest, and even the historical development of the arts teaches us that this style has mostly been peculiar to peoples at a time when they remained at a relatively lower state of civilization."

If we consider this proposition, which indeed minimizes the role which geometric style has played with peoples of advanced culture, we are faced with this fact: the style which is most perfect in its regularity, the style of the highest abstraction, the strictest exclusion of life, is peculiar to peoples at their most primitive stage of culture. Thus there must be a causal connection between primitive culture and the highest, most purely regular form of art. And we may further set up the principle that the less the human race, by virtue of its spiritual perception, is on friendly and trustful terms with the external object, the more powerful is the dynamic force from which that highest abstract beauty springs.

Not that primitive man sought more strenuously for regularity in nature or felt regularity more strongly in it, quite the contrary: because he stands so lost and spiritually helpless among the things of the external world, because he feels only mystery and arbitrariness in the connection and interplay of external phenomena, the impulse is so strong in him to release the things of the external world from their arbitrariness and obscurity, to give them the value of necessity and the value of regularity. To make use of a bold comparison: in primitive man, as it were, the instinct for the "thing in itself" is most powerful. The increasing spiritual domination over the external world and the force of habit signify a deadening, a dulling of this instinct. Only after the human spirit, in an evolution of thousands of years, has traversed the whole path of rationalistic understanding, there awakens anew in man, as he gives up the attempt at ultimate knowledge, the feeling for the "thing in itself." What was previously instinct is now the final product of understanding. Cast down from the pride of knowledge, man now stands again quite as lost and helpless in face of the cosmos as primitive man, after he has recognized "that this visible world in which we find ourselves is the work of Maya, a spell, an appearance without consistency and in itself without substance, to be compared to an optical illusion or a dream, a veil which surrounds the human consciousness, a something of which it is as false and as true to say 'that it is, as that it is not.' " (Schopenhauer, *Kritik der Kantischen Philosophie.*)

But this perception was artistically unfruitful, since man had already become an individual and had released himself from the mass. Only the dynamic force which resides in an undifferentiated mass held together by a common instinct could have created those forms of the highest abstract beauty. The individual standing alone was too weak for such abstraction.

We would misinterpret the psychological conditions of the origin of this abstract art-form if we were to say that the yearning for regularity made

men consciously grasp at geometrical regularity, for this would presuppose
an intellectual preoccupation with geometrical form, would make it appear
a product of deliberation and calculation. We are much more justified in
assuming that here we have a purely instinctive creation, that the tendency
to abstraction has created this form with elementary necessity without the
intervention of the intellect. Just because the intellect had not yet disturbed the instinct, the innate disposition toward regularity could find
abstract expression. . . .

These abstract regular forms are thus the only and the highest forms in
which man can rest in face of the immense confusion of the cosmos. . . .
The plain and simple line and its elaboration with purely geometrical
regularity must have offered the greatest possibility of happiness for men
disturbed by the obscurity and confusion of phenomena. For here the last
vestige of connection with and dependence upon life is wiped out; here the
highest absolute form, the purest abstraction is attained; here there is law,
there is necessity, where otherwise the arbitrariness of the organic prevails.
But such abstraction does not now serve as the prototype of any natural
object. "From the natural object the geometrical line is distinguished just
by this, that it does not stand in the context of nature. What constitutes its
essence belongs indeed to nature; the mechanical forces are forces of nature.
But in the geometrical line and geometrical forms they are taken altogether
out of the context of nature and the endless interplay of natural forces and
accentuated for themselves." (Lipps, *Aesthetik*, p. 249.)

This pure abstraction could naturally never be attained when an actual
natural prototype was the model. Therefore the question arises: How does
the impulse to abstraction stand in relation to external objects? We have
already emphasized that it was not the imitative instinct—the history of the
imitative instinct is something else than the history of art—that required the
artistic rendering of a natural prototype. Instead we see in this abstract art
the effort to release the individual external object, so far as it arouses a
special interest, from its connection with and dependence on other things,
to snatch it from the stream of transiency, to make it absolute. . . .

A decisive consequence of such an artistic purpose was on the one hand
the approximation to flat representation, and on the other hand strict suppression of the representation of space and exclusive rendering of the
individual form.

Men were impelled toward flat representation because three-dimensional-
ity is the greatest obstacle to a grasp of the object in its self-enclosed
material individuality. Its perception as three-dimensional requires a
sequence of connected moments of perception in which the separate individuality of the object dissolves. Then too, on the other hand, the dimensions of depth betray themselves only by foreshortenings and shadows;
hence their comprehension requires a strong co-operation of understanding
and habit. Thus in both respects the independence of outer things is
disturbed by a subjective interpretation whose avoidance was as far as
possible the task of the peoples of ancient culture.

The suppression of space-representation was for this reason a dictate of
the tendency to abstraction; because it is space itself which connects things
with one another, which gives them their relativity in the cosmos, and

because space does not permit itself to be individualized. Thus so far as a sensible object is still dependent on space, it cannot appear to us in its isolated material individuality. All effort was thus directed to the individual form redeemed from space.

Now if we repeat the formula which we found as the basis of empathic experience: "Esthetic enjoyment is objectified self-enjoyment," we are at once aware of the polar opposition between these two forms of esthetic enjoyment [that is, abstraction and empathy]. On the one hand, the I as a disturbing force, an obstacle to the happiness that might be found in the work of art; on the other hand, the inmost connection between the I and the work of art, which takes all its life from the I alone.

This dualism of esthetic experience . . . is not final. These two poles are only different expressions of one common need, which reveals itself to us as the deepest and ultimate essence of all esthetic experience: that is the need of self-privation.

In the tendency to abstraction, the intensity of the impulse of self-privation is much greater and more consistent. Here it is characterized, not as in the case of the need for empathy as a tendency to part with one's separate individuality, but as a tendency, in the contemplation of something necessary and immutable, to escape from the accidental in human existence in general, from the apparent arbitrariness of organic existence. Life as such is felt as the disturber of esthetic enjoyment.

That even the need for empathy, as the starting-point of esthetic experience, represents at bottom an impulse to self-privation, will be all the more incomprehensible to us at first glance since we still have ringing in our ears that formula: "Esthetic enjoyment is objectified self-enjoyment." For these words assert that the process of empathy represents a self-affirmation, an affirmation of the universal will to activity which is in us. "We have always a need for self-exercise. This is indeed the fundamental need of our nature." But while we empathically project our will to activity into another object, we are *in* that other object. We are released from our individual existence so long as we with our inner impulse to experience are absorbed in an external object, in an external form. We feel as if our individuality were flowing within fixed limits as against the limitless differentiation of the individual consciousness. In this self-objectification lies self-privation. This affirmation of our individual need of activity represents at the same time a restriction of its illimitable possibilities, a denial of its boundless differentiations. We rest with our inner impulse to activity within the limits of this objectification. "Thus in empathy I am not the real I, but am inwardly released from this ego; that is, I am released from all that I am apart from the contemplation of form. I am only this ideal I, this contemplating I." (Lipps, *Aesthetik*, p. 247.) Common parlance speaks pertinently of a losing of the self in the contemplation of a work of art.

Thus in this sense it cannot be too strongly emphasized that all esthetic enjoyment, as perhaps even all human feeling of happiness in general, is to be traced back to the impulse of self-privation as its deepest and ultimate essence. . . .[6]

—*Abstraktion und Einfülung* (1908; twelfth edition, 1921, translated by Bernard Freyd and Melvin Rader)

NOTES

1. Gottfried Semper (1803–1879) is often referred to as a leading exponent of "esthetic materialism," but this term is a misnomer when applied to his doctrine as a whole. His principal work, *Der Stil in den technischen und tektonischen Künsten, oder Praktische Aesthetik,* 2 Vols., 1860–1863, is remarkable for its scope and profundity. (Editor's note.)

2. My work at many points is based on the view of Riegl, as laid down in *Stilfragen* (1893) and in *Spätrömischen Kunstindustrie* (1901). An acquaintance with these works is very desirable, even if not absolutely necessary, for understanding my work. Even though the present writer does not agree with Riegl in all points, he stands on the same ground so far as the method of investigation is concerned, and owes to him the greatest stimulation.

3. *Cf.* Heinrich Wölfflin: "To deny a technical origin of particular forms, is naturally very far from my intention. The nature of the material, the mode of its working, the construction are never without influence. But what I should maintain—particularly as against several recent tendencies—is this, that technique never creates a style, but where we speak of art a definite feeling of form is always the primary element. The technically produced forms must not contradict this feeling of form; they can continue to exist only where they accommodate themselves to the form-taste which is already present." (*Renaissance und Barock,* 2nd ed., p. 57.)

4. That we today can empathize ourselves even into the form of a pyramid is not to be denied, and in general the possibility of an empathy into abstract forms, of which much will be said later, should not be denied. But everything contradicts the supposition that this impulse of empathy was effective in the creators of the pyramidal form. . . .

5. In this connection we may recollect that the fear of space manifests itself clearly in Egyptian architecture. By countless columns, which have no constructive function, it was sought to destroy the impression of free space and to steady man's helpless gaze. *Cf.* Riegl, *Spätrömische Kunstindustrie,* Chap. I.

6. Schopenhauer's esthetics offers an analogy to such a conception. For Schopenhauer the happiness of esthetic contemplation consists in just this, that in it man is released from his individuality, from his will, and remains only as a pure subject, as a clear mirror of the object. "And just thereby is the one engaged in such contemplation no longer an individual, for this individual has in just such contemplation lost himself: but he is the pure, will-less, painless, timeless subject of perception." (*Cf.* the third book of *The World as Will and Idea.*)

EDWARD BULLOUGH

Psychical Distance

3. The variability of Distance.
4. Distance as the psychological formulation of the antirealism of Art: naturalistic and idealistic Art.
5. Distance as applied to the antithesis "sensual" and "spiritual."
6. Distance as applied to the antithesis "individualistic" and "typical."

I

1. The conception of "Distance" suggests, in connection with Art, certain trains of thought by no means devoid of interest or of speculative importance. Perhaps the most obvious suggestion is that of *actual spatial* distance, that is, the distance of a work of Art from the spectator, or that of *represented spatial* distance, that is, the distance represented within the work. Less obvious, more metaphorical, is the meaning of *temporal* distance. The first was noticed already by Aristotle in his *Poetics;* the second has played a great part in the history of painting in the form of perspective; the distinction between these two kinds of distance assumes special importance theoretically in the differentiation between sculpture in the round, and relief-sculpture. Temporal distance, remoteness from us in point of time, though often a cause of misconceptions, has been declared to be a factor of considerable weight in our appreciation.

It is not, however, in any of these meanings that "Distance" is put forward here, though it will be clear in the course of this essay that the above mentioned kinds of distance are rather special forms of the conception of Distance as advocated here, and derive whatever *esthetic* qualities they may possess from Distance in its general connotation. This general connotation is "Psychical Distance."

A short illustration will explain what is meant by "Psychical Distance." Imagine a fog at sea: for most people it is an experience of acute unpleasantness. Apart from the physical annoyance and remoter forms of discomfort such as delays, it is apt to produce feelings of peculiar anxiety, fears of invisible dangers, strains of watching and listening for distant and unlocalized signals. The listless movements of the ship and her warning calls soon tell upon the nerves of the passengers; and that special, expectant, tacit anxiety and nervousness, always associated with this experience, make a fog the dreaded terror of the sea (all the more terrifying because of its very silence and gentleness) for the expert seafarer no less than for the ignorant landsman.

Nevertheless, a fog at sea can be a source of intense relish and enjoyment. Abstract from the experience of the sea fog, for the moment, its danger and practical unpleasantness, just as every one in the enjoyment of a mountain-climb disregards its physical labor and its danger (though, it is not denied, that these may incidentally enter into the enjoyment and enhance it); direct the attention to the features "objectively" constituting the phenomenon—the veil surrounding you with an opaqueness as of transparent milk, blurring the outline of things and distorting their shapes into weird grotesqueness; observe the carrying-power of the air, producing the impression as if you could touch some far-off siren by merely putting out your hand and letting it lose itself behind that white wall; note the curious creamy smoothness of the water, hypocritically denying as it were any suggestion of danger; and, above all, the strange solitude and remoteness from the world, as it can be found only on the highest mountain tops; and the experience may acquire, in its uncanny mingling of repose and terror, a flavor of such concentrated poignancy and delight as to contrast sharply with the blind and distempered anxiety of its other aspects. This contrast, often emerging with startling suddenness, is like a momentary switching on of some new current, or the passing ray of a brighter light, illuminating the outlook upon perhaps the most ordinary and familiar objects—an impression which we experience sometimes in instants of direst extremity, when our practical interest snaps like a wire from sheer over-tension, and we watch the consummation of some impending catastrophe with the marveling unconcern of a mere spectator.

It is a difference of outlook, due—if such a metaphor is permissible—to the insertion of Distance. This Distance appears to lie between our own self and its affections, using the latter term in its broadest sense as anything which affects our being, bodily or spiritually, for example, as sensation, perception, emotional state or idea. Usually, though not always, it amounts to the same thing to say that the Distance lies between our own self and such objects as are the sources or vehicles of such affections.

Thus, in the fog, the transformation by Distance is produced in the first instance by putting the phenomenon, so to speak, out of gear with our practical, actual self; by allowing it to stand outside the context of our personal needs and ends—in short, by looking at it "objectively," as it has often been called, by permitting only such reactions on our part as emphasize the "objective" features of the experience, and by interpreting even our "subjective" affections not as modes of *our* being but rather as characteristics of the phenomenon.

The working of Distance is, accordingly, not simple, but highly complex. It has a *negative*, inhibitory aspect—the cutting-out of the practical sides of things and of our practical attitude to them—and a *positive* side—the elaboration of the experience on the new basis created by the inhibitory action of Distance.

2. Consequently, this distanced view of things is not, and cannot be, our normal outlook. As a rule, experiences constantly turn the same side towards us, namely, that which has the strongest practical force of appeal. We are not ordinarily aware of those aspects of things which do not touch us immediately and practically, nor are we generally conscious of impressions apart from our own self which is impressed. The sudden view of things from their reverse, usually unnoticed, side, comes upon us as a revelation, and such revelations are precisely those of Art. In this most general sense, Distance is a factor in all Art.

3. It is, for this very reason, also an esthetic principle. The esthetic contemplation and the esthetic outlook have often been described as "objective." We speak of "objective" artists as Shakespeare or Velasquez, of "objective" works or art forms as Homer's *Iliad* or the drama. It is a term constantly occurring in discussions and criticisms, though its sense, if pressed at all, becomes very questionable. For certain forms of Art, such as lyrical poetry, are said to be "subjective"; Shelley, for example, would usually be considered a "subjective" writer. On the other hand, no work of

Art can be genuinely "objective" in the sense in which this term might be applied to a work on history or to a scientific treatise; nor can it be "subjective" in the ordinary acceptance of that term, as a personal feeling, a direct statement of a wish or belief, or a cry of passion is subjective. "Objectivity" and "subjectivity" are a pair of opposites which in their mutual exclusiveness when applied to Art soon lead to confusion.

Nor are they the only pair of opposites. Art has with equal vigor been declared alternately "idealistic" and "realistic," "sensual" and "spiritual," "individualistic" and "typical." Between the defense of either terms of such antitheses most esthetic theories have vacillated. It is one of the contentions of this essay that such opposites find their synthesis in the more fundamental conception of Distance.

Distance further provides the much needed criterion of the beautiful as distinct from the merely agreeable.

Again, it marks one of the most important steps in the process of artistic creation and serves as a distinguishing feature of what is commonly so loosely described as the "artistic temperament."

Finally, it may claim to be considered as one of the essential characteristics of the "esthetic consciousness"—if I may describe by this term that special mental attitude towards, and outlook upon, experience, which finds its most pregnant expression in the various forms of Art.

II

Distance, as I said before, is obtained by separating the object and its appeal from one's own self, by putting it out of gear with practical needs and ends. Thereby the "contemplation" of the object becomes alone possible. But it does not mean that the relation between the self and the object is broken to the extent of becoming "impersonal." Of the alternatives "personal" and "impersonal" the latter surely comes nearer to the truth; but here, as elsewhere, we meet the difficulty of having to express certain facts in terms coined for entirely different uses. To do so usually results in paradoxes, which are nowhere more inevitable than in discussions upon Art. "Personal" and "impersonal," "subjective" and "objective" are such terms, devised for purposes other than esthetic speculation, and becoming loose and ambiguous as soon as applied outside the sphere of their special meanings. In giving preference therefore to the term "impersonal" to describe the relation between the spectator and a work of Art, it is to be noticed that it is not impersonal in the sense in which we speak of the "impersonal" character of Science, for instance. In order to obtain "objectively valid" results, the scientist excludes the "personal factor," that is, his personal wishes as to the validity of.his results, his predilection for any particular system to be proved or disproved by his research. It goes without saying that all experiments and investigations are undertaken out of a personal interest in the science, for the ultimate support of a definite assumption, and involve personal hopes of success; but this does not affect the "dispassionate" attitude of the investigator, under pain of being accused of "manufacturing his evidence."

1. Distance does not imply an impersonal, purely intellectually interested

relation of such a kind. On the contrary, it describes a *personal* relation, often highly emotionally colored, but of a *peculiar character*. Its peculiarity lies in that the personal character of the relation has been, so to speak, filtered. It has been cleared of the practical, concrete nature of its appeal, without, however, thereby losing its original constitution. One of the best-known examples is to be found in our attitude towards the events and characters of the drama: they appeal to us like persons and incidents of normal experience, except that that side of their appeal, which would usually affect us in a directly personal manner, is held in abeyance. This difference, so well known as to be almost trivial, is generally explained by reference to the knowledge that the characters and situations are "unreal," imaginary. . . . But, as a matter of fact, the "assumption" upon which the imaginative emotional reaction is based is not necessarily the condition, but often the consequence, of Distance; that is to say, the converse of the reason usually stated would then be true: namely, that Distance, by changing our relation to the characters, renders them seemingly fictitious, not that the fictitiousness of the characters alters our feelings toward them. It is, of course, to be granted that the actual and admitted unreality of the dramatic action reinforces the effect of Distance. But surely the proverbial unsophisticated yokel whose chivalrous interference in the play on behalf of the hapless heroine can only be prevented by impressing upon him that "they are only pretending," is not the ideal type of theatrical audience. The proof of the seeming paradox that it is Distance which primarily gives to dramatic action the appearance of unreality and not *vice versa*, is the observation that the same filtration of our sentiments and the same seeming "unreality" of *actual* men and things occur, when at times, by a sudden change of inward perspective, we are overcome by the feeling that "all the world's a stage."

2. This personal but "distanced" relation (as I will venture to call this nameless character of our view) directs attention to a strange fact which appears to be one of the fundamental paradoxes of Art: it is what I propose to call "the antinomy of Distance."

It will be readily admitted that a work of Art has the more chance of appealing to us the better it finds us prepared for its particular kind of appeal. Indeed, without some degree of predisposition on our part, it must necessarily remain incomprehensible, and to that extent unappreciated. The success and intensity of its appeal would seem, therefore, to stand in direct proportion to the completeness with which it corresponds with our intellectual and emotional peculiarities and the idiosyncrasies of our experience. The absence of such a concordance between the characters of a work and of the spectator is, of course, the most general explanation for differences of "tastes."

At the same time, such a principle of concordance requires a qualification, which leads at once to the antinomy of Distance.

Suppose a man who believes that he has cause to be jealous about his wife, witnesses a performance of *Othello*. He will the more perfectly appreciate the situation, conduct and character of Othello, the more exactly the feelings and experiences of Othello coincide with his own—at least he *ought* to on the above principle of concordance. In point of fact, he will probably do anything but appreciate the play. In reality, the concordance will merely render him acutely conscious of his own jealousy; by a sudden reversal of perspective he will no longer see Othello apparently betrayed by Desdemona, but himself in an analogous situation with his own wife. This reversal of perspective is the consequence of the loss of Distance.

If this be taken as a typical case, it follows that the qualification required is that the coincidence should be as complete as is compatible with maintaining Distance. The jealous spectator of *Othello* will indeed appreciate and enter into the play the more keenly, the greater the resemblance with his own experience—*provided* that he succeeds in keeping the Distance between the action of the play and his personal feelings: a very difficult performance in the circumstances. It is on account of the same difficulty that the expert and the professional critic make a bad audience, since their expertness and critical professionalism are *practical* activities, involving their concrete personality and constantly endangering their Distance. (It is, by the way, one of the reasons why Criticism is an art, for it requires the constant interchange from the practical to the distanced attitude and *vice versa*, which is characteristic of artists.)

The same qualification applies to the artist. He will prove artistically most effective in the formulation of an intensely *personal* experience, but he can formulate it artistically only on condition of a detachment from the experience *qua personal*. Hence the statement of so many artists that artistic formulation was to them a kind of catharsis, a means of ridding themselves of feelings and ideas the acuteness of which they felt almost as a kind of obsession. Hence, on the other hand, the failure of the average man to convey to others at all adequately the impression of an overwhelming joy or sorrow. His personal implication in the event renders it impossible for him to formulate and present it in such a way as to make others, like himself, feel all the meaning and fullness which it possesses for him.

What is therefore, both in appreciation and production, most desirable is the *utmost decrease of Distance without its disappearance.*

3. Closely related, in fact a presupposition to the "antinomy," is the *variability of Distance.* Herein especially lies the advantage of Distance compared with such terms as "objectivity" and "detachment." Neither of them implies a *personal* relation—indeed both actually preclude it; and the mere inflexibility and exclusiveness of their opposites render their application generally meaningless.

Distance, on the contrary, admits naturally of degrees, and differs not only according to the nature of the *object*, which may impose a greater or smaller degree of Distance, but varies also according to the *individual's capacity* for maintaining a greater or lesser degree. And here one may remark that not only do *persons differ from each other* in their habitual measure of Distance, but that the *same individual differs* in his ability to maintain it in the face of different objects and of different arts.

There exist, therefore, two different sets of conditions affecting the degree of Distance in any given case: those offered by the object and those realized by the subject. In their interplay they afford one of the most extensive explanations for varieties of esthetic experience, since loss of Distance, whether due to the one or the other, means loss of esthetic appreciation.

In short, Distance may be said to be *variable both according to the distancing-power of the individual, and according to the character of the object.*

There are two ways of losing Distance: either to "under-distance" or to "over-distance." "Under-distancing" is the commonest failing of the *subject,* an excess of Distance is a frequent failing of Art, especially in the past. Historically it looks almost as if Art had attempted to meet the deficiency of Distance on the part of the subject and had overshot the mark in this endeavor. It will be seen later that this is actually true, for it appears that over-distanced Art is specially designed for a class of appreciation which has difficulty to rise spontaneously to any degree of Distance. The consequence of a loss of Distance through one or other cause is familiar: the verdict in the case of under-distancing is that the work is "crudely naturalistic," "harrowing," "repulsive in its realism." An excess of Distance produces the impression of improbability, artificiality, emptiness or absurdity.

The individual tends, as I just stated, to under-distance rather than to lose Distance by over-distancing. *Theoretically* there is no limit to the decrease of Distance. In theory, therefore, not only the usual subjects of Art, but even the most personal affections, whether ideas, percepts, or emotions, can be sufficiently distanced to be esthetically appreciable. Especially artists are gifted in this direction to a remarkable extent. The average individual, on the contrary, very rapidly reaches his limit of decreasing Distance, his "Distance-limit," that is, that point at which Distance is lost and appreciation either disappears or changes its character.

In the *practice,* therefore, of the average person, a limit does exist which marks the minimum at which his appreciation can maintain itself in the esthetic field, and this average minimum lies considerably higher than the Distance-limit of the artist. It is practically impossible to fix this average limit, in the absence of data, and on account of the wide fluctuations from person to person to which this limit is subject. But it is safe to infer that, in art practice, explicit references to organic affections, to the material existence of the body, especially to sexual matters, lies normally below the Distance-limit, and can be touched upon by Art only with special precautions. Allusions to social institutions of any degree of personal importance —in particular, allusions implying any doubt as to their validity—the questioning of some generally recognized ethical sanctions, references to topical subjects occupying public attention at the moment, and such like, are all dangerously near the average limit and may at any time fall below it, arousing, instead of esthetic appreciation, concrete hostility or mere amusement.

This difference in the Distance-limit between artists and the public has been the source of much misunderstanding and injustice. Many an artist has seen his work condemned, and himself ostracized for the sake of so-called "immoralities" which to him were *bona fide* esthetic objects. His power of distancing, nay, the necessity of distancing feelings, sensations, situations which for the average person are too intimately bound up with his concrete existence to be regarded in that light, have often quite unjustly earned for him accusations of cynicism, sensualism, morbidness, or frivolity. The same misconception has arisen over many "problem plays" and "problem novels" in which the public have persisted in seeing nothing but a supposed "problem" of the moment, whereas the author may have been —and often has demonstrably been—able to distance the subject matter sufficiently to· rise above its practical problematic import and to regard it simply as a dramatically and humanly interesting situation.

The variability of Distance in respect to Art, disregarding for the moment the subjective complication, appears both as a general feature in Art, and in the differences between the special arts.

It has been an old problem why the "arts of the eye and of the ear" should have reached the practically exclusive predominance over arts of other senses. Attempts to raise "culinary art" to the level of a Fine Art have failed in spite of all propaganda, as completely as the creation of scent or liquor "symphonies." There is little doubt that, apart from other excellent reasons of a partly psycho-physical, partly technical nature, the actual, *spatial distance* separating objects of sight and hearing from the subject has contributed strongly to the development of this monopoly. In a similar manner *temporal remoteness* produces Distance, and objects removed from us in point of time are *ipso facto* distanced to an extent which was impossible for their contemporaries. Many pictures, plays, and poems had, as a matter of fact, rather an expository or illustrative significance—as for instance much ecclesiastical Art—or the force of a direct practical appeal— as the invectives of many satires or comedies—which seem to us nowadays irreconcilable with their esthetic claims. Such works have consequently profited greatly by lapse of time and have reached the level of Art only with the help of temporal distance, while others, on the contrary, often for the same reason have suffered a loss of Distance, through *over*-distancing.

Special mention must be made of a group of artistic conceptions which present excessive Distance in their form of appeal rather than in their actual presentation—a point illustrating the necessity of distinguishing between distancing an object and distancing the appeal of which it is the source. I mean here what is often rather loosely termed "idealistic Art," that is, Art springing from abstract conceptions, expressing allegorical meanings, or illustrating general truths. Generalizations and abstractions suffer under this disadvantage that they have too much general applicability to invite a personal interest in them, and too little individual concreteness to prevent them applying to us in all their force. They appeal to everybody and therefore to none. An axiom of Euclid belongs to nobody, just because it compels every one's assent; general conceptions like Patriotism, Friendship, Love, Hope, Life, Death, concern as much Dick, Tom and Harry as myself, and I, therefore, either feel unable to get into any kind of personal relation to them, or, if I do so, they become at once, emphatically and concretely, *my* Patriotism, *my* Friendship, *my* Love, *my* Hope, *my* Life and Death. By mere force of generalization, a general truth or a universal ideal is so far distanced from myself that I fail to realize it concretely at all, or, when I do so, I can realize it only as part of my *practical actual being*, that is, it falls below the Distance-limit altogether. "Idealistic Art" suffers consequently under the peculiar difficulty that its excess of Distance turns generally into an *under*-distanced appeal—all the more easily, as it is the usual failing of the subject to *under-* rather than to *over*-distance.

The different special arts show at the present time very marked variations in the degree of Distance which they usually impose or require for their appreciation. Unfortunately here again the absence of data makes itself felt and indicates the necessity of conducting observations, possibly experiments, so as to place these suggestions upon a securer basis. In one single art, namely, the *theater*, a small amount of information is available, from an unexpected source, namely the proceedings of the censorship committee,[1] which on closer examination might be made to yield evidence of interest to the psychologist. In fact, the whole censorship problem, as far as it does not turn upon purely economic questions, may be said to hinge upon Distance; if every member of the public could be trusted to keep it, there would be no sense whatever in the existence of a censor of plays. There is, of course, no doubt that, speaking generally, theatrical performances *eo ipso* run a special risk of a loss of Distance owing to the material presentment[2] of its subject-matter. The physical presence of living human beings as vehicles of dramatic art is a difficulty which no art has to face in the same way. A similar, in many ways even greater, risk confronts *dancing*: though attracting perhaps a less widely spread human interest, its animal spirits are frequently quite unrelieved by any glimmer of spirituality and consequently form a proportionately stronger lure to under-distancing. In the higher forms of dancing technical execution of the most wearing kind makes up a great deal for its intrinsic tendency towards a loss of Distance, and as a popular performance, at least in southern Europe, it has retained much of its ancient artistic glamour, producing a peculiarly subtle balancing of Distance between the pure delight of bodily movement and high technical accomplishment. In passing, it is interesting to observe (as bearing upon the development of Distance), that this art, once as much a fine art as music and considered by the Greeks as a particularly valuable educational exercise, should—except in sporadic cases—have fallen so low from the pedestal it once occupied. Next to the theater and dancing stands *sculpture*. Though not using a *living* bodily medium, yet the human form in its full spatial materiality constitutes a similar threat to Distance. Our northern habits of dress and ignorance of the human body have enormously increased the difficulty of distancing Sculpture, in part through the gross misconceptions to which it is exposed, in part owing to a complete lack of standards of bodily perfection, and an inability to realize the distinction between sculptural form and bodily shape, which is the only but fundamental point distinguishing a statue from a cast taken from life. In *painting* it is apparently the form of its presentment and the usual reduction in scale which would explain why this art can venture to approach more closely than sculpture to the normal Distance-limit. As this matter will be discussed later in a special connection this simple reference may suffice here.

Music and *architecture* have a curious position. These two most abstract of all arts show a remarkable fluctuation in their Distances. Certain kinds of music, especially "pure" music, or "classical" or "heavy" music, appear for many people over-distanced; light, "catchy" tunes, on the contrary, easily reach that degree of decreasing Distance below which they cease to be Art and become a pure amusement. In spite of its strange abstractness which to many philosophers has made it comparable to architecture and mathematics, music possesses a sensuous, frequently sensual character: the undoubted physiological and muscular stimulus of its melodies and harmonies, no less than its rhythmic aspects, would seem to account for the occasional disappearance of Distance. To this might be added its strong tendency, especially in unmusical people, to stimulate trains of thought quite disconnected with itself, following channels of subjective inclinations —daydreams of a more or less directly personal character. *Architecture* requires almost uniformly a very great Distance; that is to say, the majority of persons derive no esthetic appreciation from architecture as such, apart from the incidental impression of its decorative features and its associations. The causes are numerous, but prominent among them are the confusion of building with architecture and the predominance of utilitarian purposes, which overshadow the architectural claims upon the attention.

4. That all art requires a Distance-limit beyond which, and a Distance within which only, esthetic appreciation becomes possible, is the *psychological formulation of a general characteristic of Art*, namely, its *anti-realistic nature*. Though seemingly paradoxical, this applies as much to "naturalistic" as to "idealistic" Art. The difference commonly expressed by these epithets is at bottom merely the difference in the degree of Distance; and this produces, so far as "naturalism" and "idealism" in Art are not meaningless labels, the usual result that what appears obnoxiously "naturalistic" to one person, may be "idealistic" to another. To say that Art is anti-realistic simply insists upon the fact that Art is not nature, never pretends to be nature and strongly resists any confusion with nature. It emphasizes the *art*-character of Art: "artistic" is synonymous with "anti-realistic"; it explains even sometimes a very marked degree of artificiality.

"Art is an imitation of nature," was the current art-conception in the eighteenth century. It is the fundamental axiom of the standard-work of that time upon esthetic theory by the Abbé Du Bos, *Réflexions critiques sur la poésie et la peinture*, 1719; the idea received strong support from the literal acceptance of Aristotle's theory of μίμησις [imitation] and produced echoes everywhere, in Lessing's *Laocoön* no less than in Burke's famous statement that "all Art is great as it deceives." Though it may be assumed that since the time of Kant and of the Romanticists this notion has died out, it still lives in unsophisticated minds. Even when formally denied, it persists, for instance, in the belief that "Art idealizes nature," which means after all only that Art copies nature with certain improvements and revisions. Artists themselves are unfortunately often responsible for the spreading of this conception. Whistler indeed said that to produce Art by imitating nature would be like trying to produce music by sitting upon the piano, but the selective, idealizing imitation of nature finds merely another support in such a saying. Naturalism, pleinairism, impressionism—even the guileless enthusiasm of the artist for the works of nature, her wealth of suggestion, her delicacy of workmanship, for the steadfastness of her guidance, only produce upon the public the impression that Art is, after all, an imitation of nature. Then how can it be anti-realistic? The antithesis, Art *versus* nature, seems to break down. Yet if it does, what is the sense of Art?

Here the conception of Distance comes to the rescue. The solution of the dilemma lies in the "antinomy of Distance" with its demand: utmost decrease of Distance without its disappearance. The simple observation that Art is the more effective, the more it falls into line with our predisposi-tions which are inevitably molded on general experience and nature, has always been the original motive for "naturalism." "Naturalism," "impres-sionism" is no new thing; it is only a new name for an innate leaning of Art, from the time of the Chaldeans and Egyptians down to the present day. Even the Apollo of Tenea apparently struck his contemporaries as so startlingly "naturalistic" that the subsequent legend attributed a super-human genius to his creator. A constantly closer approach to nature, a perpetual refining of the limit of Distance, yet without overstepping the dividing line of art and nature, has always been the inborn bent of art. To deny this dividing line has occasionally been the failing of naturalism. But no theory of naturalism is complete which does not at the same time allow for the intrinsic idealism of Art: for both are merely degrees in that wide range lying beyond the Distance-limit. To imitate nature so as to trick the spectator into the deception that it is nature which he beholds, is to for-sake Art, its anti-realism, its distanced spirituality, and to fall below the limit into sham, sensationalism, or platitude.

But what, in the theory of antinomy of Distance requires explanation is the existence of an *idealistic, highly distanced* Art. There are numerous reasons to account for it; indeed in so complex a phenomenon as Art, single causes can be pronounced almost *a priori* to be false. Foremost among such causes which have contributed to the formation of an idealistic Art appears to stand the subordination of Art to some extraneous purpose of an impressive, exceptional character. Such a subordination has consisted —at various epochs of Art history—in the use to which Art was put to subserve commemorative, hieratic, generally religious, royal or patriotic functions. The object to be commemorated had to stand out from among other still existing objects or persons; the thing or the being to be wor-shiped had to be distinguished as markedly as possible from profaner objects of reverence and had to be invested with an air of sanctity by a removal from its ordinary context of occurrence. Nothing could have assisted more powerfully the introduction of a high Distance than this attempt to differentiate objects of common experience in order to fit them for their exalted position. Curious, unusual things of nature met this tendency half-way and easily assumed divine rank; but others had to be distanced by an exaggeration of their size, by extraordinary attributes, by strange combinations of human and animal forms, by special insistence upon particular characteristics, or by the careful removal of all noticeably individualistic and concrete features. Nothing could be more striking than the contrast, for example, in Egyptian Art between the monumental, stereotyped effigies of the Pharaohs, and the startlingly realistic rendering of domestic scenes and of ordinary mortals, such as "the Scribe" or "the Village Sheik." Equally noteworthy is the exceeding artificiality of Russian ikon-painting with its prescribed attributes, expressions and gestures. Even Greek dramatic practice appears to have aimed, for similar purposes and in marked contrast to our stage-habits, at an increase rather than at a decrease of Distance. Otherwise Greek Art, even of a religious type, is remarkable for its *low* Distance value; and it speaks highly for the esthetic capacities of the Greeks that the degree of realism which they ventured to impart to the representations of their gods, while humanizing them, did not, at least at first,[3] impair the reverence of their feelings towards them. But apart from such special causes, idealistic Art of great Distance has appeared at intervals, for apparently no other reason than that the great Distance was felt to be essential to its *art*-character. What is noteworthy and runs counter to many accepted ideas is that such periods were usually epochs of a low level of general culture. These were times, which, like childhood, required the marvelous, the extraordinary, to satisfy their artistic longings, and neither realized nor cared for the poetic or artistic qualities of ordinary things. They were frequently times in which the mass of the people were plunged in ignorance and buried under a load of misery, and in which even the small educated class sought rather amusement or a pastime in Art; or they were epochs of a strong practical common sense too much concerned with the rough-and-tumble of life to have any sense of its esthetic charms. Art was to them what melodrama is to a section of the public at the present time, and its wide Distance was the safeguard of its artistic character. The flowering periods of Art have, on the contrary, always borne the evidence of a narrow Distance. Greek Art, as just mentioned, was realistic to an extent which we, spoilt as we are by modern developments, can grasp with difficulty, but which the contrast with its oriental contemporaries sufficiently proves. During the Augustan period— which Art historians at last are coming to regard no longer as merely "degenerated" Greek Art—Roman Art achieved its greatest triumphs in an almost naturalistic portrait-sculpture. In the Renaissance we need only think of the realism of portraiture, sometimes amounting almost to cynicism, of the *désinvolture* with which the mistresses of popes and dukes were posed as madonnas, saints and goddesses apparently without any detriment to the esthetic appeal of the works, and of the remarkable interpenetration of Art with the most ordinary routine of life, in order to realize the scarcely perceptible dividing line between the sphere of Art and the realm of practical existence. In a sense, the assertion that idealistic Art marks periods of a generally low and narrowly restricted culture is the converse to the oft-repeated statement that the flowering periods of Art coincide with epochs of decadence: for this so-called decadence represents indeed in certain respects a process of disintegration, politically, racially, often nationally, but a disruption necessary to the formation of larger social units and to the breakdown of outgrown national restrictions. For this very reason it has usually also been the sign of the growth of personal independence and of an expansion of individual culture.

To proceed to some more special points illustrating the distanced and therefore anti-realistic character of art—both in subject matter and in the form of presentation Art has always safeguarded its distanced view. Fanciful, even phantastic, subjects have from time immemorial been the accredited material of Art. No doubt things, as well as our view of them, have changed in the course of time: *Polyphemus* and the *Lotus-Eaters* for the Greeks, the *Venusberg* or the *Magnetic Mountain* for the Middle Ages were less incredible, more realistic than to us. But *Peter Pan* or *L'Oiseau Bleu* still appeal at the present day in spite of the prevailing note of realism of our time. "Probability" and "improbability" in Art are not to be measured by their correspondence (or lack of it) with actual experience. To do so had involved the theories of the fifteenth to the eighteenth centuries in endless contradictions. It is rather a matter of *consistency* of Distance. The note of realism, set by a work as a whole, determines *intrinsically* the greater or smaller degree of fancy which it permits; and consequently we feel the loss of Peter Pan's shadow to be infinitely more probable than some trifling improbability which shocks our sense of proportion in a naturalistic work. No doubt also, fairy tales, fairy plays, stories of strange adventures were primarily invented to satisfy the craving of curiosity, the desire for the marvelous, the shudder of the unwonted and the longing for imaginary experiences. But by their mere eccentricity in regard to the normal facts of experience they cannot have failed to arouse a strong feeling of Distance.

Again, certain conventional subjects taken from mythical and legendary traditions, at first closely connected with the concrete, practical life of a devout public, have gradually, by the mere force of convention as much as by their inherent anti-realism, acquired Distance for us today. Our view of Greek mythological sculpture, of early Christian saints and martyrs must be considerably distanced, compared with that of the Greek and medieval worshiper. It is in part the result of lapse of time, but in part also a real change of attitude. Already the outlook of the Imperial Roman had altered, and Pausanias shows a curious dualism of standpoint, declaring the Athene Lemnia to be the supreme achievement of Phidias's genius, and gazing awe-struck upon the roughly hewn tree trunk representing some primitive Apollo. Our understanding of Greek tragedy suffers admittedly under our inability to revert to the point of view for which it was originally written. Even the tragedies of Racine demand an imaginative effort to put ourselves back into the courtly atmosphere of red-heeled, powdered ceremony. Provided the Distance is not too wide, the result of its intervention has everywhere been to enhance the *art*-character of such works and to lower their original ethical and social force of appeal. Thus in the central dome of the Church (Sta Maria dei Miracoli) at Saronno are depicted the heavenly hosts in ascending tiers, crowned by the benevolent figure of the Divine Father, bending from the window of heaven to bestow His blessing upon the assembled community. The mere realism of foreshortening and of the boldest vertical perspective may well have made the naïve Christian of the sixteenth century conscious of the Divine Presence—but for us it has become a work of Art.

The unusual, exceptional, has found its especial home in tragedy. It has always—except in highly distanced tragedy—been a popular objection to it

that "there is enough sadness in life without going to the theater for it."
Already Aristotle appears to have met with this view among his contemporaries clamoring for "happy endings." Yet tragedy is not sad; if it
were, there would indeed be little sense in its existence. For the tragic is
just in so far different from the merely sad, as it is distanced; and it is
largely the exceptional which produces the Distance of tragedy: exceptional
situations, exceptional characters, exceptional destinies and conduct. Not
of course, characters merely cranky, eccentric, pathological. The exceptional element in tragic figures—that which makes them so utterly different
from characters we meet with in ordinary experience—is a consistency of
direction, a fervor of ideality, a persistence and driving-force which is far
above the capacities of average men. The tragic of tragedy would, transposed into ordinary life, in nine cases out of ten, end in drama, in comedy,
even in farce, for lack of steadfastness, for fear of conventions, for the dread
of "scenes," for a hundred-and-one petty faithlessnesses toward a belief or
an ideal: even if for none of these, it would end in a compromise simply
because man forgets and time heals.[4] Again, the sympathy which aches
with the sadness of tragedy is another such confusion, the under-distancing
of tragedy's appeal. Tragedy trembles always on the knife-edge of a *personal* reaction, and sympathy which finds relief in tears tends almost always
towards a loss of Distance. Such a loss naturally renders tragedy unpleasant
to a degree: it becomes sad, dismal, harrowing, depressing. But real tragedy
(melodrama has a very strong tendency to speculate upon sympathy),
truly appreciated, is not sad. "The pity of it—oh, the pity of it," that
essence of all genuine tragedy is not the pity of mild, regretful sympathy.
It is a chaos of tearless, bitter bewilderment, of upsurging revolt and rapturous awe before the ruthless and inscrutable fate; it is the homage to the
great and exceptional in the man who in a last effort of spiritual tension
can rise to confront blind, crowning Necessity even in his crushing defeat.

As I explained earlier, the form of presentation sometimes endangers
the maintenance of Distance, but it more frequently acts as a considerable
support. Thus the bodily vehicle of *drama* is the chief factor of risk to
Distance. But, as if to counterbalance a confusion with nature, other features of stage-presentation exercise an opposite influence. Such are the general theatrical *milieu*, the shape and arrangement of the stage, the artificial
lighting, the costumes, *mise-en-scène* and make-up, even the language,
especially verse. Modern reforms of staging, aiming primarily at the removal
of artistic incongruities between excessive decoration and the living figures
of the actors and at the production of a more homogeneous stage-picture,
inevitably work also towards a greater emphasis and homogeneity of Distance. The history of staging and dramaturgy is closely bound up with the
evolution of Distance, and its fluctuations lie at the bottom not only of the
greater part of all the talk and writing about "dramatic probability" and
the Aristotelian "unities," but also of "theatrical illusion." In *sculpture*, one
distancing factor of presentment is its lack of color. The esthetic, or rather
inesthetic effect of realistic coloring, is in no way touched by the contro-
versial question of its use historically; its attempted resuscitation, such as
by Klinger, seems only to confirm its disadvantages. The distancing use
even of pedestals, although originally no doubt serving other purposes, is

evident to anyone who has experienced the oppressively crowded sensation of moving in a room among life-size statues placed directly upon the floor. The circumstance that the space of statuary is the same space as ours (in distinction to relief sculpture or painting, for instance) renders a distancing by pedestals, that is, a removal from our spatial context, imperative.[5] Probably the framing of *pictures* might be shown to serve a similar purpose—though paintings have intrinsically a much greater Distance— because neither their space (perspective and imaginary space) nor their lighting coincides with our (actual) space or light, and the usual reduction in scale of the represented objects prevents a feeling of undue proximity. Besides, painting always retains to some extent a *two*-dimensional character, and this character supplies *eo ipso* a Distance. Nevertheless, life-size pictures, especially if they possess strong relief, and their light happens to coincide with the actual lighting, can occasionally produce the impression of actual presence which is a far from pleasant, though fortunately only a passing, illusion. For decorative purposes, in pictorial renderings of vistas, garden-perspectives and architectural extensions, the removal of Distance has often been consciously striven after, whether with esthetically satisfactory results is much disputed.

A general help towards Distance (and therewith an anti-realistic feature) is to be found in the "unification of presentment"[6] of all art-objects. By unification of presentment are meant such qualities as symmetry, opposition, proportion, balance, rhythmical distribution of parts, light-arrangements, in fact all so-called "formal" features, "composition" in the widest sense. Unquestionably, Distance is not the only, nor even the principal function of composition; it serves to render our grasp of the presentation easier and to increase its intelligibility. It may even in itself constitute the principal esthetic feature of the object, as in linear complexes or patterns, partly also in architectural designs. Yet, its distancing effect can hardly be underrated. For, every kind of visibly intentional arrangement or unification must, by the mere fact of its presence, enforce Distance, by distinguishing the object from the confused, disjointed, and scattered forms of actual experience. This function can be gauged in a typical form in cases where composition produces an exceptionally marked impression of artificiality (not in the bad sense of that term, but in the sense in which all art is artificial); and it is a natural corollary to the differences of Distance in different arts and of different subjects, that the arts and subjects vary in the degree of artificiality which they can bear. It is this sense of artificial finish which is the source of so much of that elaborate charm of Byzantine work, of Mohammedan decoration, of the hieratic stiffness of so many primitive madonnas and saints. In general the emphasis of composition and technical finish increases with the Distance of the subject matter: heroic conceptions lend themselves better to verse than to prose; monumental statues require a more general treatment, more elaboration of setting and artificiality of pose than impressionistic statuettes like those of Troubetzkoi; an ecclesiastic subject is painted with a degree of symmetrical arrangement which would be ridiculous in a Dutch interior, and a naturalistic drama carefully avoids the tableau impression characteristic of a mystery play. In similar manner the variations of Distance in the arts go hand in hand with a visibly greater predominance of composition and "formal" elements, reaching a climax in architecture and music. It is again a matter of "consistency of Distance." At the same time, while from the point of view of the artist this is undoubtedly the case, from the point of view of the public the emphasis of composition and technical finish appears frequently to relieve the impression of highly distanced subjects by *diminishing the Distance of the whole.* The spectator has a tendency to see in composition and finish merely evidence of the artist's "cleverness," of his mastery over his material. Manual dexterity is an enviable thing to possess in every one's experience, and naturally appeals to the public *practically*, thereby putting it into a directly personal relation to things which intrinsically have very little personal appeal for it. It is true that this function of composition is hardly an esthetic one: for the admiration of mere technical cleverness is not an artistic enjoyment, but by a fortunate chance it has saved from oblivion and entire loss, among much rubbish, also much genuine Art, which otherwise would have completely lost contact with our life.

5. This discussion, necessarily sketchy and incomplete, may have helped to illustrate the sense in which, I suggested, Distance appears as a fundamental principle to which such antitheses as idealism and realism are reducible. The difference between "idealistic" and "realistic" Art is not a clear-cut dividing-line between the art-practices described by these terms, but is a difference of degree in the Distance-limit which they presuppose on the part both of the artist and of the public. A similar reconciliation seems to me possible between the opposites "sensual" and "spiritual," "individual" and "typical." That the appeal of Art is sensuous, even sensual, must be taken as an indisputable fact. Puritanism will never be persuaded, and rightly so, that this is not the case. The sensuousness of Art is a natural implication of the "antinomy of Distance," and will appear again in another connection. The point of importance here is that the whole sensual side of Art is purified, spiritualized, "filtered" as I expressed it earlier, by Distance. The most sensual appeal becomes the translucent veil of an underlying spirituality, once the grossly personal and practical elements have been removed from it. And—a matter of special emphasis here—*this spiritual aspect of the appeal is the more penetrating, the more personal and direct its sensual appeal would have been* BUT FOR THE PRESENCE OF DISTANCE. For the artist, to trust in this delicate transmutation is a natural act of faith which the Puritan hesitates to venture upon: which of the two, one asks, is the greater idealist?

6. The same argument applies to the contradictory epithets "individual" and "typical." A discussion in support of the fundamental individualism of Art lies outside the scope of this essay. Every artist has taken it for granted. Besides it is rather in the sense of "concrete" or "individualized," that it is usually opposed to "typical." On the other hand, "typical," in the sense of "abstract," is as diametrically opposed to the whole nature of Art, as individualism is characteristic of it. It is in the sense of "generalized" as a "general human element" that it is claimed as a necessary ingredient in Art. This antithesis is again one which naturally and without mutual sacrifice finds room within the conception of Distance. Historically the "typical" has had the effect of counteracting *under*-distancing as much as

the "individual" has opposed *over*-distancing. Naturally the two ingredients have constantly varied in the history of Art; they represent, in fact, two sets of conditions to which Art has invariably been subject: the personal and the social factors. It is Distance which on one side prevents the emptying of Art of its concreteness and the development of the typical into abstractness; which, on the other, suppresses the directly personal element of its individualism; thus reducing the antitheses to the peaceful interplay of these two factors. It is just this interplay which constitutes the "antinomy of Distance."

—*British Journal of Psychology*, Volume V (1913)

NOTES

1. Report from the Joint Select Committee of the House of Lords and the House of Commons on the Stage Plays (Censorship), 1909.
2. I shall use the term "presentment" to denote the manner of presenting, in distinction to "presentation" as that which is presented.
3. That this practice did, in course of time, undermine their religious faith, is clear from the plays of Euripides and from Plato's condemnation of Homer's mythology.
4. The famous "unity of time," so senseless as a "canon," is all the same often an indispensible condition of tragedy. For in many a tragedy the catastrophe would be even intrinsically impossible, if fatality did not overtake the hero with that rush which gives no time to forget and none to heal. It is in cases such as these that criticism has often blamed the work for "improbability"—the old confusion between Art and nature—forgetting that the death of the hero is the convention of the art-form, as much as grouping in a picture is such a convention and that probability is not the correspondence with average experience, but consistency of Distance.
5. An instance which might be adduced to disprove this point only shows its correctness on closer inspection: for it was on purpose and with the intention of removing Distance, that Rodin originally intended his *Citoyens de Calais* to be placed, without pedestals, upon the marketplace of that town.
6. See note 2, *ante*.

KENNETH CLARK

The Naked and the Nude

The English language, with its elaborate generosity, distinguishes between the naked and the nude. To be naked is to be deprived of our clothes, and the word implies some of the embarrassment most of us feel in that condition. The word "nude," on the other hand, carries, in educated usage, no uncomfortable overtone. The vague image it projects into the mind is not of a huddled and defenseless body, but of a balanced, prosperous, and confident body: the body re-formed. In fact, the word was forced into our vocabulary by critics of the early eighteenth century to persuade the artless islanders that, in countries where painting and sculpture were practiced and valued as they should be, the naked human body was the central subject of art.

For this belief there is a quantity of evidence. In the greatest age of painting, the nude inspired the greatest works; and even when it ceased to be a compulsive subject it held its position as an academic exercise and a demonstration of mastery. Velásquez, living in the prudish and corseted court of Philip IV and admirably incapable of idealization, yet felt bound to paint the *Rokeby Venus*. Sir Joshua Reynolds, wholly without the gift of formal draftsmanship, set great store by his *Cymon and Iphigenia*. And in our own century, when we have shaken off one by one those inheritances of Greece which were revived at the Renaissance, discarded the antique armor, forgotten the subjects of mythology, and disputed the doctrine of imitation, the nude alone has survived. It may have suffered some curious transformations, but it remains our chief link with the classic disciplines. When we wish to prove to the Philistine that our great revolutionaries are really respectable artists in the tradition of European painting, we point to their drawings of the nude. Picasso has often exempted it from that savage metamorphosis which he has inflicted on the visible world and has produced a series of nudes that might have walked unaltered off the back of a Greek mirror; and Henry Moore, searching in stone for the ancient laws of its material and seeming to find there some of those elementary creatures of whose fossilized bones it is composed, yet gives to his constructions the same fundamental character that was invented by the sculptors of the Parthenon in the fifth century before Christ.

These comparisons suggest a short answer to the question, "What is the nude?" It is an art form invented by the Greeks in the fifth century, just as opera is an art form invented in seventeenth-century Italy. The conclusion is certainly too abrupt, but it has the merit of emphasizing that the nude is not the subject of art, but a form of art.

It is widely supposed that the naked human body is in itself an object upon which the eye dwells with pleasure and which we are glad to see depicted. But anyone who has frequented art schools and seen the shapeless, pitiful model that the students are industriously drawing will know this is an illusion. The body is not one of those subjects which can be made into art by direct transcription—like a tiger or a snowy landscape. Often in looking at the natural and animal world we joyfully identify ourselves with what we see and from this happy union create a work of art. This is the process students of esthetics call empathy, and it is at the opposite pole of creative activity to the state of mind that has produced the nude. A mass of naked figures does not move us to empathy, but to disillusion and dismay. We do not wish to imitate; we wish to perfect. We become, in the physical sphere, like Diogenes with his lantern looking for an honest man; and, like him, we may never be rewarded. Photographers of the nude are presumably engaged in this search, with every advantage; and having found a model who pleases them, they are free to pose and light her in conformity with their notions of beauty; finally, they can tone down and accentuate by retouching. But in spite of all their taste and skill, the result is hardly ever satisfactory to those whose eyes have grown accustomed to the harmonious simplifications of antiquity. We are immediately disturbed by wrinkles, pouches, and other small imperfections, which, in the classical scheme, are eliminated. By long habit we do not judge it as a living organism, but as a design; and we discover that the transitions are inconclusive, the outline is faltering. We are bothered because the various parts of the body cannot be perceived as simple units and have no clear relationship to one another. In almost every detail the body is not the shape that art had led us to believe it should be. Yet we can look with pleasure at photographs of trees and animals, where the canon of perfection is less strict. Consciously or unconsciously, photographers have usually recognized that in a photograph of the nude their real object is not to reproduce the naked body, but to imitate some artist's view of what the naked body should be. Rejlander was the most Philistine of the early photographers, but, perhaps without knowing it, he was a contemporary of Courbet, and with this splendid archetype somewhere in the background he produced one of the finest (as well as one of the first) photographs of the nude. He succeeded partly because his unconscious archetype was a realist. The more nearly ideal the model, the more unfortunate the photographs that try to imitate it—as those in the style of Ingres or Whistler prove.

So that although the naked body is no more than the point of departure for a work of art, it is a pretext of great importance. In the history of art, the subjects that men have chosen as nuclei, so to say, of their sense of order have often been in themselves unimportant. For hundreds of years, and over an area stretching from Ireland to China, the most vital expression of order was an imaginary animal biting its own tail. In the Middle Ages drapery took on a life of its own, the same life that had inhabited the twisting animal, and became the vital pattern of Romanesque art. In neither case had the subject any independent existence. But the human body, as a nucleus, is rich in associations, and when it is turned into art these associations are not entirely lost. For this reason it seldom achieves the concentrated esthetic shock of animal ornament, but it can be made expressive of a far wider and more civilizing experience. It is ourselves and arouses memories of all the things we wish to do with ourselves; and first of all we wish to perpetuate ourselves.

This is an aspect of the subject so obvious that I need hardly dwell on it; and yet some wise men have tried to close their eyes to it. "If the nude," says Professor Alexander, "is so treated that it raises in the spectator ideas or desires appropriate to the material subject, it is false art, and bad morals." This high-minded theory is contrary to experience. In the mixture of memories and sensations aroused by Rubens' *Andromeda* or Renoir's *Bather* are many that are "appropriate to the material subject." And since these words of a famous philosopher are often quoted, it is necessary to labor the obvious and say that no nude, however abstract, should fail to arouse in the spectator some vestige of erotic feeling, even though it be only the faintest shadow—and if it does not do so, it is bad art and false morals. The desire to grasp and be united with another human body is so fundamental a part of our nature that our judgment of what is known as "pure form" is inevitably influenced by it; and one of the difficulties of the nude as a subject for art is that these instincts cannot lie hidden, as they do, for example, in our enjoyment of a piece of pottery, thereby gaining the force of sublimation, but are dragged into the foreground, where they risk upsetting the unity of responses from which a work of art derives its independent life. Even so, the amount of erotic content a work of art can hold in solution is very high. The temple sculptures of tenth-century India are an undisguised exaltation of physical desire; yet they are great works of art because their eroticism is part of their whole philosophy.

Apart from biological needs, there are other branches of human experiences of which the naked body provides a vivid reminder—harmony, energy, ecstasy, humility, pathos; and when we see the beautiful results of such embodiments, it must seem as if the nude as a means of expression is of universal and eternal value. But this we know historically to be untrue. It has been limited both in place and in time. There are naked figures in the paintings of the Far East; but only by an extension of the term can they be called nudes. In Japanese prints they are part of *ukioye*, the passing show of life, which includes, without comment, certain intimate scenes usually allowed to pass unrecorded. The idea of offering the body for its own sake, as a serious subject of contemplation, simply did not occur to the Chinese or Japanese mind, and to this day raises a slight barrier of misunderstanding. In the Gothic North the position was fundamentally very similar. It is true that German painters in the Renaissance, finding that the naked body was a respected subject in Italy, adapted it to their needs, and evolved a remarkable convention of their own. But Dürer's struggles show how artificial this creation was. His instinctive responses were curiosity and horror, and he had to draw a great many circles and other diagrams before he could brace himself to turn the unfortunate body into the nude.

Only in countries touching on the Mediterranean has the nude been at home; and even there its meaning was often forgotten. The Etruscans, owing three quarters of their art to Greece, never abandoned a type of tomb figure in which the defunct man displays his stomach with a complacency that would have shocked a Greek profoundly. Hellenistic and Roman art produced statues and mosaics of professional athletes who seem satisfied with their monstrous proportions. More remarkable still, of course, is the way in which the nude, even in Italy and Greece, is limited by time. It is the fashion to speak of Byzantine art as if it were a continuation of Greek; the nude reminds us that this is one of the refined excesses of specialization. Between the Nereids of late Roman silver and the golden doors of Ghiberti the nudes in Mediterranean art are few and insignificant —a piece of modest craftsmanship like the Ravenna ivory *Apollo and Daphne*, a few *objets de luxe*, like the Veroli Casket, with its cartoon-strip Olympus, and a number of Adams and Eves whose nakedness seldom shows any memory of antique form. Yet, during a great part of that millennium, the masterpieces of Greek art had not yet been destroyed, and men were surrounded by representations of the nude more numerous and, alas, infinitely more splendid than any that have come down to us. As late as the tenth century the *Knidian Aphrodite* of Praxiteles, which had been carried to Constantinople, it is said, by Theodosius, was praised by the Emperor Constantine Porphyrogenitus; and a famous bronze copy of it is mentioned by Robert de Clari in his account of the taking of Constantinople by the Crusaders. Moreover, the body itself did not cease to be an object of interest in Byzantium: this we may deduce from the continuation of the race. Athletes performed in the circus; workmen, stripped to the waist, toiled at the building of St. Sophia. There was no want of opportunity for artists. That their patrons did not demand representations of the nude during this period may be explained by a number of reasonable-looking causes—fear of idolatry, the fashion for asceticism, or the influence of Eastern art. But in fact such answers are incomplete. The nude had ceased to be the subject of art almost a century before the official establishment of Christianity. And during the Middle Ages there would have been ample opportunity to introduce it both into profane decoration and into such sacred subjects as show the beginning and the end of our existence.

Why, then, does it never appear? An illuminating answer is to be found in the notebook of the thirteenth-century architect, Villard de Honnecourt. This contains many beautiful drawings of draped figures, some of them showing a high degree of skill. But when Villard draws two nude figures in what he believes to be the antique style the result is painfully ugly. It was impossible for him to adapt the stylistic conventions of Gothic art to a subject that depended on an entirely different system of forms. There can be few more hopeless misunderstandings in art than his attempt to render that refined abstraction, the antique torso, in terms of Gothic loops and pothooks. Moreover, Villard has constructed his figures according to the pointed geometrical scheme of which he himself gives us the key on another page. He evidently felt that the divine element in the human body must be expressed through geometry. Cennino Cennini, the last chronicler of medieval practice, says, "I will not tell you about irrational animals, because I have never learned any of their measurements. Draw them from nature, and in this respect you will achieve a good style." The Gothic artists could draw animals because this involved no intervening abstraction. But they could not draw the nude because it was an idea: an idea that their philosophy of form could not assimilate.

As I have said, in our Diogenes search for physical beauty our instinctive desire is not to imitate but to perfect. This is part of our Greek inheritance, and it was formulated by Aristotle with his usual deceptive simplicity. "Art," he says, "completes what nature cannot bring to a finish. The artist gives us knowledge of nature's unrealized ends." A great many assumptions underlie this statement, the chief of which is that everything has an ideal form of which the phenomena of experience are more or less corrupted replicas. This beautiful fancy has teased the minds of philosophers and writers on esthetics for over two thousand years, and although we need not plunge into a sea of speculation, we cannot discuss the nude without considering its practical application, because every time we criticize a figure, saying that a neck is too long, hips are too wide or breasts too small, we are admitting, in quite concrete terms, the existence of ideal beauty. Critical opinion has varied between two interpretations of the ideal, one unsatisfactory because it is too prosaic, the other because it is too mystical. The former begins with the belief that although no individual body is satisfactory as a whole, the artist can choose the perfect parts from a number of figures and then combine them into a perfect whole. Such, we are told by Pliny, was the procedure of Zeuxis when he constructed his *Aphrodite* out of the five beautiful maidens of Kroton, and the advice reappears in the earliest treatise on painting of the post-antique world, Alberti's *Della Pittura*. Dürer went so far as to say that he had "searched through two or three hundred." The argument is repeated again and again for four centuries, never more charmingly than by the French seventeenth-century theorist, Du Fresnoy, whom I shall quote in Mason's translation:

> For tho' our casual glance may sometimes meet
> With charms that strike the soul and seem complete,
> Yet if those charms too closely we define,
> Content to copy nature line for line,
> Our end is lost. Not such the master's care,
> Curious he culls the perfect from the fair;
> Judge of his art, thro' beauty's realm he flies,
> Selects, combines, improves, diversifies;
> With nimble step pursues the fleeting throng,
> And clasps each Venus as she glides along.

Naturally, the theory was a popular one with artists: but it satisfies neither logic nor experience. Logically, it simply transfers the problem from the whole to the parts, and we are left asking by what ideal pattern Zeuxis accepted or rejected the arms, necks, bosoms, and so forth of his five maidens. And even admitting that we do find certain individual limbs or features that, for some mysterious reason, seem to us perfectly beautiful, experience shows us that we cannot often recombine them. They are right in their setting, organically, and to abstract them is to deprive them of that rhythmic vitality on which their beauty depends.

To meet this difficulty the classic theorists of art invented what they called "the middle form." They based this notion on Aristotle's definition of nature, and in the stately language of Sir Joshua Reynolds' *Discourses* it seems to carry some conviction. But what does it amount to, translated into plain speech? Simply that the ideal is composed of the average and the habitual. It is an uninspiring proposition, and we are not surprised that Blake was provoked into replying, "All Forms are Perfect in the Poet's Mind but these are not Abstracted or compounded from Nature, but are from the Imagination." Of course he is right. Beauty is precious and rare, and if it were like a mechanical toy, made up of parts of average size that could be put together at will, we should not value it as we do. But we must admit that Blake's interjection is more a believer's cry of triumph than an argument, and we must ask what meaning can be attached to it. Perhaps the question is best answered in Crocean terms. The ideal is like a myth, in which the finished form can be understood only as the end of a long process of accretion. In the beginning, no doubt, there is the coincidence of widely diffused desires and the personal tastes of a few individuals endowed with the gift of simplifying their visual experiences into easily comprehensible shapes. Once this fusion has taken place, the resulting image, while still in a plastic state, may be enriched or refined upon by succeeding generations. Or, to change the metaphor, it is like a receptacle into which more and more experience can be poured. Then, at a certain point, it is full. It sets. And, partly because it seems to be completely satisfying, partly because the mythopoeic faculty has declined, it is accepted as true. What both Reynolds and Blake meant by ideal beauty was really the diffused memory of that peculiar physical type developed in Greece between the years 480 and 440 B.C. which in varying degrees of intensity and consciousness furnished the mind of Western man with a pattern of perfection from the Renaissance until the present century.

Once more we have returned to Greece, and it is now time to consider some peculiarities of the Greek mind that may have contributed to the formation of this indestructible image.

The most distinctive is the Greek passion for mathematics. In every branch of Hellenic thought we encounter a belief in measurable proportion that, in the last analysis, amounts to a mystical religion; and as early as Pythagoras it had been given the visible form of geometry. All art is founded on faith, and inevitably the Greek faith in harmonious numbers found expression in their painting and sculpture; but precisely how we do not know. The so-called canon of Polykleitos is not recorded, and the rules of proportion that have come down to us through Pliny and other ancient writers are of the most elementary kind. Probably the Greek sculptors were familiar with a system as subtle and elaborate as that of their architects, but we have scarcely any indication as to what it was. There is, however, one short and obscure statement in Vitruvius that, whatever it meant in antiquity, had a decisive influence on the Renaissance. At the beginning of the third book, in which he sets out to give the rules for sacred edifices, he suddenly announces that these buildings should have the proportions of a man. He gives some indication of correct human proportions and then throws in a statement that man's body is a model of proportion because with arms or legs extended it fits into those "perfect" geometrical forms, the square and the circle. It is impossible to exaggerate what this simple-looking proposition meant to the men of the Renaissance. To them it was far more than a convenient rule: it was the foundation of a whole philosophy. Taken together with the musical scale of Pythagoras, it seemed to offer exactly that link between sensation and order, between an organic and a geometric basis of beauty, which was (and perhaps remains) the philosopher's stone of esthetics. Hence the many diagrams of figures standing in squares or circles that illustrate the treatises on architecture or esthetics from the fifteenth to the seventeenth century.

Vitruvian man, as this figure has come to be called, appears earlier than Leonardo da Vinci, but it is in Leonardo's famous drawing in Venice that he receives his most masterly exposition; also, on the whole the most correct, for Leonardo makes only two slight deviations from Vitruvius, whereas most of the other illustrations follow him very sketchily. This is not one of Leonardo's most attractive drawings, and it must be admitted that the Vitruvian formula does not provide any guarantee of a pleasant-looking body. The most carefully worked-out illustration of all, in the Como Vitruvius of 1521, shows an ungraceful figure with head too small and legs and feet too big. Especially troublesome was the question of how the square and the circle, which were to establish the perfect form, should be related to one another. Leonardo, on no authority that I can discover, said that in order to fit into a circle the figure should stretch apart his legs so that he was a fourteenth shorter than if they were together. But this arbitrary solution did not please Cesariano, the editor of the Como Vitruvius, who inscribed the square in the circle, with unfortunate results. We see that from the point of view of strict geometry a gorilla might prove to be more satisfactory than a man.

How little systematic proportion alone can be relied on to produce physical beauty is shown by Dürer's engraving known as the *Nemesis* or *Large Fortune*. It was executed in 1501, and we know that in the preceeding year Dürer had been reading Vitruvius. In this figure he has applied Vitruvian principles of measurement down to the last detail: according to Professor Panofsky, even the big toe is operative. He has also taken his subject from a work by Poliziano, the same humanist poet who inspired Botticelli's *Birth of Venus* and Raphael's *Galatea*. But in spite of these precautions he has not achieved the classical ideal. That he did so later was owing to the practice of relating his system to antique figures. It was not his squares and circles that enabled him to master classical proportions, but the fact that he applied them to memories of the *Apollo Belvedere* and the *Medici Venus*—forms "perfected in the poet's mind." And it was from these, in the end, that he derived the beautiful nude figure of Adam in his famous engraving of the *Fall*.

Francis Bacon, as we all know, said, "There is no excellent beauty that hath not some strangeness in the proportion. A man cannot tell whether Apelles or Albert Dürer were the more trifler; where of the one would make a personage by geometrical proportions: the other by taking the best part out of divers faces to make one excellent." This very intelligent observation is unfair to Dürer, and suggests that Bacon, like the rest of us, had not read his book on human proportions, only looked at the plates. For, after 1507, Dürer abandoned the idea of imposing a geometrical scheme on the body, and set about deducing ideal measurements from nature, with a result, as may be imagined, somewhat different from his analyses of the antique; and in his introduction he forcefully denies the claim that he is providing a standard of absolute perfection. "There lives no man upon earth," he says, "who can give a final judgment upon what the most beautiful shape of a man may be; God only knows that. . . . 'Good' and 'better' in respect of beauty are not easy to discern, for it would be quite possible to make two different figures, neither conforming with the other, one stouter, the other thinner, and yet we might scarce be able to judge which of the two excelled in beauty."

So the most indefatigable and masterly constructor of ideal proportions abandoned them halfway through his career, and his work, from the

Nemesis onward, is a proof that the idea of the nude does not depend on analyzable proportions alone. And yet when we look at the splendidly schematized bodies of Greek sculpture, we cannot resist the conviction that some system did exist. Almost every artist or writer on art who has thought seriously about the nude has concluded that it must have some basis of construction that can be stated in terms of measurement; and I myself, when trying to explain why a photograph did not satisfy me, said that I missed the sense of simple units clearly related to one another. Although the artist cannot construct a beautiful nude by mathematical rules, any more than the musician can compose a beautiful fugue, he cannot ignore them. They must be lodged somewhere at the back of his mind or in the movements of his fingers. Ultimately he is as dependent on them as an architect.

Dipendenza [dependency]: that is the word used by Michelangelo, supreme as a draftsman of the nude and as an architect, to express his sense of the relationship between these two forms of order. And in the pages that follow I often make use of architectural analogies. Like a building, the nude represents a balance between an ideal scheme and functional necessities. The figure artist cannot forget the components of the human body, any more than the architect can fail to support his roof or forget his doors and windows. But the variations of shape and disposition are surprisingly wide. The most striking instance is, of course, the change in proportion between the Greek and the Gothic idea of the female body. One of the few classical canons of proportion of which we can be certain is that which, in a female nude, took the same unit of measurement for the distance between the breasts, the distance from the lower breast to the navel, and again from the navel to the division of the legs. This scheme we shall find carefully maintained in all figures of the classical epoch and in most of those which imitated them down to the first century. Contrast a typical Gothic nude of the fifteenth century, the *Eve* in the Vienna gallery attributed to Memlinc. The components are—naturally—the same. The basic pattern of the female body is still an oval, surmounted by two spheres; but the oval has grown incredibly long, the spheres have grown distressingly small. If we apply our unit of measurement, the distance between the breasts, we find that the navel is exactly twice as far down the body as it is in the classic scheme. This increased length of body is made more noticeable because it is unbroken by any suggestion of ribs or muscles. The forms are not conceived as individual blocks, but seem to have been drawn out of one another as if they were made of some viscous material. It is usual to speak of this kind of Gothic nude as "naturalistic," but is Memlinc's *Eve* really closer to the average (for this is what the word means) than the antique nude? Such, at all events, was certainly not the painter's intention. He aimed at producing a figure that would conform to the ideals of his time, that would be the kind of shape men liked to see; and by some strange interaction of flesh and spirit this long curve of the stomach has become the means by which the body has achieved the ogival rhythm of late Gothic architecture.

A rather less obvious example is provided by Sansovino's *Apollo* on the Loggetta in Venice. It is inspired by the *Apollo Belvedere*, but although

Sansovino, like all his contemporaries, thought that the antique figure was of unsurpassable beauty, he has allowed himself a fundamental difference in his construction of the body. We may describe this by saying that the antique male nude is like a Greek temple, the flat frame of the chest being carried on the columns of the legs; whereas the Renaissance nude is related to the architectural system that produced the central-domed church; so that instead of the sculptural interest depending on a simple, frontal plane, a number of axes radiate from one center. Not only the elevations but, so to say, the ground plans of these figures would have an obvious relationship to their respective architectures. What we may call the multiple-axis nude continued until the classicistic revival of the eighteenth century. Then, when architects were reviving the Greek-temple form, sculptors once more gave to the male body the flatness and frontality of a frame building. Ultimately the *dipendenza* of architecture and the nude expresses the relationship we all so earnestly desire between that which is perfected by the mind and that which we love. Poussin, writing to his friend Chantelou in 1642, said, "The beautiful girls whom you will have seen in Nîmes will not, I am sure, have delighted your spirit any less than the beautiful columns of Maison Carrée; for the one is no more than an old copy of the other." And the hero of Claudel's *Partage de midi*, when at last he puts his arms round his beloved, utters, as the first pure expression of his bliss, the words "O Colonne!"

So our surmise that the discovery of the nude as a form of art is connected with idealism and faith in measurable proportions seems to be true, but it is only half the truth. What other peculiarities of the Greek mind are involved? One obvious answer is their belief that the body was something to be proud of, and should be kept in perfect trim.

We need not suppose that many Greeks looked like the *Hermes* of Praxiteles, but we can be sure that in fifth-century Attica a majority of the young men had the nimble, well-balanced bodies depicted on the early red-figure vases. On a vase in the British Museum is a scene that will arouse sympathy in most of us, but to the Athenians was ridiculous and shameful —a fat youth in the gymnasium embarrassed by his ungraceful figure, and apparently protesting to a thin one, while two young men of more fortunate development throw the javelin and the discus. Greek literature from Homer and Pindar downward contains many expressions of this physical pride, some of which strike unpleasantly on the Anglo-Saxon ear and trouble the minds of schoolmasters when they are recommending the Greek ideal of fitness. "What do I care for any man?" says the young man Kritobalos in the *Symposium* of Xenophon: "I am beautiful." And no doubt this arrogance was increased by the tradition that in the gymnasium and the sportsground such young men displayed themselves totally naked.

The Greeks attached great importance to their nakedness. Thucydides, in recording the stages by which they distinguished themselves from the barbarians, gives prominence to the date at which it became the rule in the Olympic games, and we know from vase paintings that the competitors at the Panathenaic festival had been naked ever since the early sixth century. Although the presence or absence of a loincloth does not greatly affect questions of form, and in this study I shall include figures that are lightly draped, psychologically the Greek cult of absolute nakedness is of great importance. It implies the conquest of an inhibition that oppresses all but the most backward people; it is like a denial of original sin. This is not, as is sometimes supposed, simply a part of paganism: for the Romans were shocked by the nakedness of Greek athletes, and Ennius attacked it as a sign of decadence. Needless to say, he was wide of the mark, for the most determined nudists of all were the Spartans, who scandalized even the Athenians by allowing women to compete, lightly clad, in their games. He and subsequent moralists considered the matter in purely physical terms; but, in fact, Greek confidence in the body can be understood only in relation to their philosophy. It expresses above all their sense of human wholeness. Nothing that related to the whole man could be isolated or evaded; and this serious awareness of how much was implied in physical beauty saved them from the two evils of sensuality and estheticism.

At the same party where Kritobalos brags about his beauty Xenophon describes the youth Autolykos, victor of the Pankration, in whose honor the feast was being given. "Noting the scene," he says, "the first idea to strike the mind is that beauty has about it something regal; and the more so if it chance to be combined (as now in the person of Autolykos) with modesty and self-respect. Even as when a splendid object blazes forth at night, the eyes of men are riveted, so now the beauty of Autolykos drew on him the gaze of all; nor was there one of those onlookers but was stirred to his soul's depth by him who sat there. Some fell into unwonted silence, while the gestures of the rest were equally significant."

This feeling, that the spirit and body are one, which is the most familiar of all Greek characteristics, manifests itself in their gift of giving to abstract ideas a sensuous, tangible, and, for the most part, human form. Their logic is conducted in the form of dialogues between real men. Their gods take visible shape, and on their appearance are usually mistaken for half-familiar human beings—a maidservant, a shepherd, or a distant cousin. Woods, rivers, even echoes are shown in painting as bodily presences, solid as the living protagonists, and often more prominent. Here we reach what I take to be the central point of our subject: "Greek statues," said Blake, in his *Descriptive Catalogue*, "are all of them representations of spiritual existences, of gods immortal, to the mortal, perishing organ of sight; and yet they are embodied and organized in solid marble." The bodies were there, the belief in the gods was there, the love of rational proportion was there. It was the unifying grasp of the Greek imagination that brought them together. And the nude gains its enduring value from the fact that it reconciles several contrary states. It takes the most sensual and immediately interesting object, the human body, and puts it out of reach of time and desire; it takes the most purely rational concept of which mankind is capable, mathematical order, and makes it a delight to the senses; and it takes the vague fears of the unknown and sweetens them by showing that the gods are like men and may be worshiped for their life-giving beauty rather than their death-dealing powers.

To recognize how completely the value of these spiritual existences depends on their nudity, we have only to think of them as they appear, fully clothed, in the Middle Ages or early Renaissance. They have lost all their meaning. When the Graces are represented by three nervous ladies hiding behind a blanket, they no longer convey to us the civilizing influence of beauty. When Herakles is a lumbering *Landsknecht* weighed down by fashionable armor, he cannot increase our sense of well-being by his own superabundant strength. Conversely, when nude figures, which had been evolved to express an idea, ceased to do so, and were represented for their physical perfection alone, they soon lost their value. This was the fatal legacy of neoclassicism, and Coleridge, who lived through the period, summed up the situation in some lines he added to the translation of Schiller's *Piccolomini*:

> The intelligible powers of ancient poets,
> The fair humanities of old religion,
> The Power, the Beauty and the Majesty,
> That had their haunts in dale or piney mountain,
> . . . all these have vanished.
> They live no longer in the faith of reason.

The academic nudes of the nineteenth century are lifeless because they no longer embodied real human needs and experiences. They were among the hundreds of devalued symbols that encumbered the art and architecture of the utilitarian century.

The nude had flourished most exuberantly during the first hundred years of the classical Renaissance, when the new appetite for antique imagery overlapped the medieval habits of symbolism and personification. It seemed then that there was no concept, however sublime, that could not be expressed by the naked body, and no object of use, however trivial, that would not be better for having been given human shape. At one end of the scale was Michelangelo's *Last Judgment*; at the other the door knockers, candelabra, or even handles of knives and forks. To the first it might be objected—and frequently was—that nakedness was unbecoming in a representation of Christ and His saints. This was the point put forward by Paolo Veronese when he was tried by the Inquisition for including drunkards and Germans in his picture of the marriage of Cana: to which the chief inquisitor gave his immortal reply, "Do you not know that in these figures by Michelangelo there is nothing that is not spiritual—*non vi è cosa se non de spirito?*" And to the second it might be objected—and frequently is—that the similitude of the naked Venus is not what we need in our hand when we are cutting up our food or knocking at a door, to which Benvenuto Cellini would have replied that since the human body is the most perfect of all forms we cannot see it too often. In between these two extremes was that forest of nude figures, painted or carved, in stucco, bronze, or stone, which filled every vacant space in the architecture of the sixteenth century.

Such an insatiable appetite for the nude is unlikely to recur. It arose from a fusion of beliefs, traditions, and impulses very remote from our age of essence and specialization. Yet even in the new self-governing kingdom of the esthetic sensation the nude is enthroned. The intensive application of great artists has made it into a sort of pattern for all formal constructions, and it is still a means of affirming the belief in ultimate perfection. "For soule is forme, and doth the bodie make," wrote Spenser in his *Hymne in Honour of Beautie*, echoing the words of the Florentine Neoplatonists, and although in life the evidence for the doctrine is inconclusive, it is perfectly applicable to art. The nude remains the most complete example of the transmutation of matter into form.

Nor are we likely once more to cut ourselves off from the body, as in the ascetic experiment of medieval Christianity. We may no longer worship it, but we have come to terms with it. We are reconciled to the fact that it is our lifelong companion, and since art is concerned with sensory images the scale and rhythm of the body is not easily ignored. Our continuous effort, made in defiance of the pull of gravity, to keep ourselves balanced upright on our legs affects every judgment on design, even our conception of which angle shall be called "right." The rhythm of our breathing and the beat of our hearts are part of the experience by which we measure a work of art. The relation of head to body determines the standard by which we assess all other proportions in nature. The disposition of areas in the torso is related to our most vivid experiences, so that, abstract shapes, the square and the circle, seem to us male and female; and the old endeavor of magical mathematics to square the circle is like the symbol of physical union. The starfish diagrams of Renaissance theorists may be ridiculous, but the Vitruvian principle rules our spirits, and it is no accident that the formalized body of the "perfect man" became the supreme symbol of European belief. Before the *Crucifixion* of Michelangelo we remember that the nude is, after all, the most serious of all subjects in art; and that it was not an advocate of paganism who wrote, "The Word was made flesh, and dwelt among us . . . full of grace and truth."

—*The Nude* (1956)

JOHN HOSPERS

The Esthetic Attitude

Before considering the aesthetic questions that occur in the philosophy of art, we should consider the question, What is it to view (listen to, etc.) an object aesthetically?, since in the absence of the experience of aesthetic objects, none of the other questions would arise. Is there an aesthetic way of looking at things, and if so, what distinguishes it from other ways of experiencing these things? On this question there have been many different views, usually overlapping but still distinguishable.

Aesthetic and Nonaesthetic Attitudes

The aesthetic attitude, or the "aesthetic way of looking at the world," is most commonly opposed to the *practical* attitude, which is concerned only with the utility of the object in question. The real estate agent who views a landscape only with an eye to its possible monetary value is not viewing the landscape aesthetically. To view a landscape aesthetically one must "perceive for perceiving's sake," not for the sake of some ulterior purpose. One must savor the experience of perceiving the landscape itself, dwelling on its perceptual details, rather than using the perceptual object as a means to some further end.

> The needs of our actual life are so imperative, that the sense of vision becomes highly specialized in their service. With an admirable economy we learn to see only so much as is needful for our purposes; but this is in fact very little, just enough to recognize and identify each object or person; that done, they go into an entry in our mental catalogue and are no more really seen. In actual life the normal person really only reads the labels as it were on the objects around him and troubles no further. Almost all the things which are useful in any way put on more or less this cap of invisibility. It is only when an object exists in our lives for no other purpose than to be seen that we really look at it, as for instance at a China ornament or a precious stone, and towards such even the most normal person adopts to some extent the artistic attitude of pure vision abstracted from necessity. (Roger Fry, *Vision and Design*, pp. 24–25)

One might object, of course, that even in aesthetic contemplation we are regarding something not "for its own sake" but for the sake of something else, namely, enjoyment. We would not continue to attend to the perceptual object if doing so were not enjoyable; hence, is not enjoyment the end in the aesthetic case? One may indeed so describe it, and perhaps the terminology of "perceiving for its own sake" is a misleading one. Still, there is a difference between savoring the perceptual experience itself and merely using it for purposes of identification, classification, or further action, as we commonly do in daily life when we do not really look at the tree but perceive it only clearly enough to identify it as a tree and then walk around it if it is in our path. The distinction remains, and only the mode of describing it is subject to clarification.

The aesthetic attitude is also distinguished from the cognitive. Students who are familiar with the history of architecture are able to identify quickly a building or a ruin, in regard to its time and place of construction, by means of its style and other visual aspects. They look at the building primarily to increase their knowledge and not to enrich their perceptual experience. This kind of ability may be important and helpful (in passing examinations, for example), but it is not necessarily correlated with the ability to enjoy the experience of simply viewing the building itself. The analytical ability may eventually enhance the aesthetic experience, but it may also stifle it. People who are interested in the arts from a professional or technical aspect are particularly liable to be diverted from the aesthetic way of looking to the cognitive. This leads us directly into a further distinction.

The aesthetic way of looking is also antipathetic to the personal, in which the viewer, instead of regarding the aesthetic object so as to absorb what it has to offer him, considers its relation to himself. Those who do not listen to music but use it as a springboard for their own personal reveries provide an example of this nonaesthetic hearing that often passes for listening. In Edward Bullough's famous example, the man who goes to see a performance of *Othello* and instead of concentrating on the play thinks only of the similarity of Othello's situation to his own real life situation with his wife, is not viewing the play aesthetically. His attitude is one of personal involvement; it is a personalized attitude, and the personalization inhibits whatever aesthetic response the viewer may otherwise have had. In viewing something aesthetically we respond to the aesthetic object and what it has to offer us, not to its relation to our own lives. (The latter often occurs, and it is not necessarily undesirable, but it should be sharply distinguished from the aesthetic response.)

The formula "we should not get personally involved" is sometimes used to describe this criterion, but this too is misleading. It does not mean that a playgoer may not identify with the characters in the play or be vitally interested in what happens to them; it only means that he must not make any personal involvement he may have with the characters or the problems in the play substitute for a careful viewing of the play itself. We can see the difference clearly if we contrast the situation of being involved in a shipwreck with viewing a newsreel of it or a movie about it. In the first case we would do what we could to save our own lives and assist others. In the second case, however, we know that whatever disastrous events occurred have already happened and there is nothing we can do about it now, and realizing this, our tendency to respond to the situation with action is automatically cut off. However much we may identify with the sufferers, we are not personally involved in any sense that is geared to action.

It is evident from the above criteria that many types of responses to objects, including to works of art, are excluded from the realm of the aesthetic. For example, pride of ownership may interfere with the aesthetic response. The person who responds enthusiastically to the playing of a symphony before guests on his own stereo set, but fails to respond to the playing of the same symphony on an identical recording set in his neighbor's house, is not responding aesthetically. The antiquarian or the museum directors who, in choosing a work of art, must attend to historical value, prestige, age, and so on, may be partly influenced by an estimate of its aesthetic value, but his attention is necessarily diverted to nonaesthetic factors. Similarly, if a person values a play or novel because he can glean from it items of information concerning the time and place about which it was written, he is substituting an interest in acquiring knowledge for an interest in aesthetic experience. If a person favors a work of art because it offers moral edification or "supports the right cause," he is confusing a moral attitude with the aesthetic, which is also true if he condemns it on moral grounds and fails to separate this condemnation from his aesthetic evaluation of it. (This is particularly likely to occur with persons who never really view an object aesthetically at all, but simply as a vehicle for propaganda, whether moral, political, or otherwise.)

OTHER CRITERIA OF THE AESTHETIC ATTITUDE

Still other terms have been employed to define the aesthetic attitude. "Detachment," for example, is an attitude which is said to distinguish the aesthetic from the nonaesthetic way of looking at things, but this term seems to be more misleading than useful. Like the phrase "not being personally involved," it sounds as though the viewer is not supposed to care greatly about what goes on in the drama or the symphony, whereas there is a sense (as we have seen) in which we are very much involved with the fate of Oedipus when we witness *Oedipus Rex*. We are detached only in the sense in which we know that it is a drama and not real life (although it may be a drama about real life), and that what is on the other side of the footlights is a different world, to which we are not supposed to respond as we do to the practical world around us. In this sense we *are* "detached," but not in the sense of failure to identify with the characters or to be totally absorbed in the drama.

The term "disinterested" is also widely employed to describe the aesthetic attitude. Disinterestedness is a quality of a good judge and occurs when he is impartial. The judge may be personally involved in the sense that he cares deeply about the disposition of a case (for example, who will get custody of the children in a divorce case), but in deciding the case, he must not be personally involved in the sense of letting his personal feelings and sympathies sway him or prejudice him one way or the other. Impartiality in moral and legal matters certainly characterizes what has been called "the moral point of view," but it is far from clear in what way we are supposed to be disinterested (that is, impartial) when we look at a painting or listen to a concert. Impartial as between what conflicting parties? "Judging impartially" makes sense, but what of looking or listening impartially? "Impartial" is a term geared to situations in which there is a conflict between opposing parties in a dispute, but it does not appear to be a very useful term when one is attempting to describe the aesthetic way of looking at things.

Internal and External Relations

A somewhat less misleading way of describing the aesthetic experience is in terms of internal versus external relations. When we are viewing a work of art or nature aesthetically, we concentrate on internal relations only, that is, on the aesthetic object and its properties, and not on its relation to ourselves or even its relation to the artist who created it or to our knowledge of the culture from which it sprang. Most works of art are quite complex and require our full attention. The aesthetic state is one of close and complete concentration. Intense perceptual awareness is required, and the aesthetic object and the various relations within it (that is, internal to it) must be the sole focus of our attention. The student who is not accustomed to viewing a nude human figure may be so distracted by seeing nude goddesses in a painting that he cannot view the painting aesthetically. Because of his own impulses, he is bothered by external relations (that is, relations external to the work of art) so that he cannot properly focus his attention upon the object and the perceptual relations internal to it. Sometimes the freedom from awareness of external relations is labeled "aesthetic distance" or "psychical distance," but again, this term may be more misleading than helpful because of the metaphorical use of the term "distance," which implies that we should somehow keep the aesthetic object at arm's length. Moreover, while it may be said that the spectator who identifies with Othello is suffering from lack of distance, the person who is just feeling his way in the appreciation of an art form that is new to him (such as a symphony, when he is not accustomed to hearing more than one melody at a time) may be said to be suffering from too much distance. The meaning of the metaphor "distance" has shifted: in the first case, it refers to the nonpractical way of viewing and in the second case, to lack of familiarity, which is a different matter entirely. (Ambiguities of this type run through Edward Bullough's famous paper "Psychical Distance" and render the use of the term "distance" more confusing than helpful, because the same word is used to cover several different types of attitude which must be carefully distinguished.)

The Phenomenal Object

Several other attempts to distinguish the aesthetic way of looking at the world from all others have been suggested, either by reference to the attitude itself or by restricting the kind of objects toward which the attitude should be taken.

Aesthetic attention is always to the phenomenal object, not to the physical object (Monroe C. Beardsley, *Aesthetics*, Ch. 1). Without the presence of a physical object, such as paint on canvas, we would not of course perceive any painting, but the attention must be focused on the perceived characteristics, not on the physical characteristics which make the perceived ones possible. Thus, we should concentrate on the color combinations in the painting, but not on the way the paints had to be mixed in order to produce this color, nor anything else involving the chemistry of paints. The latter has to do with the physical basis of the perceptual (i.e., phenomenal) object, rather than with the visual percept itself. Similarly, we may be disturbed because we cannot hear all the instruments in the orchestra from a certain spot in the auditorium, and this is relevant to aesthetic perception because it involves what we hear (or fail to hear). But the investigation of the physical cause of this failure is strictly a physical enterprise, involving a technical knowledge of acoustics; and acoustics is a branch of physics, not of music.

This distinction is surely an important one and serves at least the useful negative function of eliminating certain kinds of attention as being nonaesthetic (such as that of the engineer when he is attempting to remedy the acoustics of an auditorium). That which cannot be perceived (seen, heard, etc.) is not relevant to aesthetic perception because it makes no difference to the nature of the "sensuous presentation" before us. The fact that the painter had to use a very difficult method to get his painting to look "shimmering" is not a relevant aesthetic consideration; it may lead us to admire the painter for undertaking a difficult task, but not to admire the painting itself any more than we did before. However, the fact that the completed painting, as perceived by us, has a "shimmering" look, is aesthetically relevant, for this is a part of what we perceive. But it is still not entirely clear what precisely the criterion includes or excludes. When I focus attention on the color combinations in a painting, or on the harmony of the shapes, I am clearly attending to perceptual phenomena; but what if I also enjoy the painting because of its prevailing mood? or music, not because it is fast or slow, but because it is sad? or dislike a poem because it is sentimental, maudlin, or "phony"? Are these, or is the apprehension of these, aesthetic? Although they are not characteristics of the physical object, are they to be classified as phenomenal?

Indeed, there has been considerable controversy over whether aesthetic attention is limited to the perceptual at all. In the case of perceiving the color combination or the formal arrangement of parts in a painting, it is certainly so; we are concentrating on the perceived (or at any rate perceivable) qualities of the aesthetic object. But must there be, in every case, a perceptual object at all in order for aesthetic attention to be possible? Granted that if we savor the intense color, shape, contour, and even the apparent delicacy and grace of a rose, this is perceptual, while if we attend to its hardiness or disease-resistant qualities, this is not; so far the distinction seems clear. But when we say that a symphony is heroic, that a play is melodramatic, and that a painting is suffused with *joie de vivre*, is not the kind of attention that results in this description aesthetic also? Yet it is difficult to see how the "heroic quality" is perceptual. To be sure, we apprehend it, if at all, by means of noting the music's perceived qualities, but it is also through perception that we are aware of an object's physical qualities, which are not supposed to be relevant to aesthetic attention.

When we enjoy or appreciate the elegance of a mathematical proof, it would surely seem that our enjoyment is aesthetic, although the object of that enjoyment is not perceptual at all: it is the complex relation among abstract ideas or propositions, not the marks on paper or the blackboard, that we are apprehending aesthetically. It would seem that the appreciation of neatness, elegance, or economy of means is aesthetic whether it occurs in a perceptual object (such as a sonata) or in an abstract entity (such as a logical proof), and if this is so, the range of the aesthetic cannot be limited to the perceptual.

Moreover, what of the art of literature? No one would wish to say that our appreciation of literature is nonaesthetic, and yet the "aesthetic object" in the case of literature does not consist of visual or auditory percepts. It is not sounds or marks on paper, but their *meanings* that constitute the medium of literature, and meanings are not concrete objects or percepts. In this respect, the distinction between literature and all the other arts is a very great one, so much so that the auditory and visual arts have been called sensory arts (consisting of sensuous presentations to the eye or ear), as distinguished from literature, which is an ideo-sensory art (T. E. Jessop, "The Definition of Beauty," *PAS*, Vol. 33, 1932–1933, 170–171). Because the reading of the words evokes sensuous images in the minds of readers, so that there are percepts after all (imagined ones, but still sensuous, as in dreams), it has been suggested that literature *is* actually sensory. This suggestion, however, is hardly plausible, for many readers can read appreciatively and intelligently without having any visual or other images evoked in their minds. Is the attention of such readers therefore to be dismissed as being nonaesthetic? It would appear that the reader of literature must, at the very least, focus attention upon words and their meanings (some would say, on words only as vehicles for their meanings), but these are not percepts in the way that colors, shapes, sounds, tastes, and smells are. The inclusion of literature in the category of the perceptual by means of some image evocation theory constitutes a desperate attempt to make the facts fit a theory. However, the dismissal of literature as not being the object of aesthetic attention because of its nonperceptual character would seem to be a prime case of throwing the baby out with the bath water.

Sense Modality

Within the sense domain, attempts have been made to restrict the area of aesthetic attention by means of sense modality—specifically, to include vision and hearing as acceptable and to dismiss smell, taste, and touch (the "lower" senses) as unacceptable for aesthetic attention. But this suggestion also seems doomed to failure. What reason could be offered for denying that the enjoyment of smell, taste, and touch is aesthetic? Is not the savoring of the smell of a rose or the taste of a wine aesthetic? We can enjoy tastes and smells just as we enjoy sights and sounds—for their own sakes alone, or, if one prefers, for the sake of enjoyment only. It is true that works of art have not, on the whole, been produced in sensuous media other than the visual and auditory; for example, we do not have "smell symphonies." There are various reasons for this: (1) It is more difficult in this instance to separate the practical from the nonpractical—for example, to separate the enjoyment of food because we are hungry from the enjoyment of it because it tastes good. The "lower" senses are so closely connected with the fulfillment of bodily needs that it is difficult to isolate the strictly aesthetic enjoyment derived from them. (In the case of a wine, however, it may be argued that we do not ordinarily drink it because we are thirsty, but simply because we enjoy it for its own sake.) (2) Perceptually, even if not physically, the data of the "lower" senses are less complex, so that the perceived elements do not lend themselves to the complex formal arrangement that is so characteristic of works of art. In a series of smells and tastes, there is a "before" and "after," but not much beside this strictly serial order—that is, there is no "harmony" or "counterpoint." Colors and sounds, however, fall into a complex order, enabling us to make fine distinctions between countless visual and auditory sensations. This type of distinction makes possible the apprehension of a great formal complexity in works of visual and auditory art which it is impossible for human perceivers to apprehend in the other sense modalities. In this instance, we refer to a phenomenal rather than to a physical order, for there are exact physical correlates for experienced smells just as there are for sounds (pitch, volume, timbre) and colors (hue, saturation, brightness). But if precise distinctions among these sensory data cannot be made in the case of smell and taste, they are unavailable for the use of human perceivers, even though an exact order of physical correlates exists equally for all of them.

Denials of Distinct Aesthetic Attitude

Some writers have despaired of finding any criteria at all for distinguishing an aesthetic attitude from other kinds of attitudes. For example, some aestheticians have denied that there is any distinctively aesthetic attitude at all (J. O. Urmson, "What Makes a Situation Aesthetic?" *PAS*, Suppl. Vol. 31, 1957). They find the distinguishing characteristic of the aesthetic not in any attitude, experience, or mode of attention that observers may have, but in the reasons they give to support their judgments—that is, aesthetic reasons, moral reasons, economic reasons, and so forth. Although most aestheticians agree that there are distinctively aesthetic reasons, they go further and hold that these reasons presuppose a type of attitude or attention that is given to objects (that is, a way of perceiving) which, although difficult to identify precisely and even more difficult to explain verbally without being misleading, does exist and distinguishes this one mode of attention from all others. It has also been held that there is no such thing as a distinctively aesthetic attitude, unless one simply defines it as "paying close attention" to the work of art (or nature) in question (George Dickie, "The Myth of the Aesthetic Attitude," *American Philosophical Quarterly*, Vol. 1, No. 1, 1964, 56–65). There is no special kind of attention to objects that can be called aesthetic; there is only "paying close attention to the qualities of the object" as against failure to do so. According to this view, we may come to a work of art with various motives that can be distinguished from one another, but there is no special type of attention in the witnessing of a play that distinguishes, for example, the spectator from the play producer or the playwright in search of ideas: the type of attention is the same in all cases, that is, all should concentrate carefully upon the aesthetic object. The distinction between viewing aesthetically and nonaesthetically becomes strictly a motivational distinction, not a perceptual one.

—*The Encyclopedia of Philosophy* (1967)

CHAPTER

11

The Response
of the Critic

Criticism is commonly understood to involve both interpretation and
assessment. Goethe, combining the two, said that the critic should seek to
answer three questions: What was the artist trying to do? Did he succeed in
doing it? Was it worth doing? This prescription has been challenged
by literary critic William K. Wimsatt, Jr., and philosopher Monroe C.
Beardsley in "The Intentional Fallacy" (1946). Rather than reprint this
famous essay, which is concerned primarily with literature, I reproduce
below an article by John Kemp (1920–   ), Professor of Philosophy
at the University of Leicester, who extends the theory of "the intentional
fallacy" beyond literature to art in general. The "fallacy" is to interpret
and judge the work of art by the intention of the artist. "It is
always," Kemp remarks, "what is done that we have to judge," and "not
what the artist intended, but perhaps failed to do."

In sharp contrast to the anti-intentionalist position, Lucien Goldmann
(1913–   ) insists upon a contextualist interpretation of the work of
art. Born in Rumania, he was educated at Bucharest, Vienna, Zurich,
and Paris, and has taught at the University of Brussels and the École
Pratique des Hautes Études in Paris. This cosmopolitan background is
reflected in the eclectic nature of his thought, drawing upon the
"dialectical materialism" of Karl Marx, the theory of "world-visions"
(*Weltanschauungs*) of Wilhelm Dilthey (1833–1911), and the structuralism
of Jean Piaget (with whom he worked in Geneva). Common to Marx,
Dilthey, and Piaget is the stress upon structure and context, the
integral relation of part to whole. Goldmann makes this emphasis the
cornerstone of his critical method. In his remarkable book *The Hidden
God*, an interpretation of Pascal and Racine, he contends that
philosophical and artistic works convey their real meaning to us but can
be fully understood only when they are seen as integral to the lives and
social milieus of their creators.

Goldmann agrees with the statement of Marx: "The mode of production of material life determines the general character of the social, political and spiritual processes of life." Among these spiritual processes are art and literature. The influence of economic conditions and class status upon the artist and his work is filtered through an ideological screen, which Goldmann (following the lead of Dilthey) calls a "world vision." "The tragic vision of life," for example, is a social creation of many artists and thinkers, whose individual works are intelligible only within its context. The value of a work of art is to be judged not only in terms of the formalist criterion of internal coherence but also by the contextualist criterion of "degree of realism." By "realism" Goldmann means "the richness and complexity of the real social relationships which are reflected in the imaginary world created by the artist or writer."

The emphasis on the individual and the uniqueness of his works in the writings of George Boas (1891–), professor emeritus of philosophy at the Johns Hopkins University, stands in contrast to Goldmann's stress on economic class and cultural context. In numerous articles and books, Boas has advanced a pluralistic interpretation of the arts. His defense of the "unintelligibility" of contemporary art reminds one of the words of Nietzsche's Zarathustra: "This is *my* way; what is yours? As for *the* way, it does not exist." These words might be taken as the keynote of "modernist art," so baffling to those who wish to pigeonhole and categorize. In defending works that are so completely individualized and concrete that they elude traditional methods of classification, Boas seeks not only to characterize the modern movement in art but to answer those who attack it. His pluralism does not make the task of the critic any easier, but it does help to liberate criticism from stereotypes and dogmatisms.

When Boas presented his presidential address to the American Society of Aesthetics in 1950, some of the more extreme tendencies in avant-garde art had not yet appeared. Clement Greenberg (1909–), the eminent American art critic, delivered his lecture at Brandeis University twenty years later, after Abstract Impressionism, Op and Pop, Minimalist and *informel* art, and surprises galore had been thrust on a bewildered public. Amid all this novelty the question arises as to whether there are any general and enduring standards of esthetic judgment. Greenberg thinks there are. In comparison to Boas' address, his is a later and, in some ways, a more conservative reaction to "modernist art." Although he distinguishes between the academic artist and the superior, truly original artist, he rejects the advanced-gardist rhetoric about "total liberation" and absolute novelty and reasserts the importance of expectation and continuity.

"The issue remains quality:" he says, "that is, to endow art with greater capacity to move you." To do this it is not enough to put a thing into a public art context, as Duchamp did when he displayed a urinal in an art exhibit. Nor is it sufficient to have surprise for the sake of surprise. "Art depends on expectation and its satisfaction. It moves and satisfies you in a heightened way by surprising expectation." If the surprise is achieved in disregard of artistic expectations, or in response only to rudimentary ones, it sinks to the level of very minimal art, soon turning to the ashes of boredom. But if the creation is under the control of expanded *artistic* expectations, the "surprise not only enhances esthetic satisfaction, but also becomes a self-renewing and more or less permanent surprise—as all superior art shows." To provide the context for this kind of surprise, continuity of tradition and cultivation of taste are as indispensable now as ever they were. Although Greenberg is mainly concerned with avant-gardism in painting and sculpture, his critique is applicable to all-out, way-out works in music, literature, and other art genders.

The position that there are general standards of esthetic judgment is also maintained by Monroe C. Beardsley (1915–   ), professor of philosophy at Temple University and author of important works in esthetics. The problem, as he sees it, is this: "Do critical reasons have a kind of generality of application, so that it makes sense to try to formulate principles of criticism?" He defends "the General Criterion Theory" and answers some skeptical arguments. "A general criterion," he points out, is "a feature that helps to make the work of art good or bad, better or worse; it adds to or detracts from its esthetic goodness." To cite such a criterion in support of a critical evaluation is to give a reason for that judgment. There are two possibilities in the skeptical position: (1) that there are no *general* reasons, only reasons that hold for particular cases, or (2) that there are no valid critical criteria and hence no genuine reasons at all. Beardsley answers both contentions, but devotes most of his argument to the first, more moderate position, exemplified, for example, by William Kennick's well-known essay, "Does Traditional Aesthetics Rest on a Mistake?"[1] His discussion of the universalizability of esthetic judgments touches on some of the liveliest controversies in contemporary critical theory.

Stephen Coburn Pepper (1891–1972), professor emeritus of philosophy at the University of California, recognizes diverse standards of critical judgment, but believes that each standard may be applied with a fair degree of objectivity. A significant standard does not reflect mere personal taste, but springs from a comprehensive orientation toward reality, a philosophical *Weltanschauung* or world hypothesis. He distinguishes four relatively adequate world hypotheses, which he calls mechanism, contextualism, organicism, and formism. Mechanism also goes by the name of "naturalism" or "materialism"; contextualism is usually called "pragmatism" or "instrumentalism"; organicism is most fully expressed in "absolute idealism"; formism, with its emphasis upon universals or similarities, is often called "realism" or "Platonic idealism." In his discussion of esthetic criticism, Pepper cites Santayana as an example of a mechanist, Dewey as a contextualist, Bosanquet as an organicist, and Aristotle as a formist. The mechanist asks of the work that it give pleasure; the contextualist, that it exhibit vividness of quality; the organicist, that it be a rich and well-integrated unity; the formist, that it typify the normal or universal. In his *Principles of Art Appreciation*, Pepper employed the "mechanist" criterion of pleasure; and in his *Aesthetic Quality* and the selection in this anthology, from *The Basis of*

Criticism in the Arts, he skillfully elaborated the contextualist standard: How vivid and intense and deep is the experience yielded by the work of art?

In a remarkable article, "Autobiography of an Aesthetics," in *The Journal of Aesthetics and Art Criticism* (Spring 1970), Pepper outlines his whole development as an esthetician, including the reformulations and additions in his book, *Concept and Quality* (1967). The masterly sweep of his achievement is very impressive.

NOTE

1. This essay appeared in *Mind*, Vol. 67 (1958).

JOHN KEMP

The Work of Art and the Artist's Intentions

I

In this paper I shall discuss the question whether the understanding and appreciation of a work of art require us to have a knowledge of the intentions of the artist. It is a question which has received divergent, not to say diametrically opposed, answers from philosophers and critics. For example, in a recent American collection of "readings" in aesthetics,[1] we find in close juxtaposition an essay by W. K. Wimsatt and M. C. Beardsley (pp. 275–88), which argues that the critic has no concern with the artist's intentions, and an article by H. D. Aiken (pp. 295–305), which maintains that a work of art cannot be properly understood or interpreted without reference to the artist's intentions. Such downright opposition as this is perhaps commoner in philosophy than in most other disciplines, and it can often be to a large extent resolved by a process of philosophical analysis, which shows that much or all of the disagreement occurs because the parties to it are using the same word or words in different ways. However, I do not think that this particular disagreement can be totally resolved in this way; and I think, as will appear from my later arguments, that the first of these two views is much more nearly right than the second. But some preliminary analysis is necessary if we are to make any progress towards answering the question before us.

A perfectionist might say, as Socrates would doubtless have said, that we cannot begin to answer the question until we have given a precise and accurate account of the terms "artist" and "work of art"; but the problems connected with these concepts are too complex to allow of serious treatment in the introductory stages of a short article. It is sufficient to say that the word "artist" is here used to denote such people as painters, sculptors, poets, novelists and composers, and that the expression "work of art" is used to mean such things as statues, paintings, poems, novels and symphonies. The enormous difficulties that are concealed by this short method of dealing with the problem need not trouble us unduly here. It should be noticed, however, that I am using both "artist" and "work of art" in a neutral sense, so as to include bad and indifferent painters, poets, etc., and bad and indifferent paintings, poems, etc., as well as good ones; I am not using them in an honorific sense, although they are frequently, and quite properly, so used.

The part of our question which stands most in need of discussion is the concept of intention itself; but a brief reference must first be made to the notions of understanding and appreciating. I am primarily concerned in this paper with the idea of understanding or interpreting a work of art; with seeing (either literally or metaphorically) what is in it, what are its properties and its structure. Questions of understanding and interpretation are methodologically prior to questions of appreciation and evaluation, in the sense that we have to have an adequate knowledge and understanding of what it is that we are assessing before we can hope to arrive at a correct assessment of it. They are also logically prior, in the sense that we cannot even begin to make an assessment of it until we have some idea of what the word "it" refers to. If the main thesis of this paper is correct, some important conclusions about artistic evaluation and appreciation follow from it; but I do not try to draw them here.

II

Talk about intention or intentions may take a number of different forms, but for our purpose two distinctions may be mentioned.[2] First, there is the distinction between intentional and unintentional action (relevant here is the whole family of such words as "inadvertent," "involuntary" and "accidental"). Secondly, and more important, there is the distinction between a man's intention in the sense of that which he intends, or sets himself, to do, and his intention in the sense of that which he intends or hopes to achieve as a result of doing what he does. If someone strikes middle C on a piano, we may ask: "What did he intend to do?" meaning, for example: "Did he intend to strike middle C, or some other note, or did he perhaps not intend to strike a note at all?" This first sense of "intend" or "intention" I shall refer to as "immediate intention." An example of the second sense (which I shall call "ulterior intention") is provided if we assume that the man who struck middle C intended to do so (in the first sense), and ask what was his intention or purpose in striking it. The first question asked what his immediate intention was: the second is one way (though not the only way) of asking why he formed the intention that he did.

In the field of action in general this distinction is sometimes difficult to make in a clear-cut fashion—in much the same way, and for much the same reasons, there is often a difficulty in deciding where precisely to draw the distinction between an act and its consequences. One might perhaps be tempted to say of a successful murderer that his immediate intention was to pull the trigger of a loaded gun aimed at his victim and that his ulterior intention was, by so doing, to bring about his victim's death: from another point of view one might prefer to say that his immediate intention was to kill his victim (and his ulterior intention, perhaps, to inherit some of his money). Fortunately, however, this difficulty scarcely arises as far as the distinction between the immediate and ulterior intentions of the artist is concerned, nor, in general, where making, as opposed to doing, is in question. It is relatively easy to distinguish the making of something from the consequences of making it, and the intention to make something from the intention with which, or the purpose for which, one makes it; it is equally easy to distinguish the intention to paint a picture from the intention with which one paints it.

III

The distinction between intentional and unintentional action need not detain us long in this context. We cannot discount an unpleasant clash of colours in a painting on the ground that it was unintentional—that the artist did not mean or intend it, or that he had not noticed it (except perhaps in the trivial sense that a painter may have splashed some paint on to his canvas without noticing it; but even here one could hardly ignore this if the painter had let the work go without cleaning it off). It is worth noticing that the predicates "intentional" and "unintentional" may be applied at different levels; for example, colour A in this place and colour B in that may both be intentional, and yet the clash or harmony or, in general, the relation between them may not be, if the painter has not seen it or paid any attention to it. Moreover within the category of the unintentional we must distinguish that which is contrary to a man's intention from that which merely fails to form a part of it. In any painting there will be some things that are non-intentional, some aspects of design or significance which the painter will not have thought about and *a fortiori* will not have intended; and the greater the painting the more numerous and important these non-intentional features are likely to be—indeed, one of the criteria of greatness in art is that later generations continually find in a work fresh features to study and admire even though the existence of these features was not apparent either to the artist or to his contemporaries. On the other hand most great or successful works of art will contain little or nothing that is counter-intentional; for the existence of counter-intentional features is normally a sign of failure or of artistic mediocrity or badness (though some great works may be faulty in so far as they are magnificent attempts which do not entirely succeed).

But for our purpose the important distinction is that between the two senses of the word "intention." Many, at least, of those who have asserted that in order to understand a work of art we must first discover the artist's intention have either not noticed, or have not paid enough attention to, this distinction. We may take as an example some remarks of Arnold Hauser in his stimulating book *The Philosophy of Art History* (1959). One of the features which, according to Hauser, distinguishes an artist's work from that of a mathematician or a scientist is that his achievement, unlike theirs, cannot be separated from the process by which he achieved it. "There is only an incidental connection between Newton and the law of gravity, and nothing we might discover about Pythagoras could make any difference to the meaning of his theorem. All traces of the struggle to achieve an intellectual creation are obliterated in the final product" (p. 169). This is not so, he thinks, in artistic creation; to try to understand the work of art is, in effect, to try to identify oneself as closely as possible with the intention of the artist. Without this attempt we are reduced to conceiving of the work of art as a meaningless series of formal patterns. "Considered as mere movements, the manœuvres of football players are unintelligible and, in the long run, boring. For a time one can find a certain pleasure in their speed and suppleness—but how meaningless are these qualities compared with those noted by the expert observer who understands the object of all this running, jumping, and pushing. If we do not know or even want to know the aims that the artist was pursuing through his work—his aims to inform, to convince, to influence people— then we do not get much further in understanding his art than the ignorant spectator who judges the football simply by the beauty of the players' movements. A work of art is a communication; although it is perfectly true that the successful transmission of this requires an outward form at once effective, attractive, faultless, it is no less true that this form is insignificant apart from the message it communicates" (*ibid.*, p. 5).

Two points here require comment; Hauser's insistence on the connection between intention and significance, and his claim that art is communication.

The analogy between understanding the movements of the footballers and understanding the various paint-marks on a canvas is, in the form in which Hauser uses it, an unfortunate one. The footballers' movements admittedly make sense only if one knows something about the objectives to which they are directed, and above all about the main objective, to score more goals than one's opponents. All footballing activities, however varied, have this relatively simple purpose or objective; and it is according as they contribute to the achievement of the objective that they are valued (though they may have other, *e.g.* aesthetic or technical, value as well). But there is no such general objective common to all artists; and even if there were, it would not explain how one painting differs from another— which is more interesting and important, from almost every point of view, than the way in which one painting resembles another. Moreover, Hauser is clearly failing to distinguish the artist's ulterior from his immediate intention. An artist's ulterior intention is completely irrelevant to the understanding and appreciation of his work; that Beethoven wrote the *Missa Solemnis* primarily in order to deepen religious feeling in its hearers is as artistically irrelevant as the fact that he wrote some of his other works primarily in order to make money. (In much the same way the discovery of the meaning of "The cat is on the mat" is not dependent on our knowing anything about the speaker's purpose in saying it; he may say it in order to communicate some information or misinformation, but he may, if he is a small child, say it in order to show off his powers of linguistic expression. In either case the meaning of the words is the same.)

But what is the relevance of an artist's immediate intention? Two types of question may be asked about intention of this kind: (a) What sort of work, as a whole, is the artist intending to create? and (b) What does the artist intend this particular feature of the work to contribute to the whole? But although answers to these questions may be interesting and, for some purposes, important, they are neither necessary nor sufficient for artistic understanding and appreciation. They are obviously not sufficient; for whatever the artist may have intended to do, it is possible that he failed to carry out his intention. But they are not necessary either; for it is what the artist has actually done that counts, not what he intended to do (whether or not that differs from what he has actually done). That is, not merely cannot we count the things which the artist intended to do but did not; we cannot discount the things which he did not intend to do but did (we cannot discount the non-intentional any more than we can discount the counter-intentional). It is true that we may ask such questions as: "Why did the painter paint a line of this particular shape and colour in this particular place?" or "Why did the dramatist introduce this particular character into his play at this particular point?" But although critics frequently ask questions of this kind, the answers they give are almost invariably answers to a quite different kind of question, *viz.* "What does this line contribute to the painting?" or "What does this character contribute to the play?"—*i.e.* they are really interested in discovering the actual function of the line or character, not the function which the artist or dramatist intended it to have. Exceptions to this occur either (a) when the writer is primarily interested in the psychological aspects of the artist's biography—a perfectly legitimate interest, but not equivalent to an interest in his art—or (b) when the writer is a victim of the myth that the artist's intentions are paramount, and so thinks that he must talk about them if he is to talk convincingly about the work of art.

There is one apparent exception to the general irrelevance of intentions. We may sometimes find it useful to know what an artist intended to do, to the extent that knowing that he intended to do X may lead, or help, us to see that in fact he has done X—*i.e.* a knowledge of his intentions may lead us to see things about the work of art that we might not otherwise have noticed. However, the apparent exception is not a real one; for although such a procedure may enable us to see something in the work of art that we had not noticed, that "something" must have been objectively there in order for it to be noticed, and therefore the nature and meaning of the work of art still remains to be discovered from observation and study of the work itself.

IV

To turn now to the question of communication—the artist is indeed in a sense a communicator and it is natural to hold that, since he is doing the communicating, he is somehow in an authoritative position as regards the nature of what he is communicating. There are, however, two serious objections to this view.

In the first place, although the artist may appear to be in an authoritative position in the sense that he knows what he wants to communicate, it is still possible that he will not succeed in his attempt to communicate this. It is important to distinguish between the meaning which someone intends to convey to his audience and the meaning which he actually does convey to it. And even if we know what he is trying to convey, even if we can infer from what he says or paints that this is what he is trying to convey, nevertheless what he writes or paints may still fail to convey it. (Mrs. Malaprop provides a useful analogy here. We know what she intends to convey by "Sure, if I reprehend anything in this world it is the use of my oracular tongue, and a nice derangement of epitaphs!" But she does not say what she means; and it is what the artist says that counts towards the interpretation of his work, not what he meant, or meant to say.) To put the point in a slightly different way, what a man means to say or do is one thing and what is meant by, the meaning of, what he says or does is another. The two may coincide, or they may be opposed (as with Mrs. Malaprop); but often, and in complex statements or expressions always, even where there is no opposition the latter will have a wider range or scope than the former.

Secondly, communication by means of a work of art differs in a vitally important respect from communication by means of conversation. If it is discovered that the speaker's words in a conversation do not convey his meaning clearly or adequately, these words can be corrected or modified; and a similar corrective process can also occur, even though with more practical difficulty, with the writing of letters. Now in poetry or painting or art in general correction of a kind is obviously possible and it can take place after the publication of the original version, not merely during the original creative process. Nevertheless, although a corrected or revised version of a painting or a poem may perhaps be said to express the painter's or poet's intention better than the earlier version did, the first version, once it has been published, *is* the painting or poem. Words used in a conversation may be thought of as tentative and susceptible of improvement, and as still therefore, in a sense, under the control of the speaker; but a published work of art has been, as it were, detached from the artist, and he has sent it out into the world, with the result that later versions do not necessarily cancel earlier published ones as later cancel earlier in the working-out stage before publication and as later conversational remarks may cancel earlier ones. If Keats had published *Endymion* with "A thing of beauty is a constant joy" as the first line, it is by that line, among others, that the poem would have had to be judged, even by those who knew or suspected that Keats was dissatisfied with it. Even if the corrected version may be said, in a sense, to represent the artist's original intention better than the original version does, this original version still is the work of art (or part of it).[3] It is true that Keats might have said, after writing the first version and before thinking of the second: "This isn't quite what I intended" (though it might be more natural to say: "This isn't quite what I want"); but it does not follow that there was something concrete and definite which he intended or wanted, and which this first version fails to be. After composing the final version he can say: "That's more like it, that's what I was looking for"; meaning, in effect, that he no longer feels any uneasiness or dissatisfaction with the verse. But he cannot say that this second version is what he intended if the word "intended" is meant to refer to his intention as it was at a time before he had thought of the revised version.

One reason, I suspect, why so many philosophers and critics have paid exaggerated respect to the artist's intentions is that they devote most of their attention to worth-while paintings or poems (to works of art in the honorific sense of that term). With such works it is fair to conclude that things are for the most part as the painter, poet, etc., intended them to be,[4] to the extent that he could not see any way of improving them and perhaps could not reasonably be expected to do so. But if we extend our view to include mediocre and bad paintings or poems, we shall often find that the mediocrity or badness is due in large part to the artist's failure to match his achievement to his intentions, coupled either with an inability to see anything wrong with his work or with an inability to do anything to remedy the failure that he does see. Sometimes, if the intention is almost superhuman and the achievement magnificent by human standards, we may regard a failure of this kind as a fine work of art; more often, if the intention is one which we do not regard as being particularly difficult to achieve, we regard the failure as a sign of incompetence or mediocrity. But it is always what is done that we have to judge, not what the artist intended, but perhaps failed, to do.

V

Art forms of one particular type present special problems in relation to the artist's intentions, *viz.* those, like music and drama, which require some sort of performance before they are fully constituted works of art. The composer of a symphony, for example, may issue instructions to the performers, and these instructions may not unreasonably be regarded as, in a sense, expressing his intentions. We might say that they represent his intentions as to how the symphony should be played, as opposed to his intentions as to the kind of symphony it should be and to his intentions as to the functions of the various parts and aspects of the symphony. It is impossible, however, to make this distinction a rigid one; for some instructions are clearly an integral part of the work, even if others are not. We cannot change a number of Beethoven's *fortissimos* to *pianissimos*, or *allegros* to *adagios*, without drastically alerting the character of the music. On the other hand some of a composer's instructions may be so thoroughly rooted in the limitations and conventions of his own day that modern performances may justifiably ignore or amend them and still claim to be presenting Beethoven's *Eroica* (say), as opposed to Beethoven's *Eroica* arranged or adapted by X. We may compare here the re-orchestrations by Sargent and others of Handel's *Messiah*. It is sometimes said that such re-orchestration is justified because Handel would have done something like it if he had had the physical resources; or, conversely, that it is unjustified because, whatever resources Handel had had, he would have strongly disapproved of anything like this. But counterfactual and posthumous references to Handel's intentions or wishes are pointless and irrelevant; the only way to judge is by taking note of the way the revised version sounds. If it sounds magnificent but very unlike the original, then, however justifiable its performance may be, it cannot be regarded as Handel's *Messiah tout court*, but must be thought of as Handel's *Messiah* arranged by any or all of Mozart, Prout and Sargent.

But wherever we draw the line between Beethoven's *Eroica* Symphony and Beethoven's instructions to conductors and instrumentalists for playing it, and whatever we say about the "ontological status" of a symphony (or of any other work of art that requires to be constituted, or re-constituted, by performance), the remarks which I have made about the irrelevance of the artist's intentions will, if they are correct, apply just as much to a piece of music (and, *mutatis mutandis*, to a play) as to a painting or a poem.

—*The British Journal of Aesthetics*, Vol. 4 (1964)

NOTES

1. M. Weitz (ed.), *Problems in Aesthetics* (1959).
2. For a valuable discussion of intention in general, without specific references to art, see G. E. M. Anscombe, *Intention* (1957).
3. There is of course a difference between paintings and poems, in that one cannot alter a painting without destroying the original version, whereas two or more versions of a poem may be studied side by side; but this difference does not give rise to any serious philosophical problems here.
4. This does not, of course, rule out the operation of unconscious factors in the activity of the artist.

LUCIEN GOLDMANN

The Whole and the Parts

I set out from the fundamental principle of dialectical materialism, that the knowledge of empirical facts remains abstract and superficial so long as it is not made concrete by its integration into a whole; and that only this act of integration can enable us to go beyond the incomplete and abstract phenomenon in order to arrive at its concrete essence, and thus, implicitly, at its meaning. I thus maintain that the ideas and work of an author cannot be understood as long as we remain on the level of what he wrote, or even of what he read and what influenced him. Ideas are only a partial aspect of a less abstract reality: that of the whole, living man. And in his turn, this man is only an element in a whole made up of the social group to which he belongs. An idea which he expresses or a book which he writes can acquire their real meaning for us, and can be fully understood, only when they are seen as integral parts of his life and mode of behaviour. Moreover, it often happens that the mode of behaviour which enables us to understand a particular work is not that of the author himself, but that of a whole social group; and, when the work with which we are concerned is of particular importance, this behaviour is that of a whole social class.

The multiple and complex phenomenon of the relationship which each individual has with his fellows often separates his daily life as a member of society from his abstract ideas or his creative imagination, so that the relationship which he has with his social group may be too indirect for it to be analysable with any degree of accuracy. In cases such as these—which are numerous—it is difficult to understand a work if one comes to it through a study of the author's life. What he intended to say, and the subjective meaning which his books had for himself, do not always coincide with their objective meaning, and it is this which is the first concern of the philosophically-minded historian. For example, Hume was not himself a thorough-going sceptic, but the empiricism to which his work gave rise does lead to an attitude of complete scepticism. Descartes believed in God, but Cartesian rationalism is atheistic. It is when he replaces the work in a historical evolution which he studies as a whole, and when he relates it to the social life of the time at which it was written—which he also looks upon as a whole—that the enquirer can bring out the work's objective meaning, which was often not completely clear for the author himself. . . .

. . . The historian of literature or of philosophy begins with a series of empirical facts consisting of the texts which he is going to study. He can approach them in one of three ways: by methods of textual analysis which I shall call "positivistic"; by intuitive methods based upon feelings of personal sympathy and affinity; or, finally, by dialectical methods. Leaving aside for the moment the second group, which in my view is not properly scientific, there is only one criterion which enables us to separate the dialectical from the positivistic approach: the two methods consider the actual texts to be both the starting-point and the conclusion of their researches, but whereas one method offers the opportunity of understanding the more or less coherent meaning of these texts, the other does not.

The concept already mentioned of the relationship between the whole and the parts immediately separates the traditional methods of literary scholarship, which frequently pay insufficient attention to the obvious factors revealed by psychology and by the study of society, from the dialectical method. The actual writings of an author, in fact, constitute only a sector of his behaviour, a sector depending upon a highly complex physiological and psychological structure which undergoes great changes during his life.

Moreover, there is an even greater though similar variety in the infinite multiplicity of the particular situations in which an individual can be placed during the course of his existence. Certainly, if we had a complete and exhaustive knowledge of the psychological structure of the author in question and of his daily relationship with his environment, we should be able, if not wholly then at least partially, to understand his work through his life. The acquisition of such knowledge is, however, both for the present and in all probability for the future, a Utopian dream. Even when we are dealing with people alive at the present day, whom we can test and examine in the laboratory, we can only achieve a more or less fragmentary view of any particular individual. This is even more the case when the man we are trying to study has been dead for a long time, and when the most detailed research will reveal only a superficial and fragmentary image of him. At a time when, thanks to the existence of psycho-analysis, of Gestalt psychology, of the work of Jean Piaget, we have a better awareness than ever of the extreme complexity of the human individual, there is something paradoxical in any attempt to understand the work of Pascal, Plato or Kant by a study of their life. However great the apparent rigour with which research is conducted, any conclusion is bound to remain extremely arbitrary. We must certainly not exclude the study of biographical details, since these often provide extremely useful information. However, it will always remain merely a partial and auxiliary method which must never be used as the final basis for any explanation.

Thus, the attempt to go beyond the immediate text by incorporating it into the author's life is both difficult and unlikely to provide reliable results. Should we therefore go back to the positivistic approach, and concentrate on everything implied by a "complete study of the text"?

I do not think so, for any purely textual study comes up against obstacles which cannot be overcome until the work has been fitted into the historical whole of which it forms part.

First of all, how is the "work" of an author to be defined? It is everything which he ever wrote, including letters, notes and posthumous publications? Or is it only the works that he himself completed during his lifetime and intended for publication?

The arguments in favour of one or the other of these two attitudes are well known. The principal difficulty lies in the fact that not everything which an author writes is equally important for an understanding of his work. On the one hand, there are texts which can be explained by personal and accidental circumstances, and which consequently offer at most a biographical interest; on the other, there are essential texts, without which his work simply cannot be understood. Moreover, the historian's task is made all the more difficult by the fact that an author's letters and rough notes may contain some of the really essential texts, while certain sections of his published work may have little more than an anecdotal interest. This brings us face to face with one of the fundamental difficulties of any form of scientific investigation: the need to distinguish the essential from the accidental, a problem which has preoccupied philosophers from Aristotle to Husserl, and to which we must find a genuinely scientific answer.

There is a second difficulty which is no less important than the first. It is that, at first sight at least, the meaning of some texts is by no means certain and unambiguous. Words, sentences and phrases which are apparently similar, and in some cases even identical, can nevertheless have a different meaning when used in a different context. Pascal was well aware of this when he wrote: 'Words arranged differently compose different meanings, and meanings arranged differently produce different effects' (fr. 23,E.944).[1]

> Let it not be said that I have said nothing new: I have presented the matter in a different way. When men play tennis, they both use the same ball, but one places it better than the other.
>
> I would just as much prefer people to say that I have used old words—as if the same ideas did not make up a different body of discourse when they are differently arranged, in the same way as the same words present different ideas when they are differently arranged (fr. 22, E.4).

. . . The difficulties presented by the relationship between an author's life and his work, far from suggesting that we should go back to simply studying the text, encourage us to keep moving forward in the original direction, going not only from the text to the individual, but from the individual to the social group of which he forms part. For when we look at them more closely the difficulties raised both by a consideration of the text and by a study of the author's life are basically the same and have the same epistemological basis. For since the individual facts which we encounter are inexhaustible in their variety and multiplicity, any scientific study of them must enable us to separate the accidental from the essential elements in the immediate reality which presents itself to our experience. Leaving on one side the problem presented by the physical sciences, where the situation is different, it is my contention that, in the study of man, we can separate the essential from the accidental only by integrating the individual elements into the overall pattern, by fitting the parts into the whole. This is why, although we can never actually reach a totality which is no longer an element or part of a greater whole, the methodological problem, as far as the humanities or the science of man is concerned, is principally this: that of dividing the immediately available facts into relative wholes which are sufficiently autonomous to provide a framework for scientific investigation. If, however, for the reasons that I have just given, neither the individual work nor the personality of the author are sufficiently autonomous wholes to provide such a framework, we still have the possibility that the group, especially if studied from the point of view of its division into social classes, might perhaps constitute a reality which could enable us to overcome the difficulties met with either on the plane of the individual text or on that of the relationship between the author's life and his work.

It is more convenient to reverse the order in which the two original difficulties were first mentioned, and begin by asking: how can we define the meaning either of a particular text or of a fragment? The reply is provided by our earlier analysis: by fitting it into the coherent pattern of the work as a whole. . . .

The historian of art or literature has an immediate and direct criterion: that of aesthetic value. Any attempt to understand Goethe's work can leave on one side minor texts such as *The Citizen General*, and any attempt to understand Racine's work can dispense with studying *Alexandre* or *La Thébaide*. But apart from the fact that, once isolated from any conceptual or explanatory framework, the criterion of artistic validity is arbitrary and subjective,[2] it has the additional disadvantage of being quite inapplicable to works of philosophy or theology.

It thus follows that the history of philosophy and literature can become scientific only when an objective and verifiable instrument has been created which will enable us to distinguish the essential from the accidental elements in a work of art; the validity of this method will be measured by the fact that it will never proclaim as accidental works which are aesthetically satisfying. In my view, such an instrument is to be found in the concept of the *world vision*.

In itself, this concept is not dialectical in origin, and has been widely used by Dilthey and his school. Unfortunately, they have done so in a very vague way, and have never succeeded in giving it anything like a scientific status. The first person to use it with the accuracy indispensable to any instrument of scientific research was George Lukàcs, who employed it in a number of works whose methods I have tried to describe elsewhere.[3]

What is a *world vision*? It is not an immediate, empirical fact, but a conceptual working hypothesis indispensable to an understanding of the way in which individuals actually express their ideas. Even on an empirical plane, its importance and reality can be seen as soon as we go beyond the ideas of work of a single writer, and begin to study them as part of a whole. For example, scholars have long since noted the similarities which exist between certain philosophical systems and certain literary works: Descartes and Corneille, Pascal and Racine, Schelling and the German romantics, Hegel and Goethe. What I shall try to show in this book is that similarities can be found not only in the detail of the particular arguments put forward but also in the general structure of texts as apparently dissimilar as the critical writings of Kant and the *Pensées* of Pascal.

On the plane of personal psychology, there are no people more different than the poet, who creates particular beings and things, and the philosopher, who thinks and expresses himself by means of general concepts. Similarly, it is difficult to imagine two beings more dissimilar in every aspect of their lives than Kant and Pascal. Thus, if most of the essential elements which make up the schematic structure of the writings of Kant, Pascal and Racine are similar in spite of the differences which separate these authors as individuals, we must accept the existence of a reality which goes beyond them as individuals and finds its expression in their work. It is this which I intend to call the *world vision*, and, in the particular case of the authors to be studied in this book, the *tragic vision*.

It would be wrong, however, to look upon this world vision as a metaphysical concept or as one belonging purely to the realm of speculation. On the contrary, it forms the main concrete aspect of the phenomenon which sociologists have been trying to describe for a number of years under the name of collective consciousness, and the analysis which I shall now undertake will enable us to reach a clearer understanding of the notion of coherence.

The psycho-motor behaviour of every individual stems from his relationship with his environment. Jean Piaget has broken down the effect of this relationship into two complementary operations: the assimilation of the environment into the subject's scheme of thought and action and the attempt which the individual makes to accommodate this personal scheme to the structure of his environment when this cannot be made to fit into his plans.[4]

The main error of most psychological theories has been to concentrate too frequently on the individual as absolute and sole reality, and to study other men only in so far as they play the part of *objects* in the individual's ideas and activities. This atomistic view of the individual was shared by the Cartesian or Fichtean concept of the Ego, by the neo-Kantians and the phenomenologists with their idea of the "transcendental Self," by Condillac and his theory of the animated statue and by other thinkers. Now this implicit concept of man primarily as an isolated individual, which dominates modern non-dialectical philosophy and psychology, is quite simply wrong. The simplest empirical observation is enough to reveal its inaccuracy. Almost no human actions are performed by isolated individuals for the subject performing the action is a group, a "We," and not an "I," even though, by the phenomenon of reification, the present structure of society tends to hide the "We" and transform it into a collection of different individuals isolated from one another. There is indeed another possible relationship between men apart from that of subject to object, and the "I" to the "you"; this is the communal relationship which I shall call the "We," the expression which an action assumes when it is exercised on an object by a group of men acting in common.

Naturally, in modern society every individual is engaged in a number of activities of this type. He takes part in different activities in different groups, with the result that each activity has a greater or lesser influence on his consciousness and behaviour. The groups to which he belongs, and which may perform communal activities, can be his family, his country, his professional or economic association, an intellectual or religious community and so on. For purely factual reasons that I have expressed elsewhere,[5] the most important group to which an individual may belong, from the point of view of intellectual and artistic activity and creation, is that of the social class, or classes, of which he is a member. Up to the present day, it is class, linked together by basic economic needs, which has been of prime importance in influencing the ideological life of man, since he has been compelled to devote most of his thought and energy either to finding enough to live on or, if he belonged to a ruling class, to keeping his privileges and administering and increasing his wealth.

As I have already said, an individual can doubtless separate his ideas and intellectual aspirations from his daily life; the same is not true of social groups, for as far as they are concerned, their ideas and behaviour are rigorously and closely related. The central thesis of dialectical materialism does nothing more than affirm the existence of this relationship and demand that it should be given concrete recognition until the day when man succeeds in freeing himself from his slavery to economic needs on the plane of his daily behaviour.

However, not all groups based on economic interests necessarily constitute social classes. In order for a group to become a class, its interests must be directed, in the case of a "revolutionary" class, towards a complete transformation of the social structure or, if it is a "reactionary" class, towards maintaining the present social structure unchanged. Each class will then express its desire for change—or for permanence—by a complete vision both of what the man of the present day is, with his qualities and failings, and of what the man of the future ought to be, and of what relationship he should try to establish with the universe and with his fellows.

What I have called a "world vision" is a convenient term for the whole complex of ideas, aspirations and feelings which links together the members of a social group (a group which, in most cases, assumes the existence of a social class) and which opposes them to members of other social groups.

This is certainly a highly schematic view, an extrapolation made by the historian for purposes of convenience; nevertheless, it does extrapolate a tendency which really exists among the members of a certain social group, who all attain this class consciousness in a more or less coherent manner. I say "more or less," because even though it is only rarely that an individual is completely and wholly aware of the whole meaning and direction of his aspirations, behaviour and emotions, he is nevertheless always relatively conscious of them. In a few cases—and it is these which interest us—there are exceptional individuals who either actually achieve or who come very near to achieving a completely integrated and coherent view of what they and the social class to which they belong are trying to do. The men who express this vision on an imaginative or conceptual plane are writers and philosophers, and the more closely their work expresses this vision in its complete and integrated form, the more important does it become. They then achieve the maximum possible awareness of the social group whose nature they are expressing.

These ideas should be enough to show how a dialectical conception of social life differs from the ideas of traditional psychology and sociology. In a dialectical conception the individual ceases to be an atom which exists in isolation and opposition to other men and to the physical world, and the "collective consciousness" ceases to be a static entity which stands above and outside particular individuals. The collective consciousness exists only in and through individual consciousnesses, but it is not simply made up of the sum of these. In fact, the term "collective consciousness" is not a very satisfactory one, and I myself prefer that of "group consciousness," accompanied in each case, as far as that is possible, by the description of the group in question: family, professional, national, class. This group consciousness is the tendency common to the feelings, aspirations and ideas of the members of a particular social class; a tendency which is developed as a result of a particular social and economic situation, and which then gives rise to a set of activities performed by the real or potential community constituted by this social class. The awareness of this tendency varies from one person to another, and reaches its height only in certain exceptional individuals or, as far as the majority of the group is concerned, in certain privileged situations: war in the case of national group consciousness, revolution for class consciousness, etc. It follows from this that exceptional individuals can give a better and more accurate expression to the collective consciousness than the other members of the group, and that consequently we must reverse the traditional order in which historians have studied the problem of the relationship between the individual and the community. For example, scholars have often tried to determine to what extent Pascal was or was not a Jansenist. But both those who said that he was and those who said that he was not were in agreement as to how the question should be asked. Both agreed that it had the following meaning: "To what extent did his ideas coincide with those of Antoine Arnauld, Nicole and other well-known thinkers who were universally acknowledged to be Jansenists?" In my view, the question should be asked the other way round: we must first of all establish what Jansenism was as a social and ideological phenomenon; we must then decide what are the characteristics of a consistently "Jansenist" attitude; and we must then compare the writings of Nicole, Arnauld and Pascal to this conceptual prototype of Jansenism. This will enable us to reach a much better understanding of the objective meaning of the work of each of these three men, each with his own particular limitations; we shall then see that on the literary and ideological plane the only really thorough-going Jansenists were Pascal and Racine, and perhaps Barcos, and that it is by reference to what they wrote that we should judge to what extent Arnauld and Nicole were Jansenist thinkers.

Is this not an arbitrary method? Could we not do without the Jansenism of Nicole and Arnauld and the idea of the "world vision"? I know of only one reply to this objection: "By their fruits Ye shall know them." Such a method is justified if it enables us to reach a better understanding of the particular works in question: the *Pensées* of Pascal and the tragedies of Racine.

This takes us back to our starting-point: any great literary or artistic work is the expression of a world vision. This vision is the product of a collective group consciousness which reaches its highest expression in the mind of a poet or a thinker. The expression which his work provides is then studied by the historian who uses the idea of the world vision as a tool which will help him to deduce two things from the text: the essential meaning of the work he is studying and the meaning which the individual and partial elements take on when the work is looked at as a whole.

I will add that the historian of literature and philosophy should study not only world visions in the abstract but also the concrete expressions which these visions assume in the everyday world. In studying a work he should not limit himself to what can be explained by presupposing the existence of such and such a vision. He must also ask what social and individual reasons there are to explain why this vision should have been expressed in this particular way at this particular time. In addition, he should not be satisfied with merely noting the inconsistencies and variations which prevent the work in question from being an absolutely coherent expression of the world vision which corresponds to it; such inconsistencies and variations are not merely facts which the historian should note; they are problems which he must solve, and their solution will lead him to take into account not only the social and historical factors which accompanied the production of the work but also, more frequently, factors related to the life and psychological make-up of the particular author. It is in this context that these factors should be studied, for they constitute elements which, although accidental, should not be ignored by the historian. Moreover, he can understand them only by reference to the essential structure of the object under investigation.

It must be added that the dialectical method just described has already been spontaneously applied, if not by historians of philosophy, then at least by philosophers themselves when they wanted to understand the work of their predecessors. This is true of Kant, who is perfectly aware, and says so in so many words, that Hume is not a complete sceptic and is not consistently empirical in his outlook, but who nevertheless discusses him as if this were the case. He does so because what he is trying to do is to reach the philosophical doctrine (what I have called the "world vision"), which gives its meaning and significance to Hume's position. Similarly, in the dialogue between Pascal and Monsieur de Saci (which, although a transcription by Fontaine, is probably very close to the original text) we find two similar examples of a deformation of another writer's ideas. Pascal doubtless knew that Montaigne's position was not that of consistent and rigorous scepticism. Nevertheless, for exactly the same reasons that Kant slightly distorts Hume's position, he does treat him as if this were the case: because what he is trying to do is discuss a specific philosophical position and not analyse the actual meaning of a text. Similarly, we also see him attributing to Montaigne the hypothesis of the malign demon—a mistake from a strictly textual point of view, but one that can be justified on philosophical grounds, since for its real author, Descartes, this hypothesis was merely a provisional supposition whose aim was to summarise and carry to its logical conclusion the sceptical position that he wants to refute.

Thus, the method which consists of going from the actual text to the conceptual vision, and then returning from this vision to the text again, is not an innovation of dialectical materialism. The improvement which dialectical materialism makes upon this method lies in the fact that by integrating the ideas of a particular individual into those of a social group, and especially by analysing the historical function played in the genesis of ideas by social classes, it provides a scientific basis for the concept of world vision, and frees it from any criticism that it might be purely arbitrary, speculative and metaphysical.

These few pages were needed to clarify the general characteristics of the method which I intended to use. I should now merely add that since a "world vision" is the psychic expression of the relationship between certain human groups and their social or physical environment, the number of such visions which can be found in any fairly long historical period is necessarily limited.

However many and varied the actual historical situations in which man may find himself can be, the different world visions that we encounter nevertheless express the reaction of a group of beings who remain relatively constant. A philosophy or work of art can keep its value outside the time and place where it first appeared only if, by expressing a particular human situation, it transposes this on to the plane of the great human problems created by man's relationship with his fellows and with the universe. Now since the number of coherent replies that can be given to these problems is limited[6] by the very structure of the human personality, each of the replies given may correspond to different and even contradictory historical situations. This explains both the successive rebirths of the same idea which we find in the world of history, art and philosophy and the fact that, at different times, the same vision can assume different aspects; it can be sometimes revolutionary, sometimes defensive, reactionary and conservative, and sometimes even decadent.

This statement is, of course, true only so long as the concept of the world vision is considered in the abstract, as an attempt to solve certain fundamental human problems and to give each of them its own importance. As we move away from the abstract idea of the world vision, so we find that the individual details of each vision are linked to historical situations localised in place and time, and even to the individual personality of the writer or thinker in question.

Historians of philosophy are justified in accepting the notion of Platonism as valid when it is applied to Plato himself, to Saint Augustine, to Descartes and to certain other thinkers. The same thing is true of mysticism, empiricism, rationalism, the tragic vision and other expressions of the "world vision," as long as the following condition is held in mind: that setting out both from the general characteristics shared by Platonism as a world vision and from the elements which the historical situation of fourth-century Athens, sixth-century Carthage and seventeenth-century France have in common, historians try to discover what was peculiar to each of these three situations, how these peculiarities were reflected in the work of Plato, Saint Augustine and Descartes, and, finally, if they wish to present a really complete study, how the personality of each of these thinkers expressed itself in his work.

I will add that, in my view, the principal task of the historian of art or philosophy lies in describing the nature of the different world visions which may exist; that once he has done this, he will have made an essential contribution to any truly scientific and philosophical view of man; and that this is a task which has scarcely even begun. Like the great systems in the world of the physical sciences, it will be the eventual achievement of a whole series of particular studies whose own individual meaning it will then make clearer and more precise. . . .

I have already said that the dialectical aesthetic sees every work of art as the expression, in the specific language of literature, painting, music or sculpture, etc., of a world vision; and that, as we would expect, this vision also expresses itself on numerous other philosophical and theological levels, as well as on that of men's everyday actions and activity. The essential criteria by which the aesthetic of dialectical materialism judges the value of any expression of a world vision are the inner coherence of the work of art and especially the coherence between form and content. It also, however, has another criterion, corresponding on the philosophical plane to that of truth, and which enables a hierarchy of values to be set up between the different aesthetic expressions of world visions. This criterion is what the artistic theories of dialectical materialism call the "degree of realism," implying by this the richness and complexity of the real social relationships which are reflected in the imaginary world created by the artist or writer. Finally, precisely because the dialectical aesthetic accepts realism as the next most important criterion after coherence, it takes its stand on a classical aesthetic which refuses to admit any formal, autonomous element which is not justified by a particular function, either—as in architecture for example—in the utilisation of the object or in the expression of the reality of a committed, essential man.

—*The Hidden God* (1955; translated by Philip Thody, 1964)

NOTES

1. Pascal's *Pensées* are quoted in the Brunschvicg edition by Goldmann, and the number of the fragment refers to this edition. The second number, indicated by a capital E, refers to the Lafuma edition, which is followed in the Everyman Library translation. (Editor's note)

2. And this is also true for reasons which are to a very great extent social. At any one historical period the sensibility of the members of any particular social class, and also of the intellectuals in general, is more receptive to some works than to others. It is for this reason that most studies written at the present day on Corneille, Hugo or Voltaire are to be read with a certain amount of caution. This is not the case with irrationalistic or even with tragic texts, whose aesthetic value can be clearly perceived by the modern intellectual even when their objective meaning is only imperfectly understood.

3. See Lucien Goldmann, "Matérialisme dialectique et Histoire de la philosophie," in *Revue philosophique de France et de l'étranger*, 1948, No. 46; and Goldmann, *Sciences humaines et Philosophie* (1952).

4. Marx said the same thing in a passage from *Das Capital* which Piaget reproduced in his latest work: "Primarily, labour is a process going on between man and nature, a process in which man, through his own activity, initiates, regulates and controls the material exchanges between himself and nature. He confronts nature as one of her own forces, setting in motion arms and legs, head and hands, in order to appropriate nature's productions in a form suitable to his own wants. By thus acting on the external world and changing it, he at the same time changes his own nature" (Part Three, Chapter Five, Eden and Cedar Paul's translation in the Everyman edition, 1930).

5. Cf. Lucien Goldmann, *Sciences humaines et Philosophie*.

6. Although we are, today, very far from having indicated with any degree of scientific precision where such a limit might lie. The scientific elaboration of a typology of world visions has scarcely even begun.

GEORGE BOAS

In Defense of the Unintelligible[1]

One of the most usual complaints against the contemporary arts is that they are unintelligible. One is confronted with a canvas covered with lines and colors going every which way, of fragmented human beings and other animals, of bits of crockery, cloth, and paper, and one has no point of reference by which one may judge either the excellence or even the meaning of the visual chaos before one's eyes. This was not so in the days of Raphael. Or one picks up what is ostensibly a poem and is confronted with snatches of whole sentences, words unrelated by the rules of grammar or syntax, exclamations, questions, bits of quotations from the classics, even disconnected syllables of words, and one is hard put to it to make sense out of the jumble. Such poems, if they are poems, we are told, resemble more than anything else the output of the celebrated battalion of monkeys before their typewriters. Or again, and this will be my last example, one goes to a concert and one's ears are assailed by howling, screeching, moaning, and whistling coming out of a collection of instruments, and no sound or group of sounds seems to be related to any others—no tonics, no dominants, not even any keys. All this, we are informed by those who say they know, is deliberate mystification, the foals of nightmares, sheer delight in horror for its own sake, the cult of ugliness. But, we are also informed, the really great artists of the past worshipped the beautiful and, what is more, were easily understood by any man of sensibility who saw, read, or heard their works.

Out of this welter of abuse let us select one point, the criticism that contemporary works of art are unintelligible. I think that I know what it is to be intelligible and what conditions a symbol must fulfill in order to be intelligible. Only common nouns and adjectives, and sentences containing them are intelligible. Proper nouns are not intelligible. Thus symbols in order to be intelligible have to be the equivalent of generic terms. If I say, *This is a picture*, I am talking intelligible English, but if I say, *Aucassin and Nicolette*, I am unintelligible, for I have made no assertion. In fact, my hearer does not even know what I am referring to, for though he might think that I was naming a medieval romance, I might after all be simply referring to a water-color by Demuth representing two chimneys. To give the name of something, except when one is answering a question, is not to say anything.

It is an old story in elementary courses in logic that our nouns differ in denotation and connotation. Such words as *World War II, The American Society for Aesthetics, The Lord Nelson Mass*, refer to one object or incident or event. They are simply names whose meaning, in the usual sense of meaning cannot be expanded into a declarative sentence. One may of course describe each of the things they name and identify them in a variety of ways. One can tell when they occurred, what their causes were, what their purposes were, if they had any, and so on. But the meaning of these names is simply their referents. There is, to be sure, another common use of the word "meaning" which would not be the denotation of these names. It would be the emotional effect of the objects to which they refer when one thinks about them or experiences them directly. But this varies to such an extent among individuals, that it cannot be the meaning of their names if one wants to use the word "meaning" for something which is communicable. If, for instance, John Doe when he hears the word, *World War II*, thinks of heroism, glory, promotion, medals, fogies, and a fat bonus, and Richard Roe thinks of misery, mud, K-rations, loneliness, boredom, obscenity, and oratory, the word has become so ambiguous as to have become useless as a means of identification. Please note that I am not maintaining either that individuals do not use the proper names in this way or that they all ought to feel the same emotions when they hear a given proper name. Certainly conversation would be greatly clarified and a good deal cooler, too, if each event and thing aroused the same emotions in all people. But the fact is that they do not. It is also true that people discuss their emotions as if they were the proper emotions for all people to experience, given a certain stimulus. The man who is bored to death by Goethe's *Faust,* and your president, alas, is one such, cannot understand why other people should think it so lofty, noble, profound, stimulating, and indeed epoch-making. One would like other people to have the same emotions as one has oneself. To laugh, weep, and be bored in company is the pathetic goal of most lives, provided that the target of one's laughter, tears, and boredom is not one's companions. But all this is beside the point. The point is that before one can discuss the object and event to which a proper name refers, one must expand that name into a series of statements made about its denotation and such statements will perforce use common nouns, or universals. In other words intelligibility varies directly with abstractness: the more abstract a statement, the more intelligible, so that mathematics becomes the most intelligible of subject matters. Even so elementary a sentence as, *I see a cat,* may require elucidation: what is the ego which sees; what does vision consist in; how much of the cat does one see; and what particularly feline, or symbolic feline, is one seeing? But no such questions could arise over the statement, *Things equal to the same thing are equal to each other.* To ask, *What things?* would meet with ridicule even at the hands of metaphysicians.

This, I should imagine, would be granted by everyone. No one is ever in doubt of the meaning of an algebraic formula or a theorem in geometry. Such statements have a maximum of intelligibility for the very fact that they consist entirely of variables. When one says that the square of the sum of two numbers is equal to the square of the first plus twice the product of the two plus the square of the second, no one replies that this might be so in South Africa but could hardly be expected to hold good in North Carolina; or that it would all depend on whether one was a capitalist or a working man or had been brought up in a polygamous society. Nor would anyone hearing the formula exclaim, *How delightful!* or *How monotonous!* or *What an exquisite combination of unity and variety!* At least no one would in a course in algebra. But let two people listen to one of the Rasoumovsky Quartets and immediately the interpretations differ. If this needs confirmation, read the program notes printed on the record albums.

The question boils down to that of trying to translate into words something which is not intelligible. I am asserting that a work of art is intelligible only to the extent that it resembles another work of art. In that respect it is exactly like a human being. One can hear the name, *Abraham Lincoln,* and know to whom it refers. But as soon as one tries to elucidate the meaning of the name, other than by pointing to the man who bore it, one is involved in a futile chase. The reason is that "meaning" now will be interpreted as significance or historical importance, involving an evaluation more or less personal. What Lincoln stood for depends entirely on the system of relations into which one is trying to integrate him and there is no general agreement which will help one choose. For he stood at the intersection of so many systems of reference that no single human being could grasp them all. One is constantly discovering new things about him which make him more interesting, things bad as well as good, and the possibility of saying that at last one has discovered the real Lincoln, in the sense of a set of statements which are all true as well as exhaustive of his personality, recedes farther and farther beyond one's grasp. For surely we have learned that it is of the essence of human personality to be complex and full of inconsistencies, and the peculiar set of elements which make up any one individual is probably never repeated. That is why it is wisest to use a proper name and find out as much as one can about the person to which it refers, rather than first to select one set of traits and say that these are the essential person, meaning nothing more in actual practice than that these traits are those which one can classify under some rubric established by psychologists in the past whom one has happened to read and whose conclusions will no doubt be superseded as soon as one has finished reading them.

That such remarks could be made about any work of art is so obvious that it requires no proof here. Works of art, like people, demand interpretation; such interpretation will be made by people and cannot be directly established by rules, by dictionaries, or by the writings of authorities. This is, I imagine, about what Croce has been saying for some years now, though my language and philosophy are scarcely his. I admit that our interpretations depend to a great extent upon tradition, since they are always made verbally and we inherit and do not invent our vocabularies. Much interpretation consists in making a new situation fit into an old classification, a problem which we are used to in courts of law. When a man does something which other people do not approve of, he has to be charged with a crime or misdemeanor which already is on the books. But if one thinks that the name of the crime or misdemeanor was invented to cover all things which human beings might do, one attributes a degree of foresight to the human race which only God could possess. But in the field of aesthetics, critics are outraged when an analogous situation arises. They have on their books such words as *tragedy, comedy, landscape, still-life, sonata-form,* and *fugue,* and instead of saying that the composer, to take but one example, must have written a sonata or a fugue, because those are the words we possess to name what the composer has written, the critic points out that the composer has not written a sonata or a fugue but should have. In a court of law, an acquittal would be in order; in a court of aesthetics, a conviction follows.

I should like at this place to insert a bit of speculation. It has been pointed out by historians of language that primitive languages are concrete and that as they grow they become more and more simplified and hence abstract. A savage will have fifteen or twenty words which we translate "knife." But he has no generic word for "knife." Consequently, if one tried to say in his language, "Is your knife sharp?" it would be impossible.

For a man's knife and a woman's knife and a knife for scaling fish and a knife for stabbing enemies and so on would all be named by different words and the savage would see no similarity in all these different objects which would justify calling them all by the same generic name. So the Japanese have one word for one's own wife and another for the wife of someone else; nor is there any general word for "wife." We too have remnants of this sort of thing: we have no general word for the siblings of our parents. We can classify their sisters as our aunts and their brothers as uncles, but how can we talk about both their brothers and sisters in one word?

But oddly enough, though primitive speech is highly concrete, primitive painting and sculpture seem to be highly abstract. At times they resemble pictographs with only that degree of individuality that exists in handwriting. We find much the same thing in the drawings of some children who ask, *How do you draw a man?* That there is a way to draw a man, any man, is something that would never occur to a sophisticated modern painter, though it is true that vestiges of such rituals are to be found in all. In fact, it is doubtful whether anyone will ever understand artistry who overlooks the effects of ritualization in any art. But it is certainly true that in what we call primitive art abstraction is much more noticeable than in a highly developed art. If now one turns to classical Greece, one observes that as philosophy and science developed and language became capable of expressing the abstractions demanded by these disciplines, Greek sculpture—and probably painting too, if one may judge from the vases—became more concrete. The realism which Professor Rhys Carpenter has found evolving steadily in the history of Greek art marches step by step with the increasing generality of the Greek vocabulary. One has only to think of the inventions of Aristotle to name his new concepts, *essence, accident, potentiality, cause, quality,* and so on, words which we have to transliterate from the Latin equivalents, so awkward is the original Greek, and to think at the same time of fourth century Greek sculpture and vase-painting, and the contrast will be clear. Our thinking would fail if such words were taken away from us; our mathematics, physics, chemistry, and indeed all our sciences depend upon our ability to express degrees of abstraction which our fathers saw no need for.

But our painting, and I think that this holds true of much of our sculpture and poetry, has become more and more individualized or concrete. Even so-called abstract paintings are hardly all alike. They may look at times like geometrical illustrations, but they do not illustrate geometrical theorems. Each is as specific as a portrait. And if my speculation is well founded, that is what is to be expected. We no longer have to look at a picture to see what *mankind* is like; we get better information from books on anthropology and psychology. Our interest in the particular, not in the general, is satisfied by our paintings and only those people who have no interest in the particular, in what differentiates rather than in what integrates, are bewildered by them. But such people are precisely those who are innocent of philosophy or who still think of philosophy as it was before the twentieth century. They have retained in their prejudices the principles of an epoch before the development of modern science, that is, before the acceptance of time and multiplicity as things not to be explained away. Consequently they expect a painting made in 1950 to resemble one made in 1850. But by 1850 the revolution in thinking had already begun and it was not long before Monet was painting not merely the cathedral of Rouen or the poplars along the Seine, but the cathedral and the poplars at various hours of the day. It was as if the painter were anticipating one of the major shifts in science, the shift from the stable and unchanging material object to the fugitive object, one of whose dimensions is time.

That Monet's practice, scandalous as it was, did not horrify people more is probably due to his method of objectively seeing a real physical thing and trying to represent it as faithfully as possible. Once a spectator caught on, he could see what Monet saw. It took, to be sure, at least a quarter of a century before the scandal ceased to be one, but by now Monet no longer seems outrageous; on the contrary he seems old-fashioned. It was not very long, however, before painters as well as other artists began raising the question of what seeing consisted in. What Monet would have called objective seeing is scarcely what Picasso would have called it, for Monet still believed that everyone could see as he saw. And indeed if a person is willing to suppress enough of his mind, he can always identify himself with anyone else and thus select that which is common to two experiences. Though there was a lot more individuality in his vision than in that of the followers of Raphael, none of whom seem to have looked at anything with their own eyes, yet it was still possible to maintain that there was a purely visual object which the impressionist could reproduce. That such an object exists can no more be doubted than that a physicist can measure the wave lengths which are correlated with any given color. But nevertheless the purely visual object, in the sense of that which is selected by the eye alone at a certain moment of the day, is more concrete than the visual object as it would theoretically appear under some standard lighting, and more abstract than it would appear if the whole human being were seeing it with his whole mind, not simply his retina.

It is no discovery of mine that any way of representing things will seem right and natural and proper once one has become accustomed to it. I suppose that the Egyptians thought it right and proper and natural to represent things in profile, with the exception of the human eye and shoulders. We may talk with a sneer about mere habit, but habit is not so mere as all that; its compulsive force is one of the most potent things in history. The habits of society, which we call tradition, acquire a sanctity which is overwhelming to the individual, and a violation of tradition may bring about feelings of guilt whose consequences are too terrible to be dwelt upon in an after-dinner address. It should not be forgotten by aestheticians that the harmonizing of experiences has to be learned. Surely nobody in this room can have forgotten his childhood feeling of uniqueness. That other people feel as one does oneself is a discovery of great emotional power. It is never quite fully believed, I should imagine, and when it takes on plausibility, that plausibility is acquired by the sacrifice of one's own contributions to one's experiences. One can learn to suppress oneself to an amazing extent, as anyone who has ever served in the armed forces soon finds out. Indeed education is largely a process of standardization, which is self-suppression, through the imposition of correct speech, correct manners, and above all the correct curriculum interpreted in the correct way. We begin very early in life to repress our individual likings and dislikings and modes of self-expression in order to conform to the social pattern which our parents, siblings, friends, and school teachers have the authority to impose upon us. I am not objecting to this since I appreciate the need for a certain conformity in living. Rituals often liberate the imagination by making certain practices automatic. But at the same time one should not overlook precisely what a ritual is and must not confuse it with natural law. There will always be a swing between ritual and spontaneity, as some of the German romanticists saw; the problem is to keep the balance.

In the case of seeing, a man may either see with his whole mind or not. He may see with his emotions or he may suppress them. If he is sufficiently unaware of what he is doing, he may simply incorporate the emotions which are traditionally associated with things into his paintings and think that he is seeing objectively. Swans, willow trees, and Victorian maidens are to such people graceful, and graceful they will be world without end until someone sees a swan on land, a willow tree pollarded, a Victorian maiden eating corn on the cob. So mountains will frown and the ocean will crash against stern and rock-bound coasts and children will be innocent and soldiers will be boys and even Agrippina will express a mother's love. But this is nothing more than the freezing of experience into hieroglyphs, rejecting the vitality of the natural world and seeing only its mechanical exterior. But if a painter becomes suddenly aware of his freedom to associate untraditional emotions with the things of his visual world and if he actually does express those feelings, then his paintings will appear to be shockingly novel, not to say horrible or revolting. People will look at them and wonder how anyone could be so disgusting, will ask whether the painter is not trying to make fun of them, or, if they are modest people, will say simply that they do not understand. In such a sentence as this, the word "understand" means "to feel the same feelings." But the greater question is why anyone should expect to. Few things differentiate people more than their emotional responses, even though they have been educated in the same schools and have learned the same technique of repression.

Now let us assume that we are painters or poets and that we have had an experience which we believe to be valuable at least to us and that we wish to express that experience in all its individuality and concreteness. To do this we do not try to make it as similar to the experiences of other people as possible but to emphasize its peculiarities. So if we are trying to write a biography, we do not select those details of a man's life which are exactly like the details of everyone else's life and dwell on them. But the more successful we are in our striving for the concrete, the more unintelligible we become. This is unavoidable. If there are other people who have enough good-will to make an effort towards sympathy, they will at least understand what we are trying to achieve and though their comprehension of our aims will not, to be sure, bridge the gap between their personality and ours, our works of art will at least seem less monstrous and bizarre to them.

Since the beginning of the twentieth century certain new ways of thinking have arisen which cannot fail to have had some influence on almost all of us. I refer to the work of Freud, Einstein, the Curies, Bergson, statistical mechanics, and symbolic logic, to mention only items outside the world of aesthetics. The contribution of Freudian psychology with its emphasis upon the contributions of Unconscious would have sufficed—could it have arisen in isolation from everything else—to have changed men's minds about the processes of artistry and especially about what the eye selects. But it did not arise alone and I doubt whether there is any subject which has been developed since 1905 which could have been understood in 1880. And as knowledge of the external world dissolved into a series of equations, so the perceptions of that world hardened into a cluster of associations some of which took on a new and strange and for that reason alone horrible significance. It is noticeable that the hostile critics of what is called modern art are not left cold and untouched by it. On the contrary, unless my experience is peculiar, they begin frothing at the mouth, their eyeballs protrude from their sockets, their tongues grow thick and they pour forth a stream of denunciation which not even Jeremiah could have equaled. A work of art so powerfully stimulating may be unintelligible, but it is not ineffectual.

I should therefore surmise that what we have in such pictures, poems, and sculptures, is experience so completely individualized and concrete that it eludes our traditional methods of classification and by that very fact becomes incomprehensible. Regardless of what aesthetic theorists may have said in the past, people persist in looking at works of art with their whole minds and not with some special faculty called aesthetic perception. They therefore are doomed to fail when they attempt to find in what is unique those elements which are not unique, to apply as a standard of excellence conformity to rules which are no longer applicable. No rule in any event is applicable except to a class of objects or events; rules are generic descriptions and while they can measure deviation from a norm, they cannot condemn it. Yet the tendency to act as if the business of human beings was to conform to generic behavior persists and I suspect that the persistence is grounded in our passion for praising and blaming. I admit that we would all be easier prey for the psychologists, moralists, and aesthetic critics if we were all alike and if our works of art were so highly standardized that they could as well have been produced by machines. But our mission in life does not seem to be that of making psychology easy and if we are a wayward lot, that is the cross which students of our behavior will have to bear with resignation.

Before leaving you in peace, let me admit that everyone must realize that any such label as *modern art* is misleading. The arts of today are more stratified and various than those of any other time, for nothing to speak of has ever been lost. Painters of 1950 vary from those who imitate Bonnat to those who imitate Picasso; there are poets who still write in the idiom of Tennyson and sculptors whose work if dug up would be identified with the school of Puech. Furthermore what I have said about concrete experience must be qualified—and severely qualified—by the observation that any experience when filtered through a man's imagination in the form of verbal or plastic expression is bound to lose its concreteness to a certain extent, for the expressive vocabularies are to a large extent acquired by learning. From the spectator's point of view works of art also will lose individuality, for they will require interpretation, and one can interpret a symbol only in a language which one has already learned and which is therefore over-individual. But one may make one generalization which is as true as most generalizations about human affairs. In language we are reaching a maximum of univalence, thanks to the mathematicians and semanticists. But we are compensating for that rigidity in the arts and the emotional shock of bewilderment is in itself a blessing. Personally I should think that the public would be happy to find a field which they do not understand. Have we not heard that the love of wisdom begins in wonder? Why do we complain when a group of artists gives us something to wonder about? Have we forgotten the many essays on the mystery of beauty, beauty which seemed to increase in value in proportion to its mysteriousness? If by "beauty" one means the quality of certain academic paintings, then let us admit that beauty is as dead as Pan and that the artists of today are expressing a new value to take its place, whatever name one wishes to give it. It is the value of the immediate presence of a concrete experience, by which I mean, for instance, not simply the cathedral of Rouen seen on a sunny day at noon, but the cathedral seen by such and such a person in his own way, with all his devotion or hatred for it externalized, in fragments, if necessary, as his mind turns from the divinity which is believed to inhabit it to the tyranny and persecution which its administrators have practiced, with a clash of color as conflicting as the emotions which it stimulates, with evocations of the saints and martyrs associated with it. . . .

Let us remember that western Europe has been educated in a religion whose heart is an incomprehensible mystery, the horror of which is attenuated only by having been seen so often in the last two thousand years. Horror in the last resort is simply that which horrifies us. A man from Mars, or even from Tahiti, might be horrified by seeing young girls in white dresses wearing round their neck as jewels little duplicates of a Roman instrument of torture. We seem to be able to endure the sight with equanimity. I do not therefore believe that the expressions of revulsion in which some critics indulge at the sight of paintings which they admittedly do not understand signify anything more than their own narrowness of mind. It is true that the nineteenth century now seems in many ways to have been incredibly optimistic; its leaders thought that they had finally understood all problems and that there were no *terrae incognitae*. Well, the twentieth century has suddenly changed all that and there seem to be more worlds to conquer than our fathers dreamed of. The universe has grown in many ways more mysterious, rather than less, and this is especially true as far as human affairs are concerned. So long as the human eye was simply a retina on whose passive surface the light rays made their impressions, pictures were easily enough painted and understood. But now we know that between the retina and the paint brush lies an enormous complex of hate and longing and dread and hunger, of fears emerging from infancy and childhood, of desires to placate, to annoy, to kill, to create. What folly then to preach an aesthetic creed based upon an obsolete psychology! Does anyone really believe that any artist worth his salt would pay the slightest attention to such scoldings? Critics by tradition have the pretension of deciding what is good and what is bad, but aestheticians at least might be expected to study works of art rather than to praise and blame them. It is obvious that one cannot understand the unintelligible. But it is next to obvious that one can understand why it is unintelligible. If to be intelligible means to be translatable into words, then there are plenty of unintelligibles in the universe. But man can appreciate what he does not understand, as he can love his wife and children. We have known for centuries why certain things occur; we have never known whether they will occur or not. We can always state the conditions under which events will happen; that they will happen is never certain. If one prefer the jargon of the schools, the *what* is intelligible, not the *that*, and there has never yet been perfected a system of philosophy which could explain why any general rule was exemplified, if indeed the question has any meaning. It is always possible of course to classify everything, if classification is of interest. The great question is whether the main purpose of the modern artist is to exemplify generic traits of some imaginary class or to produce an individual object.

—*The Journal of Aesthetics and Art Criticism*, Vol. 9 (1950–1951)

NOTE

1. Presidential address at the annual meeting of the American Society for Aesthetics in Durham, N.C., October 20, 1950.

CLEMENT GREENBERG

Counter-Avant-Garde[1]

Das Gemeine lockt jeden: siehst du in
Kürze von vielen.
Etwas geschehen, sogleich denke nur:
dies ist gemein.[2]
Goethe: *Venetian Epigrams*

The case of what passes nowadays for advanced-advanced art has its fascination. This isn't owed to the quality of the art; rather it has to do with its very lack of quality. The fascination is more historical, cultural, theoretical than it is esthetic. Not that no advanced art of superior quality is being produced at this time. It is, in the usual relatively small quantities. But it's not that kind of art that I call advanced-advanced art. Nor does superior art, in any case, have the kind of fascination I'm speaking of, which offers far more challenge to understanding than to taste. Here, understanding requires going to origins.

As we know, the production of art in the West divided itself over a century ago into advanced or avant-garde on one side and academic, conservative, or official on the other. All along there had been the few artists who innovated and the many who didn't. And all along the highest qualities of art had depended in crucial part on the factor of newness or originality. But never before the 1860's in France had the difference between decided newness and everything else shown itself so strikingly in high art. Nor had innovation ever before been resisted so stubbornly by the cultivated art public.

That was when the present notion of the avant-garde was born. . . . For a while this notion did not correspond to a readily identifiable or definable entity. You might paint in imitation of the Impressionists or write verse like a Symbolist, but this did not mean necessarily that you had joined something called the avant-garde. It wasn't there definitely enough to join. You could join bohemia, but bohemia antedated the avant-garde and meant a way of life, not a way of art. The avant-garde was something constituted from moment to moment by artists—a relative few in each moment—going towards what seemed the improbable. It was only after the avant-garde, as we now recognize it, had been under way for some fifty years that the notion of it seemed to begin to correspond to a fixed entity with stable attributes. It was then that the avant-garde came into focus as something that could be joined. That was also when it first began to look like something really worth joining; by then enough people had awakened to the fact that every major painter since Manet, and every major poet since Baudelaire (at least in France), entered the maturity of his art as a "member" of the avant-garde. At this point, too, innovation and advancedness began to look more and more like given, categorical means to artistic significance apart from esthetic quality.

The Italian Futurists may not have been the very first individuals to see the avant-garde and advancedness in this light, but they were the first to make the avant-garde, as seen in this light, a viable, on-going notion and classification. They were the first to think in terms of avant-garde*ness*, and to envisage newness in art as an end in itself; and they were the first group to adopt a program, posture, attitude, stance that was consciously "avant-garde."

It was no accident (to talk as Marxists used to) that Futurism became the first manifestation connected with the avant-garde to win public attention more or less immediately, and that "Futuristic" became the popular adjective for modernist art. The Futurists announced, spelled out, and illustrated their intention of pursuing the new as no intention associated with avant-garde art had ever been before. (The sensation made at the New York Armory show in 1913 by Marcel Duchamp's *Nude Descending a Staircase*, which resembles Futurist versions of Analytical Cubism, is a case in point: this work gave people enough cues to permit them to watch themselves being startled by the "new"—as they could not do with Picasso's, Braque's, Léger's, or even Matisse's newnesses in that same exhibition.)

The Futurists discovered avant-gardeness, but it was left to Duchamp to create what I call avant-gard*ism*. In a few short years after 1912 he laid down the precedents for everything that advanced-advanced art has done in the fifty-odd years since. Avant-gardism owes a lot to the Futurist vision, but it was Duchamp alone who worked out, as it now looks, every implication of that vision and locked advanced-advanced art into what has amounted to hardly more than elaborations, variations on, and recapitulations of his original ideas.

With avant-gardism, the shocking, scandalizing, startling, the mystifying and confounding, became embraced as ends in themselves and no longer regretted as initial side-effects of artistic newness that would wear off with familiarity. Now these side-effects were to be built in. The first bewildered reaction to innovative art was to be the sole and appropriate one; the avant-gardist work—or act or gesture—was to hold nothing latent, but deliver itself immediately. And the impact, more often than not, was to be on cultural habits and expectations, social ones too, rather than on taste. At the same time newness, innovation, originality itself was to be standardized as a category into which a work, an act, a gesture, or an attitude could insert itself by displaying readily recognizable and generally identifiable characteristics or stimuli. And while the conception of the new in art was narrowed on one side to what was obviously, ordinarily, or only ostensibly startling, it was expanded on the other to include the startling in general, the startling as sheer phenomenon or sheer occurrence.

All along the avant-garde had been accused of seeking originality for its own sake. And all along this had been a meaningless charge. As if genuine originality in art could be envisaged in advance, and could ever be attained by mere dint of willing. As if originality had not always surprised the original artist himself by exceeding his conscious intentions. It's as though Duchamp and avant-gardism set out, however, deliberately to confirm this accusation. Conscious volition, deliberateness, plays a principal part in avant-gardist art: that is, resorting to ingenuity instead of inspiration, contrivance instead of creation, "fancy" instead of "imagination"; in effect, to the known rather than the unknown. The "new" as known beforehand—the general look of the "new" as made recognizable by the avant-garde past—is what is aimed at, and because known and recognizable, it can be willed. Opposites, as we know, have a way of meeting. By being made into the idea and notion of itself, and established as a fixed category, the avant-garde is turned into its own negation. The exceptional enterprise of artistic innovation, by being converted into an affair of standardized categories, of a set of "looks," is put within reach of uninspired contrivance. Avant-gardism was not all there was to Futurism, Dada, or Duchamp—even to the post-1912 Duchamp. It's far from being all there was to Surrealism either, though Surrealism did more even than Futurism to popularize avant-gardism. But it's doubtful whether even in Surrealism's heyday, in the latter 1920's and in the 1930's, avant-gardism took hold in artistic practice as thoroughly as it had among a few adventurous or would-be adventurous artists at the time of Dada. For all the designed "aberrations" of Surrealist art, there was hardly a Surrealist artist of consequence who sacrificed his *taste* to the sole effect of the innovative.

In the latter 1940's and in the 1950's, when Abstract Expressionism and art informel were in the ascendant, avant-gardism receded even further from actual artistic practice. The worst of the artists caught up in these tendencies (and they were legion) as well as the best (they were a handful) were genuinely avant-garde, not avant-gardist, in aspiration, whether they knew it or not. They wanted their works to function as art in the "traditional" sense that avant-gardism often professed to repudiate.

This may sound surprising to some people. If so, it's because they haven't looked closely enough at Abstract Expressionist or informel painting and/or because they've taken on faith too much of what's been written and said about it. (The very term, art informel, expresses and forces a misunderstanding, not to mention "Action Painting.")

Almost all new manifestations of art get misunderstood in the first attempts to explain them, and usually they stay misunderstood for a good while after. This was so long before the avant-garde appeared, but it has become ever so much more so since then. With avant-gardism, however, there has come forced misunderstanding—aggressive, inflated, pretentious misunderstanding. Avant-gardism, even today, is planted deeper and more broadly in the talk and writing about art than in its practice. And it planted itself in the talk and the writing earlier, appearing in Apollinaire's art criticism before it ever did in Futurist practice or attitudinizing. What Apollinaire wrote on behalf of Cubism foretold in many respects what was later written on behalf of Dada, Surrealism—and Abstract Expressionism. The palaver of the 1950's about absolute spontaneity, about the liberation from all formal constraints, and about breaking with the whole past of art —all this wasn't just part of the ordinary muddlement that has affected talk about art ever since people first tried to account for it. It emerged, as applause, only with avant-gardist rhetoric. Maybe the most constant topic of avant-gardist rhetoric is the claim made with each new phase of avant-garde, or seemingly avant-garde, art that the past is now being finally closed out and a radical mutation in the nature of art is taking place after which art will no longer behave as it has heretofore. As it happens, this was already said more or less about Impressionism in its time, and it was also said about every next step of modernist art—but it was said then only in condemnation and opposition. Not till around 1910 did the same thing begin to be said in praise and welcome. Again—as with the business of pursuing originality for its own sake—it was as though avant-gardism were trying deliberately to confirm a standard charge against the avant-garde.

A key figure in the Abstract Expressionist situation was Jackson Pollock. I mean a key figure—aside from the value of his art—as looked back at in the light of what has most conspicuously happened in art since Abstract Expressionism. Pollock's all-over "drip" paintings of 1947–50 were in their time taken for arbitrary effusions by his fellow-Abstract Expressionists as well as by almost everybody else. These fellow-artists may have basked in avant-gardist rhetoric about total "liberation," and they may have indulged in that kind of rhetoric themselves, but—as I've said—at bottom they still believed in, and acted on, painting as a discipline oriented to esthetic values. Because they could discern little or nothing of these in Pollock, they did not consider him to be a "real" painter, a painter who knew how to paint, like a de Kooning, a Kline, or a Rothko; they saw him, rather, as a freakish apparition that might signify something in terms of cultural drama but hardly anything in those of art proper. The younger artists who in the 1960's displaced the Abstract Expressionists on what's called the "scene" likewise saw Pollock's middle-period painting as freakish and inartistic, but instead of deploring that, they hailed it. They could no more "read" Pollock than their predecessors could, but they admired him all the more precisely because of that. And as the 1960's wore along and art went further and further out, Pollock's reputation became more and more a hallowed one, second only to Duchamp's in the pantheon of avant-gardism.

The conclusions the avant-gardist artists of the 1960's drew from their inability to grasp the art in Pollock got acted on in much the same way as those which Duchamp had drawn almost fifty years earlier from his inability to recognize the whole of the art in Cubism. He would seem to have attributed the impact of Cubism—and particularly of Picasso's first collage-constructions—to what he saw as its startling difficulty; and it's as though the bicycle wheel mounted upside down on a stool and the store-bought bottle rack he produced in 1913 were designed to go Picasso one better in this direction. Young artists in the 1960's, reasoning in a similar way from their misconception of Pollock's art, likewise concluded that the main thing was to look difficult, and that the startlingly difficult was sure to look new, and that by looking newer and newer you were sure to make art history. To repeat: it wasn't Abstract Expressionist art as such that helped bring on the great resurgence of avant-gardism in the 60's, but the misconceptions of it propagated by avant-gardist rhetoric and welcomed and maintained by younger artists of retarded, academic taste.

"Academic" is an unhelpful term unless constantly re-defined and re-located. One of the notable things done by Charles W. Millard, in an article called "Dada, Surrealism, and the Academy of the Avant-Garde" which appeared in *Hudson Review* of Spring 1969, was to define and locate academicism as an aggressive tendency inside the precincts of the avant-garde, and not just a matter of imitativeness or belatedness. Mr. Millard specifies Dada and Surrealism as being in part an effort to "modify modernism, to make it 'easier,' and to reintroduce literary content." I would add that Dada and Surrealism, insofar as they were avant-gardist (Mr. Millard doesn't use this label), constituted a first attempt not just to modify, but to capture the avant-garde—from within as it were—in order to turn it against itself.

Academic qualms are omnipresent, like mold spores in the air. They arise from the need for security, which artists feel as much as other human beings do. Until recently any kind of art in which this need predominated declared itself more or less openly as academic. There were, of course, degrees and degrees; and it never was, and never will be, easy to distinguish among them. Yet when we look back it seems that it used to be easier to do so than it is now, when so many sheep have taken to wearing wolf's clothing.

In the 1950's old-time, self-evident academic art began to be pushed from the current foreground of the larger art public's attention by Abstract Expressionism and *art informel*. It was left to Pop art, however, to finish the job, in the early 1960's, and Pop art was able to finish it because it was more essentially, and viably, academic than Abstract Expressionism had ever been, even in its last and worst days. The current foreground was the natural habitat of academic art, and it was a habit, moreover, that wouldn't tolerate any other kind of art. Having been thrust from that habitat in all its old guises, academic art rushed back in new ones. This marked the beginning of the present revival of avant-gardism. In the meantime the public attracted by whatever could be considered advanced art had grown enormously, so that by the early 60's it had come to coincide to all intents and purposes with the public for contemporary art in general. But this public, while it had a great appetite for the look of the advanced, turned out to have no more real stomach for the substance of it than any previous art public had.

Like Assemblage and Op, Pop art remained too tamely artistic, too obviously tasteful, to maintain for long the advanced-advanced look that avant-gardist art needed in order to be plausible. If academic sensibility were to continue to disguise itself effectively it would have to wear a much more physically, phenomenally new look, a more opaque and "difficult" one. Innovation was not supposed to be all that easy on taste. Again Duchamp was consulted, this time less for his "Pop" irony than for his vision of the all-out far-out—art beyond art, beyond anti-art and non-art. This was what the past triumphs of the classic avant-garde, from Manet to Barnett Newman, had now—with help from avant-gardist rhetoric—prepared a new middlebrow consciousness for.

Academic sensibility has taken to cavorting in ways that seem to defy and deny all past notions of the academic. Doesn't the academic depend, always on the tried and proven and isn't every sort of untried and unproven thing being adventured with here? Well, just as there's almost nothing that can't (under sufficient pressure of both taste and inspiration) be turned into high and original art, so there's almost nothing that can't be turned immediately into academic (or less than academic) art: nothing that can't be conventionalized on the spot, including unconventionality itself. It's one of avant-gardism's great theoretical services to have demonstrated that the look, at least, of the unconventional, the adventurous, the advanced, can be standardized enough to be made available to the tritest sensibility.

But you can still wonder exactly why it is that all the phenomenal, configurational, and physical newness that abounds in art today should evince so little genuinely artistic or esthetic newness—why most of it comes out so banal, so empty, so unchallenging to taste. In the past phenomenal newness used almost always to coincide with authentic artistic newness—in Giotto's or Donatello's case, really, as much as in Brancusi's or Pollock's. Why does the equation between phenomenal and esthetic newness no longer seem to hold today?

In some part this question resolves itself into one of context. All art depends in one way or another on context, but there's a great difference between an esthetic and a non-esthetic context. The latter can range from the generally cultural through the social and political to the merely sexual. From the start avant-gardist art resorted extensively to effects depending on an extraesthetic context. Duchamp's first Readymades, his bicycle wheel, his bottlerack, and later on his urinal, were not new at all in configuration; they startled when first seen only because they were presented in a fine-art context, which is a purely cultural and social, not an esthetic or artistic context. (It doesn't matter in this connection that the "influence" of Cubism can be detected in the choice of the bicycle wheel and the bottle-rack.) But of "context" art, more a little later.

There are, however, other varieties of avant-gardist art that do not rely on extrinsic context, and which do aim at intrinsic visual or situational originality: Minimal art (which is not altogether avant-gardist), tech-nological, "funky," earth, "process," "systems," etc., etc. These kinds of art more emphatically pose the question of why phenomenal novelty, and especially spectacular phenomenal novelty, seems to work nowadays so differently from the way it used to.

Among the many things that highly original art has always done is con-vert into art what seems to be non-art. Avant-garde art called attention to this supposed conversion in more obvious and striking ways than any art before it had—at least any urban art. It was as though the line between art and supposed non-art receded faster for the avant-garde, and that at the same time the latter had to push harder and harder against that line. As I've already said: to most people at the time, the first full-blown Impres-sionist paintings seemed to break with everything previously considered pictorial art and to remain "non-art" objects; this, the "non-art" reaction, was provoked by every subsequent move of modernist art and, like other such standard reactions to it, was finally adopted by avant-gardism as something to be welcomed.

But Duchamp's Readymades already showed that the difference between art and non-art was a conventionalized, not a securely experienced differ-ence. (As they also showed that the condition of being art was not neces-sarily an honorific one.) Since then it has become clearer, too, that any thing that can be experienced at all can be experienced esthetically; and that any thing that can be experienced esthetically can also be experienced as *art*. In short, art and the esthetic don't just overlap, they coincide (as Croce suspected, but didn't conclude). The notion of art, put to the strictest test of experience, proves to mean not skilful making (as the ancients defined it), but an act of mental distancing—an act that can be performed even without the help of sense perception. Any and everything can be subjected to such distancing, and thereby converted into something that takes effect as art. There turns out, accordingly, to be such a thing as art at large, art that is realized or realizable everywhere, even if for the most part inadvertently, momentarily, and solipsistically: art that is private, "raw," and unformalized (which doesn't mean "formless," of which there is no such thing). And because this art can and does feed on anything within the realm of conceivability, it is virtually omnipresent among human beings.

This "raw," ubiquitous art doesn't as a rule move anybody more than minimally on the esthetic level, however much it might do so on the level of consolation or therapy or even of the "sublime." It's literally and truly minimal art. And it's able to remain that because in its usual privacy it is sheltered from the pressure of expectations and demands. Art starts from expectation-and-satisfaction, but only under the pressure of heightened expectation—expectation as schooled and heightened by sufficient esthetic experience—does art lift itself out of its "raw" state, make itself communicable, and become what society considers to be art proper, public art.

Duchamp's "theoretical" feat was to show that "raw" art could be formalized, made public, simply by setting it in a formalized art situation, and without trying to satisfy expectations—at least not in principle. Since Duchamp this formalizing of "raw" art by fiat has become a stereotype of avant-gardist practice, with the claim being made, always, that new areas of non-art are being won for art thereby. All this has actually amounted to, however, is that public attention is called to something that was art to begin with, and banal as that, and which is made no more intrinsically interesting by being put into a recognized art context. New areas are thereby won not for art, but only for bad formalized art. The esthetic expectations to which art by fiat is directed are usually rudimentary. Surprise, which is an essential factor in the satisfaction of more than minimal esthetic expectations, is here conceived of in relation mainly to non-esthetic ones, and derives only from the act of offering something as formalized art that's otherwise taken to be, and expected to be, anything but art—like a bicycle wheel or a urinal, a littered floor, or the temperature multiplied by the barometric pressure in a hundred different places at the same time or at a thousand different times. (Or else the surprise comes from reproducing or representing objects in incongruous materials or sizes, or from affixing incongruous objects to pictures, or from offering reproductions of photographs as paintings, and so on, with the stress being always put on incongruity in the "material mode." And though there's nothing that says that *stressed* incongruity can't be an integral esthetic factor, it has hardly ever managed to be that so far except in literature.)

The issue for art is not merely to extend the limits of what's considered art, but to increase the store of what's experienced as "good and better" art. This is what extending the "limits" of art meant for the classic avant-garde. The issue remains quality: that is, to endow art with greater capacity to move you. Formalization by itself—putting a thing in a public art context—does not do this, or does it only exceptionally. Nor does surprise for the sake of surprise do this. Art, as I've said, depends on expectation and its satisfaction. It moves and satisfies you in a heightened way by surprising expectation; but it does not do so by surprising expectation *in general;* it does what it does best by surprising expectations that are of a certain order. By conforming to these even as it jars them, artistic surprise not only enhances esthetic satisfaction, but also becomes a self-renewing and more or less permanent surprise—as all superior art shows.

Superior art comes, almost always, out of a tradition—even the superior art that comes early—and a tradition is created by the interplay of expectation and satisfaction through surprise as this interplay operates not only within individual works of art, but between them. Taste develops *as* a context of expectations based on experience of previously surprised expectations. The fuller the experience of this kind, the higher, the more truly sophisticated the taste. At any given moment the most sophisticated, the best taste with regard to the new art of that moment is the taste which implicitly asks for new surprises, and is ready to have its expectations revised and expanded by the enhanced satisfactions which these may bring. Only the superior artist responds to this kind of challenge, and major art proceeds as one frame of expectations evolves out of, and includes, another. (Need I remind anyone that this evolution, for all its cumulativeness, does not necessarily mean "progress"—any more than the word, "evolution," itself does?)

The superior artist acquires his ambition from, among other things, the experience of his taste, his own taste. No artist is known—at least not where the evidence is clear enough—to have arrived at important art without having effectively assimilated the best new art of the moment, or moments, just before his own. Only as he grasps the expanded expectations created by this best new art does he become able to surprise and challenge them in his own turn. But his new surprises—his innovations—can never be total, utterly disconcerting; if they were, the expectations of taste would receive no satisfaction at all. To repeat: . . . surprise demands a context. According to the record, new and surprising ways of satisfying in art have always been connected closely with immediately previous ways, no matter how much in opposition to these ways they may look or actually have been. (This holds for Cavallini and Giotto as well as for David and Manet, and for the Pisanos as well as for Picasso as constructor and sculptor.) There have been no great vaults "forward," no innovations out of the blue, no ruptures of continuity in the high art of the past—nor have any such been witnessed in our day. Ups and downs of quality, yes, but no gaps in *stylistic* evolution or nonevolution. (Continuity seems to belong to the human condition in general, not just to the artistic one.)

The academic artist tends, in the less frequent case, to be one who grasps the expanded expectations of his time, but complies with these too patly. Far more often, however, he is one who is puzzled by them, and who therefore orients his art to expectations formed by an earlier phase of art. The unique historical interest of Duchamp's case lies in his refusal, as an academic artist of the second kind, to follow this second way, and in his deciding, instead, to wreak his frustration on artistic expectations in general. As well as by scrambling literary and cultural with visual contexts he tried to disconcert expectation by dodging back and forth between pictorial and sculptural ones (as he must have thought Picasso was doing in his collage-constructions).[3] Again, there's nothing necessarily wrong or qualitatively compromising in the juggling of expectations between one medium and another. The classic avant-garde's emphasis on "purity" of medium is a time-bound one and no more binding on art than any other time-bound emphasis. What's been wrong in the avant-gardist juggling of expectations is that the appeal from one frame of expectations to another has usually been away from the most sophisticated expectations working in one medium to less sophisticated ones operating in some other. It's a lesser pressure of literary taste that the Pop artist appeals to as against a higher pressure of pictorial or sculptural taste; it's a lower pressure of pictorial taste that the Minimalist artist appeals to as against a higher pressure of sculptural taste. The invoking of the literally three-dimensional in a two-dimensional context (as in the shaped canvas), and of the two-dimensional in a three-dimensional context (though there are strong exceptions here) has meant, in general, the attempt to evade the highest going pressures of taste, and at the same time to disguise this. Which is maybe the most succinct way of all of describing avant-gardism in any of the arts—those of literature and music and architecture as well as of painting and sculpture.

For good reasons, the drift of avant-gardist medium-scrambling in visual art has been more and more towards the non-pictorial and three-dimensional. Now that utter abstractness is taken for granted, it has become more difficult to approach the "limits" of art in a pictorial context; now everything and anything two-dimensional states itself automatically as pictorial—a stretch of mud (in bas-relief) as well as a blank wall or blank canvas—and thus exposes itself immediately and nakedly to pictorial taste. (Some awareness of this lies behind the recent cry that painting is "finished.") On the other hand, taste, even the best taste, appears to function far more uncertainly nowadays in the area of the three-dimensional than in that of the two-dimensional. The difference between abstract sculpture (or "object"-making) and "non"-art still seems relatively tenuous. Experience of sculpture has not yet produced an order of expectations that would help the eye firmly separate abstract sculpture not only from architecture and utilitarian design, but even from three-dimensional appearances at large. (This may help account for the repeated disappointments of abstract sculpture so far.) Something like a break in the continuity of sculptural taste has appeared: something that looks, even, like a vacuum of taste. This ostensible vacuum has come in opportunely for academic sensibility that wants to mask itself. Here is the chance to escape not just from strict taste, but from taste as such. And it's in this vacuum that avant-gardist art has produced, and performed, its most daring and spectacular novelties. But this vacuum also explains, finally, why they all come out so un-new, why phenomenal and configurational innovation doesn't coincide the way it used to with the genuinely artistic kind.

Art that realizes—and formalizes—itself in disregard of artistic expectations of any kind, or in response only to rudimentary ones, sinks to the level of that unformalized and infinitely realizable, sub-academic, sub-*kitschig* art—that sub-art which is yet art—whose ubiquitousness I called attention to earlier. This kind of art barely makes itself felt, barely differentiates itself, as art because it has so little capacity to move and elate you. Nor can any amount of phenomenal or configurational novelty increase this capacity in the absence of the control of informed expectations. Ironically enough, this very incapacity to move, or even interest, you— except as a momentary apparition—has become the most prized, the most definitive feature of up-to-date art in the eyes of many art-followers. Some recent art that happens not at all to be avant-gardist in spirit gets admired precisely when it fails to move you and because of what makes it fail to do so.

But to adapt that saying of Horace's again: you may throw taste out by the most modern devices, but it will still come right back in. Tastefulness —abject good taste, academic taste, "good design"—leaks back constantly into the furthest-out as well as furthest-in reaches of the vacuum of taste.

The break in continuity gets steadily repaired. Finally it turns out that there has not really been a break, only the illusion of one. In the showdown abstract sculpture does get *seen*, and does get judged. The vacuum of taste collapses.

The inexorability with which taste pursues is what avant-gardist art in its very latest phase is reacting to. It's as though Conceptualist art in all its varieties were making a last desperate attempt to escape from the jurisdiction of taste by plumbing remoter and remoter depths of sub-art—as though taste might not be able to follow that far down. And also as though boredom did not constitute an esthetic judgment.

—Art International, Vol. 15 (1971)

NOTES

1. This is a revised and much expanded version of an Adolph Ullman Lecture given at Brandeis University, in Waltham, Massachusetts, on 13 May 1970.

2. *Translation:* What's ordinary attracts everybody; when you see something going over fast with lots of people, then just think: that's ordinary.

3. In all fairness to Duchamp as an artist I should point out that he did several things—the "straight" painting. *Network of Stoppages*, of 1914, and the *Glasses* of a little later date—that achieve genuinely large, even major quality, and that are also prophetic in the way that they make a virtue out of their opposition to Synthetic Cubism. In those years, Duchamp could fall into inspiration.

MONROE C. BEARDSLEY

*On the Generality of Critical Reasons**

If giving reasons for an assertion consists in making other assertions and also asserting that they support it, then critics evidently give reasons for their judgments of art. To doubt this is to urge a stricter concept of reason-giving, according to which not every proposition that is alleged to be a reason actually is one. But then, using the narrower definition, we can still say that critics wish to give reasons, and think they are doing so, whether or not they succeed. Whichever way we put it, the critic implicitly makes the same essential claim: namely, that his judgments can be supported in some way by other propositions.

This claim is challenged by the Critical Skeptic. The form of his challenge depends on the latitude given to the term "reason," but its substance is the same. A few years ago, a colleague of mine and I engaged in correspondence with an English gentleman, author of a monograph entitled *Shakespeare's Hyphens*,[1] who pointed out to us that Shakespeare used a great many hyphenated words and that this practice was also followed by Walt Whitman and Dylan Thomas. Our correspondent argued at one point: the more hyphens, the greater the poet. Now, suppose a critic were to propose the following: This poem is poor, because it is deficient in hyphens. We may choose to say that this is not a reason at all, because it is so wildly irrelevant; in this sense of "reason," the skeptic's position is that no reasons can be given for critical judgments. On the other hand, we may take a more charitable view, and call this a reason simply because it is offered as one; in this broad sense, the skeptic's position is that no good, or cogent, reasons can be given for critical judgments.

The critical skeptic may remind us of Wordsworth's assurance, in his 1800 Preface, that he was not "principally influenced by the selfish and foolish hope of *reasoning* him [i.e., the reader] into an approbation of these particular Poems."[2] Now this was a somewhat peculiar remark in the first place. The hope of reasoning someone into an approbation might conceivably be "selfish" (if Wordsworth were merely aiming to increase his royalties), but it is "foolish" only if we take "approbation" in the sheer sense of *liking*. "How can anyone be *argued* into liking Wordsworth's 'We are Seven'?" the skeptic asks. But I should think that the aim of the reasoner—that is, the critic armed with reasons—is not to get people to *like* the poem, but to get them to acknowledge that it is good. And the question is whether his reasons—or alleged reasons are of service to him in this enterprise.

I don't think that the skeptic's position, Cartesian though it may in some respects appear, can be disposed of by a simple appeal to paradigm cases. We might try this argument against him: Granted that the number of hyphens does not make a poem poor (or good), still that's not the sort of thing critics usually say. Consider a principle enunciated by Cleanth Brooks:

A poem, then, to sum up, is to be judged, not by the truth or falsity as such, of the idea which it incorporates, but rather by its character as drama—by its coherence, sensitivity, depth, richness, and tough-mindedness.[3]

Now, suppose the critic says, "This poem is poor because it is incoherent." If that is not a good reason for condemning a poem, what *could* be a good reason? Doesn't critical skepticism imply that the expression "good reason" has no application at all in critical discourse? But surely this term must have some application, or we would never have learned how to use it.

If this sort of argument is ever persuasive, I'm afraid that aesthetics is the last place in which to employ it. Probably a fair number of philosophers would be quite ready to label the whole body of critical reasoning a misuse of language. Let us assume that there must be *some* examples of good reasons, if we can speak intelligibly of good reasons; but it might well be that all of the examples are to be found in other fields than criticism, and that none of the arguments in, say, *The Well Wrought Urn*, come near to meeting the high standards that are exemplified in legal reasoning, or ethics, or the game-theory of nuclear deterrence. No—if we are going to be able to make sense of what the critic does when he gives reasons, and back him up with a philosophical account of how those reasons really work, we must grapple more closely with the skeptic's arguments.

I

The general problem of justifying the critic's appeal to reasons is, of course, large and complex. I propose to deal with only one of its parts—but one that has received some attention in the past few years.

To pass over a number of preliminary matters, let me first say that I hold that the critic does make value judgments and does sometimes adequately support them by good reasons. A reason is some descriptive or interpretive proposition about the work under consideration—"The poem is incoherent," for example. Thus a reason always cites some property of the work, and we may say that this property is then employed as a *criterion of value* by the critic who presents that reason. Criteria cited in reasons supporting favorable judgments are merits; criteria cited on behalf of unfavorable judgments are defects. If the critic says, "This poem is poor because (among other things) it is incoherent," then he is treating incoherence as a poetic defect. A critical criterion is thus a feature that helps to make the work good or bad, better or worse; it adds to or detracts from its esthetic goodness.

This is the position that the skeptic rejects. He holds that, in the sense proposed, there are no criteria of aesthetic value, that is, of goodness or badness in poems, paintings, plays, music, etc. Some skeptics like to invoke John Wisdom's distinction, in another context, between what he called "dull" and "interesting" ways of talking about art. A book about art, says Wisdom, "is dull when it tries to set out in general terms what makes a good picture good" by giving "rules" or "canons."[4] This, by itself, is something of an obiter dictum, but it can be given plausible and perhaps rather convincing support.

If one proposition is a reason for another, in the sense of actually supporting it, then there must be a logical connection of some sort between them. And, being a logical connection, it must relate general concepts in an abstract way. Thus, for example, if a certain degree of sharpness is a merit in knives (we can think of a particular sort of knife, such as the butcher's), then to say that a knife has that degree of sharpness must *always* be a reason to support the conclusion that it is good, and it must apply to *all* knives of the relevant sort. This reason may not be enough to *prove* that the knife is good, since the merit may be outweighed by serious defects, but sharpness to that degree will always make its contribution to the goodness of the knife. It will, at least, never be a fault in a knife: that is, we cannot say, "That knife is poor, just because it is exactly that sharp." And, of two knives similar in all other respects, if one is sharp and the other is not, the former will be a better knife than the other. Thus sharpness is a *general* merit in knives.

Generality of this sort appears to be essential to reasons in the logical sense, and if critical criteria are defined as features citable in reasons, then there must be an important sense in which such criteria are general, too.

Thus the view that there *are* reasons that support the critic's judgment entails the view that there are general criteria of evaluation. Let us call this view the General Criterion Theory. It is a main target of the critical skeptic's attack.

As my main text for examination, I shall select the very forthright statement by Mr. William E. Kennick, in his article, "Does Traditional Aesthetics Rest on a Mistake?"[5] In this article, Mr. Kennick holds that there are no "general rules, standards, criteria, canons, or laws applicable to all works of art by which alone such critical appraisals can be supported" (329). And he goes on to say this:

> Ordinarily we feel no constraint in praising one novel for its verisimilitude, another for its humour, and still another for its plot or characterization. . . . Botticelli's lyric grace is his glory, but Giotto and Chardin are not to be condemned because their poetry is of another order. . . . Different works of art are, or may be, praiseworthy or blameworthy for different reasons, and not always for the same reasons. A quality that is praiseworthy in one painting may be blameworthy in another; realism is not always a virtue, but this does not mean that it is not sometimes a virtue (331).[6]

The problem, then, is this: Do critical reasons have a kind of generality of application, so that it makes sense to try to formulate principles of criticism? I believe they do. Mr. Kennick, like a number of other recent writers, believes they do not. Now, if they do not, there are two possibilities. Some philosophers, including Mr. Kennick, hold that we can still talk of giving reasons in particular cases (that is, supporting the judgment that this or that poem is good or poor), without committing ourselves to any general principles at all. Others, however, hold (and I think with more reason) that some form of generality is essential to reason-giving and, therefore, that if there are no general criteria, there can be no critical criteria at all. My aim is to examine the arguments against the General Criterion Theory.

Before coming to them, however, it may be helpful to remind ourselves that the issue has two close analogues in other fields of philosophy, no less troublesome elsewhere than this is here. First, there is the problem of the universalizability of ethical judgments. Some writers have contended that it is precisely the difference between ethical judgment and critical judgment that one is general and the other is not,[7] but there does seem to be a similar problem in ethics. When we blame a man for not keeping an appointment, are we committed to the universalization of an implicit principle? Most moral philosophers would say we are; and the principle is something like: Anyone else in circumstances that do not differ in relevant ways from this one would be equally to blame. The problem is to provide an adequate criterion of relevance, without circularity. We want to say, for example, that having a different color skin is not relevant, while having been knocked down by a truck *is* relevant. Is there an analogous kind of implicit commitment involved in criticism? (And I don't mean when we blame the painter, but when we set a low estimate on his work.)

Second, there is the problem of the relation between singular causal statements and general laws. According to the traditional view, singular causal statements (such as, "Dropping caused that pitcher to break") are, and must be, applications of universal lawlike statements, even if we cannot formulate the latter completely ("Whenever a pitcher of this sort is dropped in this way, it will break"). But in recent years some philosophers have suggested that we may be able to know singular causal statements, without relying on *any* general laws. Historical explanations are sometimes alleged to be of this sort. I would be happy to avoid this broad and complicated issue, but there is more than an analogy between my aesthetic problem and the causal problem: the former is in fact a special case of the latter. For, speaking very sketchily, I conceive the peculiar aesthetic goodness of a work of art to consist of its capacity to provide experiences with certain desirable qualities; and the criteria of critical evaluation are simply features that tend to contribute to or detract from this capacity. Hence, according to my theory, there is a causal relationship involved in the notion of critical criteria. And since I side with those who think that some generalized lawful relationships are essential to individual causal actions, by the same token I must suppose that a criterion can be relevant to the value of a particular work of art only if some generality of bearing lurks (so to speak) in the background.

II

A fundamental point alleged against the General Criterion Theory is that works of art are unique. Frequent repetition has not worn off the oddness of this statement. It can be construed in several ways—of which the most sensible are the most pointless. Mary Mothersill and Ruby Meager have analyzed and criticized it very effectively, and I need not review what they have said.[8] No doubt works of art—if we confine our attention to the good ones—tend to have a comparatively high degree of individuality, at least as compared with knives and typewriters. Because there are many human acts that may be called acts of promise-keeping, we can speak of general moral rules. But perhaps there are no genuine classes of aesthetic objects, such as poems and paintings (this seems to be the extreme neo-Crocean view)—or perhaps the members of each class differ so much from one another that no features can be found that are desirable in all or most of them.

But there *are* genuine classes of aesthetic objects, and their members share important properties. I don't see why we cannot admit that visual designs vary enormously in many ways, without denying that certain fundamental laws of perception may be at work in all of them. I should think that people and their moral predicaments are at least as different as poems, yet we can say that courage is a virtue in anyone in whom it may be found.

There is an interesting phrase that turns up here and there. For example: "A good critic is one who can discern the *peculiar* excellence of a particular work."[9] Now what is meant by "the peculiar excellence" of a work? If it means (as I should think it must) an excellence that no other existing work happens to have—then of course many works do have peculiar excellences. (Many also have excellences that are not peculiar to them.) But the existence of such excellences does not in any way contradict the General Criterion Theory. On the other hand, if it means instead a quality that is an excellence in this work, but that, if it appeared in any other work, could *not* be an excellence—then I have seen no convincing proof that there are "peculiar excellences" in this sense.

Let us now turn back to Mr. Kennick's propositions and examples. I think his paper contains at least four distinguishable arguments against the General Criterion Theory, each going a little beyond the previous one.

The first argument is this: the General Criterion Theory can't be true because there are no single features of poetry, for example, that are either necessary or sufficient conditions of goodness.[10] That no single feature is sufficient I am prepared to grant at once. That there is no necessary feature I am not prepared to grant without qualification: for example, I have argued that some degree of coherence is a necessary condition of being a poem at all, and a fortiori of being a good poem.[11] I suppose, however, that it could be replied, by way of putting this qualification in its place, that no *special* degree of coherence is necessary to make a poem a good poem. In any case, I shall waive my objection and concede for the sake of argument that there are no necessary or sufficient single conditions of poetic goodness. Does it follow that the General Criterion Theory is wrong?

The answer seems sufficiently obvious. Though a given feature may be present in some poor poems and absent from some good ones, so that it neither guarantees poetic goodness nor is indispensable to it, nevertheless it may contribute to the goodness of any poem that contains it and, thus, may be citable as a merit wherever it can be found. A man may be good without being magnanimous, and he may be magnanimous without being good; but that doesn't show that magnanimity is not a virtue in anyone who has it, and to the degree in which he has it. So, too, not every good poem has "depth," to recall one of the terms quoted from Cleanth Brooks above, and not every deep poem is good—yet depth may always be a good thing, as far as it goes.

The second argument given by Mr. Kennick involves a shift of ground: What if different features are merits in different contexts?—humor in one case, he suggests, tragic intensity in another. Or lyric grace in one painting, heroic strength in another. Does this refute the possibility of general criteria? I think not. Lyric grace may nevertheless always be a good thing when it can be had, and heroic strength likewise—only it may turn out that they cannot both be had in the same painting, or not without being watered down or confused. The General Criterion Theory certainly need not deny that there are qualitatively different merits that cannot always be combined. We admire one person's physical courage and another person's sensitivity to others, but we find few, if any, who combine both of these virtues to a high degree. So with two of Brooks's criteria—"sensitivity" and "tough-mindedness": poems that excel in one of these are perhaps not likely to excel in the other.

The third argument is also Mr. Kennick's—and this time he belongs to a larger company.[12] What if there are features that are merits in some works, but not merits at all in other works? Take realism, Mr. Kennick suggests: sometimes it is a merit, sometimes not. But this does not tell against the General Criterion Theory if we complicate the theory in an easy and convenient way. There are features of poems, and there are pairs and clusters of features. And some contribute value, so to speak, on their own, while others do so only in combination. This principle has an application in many walks of life, as G. E. Moore pointed out some time ago. It's like saying that you don't want butter without bread, or bread without butter, but only the two together. We can say that bread is not desirable, and butter is not desirable, but bread-and-butter is desirable; or we can say that butter is sometimes desirable (namely, when there's bread) and sometimes not (namely, when there isn't).

Thus we should not be surprised to find specific features that may be good in one poem but neutral in another: their goodness depends upon association with other cooperative features. Mr. Kennick's example, realism, is a broad notion, so it's not clear exactly what sort of judgment he has in mind when he says that "Realism is not always a virtue." In some of its senses, I'm not sure that realism is *ever* a strictly literary virtue (or, as I would prefer to say, merit—Mr. Kennick's moralistic terms "virtue" and "blameworthy" do not seem to me appropriate to the critical context). But a critic might justifiably cite an author's· discriminating ear for four-letter words as a merit in, say, *Tropic of Cancer*, where certain types of situation and character are present, though he would not, of course, wish to say that their introduction would improve *The Wings of the Dove* or *The Mill on the Floss*.

III

The fourth argument against the General Criterion Theory takes us a little beyond the third—though, in fact, the examples I have just given would serve for it as well. Suppose there are features that are merits in one work and actually *defects* in another. The touch of humor that is just right in one play is just exactly wrong in another—and so with the four-letter words. How then can there be any general criteria, or true propositions of the form: "Humor is always a good-enhancing feature"? The General Criterion Theory can meet this objection by one more complication that is natural and sensible. Some criteria are subordinate to others, as constituting their perceptual conditions. For example, suppose the touch of humor (the grave-digger's gags, the drunken porter at the gate) is a merit in one context because it heightens the dramatic tension, but a defect in another context, where it lets the tension down. Then we may admit that the touch of humor is not a general merit, but only because we also admit that something else *is* a general merit (in a play, that is)—namely, high dramatic tension. Remember that this does not mean that dramatic tension is either a necessary or sufficient condition of being a good play, nor does it mean that this desirable feature can be combined with all other desirable features, nor does it mean that all plays that lack a high degree of it would necessarily become better by increasing it, for some plays might thereby lose some other quality that especially adorns them. The point is that the General Criterion Theory can easily take account of such varia-tions as the skeptic points out—providing it is allowed to fall back upon more general and, so to speak, more fundamental criteria.

We may distinguish two ranks of critical criteria, then, in the following way: Let us say that the properties *A, B, C* are the *primary* (*positive*) *criteria* of aesthetic value if the addition of anyone of them or an increase in it, without a decrease in any of the others, will always make the work a better one. And let us say that a given property *X* is a *secondary* (*positive, criterion* of aesthetic value if there is a certain set of other properties such that, whenever they are present, the addition of *X* or an increase in it will always produce an increase in one or more of the primary criteria.

Notice that each of these definitions is formulated in such a way that it contains the word "always" in an important position and, therefore, that they both define *general* criteria in an important sense. But the secondary criteria are subordinate and conditional: it is only in certain contexts that, for example, elegant variation is a fault of style. (However, some of these secondary criteria are quite broad in their relevance.) The primary criteria, on the other hand, always contribute positively to the value of a work, in so far as they are present. And their absence is always a deficiency, however it may be made up in other ways. Thus I think that Paul Ziff is precisely correct when he says:

> Some good paintings are somewhat disorganized; they are good in spite of the fact that they are somewhat disorganized. But no painting is good because it is disorganized, and many are bad primarily because they are disorganized.[13]

Disorganization, by this exact description, is a primary (negative) critical criterion.

There is a danger that such a discussion as this may unintentionally confirm John Wisdom's remark that talk about "canons" and "rules" is "dull." I don't insist that it is interesting—only that it is possible and rea-sonable. The act of judging—in the sense of appraising—works of art is certainly not a purely intellectual act, and many elements of talent and training are required to perform it well. But it is, in part, a rational act, for it involves reasoning.

—*Journal of Philosophy*, Vol. 59 (1962)

NOTES

* This paper was presented at the Northwest Division of the American Society for Aesthetics, Washington State University, April 20–21, 1962.

1. L. C. Thompson, *Shakespeare's Hyphens* (London: Amalgamated Authors).

2. Preface to the *Lyrical Ballads* (1800), in *Complete Poetical Works* (Boston: Houghton Mifflin, 1911), vol. X, p. 5.

3. *The Well Wrought Urn* (New York: Reynal and Hitchcock, 1947), p. 229.

4. See his paper in the symposium on "Things and Persons," *Proceedings of the Aristotelian Society*, Supplement, 22 (1948): 207.

5. *Mind*, 67 (1958): 317–334.

6. Cf. Mary Mothersill, "Critical Reasons," *Philosophical Quarterly*, 11 (1961): 74–79; this is a reply to Dorothy Walsh, "Critical Reasons," *Philosophical Review*, 69 (1960): 386–393: "There is *no* characteristic which is amenable to independent explanation and which by its presence enhances the aesthetic value of paintings or of any sub-class of paintings"(77).

7. The writer most often quoted is Stuart Hampshire, "Logic and Appreciation," in William Elton, ed., *Aesthetics and Language* (Oxford: Blackwell, 1954).

8. See Ruby Meager, "The Uniqueness of a Work of Art," *Proceedings of the Aristotelian Society*, 59 (1959): 49–70, and Mary Mothersill, " 'Unique' as an Aesthetic Predicate," *Journal of Philosophy*, 58 (1961): 421–437. Cf. Albert Tsugawa, "The Objectivity of Aesthetic Judgments," *Philosophical Review*, 70 (1961): 3–22, esp. 11–12.

9. See Mary Mothersill, *op. cit.*, 428; this sentence appears in her formulation of the argument for the less radical form of the Autonomy Theory.

10. This seems to be the main point of A. G. Pleydell-Pearce, "On the Limits and Use of 'Aesthetic Criteria,' " *Philosophical Quarterly*, 9 (1959): 29–45.

11. See "The Definitions of the Arts," *Journal of Aesthetics and Art Criticism*, 20 (Winter, 1961): 175–187.

12. For example, Helen Knight, "The Use of 'Good' in Aesthetic Judgments," in William Elton, ed., *op. cit.*, pp. 155–156; J. A. Passmore, "The Dreariness of Aesthetics," *ibid.*, 49, 51–52; J. Kemp, "Generalization in the Philosophy of Art," *Philosophy*, 33 (1958): 152.

13. "Reasons in Criticism," in Israel Schleffler, ed., *Philosophy and Education* (Boston: Allyn and Bacon, 1958), p. 220.

STEPHEN C. PEPPER

Contextualistic Criticism

The mechanistic criticism, . . . springing as it does from a world hypothesis founded on the space-time field, lays great stress on the location of things. So, it locates a work of art as a physical object outside of an organism, and describes the path of stimulation from the physical object to the organism, and locates the value of the work among the responses of the organism in the form of pleasures correlated with these responses. The direct objects of esthetic value, however, turn out to be sensations and images stimulated by the external object or associated with it. The human body and the boundaries of the body are accordingly prominent features in this type of criticism, for the values are conceived as centered in the body and confined within it.

When we turn to contextualism, all this is changed. The most striking feature of contextualism is the relative insignificance of the boundaries of the human body. The body becomes simply a constant detail in a man's changing environment somewhat like the clothes he wears and the profession he follows. The basic concept of contextualism is a context of activity. The word "situation" has recently been suggested for this idea by Otis Lee in an article entitled "Value and the Situation,"[1] which is one of the clearest and most consistent statements yet to appear of this relatively new concept in philosophy. The concept of situations, he writes, "enables us to understand how values are objective, as common men believe them to be, and at the same time concrete, specific, and inherent in the process of . . . experience."[2]

By saying that "values are objective," he means precisely that they are not like a mechanist's conception of values confined to individual subjects, organisms, bodies, but are spread over a whole environmental situation.

> A situation [he continues] includes both agents and circumstances, so action and the situation go together. The agent is faced by circumstances within the situation, and the act is his response to the problem they present. Through it the total situation, including both agent and circumstances, is changed in some way. There are three characteristics of the situation which make it important for the understanding of value: its unity, value potentialities, and problematic nature.
>
> The situation is one. It is a natural fact with a natural unity, not a construct made and existing only in the mind. It is not an assemblage of people, things, events, qualities and relations, pleasures, pains, and interests, combined in and by the perspective of some given individual. All these are among its constituents, but it is itself an independent unit. Its unity is constituted by a characteristic quality, which is unique in each situation, though when we describe it we must use words which do or might apply to other situations as well—words such as cheerful, dynamic, hostile, peaceful, stimulating, competitive, and promising.
>
> Language recognizes its existence. We say of people, "They found themselves in an unusual situation, which afforded exceptional opportunities," or, "His situation was desperate." We do not deal with the universe at large; neither do we deal with single things, events, or persons in succession. We are always acting within a limited setting which includes various circumstances, and probably other actors in addition to ourselves. In this sense the situation, including both agent or agents and the circumstances confronting him or them, is the unit of experience. Moreover, it has value quality, as is suggested by such descriptive words as those above: cheerful, dynamic, and hostile.[3]

This description seems to come from another world than Santayana's. In a certain sense it does come from another world. It comes from a basically different way of handling the world's evidence, from a different world hypothesis. Contextualism is the youngest of the relatively adequate world views and is still in its tentative stages. But through the work of James and Peirce, Schiller and Bergson, Mead and Dewey, and many others it has already had a great influence on contemporary thought. It has produced operationalism in science, instrumentalism in logic, and a new kind of objective relativism in ethics and social theory. Its influence on esthetic theory is equally pronounced, though I do not know by what name to call it other than contextualistic esthetics.

Esthetic experience is obviously to be found, on such a view, in a human situation. It has been uniformly identified, moreover, by competent contextualists with the qualitative side of a situation. As Otis Lee points out, every situation has its unique quality. There is pretty general agreement that the esthetic character of a situation consists in the perception of its quality. Whether there should be any further qualification of the field depends on the question of its congruence with the field of the test common sense definition, referred to in the first lecture.[4] And the field of humanly intuited qualities of events does seem too wide. Even when narrowed to vividly intuited quality, it includes toothaches and other involuntarily endured pains which common sense would never tolerate as positive esthetic values. Accordingly, I suggest for the contextualistic definition of the esthetic field: *voluntary vivid intuitions of quality.*

This appears to me a better definition than that of "enjoyable intuitions of quality" implied occasionally by contextualists, though it comes to much the same thing. Men will not voluntarily remain long in a painful experience. They turn it into a practical situation and seek means to get out of it. A voluntary intuition of vivid quality is either pleasant or finds something so satisfying in the situation that it absorbs the pain. But if one wants to get at the particular force of contextualistic criticism, he does better not to think about the pleasure (leave that to the mechanist) but about the experience. The contextualist is a gourmand for experience. The stress is on the experience, the unique quality of the experience, and it is this that is quantified to give the contextualistic esthetic standard. *The more vivid the experience and the more extensive and rich its quality, the greater its esthetic value.* Whatever pleasure it contains is incidental, merely a contribution to the situation from an organism involved in it. As Otis Lee said, "Pleasures, pains, and interests . . . are among its constituents, but it is itself an independent unit." Value lies in the situation as a whole, and the esthetic value lies in the intensity and extensity of its quality. Irwin Edman in his *Arts and the Man*[5] states the view beautifully in these words,

> Whatever experience may portend or signify, veil or reveal, it is irretrievably there. It may be intensified and heightened or dulled and obscured. It may remain brutal and dim and chaotic; it may become meaningful and clear and alive. For a moment in one aspect, for a lifetime in many, experience may achieve lucidity and vividness, intensity and depth. To effect such an intensification and clarification of experience is the province of art.[6]

Intensity and depth of experience—that is the contextualistic standard of beauty.

And let me say again that the evidential support for this definition of esthetic value lies not alone in what it can do in the esthetic field, but in its conformity with a mode of handling all evidence according to the contextualistic world hypothesis. Its success in the esthetic field contributes to the evidence for the contextualistic world hypothesis, but the success of this world hypothesis in other fields gives at the same time a wide corroborative support to the empirical justification of this definition.

Now I will expand some of the esthetic implications of this view, and show their bearing on the judgment of a work of art. These may be brought out by a series of contrasts. I will arrange them in a pair of columns:

Quality *vs.* Relations
Intuition *vs.* Analysis
Fusion *vs.* Diffusion
Unity *vs.* Detail

The left hand column represents the esthetic features of a situation; the right hand column, the analytical features which are for the most part the practical also. Every human situation has a certain proportion of both of these sets of features. For it is the quality that determines the unity and range of a situation (at least esthetically) and it is the fused details and relations that determine the content. There is accordingly no sharp line in experience between the esthetic and the non-esthetic. Esthetic value runs out into all life, though it runs pretty thinly through much of it. It is characteristic of contextualistic esthetics that there is no negative esthetic value. Beauty is found in a vivid realization of the quality of a situation, and, where vivid realization fails, beauty is absent. What we call ugliness, on this view, is a drab or painful situation calling for practical action, which we deplore because we feel morally that it ought to be beautiful. Ugliness is moral disapproval of the absence of esthetic value in a situation. It is an ethical rather than an esthetic evaluation. But this moral judgment is very close to the esthetic. And it is another characteristic of contextualistic point of view not to admit of sharp lines between different spheres of judgment. So one is at a loss to say of Dewey's *Art as Experience*, which has proved quite justifiably the most influential esthetic work in contextualistic literature, whether it is mainly a book in esthetics or in ethics. It is a crusade against all manner of attitudes and customs and social conditions which stand in the way of our getting the fullest realization of our environment and our lives.

But to return to our two columns of contrasted features of a situation. These will require explanation for any one not familiar with them. Yet in a fundamental sense they defy explanation, since they are basic categories in this world hypothesis. They are ultimate concepts in terms of which other concepts are explained in contextualism. There is nothing one can do but point to them. So that is what I shall try to do by means of a stanza from a lyric of Coleridge's:

A sunny shaft did I behold
From sky to earth it slanted;
And poised therein a bird so bold—
Sweet bird, thou wert enchanted.
—"Glycine's Song"

Now if you permit the image to form from this lyric and the words and the rhythm to have their way, something will surely have happened between you and these sounds in the brief time of my reading the verses. Whatever the quality of the previous moments in the context of this lecture room with the blackboard behind me and this desk in front and these seats and the listeners and the concepts of a theory being expounded, I am sure Coleridge's verses brought in an event with quite a different color. Well, that is what the contextualist means by quality. It is the character, the mood, and you might almost say, the personality of an event. You will not find it easy to give an adequately descriptive name to this stanza. "Cheerful," "optimistic," "anticipative"—these touch upon the quality of Coleridge's lines, but do not name it. It requires a proper name. That is what Otis Lee meant by speaking of a characteristic quality, "which is unique in each situation." If you wish to carry this principle of uniqueness to the limit, you will say that every one of us in the room had a different event with a different quality, and that for each one of us at another reading these verses will have yet another quality. As Dewey says, "A new poem is created by every one who reads poetically. . . . Every individual brings with him . . . a way of seeing and feeling that in its interaction with old material creates something new, something previously not existing in experience."[7] There is a truth in this insight never to be forgotten. There is an ultimate, irreducible relativity of contexts. Two situations never exactly repeat. It is the relativism of contextualism. But at the same time and by the same principle there is a connectedness of contexts, which is reflected in the qualities of the connected events. There is a family likeness among the qualities of my own separate readings of this poem, and without much question also among the qualities of your several simultaneous events in listening to it just now. So, it is possible to speak with a fairly high degree of approximation to agreement of *the* quality of the poem. We shall have more to say about this matter later; but for the present let it rest at this, that while technically it is true that the quality of every event is unique and unrepeated, practically the large amount of identity of context in the perception of a work of art renders the differences relatively negligible, so that it is practically correct to speak of an identical quality running through our technically different situations.

That, then, is what quality is. It is what you experienced as the total character of the reading of those lines. Next observe that this character is derived from a fusion of the characters of the details interrelated within the stanza. Just single out the image of the bird poised in the shaft of light. That is a remarkably clear-cut unity. But see what goes to make it up. Observe some of the phrases and the words. Consider "sunny shaft" and "slanted" and "from sky to earth" (notice, not from earth to sky), and "I behold" just preceding "from sky" and suggesting looking up, and "poised therein," and "bold sweet bird," and "enchanted." It is an event magically, momentarily caught and crystalized and shaped into one unified image character. But on analysis we see that the character of the image grows out of a fusion, the cementing together or the interpenetration of the interrelated details.

Get the quality of "sunny shaft" by itself. Isolated as a separate event quoted out of its context, it has its own quality. And get the quality of "bold sweet bird." And then put them both back into their context in the total image, and do you not see that something has happened to them in their union in the total texture? That is their fusion. It is like the separate notes of a chord which fuse in the specific character of the chord, which yet is made out of the very characters of the notes that compose it. Fusion is thus pointed to as something ultimate, and unanalyzable, and immediate.

Now, let us see what all this comes to. Our little piece of analysis has succeeded in bringing out every term set down in the two contrasted columns. A situation or event is a unity with details. If we intuit the unity of it, as we did in the original reading, we get the quality of the event by a fusion of its interrelated details. If we analyze it to find the relations of its details, we diffuse the unity and lose the quality of the whole, or at least diminish its vividness in following out the details. Do you see that too? For we have done both. We have both synthesized and analyzed. We have had a first intuition of the total quality, and then we have partially analyzed the relations of the details which entered into it.

It must now be clear that the four terms in each column all go together, and amount to so many ways of designating either the wholeness or the composition of a situation.

It appears further that the two columns are correlative to each other. There is no such thing as a situation having a quality without interrelated details to make it up. And there is no such thing as an analysis of details unless there is a total situation to be analyzed into its details. Moreover, the two columns are inversely related: the greater the fusion and the intuition of the quality of the whole, the less the analytical sense of the separate details and their relations and *vice versa*. Moreover, there are all degrees of cognition from total fusion through the various proportions of intuition and analysis to complete analysis with just enough sense of the unity of the situation to give the analysis significance. Finally, vividness of quality is, with certain exceptions, associated with fusion and intuition, and loss of vividness with attention to relations and analysis.[8]

Of the four terms named in the first or esthetic column, fusion is the one likely to give most trouble and is, in a way, the key to the others. It is the process which connects the two columns by transmitting the separate details of the analytical situation into the unified quality of the esthetic situation. It is ignored, disparaged, or explained away by most other world hypotheses—called merely subjective, a result of insufficient analysis, mere vagueness, or nothing but a lot of undiscriminated elements. In rebuttal the contextualist points to it as an ultimate categorial fact of immediacy. He insistently repeats that it cannot be explained away because it is something in terms of which he explains other things. And for that very reason it cannot be explained. One cannot explain an ultimate fact. . . .

But even if it cannot be explained, we can say things about it. For, of course, fusion is not explained by pointing out that the quality of a fusion is made up of the qualities of the details fused. The whole point about a fusion is that it results in a quality different from the qualities of any of its constituents. Once more I refer you back to Coleridge's lines read as a whole and our later analysis of its details. The quality of the fusion is different from the sum of the qualities of its analyzed factors. It is an emergent. Or to say the same thing in reverse and in a way that is perhaps more familiar, analysis always destroys something. It begins by destroying the vividness of the quality of the whole and may end by destroying the esthetic whole.

Now, so far as the relevance of fusion to the esthetic values is concerned, it is, I believe, equivalent to emotional perception. You remember William James identified emotion with the fusion (that was his own word) of organic and kinesthetic sensations. There is no very good reason why he should not have included the external sensations also when these are present. Actually, in any emotional reaction there is no clear separation of visual, auditory, or tactile sensations from the internal and dynamic ones. The sound of thunder is with difficulty distinguished from its fearfulness. The sound is fused with all the other things which W. B. Cannon shows enter into fear. Moreover, there are funded memories entering in. The fusion of all these makes up the specific fear of thunder. This basic insight of the James-Lange theory of emotion appears to hold in spite of all the criticisms of it. Only, what James should have stressed was not the kind of sensations that make an emotional quality, but the manner of their appearance, their fusion. In short, vividly fused experience is, for esthetic purposes at least, a very convenient definition of emotional experience. When the fusion is massive and unmistakably draws in the dynamic tensions of instinctive action, no one would hesitate to call it emotional. The importance of this comment is to suggest that the contextualistic account is the one that particularly takes care of the emotional aspect of esthetic experience, and does so inconspicuously, realistically, and without the sentimentality and mythology of mysticism which parades its emotionality. It is symptomatic that Dewey frequently chooses the word "seizure" to designate the highest esthetic experience. It is an experience in which a total situation is absorbed in a vivid fused satisfying quality.

How may vividness of quality be increased? This is best discovered by observing what produces its opposite. There are chiefly three causes for the reduction of vividness: (1) habit, convention, tradition, and the like; (2) practical activity in achieving goals; and (3) analysis.

Habit simply dulls experience and reduces it to routine. Practical activity ordinarily drains off vividness of quality by its urgency to attain its goal, or by producing a problem to solve which turns the attention away from the felt character of a situation to a solution in the future and escapes from the present. It also leads to analysis of the situation, in search for the means of solution, and the devivifying effect of analysis we have already brought out.

These then, one would think, should be scrupulously avoided in pursuit of esthetic values. But one of the paradoxes of contextualism is that the last two, practical activity and analysis, when carefully applied, can be powerful agents for increasing quality. Human conflict, which is the greatest source of practical problems, is a potent means of intensifying experience by breaking up the dullness of routine, provided only the impulses involved can be held in contemplation and restrained from seeking practical solution. And analysis has a great capacity for increasing the spread of a vivid situation by exhibiting its structure and the details of its organization.

The ways in which artists have learned to increase the vividness of quality by the discreet use of conflict, and to increase the spread of quality by the organization of details, are known as the artists' techniques. The latter, the principles of composition, of design, pattern, and the intrinsic orders of sense materials are much better known to writers of esthetics and criticism than the former—that is, the techniques of conflict. (Incidentally, notice how considerations of sense materials come up last in contextualistic esthetics rather than first as in the mechanistic. The normal structure of a mechanistic book on esthetics is from the elements to the wholes; that of a contextualistic book from the wholes to the details.[9]) It should not be said that the techniques of design and pattern are less important to the contextualistic critic than those of vivification through conflict, but certainly attention to the handling of conflict for esthetic purposes is a peculiar contribution of contextualism.

It is remarkable how few contextualistic writers on art have noticed this. They tend to veer off after a good start in contextualism toward an integrative, organistic theory of art. If esthetic value is a matter of vividness of quality, there is virtue in integration as a means of increasing the spread of quality through massive organization. This is an old story, the old story of harmonious unity. But it is something new in esthetic theory to discover the esthetic value of conflict. This side of his theory is what a contextualist should exploit. The integration he should stress is an integration of conflicts.

The techniques for the esthetic use of conflict have been very little explored. The concept of "psychical distance" marks about the limit of it— that is, the idea that a man cannot get esthetic value out of an experience that draws upon his emotions unless he can maintain an attitude that will keep these emotions from bolting into action. You can appreciate a storm as long as you are not prompted to look for a lifeboat, and you can appreciate Hamlet as long as he does not remind you too much of your own personality problems. That is about as far as criticism along these lines has gone. But very few have noticed the reverse of this idea, which is much the more interesting, that in proportion as these conflicts do touch you (to the point of not precipitating action) the esthetic value of the experience is increased.

This fact has two important esthetic bearings. For one thing, it explains in large degree the force of tragedy in art. Most of what we have taken to be our greatest art is outright tragedy or contains tragic portions. To a hedonist this is a mystery. Why in the temple of pleasure do we set up a god of sorrow? A contextualist explains that when the center of esthetic interest is placed on vivid realization of experience, then the attraction of the artist to tragic subject matter is seen as inevitable. Conflicts of instinctive impulse and social interest stir our awareness of experience to the deepest, and the further they can be carried in a work of art towards their full tragic import the more vivid our realization. Tragedy in art then becomes no paradox.

The second bearing of the use of conflict in art is ethical. We now begin to understand how moral values enter into art. For in spite of the hedonists' efforts like that of the early Santayana to separate morality from art as something purely negative, or, like that of Pater to seek to identify moral and esthetic values, we recoil and feel that the relation is not so simple. The conviction persists that the ethical values are different from the esthetic, and that nevertheless in the most serious art they somehow get intimately involved with each other. Now we see that this is indeed the case, and why it happens. An artist seeks out social issues because they reflect conflicts and are sources of vivid realization of experience. In this way, an artist becomes a more powerful moral influence than a social reformer. For he possesses the techniques for making us vividly aware of our problems and cultivates a keenness of perception for precisely what are the sources of human conflict. Think how many essays were written with mild effect about the farm labor problem in America until Steinbeck came out with *The Grapes of Wrath.* Then for the first time the problem became vivid through the technique of an artist.

Dewey's prevailing message that art should get closer to living and that it grows weak when it is taken as luxury and entertainment and separated from the main stream of practical everyday contemporary living, is contextualistically sound. And a corollary of this principle is that art is perennially contemporary. So far as art depends on culture and not upon instinct, the art of one age cannot be vividly repeated in another, and, if the art of an earlier age appeals to a later, it is often for other than the original reasons, so that as contextualists repeat, sometimes too insistently, critics are required in each age to register the esthetic judgments of that age.

We can already see what is expected of the critic on the contextualistic view. He is to judge the degree of realization of experience achieved by an artist—the vividness and the spread of it. He will consider whether the artist has made the most of his emotional material, or has gone beyond the limits of esthetic endurance and destroyed esthetic distance. He will show the relation of the work to its social context. He will consider the suitability of the structure of the work. And for the benefit of the spectator he will analyze the structure and exhibit its details, so that these will not be missed and may be funded in the full realization of the work in its total fused quality.

So much we see of what the critic is expected to do. But we have not yet seen what a work of art is on this view. And until we have, we cannot entirely comprehend the critic's rôle. For the description of the nature of a work of art furnished by a consistent application of the contextualistic approach is one of the special contributions of this theory. With that description and its bearing on criticism, I shall conclude this lecture.

The perception of a work of art is clearly the awareness of the quality of a situation. There are obviously two main factors in the situation of perceiving a work of art, and it is the relation of these two factors through successive perceptions of the identical work that is to be noticed. I think I can make this situation, or rather the succession of situations, clearer by a diagram. The two main factors are, first, what we ordinarily call the physical work of art—that is, the stone or bronze of a statue, the canvas and pigments of painting, the score of a piece of music, the paper and print of a book—and, second, the spectator. Here is the diagram:

Physical
Work of Art

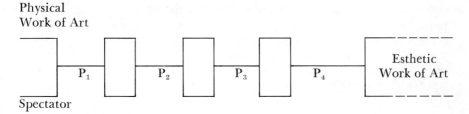

Spectator

The upper line represents the physical work of art, the lower line the spectator. If you follow these along, you will see they are both continuous lines. When they come together at P_1, P_2, P_3 . . . we have perceptual situations. Suppose we think of a picture, say El Greco's "Toledo" in the Metropolitan Museum. The physical picture has had a long continuous history since El Greco laid the pigments on the canvas. And, supposing I am the spectator, so have I as an organism and personality had a long continuous history—though not so long. When I first saw the "Toledo," that was P_1. Some time later I saw it again, P_2, and so on. And I hope to see it yet many times to come, which is the meaning of the dotted lines.

Now whatever the nature of the physical work of art apart from the spectator, we know it has not the quality of the perceived picture, for the quality of the perception includes colors and line movements and clouds and hills and city walls and these require the action of a spectator in the situation before they can appear. Similarly the quality of that El Greco did not exist for the spectator, for me, till I first came in contact with the physical picture in the Metropolitan Museum. The quality of the "Toledo," then, arises out of a situation to which the physical work of art and the spectator are both contributing. It requires the two in contact to produce the perception and realize the quality. It is true that the spectator can, once he has perceived the picture, bring up the memory of it, but we shall not here concern ourselves with this phase of the matter nor with photographs or other possible reproductions of the original. Strictly speaking, the quality of the picture is only realized on the occasions when it is actually perceived. Each such experience is an esthetic experience.

But the next point is the important one. Normally each successive perception funds the previous one and adds something new not perceived before. Some new detail comes out, some line carries through as not observed before, some shape is seen as a contrast or subtle variation of another. These potentialities were in the picture from the beginning, but now for the first time I see them. And so the picture increases in breadth and vividness of quality from perception to perception. Not that there is a steady increase. Sometimes I am fatigued and see and feel it less than at earlier times. And sometimes I analyze it and voluntarily reduce quality for that perception in order to fund the results of the analysis in future perceptions and so increase the quality. But in general and over a number of perceptions, the realization of the work increases.

What all this means is that the esthetic work of art is the cumulative succession of intermittent perceptions. It is $P_1 + P_2 + P_3 + ...$ The esthetic work of art is not continuous but intermittent. This fact has rarely been given sufficient attention. But the intermittency and fugitive nature of the esthetic work of art does not stand in the way of a high degree of objectivity in the esthetic judgment of it. For the potentiality of the cumulative series of perceptions and of the ideal of the fully realized and funded perception at the end of the series lies in the actual continuity of the physical work of art. It lies in this and in the continuity of each spectator and in the considerable degree of uniformity in the perceptive capacities of different spectators.

The only adequate judgment of a work of art, therefore, is one based on the fullest realization of it, on a perception which contains the funded experiences of many preceding perceptions. An initial perception is superficial and untrustworthy unless the spectator has had much experience with similar works, or unless the work is clearly very simple and requires no further experience. Moreover, any one man's judgment of a very rich work of art is likely to need supplementation from that of another. For every spectator has his blind spots, and, to reach a complete judgment of a work of art, many men are needed in order to draw out its total capacity of realization. A complete esthetic work of art thus becomes an ideal, realizable in the lesser works but perhaps rarely fully realized in the greater— possibly not even by the creating artist himself so many possibilities of realization may unconsciously enter in. It is that ideal final perception which rolls up all that is relevant in the line of preceding perceptions and intuits the whole potentiality of the physical work of art in a total vivid seizure.

This conception of the esthetic work of art as a succession of cumulative perceptions leading up to a total funded perception which realizes the full appreciative capacities of the physical object seems to me the soundest and most fruitful to have appeared. It can be adapted to other points of view in esthetics, but it generates spontaneously only out of the contextualistic.

Ironically, the contextualist himself does not seem to be able to make the most of it. He is so impressed with evidences of historical change and cultural influences and the shifting contexts of value that he cannot easily bring himself to accept any degree of permanence in esthetic values. I would be far from asserting that beauty is eternal. But on the evidence of the other three world hypotheses I am convinced that there is much more permanence in the world than the contextualist admits. And I believe that the capacity of a great work of art to be appreciated exists as long as the physical work exists and there are men to perceive it. So far as a work of art appeals to our common instincts and our deepest emotions, it can move men of whatever age or culture. It may from accident of language and fashion and national or religious bigotry come in and out of popularity, but there it is ready to move the common man or the student who will put himself in contact with it. Potentially, the contextualist has given us an empirical basis for this belief.

But even if the contextualist does not care to take full advantage of his discovery, he has uncovered a new function for the critic. That is to contribute as far as he can to the complete realization of great works of art. The critic acquires a sort of creative function. It is something more than giving an expert judgment on the esthetic value of the work. It is an act of producing the values latent therein. And it requires the coöperation of many perceptive men to do this, since the capacities of a great work of art for esthetic appreciation can rarely be compassed by one man alone. Many men contribute their perceptions and gradually the full potential perception comes to light. When this is achieved, the esthetic work of art has attained its final judgment.

If the contextualist himself displays a skepticism about final judgments

of any kind, we will respect his testimony, but we will balance it against
that of other men of equal competence in handling the evidence. . . .
                                        —*The Basis of Criticism in the Arts* (1946)

NOTES

1. *The Journal of Philosophy*, XLI (1944), 337–360.
2. *Ibid.*, p. 337.
3. *Ibid.*, pp. 338–339.
4. Professor Pepper is here referring to the following remarks: "In the esthetic
field . . . it is generally acknowledged that the poems, pictures, statues, musical
compositions of the great artists are esthetic materials, and also many buildings
such as medieval cathedrals, and fondly made tools like paddles and baskets and
pottery of primitive peoples, and dance and ritual, and also certain perceptions
of nature like the sea and starry nights and sunsets and pleasant pastures and
groves and sometimes fear-inspiring scenes like storms and waterfalls. . . . To
deny that these are works of art or objects of beauty would be regarded by most
men as contrary to common sense. As objects and experiences commonly denoted
as beautiful or esthetic these may be taken as the common ostensive reference
of these terms. Hereby we have a common sense ostensive definition of the esthetic
field." (Editor's note.)
5. *Arts and the Man; A Short Introduction to Esthetics* (New York: W. W.
Norton & Co., 1939).
6. *Ibid.*, p. 12.
7. *Art as Experience* (New York: Minton, Balch & Co., 1934), p. 108.
8. There seem to be two main exceptions: First, states of alertness, where in
preparing to solve or meet a situation one is keenly observant of the details of
the situation. In an emergency, for instance, perception is, for a man who keeps
his head, very vivid and at the same time analytical. It is as though an organism
could under conditions of emergency calling for exceptional output of energy be
at once intuitive and analytical. The contrast between the two attitudes is here
partially dissolved and we have almost the two in one. . . . (*Cf.* L. E. Hahn, *A
Contextualistic Theory of Perception* [University of California Press, 1942], pp.
120–121.)
The second exception is of an opposite nature, where through habit vividness
is dulled though the fused intuition of the quality of the situation is undoubtedly
there. This is the way we meet familiar objects about the town, familiar faces
about the house.
But barring states of alertness and habit, then for all states of ordinary perception the correlation of vividness of quality with fusion, and of the loss of vividness
in the quality of a total situation with analysis and diffusion seems to hold good.
9. Compare, for instance, Santayana's *Sense of Beauty* with Pepper's *Aesthetic
Quality*.

CHAPTER
12
The Response
of the Community

FRIEDRICH SCHILLER: Esthetic Play and Human Liberation
KARL MARX: Art and History
MAX RAPHAEL: Economic Base and Artistic Superstructure
LEWIS MUMFORD: The Esthetic Assimilation of the Machine
IAN McHARG: Design with Nature

We turn in this concluding chapter of Part Three to the response of the community to art and esthetic experience. There is no better introduction to this subject than the treatise *On the Aesthetic Education of Man* (1795) by the German poet-philosopher, Friedrich Schiller (1759–1805). The psychological basis of his theory is the relation between three instinctive drives—the sensuous drive of bodily needs (*Stofftrieb*), the form-giving drive of reason (*Formtrieb*), and the play-drive of imagination (*Spieltrieb*). The first two drives tend to conflict, and the third drive, imaginative play, mediates between and harmonizes them.

Schiller maintained that the source of both play and art is overflowing energy. Even when a lion, for example, is not hungry or mad, it playfully expends its surplus energy through roaring. Similarly, the imagination of man enjoys its native power and liberty, although there is perhaps no outward gain to be achieved. Esthetic play, however, requires order and control. Man's esthetic taste directs the spontaneous flow of imagery in which imaginative play consists. Art is thus form imposed by taste upon playful imagistic activity. As in all the higher forms of play, there is a fusion of impulse and law; the rational part of man's nature is united harmoniously with the imaginative and the sensuous. Hence, Schiller is able to say, "Man only plays when in the full meaning of the word he is a man, and he is only completely a man when he plays."

In the opening sentences of the Twenty-Seventh Letter reproduced below, Schiller refers to "semblance" (*Schein*), a concept basic to his esthetics. Semblance is sheer appearance, recognized as such and enjoyed for its own sake. Imagination is the power to distinguish semblance from reality, to abide with it in contentment and without deception, and to create an imaginary world—a realm of semblance—with its independent principles of construction and internal coherence. "Indifference to reality and interest in semblance," Schiller declares, "may be regarded as a genuine enlargement of humanity and a decisive step toward culture." (XXVI, 4). Only when the "constraint of need" is replaced by sufficient leisure and abundance is the rich flowering of human nature possible. In addition, there must be the free play and reconciliation of the diverse sides of human nature, the formal and the sensuous drives balanced and harmonized through the reconciling power of imagination.

The greatest of all revolutionary thinkers, Karl Marx (1818–1883), was strongly influenced by these ideas of Schiller. Some of the concepts that appear in the excerpts from Marx—the sense of estrangement from one's own self and the surrounding world, the dehumanizing effect of the extreme division of labor, the ideal of the all-round man, the vital link between freedom and esthetic activity—were eloquently voiced in the *Letters On the Aesthetic Education of Man.* But Marx, unlike Schiller, sought to ground these ideas on "a materialistic interpretation of history." According to this interpretation, society has an economic ("material") foundation upon which the culture and social institutions— law, politics, religion, manners, science, art—are constructed. All these spheres causally interact with one another, but it is an interaction of *unequal* forces, of which the economic, in the long run, is by far the most powerful.

Marx distinguishes between "the forces of production," such as labor power and technology, and "the relations of production," such as the class structure and the institutions of property. The forces, under the spur of technology, develop more rapidly than the relations, which are held back by vested interests. The result is an incongruous combination of fast and slow changes, the productive forces being fettered and perverted by the stifling relations. When the resultant conflict becomes very acute, a revolutionary transformation of the class structure ensues, accompanied by a clash of political and cultural ideologies, including the aesthetic. As a consequence of revolution, there are profound changes in art and all other forms of culture.

Although Marx insists on the decisive role of economic causes in this transformation, he avoids an extreme economic determinism. He recognizes that artistic development is not entirely dependent on, or proportionate to, economic development. Rejecting the doctrine that esthetic value is completely relative to the economic system, he was too much the lover of the Greek classics to suppose that their value disappeared with the ancient slave economy.

Marx regards the alienation of modern man in his esthetic and artistic life as a phase of the total alienation produced by the capitalist system of production. Under this system, he charges, material forces tyrannize over human beings, human life is reduced to a material level, and men are estranged from one another and from their species-nature.

The essence of man, he thinks, is not, as Aristotle and Hegel supposed, that he is a *rational* animal, but that he is a *productive* and *creative* animal. This species-nature, embodying the deepest human needs and potentialities, is created by man himself in the historical process. Strongly insisting on the sensory and passional nature of man, Marx holds that external nature is man's larger "body" and should serve his needs and ends. Apparently, what he means is that nature, as intellectually knowable and esthetically enjoyable, is a kind of extension of man's species-being. Nature so understood shares a common essence with humanity, and as man's being is creatively enriched, nature is humanized and man is naturalized. This ideal of symbiotic harmony with nature is definitely esthetic in tone. Its realization awaits the achievement of a classless society in which "socialized mankind, the associated producers, regulate their interchange with nature rationally, bring it under their common control, instead of being ruled by it as by some blind power, and accomplish their task with the least expenditure of energy and under such conditions as are proper and worthy of human beings." (*Capital*, III).

I have appended to the passages from Marx a brief excerpt from Max Raphael (1889–1952). Born in West Prussia and living in Switzerland, France, and America, this wandering scholar probed deeply into the meaning of art and its relation to Marxism. In an introduction to Raphael's posthumous book, *The Demands of Art*, Herbert Read writes:

> Raphael is exactly the kind of philosopher of art that the world most needs—a man of great scholarship and equal sensibility, a man who believed in the future but realized that the world is changing and must be changed; one who was passionately convinced that the quality of life in the new society that would emerge must depend on "the ever-renewed creative act, the active dialogue between spirit and matter," and that in this transformation of living energies, art is the most effective weapon.

The distinguished American critic and social philosopher Lewis Mumford (1895–   ), has been inspired by a similar hope and ideal of human liberation. In his *Technics and Civilization* (1934) he divides "the development of the machine and the machine civilization into three successive but overlapping and interpenetrating phases: eotechnic, paleotechnic, neotechnic. . . . Speaking in terms of power and characteristic materials, the eotechnic phase is a water-and-wood complex, the paleotechnic phase is a coal-and-iron complex, and the neotechnic phase is an electric-and-alloy complex." Each phase has the most profound social ramifications, involving art, religion, and all humane pursuits. Beginning with the eotechnic phase, whose goal was at first a greater intensification of life, the rift between mechanization and humanization has gradually widened, until it has reached its climax in the "smoke-pall, air-sewage, and disorder" of some of our modern industrial cities. But new cleanliness and beauty is made possible by electricity and modern materials (for example, "the steel frame construction in architecture, which permits the fullest use of glass and the most complete utilization of sunlight").

When these new resources are finally controlled by humane social planning, and the biological and social sciences come to maturity, a new phase will begin—the "biotechnic": "Life, which has always paid the fiddler, now begins to call the tune." But before we can enter into this higher stage, art must be enriched by the machine, and the machine in turn humanized by art. The political and economic order necessary to effect this profound transformation Mumford calls "basic communism," but his ideal is that of a free society very different from that of the so-called communist states.

Mumford's *Technics and Civilization* is more optimistic in tone than his later books, such as the two-volume work *The Myth of the Machine* (1967, 1970), which emphasizes the dehumanizing effects of technology. The massive forces of change are moving toward an organizational gigantism and standardization that undermine the values of individuality. But Mumford refuses to be a prophet of doom, maintaining that the dreadful miscarriages of our civilization are not inevitable, but can, with understanding and resolute action, be overcome or avoided.

Tragedy and hope! These are the dominant notes of our ambivalent civilization, and these are the notes struck by Ian McHarg (1920–   ), professor of landscape architecture and urban planning at the University of Pennsylvania. As author of a comprehensive landscape plan for Washington, D. C., and other urban or regional plans, he has grappled with the basic problems of ecology and environmental reconstruction. In the selection reproduced in this chapter, he contrasts the beauty of his native Scotland, which he knew as a boy, with the smog, water-pollution, urban sprawl, and bulldozed devastation of industrialized America. The threat of worse ecological catastrophe can be averted only by a profound transmutation of values and national priorities. McHarg calls for a new philosophy of life, almost a new religion, turning sharply away from man's ruthless domination of nature toward a symbiotic harmony with the natural environment. Art and esthetics are caught up in a much larger context than is normally encountered.

FRIEDRICH SCHILLER

Esthetic Play and Human Liberation

1. You need have no fear for either reality or truth if the lofty conception of aesthetic semblance which I put forward in the last Letter were to become universal. It will not become universal as long as man is still uncultivated enough to be in a position to misuse it; and should it become universal, this could only be brought about by the kind of culture which would automatically make any misuse of it impossible. To strive after autonomous semblance demands higher powers of abstraction, greater freedom of heart, more energy of will, than man ever needs when he confines himself to reality; and he must already have left this reality behind if he would arrive at that kind of semblance. How ill-advised he would be, then,

to take the path towards the ideal in order to save himself the way to the real! From semblance as here understood we should thus have little cause to fear for reality; all the more to be feared, I would suggest, is the threat from reality to semblance. Chained as he is to the material world, man subordinates semblance to ends of his own long before he allows it autonomous existence in the ideal realm of art. For this latter to happen a complete revolution in his whole way of feeling is required, without which he would not even find himself on the way to the ideal. Wherever, then, we find traces of a disinterested and unconditional appreciation of pure semblance, we may infer that a revolution of this order has taken place in his nature, and that he has started to become truly human. Traces of this kind are, however, actually to be found even in his first crude attempts at embellishing his existence, attempts made even at the risk of possibly worsening it from the material point of view. As soon as ever he starts preferring form to substance, and jeopardizing reality for the sake of semblance (which he must, however, recognize as such), a breach has been effected in the cycle of his animal behaviour, and he finds himself set upon a path to which there is no end.

2. Not just content with what satisfies nature, and meets his instinctual needs, he demands something over and above this: to begin with, admittedly, only a superfluity of material things, in order to conceal from appetite the fact that it has limits, and ensure enjoyment beyond the satisfaction of immediate needs; soon, however, a superfluity in material things, an aesthetic surplus, in order to satisfy the formal impulse too, and extend enjoyment beyond the satisfaction of every need. By merely gathering supplies around him for future use, and enjoying them in anticipation, he does, it is true, transcend the present moment—but without transcending time altogether. He enjoys more, but he does not enjoy differently. But when he also lets form enter into his enjoyment, and begins to notice the outward appearance of the things which satisfy his desires, then he has not merely enhanced his enjoyment in scope and degree, but also ennobled it in kind.

3. It is true that Nature has given even to creatures without reason more than the bare necessities of existence, and shed a glimmer of freedom even into the darkness of animal life. When the lion is not gnawed by hunger, nor provoked to battle by any beast of prey, his idle strength creates an object for itself: he fills the echoing desert with a roaring that speaks defiance, and his exuberant energy enjoys its *self* in purposeless display. With what enjoyment of life do insects swarm in the sunbeam; and it is certainly not the cry of desire that we hear in the melodious warbling of the songbird. Without doubt there is freedom in these activities; but not freedom from compulsion altogether, merely from a certain kind of compulsion, compulsion from without. An animal may be said to be at work, when the stimulus to activity is some lack; it may be said to be at play, when the stimulus is sheer plenitude of vitality, when superabundance of life is its own incentive to action. Even inanimate nature exhibits a similar luxuriance of forces, coupled with a laxity of determination which, in that material sense, might well be called play. The tree puts forth innumerable

buds which perish without ever unfolding, and sends out far more roots, branches, and leaves in search of nourishment than are ever used for the sustaining of itself or its species. Such portion of its prodigal profusion as it returns, unused and unenjoyed, to the elements, is the overplus which living things are entitled to squander in a movement of carefree joy. Thus does Nature, even in her material kingdom, offer us a prelude of the Illimitable, and even here remove in part the chains which, in the realm of form, she casts away entirely. From the compulsion of want, or physical earnestness, she makes the transition via the compulsion of superfluity, or physical play, to aesthetic play; and before she soars, in the sublime freedom of beauty, beyond the fetters of ends and purposes altogether, she makes some approach to this independence, at least from afar, in that kind of free activity which is at once its own end and its own means.

4. Like the bodily organs in man, his imagination, too, has its free movement and its material play, an activity in which, without any reference to form, it simply delights in its own absolute and unfettered power. Inasmuch as form does not yet enter this fantasy play at all, its whole charm residing in a free association of images, such play—although the prerogative of man alone—belongs merely to his animal life, and simply affords evidence of his liberation from all external physical compulsion, without as yet warranting the inference that there is any autonomous shaping power within him.[1] From this play of freely associated ideas, which is still of a wholly material kind, and to be explained by purely natural laws, the imagination, in its attempt at a free form, finally makes the leap to aesthetic play. A leap it must be called, since a completely new power now goes into action; for here, for the first time, mind takes a hand as lawgiver in the operations of blind instinct, subjects the arbitrary activity of the imagination to its own immutable and eternal unity, introduces its own autonomy into the transient, and its own infinity into the life of sense. But as long as brute nature still has too much power, knowing no other law but restless hastening from change to change, it will oppose to that necessity of the spirit its own unstable caprice, to that stability its own unrest, to that autonomy its own subservience, to that sublime self-sufficiency its own insatiable discontent. The aesthetic play-drive, therefore, will in its first attempts be scarcely recognizable, since the physical play-drive, with its wilful moods and its unruly appetites, constantly gets in the way. Hence we see uncultivated taste first seizing upon what is new and startling—on the colourful, fantastic, and bizarre, the violent and the savage—and shunning nothing so much as tranquil simplicity. It fashions grotesque shapes, loves swift transitions, exuberant forms, glaring contrasts, garish lights, and a song full of feeling. At this stage what man calls beautiful is only what excites him, what offers him material—but excites him to a resistance involving autonomous activity, but offers him material for possible shaping. Otherwise it would not be beauty—even for him. The form of his judgements has thus undergone an astonishing change: he seeks these objects, not because they give him something to enjoy passively, but because they provide an incentive to respond actively. They please him, not because

they meet a need, but because they satisfy a law which speaks, though softly as yet, within his breast.

5. Soon he is no longer content that things should please him; he himself wants to please. At first, indeed, only through that which is his; finally through that which he is. The things he possesses, the things he produces, may no longer bear upon them the marks of their use, their form no longer be merely a timid expression of their function; in addition to the service they exist to render, they must at the same time reflect the genial mind which conceived them, the loving hand which wrought them, the serene and liberal spirit which chose and displayed them. Now the ancient German goes in search of glossier skins, statelier antlers, more elaborate drinking horns; and the Caledonian selects for his feasts the prettiest shells. Even weapons may no longer be mere objects of terror; they must be objects of delight as well, and the cunningly ornamented sword-belt claims no less attention than the deadly blade of the sword. Not content with introducing aesthetic superfluity into objects of necessity, the play-drive as it becomes ever freer finally tears itself away from the fetters of utility altogether, and beauty in and for itself alone begins to be an object of his striving. Man adorns himself. Disinterested and undirected pleasure is now numbered among the necessities of existence, and what is in fact unnecessary soon becomes the best part of his delight.

6. And as form gradually comes upon him from without—in his dwelling, his household goods, and his apparel—so finally it begins to take possession of him himself, transforming at first only the outer, but ultimately the inner, man too. Uncoordinated leaps of joy turn into dance, the unformed movements of the body into the graceful and harmonious language of gesture; the confused and indistinct cries of feeling become articulate, begin to obey the laws of rhythm, and to take on the contours of song. If the Trojan host storms on to the battlefield with piercing shrieks like a flock of cranes, the Greek army approaches it in silence, with noble and measured tread. In the former case we see only the exuberance of blind forces; in the latter, the triumph of form and the simple majesty of law.

7. Now compulsion of a lovelier kind binds the sexes together, and a communion of hearts helps sustain a connexion but intermittently established by the fickle caprice of desire. Released from its dark bondage, the eye, less troubled now by passion, can apprehend the form of the beloved; soul looks deep into soul, and out of a selfish exchange of lust there grows a generous interchange of affection. Desire widens, and is exalted into love, once humanity has dawned in its object; and a base advantage over sense is now disdained for the sake of a nobler victory over will. The need to please subjects the all-conquering male to the gentle tribunal of taste; lust he can steal, but love must come as a gift. For this loftier prize he can only contend by virtue of form, never by virtue of matter. From being a force impinging upon feeling, he must become a form confronting the mind; he must be willing to concede freedom, because it is freedom he wishes to

please. And even as beauty resolves the conflict between opposing natures in this simplest and clearest paradigm, the eternal antagonism of the sexes, so too does it resolve it—or at least aims at resolving it—in the complex whole of society, endeavouring to reconcile the gentle with the violent in the moral world after the pattern of the free union it there contrives between the strength of man and the gentleness of woman. Now weakness becomes sacred, and unbridled strength dishonourable; the injustice of nature is rectified by the magnanimity of the chivalric code. He whom no violence may alarm is disarmed by the tender blush of modesty, and tears stifle a revenge which no blood was able to assuage. Even hatred pays heed to the gentle voice of honour; the sword of the victor spares the disarmed foe, and a friendly hearth sends forth welcoming smoke to greet the stranger on that dread shore where of old only murder lay in wait for him.

8. In the midst of the fearful kingdom of forces, and in the midst of the sacred kingdom of laws, the aesthetic impulse to form is at work, unnoticed, on the building of a third joyous kingdom of play and of semblance, in which man is relieved of the shackles of circumstance, and released from all that might be called constraint, alike in the physical and in the moral sphere.

9. If in the dynamic State of rights it is as force that one man encounters another, and imposes limits upon his activities; if in the ethical State of duties Man sets himself over against man with all the majesty of the law, and puts a curb upon his desires: in those circles where conduct is governed by beauty, in the aesthetic State, none may appear to the other except as form, or confront him except as an object of free play. To bestow freedom by means of freedom is the fundamental law of this kingdom.

10. The dynamic State can merely make society possible, by letting one nature be curbed by another; the ethical State can merely make it (morally) necessary, by subjecting the individual will to the general; the aesthetic State alone can make it real, because it consummates the will of the whole through the nature of the individual. Though it may be his needs which drive man into society, and reason which implants within him the principles of social behaviour, beauty alone can confer upon him a social character. Taste alone brings harmony into society, because it fosters harmony in the individual. All other forms of perception divide man, because they are founded exclusively either upon the sensuous or upon the spiritual part of his being; only the aesthetic mode of perception makes of him a whole, because both his natures must be in harmony if he is to achieve it. All other forms of communication divide society, because they relate exclusively either to the private receptivity or to the private proficiency of its individual members, hence to that which distinguishes man from man; only the aesthetic mode of communication unites society, because it relates to that which is common to all. The pleasures of the senses we enjoy merely as individuals, without the genus which is immanent within us having any share in them at all; hence we cannot make the pleasures of sense universal, because we are unable to universalize our own individual-

ity. The pleasures of knowledge we enjoy merely as genus, and by carefully removing from our judgement all trace of individuality; hence we cannot make the pleasures of reason universal, because we cannot eliminate traces of individuality from the judgements of others as we can from our own. Beauty alone do we enjoy at once as individual and as genus, i.e., as representatives of the human genus. The good of the Senses can only make one man happy, since it is founded on appropriation, and this always involves exclusion; and it can only make this one man one-sidedly happy, since his Personality has no part in it. Absolute good can only bring happiness under conditions which we cannot presume to be universal; for truth is the prize of abnegation alone, and only the pure in heart believe in the pure will. Beauty alone makes the whole world happy, and each and every being forgets its limitations while under its spell.

11. No privilege, no autocracy of any kind, is tolerated where taste rules, and the realm of aesthetic semblance extends its sway. This realm stretches upwards to the point where reason governs with unconditioned necessity, and all that is mere matter ceases to be. It stretches downwards to the point where natural impulse reigns with blind compulsion, and form has not yet begun to appear. And even at these furthermost confines, where taste is deprived of all legislative power, it still does not allow the executive power to be wrested from it. A-social appetite must renounce its self-seeking, and the Agreeable, whose normal function is to seduce the senses, must cast toils of Grace over the mind as well. Duty, stern voice of Necessity, must moderate the censorious tone of its precepts—a tone only justified by the resistance they encounter—and show greater respect for Nature through a nobler confidence in her willingness to obey them. From within the Mysteries of Science, taste leads knowledge out into the broad daylight of Common Sense, and transforms a monopoly of the Schools into the common possession of Human Society as a whole. In the kingdom of taste even the mightiest genius must divest itself of its majesty, and stoop in all humility to the mind of a little child. Strength must allow itself to be bound by the Graces, and the lion have its defiance curbed by the bridle of a Cupid. In return, taste throws a veil of decorum over those physical desires which, in their naked form, affront the dignity of free beings; and, by a delightful illusion of freedom, conceals from us our degrading kinship with matter. On the wings of taste even that art which must cringe for payment can lift itself out of the dust; and, at the touch of her wand, the fetters of serfdom fall away from the lifeless and the living alike. In the Aesthetic State everything—even the tool which serves—is a free citizen, having equal rights with the noblest; and the mind, which would force the patient mass beneath the yoke of its purposes, must here first obtain its assent. Here, therefore, in the realm of Aesthetic Semblance, we find that ideal of equality fulfilled which the Enthusiast would fain see realized in substance. And if it is true that it is in the proximity of thrones that fine breeding comes most quickly and most perfectly to maturity, would one not have to recognize in this, as in much else, a kindly dispensation which often seems to be imposing limits upon man in the real world, only in order to spur him on to realization in an ideal world?

12. But does such a State of Aesthetic Semblance really exist? And if so, where is it to be found? As a need, it exists in every finely attuned soul; as a realized fact, we are likely to find it, like the pure Church and the pure Republic, only in some few chosen circles, where conduct is governed, not by some soulless imitation of the manners and morals of others, but by the aesthetic nature we have made our own; where men make their way, with undismayed simplicity and tranquil innocence, through even the most involved and complex situations, free alike of the compulsion to infringe the freedom of others in order to assert their own, as of the necessity to shed their Dignity in order to manifest Grace.

—*On the Aesthetic Education of Man in a Series of Letters* (1795)

NOTE

1. Most of the imaginative play which goes on in everyday life is either entirely based on this feeling for free association of ideas, or at any rate derives therefrom its greatest charm. This may not in itself be proof of a higher nature, and it may well be that it is just the most flaccid natures who tend to surrender to such unimpeded flow of images; it is nevertheless this very independence of the fantasy from external stimuli, which constitutes at least the negative condition of its creative power. Only by tearing itself free from reality does the formative power raise itself up to the ideal; and before the imagination, in its productive capacity, can act according to its own laws, it must first, in its reproductive procedures, have freed itself from alien laws. From mere lawlessness to autonomous law-giving from within, there is admittedly, still a big step to be taken; and a completely new power, the faculty for ideas, must first be brought into play. But this power, too, can now develop with greater ease, since the senses are not working against it, and the indefinite does, at least negatively, border upon the infinite.

KARL MARX

Art and History

1. THE MODE OF PRODUCTION DETERMINES THE SOCIAL, POLITICAL, AND CULTURAL PROCESSES OF LIFE

In the social production which men carry on they enter into definite relations that are indispensable and independent of their will; these relations of production correspond to a definite stage of development of their material forces of production. The sum total of these relations of production constitutes the economic structure of society—the real foundation, on which rises a legal and political superstructure and to which correspond definite forms of social consciousness. The mode of production in material life determines the social, political, and intellectual life processes in general. It is not the consciousness of men that determines their being, but, on the contrary, their social being that determines their consciousness. At a certain stage of their development, the material forces of production in society come in conflict with the existing relations of production, or—what is but a legal expression for the same thing—with the property relations within which they have been at work before. From forms of development of the forces of production these relations turn into their fetters. Then begins an epoch of social revolution. With the change of the economic foundation the entire immense superstructure is more or less rapidly transformed. In considering such transformations a distinction should always be made between the material transformation of the economic conditions of production which can be determined with the precision of natural science, and the legal, political, religious, aesthetic, or philosophic—in short, ideological—forms in which men become conscious of this conflict and fight it out. Just as our opinion of an individual is not based on what he thinks of himself, so can we not judge of such a period of transformation by its own consciousness; on the contrary this consciousness must be explained rather from the contradictions of material life, from the existing conflict between the social forces of production and the relations of production. No social order ever disappears before all the productive forces for which there is room in it have been developed; and new higher relations of production never appear before the material conditions of their existence have matured in the womb of the old society itself. Therefore, mankind always sets itself only such tasks as it can solve; since, looking at the matter more closely, we will always find that the task itself arises only when the material conditions necessary for its solution already exist or are at least in the process of formation. In broad outlines we can designate the Asiatic, the ancient, the feudal, and the modern bourgeois modes of production as so many epochs in the progress of the economic formation of society. The bourgeois relations of production are the last antagonistic form of the social process of production—antagonistic not in the sense of individual antagonism, but of one arising from the social conditions of life of the individuals; at the same time the productive forces developing in the womb of bourgeois society create the material conditions for the solution of that antagonism. This social formation constitutes, therefore, the closing chapter of the prehistoric stage of human society.

> —Introduction to *A Contribution to the Critique of Political Economy* (1859), translated by N. I. Stone (1904)

2. The Disproportion between the Development of Material and Artistic Production

It is well known that certain periods of highest development of art stand in no direct connection with the general development of society, nor with the material basis and the skeleton structure of its organization. Witness the example of the Greeks as compared with the modern nations or even Shakespeare. As regards certain forms of art, as, *e.g.*, the epos, it is admitted that they can never be produced in the world-epoch-making form as soon as art as such comes into existence; in other words, that in the domain of art certain important forms of it are possible only at a low stage of its development. If that be true of the mutual relations of different forms of art within the domain of art itself, it is far less surprising that the same is true of the relation of art as a whole to the general development of society. The difficulty lies only in the general formulation of these contradictions. No sooner are they specified than they are explained. Let us take for instance the relation of Greek art and of that of Shakespeare's time to our own. It is a well known fact that Greek mythology was not only the arsenal of Greek art, but also the very ground from which it had sprung. Is the view of nature and of social relations which shaped Greek imagination and Greek [art] possible in the age of automatic machinery, and railways, and locomotives, and electric telegraphs? Where does Vulcan come in as against Roberts & Co.; Jupiter, as against the lightning rod; and Hermes, as against the Credit Mobilier? All mythology masters and dominates and shapes the forces of nature in and through the imagination; hence it disappears as soon as man gains mastery over the forces of nature. What becomes of the Goddess Fame side by side with Printing House Square? Greek art presupposes the existence of Greek mythology, *i.e.*, that nature and even the form of society are wrought up in popular fancy in an unconsciously artistic fashion. That is its material. Not, however, any mythology taken at random, nor any accidental, unconsciously artistic elaboration of nature (including under the latter all objects, hence [also] society). Egyptian mythology could never be the soil or womb which would give birth to Greek art. But in any event [there had to be] a mythology. In no event [could Greek art originate] in a society which excludes any mythological explanation of nature, any mythological attitude towards it and which requires from the artist an imagination free from mythology.

Looking at it from another side: Is Achilles possible side by side with powder and lead? Or is the *Iliad* at all compatible with the printing press and steam press? Do not singing and reciting and the muses necessarily go out of existence with the appearance of the printer's bar, and do not, therefore, disappear the prerequisites of epic poetry?

But the difficulty is not in grasping the idea that Greek art and epos are bound up with certain forms of social development. It rather lies in understanding why they still constitute with us a source of aesthetic enjoyment and in certain respects prevail as the standard and model beyond attainment.

A man cannot become a child again unless he becomes childish. But does he not enjoy the artless ways of the child and must he not strive to reproduce its truth on a higher plane? Is not the character of every epoch revived perfectly true to nature in child nature? Why should the social childhood of mankind, where it had obtained its most beautiful development, not exert an eternal charm as an age that will never return? There are ill-bred children and precocious children. Many of the ancient nations belong to the latter class. The Greeks were normal children. The charm their art has for us does not conflict with the primitive character of the social order from which it had sprung. It is rather the product of the latter, and is rather due to the fact that the unripe social conditions under which the art arose and under which alone it could appear could never return.

—*A Contribution to the Critique of Political Economy* (1859), translated by N. I. Stone (1904)

3. ALIENATED LABOR AND FREE PRODUCTION

Since alienated labour: (1) alienates nature from man; and (2) alienates man from himself, from his own active function, his life activity; so it alienates him from the species. It makes *species-life* into a means of individual life. In the first place it alienates species-life and individual life, and secondly, it turns the latter, as an abstraction, into the purpose of the former, also in its abstract and alienated form.

For labour, *life activity, productive life*, now appear to man only as *means* for the satisfaction of a need, the need to maintain his physical existence. Productive life is, however, species-life. It is life creating life. In the type of life activity resides the whole character of a species, its species-character; and free, conscious activity is the species-character of human beings. Life itself appears only as a *means of life*.

The animal is one with its life activity. It does not distinguish the activity from itself. It is *its activity*. But man makes his life activity itself an object of his will and consciousness. He has a conscious life activity. It is not a determination with which he is completely identified. Conscious life activity distinguishes man from the life activity of animals. Only for this reason is he a species-being. Or rather, he is only a self-conscious being, i.e. his own life is an object for him, because he is a species-being. Only for this reason is his activity free activity. Alienated labour reverses the relationship, in that man because he is a self-conscious being makes his life activity, his *being*, only a means for his *existence*.

The practical construction of an *objective world*, the *manipulation* of inorganic nature, is the confirmation of man as a conscious species-being, i.e. a being who treats the species as his own being or himself as a species-being. Of course, animals also produce. They construct nests, dwellings, as in the case of bees, beavers, ants, etc. But they only produce what is strictly necessary for themselves or their young. They produce only in a single direction, while man produces universally. They produce only under the compulsion of direct physical needs, while man produces when he is free from physical need and only truly produces in freedom from such need. Animals produce only themselves, while man reproduces the whole of nature. The products of animal production belong directly to their physical bodies, while man is free in face of his product. Animals construct only in accordance with the standards and needs of the species to which they belong, while man knows how to produce in accordance with the standards of every species and knows how to apply the appropriate standard to the object. Thus man constructs also in accordance with the laws of beauty.

It is just in his work upon the objective world that man really proves himself as a *species-being*. This production is his active species-life. By means of it nature appears as *his* work and his reality. The object of labour is, therefore, the *objectification of man's species-life*; for he no longer reproduces himself merely intellectually, as in consciousness, but actively and in a real sense, and he sees his own reflection in a world which he has constructed. While, therefore, alienated labour takes away the object of production from man, it also takes away his *species-life*, his real objectivity as a species-being, and changes his advantage over animals into a disadvantage in so far as his inorganic body, nature, is taken from him.

—*Economic and Philosophical Manuscripts* (1844), translated by T. B. Bottomore (1963)

4. THE OVERCOMING OF ALIENATION

Just as *private property* is only the sensuous expression of the fact that man is at the same time an *objective* fact for himself and becomes an alien and non-human object for himself; just as his manifestation of life is also his alienation of life and his self-realization a loss of reality, the emergence of an *alien* reality; so the positive supersession of private property, i.e. the *sensuous* appropriation of the human essence and of human life, of objective man and of human *creations*, by and for man, should not be taken only in the sense of *immediate*, exclusive *enjoyment*, or only in the sense of *possession* or *having*. Man appropriates his manifold being in an all-inclusive way, and thus as a whole man. All his *human* relations to the world—seeing, hearing, smelling, tasting, touching, thinking, observing, feeling, desiring, acting, loving—in short, all the organs of his individuality, like the organs which are directly communal in form, . . . are in their objective action (their *action in relation to the object*) the appropriation of this object, the appropriation of human reality. The way in which they react to the object is the confirmation of *human reality*.[1] It is human effectiveness and human *suffering*, for suffering humanly considered is an enjoyment of the self for man.

Private property has made us so stupid and partial that an object is only *ours* when we have it, when it exists for us as capital or when it is directly eaten, drunk, worn, inhabited, etc., in short, *utilized* in some way. But private property itself only conceives these various forms of possession as *means of life*, and the life for which they serve as means is the *life* of *private property*—labour and creation of capital.

Thus *all* the physical and intellectual senses have been replaced by the simple alienation of *all* these senses; the sense of *having*. The human being had to be reduced to this absolute poverty in order to be able to give birth to all his inner wealth. . . .

The supersession of private property is, therefore, the complete *emancipation* of all the human qualities and senses. It is such an emancipation because these qualities and senses have become *human*, from the subjective as well as the objective point of view. The eye has become a *human* eye when its *object* has become a *human*, social object, created by man and destined for him. The senses have, therefore, become directly theoreticians in practice. They relate themselves to the thing for the sake of the thing, but the thing itself is an *objective human* relation to itself and to man, and vice versa.[2] Need and enjoyment have thus lost their *egoistic* character and nature has lost its mere *utility* by the fact that its utilization has become *human* utilization.

Similarly, the senses and minds of other men have become my *own* appropriation. Thus besides these direct organs, *social* organs are constituted, in the form of society; for example, activity in direct association with others has become an organ for the manifestation of life and a mode of appropriation of *human* life.

It is evident that the human eye appreciates things in a different way from the crude, non-human eye, the human *ear* differently from the crude ear. As we have seen, it is only when the object becomes a *human* object, or objective *humanity*, that man does not become lost in it. This is only possible when man himself becomes a *social* object; when he himself becomes a social being and society becomes a being for him in this object.

On the one hand, it is only when objective reality everywhere becomes for man in society the reality of human faculties, human reality, and thus the reality of his own faculties, that all *objects* become for him the *objectification of himself*. The objects then confirm and realize his individuality, they are *his own* objects, i.e. man himself becomes the object. *The manner in which these objects* become his own depends upon the *nature of the object* and the nature of the corresponding faculty; for it is precisely the *determinate character* of this relation which constitutes the specific *real* mode of affirmation. The object is not the same for the *eye* as for the *ear*, for the ear as for the eye. The *distinctive character* of each faculty is precisely its *characteristic* essence and thus also the characteristic mode of its objectification, of its *objectively real*, living *being*. It is therefore not only in thought, [VIII] but through *all* the senses that man is affirmed in the objective world.

Let us next consider the subjective aspect. Man's musical sense is only awakened by music. The most beautiful music has no meaning for the non-musical ear, is not an object for it, because my object can only be the confirmation of one of my own faculties. It can only be so for me in so far as my faculty exists for itself as a subjective capacity, because the meaning of an object for me extends only as far as the sense extends (only makes sense for an appropriate sense). For this reason, the *senses* of social man are *different* from those of non-social man. It is only through the objectively deployed wealth of the human being that the wealth of subjective *human* sensibility (a musical ear, an eye which is sensitive to the beauty of form, in short, senses which are capable of human satisfaction and which confirm themselves as human faculties) is cultivated or created. For it is not only the five senses, but also the so-called spiritual senses, the practical senses (desiring, loving, etc.), in brief, human sensibility and the human character of the senses, which can only come into being through the existence of *its* object, through humanized nature. The cultivation of the five senses is the work of all previous history. Sense which is subservient to crude needs has only a restricted meaning. For a starving man the human form of food does not exist, but only its abstract character as food. It could just as well exist in the most crude form, and it is impossible to say in what way this feeding-activity would differ from that of animals. The needy man, burdened with cares, has no appreciation of the most beautiful spectacle. The dealer in minerals sees only their commercial value, not their beauty or their particular characteristics; he has no mineralogical sense. Thus, the objectification of the human essence, both theoretically and practically, is necessary in order to *humanize* man's senses, and also to create the *human senses* corresponding to all the wealth of human and natural being.

Just as society at its beginnings finds, through the development of *private property* with its wealth and poverty (both intellectual and material), the materials necessary for this *cultural development*, so the fully constituted society produces man in all the plentitude of his being, the wealthy man endowed with all the senses, as an enduring reality. It is only in a social context that subjectivism and objectivism, spiritualism and materialism, activity and passivity, cease to be antinomies and thus cease to exist as such antinomies. The resolution of the *theoretical* contradictions is possible *only* through practical means, only through the *practical* energy of man. Their resolution is not by any means, therefore, only a problem of knowledge, but is a *real* problem of life which philosophy was unable to solve precisely because it saw there a purely theoretical problem.

—*Economic and Philosophical Manuscripts* (1844), translated by T. B. Bottomore (1963)

NOTES

1. It is, therefore, just as varied as the determinations of human nature and activities are diverse.

2. In practice I can only relate myself in a human way to a thing when the thing is related in a human way to man.

MAX RAPHAEL

Economic Base and Artistic Superstructure

The main question Marx set out to answer was: How does it come about that man is the slave of the commodities he himself produces, and how can man free himself—become human again? His answer is: Human society is the basic fact, and its basic activity, continuously repeated, is the production of its means of subsistence and the propagation of the race. There is only one science (for understanding human society), and that is history, and the first object of this science is to formulate the laws governing the process of production and its development over the generations. The ideologies of law, government, art, morality, and religion are superstructures which grow upon this real objective activity. Marx was far from denying the importance of these superstructures in the historical process.

Once they have come into existence, the state and law, morality, etc., react on the productive process; they are instruments of power in the hands of the exploiting class, and to the exploited they serve as opiates. On the basis of this insight Marx made the notorious statement: "religion is the *opium* of the people"[1]—a statement which vulgar Marxists are trying to extend to art.

This is not the place to analyze Karl Marx's theory of art.[2] I should like, however, to refer to a passage at the end of *A Contribution to the Critique of Political Economy* in which he brilliantly formulated the main, but still unsolved, problem of his own—and every—theory of art. He says:

> But the difficulty is not in grasping the idea that Greek art and epos are bound up with certain forms of social development. It rather lies in understanding why they still constitute with us a source of aesthetic enjoyment and in certain respects prevail as the standard and model beyond attainment. A man can not become a child again. . . . But does he not enjoy the artless ways of the child and must he not strive to reproduce its truth on a higher plane? Is not the character of every epoch revived perfectly true to nature in child nature? Why should the social childhood of mankind, where it had obtained its most beautiful development, not exert charm as an age that will never return? There are ill-bred children and precocious children. Many of the ancient nations belong to the latter class. The Greeks were normal children. The charm their art has for us does not conflict with the primitive character of the social order from which it had sprung. It is rather the product of the latter, and is rather due to the fact that the unripe social condiions under which the art arose and under which alone it could appear can never return.

It is perhaps no accident that Marx's manuscript breaks off at this point, for he had come to a problem which he could not solve. How can art, that is, an ideological superstructure in a specific type of economy, continue to be effective after this type of economy has ceased to exist? How can the ideological superstructure be timeless if the foundation has a finite history? Marx's answer has nothing whatever to do either with historical materialism or with Communism as a guide for changing the world. It sounds petty bourgeois, almost indistinguishable from Burckhardt's answer in his history of Greek culture, save that the latter used the term "adolescence" rather than "childhood." If such a thing as eternal charm exists despite determination by historical, economic, and social conditions, then there must also be eternal sources that correspond. And if so, history cannot be the only science and the economy its primary object. The only alternative would be to provide an accurate analysis of the spiritual process that links up historical conditions with these "eternal charms"—more accurately, with the values created by men, transcending the limits of a given epoch but not the limits of historical time in general. The phrase "eternal charm" —which is doubly untenable, both as "eternal" and as "charm"—shows how far Marx was from having solved the problem he raised so astutely. We repeat, the problem remains unsolved.

And there are good reasons for this. If we apply to the thesis that art is an ideological superstructure, its own presupposition, i.e., that of historical materialism, we find that historical materialism itself is only an ideological superstructure of a specific economic order—the capitalistic order in which all productive forces are concentrated in the economic sector. A transitional epoch always implies uncertainty: Marx's struggle to understand his own epoch testifies to this. In such a period two attitudes are possible. One is to take advantage of the emergent forces of the new order with a view to undermining it, to affirm it in order to drive it beyond itself: this is the active, militant, revolutionary attitude. The other clings to the past, is retrospective and romantic, bewails or acknowledges the decline, asserts that the will to live is gone—in short, it is the passive attitude. Where economic, social, and political questions were at stake Marx took the first attitude; in questions of art he took neither. He reflected the actual changes of his time, which is to say that he made economics the foundation of thought which it had become in fact. He did not lose sight of the further problem, but as he could not see the solution, he left it unsolved. Had he been able to show that an active attitude toward art also exists, he would have brought the understanding of art up to the level of his revolutionary position.

Whatever the deficiencies of Marx's theoretical attitude toward art may have been, he was perfectly aware that after the economic, social, and political revolution the most difficult revolution would still remain to be made—the cultural one. Nowhere did he ever exclude art, as he excluded religion, on the ground that there would be no place for it in a classless society. The pseudo-Marxists who put art on the same footing with religion do not see that religion sets limits to man's creative capacities, diverts him from the things of this world, and reconciles class antagonisms by obviously imaginary and frequently hypocritical theories of love, whereas art is an ever-renewed creative act, the active dialogue between spirit and matter; the work of art holds man's creative powers in a crystalline suspension from which it can again be transformed into living energies. Consequently, art by its very nature is no opiate; it is a weapon. Art may have narcotic effects, but only if used for specific reactionary purposes; and from this we may infer only that attempts are made to blunt it for the very reason that it is feared as a weapon. . . .

Creative instinct manifests itself with greater freedom in art than in any other domain. A creative, active study of art is therefore indispensable to awaken creative powers, to assert them against the dead weight of tradition, and to mobilize them in the struggle for a social order in which everyone will have the fullest opportunity to develop his creative capacities. The details of this social order cannot be anticipated without falling into utopian dreams. We can and we must be satisfied with the awareness that art helps us to achieve the truly just order. The decisive battles, however, will be fought at another level.

—*The Demands of Art* (1968), translated by Norbert Guterman (1968)

NOTES

1. *Contribution to the Critique of Hegel's Philosophy of Right,* Introduction.
2. [See the author's *Proudhon, Marx, Picasso: Trois études sur la sociologie de l'art.*]

LEWIS MUMFORD

The Esthetic Assimilation of the Machine

. . . In the arts, it is plain that the machine is an instrument with manifold and conflicting possibilities. It may be used to counterfeit older forms of art; it may also be used, in its own right, to concentrate and intensify and express new forms of experience. As substitutes for primary experience, the machine is worthless: indeed it is actually debilitating. Just as the microscope is useless unless the eye itself is keen, so all our mechanical apparatus in the arts depends for its success upon the due cultivation of the organic, physiological, and spiritual aptitudes that lie behind its use. The machine cannot be used as a shortcut to escape the necessity for organic experience. Mr. Waldo Frank has put the matter well: "Art," he says, "cannot become a language, hence an experience, unless it is practiced. To the man who plays, a mechanical reproduction of music may mean much, since he already has the experience to assimilate. But where reproduction becomes the norm, the few music makers will grow more isolate and sterile, and the ability to experience music will disappear. The same is true with the cinema, dance, and even sport."

Whereas in industry the machine may properly replace the human being when he has been reduced to an automaton, in the arts the machine can only extend and deepen man's original functions and intuitions. Insofar as the phonograph and the radio do away with the impulse to sing, insofar as the camera does away with the impulse to see, insofar as the automobile does away with the impulse to walk, the machine leads to a lapse of function which is but one step away from paralysis. But in the application of mechanical instruments to the arts it is not the machine itself that we must fear. The chief danger lies in the failure to integrate the arts themselves with the totality of our life-experience: the perverse triumph of the machine follows automatically from the abdication of the spirit. Consciously to assimilate the machine is one means of reducing its omnipotence. We cannot, as Karl Buecher wisely said, "give up the hope that it will be possible to unite technics and art in a higher rhythmical unity, which will restore to the spirit the fortunate serenity and to the body the harmonious cultivation that manifest themselves at their best among primitive peoples." The machine has not destroyed that promise. On the contrary, through the more conscious cultivation of the machine arts and through greater selectivity in their use, one sees the pledge of its wider fulfillment throughout civilization. For at the bottom of that cultivation there must be the direct and immediate experience of living itself: we must directly see, feel, touch, manipulate, sing, dance, communicate before we can extract from the machine any further sustenance for life. If we are empty to begin with, the machine will only leave us emptier; if we are passive and powerless to begin with, the machine will only leave us more feeble.

But modern technics, even apart from the special arts that it fostered, had a cultural contribution to make in its own right. Just as science underlined the respect for fact, so technics emphasized the importance of function: in this domain, as Emerson pointed out, the beautiful rests on the foundations of the necessary. The nature of this contribution can best be shown, perhaps, by describing the way in which the problem of machine design was first faced, then evaded, and finally solved.

One of the first products of the machine was the machine itself. As in the organization of the first factories the narrowly practical considerations were uppermost, and all the other needs of the personality were firmly shoved to one side. The machine was a direct expression of its own functions: the first cannon, the first crossbows, the first steam engines were all nakedly built for action. But once the primary problems of organization and operation had been solved, the human factor, which had been left out of the picture, needed somehow to be re-incorporated. The only precedent for this fuller integration of form came naturally from handicraft: hence over the incomplete, only partly realized forms of the early cannon, the early bridges, the early machines, a meretricious touch of decoration was added: a mere relic of the happy, semi-magical fantasies that painting and carving had once added to every handicraft object. Because perhaps the energies of the eotechnic period[1] were so completely engrossed in the technical problems, it was, from the standpoint of design, amazingly clean and direct: ornament flourished in the utilities of life, flourished often perversely and extravagantly, but one looks for it in vain among the machines pictured by Agricola or Besson or the Italian engineers[2]: they are as direct and factual as was architecture from the tenth to the thirteenth century.

The worst sinners—that is, the most obvious sentimentalists—were the engineers of the paleotechnic period. In the act of recklessly deflowering the environment at large, they sought to expiate their failures by adding a few sprigs or posies to the new engines they were creating: they embellished their steam engines with Doric columns or partly concealed them behind Gothic tracery: they decorated the frames of their presses and their automatic machines with cast-iron arabesque, they punched ornamental holes in the iron framework of their new structures, from the trusses of the old wing of the Metropolitan Museum to the base of the Eiffel tower in Paris. Everywhere similar habits prevailed: the homage of hypocrisy to art. One notes identical efforts on the original steam radiators, in the floral decorations that once graced typewriters, in the nondescript ornament that still lingers quaintly on shotguns and sewing machines, even if it has at length disappeared from cash registers and Pullman cars—as long before, in the first uncertainties of the new technics, the same division had appeared in armor and in crossbows.

The second stage in machine design was a compromise. The object was divided into two parts. One of them was to be precisely designed for mechanical efficiency. The other was to be designed for looks. While the utilitarian claimed the working parts of the structure the esthete was, so to speak, permitted slightly to modify the surfaces with his unimportant patterns, his plutonic flowers, his aimless filigree, provided he did not seriously weaken the structure or condemn the function to inefficiency. Mechanically utilizing the machine, this type of design shamefully attempted to conceal the origins that were still felt as low and mean. The engineer had the uneasiness of a parvenu, and the same impulse to imitate the most archaic patterns of his betters.

Naturally the next stage was soon reached: the utilitarian and the esthete withdrew again to their respective fields. The esthete, insisting with justice that the structure was integral with the decoration and that art was something more fundamental than the icing the pastrycook put on the cake, sought to make the old decoration real by altering the nature of the structure. Taking his place as workman, he began to revive the purely handicraft methods of the weaver, the cabinet maker, the printer, arts that had survived for the most part only in the more backward parts of the world, untouched by the tourist and the commercial traveler. The old workshops and ateliers were languishing and dying out in the nineteenth century, especially in progressive England and in America, when new ones, like those devoted to glass under William de Morgan in England, and John La Farge in America, and Lalique in France, or to a miscellany of handicrafts, such as that of William Morris in England, sprang into existence, to prove by their example that the arts of the past could survive. The industrial manufacturer, isolated from this movement yet affected by it, contemptuous but half-convinced, made an effort to retrieve his position by attempting to copy mechanically the dead forms of art he found in the museum. So far from gaining from the handicrafts movement by this procedure he lost what little virtue his untutored designs possessed, issuing as they sometimes did out of an intimate knowledge of the processes and the materials.

The weakness of the original handicrafts movement was that it assumed that the only important change in industry had been the intrusion of the soulless machine. Whereas the fact was that everything had changed, and all the shapes and patterns employed by technics were therefore bound to change, too. The world men carried in their heads, their idolum, was entirely different from that which set the medieval mason to carving the history of creation or the lives of the saints above the portals of the cathedral, or a jolly image of some sort above his own doorway. An art based like handicraft upon a certain stratification of the classes and the social differentiation of the arts could not survive in a world where men had seen the French Revolution and had been promised some rough share of equality. Modern handicraft, which sought to rescue the worker from the slavery of shoddy machine production, merely enabled the well-to-do to enjoy new objects that were as completely divorced from the dominant social milieu as the palaces and monasteries that the antiquarian art dealer and collector had begun to loot. The *educational aim* of the arts and crafts movement was admirable; and, insofar as it gave courage and understanding to the amateur, it was a success. If this movement did not add a sufficient amount of good handicraft it at least took away a great deal of false art. William Morris's dictum, that one should not possess anything one did not believe to be beautiful or know to be useful was, in the shallow showy bourgeois world he addressed, a revolutionary dictum.

But the social outcome of the arts and crafts movement was not commensurate with the need of the new situation; as Mr. Frank Lloyd Wright pointed out in his memorable speech at Hull House in 1901, the machine itself was as much an instrument of art, in the hands of an artist, as were the simple tools and utensils. To erect a social barrier between machines and tools was really to accept the false notion of the new industrialist who, bent on exploiting the machine, which they owned, and jealous of the tool, which might still be owned by the independent worker, bestowed on the machine an exclusive sanctity and grace it did not merit. Lacking the courage to use the machine as an instrument of creative purpose, and being unable to attune themselves to new objectives and new standards, the esthetes were logically compelled to restore a medieval ideology in order to provide a social backing for their anti-machine bias. In a word, the arts and crafts movement did not grasp the fact that the new technics, by expanding the role of the machine, had altered the entire relation of handwork to production, and that the exact processes of the machine were not necessarily hostile to handicraft and fine workmanship. In its modern form handicraft could no longer serve as in the past when it had worked under the form of an intensive caste-specialization. To survive, handicraft would have to adapt itself to the amateur, and it was bound to call into existence, even in pure handwork, those forms of economy and simplicity which the machine was claiming for its own, and to which it was adapting mind and hand and eye. In this process of re-integration certain "eternal" forms would be recovered: there are handicraft forms dating back to a distant past which so completely fulfill their functions that no amount of further calculation or experiment will alter them for the better. These type-forms appear and reappear from civilization to civilization; and if they had not been discovered by handicraft, the machine would have had to invent them.

The new handicraft was in fact to receive presently a powerful lesson from the machine. For the forms created by the machine, when they no longer sought to imitate old superficial patterns of handwork, were closer to those that could be produced by the amateur than were, for example, the intricacies of special joints, fine inlays, matched woods, beads and carvings, complicated forms of metallic ornament, the boast of handicraft in the past. While in the factory the machine was often reduced to producing fake handicraft, in the workshop of the amateur the reverse process could take place with a real gain: he was liberated by the very simplicities of good machine forms. Machine technique as a means to achieving a simplified and purified form relieved the amateur from the need of respecting and imitating the perversely complicated patterns of the past—patterns whose complications were partly the result of conspicuous waste, partly the outcome of technical virtuosity, and partly the result of a different state of feelings. But before handicraft could thus be restored as an admirable form of play and an efficacious relief from a physically untutored life, it was necessary to dispose of the machine itself as a social and esthetic instrument. So the major contribution to art was made, after all, by the industrialist who remained on the job and saw it through.

With the third stage in machine design, an alteration takes place. The imagination is not applied to the mechanical object after the practical design has been completed: it is infused into it at every stage in development. The mind works through the medium of the machine directly, respects the conditions imposed upon it, and—not content with a crude quantitative approximation—seeks out a more positive esthetic fulfillment. This must not be confused with the dogma, so often current, that any mechanical contraption that works necessarily is esthetically interesting. The source of this fallacy is plain. In many cases, indeed, our eyes have been trained to recognize beauty in nature, and with certain kinds of animals and birds we have an especial sympathy. When an airplane becomes like a gull it has the advantage of this long association and we properly couple the beauty with the mechanical adequacy, since the poise and swoop of a gull's flight casts in addition a reflective beauty on its animal structure. Having no such association with a milkweed seed, we do not feel the same beauty in the autogyro, which is kept aloft by a similar principle. While genuine beauty in a thing of use must always be joined to mechanical adequacy and therefore involves a certain amount of intellectual recognition and appraisal, the relation is not a simple one: it points to a common source rather than an identity.

In the conception of a machine or of a product of the machine there is a point where one may leave off for parsimonious reasons without having reached esthetic perfection: at this point perhaps every mechanical factor is accounted for, and the sense of incompleteness is due to the failure to recognize the claims of the human agent. Esthetics carries with it the implication of alternatives between a number of mechanical solutions of equal validity: and unless this awareness is present at every stage of the process, in smaller matters of finish, fineness, trimness, it is not likely to come out with any success in the final stage of design. Form follows function, underlining it, crystallizing it, clarifying it, making it real to the eye. Makeshifts and approximations express themselves in incomplete forms: forms like the absurdly cumbrous and ill-adjusted telephone apparatus of the past, like the old-fashioned airplane, full of struts, wires, extra supports, all testifying to an anxiety to cover innumerable unknown or uncertain factors; forms like the old automobile in which part after part had been added to the effective mechanism without having been absorbed into the body of the design as a whole; forms like our oversized steel-work which were due to our carelessness in using cheap materials and our desire to avoid the extra expense of calculating them finely and expending the necessary labor to work them up. The impulse that creates a complete mechanical object is akin to that which creates an esthetically finished object; and the fusion of the two at every stage in the process will necessarily be effected by the environment at large: who can gauge how much the slatternliness and disorder of the paleotechnic environment undermined good design, or how much the order and beauty of our neotechnic plants —like that of the Van Nelle factory in Roterdam—will eventually aid it? Esthetic interests cannot suddenly be introduced from without: they must be constantly operative, constantly visible.

Expression through the machine implies the recognition of relatively new esthetic terms: precision, calculation, flawlessness, simplicity, economy. Feeling attaches itself in these new forms to different qualities than those that made handicraft so entertaining. Success here consists in the elimination of the nonessential, rather than, as in handicraft decoration, in the willing production of superfluity, contributed by the worker out of his own delight in the work. The elegance of a mathematical equation, the inevitability of a series of physical inter-relations, the naked quality of the material itself, the tight logic of the whole—these are the ingredients that go into the design of machines: and they go equally into products that have been properly designed for machine production. In handicraft it is the worker who is represented: in machine design it is the work. In handicraft, the personal touch is emphasized, and the imprint of the worker and his tool are both inevitable: in machine work the impersonal prevails, and if the worker leaves any tell-tale evidence of his part in the operation, it is a defect or a flaw. Hence the burden of machine design is in the making of the original pattern: it is here that trials are made, that errors are discovered and buried, that the creative process as a whole is concentrated. Once the master-pattern is set, the rest is routine: beyond the designing room and the laboratory there is—for goods produced on a serial basis for a mass market—no opportunity for choice and personal achievement. Hence apart from those commodities that can be produced automatically, the effort of sound industrial production must be to increase the province of the designing room and the laboratory, reducing the scale of the production, and making possible an easier passage back and forth between the designing and the operative sections of the plant.

Who discovered these new canons of machine design? Many an engineer and many a machine worker must have mutely sensed them and reached toward them: indeed, one sees the beginning of them in very early mechanical instruments. But only after centuries of more or less blind and unformulated effort were these canons finally demonstrated with a certain degree of completeness in the work of the great engineers toward the end of the nineteenth century—particularly the Roeblings in America and Eiffel in France—and formulated after that by theoreticians like Reidler and Meyer in Germany. The popularization of the new esthetic awaited . . . the post-impressionist painters. They contributed by breaking away from the values of purely associative art and by abolishing an undue concern for natural objects as the basis of the painter's interest: if on one side this led to completer subjectivism, on the other it tended toward a recognition of the machine as both form and symbolic.[3] In the same direction Marcel Duchamp, for example, who was one of the leaders of this movement, made a collection of cheap, ready-made articles, produced by the machine, and called attention to their esthetic soundness and sufficiency. In many cases, the finest designs had been achieved before any conscious recognition of the esthetic had taken place. With the coming of the commercialized designer, seeking to add "art" to a product which *was* art, the design has more often than not been trifled with and spoiled. The studious botching of the kodak, the bathroom fixture, and the steam radiator under such stylicizing is a current commonplace.

The key to this fresh appreciation of the machine as a source of new esthetic forms has come through a formulation of its chief esthetic principle: the principle of economy. This principle is of course not unknown in other phases of art: but the point is that in mechanical forms it is at all times a controlling one, and it has for its aid the more exact calculations and measurements that are now possible. The aim of sound design is to remove from the object, be it an automobile or a set of china or a room, every detail, every molding, every variation of the surface, every extra part except that which conduces to its effective functioning. Toward the working out of this principle, our mechanical habits and our unconscious impulses have been tending steadily. In departments where esthetic choices are not consciously uppermost our taste has often been excellent and sure. Le Corbusier has been very ingenious in picking out manifold objects, buried from observation by their very ubiquity, in which this mechanical excellence of form has manifested itself without pretense or fumbling. Take the smoking pipe: it is no longer carved to look like a human head or does it bear, except among college students, any heraldic emblems: it has become exquisitely anonymous, being nothing more than an apparatus for supplying drafts of smoke to the human mouth from a slow-burning mass of vegetation. Take the ordinary drinking glass in a cheap restaurant: it is no longer cut or cast or engraved with special designs: at most it may have a slight bulge near the top to keep one glass from sticking to another in stacking: it is as clean, as functional, as a high tension insulator. Or take the present watch and its case and compare it with the forms that handicraft ingenuity and taste and association created in the sixteenth or seventeenth centuries. In all the commoner objects of our environment the machine canons are instinctively accepted: even the most sentimental manufacturer of motor cars has not been tempted to paint his coach work to resemble a sedan chair in the style of Watteau, although he may live in a house in which the furniture and decoration are treated in that perverse fashion.

This stripping down to essentials has gone on in every department of machine work and has touched every aspect of life. It is a first step toward that completer integration of the machine with human needs and desires which is the mark of the neotechnic phase, and will be even more the mark of the biotechnic period, already visible over the edge of the horizon. As in the social transition from the paleotechnic to the neotechnic order, the chief obstacle to the fuller development of the machine lies in the association of taste and fashion with waste and commercial profiteering. For the rational development of genuine technical standards, based on function and performance, can come about only by a wholesale devaluation of the scheme of bourgeois civilization upon which our present system of production is based.

Capitalism, which along with war played such a stimulating part in the development of technics, now remains with war the chief obstacle toward its further improvement. The reason should be plain. The machine devaluates rarity: instead of producing a single unique object, it is capable of producing a million others just as good as the master model from which the rest are made. The machine devaluates age: for age is another token of rarity, and the machine, by placing its emphasis upon fitness and adaptation, prides itself on the brand-new rather than on the antique: instead of feeling comfortably authentic in the midst of rust, dust, cobwebs, shaky parts, it prides itself on the opposite qualities—slickness, smoothness, gloss, cleanness. The machine devaluates archaic taste: for taste in the bourgeois sense is merely another name for pecuniary reputability, and against that standard the machine sets up the standards of function and fitness. The newest, the cheapest, the commonest objects may, from the standpoint of pure esthetics, be immensely superior to the rarest, the most expensive, and the most antique. To say all this is merely to emphasize that the modern technics, by its own essential nature, imposes a greater purification of esthetics: that is, it strips off from the object all the barnacles of association, all the sentimental and pecuniary values which have nothing whatever to do with esthetic form, and it focuses attention upon the object itself.

The social devaluation of caste, enforced by the proper use and appreciation of the machine, is as important as the stripping down of essential forms in the process itself. One of the happiest signs of this during the last decade was the use of cheap and common materials in jewelry, first introduced, I believe, by Lalique: for this implied a recognition of the fact that an esthetically appropriate form, even in the adornment of the body, has nothing to do with rarity or expense, but is a matter of color, shape, line, texture, fitness, symbol. The use of cheap cottons in dress by Chanel and her imitators, which was another postwar phenomenon, was an equally happy recognition of the essential values in our new economy: it at last put our civilization, if only momentarily, on the level of those primitive cultures which gladly bartered their furs and ivory for the white man's colored glass beads, by the adroit use of which the savage artist often proved to any disinterested observer that they—contrary to the white man's fatuous conceit—had gotten the better of the bargain. Because of the fact that woman's dress has a peculiarly compensatory role to play in our megalopolitan society, so that it more readily indicates what is absent than calls attention to what is present in it, the victory for genuine esthetics could only be a temporary one. But these forms of dress and jewelry pointed to the goal of machine production: the goal at which each object would be valued in terms of its direct mechanical and vital and social function, apart from its pecuniary status, the snobberies of caste, or the dead sentiments of historical emulation.

This warfare between a sound machine esthetic and what Veblen has called the "requirements of pecuniary reputability" has still another side. Our modern technology has, in its inner organization, produced a collective economy and its typical products are collective products. Whatever the politics of a country may be, the machine is a communist: hence the deep contradictions and conflicts that have kept on developing in machine industry since the end of the eighteenth century. At every stage in technics, the work represents a collaboration of innumerable workers, themselves utilizing a large and ramifying technological heritage: the most ingenious inventor, the most brilliant individual scientist, the most skilled designer contributes but a moiety to the final result. And the product itself necessarily bears the same impersonal imprint: it either functions or it does not function on quite impersonal lines. There can be no qualitative difference between a poor man's electric bulb of a given candlepower and a rich man's, to indicate their differing pecuniary status in society, although there was an enormous difference between the rush or stinking tallow of the peasant and the wax candles or sperm oil used by the upper classes before the coming of gas and electricity.

Insofar as pecuniary differences are permitted to count in the machine economy, they can alter only the scale of things—not, in terms of present production, the kind. What applies to electric light bulbs applies to automobiles: what applies there applies equally to every manner of apparatus or utility. The frantic attempts that have been made in America by advertising agencies and "designers" to stylicize machine-made objects have been, for the most part, attempts to pervert the machine process in the interests of caste and pecuniary distinction. In money-ridden societies, where men play with poker chips instead of with economic and esthetic realities, every attempt is made to disguise the fact that the machine has achieved potentially a new collective economy, in which the possession of goods is a meaningless distinction, since the machine can produce all our essential goods in unparalleled quantities, falling on the just and the unjust, the foolish and the wise, like the rain itself.

The conclusion is obvious: we cannot intelligently accept the practical benefits of the machine without accepting its moral imperatives and its esthetic forms insofar as they, too, fulfill human purposes. Otherwise both ourselves and our society will be the victims of a shattering disunity, and one set of purposes, that which created the order of the machine, will be constantly at war with trivial and inferior personal impulses bent on working out in covert ways our psychological weaknesses. Lacking on the whole this rational acceptance, we have lost a good part of the practical benefits of the machine and have achieved esthetic expression only in a spotty, indecisive way. The real social distinction of modern technics, however, is that it tends to eliminate social distinctions. Its immediate goal is effective work. Its means are standardization: the emphasis of the generic and the typical: in short, conspicuous economy. Its ultimate aim is leisure —that is, the release of other organic capacities.

The powerful esthetic side of this social process has been obscured by speciously pragmatic and pecuniary interests that have inserted themselves into our technology and have imposed themselves upon its legitimate aims. But in spite of this deflection of effort, we have at last begun to realize these new values, these new forms, these new modes of expression. Here is a new environment—man's extension of nature in terms discovered by the close observation and analysis and abstraction of nature. The elements of this environment are hard and crisp and clear: the steel bridge, the concrete road, the turbine and the alternator, the glass wall. Behind the façade are rows and rows of machines, weaving cotton, transporting coal, assembling food, printing books, machines with steel fingers and lean muscular arms, with perfect reflexes, sometimes even with electric eyes. Alongside them are the new utilities—the coke oven, the transformer, the dye vats—chemically cooperating with these mechanical processes, assembling new qualities in chemical compounds and materials. Every effective part in this whole environment represents an effort of the collective mind to widen the province of order and control and provision. And here, finally, the perfected forms begin to hold human interest even apart from their practical performances: they tend to produce that inner composure and equilibrium, that sense of balance between the inner impulse and the outer environment, which is one of the marks of a work of art. The machines, even when they are not works of art, underlie our art—that is, our organized perceptions and feelings—in the way that Nature underlies them, extending the basis upon which we operate and confirming our own impulse to order. The economic: the objective: the collective: and finally the integration of these principles in a new conception of the organic— these are the marks, already discernible, of our assimilation of the machine not merely as an instrument of practical action but as a valuable mode of life.

—*Technics and Civilization* (1934)

NOTES

1. For an explanation of the terms eotechnic, paleotechnic, neotechnic, and biotechnic, employed by Mumford, see the introductory note to this chapter. (Editor's note.)

2. Georgius Agricola is the author of *De Re Mettalica* (1546), which describes the advanced technology of the early sixteenth century. Jacques Besson wrote *Theatre des Instruments Mathématiques et Méchaniques*, an account of sixteenth-century technics. Among the Italian engineers here referred to the most famous is Leonarda da Vinci. (Editor's note.)

3. In a preceding section of his book, Mumford writes as follows: "The Cubists were perhaps the first school to overcome [the] association of the ugly and the mechanical: they not merely held that beauty could be produced through the machine: they even pointed to the fact that it had been produced. The first expression of Cubism indeed dates back to the seventeenth century: Jean Baptiste Bracelle, in 1624, did a series of Bizarreries which depicted mechanical men, thoroughly cubist in conception. This anticipated in art, as Glanvill did in science, our later interests and inventions. What did the modern Cubists do? They extracted from the organic environment just those elements that could be stated in abstract geometrical symbols: they transposed and readjusted the contents of vision as freely as the inventor readjusted organic functions: they even created on canvas or in metal mechanical equivalents of organic objects: Léger painted human figures that looked as if they had been turned in a lathe, and Duchamp-Villon modeled a horse as if it were a machine. This whole process of rational experiment in abstract mechanical forms was pushed further by the constructivists. Artists like Grabo and Moholy-Nagy put together pieces of abstract sculpture, composed of glass, metal plates, spiral springs, wood, which were the nonutilitarian equivalents of the apparatus that the physical scientist was using in his laboratory. They created in forms the semblance of the mathematical equations and physical formulæ that had produced our new environment, seeking in this new sculpture to observe the physical laws of equipose or to evolve dynamic equivalents for the solid sculpture of the past by rotating a part of the object through space." (Editor's note.)

IAN McHARG

Design with Nature

Thirty years ago the wilderness of Scotland looked inviolate to me and I would have been content to give my life to the creation of oases of delight in the heart of Glasgow or dream of a marriage of man and nature in new cities and towns. My boyhood sense of the rest of the world suggested that it was even wilder than Scotland. There were still explorers in those days and missionaries enough to build a stamp collection from their solicitations. The plight that moved me then was little enough compared to today. Then there was no threat of an atomic holocaust and no fear of radiation hazard. The population problem was one of declining birthrates and Mussolini exhorted and coerced Italian mothers to greater efforts while Presidents of France deplored an effete generation. DDT and Dieldrin were not yet festering thoughts; penicillin and streptomycin were not yet hopes. Man's inhumanity to man was commonplace in distant lands but had not achieved the pinnacle of depravity which at Belsen and Dachau a civilized nation was to achieve. Poverty and oppression were real and pervasive, and war was imminent enough so that I could conclude at seventeen that I had better be ready as a trained soldier by 1939.

Yet while the city was grim indeed, the countryside could be reached by foot, by bicycle or even for the few pennies that led to a tram terminus and the gateway to wild lands where no law of trespass constrained.

The country is not a remedy for the industrial city, but it does offer surcease and some balm to the spirit. Indeed, during the Depression there were many young men who would not submit to the indignity of the dole or its queues and who chose to live off the land, selling their strength where they could for food and poaching when they could not, sleeping in the bracken or a shepherd's bothy in good weather, living in hostels and public libraries in winter. They found independence, came to know the land and live from it, and sustained their spirit.

So, when first I encountered the problem of the place of nature in man's world it was not a beleaguered nature, but merely the local deprivation that was the industrial city. Scotland was wild enough, protected by those great conservators, poverty and inaccessibility. But this has changed dramatically in the intervening decades, so that today in Europe and the United States a great erosion has been accomplished which has diminished nature—not only in the countryside at large, but within the enlarging cities and, not least, in man as a natural being.

There are large numbers of urban poor for whom the countryside is known only as the backdrop to westerns or television advertisements. Paul Goodman speaks of poor children who would not eat carrots pulled from the ground because they were dirty, terror-stricken at the sight of a cow, who screamed in fear during a thunderstorm. The Army regularly absorbs young men who have not the faintest conception of living off the land, who know nothing of nature and its processes. In classical times the barbarians in fields and forest could only say "bar bar" like sheep; today their barbaric, sheepish descendants are asphalt men.

Clearly the problem of man and nature is not one of providing a decorative background for the human play, or even ameliorating the grim city: it is the necessity of sustaining nature as source of life, milieu, teacher, sanctum, challenge and, most of all, of rediscovering nature's corollary of the unknown in the self, the source of meaning.

There are still great realms of empty ocean, deserts reaching to the curvature of the earth, silent, ancient forests and rocky coasts, glaciers and volcanoes, but what will we do with them? There are rich contented farms, and idyllic villages, strong barns and white-steepled churches, tree-lined streets and covered bridges, but these are residues of another time. There are, too, the silhouettes of all the Manhattans, great and small, the gleaming golden windows of corporate images—expressionless prisms suddenly menaced by another of our creations, the supersonic transport whose sonic boom may reduce this image to a sea of shattered glass.

But what do we say now, with our acts in city and countryside? While I first addressed this question to Scotland in my youth, today the world directs the same question to the United States. What is our performance and example? What are the visible testaments to the American mercantile creed—the hamburger stand, gas station, diner, the ubiquitous billboards, sagging wires, the parking lot, car cemetery and that most complete conjunction of land rapacity and human disillusion, the subdivision. It is all but impossible to avoid the highway out of town, for here, arrayed in all its glory, is the quintessence of vulgarity, bedecked to give the maximum visibility to the least of our accomplishments.

And what of the cities? Think of the imprisoning gray areas that encircle the center. From here the sad suburb is an unrealizable dream. Call them no-place although they have many names. Race and hate, disease, poverty, rancor and despair, urine and spit live here in the shadows. United in poverty and ugliness, their symbol is the abandoned carcasses of automobiles, broken glass, alleys of rubbish and garbage. Crime consorts with disease, group fights group, the only emancipation is the parked car.

What of the heart of the city, where the gleaming towers rise from the dirty skirts of poverty? Is it like midtown Manhattan where twenty per cent of the population was found to be indistinguishable from the patients in mental hospitals?[1] Both stimulus and stress live here with the bitch goddess success. As you look at the faceless prisms do you recognize the home of *anomie*?

Can you find the river that first made the city? Look behind the unkempt industry, cross the grassy railroad tracks and you will find the rotting piers and there is the great river, scummy and brown, wastes and sewage bobbing easily up and down with the tide, endlessly renewed.

If you fly to the city by day you will see it first as a smudge of smoke on the horizon. As you approach, the outlines of its towers will be revealed as soft silhouettes in the hazardous haze. Nearer you will perceive conspicuous plumes which, you learn, belong to the proudest names in industry. Our products are household words but it is clear that our industries are not yet housebroken.

Drive from the airport through the banks of gas storage tanks and the interminable refineries. Consider how dangerous they are, see their cynical spume, observe their ugliness. Refine they may, but refined they are not.

You will drive on an expressway, a clumsy concrete form, untouched by either humanity or art, testament to the sad illusion that there can be a solution for the unbridled automobile. It is ironic that this greatest public investment in cities has also financed their conquest. See the scars of the battle in the remorseless carving, the dismembered neighborhoods, the despoiled parks. Manufacturers are producing automobiles faster than babies are being born. Think of the depredations yet to be accomplished by myopic highway builders to accommodate these toxic vehicles. You have plenty of time to consider in the long peak hour pauses of spasmodic driving in the blue gas corridors.

You leave the city and turn towards the countryside. But can you find it? To do so you will follow the paths of those who tried before you. Many stayed to build. But those who did so first are now deeply embedded in the fabric of the city. So as you go you transect the rings of the thwarted and disillusioned who are encapsulated in the city as nature endlessly eludes pursuit.

You can tell when you have reached the edge of the countryside for there are many emblems—the cadavers of old trees piled in untidy heaps at the edge of the razed deserts, the magnificent machines for land despoliation, for felling forests, filling marshes, culverting streams, and sterilizing farmland, making thick brown sediments of the creeks.

Is this the countryside, the green belt—or rather the greed belt, where the farmer sells land rather than crops, where the developer takes the public resource of the city's hinterland and subdivides to create a private profit and a public cost? Certainly here is the area where public powers are weakest—either absent or elastic—where the future costs of streets, sidewalks and sewers, schools, police and fire protection are unspoken. Here are the meek mulcted, the refugees thwarted.

Rural land persists around the metropolis, not because we have managed the land more wisely but because it is larger, more resistant to man's smear, more resilient. Nature regenerates faster in the country than in the city where the marks of men are well-nigh irreversible. But it still wears the imprint of man's toil. DDT is in the arctic ice, in the ocean deeps, in the rivers and on the land, atomic wastes rest on the Continental Shelf, many creatures are forever extinguished, the primeval forests have all but gone and only the uninitiated imagine that these third and fourth growth stands are more than shadows of their forebears. Although we can still see great fat farms, their once deep soils, a geological resource, are thinner now, and we might well know that farming is another kind of mining, dissipating the substance of aeons of summers and multitudes of life. The Mississippi is engorged with five cubic miles of soil each year, a mammoth prodigality in a starving world. Lake Erie is on the verge of becoming septic, New York City suffers from water shortages while the Hudson flows foully past, salt water encroaches in the Delaware, floods alternate with drought, the fruits of two centuries of land mismanagement. Forest fires, mudslides and smog become a way of life in Los Angeles, and the San Andreas Fault rises in temperature to menace San Franciscans.

The maps all show the continent to be green wild landscapes save for the sepia cities huddled on lakes and seaboards, but look from a plane as it crosses the continent and makes an idiocy of distance, see the wild green sectioned as rigorously as the city. In the great plains nature persists only in the meandering stream and the flood plain forest, a meaningful geometry in the Mondrian patterns of unknowing men.

It matters not if you choose to proceed to the next city or return to the first. You can confirm an urban destination from the increased shrillness of the neon shills, the diminished horizon, the loss of nature's companions until you are alone, with men, in the heart of the city, God's Junkyard—or should it be called Bedlam, for cacophony lives here. It is the expression of the inalienable right to create ugliness and disorder for private greed, the maximum expression of man's inhumanity to man. And so our cities grow, coalescing into a continental necklace of megalopoles, dead gray tissue encircling the nation.

Surely the indictment is too severe—there must be redeeming buildings, spaces, places, landscapes. Of course there are—random chance alone would have ensured some successful accidents. But there are also positive affirmations, yet it is important to recognize that many of these are bequests from earlier times. Independence, Carpenter and Faneuil Hall symbolize the small but precious heritage of the 18th century: the great State Houses, city halls, museums, concert halls, city universities and churches, the great urban park systems, were products of the last century. Here in these older areas you will find humane, generous suburbs where spacious men built their concern into houses and spaces so that dignity and peace, safety and quiet live there, shaded by old trees, warmed by neighborliness.

You may also see hints of a new vitality and new forms in the cities, promising resurgence. You may even have found, although I have not, an expressway that gives structure to a city, or, as I have, a parkway that both reveals and enhances the landscape. There are farmlands in good heart; there are landowners—few it is true—who have decided that growth is inevitable, but that it need not lead to despoliation but to enlargement. New towns are being constructed and concepts of regional planning are beginning to emerge. There is an increased awareness for the need to manage resources and even a title for this concern—The New Conservation. There is a widening certainty that the Gross National Product does not measure health or happiness, dignity, compassion, beauty or delight, and that these are, if not all inalienable rights, at least most worthy aspirations.

But these are rare among the countless city slums and scabrous towns, pathetic subdivisions, derelict industries, raped land, befouled rivers and filthy air.

At the time of the founding of the republic—and for millennia before—the city had been considered the inevitable residence for the urbane, civilized and polite. Indeed all of these names *say* city. It was as widely believed that rich countries and empires were inevitably built upon the wealth of the land. The original cities and towns of the American 18th century were admirable—Charleston and Savannah, Williamsburg, Boston,

Philadelphia, New Orleans. The land was rich and beautiful, canons of taste espoused the 18th-century forms of architecture and town building, a wonder of humanity and elegance.

How then did our plight come to be and what can be done about it? It is a long story which must be told briefly and, for that reason, it is necessary to use a broad brush and paint with coarse strokes. This method inevitably offends for it omits qualifying statements, employs broad generalities and often extrapolates from too slender evidence. Yet the basic question is so broad that one need not be concerned with niceties. The United States is the stage on which great populations have achieved emancipation from oppression, slavery, peonage and serfdom, where a heterogeneity of peoples has become one and where an unparalleled wealth has been widely distributed. These are the jewels of the American diadem. But the setting, the environment of this most successful social revolution, is a major indictment against the United States and a threat to her success and continued evolution.

Our failure is that of the Western World and lies in prevailing values. Show me a man-oriented society in which it is believed that reality exists only because man can perceive it, that the cosmos is a structure erected to support man on its pinnacle, that man exclusively is divine and given dominion over all things, indeed that God is made in the image of man, and I will predict the nature of its cities and their landscapes. I need not look far for we have seen them—the hot-dog stands, the neon shill, the ticky-tacky houses, dysgenic city and mined landscapes. This is the image of the anthropomorphic, anthropocentric man; he seeks not unity with nature but conquest. Yet unity he finally finds, but only when his arrogance and ignorance are stilled and he lies dead under the greensward. We need this unity to survive.

Among us it is widely believed that the world consists solely of a dialogue between men, or men and God, while nature is a faintly decorative backdrop to the human play. If nature receives attention, then it is only for the purpose of conquest, or even better, exploitation—for the latter not only accomplishes the first objective, but provides a financial reward for the conqueror.

We have but one explicit model of the world and that is built upon economics. The present face of the land of the free is its clearest testimony, even as the Gross National Product is the proof of its success. Money is our measure, convenience is its cohort, the short term is its span, and the devil may take the hindmost is the morality.

Perhaps there is a time and place for everything; and, with wars and revolutions, with the opening and development of continents, the major purposes of exploration and settlement override all lesser concerns and one concludes in favor of the enterprises while regretting the wastages and losses which are incurred in these extreme events. But if this was once acceptable as the inevitable way, that time has passed.

The pioneers, the builders of railroads and canals, the great industrialists who built the foundations for future growth were hard-driven, single-minded men. Like soldiers and revolutionaries, they destroyed much in disdain and in ignorance, but there are fruits from their energies and we share them today. Their successors, the merchants, are a different breed, more obsequious and insidious. The shock of the assassination of a President stilled for only one day their wheedling and coercive blandishments for our money. It is their ethos, with our consent, that sustains the slumlord and the land rapist, the polluters of rivers and atmosphere. In the name of profit they preempt the seashore and sterilize the landscape, fell the great forests, fill the protective marshes, build cynically in the flood plain. It is the claim of convenience for commerce—or its illusion—that drives the expressway through neighborhoods, homes and priceless parks, a taximeter of indifferent greed. Only the merchant's creed can justify the slum as a sound investment or offer tomato stakes as the highest utility for the priceless and irreplaceable redwoods.

The economists, with a few exceptions, are the merchants' minions and together they ask with the most barefaced effrontery that we accommodate our value system to theirs. Neither love nor compassion, health nor beauty, dignity nor freedom, grace nor delight are important unless they can be priced. If they are non-price benefits or costs they are relegated to inconsequence. The economic model proceeds inexorably towards its self-fulfillment of more and more despoliation, uglification and inhabition to life, all in the name of progress—yet, paradoxically, the components which the model excludes are the most important human ambitions and accomplishments and the requirements for survival.

The origins of societies and of exchange go back to an early world when man was a minor inconsequence in the face of an overwhelming nature. He bartered his surpluses of food and hides, cattle, sheep and goats and valued scarcities, gold and silver, myrrh and frankincense. But the indispensable elements of life and survival were beyond his ken and control: they could not and did not enter his value system save imperfectly, through religious views. Nor have they yet. But in the intervening millennia the valuations attributed to commodities have increased in range and precision and the understanding of the operation of the limited sphere of economics has increased dramatically. This imperfect view of the world as commodity fails to evaluate and incorporate physical and biological processes: we have lost the empirical knowledge of our ancestors. We are now unable to attribute value to indispensable natural processes, but we have developed an astonishing precision for ephemera.

It is obvious that such an institutionalized myopic prejudice will exclude the realities of the biophysical world. Its very man-centeredness ensures that those processes, essential to man's evolution and survival, will be excluded from consideration and from evaluation. We have no thought in the interminable dialogues among men for the sustaining sun, the moon and tides, the oceans and hydrologic cycle, the inclined axis of the earth and the seasons. As a society we neither know nor value the chemical elements and compounds that constitute life, and their cycles, the importance of the photosynthetic plant, the essential decomposers, the ecosystems, their constituent organisms, their roles and cooperative mechanisms, the prodigality of life forms, or even that greatest of values, the genetic pool with which we confront the future.

Yet we may soon learn. Consider the moon. It apparently lacks an atmosphere and oceans and the great inheritance of life forms which we enjoy. The costs of "terra-farming" this naked, hostile planet to that benign condition which can support life as abundantly as does the earth are considered of such a magnitude as to be inconceivable. Colonies on the moon will thus have to be small envelopes enclosing some of the essential commonplaces of earth transported as priceless and indispensable commodities. The man on the moon will know the value of these things.

But surely we need not await the confrontation with the inhospitable moon to learn a lesson so rudimentary, so well known to our ancient ancestors and as familiar to the simple societies of the world today.

Economic determinism as an imperfect evaluation of the biophysical world is only one of the consequences of our inheritance. An even more serious deficiency is the attitude towards nature and man which developed from the same source and of which our economic model is only one manifestation. The early men who were our ancestors wielded much the same scale of power over nature which Australian aboriginals do today. They were generally pantheists, animatists or animists. They tried to understand the phenomenal world and through behavior, placation and sacrifice, diminish adversity and increase beneficence. This early empiricism remains a *modus vivendi* for many tribal peoples, notably the American Indian—and conspicuously the Pueblo—today.

Whatever the earliest roots of the western attitude to nature it is clear that they were confirmed in Judaism. The emergence of monotheism had as its corollary the rejection of nature; the affirmation of Jehovah, the God in whose image man was made, was also a declaration of war on nature.

The great western religions born of monotheism have been the major source of our moral attitudes. It is from them that we have developed the preoccupation with the uniqueness of man, with justice and compassion. On the subject of man-nature, however, the Biblical creation story of the first chapter of Genesis, the source of the most generally accepted description of man's role and powers, not only fails to correspond to reality as we observe it, but in its insistence upon dominion and subjugation of nature, encourages the most exploitative and destructive instincts in man rather than those that are deferential and creative. Indeed, if one seeks license for those who would increase radioactivity, create canals and harbors with atomic bombs, employ poisons without constraint, or give consent to the bulldozer mentality, there could be no better injunction than this text. Here can be found the sanction and injunction to conquer nature—the enemy, the threat to Jehovah.

The creation story in Judaism was absorbed unchanged into Christianity. It emphasized the exclusive divinity of man, his God-given dominion over all things and licensed him to subdue the earth. While Abraham Heschel, Gustave Weigel, and Paul Tillich, speaking for Judaism and Christianity, reject the literality of this view and insist that it is an allegory, it is abundantly clear that it is the literal belief that has and does permeate the western view of nature and man. When this is understood, the conquest, the depredations and the despoliation are comprehensible, as is the imperfect value system.

From early, faintly ridiculous beginnings when a few inconsequential men proclaimed their absolute supremacy to an unhearing and uncaring world, this theme has grown. It had only a modest place in classical Greece, where it was tempered by a parallel pantheism. It enlarged during the Roman tenure but was also subject to the same constraints. When the Millennium passed without punishment it grew more confident. In the Humanism of the Renaissance it made a gigantic leap and it is somewhat poignant that the poverty of the Mediterranean today is a product of the land mismanagement that occurred during this great inflation of the human ego and the increase of man's powers over nature. The 18th century was a period of pause—the Naturalist view emerged—but it barely arrested the anthropomorphic, anthropocentric surge that swelled in the 19th century and is our full-blown inheritance today.

The Inquisition was so outraged by doubt cast upon the primacy of man and his planet that Galileo was required to rescind his certainty that the earth revolved around the sun. This same insistence upon human divinity takes hard the evidence of man's animal ancestry or indeed the history of evolution. It looks as if it will resist the evidence that man's pre-hominid ancestors might well have been feral killers whose evolutionary success can be attributed to this capacity.

If the highest values in a culture insist that man must subdue the earth and that this is his moral duty, it is certain that he will in time acquire the powers to accomplish that injunction. It is not that man has produced evidence for his exclusive divinity, but only that he has developed those powers that permit the fulfillment of his aggressive destructive dreams. He now can extirpate great realms of life: he is the single agent of evolutionary regression.

In times long past, when man represented no significant power to change nature, it mattered little to the world what views he held. Today, when he has emerged as potentially the most destructive force in nature and its greatest exploiter, it matters very much indeed. One looks to see whether with the acquisition of knowledge and powers the western attitudes to nature and to man in nature have changed. But for all of modern science it is still pre-Copernican man whom we confront. He retains the same implicit view of exclusive divinity, man apart from nature, dominant, exhorted to subdue the earth—be he Jew, Christian or agnostic.

Yet surely this is an ancient deformity, an old bile of vengeance that we can no longer tolerate. This view neither approximates reality nor does it help us towards our objectives of survival and evolution. One longs for a world psychiatrist who could assure the patient that expressions of his cultural inferiority are no longer necessary or appropriate. Man is now emancipated, he can stand erect among the creatures. His ancient vengeance, a product of his resentment at an earlier insignificance, is obsolete. The exercise of his great destructive powers are less worthy of adulation than creative skills, but they are enough for the moment to assuage the yearnings for primacy so long denied. From his position of destructive eminence he can now look to his mute partners and determine who they are, what they are, what they do, and realistically appraise the system within which he lives—his role, his dependencies—and reconstitute a cosmography that better accords with the world he experiences and which sustains him.

For me the indictment of city, suburb, and countryside becomes comprehensible in terms of the attitudes to nature that society has and does espouse. These environmental degradations are the inevitable consequence of such views. It is not incongruous but inevitable that the most beautiful landscapes and the richest farmlands should be less highly valued than the most scabrous slum and loathsome roadside stand. Inevitably an anthropocentric society will choose tomato stakes as a higher utility than the priceless and irreplaceable redwoods they have supplanted.

Where you find a people who believe that man and nature are indivisible, and that survival and health are contingent upon an understanding of nature and her processes, these societies will be very different from ours, as will be their towns, cities and landscapes. The hydraulic civilizations, the good farmer through time, the vernacular city builders have all displayed this acuity. But it is in the traditional society of Japan that the full integration of this view is revealed. That people, as we know, has absorbed a little of the best of the West and much of the worst while relinquishing accomplishments that we have not yet attained and can only envy.

In that culture there was sustained an agriculture at once incredibly productive and beautiful, testimony to an astonishing acuity to nature. This perception is reflected in a language rich in descriptive power in which the nuances of natural processes, the tilth of the soil, the dryness of wind, the burgeoning seed, are all precisely describable. The poetry of this culture is rich and succinct, the graphic arts reveal the landscape as the icon. Architecture, village and town building use natural materials directly with stirring power, but it is garden making that is the unequaled art form of this society. The garden is the metaphysical symbol of society in Tao, Shinto and Zen—man in nature.

Yet this view is not enough: man has fared less well than nature here. The jewel of the western tradition is the insistence upon the uniqueness of the individual and the preoccupation with justice and compassion. The Japanese medieval feudal view has been casual to the individual human life and rights. The western assumption of superiority has been achieved at the expense of nature. The oriental harmony of man-nature has been achieved at the expense of the individuality of man. Surely a united duality can be achieved by accounting for man as a unique individual rather than as a species, man in nature.

Let us by all means honor the attribution of dignity, even divinity, to man. But do we need to destroy nature to justify man—or even to obtain God's undivided attention? We can only be enlarged by accepting the reality of history and seeing ourselves in a non-human past, our survival contingent upon non-human processes. The acceptance of this view is not only necessary for the emancipation of western man, it is essential for the survival of all men.

If the Orient is the storehouse of the art of naturalism, it is the West that is the repository of anthropocentric art. It is a great if narrow inheritance, a glorious wealth of music and painting, sculpture and architecture. The Acropolis and Saint Peter, Autun and Beauvais, Chartres and Chambord, Ely and Peterborough—all speak of the divinity of man. But when the same views are extended and used as the structure for urban form, their illusory basis is revealed. The cathedral as the stage for a dialogue between man and God is admirable as a metaphysical symbol. When the supremacy of man is expressed in the form of the city, one seeks the evidence to support this superiority and finds only an assertion. Moreover, the insistence upon the divinity of man over nature has as its companion the insistence in the divine supremacy of some man over all men. It requires a special innocence to delight in the monumental accomplishments of the Renaissance cities, notably Rome and Paris, without appreciating that the generating impulses were more authoritarian than humanitarian—authoritarian towards nature and man.

If we lower the eyes from the wonderful, strident but innocent assertions of man's supremacy, we can find another tradition, more pervasive than the island monuments, little responsive to the grand procession of architectural styles. This is the vernacular tradition. The empiricist may not know first principles, but he has observed relations between events—he is not a victim of dogma. The farmer is the prototype. He prospers only insofar as he understands the land and by his management maintains its bounty. So too with the man who builds. If he is perceptive to the processes of nature, to materials and to forms, his creations will be appropriate to the place; they will satisfy the needs of social process and shelter, be expressive and endure. As indeed they have, in the hill towns of Italy, the island architecture of Greece, the medieval communities of France and the Low Countries and, not least, the villages of England and New England.

Two widely divergent views have been discussed, the raucous anthropocentrism which insists upon the exclusive divinity of man, his role of dominion and subjugation on one hand, and the oriental view of man submerged in nature on the other. Each view has distinct advantages, both have adaptive value. Are the benefits of each mutually exclusive? I think not; but in order to achieve the best of both worlds it is necessary to retreat from polar extremes. There is indisputable evidence that man exists in nature; but it is important to recognize the uniqueness of the individual and thus his especial opportunities and responsibilities.

If the adaptation of the western view towards this more encompassing attitude required the West to accept Tao, Shinto or Zen, there would be little hope for any transformation. However, we have seen that the vernacular of the West has many similarities to the products of oriental pantheism. There is another great bridge, the 18th-century English landscape tradition. This movement originated in the poets and writers of the period, from whom developed the conception of a harmony of man and nature. The landscape image was derived from the painters of the Campagna— Claude Lorrain. Salvator Rosa and Poussin. It was confirmed in a new aesthetic by the discovery of the Orient and on these premises transformed England from a poverty-stricken and raddled land to that beautiful landscape that still is visible today. This is a valid western tradition, it presumes a unity of man and nature, it was developed empirically by a few landscape architects, it accomplished a most dramatic transformation, it has endured. Yet the precursory understanding of natural processes that underlay it was limited. A better source is that uniquely western preoccupation, science.

Surely the minimum requirement today for any attitude to man-nature is that it approximate reality. One could reasonably expect that if such a view prevailed, not only would it affect the value system, but also the expressions accomplished by society.

Where else can we turn for an accurate model of the world and ourselves but to science? We can accept that scientific knowledge is incomplete and will forever be so, but it is the best we have and it has that great merit, which religions lack, of being self-correcting. Moreover, if we wish to understand the phenomenal world, then we will reasonably direct our questions to those scientists who are concerned with this realm—the natural scientists. More precisely, when our preoccupation is with the interaction of organisms and environment—and I can think of no better description for our concern—then we must turn to ecologists, for that is their competence.

We will agree that science is not the only mode of perception—that the poet, painter, playwright and author can often reveal in metaphor that which science is unable to demonstrate. But, if we seek a workman's creed which approximates reality and can be used as a model of the world and ourselves, then science does provide the best evidence.

From the ecological view one can see that, since life is only transmitted by life, then, by living, each one of us is physically linked to the origins of life and thus—literally, not metaphorically—to all life. Moreover, since life originated from matter then, by living, man is physically united back through the evolution of matter to the primeval hydrogen. The planet Earth has been the one home for all of its processes and all of its myriad inhabitants since the beginning of time, from hydrogen to men. Only the bathing sunlight changes. Our phenomenal world contains our origins, our history, our milieu; it is our home. It is in this sense that ecology (derived from *oikos*) is the science of the home.

George Wald once wrote facetiously that "it would be a poor thing to be an atom in a Universe without physicists. And physicists are made of atoms. A physicist is the atom's way of knowing about atoms."[2] Who knows what atoms yearn to be, but we are their progeny. It would be just as sad to be an organism in a universe without ecologists, who are themselves organisms. May not the ecologist be the atom's way of learning about organisms—and ours?

The ecological view requires that we look upon the world, listen and learn. The place, creatures and men were, have been, are now and are in the process of becoming. We and they are here now, co-tenants of the phenomenal world, united in its origins and destiny.

As we contemplate the squalid city and the pathetic subdivision, suitcase agriculture and the cynical industrialist, the insidious merchant, and the product of all these in the necklace of megalopoles around the continent, their entrails coalescing, we fervently hope that there is another way. There is. The ecological view is the essential component in the search for the face of the land of the free and the home of the brave. This work seeks to persuade to that effect. It consists of borrowings from the thoughts and dreams of other men, forged into a workman's code—an ecological manual for the good steward who aspires to art.

—*Design with Nature* (1969)

NOTES

1. See Leo Srole et al., *Mental Health in the Metropolis: The Midtown Manhattan Study* (New York: McGraw-Hill, 1962).
2. George Wald in *The Fitness of the Environment*, by Lawrence J. Henderson (Beacon Press, Boston, Massachusetts, 1958), p. xxiv.

POSTSCRIPT
Esthetic Theory

LUDWIG WITTGENSTEIN: Games and Definitions
MORRIS WEITZ: The Role of Theory in Esthetics
MAURICE MANDELBAUM: Family Resemblances and Generalization
Concerning the Arts

In the preceding chapters we have reviewed different conceptions of art. Various writers have informed us that art is imagination, expression of emotion, intuition, imaginative wish-fulfillment, enhancement of experience, creation of beauty, embodiment of values, significant form, or, with a view to the experience of the beholder, empathy, abstraction, psychical distance, or some other attitude or psychological state. In view of the breadth of art and the diversity of esthetic theories, the question of the feasibility of definition and the value of esthetic theory becomes paramount. The three essays that constitute this Postscript focus upon this problem.

Skepticism as to the possibility of a universal definition of "art" or "esthetic" is not new. As Harold Osborne points out in his book, *Aesthetics and Art Theory* (London and New York, 1970), the Scottish philosopher Thomas Reid, as early as 1785, maintained that there is no common essence either in beautiful objects or in works of art, declaring that "I am unable to conceive of any quality in all the different things that are called beautiful, that is the same in them all." Dugald Stewart, another Scottish philosopher quoted by Osborne, explicitly propounded the idea of overlapping similarities, which Wittgenstein later dubbed "family resemblances." "I shall begin by supposing," he declared, "that the letters A, B, C, D, E, denote a series of objects; that A possesses one quality in common with B; B a quality in common with C; C a quality in common with D; D a quality in common with E; while at the same time no quality can be found which belongs in common to any *three* objects in the series." Nevertheless, as he observed, the whole series may be designated by a common name. He even went so far as to propose a radical change in esthetic inquiry, substituting, in place of the search for a common essence, a study of "the natural history of the Human Mind, and . . . its natural progress in the employment of speech." In terms of ordinary language, "art" has been used in a great variety of ways, as Thomas DeQuincey's essay, "Murder as One of the Fine Arts" (1827), bears amusing witness.

The challenge to philosophical inquiry that Reid and Stewart envisaged has reached a climax in the twentieth century, especially in the work of Ludwig Wittgenstein (1889–1951). Although he was born and reared in Austria, he spent much of his lifetime in England, as a student and later as a professor at Cambridge University. His immense influence was exerted through the spell of his powerful personality and his two remarkable books, *Tractatus Logico-Philosophicus* (1921) and *Philosophical Investigations* (1953).

Richly endowed with artistic ability, Wittgenstein could design a house, mold a statue, play a clarinet, conduct an orchestra, or write an imaginary dialogue. "Topics in esthetics," declares his former student Norman Malcolm, "were perhaps the most frequent at [his] at-homes, and the depth and richness of Wittgenstein's thinking about art were very exciting."[1] Nevertheless, his published writings contain only casual references to art, and his influence is to be found mainly in his general ideas and method. As the reader peruses Wittgenstein's remarks on "games and definitions," he should consider just how the ideas apply to esthetics.

One of his remarks, as quoted by Malcolm, sums up a good deal of his philosophy: "An expression has meaning only in the stream of life."[2] The meanings of a concept, such as "beauty" or "art," can best be determined by studying its actual use by ordinary human beings as they go about the business of living. When we lay aside preconceptions and study words in their vital employment, we discover that they have no fixed meanings and no sharp edges. An example discussed in the following selection is the word "game." We can find no mark or characteristic, no "essence," that is common to all games—nothing that would permit us to encompass all games in a formula or definition.

"The meaning is the use" is Wittgenstein's famous slogan—and the uses are various and unpredictable. In actual life, words are like tools that can be employed for many different purposes: "Think of the tools in a tool-box; there is a hammer, pliers, a saw, a screwdriver, a rule, a glue-pot, glue, nails and screws.—The functions of words are as diverse as the functions of these objects."[3] Even a single word, such as "beauty," has a multiplicity of uses, and this multiplicity is not predetermined or fixed. We should therefore respect the "open texture" of language, recognizing that a word has an indefinite variety of meanings and that new and unprecedented meanings will arise as the contexts of life alter. The appropriate uses of a word in such a vital context Wittgenstein calls a "language-game" by Wittgenstein, and such "games" vary from one "form of life" to another.

These and other implications of Wittgenstein's philosophy are pointed out by Morris Weitz (1916–   ), professor of philosophy at Brandeis University and distinguished contributor to esthetics. His essay is an example of the considerable influence that Wittgenstein's ideas are exercising on the philosophy of art. He asks the question whether esthetic theory, conceived as a search for the necessary and sufficient properties of art, is possible, and he replies in the negative. Reviewing the main theories of modern esthetics, he concludes that there are no limits to the "open texture" of art and no sharp demarcation or eternal essence that a definition can formulate.

The results of his analysis are not wholly negative. Each of the classical "definitions," he believes, calls attention to an important strand of similarities in artistic works or activities, or recommends some criterion of artistic excellence. The definitions thus point to aspects of art that might otherwise be neglected or underrated. So understood, they are extremely valuable.

Underlying Weitz's argument is the supposition that overlapping similarities are the basis of these attempted definitions in esthetics. This assumption is challenged by Maurice Mandelbaum (1908–   ), professor of philosophy at the Johns Hopkins University and one of America's best known philosophers. To understand his point, let us revert to "games." What is it that makes all examples of games fall within this common category? Wittgenstein's "game" theory is not as radically nominalistic as might be supposed, since he recognizes that the one thing all games have in common *is their being games.* His analogy with *family* resemblances is based upon a genetic bond, since "family" implies a common ancestry and hence more than a resemblance—an implication that Wittgenstein apparently recognized but did not stress (see Note 11 in Mandelbaum's essay). Two human beings may closely resemble each other without being members of the same family; and two or more human beings, although they may be *very* dissimilar, are members of one family if they have the same parents.

Noting this fact, Mandelbaum emphasizes unexhibited genetic ties in analyzing games and works of art. Just as fortune-telling with cards is not a game, although it may closely resemble the game of solitaire, so a rock shaped by water erosion is not a work of art, however much it may resemble a piece of abstract sculpture. On the other hand, two very different objects may be works of art if they bear the same sort of relation to human creative activities. Using such nonmanifest genetic connections as a basis, Mandelbaum argues that Morris Weitz, Paul Ziff, and other analysts overlook or understress the relation of art to the definable human intentions and creative processes from which art springs.

NOTES

1. Norman Malcolm, *Ludwig Wittgenstein: A Memoir* (London, Oxford University Press, 1958), p. 53.
2. *Ibid.,* p. 93.
3. *Philosophical Investigations,* Section 11.

LUDWIG WITTGENSTEIN

Games and Definitions[1]

65. Here we come up against the great question that lies behind all these considerations.—For someone might object against me: "You take the easy way out! You talk about all sorts of language-games, but have nowhere

said what the essence of a language-game, and hence of language, is: what is common to all these activities, and what makes them into language or parts of language. So you let yourself off the very part of the investigation that once gave you yourself most headache, the part about the *general form of propositions* and of language."

And this is true.—Instead of producing something common to all that we call language, I am saying that these phenomena have no one thing in common which makes us use the same word for all,—but that they are *related* to one another in many different ways. And it is because of this relationship, or these relationships, that we call them all "language." I will try to explain this.

66. Consider for example the proceedings that we call "games." I mean board games, card games, ball games, Olympic games, and so on. What is common to them all?—Don't say: "There *must* be something common, or they would not be called 'games' "—but *look and see* whether there is anything common to all.—For if you look at them you will not see something that is common to *all*, but similarities, relationships, and a whole series of them at that. To repeat: don't think, but look!—Look for example at board games, with their multifarious relationships. Now pass to card games; here you find many correspondences with the first group, but many common features drop out, and others appear. When we pass next to ball games, much that is common is retained, but much is lost.—Are they all "amusing"? Compare chess with noughts and crosses. Or is there always winning and losing, or competition between players? Think of patience. In ball games there is winning and losing; but when a child throws his ball at the wall and catches it again, this feature has disappeared. Look at the parts played by skill and luck; and at the difference between skill in chess and skill in tennis. Think now of games like ring-a-ring-a-roses; here is the element of amusement, but how many other characteristic features have disappeared! And we can go through the many, many other groups of games in the same way; can see how similarities crop up and disappear.

And the result of this examination is: we see a complicated network of similarities overlapping and criss-crossing: sometimes overall similarities, sometimes similarities of detail.

67. I can think of no better expression to characterize these similarities than "family resemblances"; for the various resemblances between members of a family: build, features, color of eyes, gait, temperament, etc. etc. overlap and criss-cross in the same way.—And I shall say: "games" form a family.

And for instance the kinds of number form a family in the same way. Why do we call something a "number"? Well, perhaps because it has a—direct—relationship with several things that have hitherto been called number; and this can be said to give it an indirect relationship to other things we call the same name. And we extend our concept of number as in spinning a thread we twist fibre on fibre. And the strength of the thread does not reside in the fact that some one fibre runs through its whole length, but in the overlapping of many fibres.

But if someone wished to say, "There is something common to all these constructions—namely the disjunction of all their common properties"—I should reply, Now you are only playing with words. One might as well say, "Something runs through the whole thread—namely the continuous overlapping of those fibres."

68. "All right: the concept of number is defined for you as the logical sum of these individual interrelated concepts: cardinal numbers, rational numbers, real numbers, etc.; and in the same way the concept of a game as the logical sum of a corresponding set of sub-concepts."—It need not be so. For I *can* give the concept "number" rigid limits in this way, that is, use the word "number" for a rigidly limited concept, but I can also use it so that the extension of the concept is *not* closed by a frontier. And this is how we do use the word "game." For how is the concept of a game bounded? What still counts as a game and what no longer does? Can you give the boundary? No. You can *draw* one; for none has so far been drawn. (But that never troubled you before when you used the word "game.")

"But then the use of the word is unregulated, the 'game' we play with it is unregulated."—It is not everywhere circumscribed by rules; but no more are there any rules for how high one throws the ball in tennis, or how hard; yet tennis is a game for all that and has rules too.

69. How should we explain to someone what a game is? I imagine that we should describe *games* to him, and we might add: "This *and similar things* are called 'games.' " And do we know any more about it ourselves? Is it only other people whom we cannot tell exactly what a game is?—But this is not ignorance. We do not know the boundaries because none have been drawn. To repeat, we can draw a boundary—for a special purpose. Does it take that to make the concept usable? Not at all! (Except for that special purpose.) No more than it took the definition: 1 pace = 75 cm. to make the measure of length 'one pace' usable. And if you want to say "But still, before that it wasn't an exact measure," then I reply: very well, it was an inexact one.—Though you still owe me a definition of exactness.

70. "But if the concept 'game' is uncircumscribed like that, you don't really know what you mean by a 'game.' "—When I give the description: "The ground was quite covered with plants"—do you want to say I don't know what I am talking about until I can give a definition of a plant?

My meaning would be explained by, say, a drawing and the words "The ground looked roughly like this." Perhaps I even say "it looked *exactly* like this."—Then were just *this* grass and *these* leaves there, arranged just like this? No, that is not what it means. And I should not accept any picture as exact in *this* sense.

Someone says to me: "Show the children a game." I teach them gaming with dice, and the other says "I didn't mean that sort of game." Must the exclusion of the game with dice have come before his mind when he gave me the order?[2]

---

71. One might say that the concept 'game' is a concept with blurred

edges.—"But is a blurred concept a concept at all?"—Is an indistinct photograph a picture of a person at all? Is it even always an advantage to replace an indistinct picture by a sharp one? Isn't the indistinct one often exactly what we need?

Frege compares a concept to an area and says that an area with vague boundaries cannot be called an area at all. This presumably means that we cannot do anything with it.—But is it senseless to say, "Stand roughly there?" Suppose that I were standing with someone in a city square and said that. As I say it I do not draw any kind of boundary, but perhaps point with my hand—as if I were indicating a particular *spot*. And this is just how one might explain to someone what a game is. One gives examples and intends them to be taken in a particular way.—I do not, however, mean by this that he is supposed to see in those examples that common thing which I—for some reason—was unable to express; but that he is now to *employ* those examples in a particular way. Here giving examples is not an *indirect* means of explaining—in default of a better. For any general definition can be misunderstood too. The point is that *this* is how we play the game. (I mean the language-game with the word "game.")

72. *Seeing what is common.* Suppose I show someone various multi-colored pictures, and say: "The color you see in all these is called 'yellow ochre.' "—This is a definition, and the other will get to understand it by looking for and seeing what is common to the pictures. Then he can look *at*, can point *to*, the common thing.

Compare with this a case in which I show him figures of different shapes all painted the same color, and say: "What these have in common is called 'yellow ochre.' "

And compare this case: I show him samples of different shades of blue and say, "The color that is common to all these is what I call 'blue.' "

73. When someone defines the names of color for me by pointing to samples and saying "This color is called 'blue,' this 'green' . . ." this case can be compared in many respects to putting a table in my hands, with the words written under the color-samples.—Though this comparison may mislead in many ways.—One is now inclined to extend the comparison: to have understood the definition means to have in one's mind an idea of the thing defined, and that is a sample or picture. So if I am shown various different leaves and told "This is called a 'leaf,' " I get an idea of the shape of a leaf, a picture of it in my mind.—But what does the picture of a leaf look like when it does not show us any particular shape, but "what is common to all shapes of leaf?" Which shade is the "sample in my mind" of the color green—the sample of what is common to all shades of green?

"But might there not be such 'general' samples? Say a schematic leaf, or a sample of *pure* green?"—Certainly there might. But for such a schema to be understood as a *schema*, and not as the shape of a particular leaf, and for a slip of pure green to be understood as a sample of all that is greenish and not as a sample of pure green—this in turn resides in the way the samples are used.

Ask yourself what *shape* must the sample of the color green be? Should it be rectangular? Or would it then be the sample of a green rectangle?—So should it be "irregular" in shape? And what is to prevent us then from regarding it—that is, from using it—only as a sample of irregularity of shape?

74. Here also belongs the idea that if you see this leaf as a sample of "leaf shape in general" you *see* it differently from someone who regards it as, say, a sample of this particular shape. Now this might well be so—though it is not so—for it would only be to say that, as a matter of experience, if you *see* the leaf in a particular way, you use it in such-and-such a way or according to such-and-such rules. Of course, there is such a thing as seeing in *this* way or *that*; and there are also cases where whoever sees a sample like *this* will in general use it in *this* way, and whoever sees it otherwise in another way. For example, if you see the schematic drawing of a cube as a plane figure consisting of a square and two rhombi you will, perhaps, carry out the order "Bring me something like this" differently from someone who sees the picture three-dimensionally.

75. What does it mean to know what a game is? What does it mean, to know it and not be able to say it? Is this knowledge somehow equivalent to an unformulated definition? So that if it were formulated I should be able to recognize it as the expression of my knowledge? Isn't my knowledge, my concept of a game, completely expressed in the explanations that I could give? That is, in my describing examples of various kinds of game; showing how all sorts of other games can be constructed on the analogy of these; saying that I should scarcely include this or this among games; and so on.

76. If someone were to draw a sharp boundary I could not acknowledge it as the one that I too always wanted to draw, or had drawn in my mind. For I did not want to draw one at all. His concept can then be said to be not the same as mine, but akin to it. The kinship is that of two pictures, one of which consists of color patches with vague contours, and the other of patches similarly shaped and distributed, but with clear contours. The kinship is just as undeniable as the difference.

77. And if we carry this comparison still further it is clear that the degree to which the sharp picture *can* resemble the blurred one depends on the latter's degree of vagueness. For imagine having to sketch a sharply defined picture "corresponding" to a blurred one. In the latter there is a blurred red rectangle: for it you put down a sharply defined one. Of course —several such sharply defined rectangles can be drawn to correspond to the indefinite one.—But if the colors in the original merge without a hint of any outline won't it become a hopeless task to draw a sharp picture corresponding to the blurred one? Won't you then have to say, "Here I might just as well draw a circle or heart as a rectangle, for all the colors merge." Anything—and nothing—is right.—And this is the position you are in if you look for definitions corresponding to our concepts in esthetics or ethics.

In such a difficulty always ask yourself, How did we *learn* the meaning of this word ("good" for instance)? From what sort of examples? in what language-games? Then it will be easier for you to see that the word must have a family of meanings.

—*Philosophical Investigations* (1953), translated by G. E. M. Anscombe

NOTES

1. Wittgenstein expressed the wish that his German text always be available to the reader of his work. His publisher, Basil Blackwell of Oxford, wishes me to note that the original German text, along with the English translation, is available in the standard edition of *Philosophical Investigations*. (Editor)

2. This paragraph—here set off by lines—was written on a slip and inserted by Wittgenstein without a definite indication of where it should come in. (Editor's note.)

MORRIS WEITZ

The Role of Theory in Esthetics

Theory has been central in esthetics and still the preoccupation of the philosophy of art. Its main avowed concern remains the determination of the nature of art which can be formulated into a definition of it. It construes definition as the statement of the necessary and sufficient properties of what is being defined, where the statement purports to be a true or false claim about the essence of art, what characterizes and distinguishes it from everything else. Each of the great theories of art—Formalism, Voluntarism, Emotionalism, Intellectualism, Intuitionism, Organicism—converges on the attempt to state the defining properties of art. Each claims that it is the true theory because it has formulated correctly into a real definition the nature of art; and that the others are false because they have left out some necessary or sufficient property. Many theorists contend that their enterprise is no mere intellectual exercise but an absolute necessity for any understanding of art and our proper evaluation of it. Unless we know what art is, they say, what are its necessary and sufficient properties, we cannot begin to respond to it adequately or to say why one work is good or better than another. Esthetic theory, thus, is important not only in itself but for the foundations of both appreciation and criticism. Philosophers, critics, and even artists who have written on art, agree that what is primary in esthetics is a theory about the nature of art.

Is esthetics theory, in the sense of a true definition or set of necessary and sufficient properties of art, possible? If nothing else does, the history of esthetics itself should give one enormous pause here. For, in spite of the many theories, we seem no nearer our goal today than we were in Plato's time. Each age, each art-movement, each philosophy of art, tries over and over again to establish the stated ideal only to be succeeded by a new or revised theory, rooted, at least in part, in the repudiation of preceding ones. Even today, almost everyone interested in esthetic matters is still deeply wedded to the hope that the correct theory of art is forthcoming. We need only examine the numerous new books on art in which new definitions are proffered; or, in our own country especially, the basic text-books and anthologies to recognize how strong the priority of a theory of art is.

In this essay I want to plead for the rejection of this problem. I want to show that theory—in the requisite classical sense—is *never* forthcoming in esthetics, and that we would do much better as philosophers to supplant the question, "What is the nature of art?," by other questions, the answers to which will provide us with all the understanding of the arts there can be. I want to show that the inadequacies of the theories are not primarily occasioned by any legitimate difficulty such as, for example, the vast complexity of art, which might be corrected by further probing and research. Their basic inadequacies reside instead in a fundamental misconception of art. Esthetic theory—all of it—is wrong in principle in thinking that a correct theory is possible because it radically misconstrues the logic of the concept of art. Its main contention that "art" is amenable to real or any kind of true definition is false. Its attempt to discover the necessary and sufficient properties of art is logically misbegotten for the very simple reason that such a set and, consequently, such a formula about it, is never forthcoming. Art, as the logic of the concept shows, has no set of necessary and sufficient properties, hence a theory of it is logically impossible and not merely factually difficult. Esthetic theory tries to define what cannot be defined in its requisite sense. But in recommending the repudiation of esthetic theory I shall not argue from this, as too many others have done, that its logical confusions render it meaningless or worthless. On the contrary, I wish to reassess its role and its contribution primarily in order to show that it is of the greatest importance to our understanding of the arts.

Let us now survey briefly some of the more famous extant esthetic theories in order to see if they do incorporate correct and adequate statements about the nature of art. In each of these there is the assumption that it is the true enumeration of the defining properties of art, with the implication that previous theories have stressed wrong definitions. Thus, to begin with, consider a famous version of Formalist theory, that propounded by Bell and Fry. It is true that they speak mostly of painting in their writings but both assert that what they find in that art can be generalized for what is "art" in the others as well. The essence of painting, they maintain, is the plastic elements in relation. Its defining property is significant form, that is, certain combinations of lines, colors, shapes, volumes—everything on the canvas except the representational elements—which evoke a unique response to such combinations. Painting is definable as plastic organization. The nature of art, what it *really* is, so their theory goes, is a unique combination of certain elements (the specifiable plastic ones) in their relations. Anything which is art is an instance of significant form; and anything which is not art has no such form.

To this the Emotionalist replies that the truly essential property of art has been left out. Tolstoy, Ducasse, or any of the advocates of this theory, find that the requisite defining property is not significant form but rather the expression of emotion in some sensuous public medium. Without projection of emotion into some piece of stone or words or sounds, etc., there can be no art. Art is really such embodiment. It is this that uniquely characterizes art, and any true, real definition of it, contained in some adequate theory of art, must so state it.

The Intuitionist disclaims both emotion and form as defining properties. In Croce's version, for example, art is identified not with some physical, public object but with a specific creative, cognitive, and spiritual act. Art is really a first stage of knowledge in which certain human beings (artists) bring their images and intuitions into lyrical clarification or expression. As such, it is an awareness, non-conceptual in character, of the unique individuality of things; and since it exists below the level of conceptualization or action, it is without scientific or moral content. Croce singles out as the defining essence of art this first stage of spiritual life and advances its identification with art as a philosophically true theory or definition.

The Organicist says to all of this that art is really a class of organic wholes consisting of distinguishable, albeit inseparable, elements in their causally efficacious relations which are presented in some sensuous medium. In A. C. Bradley, in piecemeal versions of it in literary criticism, or in my own generalized adaptation of it in my *Philosophy of the Arts*, what is claimed is that anything which is a work of art is in its nature a unique complex of interrelated parts—in painting, for example, lines, colors, volumes, subjects, etc., all interacting upon one another on a paint surface of some sort. Certainly, at one time at least it seemed to me that this organic theory constituted the one true and real definition of art.

My final example is the most interesting of all, logically speaking. This is the Voluntarist theory of Parker. In his writings on art, Parker persistently calls into question the traditional simpleminded definitions of aesthetics. "The assumption underlying every philosophy of art is the existence of some common nature present in all the arts."[1] "All the so popular brief definitions of art—'significant form,' 'expression,' 'intuition,' 'objectified pleasure'—are fallacious, either because, while true of art, they are also true of much that is not art, and hence fail to differentiate art from other things; or else because they neglect some essential aspect of art."[2] But instead of inveighing against the attempt at definition of art itself, Parker insists that what is needed is a complex definition rather than a simple one. "The definition of art must therefore be in terms of a complex of characteristics. Failure to recognize this has been the fault of all the well-known definitions."[3] His own version of Voluntarism is the theory that art is essentially three things: embodiment of wishes and desires imaginatively satisfied, language, which characterizes the public medium of art, and harmony, which unifies the language with the layers of imaginative projections. Thus, for Parker, it is a true definition to say of art that it is ". . . the provision of satisfaction through the imagination, social significance, and harmony. I am claiming that nothing except works of art possess all three of these marks."[4]

Now, all of these sample theories are inadequate in many different ways. Each purports to be a complete statement about the defining features of all works of art and yet each of them leaves out something which the others take to be central. Some are circular, for example, the Bell-Fry theory of art as significant form which is defined in part in terms of our response to significant form. Some of them, in their search for necessary and sufficient properties, emphasize too few properties, like (again) the Bell-Fry definition which leaves out subject-representation in painting, or the Croce theory which omits inclusion of the very important feature of the public, physical character, say, of architecture. Others are too general and cover objects that are not art as well as works of art. Organicism is surely such a view since it can be applied to *any* causal unity in the natural world as well as to art.[5] Still others rest on dubious principles, for example, Parker's claim that art embodies imaginative satisfactions, rather than real ones; or Croce's assertion that there is nonconceptual knowledge. Consequently, even if art has one set of necessary and sufficient properties, none of the theories we have noted or, for that matter, no esthetic theory yet proposed, has enumerated that set to the satisfaction of all concerned.

Then there is a different sort of difficulty. As real definitions, these theories are supposed to be factual reports on art. If they are, may we not ask, Are they empirical and open to verification or falsification? For example, what would confirm or disconfirm the theory that art is significant form or embodiment of emotion or creative synthesis of images? There does not even seem to be a hint of the kind of evidence which might be forthcoming to test these theories; and indeed one wonders if they are perhaps honorific definitions of "art," that is, proposed redefinitions in terms of some *chosen* conditions for applying the concept of art, and not true or false reports on the essential properties of art at all.

But all these criticisms of traditional esthetic theories—that they are circular, incomplete, untestable, pseudo-factual, disguised proposals to change the meaning of concepts—have been made before. My intention is to go beyond these to make a much more fundamental criticism, namely, that esthetic theory is a logically vain attempt to define what cannot be defined, to state the necessary and sufficient properties of that which has no necessary and sufficient properties, to conceive the concept of art as closed when its very use reveals and demands its openness.

The problem with which we must begin is not "What is art?," but "What sort of concept is 'art'?" Indeed, the root problem of philosophy itself is to explain the relation between the employment of certain kinds of concepts and the conditions under which they can be correctly applied. If I may paraphrase Wittgenstein, we must not ask, What is the nature of any philosophical x?, or even, according to the semanticist, What does "x" mean?, a transformation that leads to the disastrous interpretation of "art" as a name for some specifiable class of objects; but rather, What is the use or employment of "x"? What does "x" do in the language? This, I take it, is the initial question, the begin-all if not the end-all of any philosophical problem and solution. Thus, in esthetics, our first problem is the elucidation of the actual employment of the concept of art, to give a logical description of the actual functioning of the concept, including a description of the conditions under which we correctly use it or its correlates.

My model in this type of logical description or philosophy derives from Wittgenstein. It is also he who, in his refutation of philosophical theorizing in the sense of constructing definitions of philosophical entities, has furnished contemporary esthetics with a starting point for any future progress. In his new work, *Philosophical Investigations*,[6] Wittgenstein raises as an illustrative question, What is a game? The traditional philosophical, theoretical answer would be in terms of some exhaustive set of properties common to all games. To this Wittgenstein says, let us consider what we call "games": "I mean board games, card games, ball games, Olympic games, and so on. What is common to them all?—Don't say: 'there *must* be something common, or they would not be called "games" ' but *look and see* whether there is anything common to all.—For if you look at them you will not see something that is common to *all*, but similarities, relationships, and a whole series of them at that. . . ."

Card games are like board games in some respects but not in others. Not all games are amusing, nor is there always winning or losing or competition. Some games resemble others in some respects—that is all. What we find are no necessary and sufficient properties, only "a complicated network of similarities overlapping and crisscrossing," such that we can say of games that they form a family with family resemblances and no common trait. If one asks what a game is, we pick out sample games, describe these, and add, "This and *similar things* are called 'games.' " This is all we need to say and indeed all any of us knows about games. Knowing what a game is is not knowing some real definition or theory but being able to recognize and explain games and to decide which among imaginary and new examples would or would not be called "games."

The problem of the nature of art is like that of the nature of games, at least in these respects: If we actually look and see what it is that we call "art," we will also find no common properties—only strands of similarities. Knowing what art is is not apprehending some manifest or latent essence but being able to recognize, describe, and explain those things we call "art" in virtue of these similarities.

But the basic resemblance between these concepts is their open texture. In elucidating them, certain (paradigm) cases can be given, about which there can be no question as to their being correctly described as "art" or "game," but no exhaustive set of cases can be given. I can list some cases and some conditions under which I can apply correctly the concept of art but I cannot list all of them, for the all-important reason that unforeseeable or novel conditions are always forthcoming or envisageable.

A concept is open if its conditions of application are emendable and corrigible; that is, if a situation or case can be imagined or secured which would call for some sort of *decision* on our part to extend the use of the concept to cover this, or to close the concept and invent a new one to deal with the new case and its new property. If necessary and sufficient conditions for the application of a concept can be stated, the concept is a closed one. But this can happen only in logic or mathematics where concepts are constructed and completely defined. It cannot occur with empirically-descriptive and normative concepts unless we arbitrarily close them by stipulating the ranges of their uses.

I can illustrate this open character of "art" best by examples drawn from its sub-concepts. Consider questions like "Is Dos Passos' *U. S. A.* a novel?," "Is V. Woolf's *To the Lighthouse* a novel?," "Is Joyce's *Finnegan's Wake* a novel?" On the traditional view, these are construed as factual problems to be answered yes or no in accordance with the presence or absence of defining properties. But certainly this is not how any of these questions is answered. Once it arises, as it has many times in the development of the novel from Richardson to Joyce (for example, "Is Gide's *The School for Wives* a novel or a diary?"), what is at stake is no factual analysis concerning necessary and sufficient properties but a decision as to whether the work under examination is similar in certain respects to other works, already called "novels," and consequently warrants the extension of the concept to cover the new case. The new work is narrative, fictional, contains character delineation and dialogue but (say) it has no regular time-sequence in the plot or is interspersed with actual newspaper reports. It is like recognized novels, A, B, C . . . , in some respects but not like them in others. But then neither were B and C like A in some respects when it was decided to extend the concept applied to A to B and C. Because work N + 1 (the brand new work) is like A, B, C . . . N in certain respects—has strands of similarity to them—the concept is extended and a new phase of the novel engendered. "Is N + 1 a novel?," then, is no factual, but rather a decision problem, where the verdict turns on whether or not we enlarge our set of conditions for applying the concept.

What is true of the novel is, I think, true of every sub-concept of art: "tragedy," "comedy," "painting," "opera," etc., of "art" itself. No "Is X a novel, painting, opera, work of art, etc.?" question allows of a definitive answer in the sense of a factual yes or no report. "Is this *collage* a painting or not?" does not rest on any set of necessary and sufficient properties of painting but on whether we decide—as we did!—to extend "painting" to cover this case.

"Art," itself, is an open concept. New conditions (cases) have constantly arisen and will undoubtedly constantly arise; new art forms, new movements will emerge, which will demand decisions on the part of those interested, usually professional critics, as to whether the concept should be extended or not. Estheticians may lay down similarity conditions but never necessary and sufficient ones for the correct application of the concept. With "art" its conditions of application can never be exhaustively enumerated since new cases can always be envisaged or created by artists, or even nature, which would call for a decision on someone's part to extend or to close the old or to invent a new concept. (For example, "It's not a sculpture, it's a mobile.")

What I am arguing, then, is that the very expansive, adventurous character of art, its ever-present changes and novel creations, makes it logically impossible to ensure any set of defining properties. We can, of course, choose to close the concept. But to do this with "art" or "tragedy" or "portraiture," etc., is ludicrous since it forecloses on the very conditions of creativity in the arts.

Of course there are legitimate and serviceable closed concepts in art. But these are always those whose boundaries of conditions have been drawn for a *special* purpose. Consider the difference, for example, between "tragedy" and "(extant) Greek tragedy." The first is open and must remain so to allow for the possibility of new conditions, for example, a play in which the hero is not noble or fallen or in which there is no hero but other elements that are like those of plays we already call "tragedy." The second is closed. The plays it can be applied to, the conditions under which it can be correctly used are all in, once the boundary, "Greek," is drawn. Here the critic can work out a theory or real definition in which he lists the common properties at least of the extant Greek tragedies. Aristotle's definition, false as it is as a theory of all the plays of Aeschylus, Sophocles, and Euripides, since it does not cover some of them,[7] properly called "tragedies," can be interpreted as a real (albeit incorrect) definition of this closed concept; although it can also be, as it unfortunately has been, conceived as a purported real definition of "tragedy," in which case it suffers from the logical mistake of trying to define what cannot be defined—of trying to squeeze what is an open concept into an honorific formula for a closed concept.

What is supremely important, if the critic is not to become muddled, is to get absolutely clear about the way in which he conceives his concepts; otherwise he goes from the problem of trying to define "tragedy," etc., to an arbitrary closing of the concept in terms of certain preferred conditions or characteristics which he sums up in some linguistic recommendation that he mistakenly thinks is a real definition of the open concept. Thus, many critics and estheticians ask, "What is tragedy?," choose a class of samples for which they may give a true account of its common properties, and then go on to construe this account of the chosen closed class as a true definition or theory of the whole open class of tragedy. This, I think, is the logical mechanism of most of the so-called theories of the subconcepts of art: "tragedy," "comedy," "novel," etc. In effect, this whole procedure, subtly deceptive as it is, amounts to a transformation of correct criteria for *recognizing* members of certain legitimately closed classes of works of art into recommended criteria for *evaluating* any putative member of the class.

The primary task of esthetics is not to seek a theory but to elucidate the concept of art. Specifically, it is to describe the conditions under which we employ the concept correctly. Definition, reconstruction, patterns of analysis are out of place here since they distort and add nothing to our understanding of art. What, then, is the logic of "X is a work of art"?

As we actually use the concept, "Art" is both descriptive (like "chair") and evaluative (like "good"); that is, we sometimes say, "This is a work of art," to describe something and we sometimes say it to evaluate something. Neither use surprises anyone.

What, first, is the logic of "X is a work of art," when it is a descriptive utterance? What are the conditions under which we would be making such an utterance correctly? There are no necessary and sufficient conditions but there are the strands of similarity conditions, i.e., bundles of properties, none of which need be present but most of which are, when we describe things as works of art. I shall call these the "criteria of recognition" of works of art. All of these have served as the defining criteria of the individual traditional theories of art; so we are already familiar with them. Thus, mostly, when we describe something as a work of art, we do so under the conditions of there being present some sort of artifact, made by human skill, ingenuity, and imagination, which embodies in its sensuous, public medium—stone, wood, sounds, words, etc.—certain distinguishable elements and relations. Special theorists would add conditions like satisfaction of wishes, objectification or expression of emotion, some act of empathy, and so on; but these latter conditions seem to be quite adventitious, present to some but not to other spectators when things are described as works of art. "X is a work of art and contains *no* emotion, expression, act of empathy, satisfaction, etc.," is perfectly good sense and may frequently be true. "X is a work of art and . . . was made by no one," or . . . "exists only in the mind and not in any publicly observable thing," or . . . "was made by accident when he spilled the paint on the canvas," in each case of which a normal condition is denied, are also sensible and capable of being true in certain circumstances. None of the criteria of recognition is a defining one, either necessary or sufficient, because we can sometimes assert of something that it is a work of art and go on to deny any one of these conditions, even the one which has traditionally been taken to be basic, namely, that of being an artifact: Consider, "This piece of driftwood is a lovely piece of sculpture." Thus, to say of anything that it is a work of art is to commit oneself to the presence of *some* of these conditions. One would scarcely describe X as a work of art if X were not an artifact, or a collection of elements sensuously presented in a medium, or a product of human skill, and so on. If none of the conditions were present, if there were no criteria present for recognizing something as a work of art, we would not describe it as one. But, even so, no one of these or any collection of them is either necessary or sufficient.

The elucidation of the descriptive use of "Art" creates little difficulty. But the elucidation of the evaluative use does. For many, especially theorists, "This is a work of art" does more than describe; it also praises. Its conditions of utterance, therefore, include certain preferred properties or characteristics of art. I shall call these "criteria of evaluation." Consider a typical example of this evaluative use, the view according to which to say of something that it is a work of art is to imply that it is a *successful* harmonization of elements. Many of the honorific definitions of art and its sub-concepts are of this form. What is at stake here is that "Art" is construed as an evaluative term which is either identified with its criterion or justified in terms of it. "Art" is defined in terms of its evaluative property, e.g., successful harmonization. On such a view, to say "X is a work of art" is (1) to say something which is taken *to mean* "X is a successful harmonization" (e.g., "Art *is* significant form") or (2) to say something praiseworthy *on the basis* of its successful harmonization. Theorists are never clear whether it is (1) or (2) which is being put forward. Most of them, concerned as they are with this evaluative use, formulate (2), i.e., that feature of art that *makes* it art in the praise-sense, and then go on to state (1), i.e., the definition of "Art" in terms of its art-making feature. And this is clearly to confuse the conditions under which we say something evaluatively with the meaning of what we say. "This is a work of art," said evaluatively, cannot mean "This is a successful harmonization of elements"—except by stipulation—but at most is said in virtue of the art-making property, which is taken as a (the) criterion of "Art," when "Art" is employed to assess. "This is a work of art," used evaluatively, serves to praise and not to affirm the reason why it is said.

The evaluative use of "Art," although distinct from the conditions of its use, relates in a very intimate way to these conditions. For, in every instance of "This is a work of art" (used to praise), what happens is that the criterion of evaluation (e.g., successful harmonization) for the employment of the concept of art is converted into a criterion of recognition. This is why, on its evaluative use, "This is a work of art" implies "This has P," where "P" is some chosen art-making property. Thus, if one chooses to employ "Art" evaluatively, as many do, so that "This is a work of art and not (aesthetically) good" makes no sense, he uses "Art" in such a way that he refuses to *call* anything a work of art unless it embodies his criterion of excellence.

There is nothing wrong with the evaluative use; in fact, there is good reason for using "Art" to praise. But what cannot be maintained is that theories of the evaluative use of "Art" are true and real definitions of the necessary and sufficient properties of art. Instead they are honorific definitions, pure and simple, in which "Art" has been redefined in terms of chosen criteria.

But what makes them—these honorific definitions—so supremely valuable is not their disguised linguistic recommendations; rather it is the *debates* over the reasons for changing the criteria of the concept of art which are built into the definitions. In each of the great theories of art, whether correctly understood as honorific definitions or incorrectly accepted as real definitions, what is of the utmost importance are the reasons proffered in the argument for the respective theory, that is, the reasons given for the chosen or preferred criterion of excellence and evaluation. It is this perennial debate over these criteria of evaluation which makes the history of esthetic theory the important study it is. The value of each of the theories resides in its attempt to state and to justify certain criteria which are either neglected or distorted by previous theories. Look at the Bell-Fry theory again. Of course, "Art is significant form" cannot be accepted as a true, real definition of art; and most certainly it actually functions in their esthetics as a redefinition of art in terms of the chosen condition of significant form. But what gives it its esthetic importance is what lies behind the formula: In an age in which literary and representational elements have become paramount in painting, *return* to the plastic ones since these are indigenous to painting. Thus, the role of the theory is not to define anything but to use the definitional form, almost epigrammatically, to pinpoint a crucial recommendation to turn our attention once again to the plastic elements in painting.

Once we, as philosophers, understand this distinction between the formula and what lies behind it, it behooves us to deal generously with the traditional theories of art; because incorporated in every one of them is a debate over and argument for emphasizing or centering upon some particular feature of art which has been neglected or perverted. If we take the esthetic theories literally, as we have seen, they all fail; but if we reconstrue them, in terms of their function and point, as serious and argued-for recommendations to concentrate on certain criteria of excellence in art, we shall see that esthetic theory is far from worthless. Indeed, it becomes as central as anything in esthetics, in our understanding of art, for it teaches us what to look for and how to look at it in art. What is central and must be articulated in all the theories are their debates over the reasons for excellence in art—debates over emotional depth, profound truths, natural beauty, exactitude, freshness of treatment, and so on, as criteria of evaluation—the whole of which converges on the perennial problem of what makes a work of art good. To understand the role of esthetic theory is not to conceive it as definition, logically doomed to failure, but to read it as summaries of seriously made recommendations to attend in certain ways to certain features of art.

—*The Journal of Aesthetics and Art Criticism*, Volume 15 (1956)

NOTES

1. DeWitt H. Parker, "The Nature of Art," reprinted in E. Vivas and M. Krieger, *The Problems of Aesthetics* (N.Y., 1953), p. 90.
2. *Ibid.*, pp. 93–94.
3. *Ibid.*, p. 94.
4. *Ibid.*, p. 104.
5. See M. Macdonald's review of my *Philosophy of the Arts* in *Mind*, Oct., 1951, pp. 561–564, for a brilliant discussion of this objection to the Organic theory.
6. L. Wittgenstein, *Philosophical Investigations*, (Oxford, 1953), tr. by E. Anscombe. (All quotations appear in the preceding selection, pp. 505–509—Editor's note.)
7. See H. D. F. Kitto, *Greek Tragedy*, (London, 1939), on this point.

MAURICE MANDELBAUM

Family Resemblances and Generalization Concerning the Arts

In 1954 William Elton collected and published a group of essays under the title *Aesthetics and Language*. As his introduction made clear, a common feature of these essays was the application to aesthetic problems of some of the doctrines characteristic of recent British linguistic philosophy.[1] While this mode of philosophizing has not had as pervasive an influence on aesthetics as it has had on most other branches of philosophy,[2] there have been a number of important articles which, in addition to those contained in the Elton volume, suggest the direction in which this influence runs. Among these articles one might mention "The Task of Defining a Work of Art" by Paul Ziff,[3] "The Role of Theory in Aesthetics" by Morris Weitz,[4] Charles L. Stevenson's "On 'What is a Poem' "[5] and W. E. Kennick's "Does Traditional Aesthetics Rest on a Mistake?"[6] In each of them one finds a conviction which was also present in most of the essays in the Elton volume: that it is a mistake to offer generalizations concerning the arts, or, to put the matter in a more provocative manner, that it is a mistake to attempt to discuss what art, or beauty, or the aesthetic, or a poem, *essentially* is. In partial support of this contention, some writers have made explicit use of Wittgenstein's doctrine of *family resemblances*; Morris Weitz, for example, has placed it in the forefront of his discussion. However, in that influential and frequently anthologized article, Professor Weitz made no attempt to analyze, clarify, or defend the doctrine itself. Since its use with respect to aesthetics has provided the means by which others have sought to escape the need of generalizing concerning the arts, I shall begin my discussion with a consideration of it.

I

The *locus classicus* for Wittgenstein's doctrine of family resemblances is in Part I of *Philosophical Investigations*, sections 65–77.[7] In discussing what he refers to as language-games, Wittgenstein says:

> Instead of producing something common to all that we call language, I am saying that these phenomena have no one thing in common which makes us use the same word for all—but they are *related* to one another in many different ways. And it is because of this relationship, or these relationships, that we call them all "language." (§65)

He then illustrates his contention by citing a variety of *games*, such as board games, card games, ball games, etc., and concludes:

> We see a complicated network of similarities overlapping and criss-crossing: sometimes overall similarities of detail. (§66)
>   I can think of no better expression to characterize these similarities than "family resemblances"; for the various resemblances between members of a family: build, features, colour of eyes, gait, temperament, etc., etc. overlap and criss-cross in the same way.—And I shall say: "games" form a family. (§67)

In short, what Wittgenstein aims to establish is that one need not suppose that all instances of those entities to which we apply a common name do in fact possess any one feature in common. Instead, the use of a common name is grounded in the criss-crossing and overlapping of resembling features among otherwise heterogeneous objects and activities.

Wittgenstein's concrete illustrations of the diversity among various types of games may at first make his doctrine of family resemblances extremely plausible. For example, we do not hesitate to characterize tennis, chess, bridge, and solitaire as games, even though a comparison of them fails to reveal any specific feature which is the same in each of them. Nonetheless, I do not believe that his doctrine of family resemblances, as it stands, provides an adequate analysis of why a common name, such as "a game," is in all cases applied or withheld.

Consider first the following case. Let us assume that you know how to play that form of solitaire called "Canfield"; suppose also that you are acquainted with a number of other varieties of solitaire (Wittgenstein uses "patience," i.e., "solitaire," as one instance of a form of game). Were you to see me shuffling a pack of cards, arranging the cards in piles, some face up and some face down, turning cards over one-by-one, sometimes placing them in one pile, then another, shifting piles, etc., you might say: "I see you are playing cards. What game are you playing?" However, to this I might answer: "I am not playing a game; I am telling (or reading) fortunes." Will the resemblances between what you have seen me doing and the characteristics of card games with which you are familiar permit you to contradict me and say that I am indeed playing some sort of game? Ordinary usage would not, I believe, sanction our describing fortune-telling as an example of playing a game, no matter how striking may be the resemblances between the ways in which cards are handled in playing solitaire and in telling fortunes. Or, to choose another example, we may say that while certain forms of wrestling contests are sometimes characterized as games (Wittgenstein mentions *"Kampfspiele"*)[8] an angry struggle between two boys, each trying to make the other give in, is not to be characterized as a game. Yet one can find a great many resembling features between such a struggle and a wrestling match in a gymnasium. What would seem to be crucial in our designation of an activity as a game is, therefore, not merely a matter of noting a number of specific resemblances between it and other activities which we denote as games, but involves something further.

To suggest what sort of characteristic this "something further" might possibly be, it will be helpful to pay closer attention to the notion of what constitutes a family resemblance. Suppose that you are shown ten or a dozen photographs and you are then asked to decide which among them exhibit strong resemblances.[9] You might have no difficulty in selecting, say, three of the photographs in which the subjects were markedly round-headed, had a strongly prognathous profile, rather deep-set eyes, and dark curly hair.[10] In some extended, metaphorical sense you might say that the similarities in their features constituted a family resemblance among them. The sense, however, would be metaphorical, since in the absence of a biological kinship of a certain degree of proximity we would be inclined to speak only of resemblances, and not of a *family* resemblance. What marks the difference between a literal and a metaphorical sense of the notion of "family resemblances" is, therefore, the existence of a genetic connection in the former case and not in the latter. Wittgenstein, however, failed to make explicit the fact that the literal, root notion of a family resemblance includes this genetic connection no less than it includes the existence of noticeable physiognomic resemblances.[11] Had the existence of such a *twofold* criterion been made explicit by him, he would have noted that there is in fact an attribute common to all who bear a family resemblance to each other: they are related through a common ancestry. Such a relationship is not, of course, one among the specific features of those who share a family resemblance; it nonetheless differentiates them from those who are not to be regarded as members of a single family.[12] If, then, it is possible that the analogy of family resemblances could tell us something about how games may be related to one another, one should explore the possibility that, in spite of their great dissimilarities, games may possess a common attribute which, like biological connection, is not itself one among their directly exhibited characteristics. Unfortunately, such a possibility was not explored by Wittgenstein.

To be sure, Wittgenstein does not explicitly state that the resemblances which are correlated with our use of common names must be of a sort that are directly exhibited. Nonetheless, all of his illustrations in the relevant passages involve aspects of games which would be included in a description of how a particular game is to be played; that is, when he commands us to "look and see" whether there is anything common to all games,[13] the "anything" is taken to represent precisely the sort of manifest feature that is described in rule-books, such as Hoyle. However, as we have seen in the case of family resemblances, what constitutes a *family* is not defined in terms of the manifest features of a random group of people; we must first characterize the *family* relationship in terms of genetic ties, and then observe to what extent those who are connected in this way *resemble* one another.[14] In the case of games, the analogue to genetic ties might be the purpose for the sake of which various games were formulated by those who invented or modified them, e.g., the potentiality of a game to be of absorbing non-practical interest to either participants or spectators. If there were any such common feature one would not expect it to be defined in a rule book, such as Hoyle, since rule books only attempt to tell us how to play a particular game: our interest in playing a game, and our understanding of what constitutes a game, is already presupposed by the authors of such books.

It is not my present concern to characterize any feature common to most or all of those activities which we call games, nor would I wish to argue on the analogy of family resemblances that there *must be* any such feature. If the question is to be decided, it must be decided by an attempt to "look and see." However, it is important that we look in the right place and in the right ways if we are looking for a common feature; we should not assume that any feature common to all games must be some manifest characteristic, such as whether they are to be played with a ball or with cards, or how many players there must be in order for the game to be played. If we were to rely exclusively on such features we should, as I have suggested, be apt to link solitaire with fortune-telling, and wrestling matches with fights, rather than (say) linking solitaire with cribbage and wrestling matches with weight-lifting. It is, then, my contention that Wittgenstein's emphasis on directly exhibited resemblances, and his failure to consider other possible similarities, led to a failure on his part to provide an adequate clue as to what—in some cases at least—governs our use of common names.[15]

If the foregoing remarks are correct, we are now in a position to see that the radical denigration of generalization concerning the arts, which has come to be almost a hallmark of the writings of those most influenced by recent British philosophy, may involve serious errors, and may not constitute a notable advance.

II

In turning from Wittgenstein's statements concerning family resemblances to the use to which his doctrine has been put by writers on aesthetics, we must first note what these writers are *not* attempting to do. In the first place, they are not seeking to clarify the relationships which exist among the many different senses in which the word "art" is used. Any dictionary offers a variety of such senses (e.g., the art of navigation, art as guile, art as the craft of the artist, etc.), and it is not difficult to find a pattern of family resemblances existing among many of them. However, an analysis of such resemblances, and of their differences, has not, as a matter of fact, been of interest to the writers of the articles with which we are here concerned. In the second place, these writers have not been primarily interested in analyzing how words such as "work of art" or "artist" or "art" are ordinarily used by those who are neither aestheticians nor art critics; their concern has been with the writings which make up the tradition of "aesthetic theory." In the third place, we must note that the concern of these writers has not been to show that family resemblances do in fact exist among the various arts, or among various works of art; on the contrary, they have used the doctrine of family resemblances in a *negative* fashion. In this, they have of course followed Wittgenstein's own example. The position which they have sought to establish is that traditional aesthetic theory has been mistaken in assuming that there is any essential property or defining characteristic of works of art (or any set of such properties or characteristics); as a consequence, they have contended that most of the questions which have been asked by those engaged in writing on aesthetics are mistaken sorts of questions.

However, as the preceding discussion of Wittgenstein should have served to make clear, one cannot assume that if there is any one characteristic common to all works of art it must consist in some specific, directly exhibited feature. Like the biological connections among those who are connected by family resemblances, or like the intentions on the basis of which we distinguish between fortune-telling and card games, such a characteristic might be a relational attribute, rather than some characteristic at which one could directly point and say: "It is this particular feature of the object which leads me to designate it as a work of art." A relational attribute of the required sort might, for example, only be apprehended if one were to consider specific art objects as having been created by someone for some actual or possible audience.

The suggestion that the essential nature of art is to be found in such a relational attribute is surely not implausible when one recalls some of the many traditional theories of art. For example, art has sometimes been characterized as being one special form of communication or of expression, or as being a special form of wish-fulfillment, or as being a presentation of truth in sensuous form. Such theories do not assume that in each poem, painting, play, and sonata there is a specific ingredient which identifies it as a work of art; rather, that which is held to be common to these otherwise diverse objects is a relationship which is assumed to have existed, or is known to have existed, between certain of their characteristics and the activities and the intentions of those who made them.[16]

While we may acknowledge that it is difficult to find any set of attributes —whether relational or not—which can serve to characterize the nature of a work of art (and which will not be as vulnerable to criticism as many other such characterizations have been),[17] it is important to note that the difficulties inherent in this task are not really avoided by those who appeal to the notion of family resemblances. As soon as one attempts to elucidate how the term "art" is in fact used in the context of art criticism, most of the same problems which have arisen in the history of aesthetic theory will again make their appearance. In other words, linguistic analysis does not provide a means of escape from the issues which have been of major concern in traditional aesthetics. This fact may be illustrated through examining a portion of one of the articles to which I have already alluded, Paul Ziff's article entitled "The Task of Defining a Work of Art."

To explain how the term "a work of art" is used, and to show the difficulties one encounters if one seeks to generalize concerning the arts, Professor Ziff chooses as his starting point one clear-cut example of a work of art and sets out to describe it. The work he chooses is a painting by Poussin, and his description runs as follows:

> Suppose we point to Poussin's "The Rape of the Sabine Women," as our clearest available case of a work of art. We could describe it by saying, first, that it is a painting. Secondly, it was made, and what is more, made deliberately and self-consciously with obvious skill and care, by Nicolas Poussin. Thirdly, the painter intended it to be displayed in a place where it could be looked at and appreciated, where it could be contemplated and admired. . . . Fourthly, the painting is or was exhibited in a museum gallery where people do contemplate, study, observe, admire, criticize, and discuss it. What I wish to refer to here by speaking of contemplating, studying, and observing a painting, is simply what we may do when we are concerned with a painting like this. For example, when we look at this painting by Poussin, we may attend to its sensuous features, to its "look and feel." Thus we attend to the play of light and color, to dissonances, contrasts, and harmonies of hues, values, and intensities. We notice patterns and pigmentation, textures, decorations, and embellishments. We may also attend to the structure, design, composition, and organization of the work. Thus we look for unity, and we also look for variety, for balance and movement. We attend to the formal interrelations and cross connections in the work, to its underlying structure. . . . Fifthly, this work is a representational painting with a definite subject matter; it depicts a certain mythological scene. Sixthly, the painting is an elaborate and certainly complex formal structure. Finally, the painting is a good painting. And this is to say simply that the Poussin painting is worth contemplating, studying, and observing in the way I have ever so roughly described.[18]

With reference to this description we must first note that it is clearly not meant to be anything like a complete description of the Poussin painting; it is at most a description of those aspects of that painting which are relevant to its being called a work of art. For example, neither the weight of the painting nor its insurable value is mentioned. Thus, whether because of his own preconceptions, or because of our ordinary assumptions concerning how the term "work of art" is to be used, Professor Ziff focuses attention on some aspects of the Poussin painting rather than upon others. In doing so, he is making an implicit appeal to what is at least a minimal aesthetic theory, that is, he is supposing that neither weight nor insurable value need be mentioned when we list the characteristics which lead us to say of a particular piece of painted canvas that it is a work of art. In the second place, we must note that of the seven characteristics which he mentions, not all are treated by Professor Ziff as being independent of one another; nor are all related to one another in identical ways. It will be instructive to note some of the differences among their relationships, since it is precisely here that many of the traditional problems of aesthetic theory once again take their rise.

For example, we are bound to note that Professor Ziff related the seventh characteristic of the Poussin painting to its fourth characteristic: the fact that it is a good painting is, he holds, related to the characteristics which we find that it possesses when we contemplate, observe, and study it. Its goodness, however, is not claimed to be related to its first, third, or fifth characteristics: in other words, Professor Ziff is apparently not claiming that the goodness of this particular work of art depends upon its being a painting rather than being some other sort of work of art which is capable of being contemplated, studied, etc.; nor is he claiming that its goodness is dependent upon the fact that it was intended to be hung in a place where it can be observed and studied; nor upon the fact that it is a representational painting which depicts a mythological scene. If we next turn to the question of how the goodness of this painting is related to the fact that it was "made deliberately and self-consciously, with obvious skill and care by Nicolas Poussin," Professor Ziff's position is somewhat less explicit, but what he would say is probably quite clear. Suppose that the phrase "obvious skill" were deleted from the description of this characteristic: would the fact that this painting had been deliberately and self-consciously made, and had been made with care (but perhaps not with skill), provide a sufficient basis for predicating goodness of it? I should doubt that Professor Ziff would hold that it would, since many bad paintings may be supposed to have been made deliberately, self-consciously, and with care. Yet, if this is so, how is the maker's skill related to the object's goodness? Perhaps the fact that "obvious skill" is attributed to Poussin is meant to suggest that Poussin intended that "The Rape of the Sabine Women" should possess those qualities which Professor Ziff notes that we find in it when we contemplate, study, and observe it in the way in which he suggests that it should be contemplated. If this is what is suggested by attributing skill to the artist, it is surely clear that Professor Ziff has without argument built an aesthetic theory into his description of the Poussin painting. That theory is implicit both in the characteristics which he chooses as being aesthetically relevant, and in the relations which he holds as obtaining among these characteristics.

If it be doubted that Professor Ziff's description contains at least an implicit aesthetic theory, consider the fact that in one of the passages in which he describes the Poussin painting (but which I did not include in my foreshortened quotation from that description), he speaks of the fact that in contemplating, studying, and observing this painting "we are concerned with both two-dimensional and three-dimensional movements, the balance and opposition, thrust and recoil, of spaces and volumes." Since the goodness of a painting has been said by him to depend upon the qualities which we find in it when we contemplate, study, and observe it, it follows that these features of the Poussin painting contribute to its goodness. And I should suppose that they are also included in what Professor Ziff calls the sixth characteristic of the Poussin painting, namely its "complex formal structure." Thus, presumably, the goodness of a painting does depend, in part at least, upon its formal structure. On the other hand, Professor Ziff never suggests that the goodness of the Poussin painting depends upon the fact that it is a representational painting, and that it has a mythological (or historical) subject matter, rather than some other sort of subject matter. In fact, when he discusses critics such as Kenyon Cox and Royal Cortissoz, Professor Ziff would apparently—and quite properly—wish to separate himself from them, rejecting the view that what makes a painting a good painting has any necessary relation to the fact that it is or is not a representational painting of a certain sort. Thus, Professor Ziff's account of the aesthetically relevant features of the Poussin painting, and his statements concerning the interrelationships among the various features of that painting, define a particular aesthetic position.

The position which I have been attributing to him is one with which I happen to agree. However, that fact is not of any importance in the present discussion. What is important to note is that Professor Ziff's characterization of the Poussin painting contains an implicit theory of the nature of a work of art. According to that theory, the goodness of a painting depends upon its possession of certain objective qualities, that these qualities are (in part at least) elements in its formal structure, and that the artist intended that we should perceive these qualities in contemplating and studying the painting. (Had he not had this intention, would we be able to say that he had made the object self-consciously, deliberately, *and* with skill?) Further, this implicit theory must be assumed to be a theory which is general in import, and not confined to how we should look at this one painting only. Were this not so, the sort of description of the Poussin painting which was given by Professor Ziff would not have helped to establish a clear-cut case of what is to be designated as a work of art. For example, were someone to describe the same painting in terms of its size, weight, and insurable value (as might be done were it to be moved from museum to museum), we would not thereby learn how the term "work of art" is to be used. In failing to note that his description of the Poussin painting actually did involve a theory of the nature of art, Professor Ziff proceeded to treat that description as if he had done nothing more than bring forward a list of seven independent characteristics of the painting he was examining. In so doing, he turned the question of whether there are any features common to all works of art into a question of whether one or more of these seven specific indices could be found in all objects to which the term "work of art" is applied. Inevitably, his conclusion was negative, and he therefore held that "no one of the characteristics listed is necessarily a characteristic of a work of art."[19]

However, as we have seen, Professor Ziff's description of the Poussin painting was not actually confined to noting the specific qualities which were characteristic of the pictorial surface of that painting; it included references to the relations between these qualities and the aim of Poussin, and references to the ways in which a painting having such qualities is to be contemplated by others. Had he turned his attention to examining these relationships between object, artist, and contemplator, it would assuredly have been more difficult for him to assert that "neither a poem, nor a novel, nor a musical composition can be said to be a work of art in the same sensé of the phrase in which a painting or a statue or a vase can be said to be a work of art."[20] In fact, had he carefully traced the relationships which he assumed to exist among some of the characteristics of the Poussin painting, he might have found that, contrary to his inclinations, he was well advanced toward putting forward explicit generalizations concerning the arts.

III

While Professor Ziff's argument against generalization depends upon the fact that the various artistic media are significantly different from one another, the possibility of generalizing concerning the arts has also been challenged on historical grounds. It is to Morris Weitz's use of the latter argument that I shall now turn.

In "The Role of Theory in Aesthetics" Professor Weitz places his primary emphasis on the fact that art forms are not static. From this fact he argues that it is futile to attempt to state the conditions which are necessary and sufficient for an object to be a work of art. What he claims is that the concept "art" must be treated as an open concept, since new art forms have developed in the past, and since any art form (such as the novel) may undergo radical transformations from generation to generation. One brief statement from Professor Weitz's article can serve to summarize this view:

> What I am arguing, then, is that the very expansive, adventurous character of art, its ever-present changes and novel creations, makes it logically impossible to ensure any set of defining properties. We can, of course, choose to close the concept. But to do this with "art" or "tragedy" or portraiture, etc. is ludicrous since it forecloses the very conditions of creativity in the arts.[21]

Unfortunately, Professor Weitz fails to offer any cogent argument in substantiation of this claim. The lacuna in his discussion is to be found in the fact that the question of whether a particular concept is open or closed (i.e., whether a set of necessary and sufficient conditions can be offered for its use) is not identical with the question of whether future instances to which the very same concept is applied may or may not possess genuinely novel properties. In other words, Professor Weitz has not shown that every novelty in the instances to which we apply a term involves a stretching of the term's connotation.

By way of illustration, consider the classificatory label "representational painting." One can assuredly define this particular form of art without defining it in such a way that it will include only those paintings which depict either a mythological event or a religious scene. Historical paintings, interiors, fête-champetres, and still life can all count as "representational" according to any adequate definition of this mode of painting, and there is no reason why such a definition could not have been formulated prior to the emergence of any of these novel species of the representational mode. Thus, to define a particular form of art—and to define it truly and accurately—is not necessarily to set one's self in opposition to whatever new creations may arise within that particular form.[22] Consequently, it would be mistaken to suppose that all attempts to state the defining properties of various art forms are prescriptive in character and authoritarian in their effect.

This conclusion is not confined to cases in which an established form of art, such as representational painting, undergoes changes; it can also be shown to be compatible with the fact that radically new art forms arise. For example, if the concept "a work of art" had been carefully defined prior to the invention of cameras, is there any reason to suppose that such a definition would have proved an obstacle to viewing photography or the movies as constituting new art forms? To be sure, one can imagine definitions which might have done so. However, it was not Professor Weitz's aim to show that one or another definition of art had been a poor definition; he wished to establish the general thesis that there was a necessary incompatability, which he denoted as a logical impossibility, between allowing for novelty and creativity in the arts and stating the defining properties of a work of art. He failed to establish this thesis since he offered no arguments to prove that new sorts of instantiation of a previously defined concept will necessarily involve us in changing the definition of that concept.

To be sure, if neither photography nor the movies had developed along lines which satisfied the same sorts of interest that the other arts satisfied, and if the kinds of standards which were applied in the other arts were not seen to be relevant when applied to photography and to the movies, then the antecedently formulated definition of art would have functioned as a closed concept, and it would have been used to exclude all photographers and all motion-picture makers from the class of those who were to be termed "artists." However, what would the defender of the openness of concepts hold that one should have done under these circumstances? Suppose, for example, that all photographers had in fact been the equivalent of passport photographers, and that they had been motivated by no other interests and controlled by no other standards than those which govern the making of photographs for passports and licenses: would the defender of open concepts be likely to have expanded the concept of what is to count as an art in order to have included photography? The present inclusion of photography among the arts is justified, I should hold, precisely because photography arises out of the same sorts of interest, and can satisfy the same sorts of interest, and our criticism of it employs the same sorts of standards, as is the case with respect to the other arts.

Bearing this in mind, we are in a position to see that still another article which has sometimes been cited by those who argue for the openness of the concept "a work of art" does not justify the conclusions which have been drawn from it. That article is Paul Oskar Kristeller's learned and informative study entitled "The Modern System of the Arts."[23] The way in which Professor Kristeller states the aim of his article suggests that he too would deny that traditional aesthetic theory is capable of formulating adequate generalizations concerning the arts. He states his aim in saying:

> The basic notion that the five "major arts" constitute an area all by themselves, clearly separated by common characteristics from the crafts, the sciences and other human activities has been taken for granted by most writers on aesthetics from Kant to the present day. . . .
> It is my purpose to show that this system of the five major arts, which underlies all modern aesthetics and is so familiar to us all, is of comparatively recent origin and did not assume definite shape before the eighteenth century, although it had many ingredients which go back to classical, mediaeval, and Renaissance thought.[24]

However, the fact that *the classification of the arts* has undoubtedly changed during the history of Western thought, does not of itself suggest that *aesthetic theory* must undergo comparable changes. Should this be doubted, one may note that Professor Kristeller's article does not show in what specific ways attempts to classify or systematize the arts are integral to, or are presupposed by, or are consequences of, the formulation of an aesthetic theory. This is no minor cavil, for if one examines the writers on aesthetics who are currently attacked for their attempts to generalize concerning the nature of art, one finds that they are not (by and large) writers whose discussions are closely allied to the discussions of those with whom Kristeller's article was primarily concerned. Furthermore, it is to be noted that Kristeller did not carry his discussion beyond Kant. This terminal point was justified by him on the ground that the system of the arts has not substantially changed since Kant's time.[25] However, when one recalls that Kant's work is generally regarded as standing near the beginning of modern aesthetic theory—and surely not near its end—one has reason to suspect that questions concerning "the system of the arts" and questions concerning aesthetic theory constitute distinct, and probably separate sets of questions. A survey of recent aesthetic theory bears this out. Since the time of Hegel and of Schopenhauer there have been comparatively few influential aesthetic theories which have made the problem of the diversity of art forms, and the classification of these forms, central to their consideration of the nature of art.[26] For example, the aesthetic theories of Santayana, Croce, Alexander, Dewey, Prall, or Collingwood cannot be said to have been dependent upon any particular systematic classification of the arts. In so far as these theories may be taken as representative of attempts to generalize concerning the arts, it is strange that current attacks on traditional aesthetics should have supposed that any special measure of support was to be derived from Kristeller's article.

Should one wish to understand why current discussions have overlooked the gap between an article such as Kristeller's and the lessons ostensibly derived from it, an explanation might be found in the lack of concern evinced by contemporary analytic philosophers for the traditional problems of aesthetic theory. For example, one looks in vain in the Elton volume for a careful appraisal of the relations between aesthetic theory and art criticism, and how the functions of each might differ from the functions of the other. A striking example of the failure to consider this sort of problem is also to be found in John Wisdom's often cited dicta concerning "the dullness" of aesthetic theory.[27] In examining his views one finds that the books on art which Wisdom finds *not* to be dull are books such as Edmund Wilson's *Axel's Castle*, in which a critic "brings out features of the art he writes about, or better, brings home the character of what he writes about."[28] In short, it is not theory—it is not aesthetic theory at all—that Wisdom is seeking: he happens to be interested in criticism.

I do not wish to be taken as denying the importance of criticism, nor as belittling the contribution which a thorough acquaintance with the practice of criticism in all of the arts may make to general aesthetic theory. However, it is important to note that the work of any critic presupposes at least an implicit aesthetic theory, which—as critic—it is not his aim to establish or, in general, to defend. This fact can only be overlooked by those who confine themselves to a narrow range of criticism: for example, to the criticism appearing in our own time in those journals which are read by those with whom we have intellectual, political, and social affinities. When we do not so confine ourselves, we rapidly discover that there is, and has been, an enormous variety in criticism, and that this variety represents (in part at least) the effect of differing aesthetic preconceptions. To evaluate criticism itself we must, then, sometimes undertake to evaluate these preconceptions. In short, we must do aesthetics ourselves.

However, for many of the critics of traditional aesthetics this is an option which does not appeal. If I am not mistaken, it is not difficult to see why this should have come to be so. In the first place, it has come to be one of the marks of contemporary analytic philosophy to hold that philosophic problems are problems which cannot be solved by appeals to matters of fact. Thus, to choose but a single instance, questions of the relations between aesthetic perception and other instances of perceiving—for example, questions concerning psychical distance, or empathic perception, or the role of form in aesthetic perception—are not considered to be questions with which a philosopher ought to try to deal. In the second place, the task of the philosopher has come to be seen as consisting largely of the unsnarling of tangles into which others have gotten themselves. As a consequence, the attempt to find a synoptic interpretation of some broad range of facts—an attempt which has in the past been regarded as one of the major tasks of a philosopher—has either been denigrated or totally overlooked.[29] Therefore, problems such as the claims of the arts to render a true account of human character and destiny, or questions concerning the relations between aesthetic goodness and standards of greatness in art, or an estimate of the significance of variability in aesthetic judgments, are not presently fashionable. And it must be admitted that if philosophers wish not to have to face either factual problems or synoptic tasks, these are indeed questions which are more comfortably avoided than pursued.

NOTES

1. See William Elton (ed.), *Aesthetics and Language* (Oxford, Basil Blackwell, 1954), p. 1, n. 1 and 2.

2. A discussion of this fact is to be found in Jerome Stolnitz, "Notes on Analytic Philosophy and Aesthetics," *British Journal of Aesthetics*, vol. 3 (1961), pp. 210–222.

3. *Philosophical Review*, vol. 62 (1953), pp. 58–78.

4. *Journal of Aesthetics and Art Criticism*, vol. 15 (1956), pp. 27–35.

5. *Philosophical Review*, vol. 66 (1957), 329–362.

6. *Mind*, vol. 67 (1958), pp. 317–334. In addition to the articles already referred to, I might mention "The Uses of Works of Art" by Teddy Brunius in *Journal of Aesthetics and Art Criticism*, vol. 22 (1963), pp. 123–133, which refers to both Weitz and Kennick, but raises other questions with which I am not here concerned.

7. Ludwig Wittgenstein, *Philosophical Investigations*, translated by G. E. M. Anscombe (New York, Macmillan, 1953), pp. 31–36. A parallel passage is to be found in "The Blue Book"; see *Preliminary Studies for the "Philosophical Investigations," Generally Known as The Blue and Brown Books* (Oxford, Basil Blackwell, 1958), pp. 17–18.

8. Ludwig Wittgenstein, *Philosophical Investigations*, §66, p. 31. For reasons which are obscure, Miss Anscombe translates "*Kampfspiele*" as "Olympic games."

9. In an article which is closely related to my discussion, but which uses different arguments to support a similar point, Haig Khatchadourian has shown that Wittgenstein is less explicit than he should have been with respect to the levels of determinateness at which these resemblances are significant for our use of common names. See "Common Names and 'Family Resemblances'," *Philosophy and Phenomenological Research*, vol. 18 (1957–58), pp. 341–358. (For a related, but less closely relevant article by Professor Khatchadourian see "Art-Names and Aesthetic Judgments," *Philosophy*, vol. 36 [1961], pp. 30–48.)

10. It is to be noted that this constitutes a closer resemblance than that involved in what Wittgenstein calls "family resemblances," since in my illustration the specific similarities all pertain to a single set of features, with respect to each one of which all three of the subjects directly resemble one another. In Wittgenstein's use of the notion of family resemblances there is, however, no one set of resembling features common to each member of the "family"; there is merely a criss-crossing and overlapping among the elements which constitute the resemblances among the various persons. Thus, in order to conform to his usage, my illustration would have to be made more complicated, and the degree of resemblance would become more attenuated. For example, we would have to introduce the photographs of other subjects in which, for example, recessive chins would supplant prognathous profiles among those who shared the other characteristics; some would have blond instead of dark hair, and protruberant instead of deep-set eyes, but would in each case resemble the others in other respects, etc. However, if what I say concerning family resemblances holds of the stronger similarities present in my illustration, it should hold *a fortiori* of the weaker form of family resemblances to which Wittgenstein draws our attention.

11. Although Wittgenstein failed to make explicit the fact that a genetic connection was involved in his notion of "family resemblances," I think that he did in fact presuppose such a connection. If I am not mistaken, the original German makes this clearer than does the Anscombe translation. The German text reads:

Ich kann diese Ähnlichkeiten nicht besser charakterisieren, als durch das Wort "Familienähnlichkeiten"; denn so übergreifen und kreuzen sich die verschiedenen Ähnlichkeiten, dies zwischen den Gliedern einer Familie bestehen: Wuchs, Gesichtzüge, Augenfarbe, Gang, Temperament, etc., etc. (§67).

Modifying Miss Anscombe's translation in as few respects as possible, I suggest that a translation of this passage might read:

> I can think of no better expression to characterize these similarities than "family resemblances," since various similarities which obtain among the members of a family—their build, features, color of eyes, gait, temperament, etc., etc.,—overlap and criss-cross in the same way.

This translation differs from Miss Anscombe's (which has been quoted above) in that it makes more explicit the fact that the similarities are similarities among the members of a single family, and are not themselves definitive of what constitutes a *family* resemblance.

12. Were this aspect of the twofold criterion to be abandoned, and were our use of common names to be solely determined by the existence of overlapping and criss-cross relations, it is difficult to see how a halt would ever be called to the spread of such names. Robert J. Richman has called attention to the same problem in "'Something Common'," *Journal of Philosophy*, vol. 59 (1962), pp. 821–830. He speaks of what he calls "the Problem of Wide-Open Texture," and says: "the notion of family resemblances may account for our extending the application of a given general term, but it does not seem to place any limit on this process" (p. 829.)

In an article entitled "The Problem of Model-Language Game in Wittgenstein's Later Philosophy," *Philosophy*, vol. 36 (1961), pp. 333–351, Helen Hervey also calls attention to the fact that "a family is so-called by virtue of its common ancestry" (p. 334). She also mentions (p. 335) what Richman referred to as the problem of "the wide-open texture."

13. Ludwig Wittgenstein, *Philosophical Investigations*, §66, p. 31.

14. Although I have only mentioned the existence of genetic connections among members of a family, I should of course not wish to exclude the effects of habitual association in giving rise to some of the resemblances which Wittgenstein mentions. I have stressed genetic connection only because it is the simplest and most obvious illustration of the point I have wished to make.

15. I do not deny that directly exhibited resemblances often play a part in our use of common names: this is a fact explicitly noted at least as long ago as by Locke. However, similarities in origin, similarities in use, and similarities in intention may also play significant roles. It is such factors that Wittgenstein overlooks in his specific discussions of family resemblances and of games.

16. I know of no passage in which Wittgenstein takes such a possibility into account. In fact, if the passage from "The Blue Book" to which I have already alluded may be regarded as representative, we may say that Wittgenstein's view of traditional aesthetic theories was quite without foundation. In that passage he said:

> The idea of a general concept being a common property of its particular instances connects up with other primitive, too simple, ideas of the structure of language. It is comparable to the idea that *properties* are *ingredients* of the things which have the properties; e.g., that beauty is an ingredient of all beautiful things as alcohol is of beer and wine, and that we therefore could have pure beauty, unadulterated by anything that is beautiful (p. 17).

I fail to be able to identify any aesthetic theory of which such a statement would be true. It would not, for example, be true of Clive Bell's doctrine of "significant form," nor would it presumably be true of G. E. Moore's view of beauty, since both Bell and Moore hold that beauty depends upon the specific nature of other qualities which characterize that which is beautiful.

However, it may be objected that when I suggest that what is common to works of art involves reference to "intentions," I overlook "the intentional fallacy" (see W. K. Wimsatt, Jr., and Monroe C. Beardsley, "The Intentional Fallacy," *Sewanee Review*, vol. 54 [1946], pp. 468–488). This is not the case. The phrase "the intentional fallacy" originally referred to a particular method of criticism, that is, to a method of interpreting and evaluating given works of art; it was not the aim of Wimsatt and Beardsley to distinguish art and non-art. These two problems are, I believe, fundamentally different in character. However, I do not feel sure that Professor Beardsley has noted this fact, for in a recent article in which he set out to criticize those who have been influenced by the doctrine of family resemblances he apparently felt himself obliged to define art *solely* in terms of some characteristic in the object itself (see "The Definition of the Arts," *Journal of Aesthetics and Art Criticism*, vol. 20 [1961], pp. 175–187). Had he been willing to relate this characteristic to the activity and intention of those who make objects having such a characteristic, his discussion would not, I believe, have been susceptible to many of the criticisms leveled against it by Professor Douglas Morgan and Mary Mothersill (*ibid.*, pp. 187–198).

17. I do not say *"all"* such definitions, for I think that one can find a number of convergent definitions of art, each of which has considerable merit, though each may differ slightly from the others in its emphasis.

18. *Op. cit.*, pp. 60–61. It is an interesting problem, but not germane to our present concerns, to consider whether Poussin's painting should be classified as a "mythological" painting, as Professor Ziff describes it, or whether it should be regarded as an historical painting.

19. *Ibid.*, p. 64.

20. *Ibid.*, p. 66. For example, Ziff denies that a poem can be said to be "exhibited or displayed." Yet it is surely the case that in printing a poem or in presenting a reading of a poem, the relation between the work and its audience, and the relation between artist, work, and audience, is not wholly dissimilar to that which obtains when an artist exhibits a painting. If this be doubted, consider whether there is not a closer affinity between these two cases than there is between a painter *exhibiting* a painting and a manufacturer *exhibiting* a new line of fountain pens.

21. *Op. cit.*, p. 32.

22. To be sure, if no continuing characteristic is to be found, the fact of change will demand that the concept be treated as having been an open one. This was precisely the position taken by Max Black in a discussion of the concept "science." (See "The Definition of Scientific Method," in *Science and Civilization*, edited by Robert C. Stauffer [Madison, Wisconsin, 1949].) Paul Ziff refers to the influence of Professor Black's discussion upon his own views, and the views of Morris Weitz are assuredly similar. However, even if Professor Black's view of the changes in the concept "science" is a correct one (as I should be prepared to think that it may be), it does not follow that the same argument applies in the case of art. Nor does the fact that the meaning of "science" has undergone profound changes in the past imply that further analogous changes will occur in the future.

23. *Journal of the History of Ideas*, vol. 12 (1951), pp. 496–527, and vol. 13 (1952), pp. 17–46. This study has been cited by both Elton (*op. cit.*, p. 2) and Kennick (*op. cit.*, p. 320) in substantiation of their views.

24. *Op. cit.*, vol. 12, p. 497.

25. *Op. cit.*, vol. 13, p. 43; also, pp. 4 ff.

26. One exception is to be found in T. M. Greene: *The Arts and the Art of Criticism* (Princeton, 1940). This work is cited by Kristeller, and is one of the only two which he cites in support of the view that the system of the arts has not changed since Kant's day (*op. cit.*, vol. 12, p. 497, n. 4). The other work cited by him is Paul Franke's *System der Kunstwissenschaft* (Brünn/Leipzig, 1938), which

also offers a classification of the arts, but only within a framework of aesthetic theory which could easily embrace whatever historical changes the arts undergo.

27. See "Things and Persons," *Proceedings of the Aristotelian Society, Supplementary Volume XXII* (1948), pp. 207–210.

28. *Ibid.*, p. 209.

29. For example, W. B. Gallie's "The Function of Philosophical Aesthetics," in the Elton volume, argues for "a journeyman's aesthetics," which will take up individual problems, one by one, these problems being of the sort which arise when a critic or poet gets into a muddle about terms such as "abstraction" or "imagination." For this purpose the tools of the philosopher are taken to be the tools of logical analysis (*op. cit.*, p. 35); a concern with the history of the arts, with psychology, or a direct and wide-ranging experience of the arts seems not to be presupposed.

A second example of the limitations imposed upon aesthetics by contemporary linguistic analysis is to be found in Professor Weitz's article. He states that "the root problem of philosophy itself is to explain the relation between the employment of certain kinds of concepts and the conditions under which they can be correctly applied" (*op. cit.*, p. 30).

Bibliography

References to periodicals are given in full except for the following abbreviations:

JAAC   *The Journal of Aesthetics and Art Criticism*
BJA   *British Journal of Aesthetics*
J. Phil.   *The Journal of Philosophy*
PAS   *Proceedings of the Aristotelian Society*
Phil. R.   *Philosophical Review*
Phil. and Phen. Res.   *Philosophy and Phenomenological Research*

BIBLIOGRAPHICAL SOURCES

Albert, Ethel M., and Kluckhohn, Clyde, *A Selected Bibliography on Values, Ethics, and Esthetics in the Behavioral Sciences and Philosophy, 1935–1958*, New York: Free Press, 1959.

Beardsley, Monroe C., *Aesthetics*, New York: Harcourt Brace Jovanovich, 1958 (detailed bibliographical notes at the end of each chapter).

———, *Aesthetics from Classical Greece to the Present*, New York: Macmillan, 1965 (contains bibliography of the historical development of esthetics).

Chandler, Albert R., *A Bibliography of Experimental Aesthetics, 1865–1932*, Columbus: Ohio State University Press, 1933.

Duncan, Elmer H., and others, *Selective Current Bibliography for Aesthetics and Related Fields* (published annually in JAAC).

Hammond, William, *A Bibliography of Aesthetics and the Philosophy of the Fine Arts from 1900 to 1932*, New York: McKay, 1934.

Kiell, Norman, *Psychiatry and Psychology in the Visual Arts and Aesthetics: A Bibliography*, Madison: University of Wisconsin Press, 1965.

Lucas, E. Louise, *Art Books: A Basic Bibliography of the Fine Arts*, Greenwich, Conn.: New York Graphic Society, 1968.

Paperbound Books in Print, New York, published annually. Many of the books listed in the present bibliography are available in paperbound editions.

Robb, David M., and Garrison, J. J., *Art in the Western World*, 4th ed., New York: Harper & Row, 1963 (contains bibliography on the historical development of the arts).

Tillman, Frank A., and Cahn, Steven M. (eds.), *Philosophy of Art and Aesthetics: From Plato to Wittgenstein*, New York: Harper & Row, 1969 (contains extensive bibliography).

ANTHOLOGIES

Aschenbrenner, Karl, and Isenberg, Arnold (eds.), *Aesthetic Theories: Studies in the Philosophy of Art*, Englewood Cliffs, N.J.: Prentice-Hall, 1965.

Barrett, Cyril (ed.), *Collected Papers on Aesthetics*, Oxford: Blackwell, 1965.

Beardsley, Monroe C., and Schueller, Herbert M. (eds.), *Aesthetic Inquiry: Essays on Art Criticism and the Philosophy of Art*, Belmont, Cal.: Dickenson, 1967 (essays from JAAC).

Carritt, E. F. (ed.), *Philosophies of Beauty from Socrates to Robert Bridges*, New York: Oxford, 1931.

Coleman, Francis J. (ed.), *Contemporary Studies in Aesthetics*, New York: McGraw-Hill, 1968.

Elton, William (ed.), *Aesthetics and Language*, Oxford: Blackwell, 1954.

Hofstadter, Albert, and Kuhns, Richard (eds.), *Philosophies of Art and Beauty*, New York: Modern Library, 1964.

Hook, Sidney (ed.), *Art and Philosophy*, New York: New York University Press, 1966.

Hospers, John (ed.), *Introductory Readings in Aesthetics*, New York: Free Press, 1969.

Kennick, W. E. (ed), *Art and Philosophy: Readings in Aesthetics*, New York: St. Martin's, 1964.

Kiefer, Howard E., and Munitz, Milton K. (eds.), *Perspectives in Education, Religion, and the Arts*, Albany: State University of New York Press, 1970.

Langer, Susanne K. (ed.), *Reflections on Art*, Baltimore: Johns Hopkins Press, 1958.

Levich, Marvin (ed.), *Aesthetics and the Philosophy of Criticism*, New York: Random House, 1963.

Margolis, Joseph (ed.), *Philosophy Looks at the Arts*, New York: Scribner's, 1962.

Osborne, Harold (ed.), *Aesthetics in the Modern World*, New York: Weybright and Talley, 1968 (essays from BJA).

Philipson, Morris (ed.), *Aesthetics Today*, New York: World Publishing, 1962.

Richter, Peyton E. (ed.), *Perspectives in Aesthetics: Plato to Camus*, New York: Odyssey, 1967.

Sesonske, Alexander (ed.), *What Is Art? Aesthetic Theory from Plato to Tolstoy*, New York: Oxford, 1965.

Tillman, Frank A., and Cahn, Steven M. (eds.), *Philosophy of Art and Aesthetics: From Plato to Wittgenstein*, New York: Harper & Row, 1969.

Vivas, Eliseo, and Krieger, Murray (eds.), *The Problems of Aesthetics*, New York: Holt, Rinehart and Winston, 1953.

Weitz, Morris (ed.), *Problems in Aesthetics*, 2d ed., New York: Macmillan, 1970.

HISTORY OF ESTHETICS

Beardsley, Monroe C., *Aesthetics from Classical Greece to the Present*, New York: Macmillan, 1966.

———, "Aesthetics, History of," in Paul Edwards (ed.), *Encyclopedia of Philosophy*, Vol. I, pp. 18–35, New York: Macmillan and Free Press, 1967.

Bosanquet, Bernard, *A History of Aesthetics*, London: Sonnenschein, 1892; New York: Meridian, 1957.

Carritt, E. F., *The Theory of Beauty*, 3d ed., London: Methuen, 1928 (historical and critical).

Gilbert, Katherine E., and Kuhn, Helmut, *A History of Esthetics*, 2d ed., Bloomington: Indiana University Press, 1953.

Gombrich, E. H., *In Search of Cultural History*, New York: Oxford, 1969.

Kristeller, Paul O., "The Modern System of the Arts," *Journal of the History of Ideas* 12 (1951) and 13 (1952).

Kuhn, Helmut, "Aesthetics, History of," *Encyclopedia Brittanica*, Vol. I, Chicago, 1963.

Listowel, Earl of, *Modern Aesthetics: An Historical Introduction*, London: G. Allen, 1967.

Osborne, Harold, *Aesthetics and Art Theory: An Historical Introduction*, New York: Dutton, 1970.

Saisselin, Remy G., "Critical Reflections on the Origins of Modern Aesthetics," *BJA* 4 (1964).

Saw, Ruth, and Osborne, Harold, "Aesthetics as a Branch of Philosophy," *BJA* 1 (1960–1961).

Tatarkiewicz, W., "Objectivity and Subjectivity in the History of Aesthetics," *Phil. and Phen. Res.* 24 (1963).

———, *History of Aesthetics*, 2 vols., New York: Humanities Press, 1971.

Wellek, Rene, *A History of Modern Criticism*, New Haven, Conn.: Yale University Press, 1955.

Wimsatt, William K., Jr., and Brooks, Cleanth, *Literary Criticism: A Short History*, New York: Knopf, 1957.

GENERAL

Aldrich, Virgil C., *Philosophy of Art*, Englewood Cliffs, N.J.: Prentice-Hall, 1963.

Beardsley, Monroe C., *Aesthetics*, New York: Harcourt Brace Jovanovich, 1958.

Berleant, Arnold, *The Aesthetic Field*, Springfield, Ill.: Charles C Thomas, 1970.

Berndtson, Arthur, *Art, Expression, and Beauty*, New York: Holt, Rinehart and Winston, 1969.

Carritt, E. F., *An Introduction to Aesthetics*, London: Hutchinson, 1949.

Chandler, Albert R., *Beauty and Human Nature*, New York: Appleton-Century-Crofts, 1934 (summarizes the work in experimental esthetics).

Charlton, W., *Aesthetics: An Introduction*, London: Hutchinson, 1970.

Dessoir, Max, *Aesthetics and Theory of Art*, Detroit, Mich.: Wayne University Press, 1970.

Dickie, George, *Aesthetics*, Indianapolis, Ind.: Bobbs-Merrill, 1971.

Ducasse, Curt J., *Art, the Critics, and You*, Indianapolis, Ind.: Bobbs-Merrill, 1955.

———, *The Philosophy of Art*, 2d ed., New York: Dover, 1966.

Encyclopedia of World Art, Vols. I–XV, New York: McGraw-Hill, 1959–1968 (invaluable source of articles, bibliographies, illustrations).

Jarrett, James L., *The Quest for Beauty*, Englewood Cliffs, N.J.: Prentice-Hall, 1957 (general text).

Jenkins, Iredell, *Art and the Human Enterprise*, Cambridge, Mass.: Harvard University Press, 1958.

Kainz, Friedrich, *Aesthetics, the Science*, Detroit, Mich.: Wayne University Press, 1962.

Munro, Thomas, "Aesthetics," *Encyclopedia Brittanica*, Vol. I, Chicago, 1963.

———, *The Arts and Their Interrelations*, New York: Liberal Arts Press, 1949.

———, *Toward Science in Aesthetics*, New York: Liberal Arts Press, 1956.

Ogden, C. K., Richards, I. A., and Wood, James, *The Foundations of Aesthetics*, 2d ed., New York: Lear, 1948 (short critical summaries of leading theories of beauty and art).

Saw, Ruth, *Aesthetics*, New York: Doubleday, 1971.

Sparshott, F. E., *The Structure of Aesthetics*, Toronto: University of Toronto Press, 1963.

Stolnitz, Jerome, *Aesthetics and the Philosophy of Art Criticism*, Boston: Houghton Mifflin, 1960.

Tejera, Victorino, *Art and Human Intelligence*, New York: Appleton-Century-Crofts, 1965.

Wollheim, Richard, *Art and Its Objects: An Introduction to Aesthetics*, New York: Harper & Row, 1968.

CHAPTER 1: IMITATION AND IMAGINATION

Imitation—The Relation of Art to Nature

Auerbach, Erich, *Mimesis*, Princeton, N.J.: Princeton University Press, 1953.

Bloosfeldt, Karl, *Art Forms in Nature*, London: Zwemmer, 1936.

Butcher, S. H., *Aristotle's Theory of Poetry and Fine Art*, New York: Macmillan, 1923.

Collingwood, R. G., *The Principles of Art*, Oxford: Clarendon Press, 1938, Chap. 3.

Coomaraswamy, Ananda, *The Transformation of Nature in Art*, Cambridge, Mass.: Harvard University Press, 1934.

Evans, V. Burdwood, "A Scholastic Theory of Art," *Philosophy* 8 (1933) (on Maritain).

Gass, William H., *Fiction and the Figures of Life*, New York: Knopf, 1970.

Gilbert, Katherine E., "Aesthetic Imitation and Imitators in Aristotle," *Phil. R.* 45 (1936).

Gilson, Etienne, *Painting and Reality*, New York: Pantheon, 1957.

Gombrich, E. H., *Art and Illusion: A Study in the Psychology of Pictorial Representation*, 2d ed., New York: Pantheon, 1961.

———, *Meditations on a Hobby Horse and Other Essays on the Theory of Art*, New York: Phaidon, 1963.

Hepburn, Ronald W., "Aesthetic Appreciation of Nature," BJA 3 (1963).

Jenkins, Iredell, "Art and Ontology," *Review of Metaphysics* 9 (1956).

Jessup, Bertram, and Rader, Melvin, *Art and Human Values*, New York: Appleton-Century-Crofts, forthcoming, Chap. 5.

Langer, Susanne K., *Problems of Art*, New York: Scribner's, 1927, Chap. 5.

———, *Mind: An Essay on Human Feeling*, Vol. I, Baltimore: Johns Hopkins Press, 1967.

Loewenberg, Jacob, *Dialogues from Delphi*, Berkeley: University of California Press, 1949.

Lovejoy, Arthur O., " 'Nature' as Aesthetic Norm," *Modern Language Notes* 42 (1927).

Manns, James W., "Representation, Relativism and Resemblance," *BJA* 11 (1971).

Maritain, Jacques, *Art and Scholasticism*, New York: Scribner's, 1930.

———, *Creative Intuition in Art and Poetry*, New York: Pantheon, 1953.

McKeon, Richard P., "Literary Criticism and the Concept of Imitation in Antiquity," *Modern Philology* 34 (1936).

———, "Philosophic Bases of Art and Criticism," *Modern Philology* 41 (1943).

Morris, Bertram, "Beauty and Nature," *J. Phil.* 34 (1937).

Morawski, Stefan, "Mimesis," *Semiotica* 2 (1970).

Nahm, Milton C., *Aesthetic Experience and Its Presuppositions*, New York: Harper & Row, 1946, Part I.

Noon, William T., *Joyce and Aquinas*, New Haven, Conn.: Yale University Press, 1957.

Olson, Elder (ed.), *Aristotle's Poetics and English Literature*, Chicago: University of Chicago Press, 1965.

Rader, Melvin, "The Factualist Fallacy in Aesthetics," JAAC 28 (1970).

Read, Herbert, *Education through Art*, 3d ed., New York: Pantheon, 1958, Chap. 1.

Imagination and Creativity

Alexander, Samuel, "Art and Instinct," and "Artistic Creation and Cosmic Creation," *Philosophical and Literary Pieces*, London: Macmillan, 1940.

———, *Beauty and Other Forms of Value*, London: Macmillan, 1933, Chap. 4.

Anderson, Harold H., *Creativity and Its Cultivation*, New York: Harper & Row, 1959.

Anderson, Maxwell, and others, *The Bases of Artistic Creation*, New York: Octagon, 1969.

Andrews, Michael (ed.), *Creativity and Psychological Health*, Syracuse, N. Y.: Syracuse University Press, 1961.

Arnheim, Rudolf, *Picasso's Guernica: The Genesis of a Painting*, Berkeley: University of California Press, 1962.

Bartlett, F. C., "Types of Imagination," *Journal of Philosophical Studies* 3 (1928).

Beardsley, Monroe C., "On the Creation of Art," JAAC 3 (1965).

Beloff, John, "Creative Thinking in Art and Science," BJA 10 (1970).

Blanshard, Brand, The Nature of Thought, New York: Humanities Press, 1964, Vol. II, Chaps. 23–24.

Blocker, H. Gene, "Another Look at Aesthetic Imagination," JAAC 30 (1972).

Carpenter, Rhys, and others, The Bases of Artistic Creation, New Brunswick, N.J.: Rutgers University Press, 1942.

Casey, Edward S., "Imagination: Imaging and the Image," Phil. and Phen. Res. 31 (1971).

Chipp, Herschel B. (ed.), Theories of Modern Art: A Source Book by Artists and Critics, Berkeley and Los Angeles: University of California Press, 1969 (contains bibliography).

Collingwood, R. G., The Principles of Art, Oxford: Clarendon Press, 1938, pp. 125–151, 195–280.

Dessoir, Max, Aesthetics and Theory of Art, Detroit, Mich.: Wayne University Press, 1970, Chap. 5.

Downey, June, Creative Imagination, London: Routledge, 1929.

Ecker, David, "The Artistic Process as Qualitative Problem Solving," JAAC 21 (1963).

Ghiselin, Brewster (ed.), The Creative Process, Berkeley: University of California Press, 1952.

Goldwater, Robert, and Treves, Marco (eds.), Artists on Art, New York: Pantheon, 1945.

Gotshalk, D. W., Art and the Social Order, 2d ed., New York: Dover, 1962, Chap. 3.

Gourmont, Remy de, Selected Writings, Ann Arbor: University of Michigan Press, 1966, Part II.

Guggenheimer, Richard, Creative Vision in Artist and Audience, New York: Harper & Row, 1950.

Harding, Rosamond E. M., An Anatomy of Inspiration, New York: Barnes & Noble, 1967.

Hargreaves, H. L., "The 'Faculty' of Imagination," British Journal of Psychology, Monograph Supplement, III, 1927.

Hepburn, Ronald, "Poetry and 'Concrete Imagination': Problems of Truth and Illusion," BJA 12 (1972).

Ishiguro, Hideko, "Imagination," in Bernard Williams and Alan Montefiore (eds.), British Analytical Philosophy, New York: Humanities Press, 1966.

Koestler, Arthur, The Act of Creation, New York: Macmillan, 1965.

———, Insight and Outlook, New York: Macmillan, 1949.

Langer, Susanne K., Feeling and Form, New York: Scribner's, 1953, Chap. 4.

———, Problems of Art, New York: Scribner's, 1957, Chap. 4.

Lee, H. B., "The Creative Imagination," Psychoanalytic Quarterly 18 (1949).

Lowenfeld, V., The Nature of Creative Activity, 3d ed., New York: Harcourt Brace Jovanovich, 1957.

Lowes, John Livingston, The Road to Xanadu, Boston: Houghton Mifflin, 1927.

———, Convention and Revolt in Poetry, Boston: Houghton Mifflin, 1930.

MacIver, R. M. (ed.), New Horizons in Creative Thinking, New York: Harper & Row, 1954.

Malraux, André, The Psychology of Art, New York: Pantheon, 1949.

Maslow, Abraham H., "The Creative Attitude," The Structurist 3 (1963).

Mauron, Charles, Aesthetics and Psychology, London: Hogarth, 1935.

Morgan, Charles, "The Nature of Dramatic Illusion," in Susanne K. Langer (ed.), Reflections on Art, Baltimore: Johns Hopkins Press, 1958.

Morgan, Douglas, "Creativity Today," JAAC 12 (1953).

Morris, Bertram, The Aesthetic Process, Evanston, Ill.: Northwestern University Press, 1943.

Nahm, Milton C., The Artist as Creator, Baltimore: Johns Hopkins Press, 1956.

Norton, Richard, "What is Virtuality?" JAAC 30 (1972).

Portnoy, Julius, A Psychology of Art Creation, Philadelphia: University of Pennsylvania Press, 1942.

Read, Herbert, Education through Art, 3d ed., New York: Pantheon, 1958.

———, The Forms of Things Unknown, London: Faber, 1960.

Richards, I. A., Coleridge on Imagination, New York: Harcourt Brace Jovanovich, 1935.

———, Principles of Literary Criticism, New York: Harcourt Brace Jovanovich, 1924, Chap. 32.

Sartre, Jean-Paul, Imagination: A Psychological Critique, Ann Arbor: University of Michigan Press, 1962.

———, The Psychology of Imagination, New York: Philosophical Library, 1948.

Shahn, Ben, The Shape of Content, Cambridge, Mass.: Harvard University Press, 1957.

Smith, Paul (ed.), Creativity, New York: Hastings, 1959.

Snell, Bruno, The Discovery of the Mind, New York: Harper & Row, 1960, Chaps. 6, 12.

Spearman, Charles E., *Creative Mind*, New York: Appleton-Century-Crofts, 1931.

Tomas, Vincent, "Creativity in Art," *Phil. R.* 67 (1958).

—— (ed.), *Creativity in the Arts*, Englewood Cliffs, N.J.: Prentice-Hall, 1964.

Vernon, P. E. (ed.), *Creativity*, Baltimore: Johns Hopkins Press, 1971.

Wertheimer, Max, *Productive Thinking*, rev. ed., New York: Harper & Row, 1959.

Woolf, Virginia, *Mr. Bennett and Mrs. Brown*, London: Hogarth, 1924.

CHAPTER 2: EXPRESSION OF EMOTION

Emotion and Feeling in Art

Aldrich, Virgil C., "Beauty as Feeling," *Kenyon Review* 1 (1939).

Banesch, Otto, "Art and Feeling," in Susanne K. Langer (ed.), *Reflections on Art*, Baltimore: Johns Hopkins Press, 1958.

Benson, John, "Emotion and Expression," *Phil. R.* 76 (1967).

Britton, Karl, "Feelings and Their Expression," *Philosophy* 32 (1957).

Darwin, Charles, *The Expression of Emotions in Man and Animals*, Chicago: University of Chicago Press, 1965.

Ducasse, Curt J., *Art, the Critics, and You*, Indianapolis, Ind.: Bobbs-Merrill, 1955.

——, *The Philosophy of Art*, 2d ed., New York: Dover, 1963.

Garrod, H. W., *Tolstoi's Theory of Art*, Oxford: Clarendon Press, 1935.

Garvin, Lucius, "An Emotionalist Critique of 'Artistic Truth,' " *J. Phil.* 43 (1946).

Green, O. H., "The Expression of Emotion," *Mind* 79 (1970).

Hampshire, Stuart, *Feeling and Expression*, London: Lewis, 1961.

Hare, Peter H., "Feeling Imaging and Expression Theory," *JAAC* 30 (1972).

Knox, Israel, "Tolstoi's Esthetic Definition of Art," *J. Phil.* 27 (1930).

Maude, Aylmer (ed.), *Tolstoy on Art*, London: Oxford, 1924.

Morris-Jones, Huw, "The Language of Feelings," *BJA* 2 (1962).

Nahm, Milton C., *Aesthetic Experience and Its Presuppositions*, New York: Harper & Row, 1946, Part III.

Pepper, Stephen C., *Principles of Art Appreciation*, New York: Harcourt Brace Jovanovich, 1949, Chap. 6.

Tolstoy, Leo, *What Is Art? and Essays on Art*, London: Oxford, 1925.

Stolnitz, Jerome, *Aesthetics and Philosophy of Art Criticism*, Boston: Houghton Mifflin, 1960, Chap. 7.

Todd, George F., "Expression without Feeling," *JAAC* 30 (1972).

Tomas, Vincent, "Ducasse on Art and Its Appreciation," *Phil. and Phen. Res.* 13 (1952).

Véron, Eugene, *Aesthetics*, London: Chapman & Hall, 1879.

Wimsatt, W. K., and Beardsley, Monroe C., "The Affective Fallacy," *Sewanee Review* 57 (1949).

Must Art Create Beauty?

Bosanquet, Bernard, *Three Lectures on Aesthetics*, London: Macmillan, 1923; Indianapolis, Ind.: Bobbs-Merrill, 1963, Lecture III.

Carmichael, Peter A., "The Sense of Ugliness," *JAAC* 30 (1972).

Ducasse, Curt J., "What Has Beauty to Do with Art?," *J. Phil.* 25 (1928).

Gotshalk, D. W., "Art and Beauty," *Monist* 41 (1931).

Henderson, G. P., "The Concept of Ugliness," *BJA* 6 (1963).

Montague, W. P., "Beauty Is Not All: A Plea for Esthetic Pluralism," *The Ways of Things*, New York: Prentice-Hall, 1940.

Stolnitz, Jerome, "On Ugliness in Art," *Phil. and Phen. Res.* 11 (1950).

——, "Ugliness," in Paul Edwards (ed.), *Encyclopedia of Philosophy*, Vol. 8, New York: Macmillan and Free Press, 1968.

Ushenko, A., "Beauty in Art," *Monist* 42 (1932).

CHAPTER 3: INTUITION-EXPRESSION

Abercrombie, Lascelles, "Communication versus Expression in Art," *British Journal of Psychology* 14 (1923).

Bergson, Henri, *The Creative Mind*, New York: Philosophical Library, 1946.

——, *Introduction to Metaphysics*, New York: Putnam's, 1912.

——, *Laughter: An Essay on the Meaning of the Comic*, New York: Macmillan, 1911.

Bosanquet, Bernard, "Croce's Aesthetic," *Mind* 29 (1920).

——, "Croce's Aesthetic," *Proceedings of the British Academy* 9 (1919–1920).

Bousma, O. K., "The Expression Theory of Art," in Max Black (ed.), *Philosophical Analysis*, Ithaca, N.Y.: Cornell University Press, 1950.

Brown, Merle E., *Neo-Idealistic Aesthetics: Croce, Gentile, Collingwood*, Detroit, Mich.: Wayne State University Press, 1966.

Carritt, E. F., "Croce and His Aesthetic," *Mind* 62 (1953).

——, *The Theory of Beauty*, London: Methuen, 1928, Chap. 8.

——, *What Is Beauty?*, Oxford: Clarendon Press, 1932, Chap. 6.

Cary, Joyce, *Art and Reality*, New York: Harper & Row, 1958.

Collingwood, R. G., "Art," *Speculum Mentis*, Oxford: Clarendon Press, 1924.

——, *Essays in the Philosophy of Art*, Bloomington: University of Indiana Press, 1964.

——, *The Principles of Art*, Oxford: Clarendon Press, 1938.

Croce, Benedetto, *Aesthetic as Science of Expression and General Linguistic*, 2d ed., London: Macmillan, 1922.

——, "Aesthetic," *Encyclopedia Brittanica*, 14th edition.

——, *The Breviary of Aesthetic*, Houston, Tex.: Rice Institute, 1915.

——, *The Essence of Aesthetics*, London: Heinemann, 1921.

——, *Guide to Aesthetics*, Indianapolis, Ind.: Bobbs-Merrill, 1965.

Dewey, John, *Art as Experience*, New York: Minton, Balch & Co., 1934, Chaps. 4, 5.

Donagan, Alan, "The Croce-Collingwood Theory of Art," *Philosophy* 33 (1958).

——, *The Later Philosophy of R. G. Collingwood*, Oxford: Clarendon Press, 1962.

Ducasse, C. J., *The Philosophy of Art*, 2d ed., New York: Dover, 1963, Chap. 3.

Gilbert, Katherine E., "The One and the Many in Croce's Aesthetic," in *Studies in Recent Aesthetic*, Chapel Hill: University of North Carolina Press, 1927.

Gombrich, E. H., *Art and Illusion*, New York: Pantheon, 1960, Chap. 11.

Hepburn, Ronald W., "A Fresh Look at Collingwood," BJA 3 (1963).

Hospers, John (ed.), *Artistic Expression*, New York: Appleton-Century-Crofts, 1971.

——, "The Concept of Artistic Expression," PAS 55 (1954–1955).

——, "The Croce-Collingwood Theory of Art," *Philosophy* 31 (1956).

Khatchadourian, Haig, "The Expression Theory of Art," JAAC 23 (1965).

Mayo, Bernard, "Art, Language, and Philosophy in Croce," *Philosophical Quarterly* 5 (1955).

Nahm, Milton C., "The Philosophy of Aesthetic Expression: The Crocean Hypothesis," JAAC 13 (1955).

Orsini, G. N. G., "Theory and Practice in Croce's Aesthetics," JAAC 13 (1955).

Osborne, Harold, *Aesthetics and Criticism*, London: Routledge, 1955, Chap. 7.

Pantanker, R. B., "What Does Croce Mean by 'Expression'?" BJA 2 (1962).

Santayana, George, "Croce's Aesthetics," *The Idler and His Works*, New York: Braziller, 1957.

Seerveld, Calvin G., *Benedetto Croce's Earlier Aesthetic Theories and Literary Criticism*, Kampen, Holland, 1958.

Sircello, Guy, "Perceptual Acts and the Pictorial Arts: A Defense of Expression Theory," *J. Phil.* 62 (1965).

Tomas, Vincent A., "The Concept of Expression in Art," in Joseph Margolis (ed.), *Philosophy Looks at the Arts*, New York: Scribner's, 1962.

Tormey, Alan, *The Concept of Expression*, Princeton, N. J.: Princeton University Press, 1971.

Wollheim, Richard, "Expression," *The Human Agent*, New York: St. Martin's, 1968.

——, "On Expression and Expressionism," *Revue Internationale de Philosophie* 18 (1964).

Wimsatt, William K., and Brooks, Cleanth, *Literary Criticism: A Short History*, New York: Knopf, 1957, Chap. 23 (on Croce).

CHAPTER 4: IMAGINATIVE SATISFACTION OF DESIRE

On Nietzsche

Danto, Arthur, *Nietzsche as Philosopher*, New York: Macmillan, 1965, Chap. 2.

Hanna, Thomas, *The Lyrical Existentialists*, New York: Atheneum, 1962.

Hollingdale, R. G., *Nietzsche: The Man and His Philosophy*, Baton Rouge: Louisiana State University Press, 1965.

Jaspers, Karl, *Nietzsche*, Tucson: University of Arizona Press, 1965.

Kaufmann, Walter (ed.), *Basic Writings of Nietzsche*, New York: Modern Library, 1966 (contains *The Birth of Tragedy* and *The Case of Wagner*).

——, *From Shakespeare to Existentialism*, rev. ed., New York: Doubleday, 1960 (contains five chapters on Nietzsche).

——, *Nietzsche*, Princeton, N.J.: Princeton University Press, 1950 (especially Chap. 4).

——, "Nietzsche and Rilke," *Kenyon Review* 17 (1955).

Knight, A. H. J., *Some Aspects of the Life and Works of Nietzsche*, London: Cambridge University Press, 1933.

Lea, Frank Alfred, *The Tragic Philosopher*, London: Methuen, 1957.

Ludovici, Anthony M., *Nietzsche and Art*, London: Constable, 1912.

Morgan, George Allen, *What Nietzsche Means*, Cambridge, Mass.: Harvard University Press, 1941, Chap. 8.

Nietzsche, Friedrich, *The Will to Power*, trans. by Walter Kaufmann and R. G. Hollingdale, New York: Random House, 1966, Part IV, "The Will to Power as Art."

Rosenstein, Leon, "Metaphysical Foundations of the Theories of Tragedy in Hegel and Nietzsche," JAAC 28 (1970).

Smith, John E., "Nietzsche: The Conquest of the Tragic through Art," in his *Reason and God*, New Haven, Conn.: Yale University Press, 1961.

On Freud and Related Theory

Baudouin, Charles, *Psycho-Analysis and Aesthetics*, New York: Dodd, Mead, 1924.

Bodkin, A. M., "The Relevance of Psycho-Analysis to Art Criticism," *British Journal of Psychology* 25 (1924–1925).

Bruner, Jerome S., "Freud and the Image of Man," *Partizan Review* 23 (1956).

Burke, Kenneth, "Freud and the Analysis of Poetry," *Philosophy of Literary Form*, rev. ed., New York: Random House, 1957.

———, *A Grammar of Motives*, New York: Prentice-Hall, 1945.

Caudwell, Christopher, *Further Studies in a Dying Culture*, London: Bodley Head, 1949.

———, *Illusion and Reality*, New York: International Publishers, 1948.

Costigan, Giovanni, *Sigmund Freud: A Short Biography*, New York: Macmillan, 1965.

Dalbiez, Roland, *Psychoanalytical Method and the Doctrine of Freud*, New York: Longmans, 1941.

Ehrenzweig, Anton, *The Hidden Order of Art*, Berkeley: University of California Press, 1967.

———, *The Psychoanalysis of Artistic Vision and Hearing*, New York: Braziller, 1965.

———, "A New Psychoanalytic Approach to Aesthetics," BJA 2 (1962).

Fine, R., *Freud: A Critical Revaluation of His Theories*, New York: McKay, 1962.

Fraiberg, Louis, "Freud's Writings on Art," *International Journal of Psycho-Analysis* 37 (1956).

Freud, Sigmund, *The Standard Edition of the Complete Psychological Works of Sigmund Freud*, edited by James Strachey, 24 vols., London: Hogarth, 1953–1964. See especially *Civilization and Its Discontents, Delusion and Dream, The Interpretation of Dreams, Leonardo da Vinci*, and *Wit and Its Relation to the Unconscious*.

———, *Collected Papers*, 2 vols., London: International Psycho-Analytical Press, 1925.

Fry, Roger, "The Artist and Psycho-Analysis," in Leonard and Virginia Woolf (eds.), *The Hogarth Essays*, London: Hogarth, 1924.

Gombrich, E. H., "Psychoanalysis and the History of Art," in Benjamin Nelson (ed.), *Freud and the Twentieth Century*, New York: Meridian, 1957.

Gourmont, Remy de, "Subconscious Creation," *Decadence*, New York: Harcourt Brace Jovanovich, 1921.

Graves, Robert, *The Meaning of Dreams*, London: Palmer, 1924.

———, *Poetic Unreason*, London: Palmer, 1925.

Hauser, Arnold, *The Philosophy of Art History*, New York: Knopf, 1959, Chap. 3.

Hill, J. C., "Poetry and the Unconscious," *British Journal of Medical Psychology* 4 (1924).

Hoffman, Frederick J., *Freudianism and the Literary Mind*, Baton Rouge: Louisiana State University Press, 1945.

Hyman, Stanley, "Freud and the Climate of Tragedy," *Partizan Review* 23 (1956).

Jones, Ernest, *Hamlet and Oedipus*, New York: Norton, 1940.

———, *The Life and Work of Sigmund Freud*, 3 vols., New York: Basic Books, 1953–1957.

Kris, Ernst, *Psychoanalytic Explorations in Art*, New York: International Universities, 1958.

Lawrence, D. H., *Psychoanalysis and the Unconscious*, New York: Seltzer, 1921.

Lindner, Robert (ed.), *Explorations in Psychoanalysis*, New York: Julian Press, 1953, Part III.

Mann, Thomas, *Freud, Goethe, Wagner*, New York: Knopf, 1937.

Neumann, Erich, *Art and the Creative Unconscious*, Princeton, N.J.: Princeton University Press, 1959.

Parker, DeWitt H., *The Analysis of Art*, New Haven, Conn.: Yale University Press, 1924.

Phillips, William (ed.), *Art and Psychoanalysis*, New York: Criterion, 1957.

Prescott, Frederick Clarke, *The Poetic Mind*, New York: Macmillan, 1922.

Rank, Otto, *Art and Artist*, New York: Knopf, 1932.

———, *The Myth of the Birth of the Hero*, New York: Random House, 1952.

Read, Herbert, *Art and Society*, London: Faber, 1937, Chap. 5.

——, "Psychoanalysis and Criticism," *Reason and Romanticism*, New York: Russell and Russell, 1963.

—— (ed.), *Surrealism*, London: Faber, 1936.

Sachs, Hanns, *The Creative Unconscious*, Cambridge, Mass.: Sci-Art Publishers, 1942.

Schapiro, Meyer, "Leonardo and Freud: An Art-Historical Study," *Journal of the History of Ideas* 17 (1956).

Schneider, Daniel E., *The Psychoanalyst and the Artist*, New York: Farrar, Straus, 1950.

Stekel, Wilhelm, "Poetry and Neurosis," *Psychoanalytic Review* 10 (1923).

Sterba, Richard, "The Problem of Art in Freud's Writings," *Psychoanalytic Quarterly* 9 (1940).

Stevenson, Robert Louis, "A Chapter on Dreams," in *Across the Plains with Other Memories and Essays*, New York: Scribner's, 1917.

Stokes, Adrian, "Form in Art: A Psychoanalytic Interpretation," *JAAC* 18 (1959).

——, *Painting and the Inner World*, London: Tavistock, 1963.

Thorburn, John M., *Art and the Unconscious*, London: Routledge, 1925.

——, Hannay, A. H., and Leon, P., "Artistic Form and the Unconscious," in *Modern Tendencies in Philosophy*, Aristotelian Society Supplementary Vol. 13, London, 1934.

Trilling, Lionel, "Freud and Literature," "Art and Neurosis," in *The Liberal Imagination*, New York: Doubleday, 1945.

——, "The Legacy of Freud: Literary and Aesthetic," *Kenyon Review* 2 (1940).

Vygotsky, Lev Semenovich, *The Psychology of Art*, Cambridge, Mass.: Massachusetts Institute of Technology Press, 1971, Chap. 4.

Wisdom, J. O., "Psychoanalytic Theories of the Unconscious," in Paul Edwards (ed.), *Encyclopedia of Philosophy*, New York: Macmillan and Free Press, 1937, Vol. 8, pp. 189–194 (includes bibliography).

Wollheim, Richard, "Freud and the Understanding of Art," *BJA* 10 (1970).

The Concept of Archetypes

Abell, Walter, *The Collective Dream in Art*, Cambridge, Mass.: Harvard University Press, 1957.

Bodkin, Maud, *Archetypal Patterns in Poetry*, London: Oxford, 1934.

——, *Studies of Type-Images in Poetry*, *Religion, and Philosophy*, London: Oxford, 1951.

Campbell, Joseph, *The Hero with a Thousand Faces*, New York: Noonday, 1956.

Freud, Sigmund, "The Theme of the Three Caskets," *Collected Papers*, Vol. 4, London: International Psycho-Analytical Press, 1925.

Fromm, Erich, *The Forgotten Language*, New York: Holt, Rinehart and Winston, 1951.

Frye, Northrop, "The Archetypes of Literature," *Kenyon Review* 13 (1951).

Hyman, Stanley E., "Maud Bodkin and Psychological Criticism," in *The Armed Vision*, New York: Knopf, 1948.

Jacobi, Jolan, *Complex, Archetype, Symbol in the Psychology of C. G. Jung*, Princeton, N.J.: Princeton University Press, 1959.

Jung, Carl Gustav, *The Archetypes and the Collective Unconscious*, New York: Pantheon, 1959 (in *Collected Works*, Vol. 9).

——, *Contributions to Analytical Psychology*, New York: Harcourt Brace Jovanovich, 1928.

——, *Modern Man in Search of a Soul*, New York: Harcourt Brace Jovanovich, 1934.

——, *The Spirit in Man, Art and Literature*, Princeton, N.J.: Princeton University Press, 1972.

——, and Kerenyi, C., *Essays on a Science of Mythology*, New York: Pantheon, 1949.

——, and others, *Man and His Symbols*, New York: Doubleday, 1964.

Lewis, C. Day, *The Poetic Image*, London: Oxford, 1947.

Neumann, Eric, *The Archetypal World of Henry Moore*, Princeton, N.J.: Princeton University Press, 1959.

Press, John, *The Fire and the Fountain*, New York: Oxford, 1955, Chap. 6.

Read, Herbert, *Icon and Idea*, Cambridge, Mass.: Harvard University Press, 1955.

Scott, Wilbur S. (ed.), "The Archetypal Approach," *Five Approaches of Literary Criticism*, New York: Collier, 1962.

CHAPTER 5: ENHANCEMENT OF EXPERIENCE

Dewey

Ames, Van Meter, "John Dewey as Aesthetician," *JAAC* 12 (1953).

Bernstein, Richard J., "Dewey," in Paul Edwards (ed.), *Encyclopedia of Philoso-*

phy, Vol. 2, pp. 380–385, New York: Macmillan and Free Press, 1967.

Boydston, Jo A. (ed.), *Guide to the Works of John Dewey*, Carbondale: University of Southern Illinois Press, 1970.

Croce, Benedetto, "Dewey's Aesthetics and Theory of Knowledge," JAAC 11 (1952).

——, "On the Aesthetics of Dewey," with reply by Dewey, JAAC 6 (1948).

Dewey, John, "Aesthetic Experience as a Primary Phase and as an Artistic Development," JAAC 9 (1950).

——, *Art as Experience*, New York: Minton, Balch & Co., 1934.

——, *Experience and Nature*, rev. ed., LaSalle, Ill.: Open Court, 1929.

——, "Qualitative Thought," *Philosophy and Civilization*, New York: Minton, Balch & Co., 1931.

——, and others, *Art and Education*, Merion, Pa.: Barnes Foundation, 1934.

Edman, Irwin, "Dewey and Art," in Sidney Hook (ed.), *John Dewey: Philosopher of Science and Freedom*, New York: Dial, 1950.

——, "A Philosophy of Experience as a Philosophy of Art," in *Essays in Honor of John Dewey*, New York: Holt, Rinehart and Winston, 1929.

Featherstone, Joseph, "John Dewey Reconsidered," *New Republic* 167 (July 8, 1972).

Gauss, Charles E., "Some Reflections on John Dewey's Aesthetics," JAAC 19 (1960).

Geiger, George R., *John Dewey in Perspective*, New York: Oxford, 1958 (stresses Dewey's interpretation of esthetic experience as a key to his philosophy).

Gotshalk, D. W., "On Dewey's Aesthetics," JAAC 23 (1964).

Grana, Caesar, "John Dewey's Social Art and the Sociology of Art," JAAC 20 (1962).

Jacobsen, Leon, "Art as Experience and American Visual Art Today," JAAC 19 (1960).

Kaminsky, Jack, "Dewey's Concept of an Experience," *Phil. and Phen. Res.* 17 (1957).

Kuspit, Donald P., "Dewey's Critique of Art for Art's Sake," JAAC 27 (1968).

Mathur, D. C., "Dewey's Aesthetics," *J. Phil.* 63 (1966).

Morris, Bertram, "Dewey's Aesthetics," JAAC 30 (1971).

Pepper, Stephen C., "The Concept of Fusion in Dewey's Aesthetic Theory," JAAC 12 (1953).

——, "Some Questions on Dewey's Esthetics," in Paul A. Schilpp (ed.), *The Philosophy of John Dewey*, Evanston, Ill.: Northwestern University Press, 1939.

Shearer, E. A., "Dewey's Aesthetic Theory," *J. Phil.* 32 (1935).

Thomas, M. H., *John Dewey: A Centennial Bibliography*, Chicago: University of Chicago Press, 1962.

Zink, Sidney, "The Concept of Continuity in Dewey's Theory of Esthetics," *Phil. R.* 52 (1943).

Whitehead

Morris, Bertram, "The Art-Process and the Aesthetic Fact in Whitehead's Philosophy," in Paul Schilpp (ed.), *The Philosophy of Alfred North Whitehead*, Evanston, Ill.: Northwestern University Press, 1941.

Sherburne, Donald W., *A Whiteheadean Aesthetic*, New Haven, Conn., Yale University Press, 1961.

Whitehead, Alfred North, *Adventures of Ideas*, New York: Macmillan, 1933, Chaps. 17, 18.

——, *Science and the Modern World*, New York: Macmillan, 1925, Chaps. 5, 13.

Related Theory

Brown, Harold Chapman, "Art, Action, and Affective States," in *Essays in Honor of John Dewey*, New York: Holt, Rinehart and Winston, 1929.

Brownell, Baker, *Art is Action*, New York: Harper & Row, 1939.

——, *The Human Community*, New York: Harper & Row, 1950, Part X.

Buermeyer, Laurence, *The Aesthetic Experience*, Merion, Pa.: Barnes Foundation, 1929.

Gordon, Kate, "Pragmatism in Aesthetics," *Essays Philosophical and Psychological: In Honor of William James*, New York: McKay, 1908.

Kallen, Horace M., "Beauty and Use," *Phil. R.* 48 (1939).

——, *Indecency and the Seven Arts and Other Adventures of a Pragmatist in Aesthetics*, New York: Liveright, 1930.

Krutch, Joseph Wood, *Experience and Art*, New York: Harrison Smith and Robert Haas, 1932.

Lipman, Matthew, *What Happens in Art*, New York: Appleton-Century-Crofts, 1967.

Mead, George Herbert, "The Nature of Aesthetic Experience," *International Journal of Ethics* 36 (1925–1926).

Pepper, Stephen C., *Aesthetic Quality*, New York: Scribner's, 1938.

———, "Art and Experience," *Review of Metaphysics* 12 (1958).

———, "Art and Utility," *J. Phil.* 20 (1920).

———, *The Basis of Criticism in the Arts*, Cambridge, Mass.: Harvard University Press, 1945, Chap. 3 (see present volume Chapter 11).

———, "The Concept of Fusion in Dewey's Aesthetic Theory," in *The Work of Art*, Bloomington: Indiana University Press, 1955.

———, "The Development of Contextualistic Aesthetics," *Antioch Review* 28 (1968).

Rader, Melvin, "The Artist as Outsider," *JAAC* 16 (1958).

———, "Isolationist and Contextualist Esthetics: Conflict and Resolution," *J. Phil.* 44 (1947).

CHAPTER 6: EMBODIMENT OF VALUES

Santayana

Ames, Van Meter, "Santayana at One Hundred," *JAAC* 22 (1964).

Arnett, Willard E., *Santayana and the Sense of Beauty*, Bloomington: Indiana University Press, 1955.

———, "Santayana and the Fine Arts," *JAAC* 16 (1957).

Ashmore, Jerome, "Santayana's Mistrust of the Fine Arts," *JAAC* 14 (1956).

———, *Santayana, Art, and Aesthetics*, Cleveland, Oh.: Press of Case Western Reserve University, 1966.

Boas, George, "Santayana and the Arts," in Paul Arthur Schilpp (ed.), *The Philosophy of George Santayana*, Evanston, Ill.: Northwestern University Press, 1940.

Gilbert, Katherine E., "Santayana's Doctrine of Aesthetic Expression," in *Studies in Recent Aesthetic*, Chapel Hill: University of North Carolina Press, 1927.

Henfrey, Norman (ed.), *Selected Critical Writings of George Santayana*, London: Cambridge, 1968.

Howgate, George Washburne, *George Santayana*, Philadelphia: University of Pennsylvania Press, 1938.

Olafson, Frederick A., "Santayana," in Paul Edwards (ed.), *Encyclopedia of Philosophy*, Vol. 7, pp. 280–287, New York: Macmillan and Free Press, 1967.

Santayana, George, *Interpretations of Poetry and Religion*, New York: Scribner's, 1927.

———, *The Idler and His Works and Other Essays*, New York: Braziller, 1957.

———, "The Mutability of Aesthetic Categories," *Phil. R.* 34 (1925).

———, *Obiter Scripta*, New York: Scribner's, 1936.

———, *Reason in Art*, New York: Scribner's, 1922.

———, *The Sense of Beauty*, New York: Scribner's, 1896.

Singer, Irving, *Santayana's Aesthetics: A Critical Introduction*, Cambridge, Mass.: Harvard University Press, 1957.

The Concept of Beauty

Aldrich, Virgil C., "Beauty as Feeling," *Kenyon Review* 1 (1939).

Alexander, Samuel, *Beauty and Other Forms of Value*, London: Macmillan, 1933.

Beardsley, Monroe C., *Aesthetics*, New York: Harcourt Brace Jovanovich, 1958, pp. 502–512.

Carritt, E. F., *The Theory of Beauty*, London: Methuen, 1928.

Gotshalk, D. W., "Art and Beauty," *Monist* 41 (1931).

Greene, T. M., "Beauty in Art and Nature," *Sewanee Review* 69 (1961).

Gilson, Etienne, *The Arts of the Beautiful*, New York: Scribner's, 1965.

Henderson, G. P., "An 'Orthodox' Use of the Term 'Beautiful,' " *Philosophy* 35 (1960).

Jessop, T. E., "The Definition of Beauty," *PAS* 33 (1933).

Joad, C. E. M., "The Objectivity of Beauty," *Matter, Life and Value*, London: Oxford, 1929.

Kainz, Freidrich, *Aesthetics, the Science*, Detroit, Mich.: Wayne State University Press, 1962 (relation between beauty and the aesthetic attitude).

Katkov, G., "The Pleasant and the Beautiful," *PAS* 40 (1940).

Marshall, Henry Rutgers, *The Beautiful*, New York: Macmillan, 1924.

Moore, G. E., *Ethica Principia*, Cambridge: Cambridge, 1903, Chap. 6.

Osborne, Harold, *Theory of Beauty*, London: Routledge, 1952.

Reid, Louis Arnaud, *A Study in Aesthetics*, New York: Macmillan, 1931, Chaps. 5–6, 8, 13, 14.

Stace, Walter T., *The Meaning of Beauty*, London: Richards and Toulmin, 1929.

Stolnitz, Jerome, "Beauty," in Paul Edwards, *Encyclopedia of Philosophy*, Vol. 1, pp. 263–266, New York: Macmillan and Free Press, 1967.

———, " 'Beauty': Some Stages in the History of an Idea," *Journal of the History of Ideas* 22 (1961).

Ushenko, Andrew P., "Beauty in Art," *Monist* 40 (1932).

Aesthetic Value in General

Aiken, Henry David, "A Pluralistic Analysis of Aesthetic Value," *Phil. R.* 59 (1950).

Beardsley, Monroe C., *Aesthetics*, New York: Harcourt Brace Jovanovich, 1958, Chap. 10.

———, "The Discrimination of Aesthetic Enjoyment," BJA 3 (1963).

Bradley, A. C., "The Sublime," *Oxford Lectures on Poetry*, London: Macmillan, 1909.

Bruce, John, "Art and Value," BJA 6 (1966).

Child, Arthur, "The Social Historical Relativity of Esthetic Value," *Phil. R.* 52 (1944).

Dessoir, Max, *Aesthetics and the Theory of Art*, Detroit, Mich.: Wayne State University Press, 1970, Chap. 4 (on the beautiful, sublime, tragic, ugly, and comic).

Ducasse, Curt J., *The Philosophy of Art*, 2d. ed., New York: Dover, 1963, Chap. 14.

Ekman, Rolf, "Aesthetic Value and the Ethics of Life Affirmation," BJA 3 (1963).

Findlay, J. N., "The Perspicuous and the Poignant: Two Aesthetic Fundamentals," BJA 7 (1967).

Foot, Phillipa, *Morality and Art*, London: Oxford, 1970.

Ingarden, Roman, "Artistic and Aesthetic Value," BJA 4 (1964).

Jessup, Bertram, and Rader, Melvin, *Art and Human Values*, New York: Appleton-Century-Crofts, forthcoming.

Kolnai, Aurel, "Aesthetic and Moral Experience: The Five Contrasts," BJA 11 (1971).

———, "On the Concept of the Interesting," BJA 4 (1964).

Laird, John, *The Idea of Value*, London: Cambridge, 1929.

Lee, Harold Newton, *Perception and Aesthetic Value*, Englewood Cliffs, N.J.: Prentice-Hall, 1938.

Lewis, Clarence Irving, *An Analysis of Knowledge and Valuation*, La Salle, Ill.: Open Court, 1946.

Meager, Ruby, "The Sublime and the Obscene," BJA 4 (1964).

Morawski, Stefan, "Artistic Value," *Journal of Aesthetic Education* 5 (1971).

Morris, Charles W., "Esthetics and the Theory of Signs," *Journal of Unified Science* 8 (1939) (maintains that art is a sign language of values).

———, "Science, Art, and Technology," *Kenyon Review* 1 (1939).

———, *Signification and Significance: A Study of the Relation of Signs and Values*, Cambridge, Mass.: Massachusetts Institute of Technology Press, 1964.

———, *Varieties of Human Values*, Chicago: University of Chicago Press, 1956.

Perry, Ralph Barton, *Realms of Value*, Cambridge, Mass.: Harvard University Press, 1954.

Reid, Louis Arnaud, *Meaning in the Arts*, New York: Humanities Press, 1969, Chap. 11.

———, *A Study in Aesthetics*, New York: Macmillan, 1931, Chaps. 5, 6, 8, 11.

Stolnitz, Jerome, *Aesthetics and Philosophy of Art Criticism*, Boston: Houghton Mifflin, 1960, Part V.

———, "On Aesthetic Familiarity and Aesthetic Value," *J. Phil.* 53 (1956).

———, "On Aesthetic Valuing and Evaluation," *Phil. and Phen. Res.* 13 (1953).

CHAPTER 7: THE MEDIUM AND
SENSORY CONSTITUENTS

The Medium

Alexander, Samuel, *Art and the Material*, Manchester: Manchester University Press, 1925.

Arnheim, Rudolf, *Film as Art*, Berkeley: University of California Press, 1958.

Babbitt, Irving, *The New Laokoon*, Boston: Houghton Mifflin, 1910.

Berenson, Bernard, *Aesthetics and History*, New York: Pantheon, 1948, Chap. 1 (section on materials).

Bullough, Edward, "Mind and Medium in Art," *British Journal of Psychology* 11 (1920–1921).

Church, Ralph W., *An Essay on Critical Appreciation*, Ithaca, N.Y.: Cornell University Press, 1938, Chap. 3.

Crawford, Donald W., "The Uniqueness of the Medium," *The Personalist* 51 (1970).

Doerner, Max, *The Materials of the Artist*, New York: Harcourt Brace Jovanovich, 1934.

Gilbert, Katherine E., "Bosanquet on the Artist's Medium," in *Studies in Recent Aesthetics*, Chapel Hill: University of North Carolina Press, 1927.

Greene, Theodore M., *The Arts and the Art of Criticism*, Princeton, N.J.: Princeton University Press, 1940, Part I.

Hitchcock, H. R., Jr., *In the Nature of*

Materials, New York: Duell, Sloan, & Pearce-Meredith Press, 1942 (on Frank Lloyd Wright's use of architectural materials).

Hospers, John, "Collingwood and Art Media," *Southwestern Journal of Philosophy* 2 (1971).

Lessing, G. E., *Laocoon: An Essay on the Limits of Painting and Poetry,* Indianapolis, Ind.: Bobbs-Merrill, 1962.

Lyons, Nathan (ed.), *Photographers on Photography,* Englewood Cliffs, N.J.: Prentice-Hall, 1966.

Marriott, Charles, and others, "Mind and Medium in Art," *British Journal of Psychology* 11 (1920–1921).

McLuhan, Marshall, *Understanding Media,* New York: McGraw-Hill, 1964.

Munro, Thomas, *The Arts and Their Interrelations,* New York: Liberal Arts Press, 1949.

Panofsky, Erwin, "Style and Medium in the Motion Pictures," *Critique* 1 (1947). (Reprinted in Morris Weitz, *Problems in Aesthetics,* 2d ed., New York: Macmillan, 1970).

Pauson, Marion L., "Studies in Art Media," *Tulane Studies in Philosophy* 19 (1970).

Reid, Louis Arnaud, *Meaning in the Arts,* New York: Humanities Press, 1969, Chap. 5.

———, *A Study in Aesthetics,* New York: Macmillan, 1931, pp. 164–175.

Seiberling, Frank, *Looking into Art,* New York: Holt, Rinehart and Winston, 1959, Part Two.

Stallknecht, Newton P., "Art and the Four Causes," *J. Phil.* 31 (1934).

Weitz, Morris, *Philosophy of the Arts,* Cambridge, Mass.: Harvard University Press, 1950, Chap. 7.

Esthetic Surface and Sensory Materials

Aiken, Henry, "Art as Expression and Surface," *JAAC* 4 (1945).

Berenson, Bernard, *Central Italian Painters of the Renaissance,* New York: Putnam's, 1909 (emphasis on tactile values).

Clement, W. C., "Quality Orders," *Mind* 65 (1956).

Dewey, John, *Art as Experience,* New York: Minton, Balch & Co., 1934, Chaps. 9–10.

Duncan, Elmer H., "The Aesthetic Works of D. W. Prall," *JAAC* 26 (1968) (with a bibliography on Prall).

Evans, Ralph M., *An Introduction to Color,* New York: Wiley, 1948.

Geldard, Frank A., *The Human Senses,* New York: Wiley, 1953.

Goodman, Nelson, *The Structure of Appearance,* Cambridge, Mass.: Harvard University Press, 1951, Part III.

Gotshalk, D. W., *Art and the Social Order,* Chicago: University of Chicago Press, 1947, Chap. 4.

Greene, Theodore M., *The Arts and the Art of Criticism,* Princeton, N.J.: Princeton University Press, 1940, Parts I and III.

Hartshorne, Charles, *The Philosophy and Psychology of Sensation,* Chicago: University of Chicago Press, 1934.

Herring, Frances, "Touch—The Neglected Sense," *JAAC* 7 (1949).

Katz, David, *The World of Colour,* London: Routledge, 1935.

Lippman, Mathew, *What Happens in Art,* New York: Appleton-Century-Crofts, 1967, Chaps. 3, 6.

Moore, Jared S., "The Work of Art and Its Material," *JAAC* 6 (1948).

Parkhurst, Helen Huss, *Beauty,* New York: Harcourt Brace Jovanovich, 1930, Chaps. 3 and 4.

Pepper, Stephen C., *Principles of Art Appreciation,* New York: Harcourt Brace Jovanovich, 1949, Part III.

Prall, D. W., *Aesthetic Analysis,* New York: Crowell, 1936.

———, *Aesthetic Judgment,* New York: Crowell, 1929.

Randall, John Hermann, Jr., "Qualities, Qualification, and the Aesthetic Transaction," *Nature and Historical Experience,* New York: Columbia University Press, 1958.

Santayana, George, *The Sense of Beauty,* New York: Scribner's, 1896, Part II.

Sibley, Frank, "Aesthetics and the Looks of Things," *J. Phil.* 56 (1959).

Ushenko, Andrew P., "Esthetic Immediacy," *J. Phil.* 38 (1941).

CHAPTER 8: FORM

Form in General

Abell, Walter, *Representation and Form,* New York: Scribner's, 1936.

Barnes, Albert C., "Plastic Form," in *The Art in Painting,* New York: Harcourt Brace Jovanovich, 1928.

Beardsley, Monroe C., *Aesthetics,* New York: Harcourt Brace Jovanovich, 1958, Chaps. 4–6.

Bell, Clive, *Art,* New York: Stokes, 1914.

———, *Since Cezanne,* London: Chatto & Windus, 1922.

Blanshard, Frances, *Retreat from Likeness in the Theory of Painting,* New York: Columbia University Press, 1949.

Bowers, David F., "The Role of Subject-Matter in Art," *J. Phil.* 36 (1939) (discusses interaction of form and subject matter).

British Journal of Aesthetics, Special Issue, "On Clive Bell," 5 (1965) (essays by George T. Dickie, R. K. Elliott, R. Meager, and Herbert Read).

Brion, Marcel, "Abstract Art," *Diogenes* 24 (1958).

Carpenter, Rhys, *The Esthetic Basis of Greek Art*, rev. ed., Bloomington: Indiana University Press, 1959 (on fusion of form and subject matter).

Carritt, E. F., "Art without Form?," *Philosophy* 16 (1941).

Dewey, John, *Art as Experience*, New York: Minton, Balch & Co., 1934, Chaps. 6–8.

Ducasse, C. J., *The Philosophy of Art*, 2d ed., New York: Dover, 1963, Chap. 13 and Appendix.

Ekman, Rosalind, "The Paradoxes of Formalism," *BJA* 10 (1970).

Eliot, T. S., "The Music of Poetry," in *On Poetry and Poets*, New York: Farrar, Straus, 1957.

Forster, E. M., "Art for Art's Sake," in *Two Cheers for Democracy*, New York: Harcourt Brace Jovanovich, 1951 (on the value of form).

Fry, Roger, *The Hogarth Essays*, London: Hogarth, 1924.

———, *Last Lectures*, Cambridge: Cambridge, 1939.

———, *Transformations*, London: Chatto & Windus, 1920.

———, *Vision and Design*, London: Chatto & Windus, 1920.

Gotshalk, D. W., *Art and the Social Order*, 2d ed., New York: Dover, 1962, Chap. 5.

———, "Form and Expression in Kant's Aesthetics," *BJA* 7 (1967).

Greene, Theodore M., *The Arts and the Art of Criticism*, Princeton, N.J.: Princeton University Press, 1940, Part II.

Hambidge, Jay, *Dynamic Symmetry*, New Haven, Conn.: Yale University Press, 1926.

Hiler, Hilaire, *Why Abstract?*, New York: Laughlin, 1945.

Ingarden, Roman, "The General Question of the Essence of Form and Content," *J. Phil.* 57 (1960).

Jessup, Bertram, "Aesthetic Size," *JAAC* 9 (1950).

Kepes, Gyorgy (ed.), *Structure in Art and Science*, New York: Braziller, 1965.

Lang, Berel, "Significance or Form: The Dilemma of Roger Fry's Aesthetics," *JAAC* 21 (1962).

Langer, Susanne K., *Feeling and Form*, New York: Scribner's, 1953.

———, *Mind: An Essay on Human Feeling*, Baltimore: Johns Hopkins Press, 1967, Vol. I, Chap. 7.

———, *Problems of Art*, New York: Scribner's, 1957, Chap. 4.

——— (ed.), *Reflections on Art*, Baltimore: Johns Hopkins Press, 1958 (contains a number of essays on form).

Lord, Catherine, "Organic Unity Reconsidered," *JAAC* 22 (1964).

———, "Unity with Impunity," *JAAC* 26 (1967).

Lubbock, Percy, *The Craft of Fiction*, New York: Scribner's, 1931.

Moholy-Nagy, Lazlo, *The New Vision: Fundamentals of Design*, 4th ed., New York: Wittenborn, 1947.

Munro, Thomas, *Form and Style in the Arts*, Cleveland, Oh.: Press of Case Western Reserve University, 1970.

———, *The Interrelations of the Arts*, New York: Liberal Arts Press, 1949, Chap. 9.

Parker, DeWitt H., *The Analysis of Art*, New Haven, Conn.: Yale University Press, 1926, Chaps. 2–3.

Peckham, Morse, *Man's Rage for Chaos*, Philadelphia: Chilton, 1965 (antiformalist).

Pepper, Stephen C., *Aesthetic Quality*, New York: Scribner's, 1938, Chaps. 5–8.

———, *Principles of Art Appreciation*, New York: Harcourt Brace Jovanovich, 1949, Chaps. 3–5.

Podro, Michael, "Formal Elements and Theories of Modern Art," *BJA* 6 (1966).

Prall, D. W., *Aesthetic Judgment*, New York: Crowell, 1929, Chaps. 3–12.

Pratt, Carroll C., "The Form and Function of Music," in Monroe C. Beardsley and Herbert M. Schueller (eds.), *Aesthetic Inquiry*, Belmont, Calif.: Dickenson, 1967.

Ritchie, Benbow, "The Formal Structure of the Aesthetic Object," *JAAC* 3 (1944).

Santayana, George, *The Sense of Beauty*, New York: Scribner's, 1896, Part III.

Schaper, Eva, "Significant Form," *BJA* 1 (1961).

Schapiro, Meyer, "The Nature of Abstract Art," *Marxist Quarterly* 1 (1937).

Shahn, Ben, *The Shape of Content*, Cambridge, Mass.: Harvard University Press, 1957 (title essay).

Stechow, Wolfgang, "Problems of Structure

548   Bibliography

in Some Relations between the Visual Arts and Music," JAAC 11 (1953).

Stein, Erwin, Form and Performance, New York: Knopf, 1962.

Stokes, Adrian, "Form in Art: A Psychoanalytic Interpretation," JAAC 18 (1959).

Weitz, Morris, Philosophy of the Arts, Cambridge, Mass.: Harvard University Press, 1950, Chaps. 1–3.

Whyte, Lancelot Law (ed.), Aspects of Form: A Symposium on Form in Nature and Art, Bloomington: Indiana University Press, 1966.

Woolf, Virginia, Roger Fry: A Biography, New York: Harcourt Brace Jovanovich, 1940.

Style

Ackerman, James S., and Carpenter, Rhys, Art and Archeology, Englewood Cliffs, N.J.: Prentice-Hall, 1963.

Albrecht, Milton C., Barnett, James H., and Grieff, Mason (eds.), The Sociology of Art and Literature, New York: Praeger, 1970, Part I: "Forms and Styles."

Beardsley, Monroe C., and Schueller, Herbert M. (eds.), Aesthetic Inquiry, Belmont, Calif.: Dickenson, 1967 (essays on style by James S. Ackerman, Catherine Lord, Thomas Munro, William S. Newman, and Marvin Rosenberg).

Boas, George, "Historical Periods," JAAC 11 (1953).

Carpenter, Rhys, Greek Art: A Study of the Formal Evolution of Style, London: Oxford, 1963.

Cooper, Lane (ed.), Theories of Style, New York: Macmillan, 1907.

Frank, Paul L., "Historical or Stylistic Periods?" JAAC 13 (1955).

Friedrich, Carl J., "Style as the Principle of Historical Interpretation," JAAC 14 (1955).

Gombrich, E. H., Norm and Form: Studies in the Art of the Renaissance, New York: Phaidon, 1966.

Hauser, Arnold, The Philosophy of Art History, New York: Knopf, 1959, Chap. 4.

Kroeber, A. L., Style and Civilization, Berkeley: University of California Press, 1963.

Lucas, F. L., Style, New York: Macmillan, 1955.

Miles, Josephine, "Toward a Theory of Style and Change," JAAC 22 (1963).

Munro, Thomas, Evolution in the Arts, Cleveland: Press of Case Western Reserve University, 1965.

Murry, J. Middleton, The Problem of Style, New York: Oxford, 1922.

Sachs, Curt, The Commonwealth of Art:

Style in the Fine Arts, Music and the Dance, New York: Norton, 1946.

Virden, Phil, "The Social Determinants of Art Styles," BJA 12 (1972).

Zucker, Paul, Styles in Painting, New York: Viking, 1950, especially Chap. 1.

Also style is frequently discussed in the works of such art historians as Adama van Scheltema, Franz Boas, Dilthey, Dvorak, Coellen, Focillon, Löwy, Malraux, Nohl, Riegl, Semper, Sypher, Wölfflin, and Worringer.

Form and Function

Barton, J. E., Purpose and Admiration, New York: Stokes, 1933.

Brown, Theodore M., "Greenough, Paine, Emerson, and the Organic Aesthetic," JAAC 14 (1956).

Crone, Sylvia E., "The Aesthetics of Horatio Greenough," JAAC 24 (1966).

DeZurko, Edward, Origins of Functionalist Theory, New York: Columbia University Press, 1957.

Fry, Maxwell, Art in a Machine Age, New York: Barnes & Noble, 1969.

Giedion, Siegfried, Architecture, You and Me, Cambridge, Mass.: Harvard University Press, 1958.

———, Mechanization Takes Command, New York: Oxford, 1948.

———, Space, Time, and Architecture, Cambridge, Mass.: Harvard University Press, 1941.

Gill, Eric, Beauty Looks after Herself, New York: Sheed & Ward, 1933.

Greenough, Horatio, Form and Function, Berkeley: University of California Press, 1957.

Holme, Geoffrey, Industrial Design and the Future, London: Studio Publications, 1934.

Jeanneret-Gris, Charles Edouard [Le Corbusier], Towards a New Architecture, New York: Praeger, 1970.

Kuhns, Richard, "Art and Machine," JAAC 25 (1967).

Metzger, Charles R., Emerson and Greenough, Berkeley: University of California Press, 1954.

Moholy-Nagy, Lazlo, The New Vision, New York: Wittenborn, 1964.

Mumford, Lewis, Art and Technics, New York: Columbia University Press, 1952.

Nervi, Pier Luigi, Aesthetics and Technology in Building, Cambridge, Mass.: Harvard University Press, 1965.

Parker, DeWitt H., The Analysis of Art, New Haven, Conn.: Yale University Press, 1926, Chap. 5.

Pevsner, Nikolaus, *Pioneers of the Modern Movement: From William Morris to Walter Gropius*, rev. ed., Harmondsworth, Eng.: Penguin, 1960.

———, *The Sources of Modern Architecture and Design*, New York: Praeger, 1968.

Read, Herbert, *Art and Industry*, New York: Horizon Press, 1954.

Scott, Geoffrey, *The Architecture of Humanism*, London: Constable, 1924.

Torroja, Eduardo, *Philosophy of Structures*, Berkeley: University of California Press, 1965.

Veblen, Thorstein, *The Instinct of Workmanship and the State of the Industrial Arts*, New York: Macmillan, 1914.

Wind, Edgar, *Art and Anarchy*, New York: Random House, 1969, Chap. 5.

See also the discussion of form and function in the writings of such architects as Gropius, Le Corbusier, Neutra, and Frank Lloyd Wright.

CHAPTER 9: EXPRESSIVENESS

Aiken, Henry, "The Aesthetic Relevance of Belief," *JAAC* 9 (1951).

———, "Some Notes Concerning the Aesthetic and the Cognitive," *JAAC* 13 (1955).

Aldrich, Virgil, "Pictorial Meaning and Picture Thinking," *Kenyon Review* 5 (1943).

———, "Pictorial Meaning, Picture-Thinking, and Wittgenstein's Theory of Aspects," *Mind* 67 (1958).

Amyx, Clifford, "The Iconic Sign in Aesthetics," *Journal of Philosophy* 6 (1947).

Arnheim, Rudolf, *Art and Visual Perception*, Berkeley: University of California Press, 1954.

———, *Entropy and Art: A Study of Disorder and Order*, Berkeley: University of California Press, 1971.

———, *Visual Thinking*, Berkeley: University of California Press, 1969.

Barfield, Owen, *Poetic Diction: A Study in Meaning*, London: Faber, 1928.

Beardsley, Monroe C., *Aesthetics*, New York: Harcourt Brace Jovanovich, 1958, Chaps. 3, 5–9.

Bertocci, Peter A., "Susanne K. Langer's Theory of Feeling and Mind," *Review of Metaphysics* 23 (1970).

Blocker, Gene, "The Meaning of a Poem," *BJA* 10 (1970).

Boas, George, "The Problem of Meaning in the Arts," *University of California Publications in Philosophy* 25 (1950).

Bolam, David W., and Henderson, James L., *Art and Belief*, New York: Schocken, 1969.

Bousma, O. K., "The Expression Theory of Art," in Max Black (ed.), *Philosophical Analysis*, Ithaca, N.Y.: Cornell University Press, 1950.

Brooks, Cleanth, "What Does Poetry Communicate?," *The Well Wrought Urn*, New York: Harcourt Brace Jovanovich, 1949.

Burke, Kenneth, "Semantic and Poetic Meaning," *Southern Review* 4 (1939).

Carver, G. A., *Aesthetics and the Problem of Meaning*, New Haven, Conn.: Yale University Press, 1952.

Casey, Edward S., "Expression and Communication in Art," *JAAC* 29 (1971).

Cassirer, Ernst, *An Essay on Man*, New Haven, Conn.: Yale University Press, 1944, Chap. 9.

———, *Language and Myth*, New York: Dover, 1946.

———, *Philosophy of Symbolic Forms*, 3 vols., New Haven, Conn.: Yale University Press, 1953, 1955, 1957.

Church, Joseph, *Language and the Discovery of Reality*, New York: Random House, 1961.

Daiches, David, *The Place of Meaning in Poetry*, London: Oliver & Boyd, 1935.

Foss, L., "Art as Cognitive," *Philosophy of Science* 38 (1971).

Goodman, Nelson, *Fact, Fiction, and Forecast*, Indianapolis, Ind.: Bobbs-Merrill, 1965.

Greene, Theodore M., *The Arts and the Art of Criticism*, Princeton, N.J.: Princeton University Press, 1940, Parts III and IV.

Hansen, Forest, "Langer's Expressive Form: An Interpretation," *JAAC* 27 (1968).

Heidegger, Martin, "The Origin of the Work of Art," in Albert Hofstader and Richard Kuhns (eds.), *Philosophies of Art and Beauty*, New York: Modern Library, 1964 (on art and truth).

———, *Poetry, Language, Thought*, New York: Harper & Row, 1971.

Hermeren, G., *Representation and Meaning in the Visual Arts*, New York: Humanities Press, 1971.

Hofstader, Albert, *Agony and Epitaph: Man, His Art and His Poetry*, New York: Braziller, 1970.

———, *Truth and Art*, New York: Columbia University Press, 1965.

Hungerland, Isabel Creed, "Iconic Signs and Expressiveness," *JAAC* 3 (1944).

Isenberg, Arnold, "The Esthetic Function of Language," *J. Phil.* 46 (1949).

————, "Perception, Meaning, and the Subject Matter of Art," *J. Phil.* 41 (1944).

————, "The Problem of Belief," JAAC 13 (1955).

Jessup, Bertram, "Meaning Range in the Work of Art," JAAC 12 (1954).

Jung, Carl G., and others, *Man and His Symbols*, New York: Doubleday, 1968.

Kaplan, Abraham, "Referential Meaning in the Arts," JAAC 12 (1954).

Kepes, Gyorgy, *The New Landscape in Art and Science*, Chicago: University of Chicago Press, 1956.

Langer, Susanne K., "Abstraction in Art," JAAC 22 (1964).

————, *Feeling and Form*, New York: Scribner's, 1953.

————, *Mind: An Essay on Human Feeling*, Baltimore: Johns Hopkins Press, 1967, Vol. I, Chap. 7.

————, *Philosophic Sketches*, Baltimore: Johns Hopkins Press, 1962.

————, *Philosophy in a New Key*, Cambridge, Mass.: Harvard University Press, 1942.

————, *Problems of Art*, New York: Scribner's, 1957.

Lewis, C. Day, *The Poet's Way to Knowledge*, Cambridge: Cambridge, 1957.

Morris, Charles, "Esthetics and the Theory of Signs," *Journal of Unified Science (Erkenntnis)* 8 (1939).

————, "Science, Art and Technology," *Kenyon Review* 1 (1939).

————, *Signs, Language, and Behavior*, Englewood Cliffs, N.J.: Prentice-Hall, 1946.

Mothersill, Mary, "Is Art a Language?" *J. Phil.* 62 (1965).

Nagel, Ernest, "A Theory of Symbolic Form," in *Logic without Metaphysics*, New York: Free Press, 1956.

————, Review of Langer's *Philosophy in a New Key*, *J. Phil.* 40 (1943).

Nahm, Milton C., *Aesthetic Experience and Its Presuppositions*, New York: Harper & Row, 1946, Chaps. 10–14.

Natanson, Maurice, "The Fabric of Expression," *Review of Metaphysics* 21 (1968).

Panofsky, Erwin, *Idea: A Concept in Art Theory*, Columbia: University of South Carolina Press, 1968.

————, *Meaning in the Visual Arts*, New York: Doubleday, 1955.

————, *Studies in Iconology*, New York: Oxford, 1939.

Prall, D. W., *Aesthetic Judgment*, New York: Crowell, 1929, Chap. 11.

Price, Kingsley, "Is There Artistic Truth?" *J. Phil.* 46 (1949).

Progoff, Ira, *The Symbolic and the Real*, New York: Julian Press, 1963.

Raleigh, Henry P., "Art as Communicable Knowledge," *Journal of Aesthetic Education* 5 (1971).

Reid, Louis Arnaud, *Meaning in the Arts*, New York: Humanities Press, 1970.

Rieser, Max, "The Semantic Theory of Art in America," JAAC 15 (1956).

Roberts, Louise N., "Truth in Art," *Tulane Studies in Philosophy* 19 (1970).

Rudner, Richard, "On Semiotic Aesthetics," JAAC 10 (1951).

Rudner, Richard S., and Scheffler, Israel (eds.), *Logic and Art: Essays in Honor of Nelson Goodman*, Indianapolis, Ind.: Bobbs-Merrill, 1971.

Stein, George P., *The Ways of Meaning in the Arts*, New York: Humanities Press, 1970.

Stevenson, Charles L., "Symbolism in the Non-Representational Arts," in Paul Henle (ed.), *Language, Thought, and Culture*, Ann Arbor: University of Michigan Press, 1958.

Ushenko, Andrew P., "Metaphor," *Thought* 14 (1939).

Vivas, Eliseo, "Aesthetics and Theory of Signs," *Creation and Discovery*, New York: Noonday, 1955.

Wheelwright, Philip, *Burning Fountain: A Study in the Language of Symbolism*, Bloomington: University of Indiana Press, 1968.

Walsh, Dorothy, *Literature and Knowledge*, Middletown, Conn.: Wesleyan University Press, 1969.

Musical Expressiveness

Beardsley, Monroe C., *Aesthetics*, New York: Harcourt Brace Jovanovich, 1958, Chap. 7 (with bibliographical notes).

Chavez, Carlos, *Musical Thought*, Cambridge, Mass.: Harvard University Press, 1961.

Coker, Wilson, *Music and Meaning*, New York: Free Press, 1972 (with bibliography).

Epperson, Gordon, *The Musical Symbol*, Ames: Iowa State University Press, 1967.

Gurney, Edmund, *The Power of Sound*, London: Smith, Elder & Co., 1880.

Hanslick, Eduard, *The Beautiful in Music*, New York: Liberal Arts Press, 1957 (first published in 1854).

Hindemith, Paul, *A Composer's World*, Cambridge, Mass.: Harvard University Press, 1952.

Hospers, John, *Meaning and Truth in the Arts*, Chapel Hill: University of North Carolina Press, 1946 (discusses Sullivan versus Hanslick and Gurney).

Howard, V. A., "On Musical Expression," *BJA* 11 (1971).

Howes, F., *Music and Its Meanings*, London: Oxford, 1958.

Langer, Susanne K., *Feeling and Form*, New York: Scribner's, Chaps. 7–8.

——— (ed.), *Reflections on Art*, Baltimore: Johns Hopkins Press, 1958 (contains essays on music).

Meyer, Leonard, *Emotion and Meaning in Music*, Chicago: University of Chicago Press, 1956.

———, *Music, the Arts, and Ideas*, Chicago: University of Chicago Press, 1967.

Portnoy, Julius, *Music in the Life of Man*, New York: Holt, Rinehart and Winston, 1963.

———, *The Philosopher and Music*, New York: Humanities Press, 1954.

Pratt, Carroll, *The Meaning of Music*, New York: McGraw-Hill, 1931.

Schönberg, Arnold, *Style and Idea*, New York: Philosophical Library, 1950.

Sessions, Roger, *The Musical Experience of Composer, Performer, Listener*, Princeton, N.J.: Princeton University Press, 1950.

Stravinsky, Igor, *Poetics of Music*, New York: Random House, 1959.

Sullivan, J. W. N., *Beethoven: His Spiritual Development*, New York: Knopf, 1927.

Zuckerkandle, Victor, *The Sense of Music*, Princeton, N.J.: Princeton University Press, 1959.

———, *Sound and Symbol*, New York: Pantheon, 1956.

CHAPTER 10: THE EXPERIENCE OF THE BEHOLDER

Empathy and Abstraction

Ames, V. M., "On Empathy," *Psychological Review* 52 (1943).

Anstruther-Thompson, C., *Art and Man*, London: Lane, 1924.

Carritt, E. F., *The Theory of Beauty*, London: Methuen, 1928, Chap. 11.

Ducasse, C. J., *The Philosophy of Art*, 2d ed., New York: Dover, 1963, Chap. 10.

Hulme, T. E., "Modern Art and Its Philosophy," *Speculations*, New York: Humanities Press, 1954 (similar to Worringer).

Langfeld, Herbert, *The Aesthetic Attitude*, New York: Harcourt Brace Jovanovich, 1920.

Lee, Vernon, *The Beautiful*, Cambridge: Cambridge, 1913.

———, and Anstruther-Thompson, C., *Beauty and Ugliness*, London: Lane, 1912.

Lipps, Theodor, "Empathy and Aesthetic Pleasure," in Karl Aschenbrenner and Arnold Isenberg (eds.), *Aesthetic Theories*, Englewood Cliffs, N.J.: Prentice-Hall, 1965.

———, "Empathy, Inner Imitation, and Sense-Feelings," in Melvin Rader (ed.), *A Modern Book of Esthetics*, 3d ed., New York: Holt, Rinehart and Winston, 1960.

Listowel, Earl of, *Modern Aesthetics: An Historical Introduction*, London: G. Allen, 1967, Chap. 7.

Main, A. N., "A New Look at Empathy," *BJA* 9 (1969).

Nahm, Milton C., *Aesthetic Experience and Its Presuppositions*, New York: Harper & Row, 1946, Chap. 16.

Worringer, Wilhelm, *Abstraction and Empathy*, New York: International Universities, 1953.

———, *Form in Gothic*, New York: Putnam's, 1927.

Distance and Dehumanization

Beardsley, Monroe C., "Aesthetic Experience Regained," *JAAC* 28 (1969) (compare with Dickie).

Buber, Martin, "Distance and Relation," *The Knowledge of Man*, New York: Harper & Row, 1965.

———, *I and Thou*, 2d ed., New York: Scribner's, 1937.

Bullough, Edward, *Aesthetics*, Palo Alto, Calif.: Stanford University Press, 1957.

Budel, Oscar, "Contemporary Theater and Aesthetic Distance," *Publications of the Modern Language Association of America* 76 (1961).

Casebier, Allan, "The Concept of Psychical Distance," *Personalist* 52 (1971).

Chaudbury, P. J., "Psychical Distance in Indian Aesthetics," *JAAC* 7 (1948).

Clark, Kenneth, *The Nude: A Study in Ideal Form*, New York: Pantheon, 1956.

Fry, Roger, "Some Questions in Esthetics," *Transformations*, London: Chatto & Windus, 1926.

Jarrett, James L., "On Psychical Distance," *Personalist* 52 (1971).

Langfeld, Sydney, *The Aesthetic Attitude*, New York: Harcourt Brace Jovanovich, 1920 (includes a criticism of Bullough).

Longman, Lester D., "The Concept of Psychical Distance," *JAAC* 6 (1947).

Mehlis, Georg, "The Aesthetic Problem of Distance," in Susanne K. Langer (ed.), *Reflections on Art*, Baltimore: Johns Hopkins Press, 1958.

Michelis, P. A., "Aesthetic Distance and the Charm of Contemporary Art," JAAC 18 (1959).

Pepper, Stephen C., "Emotional Distance in Art," JAAC 4 (1946).

Ortega y Gasset, Jose, *The Dehumanization of Art*, Princeton, N.J.: Princeton University Press, 1948.

Weitz, Morris, *Philosophy of the Arts*, Cambridge, Mass.: Harvard University Press, 1950, Chap. 9.

Other Interpretations

Aldrich, Virgil C., "Art and the Human Form," JAAC 29 (1971).

———, "Back to Aesthetic Experience," JAAC 24 (1966).

———, "Education for Aesthetic Vision," *Journal of Aesthetic Education* 2 (1968).

———, *Philosophy of Art*, Englewood Cliffs, N.J.: Prentice-Hall, 1963, Chap. 1.

———, "Pictorial Meaning, Picture-Thinking, and Wittgenstein's Theory of Aspects," *Mind* 67 (1958).

Beardsley, Monroe C., "The Aesthetic Point of View," in Howard E. Kiefer and Milton K. Munitz (eds.), *Perspectives in Education, Religion, and the Arts*, Albany: State University of New York Press, 1972.

Bosanquet, Bernard, *Three Lectures on Aesthetics*, London: Macmillan, 1915, Lecture 3.

Brunius, Teddy, *Theory and Taste*, Uppsala, Sweden: Almquist and Wiksell, 1969.

Buermeyer, Laurence, *The Aesthetic Experience*, Merion, Pa.: Barnes Foundation, 1924.

Clammer, John, "Defining the Aesthetic Experience," BJA 10 (1970).

Cohen, Marshall, "Appearance and the Aesthetic Attitude," *J. Phil.* 56 (1959).

Dickie, George, *Aesthetics*, Indianapolis, Ind.: Bobbs-Merrill, 1971, Chap. 5.

———, "Is Psychology Relevant to Aesthetics?," *Phil. R.* 71 (1962).

———, "The Myth of the Aesthetic Attitude," *American Philosophical Quarterly* 1 (1964).

———, "Attitude and Object: Aldrich on the Aesthetic," JAAC 25 (1966).

Ducasse, Curt J., *The Philosophy of Art*, 2d ed., New York: Dover, 1963, Chaps. 9–12.

Duncan, Elmer H., "The Ideal Aesthetic

Observer: A Second Look," JAAC 29 (1970).

Durgnat, Raymond, "Art and Audience," BJA 10 (1970).

Findlay, J. A., "The Perspicuous and the Poignant," BJA 7 (1967).

Gombrich, E. H., *Art and Illusion*, 2d ed., New York: Pantheon, Part Three.

Hahn, Lewis E., *A Contextualistic Theory of Perception*, Berkeley: University of California Press, 1942.

Hospers, John, "The Ideal Aesthetic Observer," BJA 2 (1962).

Ingarden, Roman, "Aesthetic Experience and Aesthetic Object," *Phil. and Phen. Res.* 21 (1961).

Jarrett, James L., *The Quest for Beauty*, Englewood Cliffs, N.J.: Prentice-Hall, 1957, Chap. 7.

Kolnai, Aurel, "Aesthetic and Moral Experience," BJA 11 (1971).

Langfeld, H. S., *The Aesthetic Attitude*, New York: Harcourt Brace Jovanovich, 1920 (surveys a number of theories).

Nahm, Milton C., *Aesthetic Experience and Its Presuppositions*, New York: Harper & Row, 1946.

Osborne, Harold, *The Art of Appreciation*, New York: Oxford, 1970.

Pepper, Stephen C., *Principles of Art Appreciation*, New York: Harcourt Brace Jovanovich, 1949, Part I.

Sibley, Frank, "Aesthetics and the Looks of Things," *J. Phil.* 56 (1959).

Tomas, Vincent, "Aesthetic Vision," *Phil. R.* 68 (1959).

Urmson, J. O., and Pole, David, "Symposium: What Makes a Situation Aesthetic?," PAS, Supp. Vol. 31 (1957).

Vivas, Eliseo, "A Definition of the Aesthetic Experience," *J. Phil.* 34 (1937).

Vygotsky, Leo Semenovich, *The Psychology of Art*, Cambridge, Mass.: Massachusetts Institute of Technology Press, 1971, Chaps. 2, 9.

Wittgenstein, Ludwig, *Philosophical Investigations*, New York: Macmillan, 1952, pages 193–214 (statement of Wittgenstein's theory of "seeing as" and aspects —an important influence on contemporary esthetics).

CHAPTER 11: THE RESPONSE OF THE CRITIC

Is the Intention of the Artist Relevant to Interpretation and Criticism?

Aiken, Henry, "The Aesthetic Relevance of Artists' Intentions," *J. Phil.* 52 (1955).

Beardsley, Monroe C., *Aesthetics*, New

York: Harcourt Brace Jovanovich, 1958, pp. 17–29, 66–69.

Close, A. J., "Don Quixote and the Intentionalist Fallacy," BJA 12 (1972).

Eaton, Marcia M., "Art, Artifacts, and Intentions," *American Philosophical Quarterly* 6 (1969).

Eveling, H. S., "Composition and Criticism," in Marvin Levich (ed.), *Aesthetics and the Philosophy of Criticism*, New York: Random House, 1963.

Fiedler, Leslie A., "Archetype and Signature: A Study of the Relationship between Biography and Poetry," *Sewanee Review* 60 (1952).

Gang, T. M., "Intention," in Marvin Levich (ed.), *Aesthetics and the Philosophy of Criticism*, New York: Knopf, 1963.

Gendin, S., "The Artist's Intentions," JAAC 23 (1964).

Hirsch, E. D., *Validity in Interpretation*, New Haven, Conn.: Yale University Press, 1967.

Hungerland, Isabel C., "The Concept of Intention in Art Criticism," *J. Phil.* 52 (1955).

Kuh, Katherine, *The Artist's Voice*, New York: Harper & Row, 1963.

Kuhns, Richard C., "Criticism and the Problem of Intention," *J. Phil.* 57 (1960).

Morris-Jones, Huw, "The Relevance of the Artist's Intentions," BJA 4 (1964).

Pearce, Roy Harvey, "Pure Criticism and the History of Ideas," JAAC 7 (1948).

Panofsky, Erwin, "The History of Art as a Humanistic Discipline," in T. M. Greene (ed.), *The Meaning of the Humanities*, Princeton, N.J.: Princeton University Press, 1940.

Redpath, Theodore, "Some Problems of Modern Aesthetics," in C. A. Mace (ed.), *British Philosophy in Mid-Century*, London: G. Allen, 1957.

Roma, Emilio, "The Scope of the Intentional Fallacy," *Monist* 50 (1966).

Savile, Anthony, "The Place of Intention in the Concept of Art," PAS 69 (1968–1969).

Vivas, Eliseo, "Mr. Wimsatt on the Theory of Literature," *Comparative Literature* 7 (1955).

Wimsatt, W. K., and Beardsley, Monroe C., "The Intentional Fallacy," *Sewanee Review* 45 (1946) (often reprinted).

Wilson, John (ed.), *The Faith of an Artist*, London: G. Allen, 1962.

Reflections on the Avant-Garde

Berleant, Arnold, "Aesthetics and the Contemporary Arts," JAAC 29 (1970).

Ames, Van Meter, "Is It Art?," JAAC 30 (1971).

———, "The New in Art," in Konstantin Kolenda (ed.), *Insight and Vision*, San Antonio, Tex.: Trinity University Press, 1966.

Asenjo, F. G., "The Crises in Western Music and the Human Roots of Art," JAAC 29 (1971).

Bazin, Germain, *The Avant-Garde in Painting*, New York: Simon and Schuster, 1969.

Burnham, Jack, *Beyond Modern Sculpture*, New York: Braziller, 1968.

Cavell, Stanley, "Music Decomposed," *Must We Mean What We Say?*, New York: Scribner's, 1969.

Chiari, J., *Aesthetics of Modernism*, New York: Humanities Press, 1970.

Chipp, Herschel B. (ed.), *Theories of Modern Art: A Source Book by Artists and Critics*, Berkeley and Los Angeles: University of California Press, 1969.

Greenberg, Clement, *Art and Culture*, Boston: Beacon, 1965.

———, *Avant-Garde Attitudes*, New York: Wittenborn, 1969.

Harries, Karsten, *The Meaning of Modern Art*, Evanston, Ill.: Northwestern University Press, 1968.

Jessup, Bertram, "Crisis in the Fine Arts Today," JAAC 29 (1970).

Johanson, John M., "The Avant-Garde in Architecture Today," *Arts and Society* 3 (1965).

Johnson, Russell I., "A View of Twentieth Century Expression," JAAC 28 (1970).

Kahler, Erich, *The Disintegration of Form in the Arts*, New York: Braziller, 1968.

Kaprow, Allan, *Assemblage, Environments and Happenings*, New York: Abrams, 1966.

Kepes, Gyorgy, *The New Landscape in Art and Science*, Chicago: Theobald, 1956.

Kirby, Michael, *The Art of Time: Essays on the Avant-Garde*, New York: Dutton, 1969.

McMullen, Roy, *Art, Affluence, and Alienation: The Fine Arts Today*, New York: Praeger, 1968.

Neumeyer, Alfred, *The Search for Meaning in Modern Art*, Englewood Cliffs, N.J.: Prentice-Hall, 1964.

Poggioli, R., *Theory of the Avant-Garde*, Cambridge, Mass.: Harvard University Press, 1968.

Reichardt, Jasia (ed.), *Cybernetic Serendipity: The Computer and the Arts*, New York: Praeger, 1968.

Roose-Evans, James, *Experimental Theatre*

from Stanislavsky to Today, New York: Universe Books, 1970.

Rosenberg, Harold, *The Re-Definition of Art*, New York: Horizon Press, 1972.

Rosenberg, Bernard, and Fliegel, Morris, *The Vanguard Artist*, Chicago: Quadrangle Books, 1965.

Sitney, P. Adams (ed.), *Film Culture Reader*, New York: Praeger, 1970.

Sontag, Susan, *Against Interpretation and Other Essays*, New York: Farrar, Straus, 1966.

Thomson, Virgil, *American Music since 1910*, New York: Holt, Rinehart and Winston, 1970.

Tomkins, Calvin, *The Bride and the Bachelors: The Heretical Courtship in Modern Art*, New York: Viking, 1965.

Yates, Peter, *Twentieth Century Music*, New York: Pantheon, 1967, Part II.

Youngblood, Gene, *Expanded Cinema*, New York: Dutton, 1970.

Zucker, Wolfgang M., "The Artist as Rebel," JAAC 27 (1969).

Critical Methods and Standards

Abercrombie, Lascelles, *The Principles of Literary Criticism*, London: Gollancz, 1932.

———, *The Theory of Poetry*, New York: Harcourt Brace Jovanovich, 1926.

Alexander, Samuel, "Beauty and Greatness in Art," PAS 30 (1929–1930).

Arnheim, Rudolf, "What Is a Critic?," *Saturday Review* 48 (1965).

Bartlett, Ethel M., *Types of Aesthetic Judgment*, London: G. Allen, 1937.

Beardsley, Monroe C., *Aesthetics*, New York: Harcourt Brace Jovanovich, 1958, Chaps. 1–2, 10–12.

———, "The Discrimination of Aesthetic Enjoyment," BJA 3 (1963).

———, "The Classification of Critical Reasons," *Journal of Aesthetic Education* 2 (1968).

———, "Modes of Interpretation," *Journal of the History of Ideas* 32 (1971).

———, *The Possibility of Criticism*, Detroit, Mich.: Wayne State University Press, 1970.

Blackmur, R. P., and others, *Lectures in Criticism*, New York: Pantheon, 1949.

Boas, George, *The Heaven of Invention*, Baltimore: Johns Hopkins Press, 1963.

———, *A Primer for Critics*, Baltimore: Johns Hopkins Press, 1937.

———, *Wingless Pegasus*, Baltimore: Johns Hopkins Press, 1950.

Cargill, Oscar, *Toward a Pluralistic Criti-cism*, Carbondale, Ill.: University of Southern Illinois Press, 1965.

Cavell, Marcia, "Critical Dialogue," *J. Phil.* 67 (1970).

Child, Arthur, "The Social-Historical Relativity of Esthetic Value," *Phil. R.* 53 (1944).

Church, Ralph, *An Essay on Critical Appreciation*, Ithaca, N.Y.: Cornell University Press, 1938.

Cornford, C. F., "The Question of Bad Taste," BJA 8 (1968).

Crawford, Donald W., "Causes, Reasons and Aesthetic Objectivity," *American Philosophical Quarterly* 8 (1971).

Dewey, John, *Art as Experience*, New York: Minton, Balch & Co., 1934, Chap. 13.

Ducasse, Curt J., *Art, the Critics, and You*, New York: Piest, 1944.

———, *The Philosophy of Art*, 2d ed., New York: Dover, 1929, Chap. 15.

Duncan, Elmer H., "Stephen C. Pepper: A Bibliography," JAAC 28 (1970).

Eliot, T. S., *Selected Essays*, rev. ed., New York: Harcourt Brace Jovanovich, 1950 (a sampling of his many essays on criticism).

Elton, Oliver, *The Nature of Literary Criticism*, Manchester: Manchester University Press, 1935.

French, R. F. (ed.), *Music and Criticism*, Cambridge, Mass.: Harvard University Press, 1948.

Frye, Northrop, *Anatomy of Criticism*, Princeton, N.J.: Princeton University Press, 1957.

———, *The Stubborn Structure: Essays on Criticism and Society*, Ithaca, N.Y.: Cornell University Press, 1970.

Gotshalk, D. W., *Art and the Social Order*, rev. ed., New York: Dover, 1962, Chap. 8.

Grabo, Carl, *The Creative Critic*, Chicago: University of Chicago Press, 1948.

Greene, Theodore M., *The Arts and the Art of Criticism*, Princeton, N.J.: Princeton University Press, 1940.

Heyl, Bernard C., *New Bearings in Esthetics and Art Criticism*, New Haven, Conn.: Yale University Press, 1943.

———, "Relativism Again," JAAC 5 (1946).

Hook, Sydney (ed.), *Art and Philosophy*, New York: New York University Press, 1966 (contains several essays on criticism).

Jessup, Bertram, "Taste and Judgment in Aesthetic Experience," JAAC 19 (1960).

———, "What Is Great Art?," BJA 2 (1962).

———, and Rader, Melvin, *Art and Human Values*, New York: Appleton-Century-Crofts, forthcoming, Chap. 6.

Kaplan, Abraham, "On the So-Called Crisis in Criticism," JAAC 8 (1948).

Krieger, Murray, *The Play and Place of Criticism*, Baltimore: Johns Hopkins Press, 1967.

Levich, Marvin (ed.), *Aesthetics and the Philosophy of Criticism*, New York: Random House, 1963.

Lewis, C. I., *An Analysis of Knowledge and Valuation*, LaSalle, Ill.: Open Court, 1946.

Margolis, Joseph, *The Language of Art and Art Criticism*, Detroit, Mich.: Wayne University Press, 1965.

————, "The Logic of Interpretation," *Philosophy Looks at the Arts*, New York: Scribner's, 1962.

————, "Proposals on the Logic of Aesthetic Judgments," *Philosophical Quarterly* 9 (1959).

Morawski, Stefan, "On the Objectivity of Aesthetic Judgement," BJA 6 (1966).

Morris, Bertram, "The Philosophy of Criticism," *Phil. R.* 55 (1946).

Mothersill, Mary, "Critical Reasons," *Philosophical Quarterly* 2 (1961).

Nahm, Milton C., *The Artist as Creator*, Baltimore: Johns Hopkins Press, 1956, Book II.

Osborne, Harold, *Aesthetics and Criticism*, London: Routledge, 1955.

————, "Taste and Judgment in the Arts," *Journal of Aesthetic Education* 5 (1971).

Pepper, Stephen C., "Autobiography of an Aesthetic," JAAC 28 (1970).

————, *The Basis of Criticism in the Arts*, Cambridge, Mass.: Harvard University Press, 1945.

————, *Concept and Quality*, LaSalle, Ill.: Open Court, 1967.

————, "Is Non-Objective Art Superficial?," JAAC 11 (1953).

————, *Principles of Art Appreciation*, New York: Harcourt Brace Jovanovich, 1949.

————, *The Work of Art*, Bloomington: University of Indiana Press, 1955, Chaps. 2–3, 5.

Pleydell-Pearce, A. G., "Objectivity and Value in Judgments of Aesthetics," BJA 10 (1970).

Pottle, Frederick A., "The New Critics and the Historical Method," *Yale Review* 43 (1954–1955).

Pratt, Carroll C., "The Stability of Aesthetic Judgments," JAAC 15 (1956).

Ransom, John Crowe, *The New Criticism*, New York: New Directions, 1941.

Read, Herbert, *Coleridge as Critic*, London: Faber, 1949.

Rice, Philip Blair, *The Knowledge of Good and Evil*, New York: Random House, 1955, Chap. 12.

Richards, I. A., *Practical Criticism*, New York: Harcourt Brace Jovanovich, 1929.

————, *Principles of Literary Criticism*, New York: Harcourt Brace Jovanovich, 1926.

Schorer, Mark, and others, *Criticism*, New York: Harcourt Brace Jovanovich, 1948.

Scriven, Michael, "The Objectivity of Aesthetic Evaluation," *Monist* 50 (1966).

Slote, M. A., "Rationality of Aesthetic Value Judgments," *J. Phil.* 68 (1971).

Sparshott, F. E., *The Concept of Criticism*, New York: Oxford, 1967.

Stevenson, Charles L., "Interpretation and Evaluation in Aesthetics," in Max Black (ed.), *Philosophical Analysis*, Ithaca, N.Y.: Cornell University Press, 1950.

Strawson, P. F., "Aesthetic Appraisal and Works of Art," *Oxford Review* 1 (1966).

Talmor, Sascha, "The Aesthetic Judgment and Its Criteria of Value," *Mind* 78 (1969).

Walton, Kendall L., "Categories of Art," *Phil. R.* 79 (1970).

Weitz, Morris, "Criticism without Evaluation," *Phil. R.* 61 (1952).

————, *The Philosophy of the Arts*, Cambridge, Mass.: Harvard University Press, 1950, Chap. 9.

————, "Reasons in Criticism," JAAC 15 (1956).

Wellek, Rene, *Concepts of Criticism*, New Haven, Conn.: Yale University Press, 1963.

————, and Austin, Warren, *The Theory of Literature*, New York: Harcourt Brace Jovanovich, 1949.

West, Ray B. (ed.), *Essays in Modern Literary Criticism*, New York: Holt, Rinehart and Winston, 1952.

Wimsatt, W. K., *The Verbal Icon*, Lexington: University of Kentucky Press, 1954.

————, and Beardsley, Monroe C., "The Affective Fallacy," *Sewanee Review* 57 (1948).

Ziff, Paul, "Reasons in Art Criticism," in I. Scheffler (ed.), *Philosophy and Education*, Boston: Allyn and Bacon, 1958.

CHAPTER 12: THE RESPONSE OF THE COMMUNITY

Esthetic Play and Human Freedom

Ducasse, Curt J., *The Philosophy of Art*, 2d ed., New York: Dover, 1963, Chap. 7.

Garland, H. B., *Schiller*, London: Harrap, 1949.

Groos, Karl, *The Play of Animals*, New York: Appleton-Century-Crofts, 1898.

———, *The Play of Man*, New York: Appleton-Century-Crofts, 1901.

Grossman, W., "The Idea of Cultural Evolution in Schiller's *Aesthetic Education*," *Germanic Review* 34 (1959).

Hein, Hilde, "Play as an Aesthetic Concept," *JAAC* 27 (1968).

Huizinga, J., *Homo Ludens: A Study of the Play Element in Culture*, London: Routledge, 1949.

Kerry, S. S., *Schiller's Writings on Aesthetics*, Manchester: Manchester University Press, 1961.

Lange, Konrad, "Illusion in Play and Art," in Melvin Rader (ed.), *A Modern Book of Esthetics*, 3d ed., New York: Holt, Rinehart and Winston, 1960.

Lowenfeld, Margaret, *Play in Childhood*, London: Gollancz, 1935.

Marcuse, Herbert, *Eros and Civilization*, New York: Random House, 1962, Chap. 9.

Miller, R. D., *Schiller and the Ideal of Freedom*, 2d ed., New York: Oxford, 1970.

Nahm, Milton C., *Aesthetic Experience and Its Presuppositions*, New York: Harper & Row, 1946, Chap. 7.

Parker, DeWitt H., *Human Values*, New York: Harper & Row, 1931, Chap. 14.

Piaget, Jean, *Play, Dreams, and Imagination in Childhood*, New York: Norton, 1951.

Rau, Catherine, "Psychological Notes on the Play Theory of Art," *JAAC* 8 (1950).

Read, Herbert, *Education through Art*, 3d rev. ed., New York: Pantheon, 1958.

———, "The Education of Free Men," *Education for Peace*, New York: Scribner's, 1949.

Snell, Reginald, "Introduction" to his translation of Schiller, *On The Aesthetic Education of Man*, New Haven, Conn.: Yale University Press, 1954.

Schiller, Friedrich, *On the Aesthetic Education of Man in a Series of Letters*, ed. and trans. with an Introduction, Commentary, and Glossary of Terms by Elizabeth M. Wilkinson and L. A. Willoughby, Oxford: Clarendon Press, 1967 (the best translation and commentary).

Ecology and Environmental Design

"The Arts and the Human Environment," Conference, *Arts in Society* 8 (1971) (entire issue for Summer/Fall).

Banham, Reyner, *The Architecture of the Well-Tempered Environment*, Chicago: University of Chicago Press, 1969.

Basch, David, "The Uses of Aesthetics in Planning," *Journal of Aesthetic Education* 6 (1972).

Braden, William, *The Age of Aquarius: Technology and the Cultural Revolution*, Chicago: Quadrangle, 1970.

Disch, Robert (ed.), *The Ecological Conscience*, Englewood Cliffs, N.J.: Prentice-Hall, 1970.

Doxiadis, Constantine, *Architecture in Transition*, New York: Hutchinson, 1963.

Eldredge, H. Wentworth (ed.), *Taming Megalopolis*, 2 vols., New York: Doubleday, 1967.

Gropius, Walter, *Scope of Total Architecture*, New York: Harper & Row, 1955.

Gruen, Victor, *The Heart of Our Cities: The Urban Crisis, Diagnosis and Cure*, New York: Simon and Schuster, 1965.

Gutkind, E. A., *The Twilight of Cities*, New York: Free Press, 1962.

Herber, Lewis, *Crisis in Our Cities*, Englewood Cliffs, N.J.: Prentice-Hall, 1966.

Holland, Laurence B. (ed.), *Who Designs America?*, New York: Doubleday, 1966.

Howard, Ebenezer, *Garden Cities of Tomorrow*, Cambridge, Mass.: Massachusetts Institute of Technology Press, 1946 (with editorial preface by F. J. Osborn and Introduction by Lewis Mumford).

Jessup, Bertram, and Rader, Melvin, *Art and Human Values*, New York: Appleton-Century-Crofts, forthcoming, Chap. 11.

Mayfadyen, Dugald, *Sir Ebenezer Howard and the Town Planning Movement*, Cambridge, Mass.: Massachusetts Institute of Technology Press, 1971.

Mayer, Albert, *The Urgent Future*, New York: McGraw-Hill, 1967.

Mumford, Lewis, *The Culture of Cities*, New York: Harcourt Brace Jovanovich, 1938.

———, *The City in History*, New York: Harcourt Brace Jovanovich, 1961.

Nairn, Ian, *The American Landscape: A Critical View*, New York: Random House, 1968.

Nelson, George, *The Synthetic Garden*, Boston: Little, Brown, 1972 (on technology and industrial design).

Neutra, Richard, *Survival through Design*, New York: Oxford, 1954.

Osborn, Frederic J., and Wittick, Arnold, *The New Towns: The Answer to Megalopolis*, 2d ed., London: Leonard Hill, 1969.

President's Council on Recreation and

Natural Beauty, *From Sea to Shining Sea*, Washington, D.C.: United States Government Printing Office, 1968 (contains comprehensive bibliography).

Ransom, Harry S. (ed.), *The People's Architects*, Chicago: U. of Chicago Press, 1964.

Reps, John W., *The Making of Urban America: A History of City Planning in the United States*, Princeton, N.J.: Princeton University Press, 1965.

Rose, J. (ed.), *Technological Injury: The Effect of Technological Advances on Environment, Life and Society*, New York: Gordon and Breach Science Publishers, 1969.

Schneider, Kenneth R., *Destiny of Change: How Relevant Is Man in the Age of Development?*, New York: Holt, Rinehart and Winston, 1968.

Schnore, Leo F., *The Urban Scene: Human Ecology and Demography*, New York: Free Press, 1965.

Schwartz, William (ed.), *Voices for the Wilderness*, New York: Ballantine, 1969.

Scully, Vincent, *American Architecture and Urbanism*, New York: Praeger, 1969.

Shepard, Paul, and McKinley, Daniel (eds.), *The Subversive Science: Essays toward an Ecology of Man*, Boston: Houghton Mifflin, 1968.

Smith, Ralph A., and Smith, C. M., "Aesthetics and Environmental Education," *Journal of Aesthetic Education* 4 (1970).

Smith, Ralph A., "Spaceship Earth and Aesthetic Education," *Journal of Aesthetic Education* 4 (1970).

Stein, Clarence, *Toward New Towns for America*, Cambridge, Mass.: Massachusetts Institute of Technology Press, 1966.

Wagner, Richard H., *Environment and Man*, New York: Norton, 1971.

Whyte, William H., *The Last Landscape*, New York: Doubleday, 1968.

Art and the Social Order

Albrecht, Milton C., Barnett, James H., and Grieff, Mason (eds.), *The Sociology of Art and Literature*, New York: Praeger, 1970.

Battock, G., *Marcuse and Anti-Art*, New York: Dutton, 1971.

Baxandall, Lee, *Marxism and Aesthetics: A Selected Annotated Bibliography*, New York: Humanities Press, 1969.

——— (ed.), *Radical Perspectives in the Arts*, Baltimore: Penguin, 1972.

Beker, Miroslav, "Marxism and the Determinants of Critical Judgment," *JAAC* 29 (1970).

Bell, Daniel, *The Divided Society: On the Disjunction of Culture and Social Structure*, New York: Basic Books, 1972.

———, and others, "On the Third Domain —Culture 'versus' Society," *Journal of Aesthetic Education* 6 (1972) (special double issue).

Brownell, Baker, *The Human Community*, New York: Harper & Row, 1950, Part X.

Caudwell, Christopher, *English Literature: A Marxist Interpretation*, Princeton, N.J.: Princeton University Press, 1971.

———, *Further Studies in a Dying Culture*, London: Bodley Head, 1949.

———, *Illusion and Reality*, New York: International Publishers, 1948.

Chipp, Herschel B. (ed.), *Theories of Modern Art*, Berkeley: University of California Press, 1969, Part VIII: "Art and Politics."

Collingwood, R. G., *The Principles of Art*, Oxford: Clarendon Press, 1938, Chap. 14.

Comfort, Alex, *Art and Social Responsibility*, London: Falcon Press, 1946.

Eells, Richard, *The Corporations and the Arts*, New York: Macmillan, 1967.

Finkelstein, Sidney, *Art and Society*, New York: International Publishers, 1947.

Fischer, Ernst, *Art against Ideology*, London: Allen Lane, 1969.

———, *The Necessity of Art: A Marxist Approach*, Baltimore: Penguin, 1964.

Giedion, Siegfried, *Mechanization Takes Command*, New York: Oxford, 1948.

———, *Space, Time, and Architecture*, Cambridge, Mass.: Harvard University Press, 1941.

Goldmann, Lucien, "Criticism and Dogmatism in Literature," in David Cooper (ed.), *To Free a Generation*, New York: Macmillan, 1969.

———, *The Human Sciences and Philosophy*, London: J. Cape, 1969.

Gotshalk, D. W., *Art and the Social Order*, 2d ed., New York: Dover, 1962, Chaps. 9–10.

Harap, Louis, *Social Roots of the Arts*, New York: International Publishers, 1949.

Hauser, Arnold, *The Social History of Art*, 2 vols., London: Routledge, 1962.

Howe, Irving, *Politics and the Novel*, New York: Horizon Press, 1957.

Jameson, Fredric, *Marxism and Form*, Princeton, N.J.: Princeton University Press, 1972.

Jessup, Bertram, and Rader, Melvin, *Art and Human Values*, New York: Appleton-Century-Crofts, forthcoming, Chaps. 8–9, 11–13.

Kallen, Horace M., *Art and Freedom*, 2

vols., New York: Duell, Sloan & Pierce-Meredith Press, 1942.

Kavolis, Vytautas, *Artistic Expression: A Sociological Analysis*, Ithaca, N.Y.: Cornell University Press, 1968.

Kuhns, Richard, "Art and Machine," JAAC 25 (1967).

Lang, Berel, and Williams, Forrest (eds.), *Marxism and Art*, New York: McKay, 1972.

Lehmann-Haupt, Helmut, *Art under a Dictatorship*, New York: Oxford, 1954.

Lifshitz, Mikhail, *The Philosophy of Art of Karl Marx*, New York: Critics Group, 1938.

Lukacs, George, *The Historical Novel*, New York: Beacon, 1962.

———, *History and Class Consciousness*, Cambridge, Mass.: Massachusetts Institute of Technology Press, 1971 (the discussion of "reification" is basic for understanding Lukacs' esthetics).

———, *The Meaning of Contemporary Realism*, London: Merlin Press, 1963.

———, *Studies in European Realism*, New York: Grosset & Dunlap, 1964.

———, *Writer and Critic*, London: Merlin Press, 1970.

Marcuse, Herbert, "Art as a Form of Reality," in Edward F. Fry (ed.), *On the Future of Art*, New York: Viking, 1970.

———, *Counterrevolution and Revolt*, Boston: Beacon, 1972.

———, "The New Sensibility," *An Essay on Liberation*, Boston: Beacon, 1969.

———, *One Dimensional Man*, Boston: Beacon, 1964.

———, "Remarks on a Redefinition of Culture," *Daedalus* 94 (1965).

———, *Soviet Marxism*, New York: Columbia University Press, 1958 (includes critique of Soviet art and aesthetics).

Marx, Karl, *Economic and Philosophical Manuscripts*, in T. B. Bottomore (trans. and ed.), Karl Marx, *Early Writings*, London: Watts, 1963.

———, and Engels, Friedrich, *Literature and Art*, New York: International Publishers, 1947.

McMullen, Roy, *Art, Affluence, and Alienation*, New York: Praeger, 1968.

Meszaros, Istvan (ed.), *Aspects of History and Class Consciousness*, London: Routledge, 1971, Chaps. 7–9.

———, *Marx's Theory of Alienation*, London: Merlin Press, 1970, Chap. 7.

Morawski, Stefan, "The Aesthetic Views of Marx and Engels," JAAC 28 (1970).

———, "Three Functions of Art," *Arts in Society* 8 (1971).

Morris, William, *Selected Writings* (ed. by Asa Briggs), Baltimore: Penguin, 1962.

Mumford, Lewis, *Art and Technics*, New York: Columbia University Press, 1952.

———, *The Myth of the Machine*, New York: Harcourt Brace Jovanovich, Vol. 1, 1967; Vol. 2, 1970.

Parkinson, G. H. R. (ed.), *George Lukacs: The Man, His Work and His Ideas*, New York: Random House, 1970 (largely devoted to Lukacs aesthetics).

Pevsner, Nikolaus, *Pioneers of the Modern Movement: From William Morris to Walter Gropius*, rev. ed., Harmondsworth, Eng.: Penguin, 1968.

Pieper, J., *Leisure: The Basis of Culture*, New York: Pantheon, 1964.

Plekanov, George V., *Art and Social Life*, London: Lawrence and Wishard, 1953.

———, *Unaddressed Letters—Art and Social Life*, Moscow: Foreign Languages Publishing House, 1957.

Rader, Melvin, "The Artist as Outsider," JAAC 16 (1958).

———, "Marx's Interpretation of Art and Aesthetic Value," BJA 7 (1967).

Raphael, Max, *The Demands of Art*, Princeton, N.J.: Princeton University Press, 1968.

Read, Herbert, *Art and Alienation: The Role of the Artist in Society*, London: Thames and Hudson, 1967.

———, *Art and Industry*, New York: Horizon Press, 1954.

———, *Art and Society*, London: Faber, 1967.

———, *The Grass Roots of Art*, New York: Wittenborn, 1947.

———, *The Politics of the Unpolitical*, London: Routledge, 1943.

———, *The Redemption of the Robot*, New York: Trident Press, 1966.

Ruskin, John, *The Political Economy of Art*, London: Wiley, 1885.

Sewter, A. C., "The Possibilities of a Sociology of Art," *Sociological Review* 27 (1935).

Schucking, Levin, *The Sociology of Literary Taste*, 3d ed., Chicago: University of Chicago Press, 1966.

Simmel, George, *The Conflict in Modern Culture*, New York: Teachers College Press, 1968.

Smith, Hubert Llewelyn, *The Economic Laws of Art Production*, Oxford: Humphrey Milford, 1925.

Smith, Ralph A. (ed.), *Aesthetic Concepts and Education*, Urbana: University of Illinois Press, 1970.

Snell, B., *Poetry and Society*, Bloomington: Indiana University Press, 1961.

Sparshott, F. E., "Art and Society," *The Structure of Aesthetics*, Toronto: University of Toronto Press, 1963.

Trotsky, Leon, "Art and Politics," *Partizan Review* 5 (1938).

———, *Literature and Revolution*, New York: Russell and Russell, 1957.

Truitt, Willis H., "Towards an Empirical Theory of Art: A Retrospective Comment on Max Raphael's Contribution to Marxian Aesthetics," BJA 11 (1971).

———, "A Marxist Theory of Aesthetic Inquiry: The Contribution of Max Raphael," *Journal of Aesthetic Education* 5 (1971).

Wilson, Robert N., *The Arts in Society*, Englewood Cliffs, N.J.: Prentice-Hall, 1964.

——— (ed.), *The Recruitment of the Artist in Society*, Englewood Cliffs, N.J.: Prentice-Hall, 1964.

POSTSCRIPT: ESTHETIC THEORY

On the Problem of Defining Art

Beardsley, Monroe C., "The Definition of the Arts," JAAC 20 (1961).

Bywater, William G., "Who's in the Warehouse Now?," JAAC 30 (1972).

Danto, Arthur, "The Artworld," *J. Phil.* 61 (1964).

Dickie, George, "Art Narrowly and Broadly Speaking," *American Philosophical Quarterly* 5 (1968).

———, "Defining Art," *American Philosophical Quarterly* 5 (1968).

Gallie, W. B., "Art as an Essentially Contested Concept," *Philosophical Quarterly* 6 (1956).

Khatchadourian, Haig, *The Concept of Art*, New York: New York University Press, 1971.

Kahler, Erich, "What Is Art?," *Out of the Labyrinth*, New York: Braziller, 1967 (reply to Weitz).

Kennick, W. E., "Does Traditional Aesthetics Rest on a Mistake?," *Mind* 67 (1958).

Lake, Beryl, "A Study of the Irrefutability of Two Aesthetic Theories," in W. Elton (ed.), *Aesthetics and Language*, Oxford: Blackwell, 1954.

Margolis, Joseph, "Mr. Weitz and the Definition of Art," *Philosophical Studies* 9 (1958).

Mothersill, Mary, "Critical Comments, On the Arts and the Definitions of Arts," JAAC 20 (1961).

Sclafani, Richard, " 'Art,' Wittgenstein, and Open-Textured Concepts," JAAC 29 (1971.)

Sibley, Frank, "Aesthetic and Nonaesthetic," *Phil. R.* 74 (1965).

Tatarkiewcz, Wladyslaw, "What Is Art? The Problem of Definition Today," BJA 11 (1971).

Thurston, Carl, "Major Hazards in Defining Art," *J. Phil.* 44 (1947).

Zerby, Lewis K., "A Reconsideration of the Role of Theory in Aesthetics—A Reply to Morris Weitz," JAAC 16 (1957).

What Is a "Work of Art"?

Bachrach, Jay E., "Type and Token and the Identification of the Work of Art," *Phil. and Phen. Res.* 31 (1971).

Creegan, R. F., "The Significance of Locating the Art Object," *Phil. and Phen. Res.* 13 (1953).

Dufrenne, Mikel, "The Aesthetic Object and the Technical Object," JAAC 23 (1964).

Gilson, Etienne, *Painting and Reality*, New York: Pantheon, 1957, pp. 35–50.

Henze, Donald F., "Is the Work of Art a Construct?," *Journal of Philosophy* 52 (1955).

———, "The Work of Art," *J. Phil.* 54 (1957).

Khatchadourian, Haig, "Family Resemblances and the Classification of Works of Art," JAAC 28 (1969).

Ingarden, Roman, "Aesthetic Experience and Aesthetic Object," *Phil. and Phen. Res.* 21 (1961).

Jenkins, Iredell, "The Aesthetic Object," *Review of Metaphysics* 11 (1957).

MacDonald, Margaret, "Art and Imagination," PAS 53 (1953).

Margolis, Joseph, "The Identity of a Work of Art," *Mind* 67 (1959).

———, "On Disputes about the Ontological Status of Works of Art," BJA 8 (1968).

Natanson, Maurice, "Toward a Phenomenology of the Aesthetic Object," *Literature, Philosophy and the Social Sciences*, The Hague: Martinus Nijhoff, 1962.

Peltz, Richard, "Ontology and the Work of Art," JAAC 24 (1966).

Pepper, Stephen C., "Further Considerations on the Aesthetic Work of Art," *J. Phil.* 49 (1952).

———, "Supplementary Essay," *The Basis of Criticism in the Arts*, Cambridge, Mass.: Harvard University Press, 1949.

———, *The Work of Art*, Bloomington: University of Indiana Press, 1955.

Price, Kingsley, "Is a Work of Art a Symbol?," *J. Phil.* 50 (1953).

Rudner, Richard, "The Ontological Status of the Aesthetic Object," *Phil. and Phen. Res.* 10 (1950).

Sartre, Jean-Paul, "Conclusion," *The Psychology of Imagination*, New York: Philosophical Library, 1948.

Saw, Ruth, "What Is 'A Work of Art'?," *Philosophy* 36 (1961).

Stevenson, Charles L., "On 'What Is a Poem'?," *Phil. R.* 66 (1957).

Ushenko, Andrew P., *Dynamics of Art*, Bloomington: University of Indiana Press, 1953, pp. 18–25, 42–51.

Wellek, Rene, and Warren, Austin, *The Theory of Literature*, New York: Harcourt Brace Jovanovich, 1949, Chap. 12.

Zemach, Eddy M., "The Ontological Status of Art Objects," *JAAC* 25 (1966).

Zimmerman, Robert L., "Can Anything Be an Aesthetic Object?," *JAAC* 25 (1966).

Ziff, Paul, "Art and the 'Object of Art'," in William Elton (ed.), *Aesthetics and Language*, Oxford: Blackwell, 1954.

———, "The Task of Defining a Work of Art," *Phil. R.* 62 (1953).

Method in Aesthetics

Abrams, M. H., "What's the Use of Theorizing about the Arts?," in Morton W. Bloomfield (ed.), *In Search of Literary Theory*, Ithaca, N.Y.: Cornell University Press, 1972.

Barrett, C., and others, "Symposium: Wittgenstein and Problems of Objectivity in Aesthetics," *BJA* 7 (1967).

Brunius, Teddy, "The Uses of Works of Art," *JAAC* 22 (1963).

Coleman, Francis, "A Critical Examination of Wittgenstein's Aesthetics," *American Philosophical Quarterly* 5 (1968).

Danto, Arthur, "The Artworld," *J. Phil.* 61 (1964).

Elton, William (ed.), *Aesthetics and Language*, Oxford: Blackwell, 1954.

Hungerland, Isabel C., "The Logic of Aesthetic Concepts," *Proceedings and Addresses of the American Philosophical Association, 1962–1963*.

Jessup, Bertram, "Analytical Philosophy and Aesthetics," *BJA* 3 (1963).

———, and Rader, Melvin, *Art and Human Values*, New York: Appleton-Century-Crofts, forthcoming, Chap. 1.

Kadish, Mortimer, *Reason and Controversy in the Arts*, Cleveland, Oh.: Press of Case Western Reserve University, 1968.

Kennick, William E., "Theories of Art and the Artworld," *J. Phil.* 61 (1964).

Meager, Ruby, "Aesthetic Concepts," *BJA* 10 (1970).

Peltz, Richard, "Classification and Evaluation in Aesthetics: Weitz and Aristotle," *JAAC* 30 (1971).

Pepper, Stephen C., "Evaluation, Definition and Their Sanction," *JAAC* 21 (1962).

Stevenson, Charles L., "Interpretation and Evaluation in Aesthetics," in Max Black (ed.), *Philosophical Analysis*, Ithaca, N.Y.: Cornell University Press, 1950.

Stolnitz, Jerome, "Analytic Philosophy and Aesthetics," *BJA* 3 (1963).

Walton, Kendall L., "Categories of Art," *Phil. R.* 79 (1970).

Wittgenstein, Ludwig, *Lectures and Conversations on Aesthetics, Psychology and Religious Beliefs*, Berkeley and Los Angeles: University of California Press, 1966.

———, *Philosophical Investigations*, New York: Macmillan, 1953.

Zubnick, Irving L., "Phenomenology and Concept in Art," *BJA* 6 (1966).

Index